Prentice Hall Test Prep Series:
Microsoft®
Excel 2002

MOUS

Expert Level

Prentice Hall Test Prep Series:

Microsoft®
Excel 2002
MOUS
Expert Level

Marianne Fox
College of Business Administration, Butler University

Lawrence C. Metzelaar
College of Business Administration, Butler University

Prentice
Hall

Upper Saddle River, New Jersey

Library of Congress Cataloging-in-Publication Data

Fox, Marianne B.
    Microsoft Excel 2002, MOUS expert level / Marianne Fox, Lawrence C. Metzelaar.
      p. cm.—(Prentice Hall test prep series)
    ISBN 0-13-049780-0
    1. Microsoft Excel (Computer file)—Examinations—Study guides.   2. Business—
Computer programs—Examinations—Study guides.   3. Electronic spreadsheets—
Examinations—Study guides.   I. Metzelaar, Lawrence C.   II. Title.   III. Series.
    HF5548.4.M523 F678973 2002
    005.369—dc21   2002010412

Publisher and Vice President: Natalie E. Anderson
Executive Acquisitions Editor: Jodi McPherson
Senior Project Manager: Thomas Park
Assistant Editor: Melissa Edwards
Editorial Assistant: Jasmine Slowik
Media Project Manager: Cathleen Profitko
Marketing Manager: Emily Williams Knight
Production Manager: Gail Steier De Acevedo
Project Manager, Production: Tim Tate
Associate Director, Manufacturing: Vincent Scelta
Manufacturing Buyer: Tim Tate
Interior Design: Lorraine Castellano
Cover Design: Lorraine Castellano
Full-Service Composition: Impressions Book and Journal Services, Inc.
Printer/Binder: Von Hoffmann Corporation

Credits and acknowledgments borrowed from other sources and reproduced, with permission, in this textbook appear on appropriate page within the text.

Microsoft, Windows, Windows NT, MSN, The Microsoft Network, the MSN logo, PowerPoint, Outlook, FrontPage, Hotmail, and/or other Microsoft products referenced herein are either trademarks or registered trademarks of Microsoft Corporation in the United States and other countries. Screen shots and icons reprinted with permission from the Microsoft Corporation. This book is not sponsored or endorsed by or affiliated with Microsoft Corporation.

Microsoft and the Microsoft Office User Specialist logo are trademarks or registered trademarks of Microsoft Corporation in the United States and/or other countries. Pearson Education is independent from Microsoft Corporation and not affiliated with Microsoft in any manner. This text may be used in assisting students to prepare for a Microsoft Office User Specialist Exam. Neither Microsoft, its designated review company, nor Pearson Education warrants that use of this text will ensure passing the relevant exam.

Use of this Microsoft Office User Specialist Approved Courseware Logo on this product signifies that it has been independently reviewed and approved in complying with the following standards:

Acceptable coverage of all content related to the Expert Level Microsoft Office exam entitled "Excel 2002"; and sufficient performance-based exercises that relate closely to all required context, based on sampling of text.

10 9 8 7 6 5 4 3 2 1
ISBN 0-13-049780-0

Approved Courseware

What Does This Logo Mean?

It means this courseware has been approved by the Microsoft® Office User Specialist
Program to be among the finest available for learning **Microsoft® Office XP**.
It also means that upon completion of this courseware, you may be
prepared to become a Microsoft Office User Specialist.

What Is a Microsoft Office User Specialist?

A Microsoft Office User Specialist is an individual who has certified his or her skills in
one or more of the Microsoft Office desktop applications of Microsoft Word,
Microsoft Excel, Microsoft PowerPoint®, Microsoft Outlook®, Microsoft Access,
or in Microsoft Project. The Microsoft Office User Specialist Program typically
offers certification exams at the "Core" and "Expert" skill levels.[1] The Microsoft Office
User Specialist Program is the only Microsoft approved program in the world for
certifying proficiency in Microsoft Office desktop applications and Microsoft Project.
This certification can be a valuable asset in any job search or career advancement.

More Information:

To learn more about becoming a Microsoft Office User Specialist, visit **www.mous.net**.

To purchase a Microsoft Office User Specialist certification exam, visit
www.DesktopIQ.com.

To learn about other Microsoft Office User Specialist approved courseware from
Prentice Hall, visit **www.prenhall.com/phit/**.

Dedications

Marianne Fox and Lawrence Metzelaar: Excel 2002

We would like to dedicate this book to all who use it, in appreciation of your desire to learn how to learn, and your selection of our book to support those efforts.

Linda J. Bird: PowerPoint® 2002

I would like to dedicate this book to my family: Lonnie, a published author and my best supporter; and Rebecca and Sarah—articulate and awesome communicators in their own right.

Linda Ericksen: Word 2002

I would like to dedicate this book to my family: my mother Grace, my daughter Natalie, and my sisters Carol and Barbara.

Floyd Jay Winters and Julie T. Manchester: Access 2002

In total, this project required a lengthy introduction, eight Access Core chapters, eight Access Expert chapters, and a glossary. All were created from scratch with a schedule that allotted approximately one week per chapter. On top of a full teaching load, this turned out to be one of the most challenging projects of my life. As the stress mounted, I would often go to my weight room, pop in an old Queen CD, pump the volume up, and recall my 1978–1980 undefeated, championship Varsity Wrestling teams running on to the mat with the same songs blaring to the echoes of fans stomping their feet on the bleachers in rhythm to the beat. I was so proud when they voted to drop one of the weakest teams on our schedule to take on an undefeated prep school. They had faith in my ability and leadership as a coach. I want to thank them for their inspiration during a difficult yet rewarding period in my life. May all of the wrestlers from Allentown, New Jersey continue to grow and dare to succeed.
—Floyd Winters

I would like to dedicate this book to the memory of my mother, Julia Marshall Manchester.
—Julie T. Manchester

Acknowledgments

Marianne Fox and Lawrence Metzelaar: Excel 2002

We want to express our appreciation to the entire *MOUS Test Prep Series* 2002 team—other authors, editors, production staff, those in marketing who start and end the process of developing and delivering a quality text, and the entire sales force that deliver these books. Special thanks go to those with whom we were most involved on a day-to-day basis: Jodi McPherson, Executive Acquisitions Editor, for her managerial and editorial guidance as well as continual support; Thomas Park, Senior Project Manager, for his support keeping everything on track; and Tim Tate, Project Manager, Production. They continue to have our respect and gratitude for the prompt, professional, and always pleasant way in which they manage the creative process.

We also thank our colleagues at Butler University for supporting the collaborative process that was critical to the success of the *Test Prep* 2002 series and in particular: the dean of the College of Business Administration, Dr. Richard Fetter; and Chief Information Officer, Scott Kincaid and his excellent Information Resources staff.

Linda J. Bird: PowerPoint® 2002

If you've ever worked on a major project, you know that it usually requires a major team effort. Books are no exception. They're the result of a hard-working team of talented individuals. And even though most of the persons involved work behind the scenes, I'd like to publicly acknowledge their professionalism, hard work, and dedication to producing a top-quality publication.

First I'd like to thank Executive Editor Jodi McPherson for giving me the opportunity to write this book, and for her keen insights and vast knowledge about producing books for this market. I'd also like to give kudos to Managing Editors Monica Stipanov and Thomas Park for overseeing the entire series and shepherding it through production. Finally, I'd like to acknowledge Series Editors Marianne Fox and Lawrence Metzelaar for their friendship as well as for their quick and valuable feedback.

Most of all, I'd like to wholeheartedly thank my family: Lonnie, Rebecca, and Sarah—my best fans and cheerleaders throughout the entire project.

Linda Ericksen: Word 2002

I want to express my appreciation to the entire MOUS Essentials 2002 team—editors, production staff, and those in marketing who start and end the process of developing and delivering a quality text. Special thanks go to Jodi McPherson, Executive Editor; Marianne Fox and Lawrence Metzelaar, Series Editors; and Thomas Park, Project Manager for their support.

Floyd Jay Winters and Julie T. Manchester: Access 2002

We would like to give special thanks to our series editors, Marianne Fox and Lawrence Metzelaar, for their support and encouragement. Their comments, constructive criticism, and quick and nurturing feedback were absolutely invaluable. We would also like to thank our interns David Scott and Virginia Greene, who spent many hours proofing and testing our work.

About the Series Editors

Marianne Fox—Series Editor and coauthor of *Prentice Hall Test Prep Series: Microsoft Excel 2002 MOUS Core* and *Expert*

Marianne Fox is an Indiana CPA with B.S. and M.B.A. degrees in Accounting from Indiana University. For 24 years, she has enjoyed teaching full-time—initially in Indiana University's School of Business; since 1988 in the College of Business Administration at Butler University. As the co-owner of an Indiana-based consulting firm, Marianne has extensive experience consulting and training in the corporate and continuing education environments. Since 1984, she has co-authored nearly 45 computer-related books; and has given presentations on accounting, computer applications, and instructional development topics at a variety of seminars and conferences.

Lawrence C. Metzelaar—Series Editor and coauthor of *Prentice Hall Test Prep Series: Microsoft Excel 2002 MOUS Core* and *Expert*

Lawrence C. Metzelaar earned a B.S. in Business Administration and Computer Science from the University of Maryland, and an Ed.M. and C.A.G.S. in Human Problem Solving from Boston University. Lawrence has more than 37 years of experience with military and corporate mainframe and microcomputer systems. He has taught computer science and Management Information Systems (MIS) courses at the University of Hawaii, Control Data Institute, Indiana University, and Purdue University; currently, he is a full-time faculty member in the College of Business Administration at Butler University. As the co-owner of an Indiana-based consulting firm, he has extensive experience consulting and training in the corporate and continuing education environments. Since 1984, he has co-authored nearly 45 computer-related books; and has given presentations on computer applications and instructional development topics at a variety of seminars and conferences.

About the Series Authors

Linda J. Bird—Author of *Prentice Hall Test Prep Series: Microsoft PowerPoint® 2002 MOUS Comprehensive*

Linda J. Bird specializes in corporate training and support through Software Solutions, her own company. She has successfully trained users representing more than 75 businesses, including several Fortune 500 companies. Her clients have included Appalachian Electric Power Co., Goodyear, Pillsbury, Rockwell, and Shell Chemical. Her background also includes teaching at Averett College and overseeing computer training for a business training organization.

Linda has written numerous books for various publishers on PowerPoint, Word, Excel, Access, and Windows. An experienced teacher, she has also written more than 20 instructor's manuals. Additionally, she's penned more than 200 articles for *Smart Computing* and *Computer Power Users* magazines on wide-ranging computer topics—from using the Internet to troubleshooting hardware and software problems. She also writes monthly how-to columns on PowerPoint and Excel.

Linda, a graduate of the University of Wisconsin, lives on a small farm near the Great Smoky Mountains in East Tennessee, with her husband, Lonnie, and her daughters, Rebecca and Sarah. Besides authoring books, Linda home educates her daughters. When she's not writing, you can probably find her hiking in the mountains (or horseback riding) with her family.

Linda Ericksen—Author of Prentice Hall Test Prep Series: Microsoft Word 2002 MOUS Core and Expert

Linda Ericksen is the author of over 20 college-level computer textbooks on application software and the Internet, including writing her own series—*Quick Simple Microsoft Office*—for Prentice Hall. After completing both BA and MA degrees in English Literature from the University of Kentucky, Linda became a Vista volunteer in Alaska, where she began her college-level teaching career at a native Alaskan college-without-walls. She later earned an MS degree in Computer Science/Education from the University of Oregon and continued to teach at the community college and university level. Today, Linda teaches for Central Arizona College, and she teaches online for Cerro Coso Community College in California and Rio Salado Community College in Arizona.

Floyd Jay Winters—Coauthor of Prentice Hall Test Prep Series: Microsoft Access 2002 MOUS Core and Expert

Floyd Jay Winters received a BA degree from Rutgers University and an MA and an Ed. S. from Nova Southeastern University. He spent a semester sabbatical at the Harvard Graduate School. He taught three graduate level courses for Kent State University and several more graduate level courses for Nova Southeastern University in the 1980s. Floyd has been a Computer Science professor at Manatee Community College since 1986.

Floyd also coauthored *Web Collaboration Using Microsoft Office and NetMeeting*. His first textbook was *Microcomputer Troubleshooting and Maintenance*. Floyd is MOUS certified, NET+ certified, A+ certified, and he is also Cisco CCNA and CCAI certified. Before accepting his position at MCC he was the lead service technician for a computer dealer with stores in three counties. In that capacity, he was authorized and certified as a computer repair specialist by IBM and Apple. Floyd has been an active computer consultant since 1982. During the past five years, most of his consulting work has been focused on writing Microsoft Access databases for local businesses and charitable organizations.

Floyd was a varsity wrestling coach for 10 years; his teams won several championships and posted an undefeated string of 31 straight wins over a two-year period. He also was a championship youth soccer coach.

Julie T. Manchester—Coauthor of Prentice Hall Test Prep Series: Microsoft Access 2002 MOUS Core and Expert

Julie T. Manchester got her start in the computer science field in 1976, in the days of punched cards and long strings of complex job control language. She graduated from the Computer Processing Institute in East Hartford, CT. Julie has worked on IBM mainframes, programming in COBOL for such companies as Raytheon and Maryland Casualty. She worked as a project team member designing, writing, and implementing an online inventory system at Raytheon and wrote custom-tailored, data-entry and data-transmission programs for Maryland Casualty's regional offices. Julie has edited computer repair, networking, and Windows textbooks and manuals. She has designed, customized, and installed database projects for local businesses. Julie also coauthored *Web Collaboration Using Microsoft Office and NetMeeting*.

Julie earned an A.A. in Business Administration and an A.S. in Computer Science from Manatee Community College, and a B.S. in Management from University of South Florida. Julie is MOUS certified.

Contents at a Glance

Table of Contents

Prentice Hall Test Prep Series courseware is anchored in the practical and professional needs of all types of students. The MOUS titles within this series focus on preparing students to sit for the associated Core, Comprehensive, or Expert MOUS exam. Coverage of concepts and how-to steps make each text suitable for general introductory computer courses as well.

The chapters in each MOUS Prep text exactly match the skill sets—and skills being measured within each skill set—published for the associated MOUS exam. As such, it consists of skills that are built around a series of numbered, step-by-step procedures that are clear, concise, and easy to review. The end-of-chapter exercises have likewise been carefully crafted to reinforce skills and to extend what you've learned into areas beyond the explicit scope of the specific skills. Following, you'll find out more about the rationale behind each book element and how to use each to your maximum benefit.

Key Features

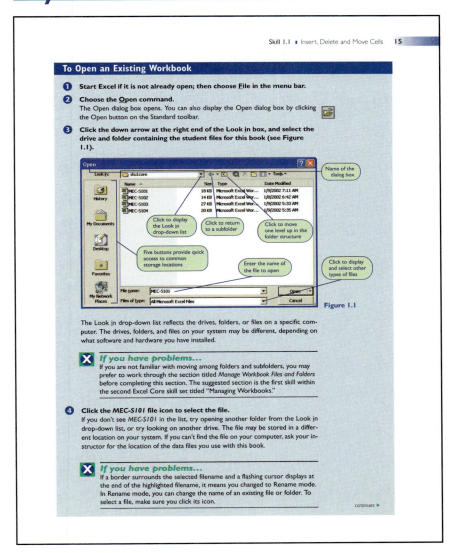

Figure 1.1

- **Step-by-Step Tutorials.** Each skill includes numbered, bold step-by-step instructions that show you how to perform the procedures in a clear, concise, and direct manner. These hands-on tutorials let you "learn by doing." A short paragraph may appear after a step to clarify the results of that step. To review the skill, you can easily scan the bold numbered steps. Accompanying data files eliminate unnecessary typing.

- **Illustrations.** Multiple illustrations add visual appeal and reinforce learning in each skill set. Each time a new button is introduced, its icon displays in the margin. Screen shots display after key steps for you to check against the results on your monitor. These figures, with ample callouts, make it easy to check your progress.

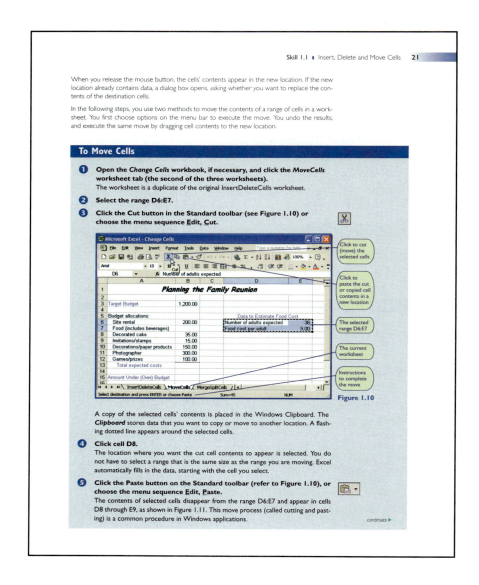

- **Notes.** Skills include three types of notes: If you have problems, Alternate Ways, and In Depth. These notes describe common problems, explain different methods for performing tasks, and provide extra tips and special hints (details provided in "How to Use This Book"). You may safely ignore these for the moment to focus on the main task at hand, or you may pause to learn and appreciate the additional information.

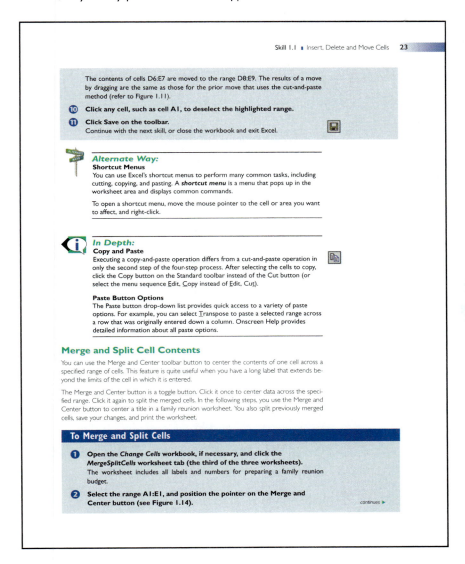

The contents of cells D6:E7 are moved to the range D8:E9. The results of a move by dragging are the same as those for the prior move that uses the cut-and-paste method (refer to Figure 1.11).

🔟 **Click any cell, such as cell A1, to deselect the highlighted range.**

⑪ **Click Save on the toolbar.**
Continue with the next skill, or close the workbook and exit Excel.

Alternate Way:
Shortcut Menus
You can use Excel's shortcut menus to perform many common tasks, including cutting, copying, and pasting. A *shortcut menu* is a menu that pops up in the worksheet area and displays common commands.

To open a shortcut menu, move the mouse pointer to the cell or area you want to affect, and right-click.

In Depth:
Copy and Paste
Executing a copy-and-paste operation differs from a cut-and-paste operation in only the second step of the four-step process. After selecting the cells to copy, click the Copy button on the Standard toolbar instead of the Cut button (or select the menu sequence Edit, Copy instead of Edit, Cut).

Paste Button Options
The Paste button drop-down list provides quick access to a variety of paste options. For example, you can select Transpose to paste a selected range across a row that was originally entered down a column. Onscreen Help provides detailed information about all paste options.

Merge and Split Cell Contents

You can use the Merge and Center toolbar button to center the contents of one cell across a specified range of cells. This feature is quite useful when you have a long label that extends beyond the limits of the cell in which it is entered.

The Merge and Center button is a toggle button. Click it once to center data across the specified range. Click it again to split the merged cells. In the following steps, you use the Merge and Center button to center a title in a family reunion worksheet. You also split previously merged cells, save your changes, and print the worksheet.

To Merge and Split Cells

❶ **Open the *Change Cells* workbook, if necessary, and click the *MergeSplitCells* worksheet tab (the third of the three worksheets).**
The worksheet includes all labels and numbers for preparing a family reunion budget.

❷ **Select the range A1:E1, and position the pointer on the Merge and Center button (see Figure 1.14).**

continues ▶

- **Summary.** A summary precedes the end-of-chapter exercises. The summary provides a brief recap of tasks learned in the skill set.

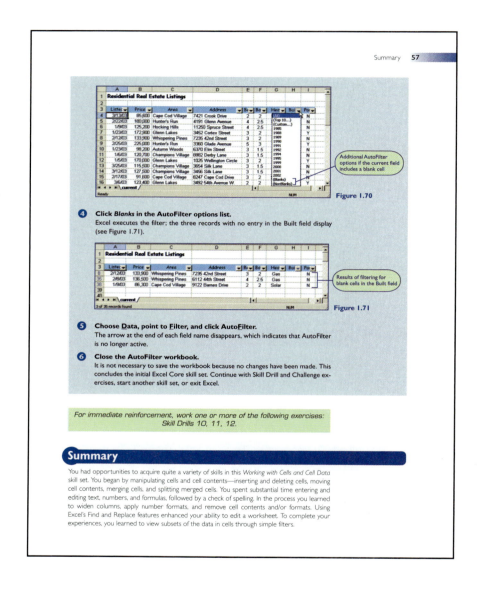

Residential Real Estate Listings

Figure 1.70

④ Click *Blanks* in the AutoFilter options list.
Excel executes the filter; the three records with no entry in the Built field display (see Figure 1.71).

Figure 1.71

⑤ Choose **D**ata, point to **F**ilter, and click Auto**F**ilter.
The arrow at the end of each field name disappears, which indicates that AutoFilter is no longer active.

⑥ Close the AutoFilter workbook.
It is not necessary to save the workbook because no changes have been made. This concludes the initial Excel Core skill set. Continue with Skill Drill and Challenge exercises, start another skill set, or exit Excel.

For immediate reinforcement, work one or more of the following exercises: Skill Drills 10, 11, 12.

Summary

You had opportunities to acquire quite a variety of skills in this *Working with Cells and Cell Data* skill set. You began by manipulating cells and cell contents—inserting and deleting cells, moving cell contents, merging cells, and splitting merged cells. You spent substantial time entering and editing text, numbers, and formulas, followed by a check of spelling. In the process you learned to widen columns, apply number formats, and remove cell contents and/or formats. Using Excel's Find and Replace features enhanced your ability to edit a worksheet. To complete your experiences, you learned to view subsets of the data in cells through simple filters.

- **End-of-Chapter Exercises.** Check out the extensive end-of-chapter exercises—at least one for each skill presented in the skill set. You'll find two levels of reinforcement: Skill Drill and Challenge (detail provided in "How to Use This Book"). Generally, each exercise is independent of other exercises, so you can complete your choices in any order. Accompanying data files eliminate unnecessary typing.

Skill Drill

Skill Drill exercises *reinforce* skills. Each skill reinforced is the same, or nearly the same, as a skill presented in the skill set. Detailed instructions are provided in a step-by-step format.

Before beginning your Excel Core Skill Set 1 Skill Drill exercises, complete the following steps:

1. Open the file named *MEC-S105*, and immediately save it as `MEC-S1drill`.

   The workbook contains thirteen sheets: an overview and twelve exercise sheets labeled SD1 through SD12.

2. Click the Overview sheet to view the organization and content of the Skill Drill workbook for Excel Core Skill Set 1.

Each exercise is independent of the others, so you may complete the exercises in any order. Be sure to save the workbook after completing each exercise. If you need a paper copy of one or more completed exercises, enter your name, centered in a header, before printing. Except for worksheets SD7 and SD9—which are large worksheets—print options have already been set to print compressed to one page and to display the filename, sheet name, and current date in a footer.

Be sure to save your changes and close the workbook if you need more than one work session to complete the desired exercises. Continue working on *MEC-S1drill* instead of starting over in the original *MEC-S105* file.

1. Move and Merge Cell Contents

You decide to change the original location of a title and subtitle on a worksheet that summarizes volunteer hours. You also want to merge and center those titles.

To move cell contents and merge cells, follow these steps:

1. If necessary, open the *MEC-S1drill* workbook; then click the SD1 sheet tab.

   The organization name *Community Volunteer Corps* displays in the range E1:G1.

2. Select the range E1:E2.

   This selects the worksheet's title and subtitle. These titles display across several columns, but are stored in the two cells in column E.

3. Click the Cut button in the toolbar (or choose Edit, Cut).

4. Click cell A3 to select the first cell in the destination range.

5. Click the Paste button in the toolbar (or choose Edit, Paste).

6. Select the range A3:F3.

7. Click the Merge and Center button in the toolbar.

   Excel centers the title Community Volunteer Corps across columns A through F.

8. Select the range A4:F4, and click the Merge and Center button.

9. Save your changes to the *MEC-S1drill* workbook.

2. Delete Cells

You maintain a worksheet that provides a 5-year trend analysis of sales. Before you enter 2003 data, you want to remove 1998 data. Deleting the column containing 1998 data would also remove labels that are needed in the worksheet. You decide to delete the cells containing 1998 data in a way that shifts data for remaining years to the left.

How to Use This Book

Each MOUS Prep book is organized by chapters—one chapter per core or expert skill set. A skill set consists of numbered skill areas that are related to that topic. Each skill within a numbered skill area presents a specific task or closely related set of tasks in a manageable chunk that is easy to assimilate and retain.

Each element in a MOUS Prep book is designed to maximize your learning experience. Following is a list of the MOUS Prep skill set elements and a description of how each element can help you:

- **Skill Set Objectives.** Starting with an objective gives you short-term, attainable goals. Using skill set objectives that closely match the titles of the step-by-step tutorials breaks down the possibly overwhelming prospect of learning several new features of an Office XP application into small, attainable, bite-sized tasks. Look over the objectives on the opening page of a chapter before you begin, and review them after completing the chapter to identify the main goals for each MOUS skill set.

- **Key Terms.** Each key term is defined during its first use within the text, and is shown in bold italic within that explanation. Definitions of key terms are also included in the Glossary.

- **Skill Set Overview.** This opening section explains the concepts and features that you will learn in the skill set.

- **If You Have Problems...** These short troubleshooting notes appear between hands-on steps. They help you anticipate or solve common problems quickly and effectively. Even if you do not encounter the problem at this time, make a mental note of it so that you know where to look when you (or others) have difficulty.

- **Alternate Way.** These notes explain a different way to perform a task. Relatively short notes display between hands-on steps or in the margin next to the associated hands-on step. Longer notes display immediately after the associated set of hands-on steps.

- **In Depth.** Many skills include "In Depth" comments. These notes provide extra tips and special hints, and they follow the related set of hands-on steps.

- **Periodic Cross-Reference to Related Exercises.** MOUS skill sets include from two to ten numbered skill areas. Therefore, some of the chapters in a text are quite long. After each numbered skill area, you find a cross reference to any Skill Drill and/or Challenge exercise(s) relating to that numbered skill area. For immediate reinforcement, work through one or more of the related exercises. Otherwise, you can continue to the next skill area.

- **Skill Drill Exercises.** Skill Drill exercises reinforce skills presented in the chapter. Each skill reinforced is the same, or nearly the same, as a skill presented within a skill set. Each exercise includes a brief narrative introduction, followed by detailed instructions in a step-by-step format.

- **Challenge Exercises.** Challenge exercises expand on or are somewhat related to skills presented in the chapter. Each exercise provides a brief narrative introduction, followed by instructions in a numbered-step format that are not as detailed as those in the Skill Drill section.

Typeface Conventions Used in This Book

Prentice Hall Test Prep uses the following conventions to make it easier for you to understand the material.

- Key terms appear in *italic and bold* the first time they are defined in a skill set.

- Monospace type appears frequently and looks `like this`. It is used to indicate text that you are instructed to key in.

- *Italic text* indicates (1) text that appears onscreen as warnings, confirmations, or general information; (2) the name of a file to be used in a skill or exercise; and (3) text from a dialog box that is referenced within a sentence, when that sentence might appear awkward if the dialog box text were not set off.

- Hotkeys are indicated by underline. Hotkeys are the underlined letters in menus, toolbars, and dialog boxes that activate commands and options, and are a quick way to choose frequently used commands and options. Hotkeys look like this: <u>F</u>ile, <u>S</u>ave.

Student Resources—Companion Website

The Web site that accompanies this book is the tool that empowers you to get the most out of this text (see Figure I.1). It provides access to all the data files for you to use as you work through the step-by-step tutorials, and the Skill Drill and Challenge exercises provided at the end of each skill set.

Figure I.1

Utilizing the Companion Website gives you access not only to the data files, but also to online study guides and Internet exercises to enhance your understanding of the software.

Accessing Student Data Files on the Companion Website

The student data files that you need to work through the skill sets can be downloaded from **www.prenhall.com/phtestprep**. Data files are provided for each chapter. The filenames correspond to the filenames called for in this book. The files are named in the following manner: The first character indicates the book series (M=MOUS); the second character denotes the application (W=Word, E=Excel, and so forth); and the third character indicates the level (C=Core or Comprehensive and E=Expert). The last four digits indicate the skill set number and the file number within the skill set. For example, the complete name for the first file in Chapter 3 (Core Skill Set 3) in the MOUS *Word* book is MWC-S301. The complete name for the third file in Chapter 14 (Expert Skill Set 7) in the MOUS *Excel* book is MEE-S703.

For the Instructor

Instructor's Resource CD-ROM

The **Instructor's Resource CD-ROM** that is available contains:

- Instructor's Manual in Word and PDF

- Solutions to all exercises from the book and Website

- PowerPoint lectures

- A Windows-based test manager and the associated test bank in Word format with over 1500 new questions

Companion Website www.prenhall.com/phtestprep

For both students and instructors, the **Companion Website** includes ancillary material to accompany the Prentice Hall Test Prep Series. Instructors will find the data and solution files, PowerPoint slides, and *Instructor's Manuals* for each application.

Prentice Hall has also formed close alliances with each of the leading online platform providers: WebCT, Blackboard, and our own Pearson CourseCompass.

 ## CourseCompass www.coursecompass.com

CourseCompass is a dynamic, interactive online course-management tool powered exclusively for Pearson Education by Blackboard. This exciting product enables you to teach market-leading Pearson Education content in an easy-to-use, customizable format.

 ## BlackBoard www.prenhall.com/blackboard

Prentice Hall's abundant online content, combined with Blackboard's popular tools and interface, result in robust Web-based courses that are easy to implement, manage, and use—taking your courses to new heights in student interaction and learning.

WebCT www.prenhall.com/webct

Course-management tools within WebCT include page tracking, progress tracking, class and student management, gradebook, communication, calendar, reporting tools, and more. GOLD LEVEL CUSTOMER SUPPORT, available exclusively to adopters of Prentice Hall courses, is provided free-of-charge upon adoption and provides you with priority assistance, training discounts, and dedicated technical support.

 ## Train & Assess IT www.prenhall.com/phit

Prentice Hall offers Performance Based Training and Assessment in one product: Train & Assess IT. The training component offers computer-based training that a student can use to preview, learn, and review Microsoft Office applications and computer literacy skills. Web- or CD-ROM delivered, the training component offers interactive, multimedia, computer-based training to augment classroom learning. Built-in prescriptive testing suggests a study path based not only on student test results but also on the specific textbook chosen for the course.

The assessment component offers computer-based testing that shares the same user interface and is used to evaluate a student's knowledge about specific topics in Word, Excel, Access, PowerPoint, Windows, Outlook, and the Internet. It does this in a task-oriented environment to demonstrate proficiency as well as comprehension of the topics by the students.

About
Excel 2002

Electronic spreadsheets are versatile tools for both personal and business use. They are designed primarily for organizing and analyzing numeric data.

An Excel file is a **workbook**, comprised of one or more worksheets. Unless you change original settings, three worksheets named Sheet1, Sheet2, and Sheet3 display in a new workbook (see Figure 0.1). You can insert as many sheets as desired, subject to the memory available on your system. You can also rename and delete sheets.

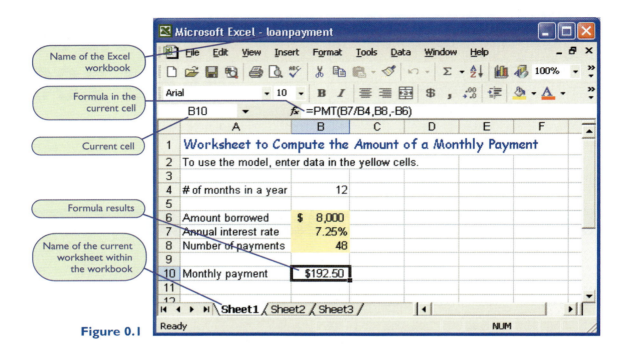

Figure 0.1

A **spreadsheet**—called a **worksheet** in Excel—is comprised of rows and columns. Each intersection of a row and a column forms a **cell**. You can enter text, a number, or a formula in a cell (refer to Figure 0.1).

An electronic worksheet enables a user to change data in one or more cells and immediately view the impact of the change on all formulas that reference the changed cells. For example, in the worksheet shown in Figure 0.1, a user can analyze the impact on the monthly payment (cell B10) that varying the amount borrowed (cell B6), the interest rate (cell B7), and/or the number of payments (cell B8) would cause.

Working through this text, you can acquire the skills to create and modify well-designed worksheets. Good worksheet design includes explanations about purposes and revisions, separate cells for data subject to change, and instructions to users. Let's begin by exploring the Excel workspace and learning how to use onscreen Help.

Explore the Excel Workspace

An Excel screen consists of a **title bar** and six additional sections: the **menu bar**, one or more **toolbars**, the **name box**, the **formula bar**, the **worksheet window**, and the **status bar**. These sections form the Excel workspace (see Figure 0.2).

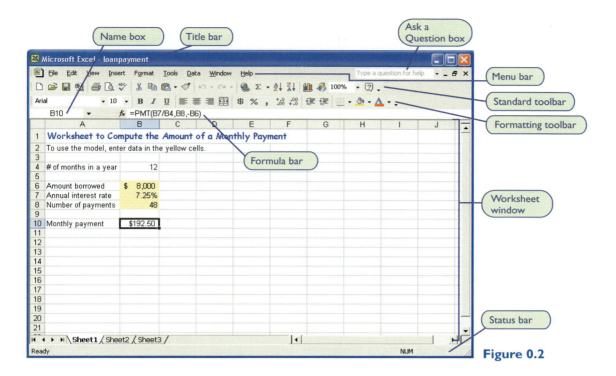

Figure 0.2

In the sample workspace, the *Formatting toolbar* displays below the *Standard toolbar* (refer to Figure 0.2). You might prefer to show only the most commonly used standard and formatting buttons on a single toolbar. You control this display by checking on or off an option titled *Show Standard and Formatting toolbars on two rows*. This option appears on the Options tab of the Customize dialog box (choose the menu sequence Tools, Customize to display the dialog box). The figures in this book show separate toolbars.

Excel features easy access to onscreen Help. For example, you can type a word or phrase in the Ask a Question box and press Enter. You can also display the *Office Assistant*, a component of onscreen Help in the form of an animated graphics image. The default image is a paper clip known as *Clippit*. In this context, *default* refers to a setting that a program uses unless you specify another setting. You learn how to access Help and how to show or hide the Office Assistant in the next section. Figures in this text do not display the Office Assistant unless its use is part of an instruction.

Explanations of Excel's screen elements are provided in a table at the end of this section. For now, launch Excel and explore the workspace.

To Start Excel and Explore the Excel Workspace

1 **Move the mouse pointer to the Start button at the left edge of the Windows taskbar; then click the left mouse button.**
The Start button's pop-up menu displays.

2 **Move the mouse pointer to the Programs menu item.**
You see a listing of available programs on your system.

3 **Move the mouse pointer to Microsoft Excel; then click the left mouse button.**

continues ▶

To Start Excel and Explore the Excel Workspace (continued)

 If you have problems...

If you don't see Microsoft Excel on the Programs submenu, move the mouse pointer over the Microsoft Office folder. Then, click the Microsoft Excel icon from the Microsoft Office submenu.

If a shortcut icon for Excel is displayed on your Windows desktop, you can also start Excel by double-clicking the icon. (If Windows was configured to use the Active Desktop, you can single-click the shortcut icon.)

Many systems are also set up to automatically display the Microsoft Office Shortcut bar on the Windows desktop. This bar contains buttons you can use to launch Microsoft Office programs, including Excel.

Excel is loaded into the computer's memory, and a blank worksheet in a new workbook displays (see Figure 0.3). The default view includes a task pane at the right side of the screen. A *task pane* provides a quick means to execute commands. The task pane that displays when you start Excel enables you to create new workbooks or to select a workbook to open from a list of files used in recent work sessions.

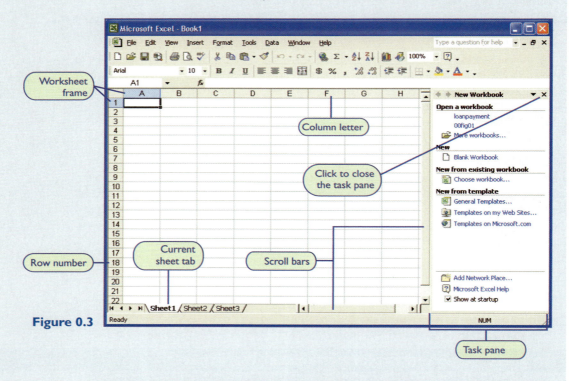

Figure 0.3

 If you have problems...

If the task pane does not display, click <u>V</u>iew on the menu bar; then click Tas<u>k</u> Pane.

4   **Click the Close button for the task pane (refer to Figure 0.3).**
You enlarged the worksheet area by closing the task pane.

5   **Move the mouse pointer to cell C6 in the worksheet, and then click the left mouse button.**
Clicking a cell selects it. An outline appears around the cell to indicate that it is the *current cell* (also called the *active cell*). The cell address C6 appears in the name box to let you know which cell is selected (see Figure 0.4). The *cell address* refers to the column and row that intersect to form the cell—in this case, column C and row 6. Typing data or executing a new action takes place at the current cell address.

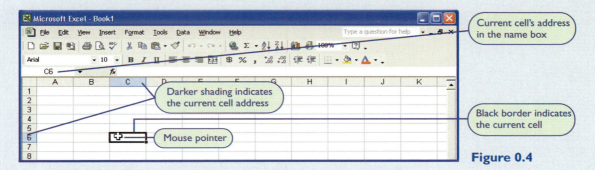

Current cell's address in the name box

Darker shading indicates the current cell address

Mouse pointer

Black border indicates the current cell

Figure 0.4

6   **Press ↓ and then press →.**
Pressing an arrow key shifts the active cell by one cell in the direction indicated on the key.

7   **Press End and then press ↓.**
The active cell is in row 65536, the last row in the worksheet.

8   **Press End and then press →.**
The active cell is IV65536, the lower-right corner of the worksheet.

9   **Press the two-key combination Ctrl+Home.**
Pressing Home while holding down Ctrl makes cell A1 the current cell. Leave the blank worksheet open for the next section, in which you use onscreen Help.

In this section, you were introduced to a number of spreadsheet basics. Table 0.1 lists and describes the screen elements illustrated in this section.

Table 0.1	Parts of the Microsoft Excel Screen
Element	**Description**
Ask a Question box	Part of the Excel onscreen Help system that appears near the right side of the menu bar. Enables you to specify a new Help topic or redisplay a previous Help topic without using the Office Assistant.
Cell	The intersection of a column and a row.
Cell address	Describes which column and row intersect to form the cell; for example, A1 is the cell address for the first cell in the first column (column A) and the first row (row 1).
Column letter	Lettered *A* through *Z, AA* through *AZ,* and so on through *IV,* up to 256 columns.
Current (or active) cell	The cell surrounded with a thick black border. The next action you take, such as typing or formatting, affects this cell.
Formatting toolbar	Provides—in button form—shortcuts to frequently used commands for changing the appearance of data.
Formula bar	Displays the contents of the current or active cell.
Menu bar	Contains common menu names that, when activated, display a list of related commands; the File menu, for example, contains such commands as Open, Close, Save, and Print.
Mouse pointer	Selects items, and positions the insertion point (cursor).
Name box	Displays the cell address of the current cell or the name of a range of cells.
Office Assistant	A component of onscreen Help in the form of an animated graphic image that can be turned on or off; brings up a list of subjects related to a question you type.
Row number	Numbered 1 through 65,536.
Scrollbars	Enable you to move the worksheet window vertically and horizontally to see other parts of the worksheet.
Sheet tab	A means to access each sheet in a workbook. Click a sheet tab to quickly move to that sheet.
Standard toolbar	Provides, in button form, shortcuts to frequently used commands including Save, Print, Cut (move), Copy, and Paste.
Status bar	Provides information about the current operation or workspace, such as displaying *CAPS* if you set Caps Lock on.
Task pane	A window that provides quick access to execute commands. For example, the task pane that displays when you open Excel enables you to create or open files. To display a task pane, select View in the menu bar and click Task Pane.

continues ▶

Table 0.1 (continued)

Element	Description
Title bar	Displays the name of the software and the name of the active workbook—either a default name, such as Book1, or a saved file.
Workbook	An Excel file that contains one or more worksheets.
Worksheet frame	The row and column headings that appear along the top and left edge of the worksheet window.
Worksheet window	Contains the current worksheet—the work area.

Get Help

Excel provides a number of onscreen Help options. The Excel program includes an Ask a Question box near the right end of the menu bar (see Figure 0.5). You can also activate the Office Assistant to help you find the answer to a specific question.

Click to select among previous search topics

Type your search topic in the Ask a Question box

Figure 0.5

Another method of accessing Help information is to use the <u>C</u>ontents tab in the Microsoft Excel Help window to scroll through general topics and related subtopics. The Help window also includes an <u>I</u>ndex tab that enables you to search on a keyword. You can also use the What's This? pointer to display a description of any feature on the screen.

In this section, you use the Ask a Question box and the <u>C</u>ontents tab in the Help window to learn about formulas. Refer to "In Depth" at the end of this section for explanations of other Help options.

To Get Help

1 **Launch Excel and display a blank worksheet, if necessary; type** `math operators` **in the Ask a Question box at the right end of the menu bar (refer to Figure 0.5).**

2 **Press** ↵Enter.
Three choices display in a pop-up box (see Figure 0.6).

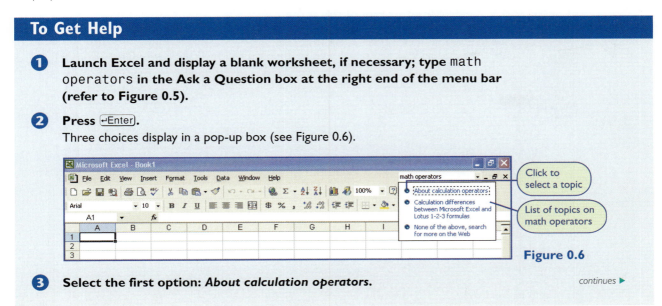

Click to select a topic

List of topics on math operators

Figure 0.6

3 **Select the first option:** *About calculation operators.*

continues ▶

To Get Help (continued)

The Microsoft Excel Help window opens and displays general information about calculation operators (see Figure 0.7).

Click to expand information on all topics

Click to expand information on a single topic

Drag the left edge of the Help topic pane to change its width

Figure 0.7

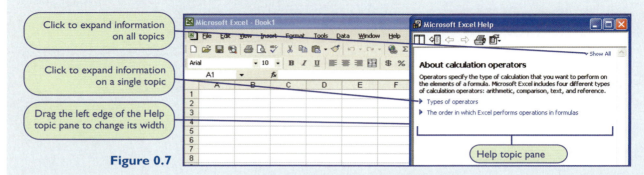

You can enlarge or reduce the width of the Help window by dragging its left edge to the left or right. Clicking a small arrowhead in front of a topic, such as the one pointing to the phrase *Types of operators*, expands the display to include information on the specific topic. Clicking the small arrowhead in front of *Show All* near the top of the Help window displays all related topics.

 ### If you have problems...

Your Help display might vary from that shown in Figure 0.7. The Help topic pane might be larger. The display might include a navigation pane with Contents, Answer Wizard, and Index tabs. These differences are possible because Excel retains the settings specified during the most recent use of onscreen Help. You can omit Step 4 if you do not want to increase the width of the Help pane. You can omit Step 6 if the Contents, Answer Wizard, and Index tabs already display in a pane to the left of the Help topic pane.

4 **Drag the left edge of the Help topic pane to the left, until it fills approximately half of the screen.**

5 **Click *Show All* near the upper-right corner of the Help window.**
Additional information displays in the Help window (see Figure 0.8).

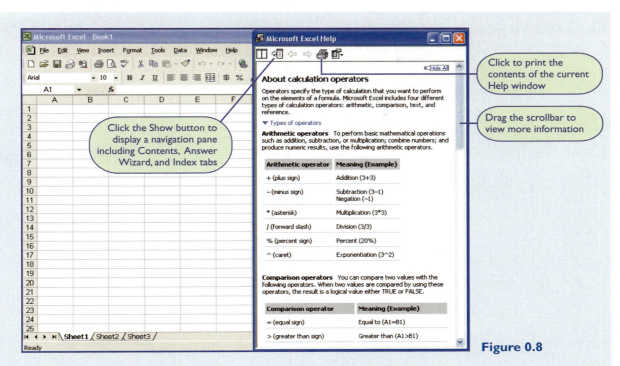

Figure 0.8

⑥ **Click the Show button near the upper-left corner of the Help window (refer to Figure 0.8).**

Clicking the Show button displays a navigation pane to the left of the current Help topic pane. The navigation pane includes Contents, Answer Wizard, and Index tabs. Excel displays a list of topics in the Contents tab (see Figure 0.9).

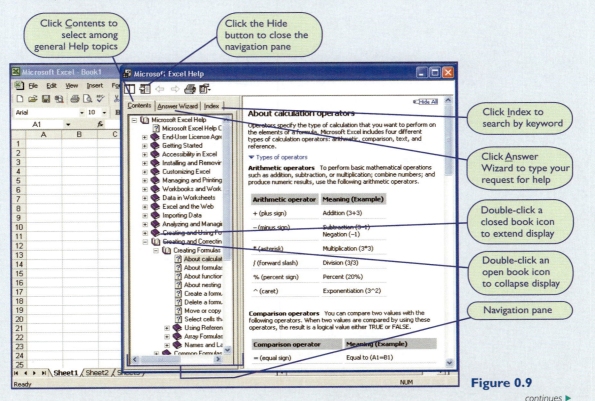

Figure 0.9

continues ▶

To Get Help (continued)

 If you have problems...
Click the <u>C</u>ontents tab in the navigation pane if it is not the current tab. If the multiple topics in Figure 0.9 do not appear in the navigation pane, double-click the closed book icon preceding *Microsoft Excel Help*, double-click the closed book icon preceding *Creating and Correcting Formulas*, and double-click the closed book icon *Creating Formulas*.

7 **Select and read Help topics of your choice from the Contents tab.**

8 **Click the Close button in the upper-right corner of the Help window.**
The Help window closes. Now keep Excel open and proceed to the first Excel Core skill set, or exit Excel by completing the next two steps.

9 **Click <u>F</u>ile on the menu bar.**
Excel displays a list of File commands (see Figure 0.10).

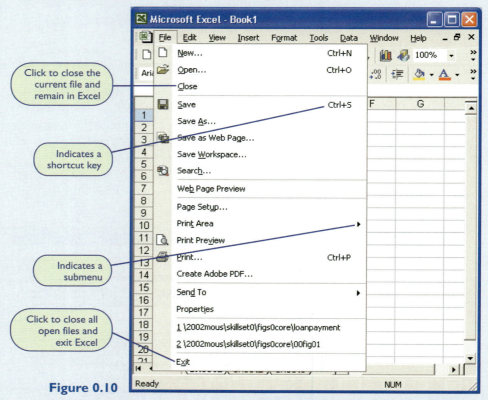

Figure 0.10

You can make a selection from a menu by typing its *hotkey*—the underlined letter—or by clicking it. Excel assigns shortcuts to frequently executed commands. A *shortcut key* enables you to execute a command by typing one or more keys instead of making selections from menus.

10 **Click E<u>x</u>it.**
Excel closes. If there are any files left open, Excel displays a dialog box that asks whether you want to save your work. Choosing <u>Y</u>es saves all open files and then closes the program. Choosing <u>N</u>o closes the program without saving the files; any work you have done since the last time you saved is erased. After you close Excel, the Windows desktop appears if no other software applications are running.

In Depth:
Displaying and Using the Office Assistant

You can use the Office Assistant instead of the Ask a Question box to display help on a specified topic. The default Office Assistant image is a paper clip named *Clippit*. If the Office Assistant image is onscreen, simply click it to open a balloon, in which you can type a question. To quickly open the Office Assistant, press F1 at any time, or click the Microsoft Excel Help button on the Standard toolbar. If the Office Assistant has been turned off, you can choose Help, Show the Office Assistant to display it.

If the Office Assistant can't find topics related to the question you type, a balloon appears, telling you so. Check to be sure you typed the question correctly, or try to be more specific; then click Search again.

To hide the Office Assistant, select the menu sequence Help, Hide the Office Assistant, or right-click the Office Assistant image and click Hide.

Other Tips on Using Help

The Index tab in the Help window includes an alphabetical listing of topics (or keywords) that you can use to find related topics. For example, if you enter the keyword Print, Excel finds dozens of topics related to the word, and displays them in the Choose a topic box. You can click a topic to select it and display its associated Help screen.

To print the contents of a Help window, click the Print button at the top of the window.

To use the What's This? pointer to display a ScreenTip about an item onscreen, choose Help, What's This, or press ⬆Shift + F1. When the pointer resembles a question mark with an arrow, click the item for which you need information.

If you can't find the information you need within Excel, you can access resources available on the World Wide Web. Assuming that you have Internet access, you can choose Help, Office on the Web to view information on Microsoft's Web site for Excel.

To display the version number of the Excel software you are using, choose Help, About Microsoft Excel.

Core Skill Set 1

Working with Cells and Cell Data

This skill set includes	
Insert, delete and move cells	▌ Open and save a workbook ▌ Insert and delete cells ▌ Move cell contents ▌ Merge and split cell contents
Enter and edit cell data including text, numbers, and formulas	▌ Enter and edit text and numbers ▌ Enter formulas and functions ▌ Apply number formats ▌ Remove cell contents and formats
Check spelling	
Find and replace cell data and formats	▌ Find and replace cell contents ▌ Find and replace cell formats
Work with a subset of data by filtering lists	▌ Filter on exact matches ▌ Filter for top and bottom records ▌ Filter for blanks and nonblanks

Skill Set Overview

s explained in the introductory section *About Excel 2002*, an Excel workbook includes one or more worksheets. Each worksheet is comprised of rows and columns, and each intersection of a row and column forms a cell.

In this skill set, you work with cells and cell data. Before you enter and edit data yourself, you learn to insert and delete cells, merge and split cells, and move cell contents. You also check spelling and use another powerful editing feature that enables you to find and replace formats as well as text. In this context, a *format* is a characteristic or attribute applied to cell contents—for example, italic or the print style Times New Roman.

The skill set concludes with multiple opportunities to view a subset of data by restricting the display to cells whose contents match specified conditions.

Skill 1.1: Insert, Delete and Move Cells

Let's do a little math! Each Excel 2002 worksheet is comprised of 256 columns and 65,536 rows. That means you have 16,777,216 cells to use in every worksheet, and there can be as many as 255 worksheets within a workbook. With so many cells available, it makes sense to focus on manipulating cells and cell contents as a starting point for developing Excel skills.

Four topics are included in this skill area: open and save a workbook, insert and delete cells, move cell contents, and merge and split cell contents.

Open and Save a Workbook

You open a file by executing a File, Open command. As in other Windows programs, you can execute a command by clicking a command on the menu bar and then clicking the command you want from the submenu. When you choose an option on the menu bar, Excel gives you the opportunity to use either short or full menus. The short menu displays an abbreviated list of commonly used commands. The full menu includes all available commands. By default, the short menu displays first; after a momentary delay, the full menu displays.

When you save a workbook, you assign the file a name and location on a disk. You can type any name you want using Windows' file-naming rules. You can include spaces as well as upper- and lowercase letters. Excel automatically stores the file in the default Excel file format, adding the XLS (Excel spreadsheet) file extension.

You save a file by executing a File, Save command or a File, Save As command. Use the Save command to save a previously saved workbook under its current name and in its current location. Use the Save As command to save a new workbook, or to save a previously saved workbook under a different name or in a different location.

Use the menu bar now to open a practice file and save it under a new name in the location of your choice. By saving under another name, you keep the original file intact.

To Open an Existing Workbook

1 **Start Excel if it is not already open; then choose <u>F</u>ile in the menu bar.**

2 **Choose the <u>O</u>pen command.**
The Open dialog box opens. You can also display the Open dialog box by clicking the Open button on the Standard toolbar.

3 **Click the down arrow at the right end of the Look <u>i</u>n box, and select the drive and folder containing the student files for this book (see Figure 1.1).**

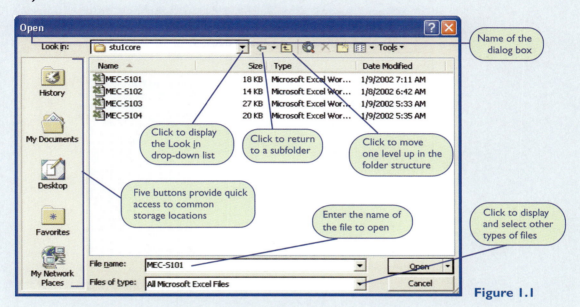

Figure 1.1

The Look <u>i</u>n drop-down list reflects the drives, folders, or files on a specific computer. The drives, folders, and files on your system may be different, depending on what software and hardware you have installed.

> **X** **If you have problems...**
> If you are not familiar with moving among folders and subfolders, you may prefer to work through the section titled *Manage Workbook Files and Folders* before completing this section. The suggested section is the first skill within the second Excel Core skill set titled "Managing Workbooks."

4 **Click the *MEC-S101* file icon to select the file.**
If you don't see *MEC-S101* in the list, try opening another folder from the Look <u>i</u>n drop-down list, or try looking on another drive. The file may be stored in a different location on your system. If you can't find the file on your computer, ask your instructor for the location of the data files you use with this book.

> **X** **If you have problems...**
> If a border surrounds the selected filename and a flashing cursor displays at the end of the highlighted filename, it means you changed to Rename mode. In Rename mode, you can change the name of an existing file or folder. To select a file, make sure you click its icon.

continues ▶

To Open an Existing Workbook (continued)

5 **Click the Open button in the lower-right corner of the Open dialog box.**
The partially completed worksheet shown in Figure 1.2 appears onscreen. Now, use the Save As command to save a copy of this file under a more descriptive file-name. The original data file is stored intact.

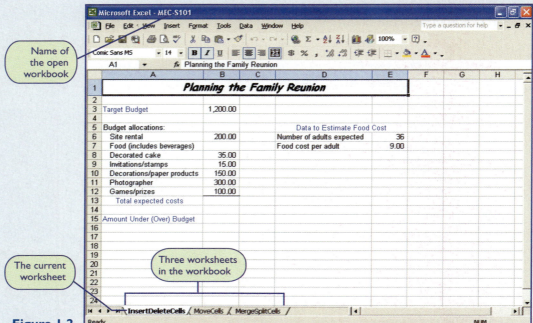

Name of the open workbook

The current worksheet

Three worksheets in the workbook

Figure 1.2

Alternate Way:
Open a File
To open a file quickly from the Open dialog box, double-click the file's icon in the list of files. If you double-click the filename instead of the file icon, however, you may end up in Rename mode.

6 **Choose the File menu again; then choose the Save As command.**
The Save As dialog box opens.

7 **In the File name text box, type** `Change Cells` **to replace** *MEC-S101.*

8 **From the Save in drop-down list, select the appropriate drive and folder for saving the new file (see Figure 1.3).**

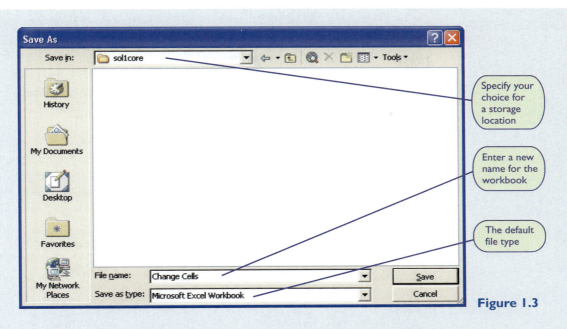

Figure 1.3

If necessary, ask your instructor where you should save the new workbook file.

9 **Click the Save button in the lower-right corner of the Save As dialog box.**

Excel saves the workbook as *Change Cells* and adds the extension .xls to the filename. The name of the file switches to *Change Cells* in the title bar at the top of the screen. There are now two identical files—the original student data file named *MEC-S101.xls* and a copy named *Change Cells.xls*. Throughout this book, you modify copies of student data files. Each original file remains intact in case you want to re-work a skill set. Keep the workbook open for the next skill.

Insert and Delete Cells

You determine the contents of a worksheet—the labels, numbers, and formulas introduced in *About Excel 2002*. A worksheet that currently provides the desired information may need sections added, deleted, or rearranged at a later date.

If you need blank cells within the existing cell content, you can insert columns or rows, as illustrated in *Core Skill 3.2 Modify Row and Column Settings*. You can also insert cells in a specified range and shift existing cell contents in that range right or down.

Make sure you understand the difference between deleting cell contents and deleting cells. You delete cell contents by selecting the range of cells and pressing (Del). The result is a set of blank cells in the selected range because adjacent cell content does not move.

You delete cells by selecting the range of cells and choosing Edit, Delete. You also specify that adjacent cell content should move left or up. The results do not include a set of blank cells because adjacent cell content shifts in the specified direction.

In the following steps, you insert a range of cells in a worksheet used to plan a family reunion. You also delete two cells in the same worksheet.

To Insert and Delete Cells

1 Check that *InsertDeleteCells* is the current worksheet in the *Change Cells* workbook (refer to the worksheet content shown in Figure 1.2).

2 Click cell D6, press and hold down the left mouse button, and drag the mouse pointer to cell E7. Release the left mouse button when the mouse pointer is in cell E7.

Several adjacent cells—called a range—are now selected (see Figure 1.4). In Excel, a **range** can be a cell or a rectangular group of adjacent cells. As you drag the mouse, the name box on the formula bar shows you how many rows and columns you are selecting; in this case, 2R x 2C, which indicates 2 rows by 2 columns. After you finish selecting the range, the entire range of selected cells is highlighted.

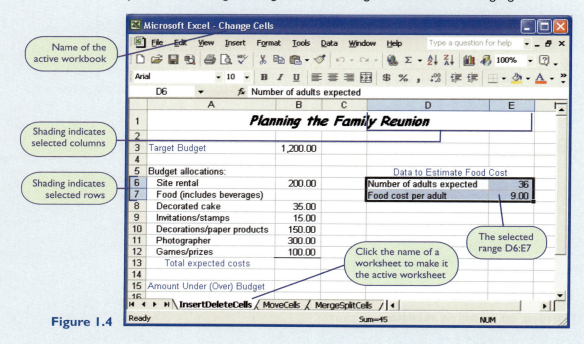

Figure 1.4

3 Choose **I**nsert from the menu bar.

The Insert menu opens to display a number of commands (see Figure 1.5).

Figure 1.5

④ Select Cells.

You can select from a menu by clicking the desired option or by typing its under-lined letter. The Insert dialog box opens, and *Shift cells down* is the selected option (see Figure 1.6).

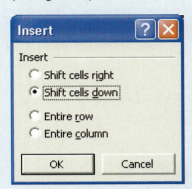

Figure 1.6

⑤ Click the OK button in the Insert dialog box.

Excel inserts cells in the selected range (see Figure 1.7).

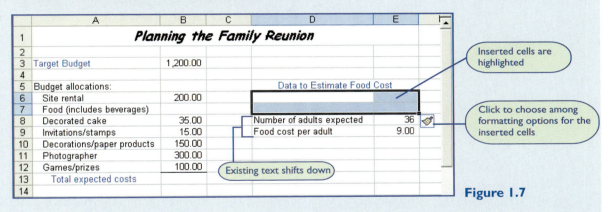

Figure 1.7

⑥ Select the range A8:B8; that is, click cell A8, press and hold down the left mouse button, drag the mouse pointer to cell B8, and release the mouse button.

The range A8:B8 is highlighted.

⑦ Choose Edit from the menu bar.

The Edit menu opens to display several options.

⑧ Select Delete.

The Delete dialog box opens, and *Shift cells up* is the selected option (see Figure 1.8).

continues ▶

To Insert and Delete Cells (continued)

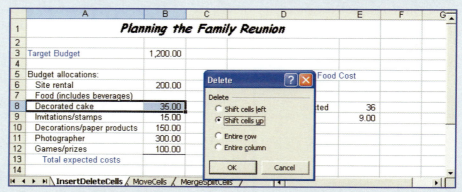

Figure 1.8

9 **Click the OK button in the Delete dialog box.**
Excel deletes cells in the selected range—the cells containing data on the budget item *Decorated cake*. Text below the deleted range shifts up (see Figure 1.9).

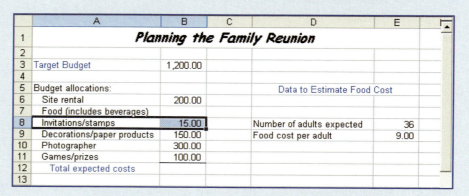

Figure 1.9

10 **Click any cell, such as cell A1, to deselect the highlighted range A8:B8.**

 11 **Click Save in the toolbar.**
Continue with the next skill, or close the workbook and exit Excel.

Move Cell Contents

You can copy or move text, numbers, and formulas from one cell (or range) to another; from one worksheet to another; and from one file to another. After a copy operation, the selected cell contents appear in two places—the original location and the new location. After a move (cut) operation, the selected cell contents appear in only the new location.

Both operations involve a four-step process if you choose a menu approach: Select the cell(s) containing the data you want to copy or move; choose either Copy or Cut from the Edit menu; position the cell pointer on the upper-left cell of the target range; and choose Edit, Paste.

A handy way to move one or more cells of data quickly is to select the cells and position the mouse pointer on any border of the cells, so the mouse pointer changes to a white arrow with a four-headed black arrow attached. Click and drag the mouse pointer to the new location. An outline of the cells that you are moving appears as you drag, and a ScreenTip shows you the current active cell (or range) where the data will appear if you release the mouse button.

When you release the mouse button, the cells' contents appear in the new location. If the new location already contains data, a dialog box opens, asking whether you want to replace the contents of the destination cells.

In the following steps, you use two methods to move the contents of a range of cells in a worksheet. You first choose options on the menu bar to execute the move. You undo the results, and execute the same move by dragging cell contents to the new location.

To Move Cells

1   **Open the *Change Cells* workbook, if necessary, and click the *MoveCells* worksheet tab (the second of the three worksheets).**
The worksheet is a duplicate of the original InsertDeleteCells worksheet.

2   **Select the range D6:E7.**

3   **Click the Cut button in the Standard toolbar (see Figure 1.10) or choose the menu sequence Edit, Cut.**

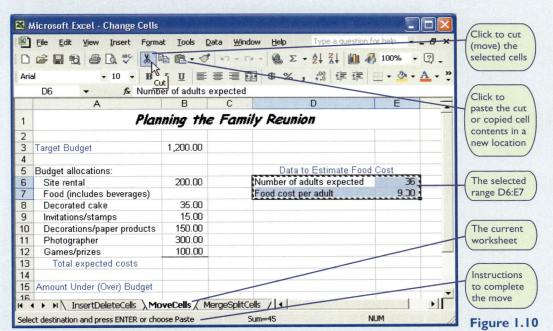

Figure 1.10

A copy of the selected cells' contents is placed in the Windows Clipboard. The *Clipboard* stores data that you want to copy or move to another location. A flashing dotted line appears around the selected cells.

4   **Click cell D8.**
The location where you want the cut cell contents to appear is selected. You do not have to select a range that is the same size as the range you are moving. Excel automatically fills in the data, starting with the cell you select.

5   **Click the Paste button on the Standard toolbar (refer to Figure 1.10), or choose the menu sequence Edit, Paste.**
The contents of selected cells disappear from the range D6:E7 and appear in cells D8 through E9, as shown in Figure 1.11. This move process (called cutting and pasting) is a common procedure in Windows applications.

continues ▶

To Move Cells (continued)

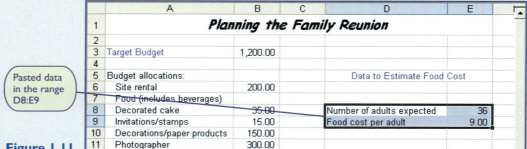

Pasted data in the range D8:E9

Figure 1.11

6 **Choose Edit, Undo Paste; press Esc to deselect the range.**
The effects of the move are reversed. Now use an alternative method to move the same cell contents.

7 **Select the range D6:E7, and then position the pointer on the bottom border of the selected cells.**
The pointer changes to a white arrow centered on smaller black arrows that point in four directions (see Figure 1.12). When this pointer is active, you can drag the selection up, down, left, or right.

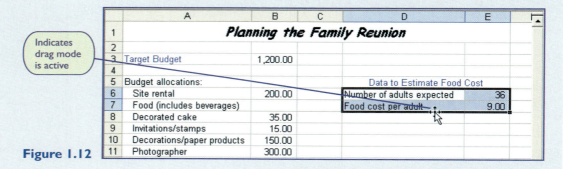

Indicates drag mode is active

Figure 1.12

8 **Hold down the left mouse button, and drag the pointer down two rows (see Figure 1.13)**

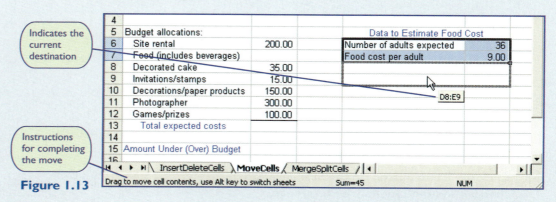

Indicates the current destination

Instructions for completing the move

Figure 1.13

9 **Release the mouse button.**

The contents of cells D6:E7 are moved to the range D8:E9. The results of a move by dragging are the same as those for the prior move that uses the cut-and-paste method (refer to Figure 1.11).

10 **Click any cell, such as cell A1, to deselect the highlighted range.**

11 **Click Save on the toolbar.**
Continue with the next skill, or close the workbook and exit Excel.

Alternate Way:

Shortcut Menus
You can use Excel's shortcut menus to perform many common tasks, including cutting, copying, and pasting. A *shortcut menu* is a menu that pops up in the worksheet area and displays common commands.

To open a shortcut menu, move the mouse pointer to the cell or area you want to affect, and right-click.

In Depth:

Copy and Paste
Executing a copy-and-paste operation differs from a cut-and-paste operation in only the second step of the four-step process. After selecting the cells to copy, click the Copy button on the Standard toolbar instead of the Cut button (or select the menu sequence Edit, Copy instead of Edit, Cut).

Paste Button Options
The Paste button drop-down list provides quick access to a variety of paste options. For example, you can select Transpose to paste a selected range across a row that was originally entered down a column. Onscreen Help provides detailed information about all paste options.

Merge and Split Cell Contents

You can use the Merge and Center toolbar button to center the contents of one cell across a specified range of cells. This feature is quite useful when you have a long label that extends beyond the limits of the cell in which it is entered.

The Merge and Center button is a toggle button. Click it once to center data across the specified range. Click it again to split the merged cells. In the following steps, you use the Merge and Center button to center a title in a family reunion worksheet. You also split previously merged cells, save your changes, and print the worksheet.

To Merge and Split Cells

1 **Open the *Change Cells* workbook, if necessary, and click the *MergeSplitCells* worksheet tab (the third of the three worksheets).**
The worksheet includes all labels and numbers for preparing a family reunion budget.

2 **Select the range A1:E1, and position the pointer on the Merge and Center button (see Figure 1.14).**

continues ▶

To Merge and Split Cells (continued)

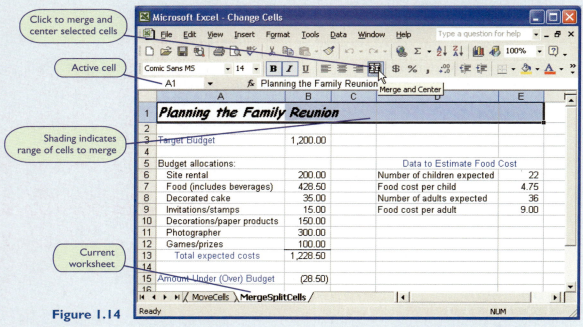

Click to merge and center selected cells

Active cell

Shading indicates range of cells to merge

Current worksheet

Figure 1.14

3 **Click the Merge and Center button (refer to Figure 1.14).**
The contents in cell A1 are centered across five cells (see Figure 1.15).

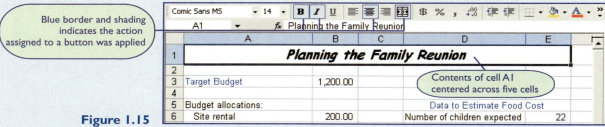

Blue border and shading indicates the action assigned to a button was applied

Contents of cell A1 centered across five cells

Figure 1.15

4 **Click cell D5.**
The contents in cell D5 are already centered across two cells (see Figure 1.16).

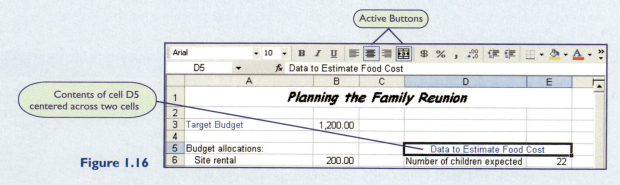

Active Buttons

Contents of cell D5 centered across two cells

Figure 1.16

5 **Click the Merge and Center button.**

The merged cells split; the phrase *Data to Estimate Food Cost* is left-aligned in cell D5.

6 **Click cell A1, and click Save in the toolbar.**
Excel saves your changes to the *MergeSplitCells* worksheet in the *Change Cells* workbook.

7 **Click Print in the toolbar (or omit this step if you do not want to print at this time).**
When you click the Print button, Excel immediately prints the current worksheet—or a portion of the current worksheet if a print area has been defined—using default print settings. In-depth coverage of printing is provided in *Core Skill 3.6, Modify Page Setup Options for Worksheets*, and *Core Skill 3.7, Preview and Print Worksheets and Workbooks*.

Continue with the next skill, or close the workbook and exit Excel.

For immediate reinforcement, work one or more of the following exercises:
Skill Drills 1, 2; Challenge 1.

Skill 1.2: Enter and Edit Cell Data Including Text, Numbers, and Formulas

The introductory section *About Excel 2002* illustrated the parts of the Excel workspace, and showed you how to move around a worksheet. Now it's time for you to enter data. Excel accepts two broad types of cell entries: constants and formulas. **Constants** can be text values (also called labels), numeric values (numbers), or date and time values. Constants do not change unless you edit them.

A **formula** produces a calculated result, usually based on a reference to one or more cells in the worksheet. The results of a formula change if you change the contents of a cell referenced in the formula.

In this skill area, you also alter the appearance of data. For example, you use the Increase Decimal and Decrease Decimal buttons in the Formatting toolbar to alter the number of decimal places a number displays. Four topics are included: enter and edit text and numbers, enter formulas and functions, apply number formats, and remove cell contents and formats.

Enter and Edit Text and Numbers

When you enter data into a cell, text aligns with the left side of the cell; and numbers, dates, and times automatically align with the right side of the cell. You can change the alignment of data at any time, as illustrated in *Skill 3.3, Modify Row and Column Formats*.

As you type, you may notice that sometimes Excel seems to anticipate what you will enter into a cell. For example, you may start typing text, and Excel automatically completes the word or phrase you have begun. This is a feature called **AutoComplete**, which compares text you are typing into a cell with text already entered in the same column. For example, if text in a cell begins with *Golf* and you start typing **G** into another cell in the same column, Excel assumes that you are entering `Golf` again. If Excel is correct, this saves you some typing. If not, just keep typing.

Let's begin by adding labels and numbers to a partially completed budget for a family reunion.

To Enter and Edit Text and Numbers

1 **Open the *MEC-S102* workbook, and save it as** Change Cell Contents.
A partially completed worksheet to plan a family reunion appears (see Figure 1.17).

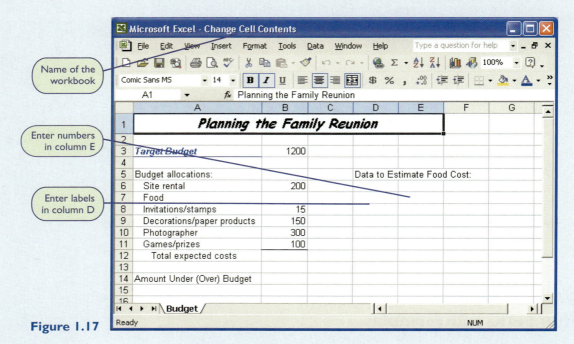

Name of the workbook

Enter numbers in column E

Enter labels in column D

Figure 1.17

2 **Click cell D6.**
A thick black border surrounds cell D6, indicating that it is the current cell.

3 **Type** Number of children **and press** ↵Enter.

 If you have problems...

If you make a mistake as you enter the text, you can make corrections the same way you do in a word-processing program. Just press Del or ←Backspace to delete the error; then continue typing. Use Del to erase text to the right of the cursor, and press ←Backspace to erase text to the left of the cursor.

If you discover a mistake after you move to another cell, click the mouse or use the arrow keys to select the cell that contains the mistake, double-click the cell to change to Edit mode, and then use ←Backspace or Del to correct the mistake. If you want to replace the entire contents of the cell, click the cell and then begin typing; the new data you enter replaces the cell's previous contents.

Excel enters the text you typed into cell D6, and cell D7 becomes the current cell (see Figure 1.18).

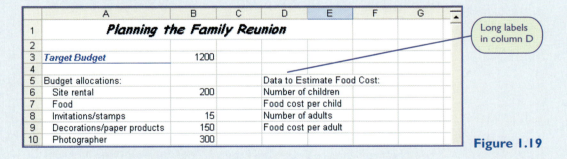

	A	B	C	D	E	F	G
1	*Planning the Family Reunion*						
2							
3	*Target Budget*	1200					
4							
5	Budget allocations:			Data to Estimate Food Cost:			
6	Site rental	200		Number of children			
7	Food						
8	Invitations/stamps	15					
9	Decorations/paper products	150					
10	Photographer	300					
11	Games/prizes	100					
12	Total expected costs						
13							

Figure 1.18

4 **Click cell D6, and look in the formula bar.**
The formula bar indicates that the entire worksheet title is stored in cell D6. Text that exceeds the width of its cell is sometimes referred to as a **long label**. Overflow text displays if the adjacent cells are blank.

5 **Click cell D7, type** Food cost per child, **and press** ↵Enter.
The new text appears left-aligned in cell D7, and cell D8 becomes the current cell.

6 **Enter the following text in the cells indicated**

Cell D8   Number of adults
Cell D9   Food cost per adult

7 **Check that your labels match those shown in Figure 1.19, and make corrections as necessary.**

	A	B	C	D	E	F	G
1	*Planning the Family Reunion*						
2							
3	*Target Budget*	1200					
4							
5	Budget allocations:			Data to Estimate Food Cost:			
6	Site rental	200		Number of children			
7	Food			Food cost per child			
8	Invitations/stamps	15		Number of adults			
9	Decorations/paper products	150		Food cost per adult			
10	Photographer	300					

Long labels in column D

Figure 1.19

8 **Click cell D6, and click in the formula bar.**
A flashing cursor displays at the end of the cell contents in the formula bar (see Figure 1.20).

continues ▶

To Enter and Edit Text and Numbers (continued)

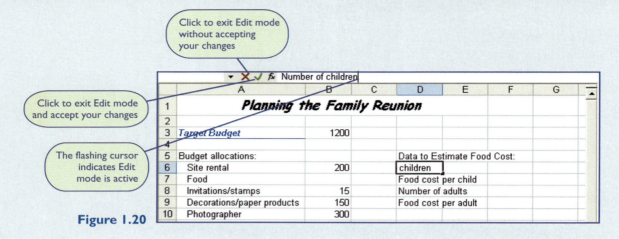

Click to exit Edit mode without accepting your changes

Click to exit Edit mode and accept your changes

The flashing cursor indicates Edit mode is active

Figure 1.20

9. **Press** Spacebar, **type** expected, **and press** ↵Enter.
   The revised label *Number of children expected* displays in cell D6.

10. **Double-click cell D8.**
    A flashing cursor displays within the cell contents in the cell (see Figure 1.21).

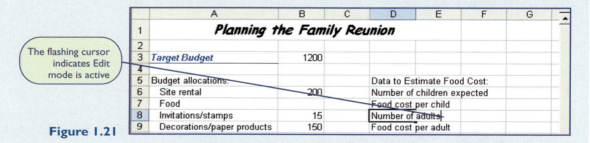

The flashing cursor indicates Edit mode is active

Figure 1.21

11. **Press** Spacebar, **type** expected, **and press** ↵Enter.
    The revised label *Number of adults expected* displays in cell D8.

12. **Click Save on the toolbar.**

The labels you entered in Column D extend into columns E and F. Before you enter the related numbers in column E, widen that column to hold its longest entry. Alternative ways to widen a column are illustrated in **Core Skill 3.3, Modify Row and Column Formats**.

To Widen a Column and Enter Numbers

1 **Position the mouse pointer between column letters D and E in the worksheet frame.**

The pointer changes to a bi-directional arrow (see Figure 1.22).

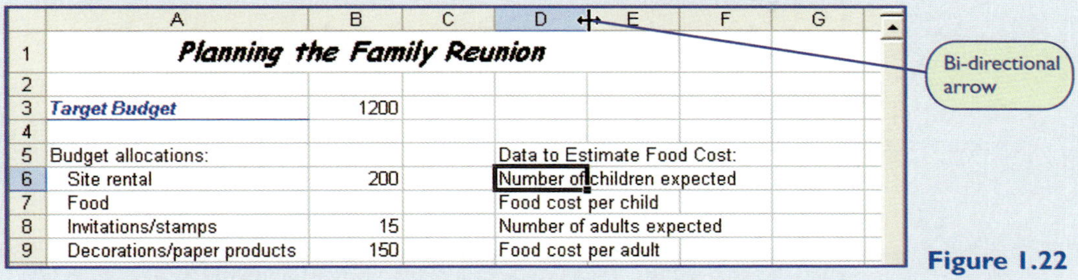

	A	B	C	D	E	F	G
1	*Planning the Family Reunion*						
2							
3	*Target Budget*	1200					
4							
5	Budget allocations:			Data to Estimate Food Cost:			
6	Site rental	200		Number of children expected			
7	Food			Food cost per child			
8	Invitations/stamps	15		Number of adults expected			
9	Decorations/paper products	150		Food cost per adult			

Bi-directional arrow

Figure 1.22

2 **Make sure that the bi-directional arrow displays between columns D and E in the worksheet frame, and double-click.**

Column D automatically widens to accommodate the longest label in the column (see Figure 1.23).

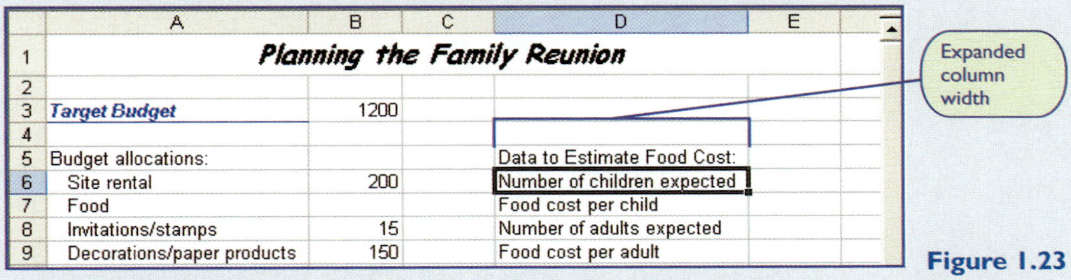

	A	B	C	D	E
1	*Planning the Family Reunion*				
2					
3	*Target Budget*	1200			
4					
5	Budget allocations:			Data to Estimate Food Cost:	
6	Site rental	200		Number of children expected	
7	Food			Food cost per child	
8	Invitations/stamps	15		Number of adults expected	
9	Decorations/paper products	150		Food cost per adult	

Expanded column width

Figure 1.23

 If you have problems...

You can use Excel's <u>U</u>ndo command on the <u>E</u>dit menu to reverse an action quickly. If you change the width of the wrong column, for example, you can use the <u>U</u>ndo command to restore the original column width.

3 **Click cell E6, type 22, and press ⏎Enter.**

4 **Enter the following numbers in the range E7:E9.**

Cell E7	4.75
Cell E8	36
Cell E9	9

5 **Check that your number entries match those shown in Figure 1.24, and make changes as necessary.**

continues ▶

To Widen a Column and Enter Numbers (continued)

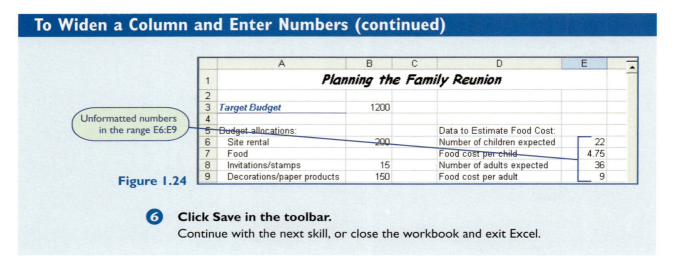

Unformatted numbers in the range E6:E9

Figure 1.24

6 **Click Save in the toolbar.**
Continue with the next skill, or close the workbook and exit Excel.

In Depth:
Using AutoFill

Using Excel's *AutoFill* feature, you can easily fill in a series of numbers, dates, or other items in a specified range.

If you want to create a sequence of consecutive entries, you can provide an example in one or two cells, select the cell(s) containing the example, and then drag the lower-right corner of the selection. The sequences can be text, numbers, or a combination of text and numbers, such as Qtr 1. For example, if you enter Jan in a cell and then use the fill handle to drag right or down eleven more cells, Excel automatically enters *Feb, Mar*... through *Dec* in the sequence of eleven cells. If you enter January in a cell as the example to start a sequence, Excel enters *February, March,*... through *December*.

You can fill data in columns as well as rows. To fill in ascending order, drag down or to the right. To fill in descending order, drag up or to the left.

If a fill sequence is to be a set of numbers incrementing by the same amount, provide a pattern in two adjacent cells, such as the number 10 in one cell and the number 20 in the next. If you select both cells and drag right or down, Excel fills the copy range with numbers incrementing by 10 (*10, 20, 30, 40,* and so on).

Using AutoFill to Enter Dates

If you fill a range of dates based on the contents of one cell, each additional date increments by one. For example, applying AutoFill to a cell containing *1/1/2003* produces the series of dates *1/1/2003, 1/2/2003, 1/3/2003,* and so forth. If you desire a different sequence, such as the last day of each month, provide a pattern in two cells. For example, if you enter 1/31/2003 in one cell and 2/28/2003 in the next cell, and then select and drag those cells, Excel continues the sequence with *3/31/2003, 4/30/2003,* and so forth.

Other AutoFill Options

If you specify a start value in one cell and then click and drag the fill handle with the right mouse button instead of the left, a shortcut menu displays with predefined increments including days, weekdays, months, and years if the start value is a date.

Excel also provides a Series dialog box that you can access by choosing Edit, Fill, Series. A variety of options that vary with the type of data set up as the start value are available.

Enter Formulas and Functions

The true power of a spreadsheet program resides in formulas. In Excel, starting an entry with an equal sign (=) identifies it as a formula rather than data to be entered in the cell.

Generally, a formula consists of arithmetic operators and references to cells. You can also include numeric values. *Arithmetic operators* include +, -, *, and / (to add, subtract, multiply, and divide, respectively). The order of the elements in a formula determines the final result of the calculation. Excel evaluates a formula from left to right, according to the order of operator precedence. For example, multiplication and division take place before addition and subtraction.

You can easily create a simple formula by typing an equation into a cell. You can also enter a cell or range of cells in a formula by clicking the cell or selecting the range of cells in the worksheet. This simplifies the process of creating a formula and also helps to ensure that you enter the correct cell addresses.

Excel provides an *AutoSum* feature that you can use to insert a formula to sum a range of cells automatically. The suggested formula is a SUM function; you can accept or edit Excel's suggestion for the range of cells to sum. A *function* is a predefined formula in Excel.

In this skill area, you complete the design of the family reunion worksheet by entering two formulas and one function. Additional opportunities to work with formulas are provided in *Core Skill 5.1, Create and Revise Formulas*. You work with a variety of functions in *Core Skill 5.2, Use Statistical, Date and Time, Financial, and Logical Functions in Formulas*.

To Enter a Formula

1 Open the *Change Cell Contents* workbook, if necessary, and click cell B7.

2 Type = (an equal sign), and click cell E6 (see Figure 1.25).

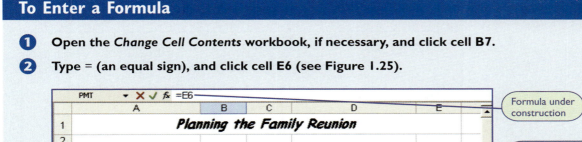

Formula under construction

Blue border around the selected cell

Blue cell reference

Figure 1.25

3 Type * (an asterisk), and click cell E7 (see Figure 1.26).

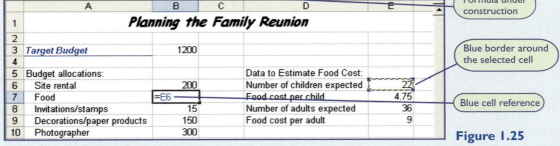

Formula under construction

Green cell reference

Green border around the second selected cell

Figure 1.26

continues ▶

To Enter a Formula (continued)

At this point, the formula computes the expected cost of food for children.

4 **Type + (a plus sign), and click cell E8.**

5 **Type * (an asterisk), and click cell E9.**

The completed formula adds the expected cost of food for adults to the expected cost of food for children (see Figure 1.27)

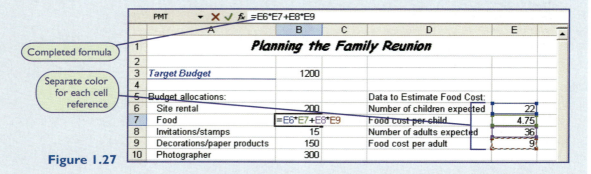

Completed formula

Separate color for each cell reference

Figure 1.27

6 **Press ⏎Enter, and click cell B7.**

The formula displays in the formula bar, and the results of the formula display in cell B7 (see Figure 1.28).

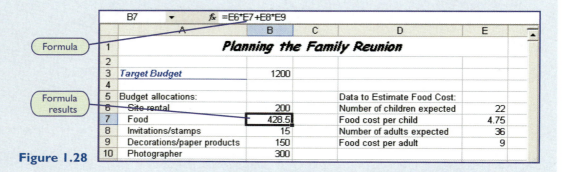

Formula

Formula results

Figure 1.28

7 **Click cell B12, and click the AutoSum button in the toolbar.**

AutoSum evaluates cells above and to the left of the current cell. Upon finding an adjacent set of consecutive cells containing values, AutoSum automatically displays the suggested range to sum (see Figure 1.29).

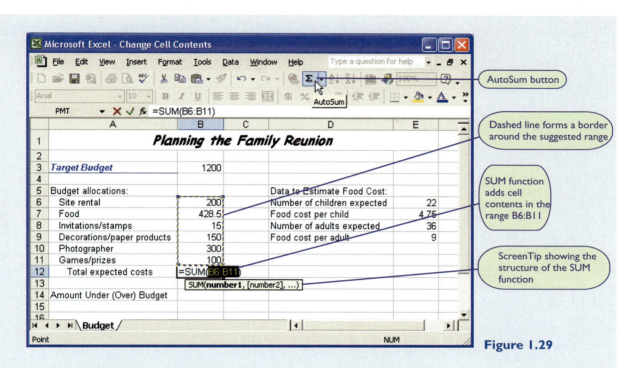

Figure 1.29

8 Press ⏎Enter **to accept the suggested function, and click cell B12.**

Excel enters the function *=SUM(B6:B11)* in cell B12, and displays *1193.5* as the calculated result (see Figure 1.30).

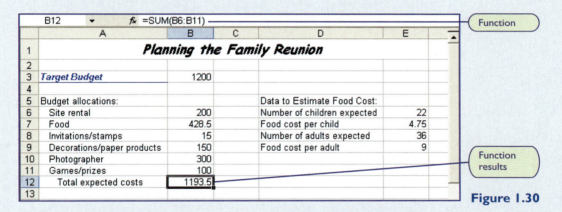

Figure 1.30

9 Click cell B14, type =B3-B12, **and press** ⏎Enter; **then click cell B14.**

The amount under budget displays in cell B14 (see Figure 1.31).

continues ▶

To Enter a Formula (continued)

B14	▼	f_x =B3-B12

	A	B	C	D	E
1		*Planning the Family Reunion*			
2					
3	*Target Budget*	1200			
4					
5	Budget allocations:			Data to Estimate Food Cost:	
6	Site rental	200		Number of children expected	22
7	Food	428.5		Food cost per child	4.75
8	Invitations/stamps	15		Number of adults expected	36
9	Decorations/paper products	150		Food cost per adult	9
10	Photographer	300			
11	Games/prizes	100			
12	Total expected costs	1193.5			
13					
14	Amount Under (Over) Budget	6.5			
15					

Formula

Formula results

Figure 1.31

⑩ Click Save on the toolbar.
Continue with the next skill, or close the workbook and exit Excel.

Apply Number Formats

When you enter a number or a formula into a cell, the entry may not appear as you hoped it would. You might type **5**, for example, but want it to look like *$5.00*. You could type the dollar sign, decimal point, and zeros; or you can have Excel automatically format the number for you. When you want to apply a standard format to a number, you format the cell in which the number is displayed.

In Excel, you can format numbers in many ways using the Number tab of the Format Cells dialog box. You usually format numbers as currency, percentages, or dates. Excel also provides toolbar buttons for three common number formats: Currency Style, Percent Style, and Comma Style.

If you want to apply a Comma or Percent style, two available methods—dialog box or toolbar button—produce the same result. However, the Currency format varies depending on whether you click the Currency Style button or use the dialog box to apply it. Excel names the toolbar button *Currency Style*, but clicking it applies the Accounting format. This disconnect has been in effect for multiple versions. You can see the difference if you work through Challenge 3 at the end of Core Skill Set 3.

In the following steps, you use the Currency Style and Comma Style buttons on the toolbar to format the display of values in the *Change Cell Contents* workbook. You also use a toolbar button to change the number of decimal places. In a subsequent set of steps, you enter a date and apply a date format.

To Format Numbers

❶ Open the *Change Cell Contents* workbook, if necessary, and click cell B3.
You want to format the first number in the column to display in a currency format.

❷ Click the Currency Style button on the Formatting toolbar (see Figure 1.32).

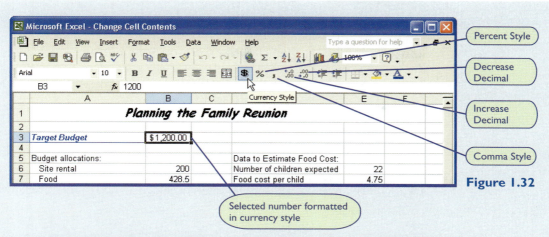

Figure 1.32

Selected number formatted in currency style

The contents of the selected cell display in the default currency format—a $ sign, a comma as the thousands separator, and two decimal places.

3 **With cell B3 still selected, click the Decrease Decimal button twice.**
Each time you click the Decrease Decimal button, Excel removes one decimal place. Clicking the button twice causes the amount in cell B3 to appear with zero decimal places (see Figure 1.33).

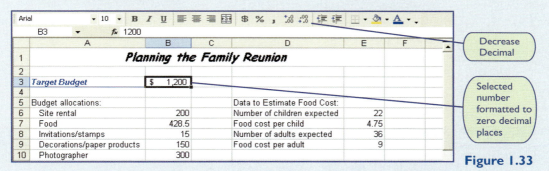

Decrease Decimal

Selected number formatted to zero decimal places

Figure 1.33

4 **Click cell B14, hold down the** Ctrl **key, click cell E7, click cell E9, and release the** Ctrl **key.**
Holding down the Ctrl key enables you to select nonadjacent cells.

5 **Click the Currency Style button.**
The three selected cells display in the default currency style (see Figure 1.34).

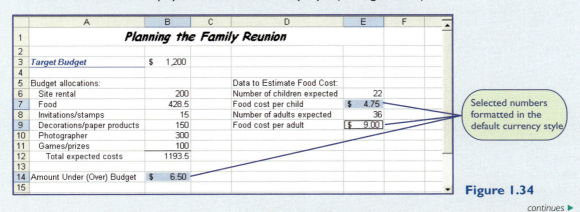

Selected numbers formatted in the default currency style

Figure 1.34

continues ▶

To Format Numbers (continued)

6 **Select cells B6:B12; then click the Comma Style button.**

The amounts for the budget allocations display with commas to indicate thousands and zero decimal places (see Figure 1.35).

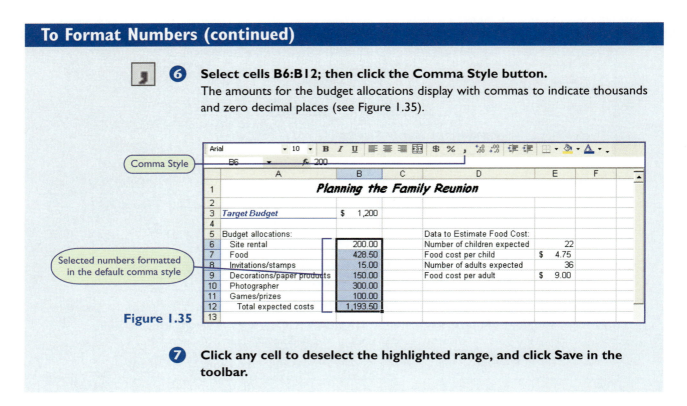

Comma Style

Selected numbers formatted in the default comma style

Figure 1.35

7 **Click any cell to deselect the highlighted range, and click Save in the toolbar.**

In the previous steps, you applied Currency and Comma formats to numbers and formula results. Now enter a date, and alter its display by applying a date format.

To Format a Date

1 **Click cell A16.**

You want to enter text that describes a date.

2 **Type** Date of last budget revision, **and press** ⏎Enter.

3 **Click cell B16, type** 5/15/2003, **and press** ⏎Enter.

The worksheet displays the date as you typed it (see Figure 1.36).

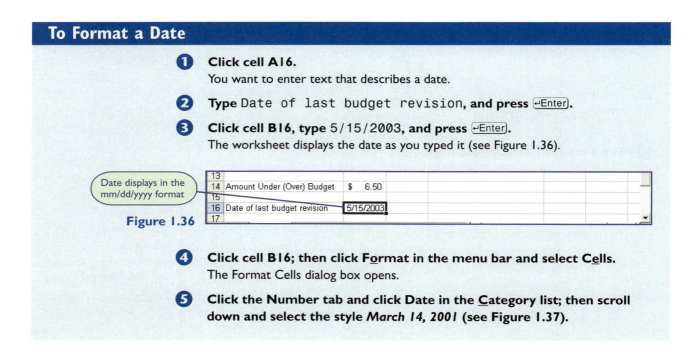

Date displays in the mm/dd/yyyy format

Figure 1.36

4 **Click cell B16; then click F̲ormat in the menu bar and select Ce̲lls.**

The Format Cells dialog box opens.

5 **Click the Number tab and click Date in the C̲ategory list; then scroll down and select the style *March 14, 2001* (see Figure 1.37).**

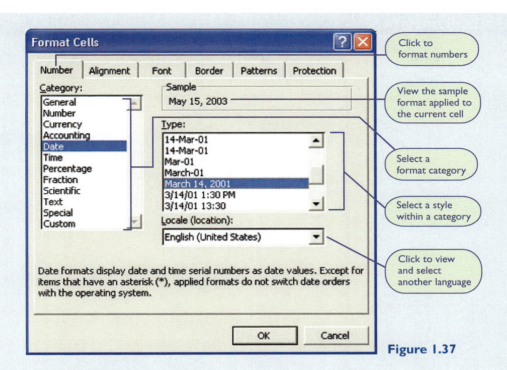

Figure 1.37

6 **Click the OK button near the lower-right corner of the Format Cells dialog box.**

The date displays in the selected format (see Figure 1.38).

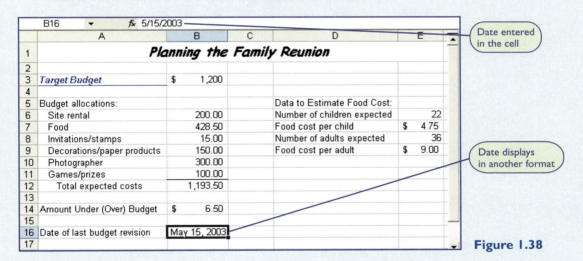

Figure 1.38

X *If you have problems…*

If ######## displays in the cell instead of the date, the column is too narrow to display the current cell's contents. Click cell B16, and then double-click in the worksheet frame between columns B and C.

7 **Repeat the process to display the Format Cells dialog box; then select the General category on the Number tab (see Figure 1.39).**

continues ▶

To Format a Date (continued)

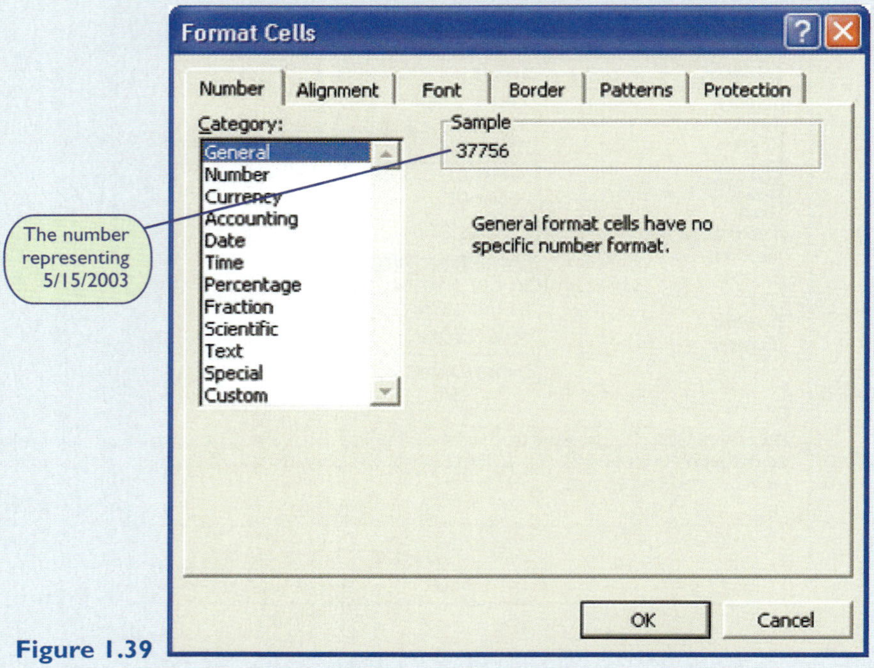

Format Cells [?] [X]

| Number | Alignment | Font | Border | Patterns | Protection |

Category:

General
Number
Currency
Accounting
Date
Time
Percentage
Fraction
Scientific
Text
Special
Custom

Sample
37756

General format cells have no specific number format.

[The number representing 5/15/2003]

OK   Cancel

Figure 1.39

The sample shows how the date in cell B16 displays if you apply a General format. Excel assigns the number 1 to January 1, 1900 and the number 2 to January 2, 1900. For each additional day, Excel increases the number by one. Therefore the 5/15/2003 date you entered is the 37,756th day since January 1, 1900.

8 **Click the OK button near the lower-right corner of the Format Cells dialog box.**

The date displays in the General format (see Figure 1.40).

[Date displays in the General format]

13			
14	Amount Under (Over) Budget	$	6.50
15			
16	Date of last budget revision		37756
17			

Figure 1.40

9 **Choose Edit, Undo Format Cells.**

Excel restores the previous date format; *May 15, 2003* displays in cell B16.

10 **Click Save in the toolbar.**

Continue with the next skill, or close the workbook and exit Excel.

Clear Contents and Formats

You can delete cell contents, but retain formats, by selecting the range of cells and pressing Del. You achieve the same results when you select the range and choose the menu sequence Edit, Clear, Contents.

To clear formats, but retain contents, select the range and choose the menu sequence Edit, Clear, Formats. You can also remove contents and formats using the menu sequence Edit, Clear, All.

In the following steps, you remove cell contents from one cell, undo the change, and then remove only formats from the same cell. After you save your changes, you print the worksheet.

To Clear Contents and Formats

1 **Open the *Change Cell Contents* workbook, if necessary, and click cell A3.**
The cell includes the label Target Budget. Formats applied to the cell include bold, italic, a blue font, and a blue bottom border.

2 **Press Del.**
The cell contents disappear, but the Bold and Italic buttons are still active (see Figure 1.41).

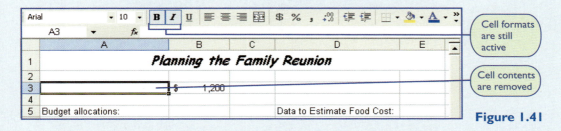

Cell formats are still active

Cell contents are removed

Figure 1.41

3 **Choose Edit, and position the pointer on the first option, Undo Clear (see Figure 1.42).**

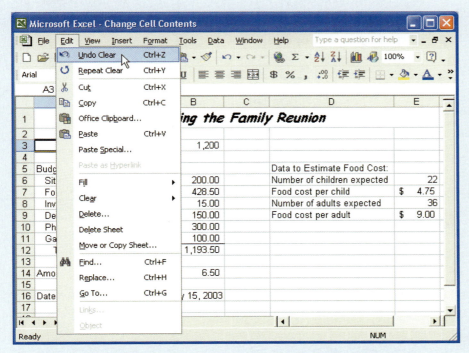

Figure 1.42

4 **Click the Undo Clear option.**
The label *Target Budget* reappears in cell A3.

5 **Choose Edit, position the pointer on Clear, and point to Formats (see Figure 1.43).**

continues ▶

To Clear Contents and Formats (continued)

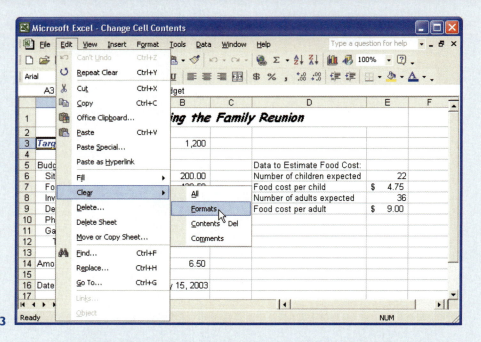

Figure 1.43

Four options are available on the Clear menu. Select <u>A</u>ll to clear contents and formats. Use the next two options to clear only formats or only contents. You learn about comments in *Core Skill 7.3, View and Edit Comments.*

6   **Click the <u>F</u>ormats option.**
The contents of cell A3 do not change, but formatting disappears (see Figure 1.44).

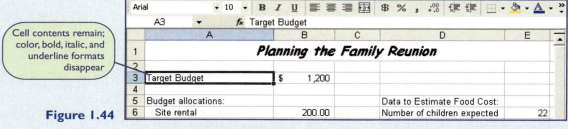

Cell contents remain; color, bold, italic, and underline formats disappear

Figure 1.44

7   **Click Save in the toolbar, and close the workbook.**
Continue with the next skill, or exit Excel.

For immediate reinforcement, work one or more of the following exercises:
Skill Drills 3, 4, 5, 6; Challenges 2, 3, 4, 5, 6.

Skill 1.3: **Check Spelling**

Microsoft Excel includes an *AutoCorrect* feature that can correct common errors as you type, such as changing *adn* to *and*. The program also includes a *spelling checker* that highlights words that are not in its dictionary. You have the option to change or ignore any highlighted word. If a highlighted word, such as a person's name or a technical term, is spelled correctly and you use the word frequently, you can add it to a custom dictionary file.

The spelling checker doesn't catch all errors. You should still read text entries carefully to see if words are missing or used incorrectly, such as using *affect* when you mean *effect*.

In the following steps, you check the spelling in a financial report.

To Check Spelling in a Worksheet

❶ Open the *MEC-S103* workbook, and save it as `Spell and Replace`.
The workbook includes three worksheets named SpellCheck, ReplaceText, and ReplaceFormats.

❷ Make sure that SpellCheck is the current worksheet, and position the pointer on the Spelling button (see Figure 1.45).

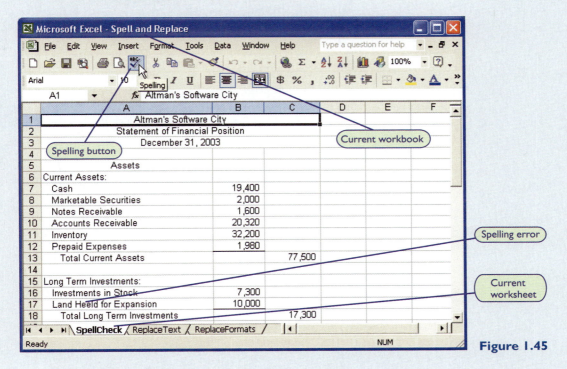

Figure 1.45

❸ Click Spelling on the toolbar (refer to Figure 1.45).
The Spelling dialog box opens; the first possible error displays in the Not in Dic-tionary box (see Figure 1.46).

continues ▶

To Check Spelling in a Worksheet (continued)

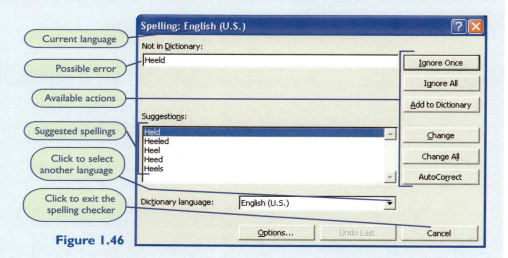

Figure 1.46

④ **Make sure that *Held* is selected in the list of suggestions, and click the Change button (refer to Figure 1.46).**
Excel changes *Heeld* to *Held* in cell A17. The next possible error *PP&E* displays in the Spelling dialog box (see Figure 1.47).

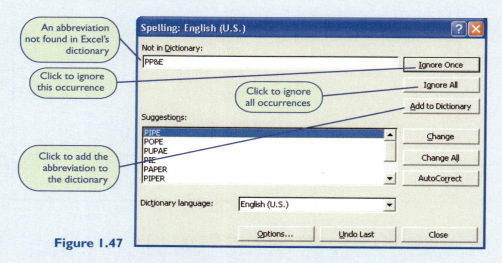

Figure 1.47

The abbreviation *PP&E* stands for Property, Plant, and Equipment—a common abbreviation in business reports. You can ignore one occurrence or all occurrences of a word not found in the dictionary, or add the word to the dictionary. Because this is a practice file, do not add the abbreviation to the dictionary.

⑤ **Click the Ignore All button in the Spelling dialog box (refer to figure 1.47).**
The next error displays. The word *Aditional* in cell A46 is not spelled correctly.

⑥ **Click the Change button in the Spelling dialog box.**
Excel changes *Aditional* to *Additional* in cell A46. A message displays that the spelling check is complete for the entire sheet (see Figure 1.48).

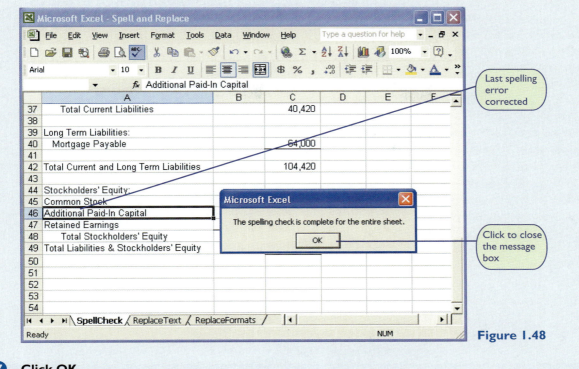

Figure 1.48

7 **Click OK.**

The message box closes.

8 **Click Save on the toolbar.**

Continue with the next skill, or close the workbook and exit Excel.

Alternate Way:

You used the Spelling button in the Standard toolbar to activate Excel's spell check feature. The same results can be achieved by pressing F7 or choosing Tools, Spelling.

In Depth:

Tips on Using the Spelling Checker

A check of spelling begins at the current worksheet cell and continues to the end of the worksheet. If you do not start the spelling checker at the beginning of the worksheet, Excel asks if you want to continue checking from the beginning. Choose *Yes* to continue a check of the entire worksheet, or choose *No* to close the spelling checker.

You can select a different language for the spell check by clicking the Options button at the bottom of the Spelling dialog box. For example, you can specify one of four English languages (Australia, Canada, U.K., and U.S) or one of two French languages (Canada and France).

You can also specify other settings by clicking the Options button. For example, you can turn off default settings to ignore words with numbers and ignore Internet and file addresses.

For immediate reinforcement, work Skill Drill 7.

Skill 1.4: **Find and Replace Cell Data and Formats**

Excel provides a variety of ways to manipulate both the content and appearance of text. Find and Replace are two options on the Edit menu that can substantially reduce editing time on large worksheets. Using the Find feature, you can search for the next occurrence of the word, number, phrase, or format you specify. Using the Replace feature, you can look for each occurrence of the word, number, phrase, or format you specify and replace each occurrence or all occurrences.

Find and Replace Cell Contents

Selecting Find or Replace from the Edit drop-down menu opens the Find and Replace dialog box. The dialog box includes two tabs: Find and Replace.

The Find tab displays a *Find what* text box in which you enter the word, number, phrase, or format you want to find. You then choose Find Next or Find All. Click the Find Next button repeatedly to jump from one occurrence to the next in the worksheet. If you click the Find All button, Excel displays a list of all the items that meet your specified criteria.

The Replace tab displays two text boxes: *Find what* and *Replace with*. After you enter your specifications in those boxes, you usually choose Replace All or Replace.

In the following steps, you use Excel's Replace feature to change all occurrences of an abbreviation to the full spelling.

To Find and Replace Cell Contents

1. **Open the *Spell and Replace* workbook, if necessary, and select the ReplaceText worksheet.**
   The ReplaceText worksheet is the second of three worksheets in the workbook. Cell A18 in that worksheet includes the abbreviation LT (see Figure 1.49).

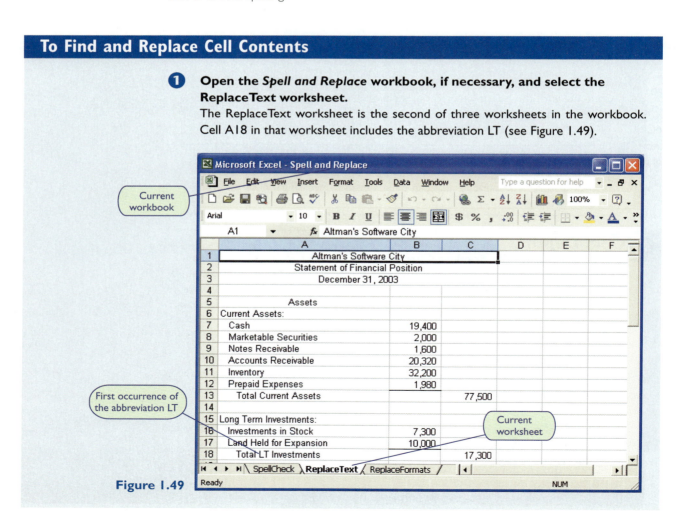

Figure 1.49

2 **Scroll down to view other occurrences of the abbreviation LT in cells A39 and A42.**

You want to replace all occurrences of the abbreviation LT with the phrase *Long Term*.

3 **Click cell A1; then choose Edit, Replace.**

The Find and Replace dialog box opens. The Replace tab is active.

 If you have problems...
You may not see Replace in the initial short list of the most recently used Edit menu choices. After a momentary delay, all Edit menu choices display. You can also click the double v symbol at the bottom of the short menu to immediately display the long menu.

4 **Enter LT in the *Find what* text box, and enter Long Term in the *Replace with* text box (see Figure 1.50).**

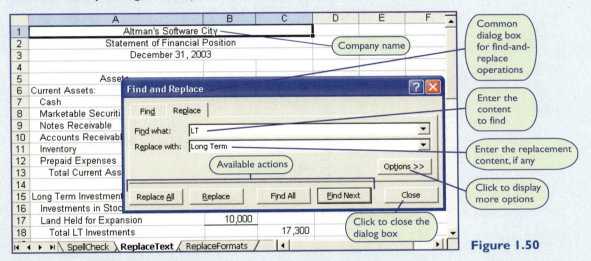

Figure 1.50

 If you have problems...
Depending on the most recent find or replace operation, your Find and Replace dialog box may include additional settings above the buttons at the bottom of the box, including Match case and Match entire cell contents. To duplicate the display in Figure 1.50, click the Options button to hide the extra options.

5 **Click the Replace All button in the lower-left corner of the dialog box (refer to Figure 1.50).**

Excel replaces all occurrences of the letters *LT* with the phrase *Long Term*. A message indicates that four replacements were made.

6 **Click OK to close the message box; close the Find and Replace dialog box, and view the results.**

The results include an unintended replacement in cell A1. Because the find condition was not case-sensitive, Excel replaced the lowercase lt in the company name (see Figure 1.51).

continues ▶

To Find and Replace Cell Contents (continued)

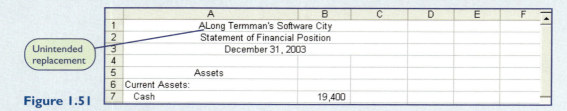

Unintended replacement

	A	B	C	D	E	F
1	ALong Termman's Software City					
2	Statement of Financial Position					
3	December 31, 2003					
4						
5	Assets					
6	Current Assets:					
7	Cash	19,400				

Figure 1.51

7 **Choose Edit, Undo Replace.**
Excels reverses the effects of the previous replace operation.

8 **Choose Edit, Replace; click the Options button near the lower-right corner of the Find and Replace dialog box.**
The dialog box expands. You can set search parameters using three drop-down lists and two check boxes.

9 **Click the Match case check box (see Figure 1.52).**

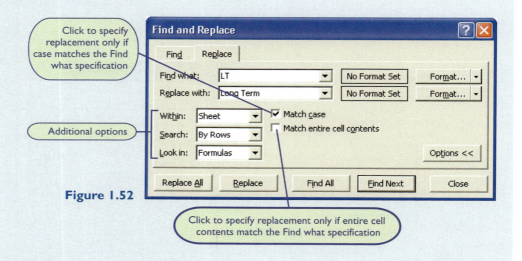

Click to specify replacement only if case matches the Find what specification

Additional options

Click to specify replacement only if entire cell contents match the Find what specification

Figure 1.52

You specified that Excel should find and replace the two-letter combination LT only if the letters are uppercase.

10 **Click Replace All.**
Excel replaces all occurrences of the uppercase letters *LT* with the phrase *Long Term*. A message indicates that three replacements were made.

11 **Click OK to close the message box; close the Find and Replace dialog box, and view the results.**
The phrase *Long Term* replaces *LT* in cells A18, A39, and A42.

12 **Save your changes to the Spell and Replace workbook.**
Continue with the next skill, or close the workbook and exit Excel.

Find and Replace Cell Formats

You can use Excel's Find and Replace feature to locate and change cell formats as well as cell contents. Click the Options button in the Find and Replace dialog box to display Format buttons and associated Preview text boxes to the right of the Find what and Replace with text boxes. Use the drop-down list for each Format button to specify the Find what and Replace with formatting.

In the following steps, you replace all occurrences of an italic format with a blue and bold format.

To Find and Replace Cell Formats

1 **Open the *Spell and Replace* workbook, if necessary, and select the ReplaceFormats worksheet.**
The ReplaceFormats worksheet is the third of three worksheets in the workbook.

2 **Scroll down to view the italic format applied to seven cells: A6, A15, A20, A26, A31, A39, and A44.**
You want to replace all occurrences of the italic format with blue and bold formats.

3 **Click cell A1; then choose Edit, Replace.**
The Find and Replace dialog box opens. The Replace tab is active.

4 **If Format buttons do not display to the right of the Find what and Replace with boxes, click the Options button.**

5 **Delete existing Find what and Replace with specifications (see Figure 1.53).**

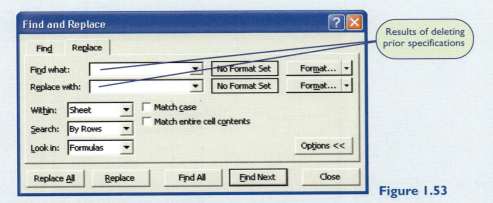

Figure 1.53

6 **Click the top Format button of two Format buttons in the upper-right corner of the Find and Replace dialog box.**
The Find Format dialog box opens.

7 **Select the Font tab, and click *Italic* in the Font style list (see Figure 1.54).**

continues ▶

To Find and Replace Cell Formats (continued)

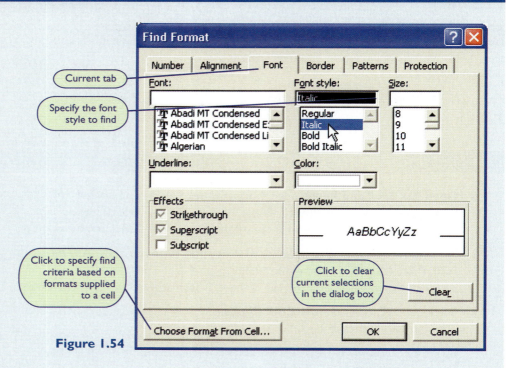

Current tab

Specify the font style to find

Click to specify find criteria based on formats supplied to a cell

Click to clear current selections in the dialog box

Figure 1.54

8 **Click OK.**
Excel displays a sample of the Find what criteria—the italic font style (see Figure 1.55).

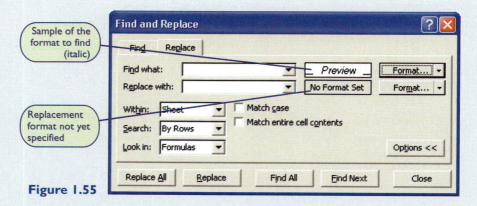

Sample of the format to find (italic)

Replacement format not yet specified

Figure 1.55

9 **Click the lower of the two Format buttons in the upper-right corner of the Find and Replace dialog box.**
The Replace Format dialog box opens.

10 **Select Bold from the Font style drop-down list, and select Blue from the Color drop-down list (see Figure 1.56).**

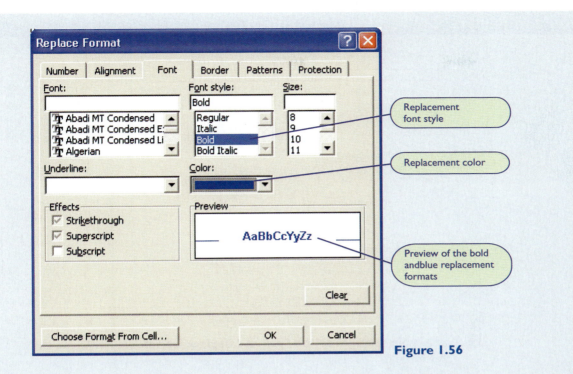

Figure 1.56

11 **Click OK.**

Excel displays a sample of the R̲eplace with criteria—bold and blue (see Figure 1.57).

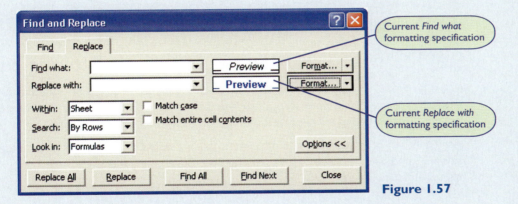

Figure 1.57

12 **Click the Replace A̲ll button in the Find and Replace dialog box.**

Excel replaces all occurrences of the italic formatting with bold and blue formatting. A message indicates that seven replacements were made.

13 **Click OK to close the message box; close the Find and Replace dialog box, and view the results (see Figure 1.58).**

continues ▶

To Find and Replace Cell Formats (continued)

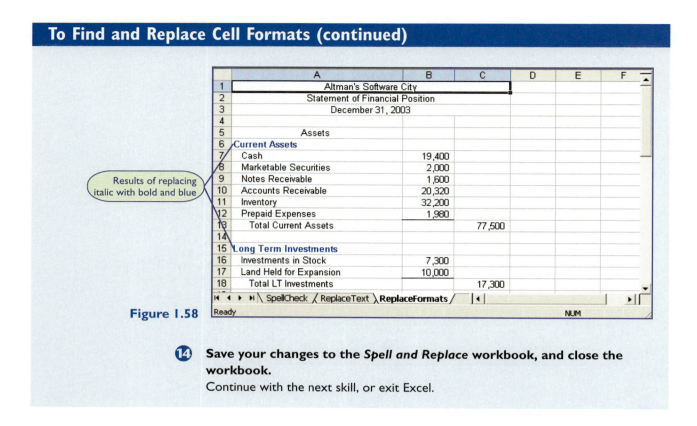

	A	B	C	D	E	F
1	Altman's Software City					
2	Statement of Financial Position					
3	December 31, 2003					
4						
5	Assets					
6	**Current Assets**					
7	Cash	19,400				
8	Marketable Securities	2,000				
9	Notes Receivable	1,600				
10	Accounts Receivable	20,320				
11	Inventory	32,200				
12	Prepaid Expenses	1,980				
13	Total Current Assets		77,500			
14						
15	**Long Term Investments**					
16	Investments in Stock	7,300				
17	Land Held for Expansion	10,000				
18	Total LT Investments		17,300			

Results of replacing italic with bold and blue

SpellCheck / ReplaceText \ **ReplaceFormats** /

Ready   NUM

Figure 1.58

14 **Save your changes to the *Spell and Replace* workbook, and close the workbook.**
Continue with the next skill, or exit Excel.

For immediate reinforcement, work Skill Drills 8 and 9.

Skill 1.5: **Work with a Subset of Data by Filtering Lists**

In general terms, you can think of a *database* as an organized collection of related data. Many database programs use a table to organize the data contained in a database file. In Excel, this concept is referred to as a *list*, which is simply a worksheet of columns and rows.

Each collection of related data in a database is called a *record*. Each record in a database contains the same parts, or *fields*. The Residential Real Estate Listings database is the list you use in this skill area (see Figure 1.59).

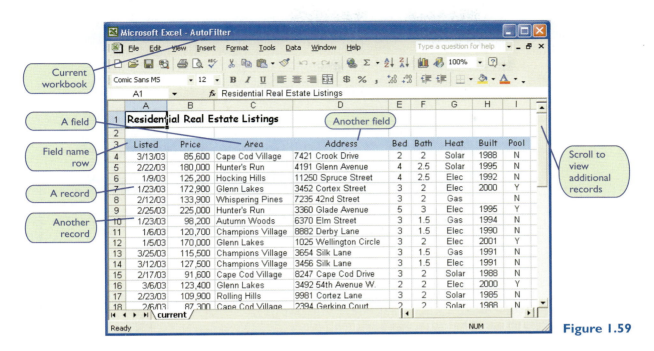

Figure 1.59

The first record in the Residential Real Estate Listings database relates to property at *7421 Crook Drive* in *Cape Cod Village* (row 4), and the second record relates to property at *4191 Glenn Avenue* in *Hunter's Run* (row 5).

The first four fields in the Residential Real Estate Listings database are the date listed (column A), the asking price (column B), the area (column C), and the address (column D).

Users of large databases with hundreds or thousands of records generally do not want to view all of the records. It's more likely that their information needs focus primarily on finding records that meet one or more conditions.

Filtering data enables you to work with a more manageable set of records. To *filter* a list means to hide all the rows except those that meet specified criteria. This is a temporary view of your list. Canceling the filter operation redisplays all the records.

Excel provides two filtering commands: AutoFilter and Advanced Filter. You can use *AutoFilter* to limit the display based on simple search conditions. *Advanced Filter* enables you to specify more complex criteria and to copy filtered records to another location.

In this skill area you use AutoFilter to set filters for exact matches. You also use the Top 10 and Blanks/NonBlanks options on the AutoFilter menu. You learn to execute more complex filters in *Expert Skill 7.2, Define and Apply Filters*.

Filter on Exact Matches

The Residential Real Estate Listings database is small and simple for practical reasons—so that you can see the results of your work while you learn Excel. In this section, you use AutoFilter to display only those records that exactly match stated criteria.

To Filter for an Exact Match

1 **Open the *MEC-0104* workbook, and save it as** AutoFilter.
The workbook contains a single worksheet that lists homes for sale (refer to Figure 1.59).

2 **Click any cell in the list range A3:I38, such as cell A4.**

3 **Choose** **D**ata **in the menu bar, and point to** **F**ilter **(see Figure 1.60).**

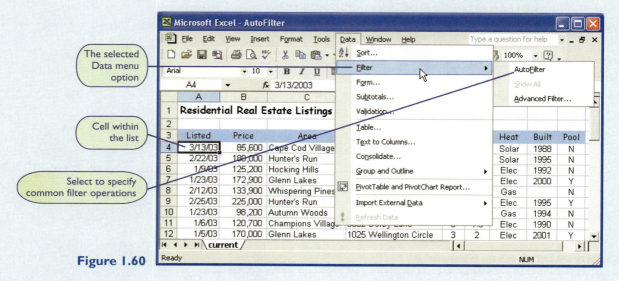

Figure 1.60

4 **Click Auto**F**ilter.**
Filter arrows appear next to each of the field names in the list (see Figure 1.61). A black filter arrow indicates that AutoFilter is active, but no filter is established.

Figure 1.61

5 **Click the filter arrow for the Area field located in cell C3.**
A drop-down list of filtering criteria appears (see Figure 1.62).

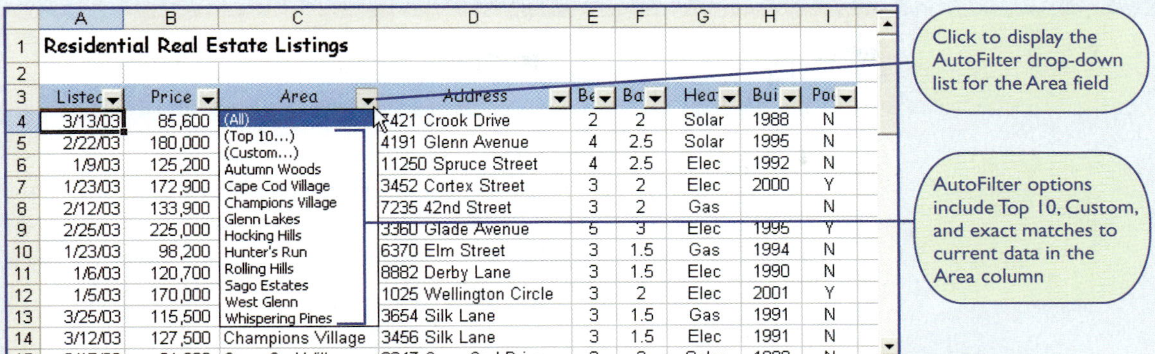

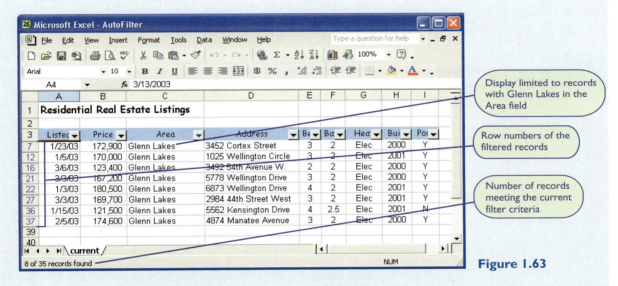

Figure 1.62

> Click to display the AutoFilter drop-down list for the Area field

> AutoFilter options include Top 10, Custom, and exact matches to current data in the Area column

6 **Click *Glenn Lakes* in the AutoFilter options list.**

Excel temporarily hides all but the eight records containing *Glenn Lakes* in the Area field (see Figure 1.63). The filter arrow next to Area is blue instead of black, indicating that there is an active filter on the field.

Figure 1.63

> Display limited to records with Glenn Lakes in the Area field

> Row numbers of the filtered records

> Number of records meeting the current filter criteria

7 **Click the filter arrow for the Bed field located in cell E3.**

The drop-down list for the Bed field opens.

8 **Click 4 in the AutoFilter options list.**

There are now one-condition filters attached to two fields. Fewer records appear because the display is limited to records that match both conditions: Glenn Lakes area and four bedrooms (see Figure 1.64).

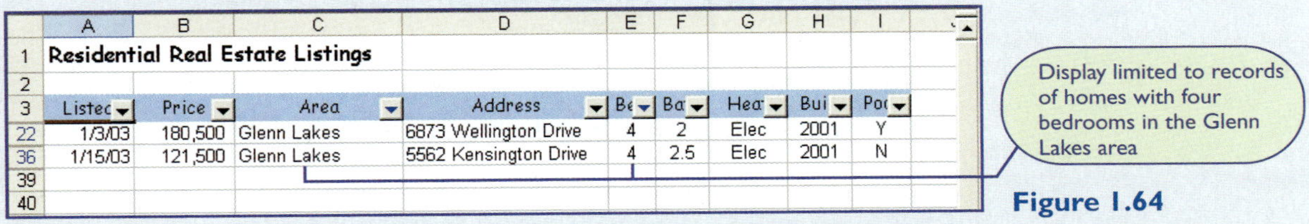

Figure 1.64

> Display limited to records of homes with four bedrooms in the Glenn Lakes area

continues ▶

To Filter for an Exact Match (continued)

⑨ Choose Data, point to Filter, and click Show All.
The two filters are removed, and all records display. AutoFilter remains active.

⑩ Choose Data, point to Filter, and click AutoFilter.
The arrow at the end of each field name disappears, which indicates that AutoFilter is no longer active. You can close the *AutoFilter* workbook now, or leave it open and continue to the next topic. It is not necessary to save the workbook because no changes have been made.

Filter for Top and Bottom Records

AutoFilter includes a Top 10 option that you can use to set a filter on fields containing numeric data. The name is somewhat misleading, because you can filter based on the bottom (lowest) amounts in a field or the top (highest) amounts.

After you select Top or Bottom, you specify a number and choose between Items or Percent. For example, you can set a filter as the Top 25 percent or the 10 lowest items.

In the following steps, you use this feature to filter records in the Residential Real Estate Listings database.

To Filter for Top and Bottom Records

① Open the *AutoFilter* workbook, if necessary.
The workbook contains a single worksheet that lists homes for sale (refer to Figure 1.59).

② Click any cell in the list range A3:I38, such as cell A4.

③ Choose Data, point to Filter, and click AutoFilter.
Filter arrows appear next to each of the field names in the list.

④ Click the filter arrow for the Price field located in cell B3.
A drop-down list of filtering criteria opens.

⑤ Click *Top 10* in the AutoFilter options list, and click the down arrow to the right of Top (see Figure 1.65).

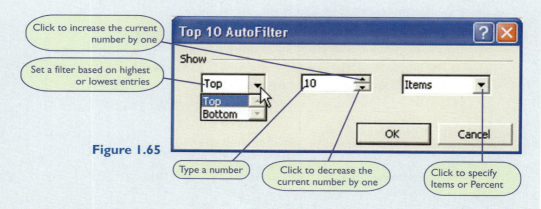

Figure 1.65

⑥ Select Bottom.

7 **Change the number in the middle box to** 5 **(see Figure 1.66).**

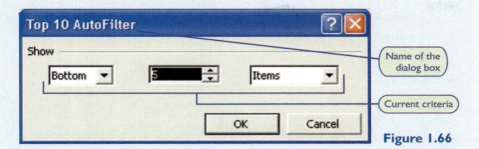

Figure 1.66

8 **Click OK.**
Excel executes the filter; the five records with the lowest values in the Price field display (see Figure 1.67).

Figure 1.67

9 **Click the filter arrow for the Price field, and select All.**
A filter is no longer set on the contents of the Price field. Excel restores display of all records.

10 **Click the filter arrow for the Listed field; then click *Top 10* in the AutoFilter options list for that field.**
Three boxes display in the Show area of the Top 10 AutoFilter dialog box.

11 **Select *Top* in the first box, enter 25 in the second box, and select *Percent* in the third box (see Figure 1.68).**

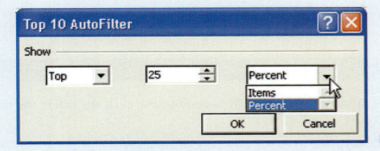

Figure 1.68

12 **Click OK.**
Excel executes the filter. Nine of 35 records display. These records contained the highest values in the Listed field (see Figure 1.69).

continues ▶

To Filter for Top and Bottom Records (continued)

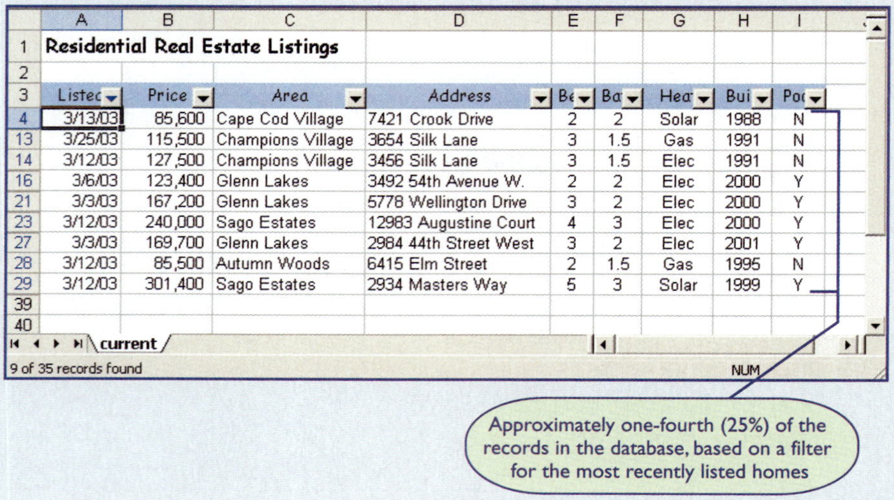

	A	B	C	D	E	F	G	H	I	
1	Residential Real Estate Listings									
2										
3	Listed	Price	Area	Address	Be	Ba	Hea	Bui	Po	
4	3/13/03	85,600	Cape Cod Village	7421 Crook Drive	2	2	Solar	1988	N	
13	3/25/03	115,500	Champions Village	3654 Silk Lane	3	1.5	Gas	1991	N	
14	3/12/03	127,500	Champions Village	3456 Silk Lane	3	1.5	Elec	1991	N	
16	3/6/03	123,400	Glenn Lakes	3492 54th Avenue W.	2	2	Elec	2000	Y	
21	3/3/03	167,200	Glenn Lakes	5778 Wellington Drive	3	2	Elec	2000	Y	
23	3/12/03	240,000	Sago Estates	12983 Augustine Court	4	3	Elec	2000	Y	
27	3/3/03	169,700	Glenn Lakes	2984 44th Street West	3	2	Elec	2001	Y	
28	3/12/03	85,500	Autumn Woods	6415 Elm Street	2	1.5	Gas	1995	N	
29	3/12/03	301,400	Sago Estates	2934 Masters Way	5	3	Solar	1999	Y	
39										
40										

current

9 of 35 records found   NUM

Figure 1.69

> Approximately one-fourth (25%) of the records in the database, based on a filter for the most recently listed homes

⑬ Choose Data, point to Filter, and click Show All.

The filter is removed, and all records display. AutoFilter remains active.

⑭ Choose Data, point to Filter, and click AutoFilter.

The arrow at the end of each field name disappears, which indicates that AutoFilter is no longer active. You can close the *AutoFilter* workbook now, or leave it open and continue to the next topic. It is not necessary to save the workbook because no changes have been made.

Filter for Blanks and NonBlanks

If AutoFilter is active, and you click the filter arrow for a field in which one or more of the cells are blank, you see two new options: Blanks, and NonBlanks. Select *Blanks* to limit display of records to those that do not contain an entry in that field. Select *NonBlanks* to limit display of records to those that do contain an entry in that field.

In the following steps, you set a filter to display records of homes for sale that do not show the year constructed.

To Filter for Blanks

① Open the *AutoFilter* workbook, if necessary, and click any cell in the list range A3:I38.

② Choose Data, point to Filter, and click AutoFilter.

③ Click the filter arrow for the Built field located in cell H3 (see Figure 1.70).

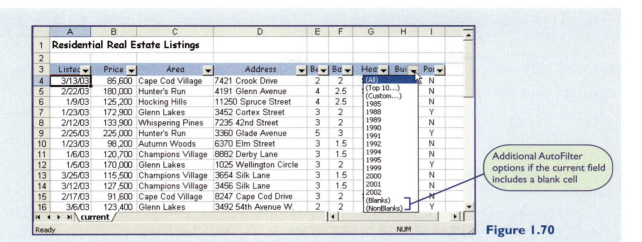

Additional AutoFilter options if the current field includes a blank cell

Figure 1.70

④ **Click *Blanks* in the AutoFilter options list.**
Excel executes the filter; the three records with no entry in the Built field display (see Figure 1.71).

Results of filtering for blank cells in the Built field

Figure 1.71

⑤ **Choose <u>D</u>ata, point to <u>F</u>ilter, and click Auto<u>F</u>ilter.**
The arrow at the end of each field name disappears, which indicates that AutoFilter is no longer active.

⑥ **Close the AutoFilter workbook.**
It is not necessary to save the workbook because no changes have been made. This concludes the initial Excel Core skill set. Continue with Skill Drill and Challenge exercises, start another skill set, or exit Excel.

For immediate reinforcement, work one or more of the following exercises:
Skill Drills 10, 11, 12.

Summary

You had opportunities to acquire quite a variety of skills in this *Working with Cells and Cell Data* skill set. You began by manipulating cells and cell contents—inserting and deleting cells, moving cell contents, merging cells, and splitting merged cells. You spent substantial time entering and editing text, numbers, and formulas, followed by a check of spelling. In the process you learned to widen columns, apply number formats, and remove cell contents and/or formats. Using Excel's Find and Replace features enhanced your ability to edit a worksheet. To complete your experiences, you learned to view subsets of the data in cells through simple filters.

Skill Drill

Skill Drill exercises *reinforce* skills. Each skill reinforced is the same, or nearly the same, as a skill presented in the skill set. Detailed instructions are provided in a step-by-step format.

Before beginning your Excel Core Skill Set I Skill Drill exercises, complete the following steps:

1. Open the file named *MEC-S105*, and immediately save it as **MEC-S1drill**.

   The workbook contains thirteen sheets: an overview and twelve exercise sheets labeled SD1 through SD12.

2. Click the Overview sheet to view the organization and content of the Skill Drill workbook for Excel Core Skill Set I.

Each exercise is independent of the others, so you may complete the exercises in any order. Be sure to save the workbook after completing each exercise. If you need a paper copy of one or more completed exercises, enter your name, centered in a header, before printing. Except for worksheets SD7 and SD9—which are large worksheets—print options have already been set to print compressed to one page and to display the filename, sheet name, and current date in a footer.

Be sure to save your changes and close the workbook if you need more than one work session to complete the desired exercises. Continue working on *MEC-S1drill* instead of starting over in the original *MEC-S105* file.

1. Move and Merge Cell Contents

You decide to change the original location of a title and subtitle on a worksheet that summarizes volunteer hours. You also want to merge and center those titles.

To move cell contents and merge cells, follow these steps:

1. If necessary, open the *MEC-S1drill* workbook; then click the SD1 sheet tab.

   The organization name *Community Volunteer Corps* displays in the range E1:G1.

2. Select the range E1:E2.

   This selects the worksheet's title and subtitle. These titles display across several columns, but are stored in the two cells in column E.

3. Click the Cut button in the toolbar (or choose <u>E</u>dit, Cu<u>t</u>).

4. Click cell A3 to select the first cell in the destination range.

5. Click the Paste button in the toolbar (or choose <u>E</u>dit, <u>P</u>aste).

6. Select the range A3:F3.

7. Click the Merge and Center button in the toolbar.

   Excel centers the title Community Volunteer Corps across columns A through F.

8. Select the range A4:F4, and click the Merge and Center button.

9. Save your changes to the *MEC-S1drill* workbook.

2. Delete Cells

You maintain a worksheet that provides a 5-year trend analysis of sales. Before you enter 2003 data, you want to remove 1998 data. Deleting the column containing 1998 data would also remove labels that are needed in the worksheet. You decide to delete the cells containing 1998 data in a way that shifts data for remaining years to the left.

To delete cells, follow these steps:

1. If necessary, open the *MEC-S1drill* workbook; then click the SD2 sheet tab.

   The organization name *Flowers Your Way* displays in cell A3.

2. Select the range B9:B25.

   This selects the 1998 column heading and data.

3. Choose Edit, Delete.

   The Delete dialog box opens, and *Shift cells left* is the selected option.

4. Click OK in the Delete dialog box.

   Excel deletes cells in the selected range. Text to the right of the deleted range shifts left.

5. Click any cell to deselect the highlighted range B9:B25.

6. Save your changes to the *MEC-S1drill* workbook.

3. Enter Text and Widen a Column

You are compiling a list of selected state names and postal codes. You already entered a worksheet title in cell A1 and narrowed column B. Now you want to enter text, and widen column A.

To enter data and change the width of a column, follow these steps:

1. If necessary, open the *MEC-S1drill* workbook; then click the SD3 sheet tab.

   The worksheet title *Selected State Codes* is already entered in cell A1.

2. Click cell A3, type **Indiana**, and press ↵Enter.

3. Enter the remaining text in columns A and B, as shown in Figure 1.72 (do not change the width of column A yet).

	A	B	C
1	Selected State Codes		
2			
3	Indiana	IN	
4	California	CA	
5	New Mexico	NM	
6	New Hampshire	NH	
7			

Figure 1.72

4. Position the mouse pointer between column letters A and B in the worksheet frame, and double-click.

   Double-clicking between columns A and B in the worksheet frame automatically widens column A to hold the longest entry—in this case, the exercise title in cell A10. However, you want column A to be just wide enough to hold the longest state name.

5. Click between column letters A and B in the worksheet frame, and drag the pointer to the left until there is very little white space between the word *Hampshire* and the right edge of cell A6; then release the mouse button.

6. Save your changes to the *MEC-S1drill* workbook.

4. Using the Subtraction Operator in a Formula

Your supervisor asked you to prepare a report summarizing sales and sales returns for the year. You decide to include a calculation of the net sales as well.

To use the subtraction operator in a formula, follow these steps:

1. If necessary, open the *MEC-S1drill* workbook; then click the SD4 sheet tab.

The worksheet title Year *2003 Summary* is already entered in cell A1.

2. Enter the remaining text and numbers shown in Figure 1.73 (text in cells A3, A4, and A5; numbers in cells B3 and B4).

	A	B	C
1	Year 2003 Summary		
2			
3	Sales	10,000	
4	Returns	200	
5	Net Sales	??	
6			

Figure 1.73

3. Click cell B5, type **=B3−B4**, and press ⏎Enter.

Check that *9800* appears in cell B5—the result of subtracting the contents of cell B4 (*200*) from the contents of cell B3 (*10000*).

4. Select the range B3:B5, and click the Comma Style button on the toolbar.

5. Click the Decrease Decimal button twice.

6. Click any cell to deselect the highlighted range, and save your changes to the *MEC-S1drill* workbook.

5. Using the Multiplication Operator in a Formula

You want to calculate the sales tax due on an item. You plan to put the tax rate in a separate cell and label it so that a user can see the current rate and easily modify it, if necessary.

To use the multiplication operator in a formula, follow these steps:

1. If necessary, open the *MEC-S1drill* workbook; then click the SD5 sheet tab.

The worksheet title *Calculating Sales Tax* is already entered in cell A1.

2. Click cell A3, type **Tax Rate**, and press →.

3. Type **5%** in cell B3, and press ⏎Enter.

4. Enter the remaining text, as shown in Figure 1.74 (text in cells B5, C5, and A6).

	A	B	C	D
1	Calculating Sales Tax			
2				
3	Tax Rate	5%		
4				
5		Price	Sales Tax	
6	Item #1	$ 160.00	??	
7				

Figure 1.74

5. Enter **160** in cell B6, and apply a Currency two decimal places format to the range B6:C6.

The number 160 displays in the Currency format with two decimal places, as shown in Figure 1.74.

6. Click cell C6, type **=B6*B3**, and press ⏎Enter.

Check that *$8.00* appears in cell C6—the result of multiplying the contents of cell B6 (*160*) by the contents of cell B3 (*5%*).

7. Save your changes to the *MEC-S1drill* workbook.

6. Using the Division Operator in a Formula

You want to compute your share of a rental fee, assuming that the cost is shared equally. You plan to enter the number of people in a separate cell and label it so that the calculation works for any fee and any number of people sharing the cost.

To use the division operator in a formula, follow these steps:

1. If necessary, open the *MEC-S1 drill* workbook; then click the SD6 sheet tab.

    The worksheet title *Calculating Cost per Person* is already entered in cell A1.

2. Enter 600 in cell A3; then format cell A3 to Currency zero decimal places.

3. Enter the remaining number and text, as shown in Figure 1.75 (number in cell A4; text in cells B3, B4, and B5).

	A	B	C	D
1	Calculating Cost per Person			
2				
3	$ 600	Rental Fee		
4	12	# of people sharing the cost		
5	??	Cost per person		
6				

Figure 1.75

4. Click cell A5, type **=A3 / A4**, and press ↵Enter.

5. Check that *50* appears in cell A5—the result of dividing the contents of cell A3 (*600*) by the contents of cell A4 (*12*).

6. Apply a Currency two decimal places format to cell A5.

7. Save your changes to the *MEC-S1 drill* workbook.

7. Check Spelling

You finished entering text, numbers, and formulas in a worksheet that generates financial reports. Now you want to check for spelling errors.

To use Excel's spelling checker, follow these steps:

1. If necessary, open the *MEC-S1 drill* workbook; then click the SD7 sheet tab.

    The organization name *Mesa Software City, Inc.* displays in cell A3.

2. Click Spelling on the toolbar.

    The Spelling dialog box opens; the first possible error *Accum* displays in the Not in Dictionary text box.

3. Click Ignore All.

    Excel retains all occurrences of *Accum*, an acceptable short form of the word *Accumulated*. The next possible error *Deprec* displays in the Not in Dictionary text box.

4. Click Ignore All.

    You bypassed changing all occurrences of *Deprec*, an acceptable short form of the word *Depreciation*. The next possible error *Addit'l* displays.

5. Click Ignore All.

    You bypassed changing *Addit'l*, an acceptable short form of the word *Additional*. The next possible error *Adminsitrative* displays.

6. Make sure that *Administrative* is selected in the list of suggestions, and click the Change button.

Excel changes *Adminsitrative* to *Administrative* in cell D71. The next possible error *Epuipment* displays.

7. Make sure that *Equipment* is selected in the list of suggestions, and click the <u>C</u>hange button.

Excel changes *Epuipment* to *Equipment* in cell D81. The next possible error *PP&E* displays in the dialog box.

8. Click <u>I</u>gnore All.

A message displays that the spelling check is complete for the entire sheet.

9. Click OK.

The message box closes.

10. Press Ctrl+Home to make cell A1 the current cell.

11. Save your changes to the *MEC-S1drill* workbook.

8. Use the Find Command

You operate a lawn mowing service, and you use an Excel worksheet to list the locations you are currently servicing. You want to change the mowing day from Tues to Weds for a customer named Sandy Bell.

To use Excel's Find command to locate the customer's record, and make the change, follow these steps:

1. If necessary, open the *MEC-S1drill* workbook; then click the SD8 sheet tab.

The worksheet title *Mowing Schedule* displays in cell A3.

2. Choose <u>E</u>dit, <u>F</u>ind.

The Find and Replace dialog box opens. The Fin<u>d</u> tab is active.

3. Clear all existing find criteria; then enter `Bell` in the Fi<u>n</u>d what text box and click Find All.

The Find and Replace dialog box expands to include the locations of four cells that contain the letters *Bell*. Three occurrences are the last names *Bellwood, Bellingham,* and *Bell*; the other is an address on *Bellflower Circle*.

4. Click the Options button to display several check boxes; then click the *Match entire cell contents* check box, and click <u>F</u>ind Next.

The first cell containing only the letters *Bell* becomes the active cell. You can achieve the same result by clicking *$B$18* in the Cell column or *Bell* in the Value column at the bottom of the dialog box.

5. Close the Find and Replace dialog box, and change the day to mow from *Tues* to **Weds** for customer Sandy Bell.

6. Save your changes to the *MEC-S1drill* workbook.

9. Use Go To and Replace Cell Formats

You finished entering text, numbers, and formulas in a worksheet that generates financial reports. There are four sections in the large worksheet: a trial balance, an Income Statement, a Statement of Retained Earnings, and a Balance Sheet. Now you want to move around the large worksheet using Excel's Go To feature. After you view several occurrences of blue text applied to cells containing the firm's name, you decide to replace the color with a different print style.

To go to specific cells, and then replace cell formats, follow these steps:

1. If necessary, open the *MEC-S1drill* workbook; then click the SD9 sheet tab.

The organization's name *Mesa Software City, Inc.* displays blue in cell A3.

2. Choose Edit, Go To (or press F5).

The Go To dialog box opens.

3. Type **D53** in the Reference text box, and click OK.

The company name displays in blue in cell D53, the current cell.

4. Scroll down and to the right to view the rest of the Income Statement and the next occurrence of the company name in blue—cell G87.

5. Choose Edit, Go To (or press F5).

The Go To dialog box opens.

6. Type **L115** in the Reference text box, and click OK.

Cell L115 becomes the active cell. You see another occurrence of the company name in blue in cell I96.

7. Press Ctrl+Home to make cell A1 the current cell.

8. Choose Edit, Replace; if Format buttons do not display to the right of the Find what and Replace with boxes, click the Options button.

9. Delete existing *Find what* and *Replace with* specifications, if any.

10. Click the top Format button of two Format buttons in the upper-right corner of the Find and Replace dialog box.

The Find Format dialog box opens.

11. Click the *Choose Format From Cell* button in the lower-left corner of the dialog box; then click cell A3.

Excel displays a sample of the Find what criteria—the blue font color.

12. Click the lower of the two Format buttons in the upper-right corner of the Find and Replace dialog box.

The Replace Format dialog box opens.

13. Select the Font tab; then specify a Comic Sans MS font and a 12-point size.

14. Click the Color drop-down list and select Automatic; then click OK.

Excel displays a sample of the *Replace with* criteria in the Find and Replace dialog box.

15. Click the Replace All button.

Excel replaces all occurrences of blue applied to cell contents with a 12-point black Comic Sans MS font. A message indicates that four replacements were made.

16. Click OK to close the message box; close the Find and Replace dialog box, and view the results.

17. Save your changes to the *MEC-S1drill* workbook.

10. Filter for an Exact Match

You work for Indy 500 Motor Works, and you maintain in list form the results of customer surveys on vehicle rentals. As you begin to analyze the data in your list, you want to focus on selected data. For example, you want to limit the display to records of compact car rentals.

To filter for an exact match using one criterion, follow these steps:

1. If necessary, open the *MEC-S1drill* workbook; then click the SD10 sheet tab.

The worksheet includes thirty records comprised of data taken from customer surveys the first quarter of 2003.

2. Click any cell within the list range A6:L36.

3. Choose Data, Filter, AutoFilter.

4. Click the arrow for the Car Size field.

5. Select *Compact* from the drop-down list.

Make sure that the display is limited to records of compact car rentals.

6. Save your changes to the *MEC-S1drill* workbook.

11. Limit Filter Results to a Specific Number

You work for Indy 500 Motor Works, and you maintain in list form the results of customer surveys on vehicle rentals. You want to find the five highest values in the Rental Cost field.

To filter your list using a specific number in Top 10 AutoFilter settings, follow these steps:

1. If necessary, open the *MEC-S1drill* workbook; then click the SD11 sheet tab.

The worksheet includes thirty records comprised of data taken from customer surveys the first quarter of 2003.

2. Turn on AutoFilter.

3. Select the *Top 10* option from the drop-down list for the Rental Cost field.

4. Change the number of items from 10 to **5**, and click OK to activate the filter.

5. Make sure that the display is limited to records with the top five values in the Rental Cost field.

In this case, six records display because two records have the same $182 value.

6. Save your changes to the *MEC-S1drill* workbook.

12. Limit Filter Results to a Percent

You work for Indy 500 Motor Works, and you maintain in list form the results of customer surveys on vehicle rentals. You want to limit display to the top 10 percent based on values in the Rental Cost field.

To set the desired filter, follow these steps:

1. If necessary, open the *MEC-S1drill* workbook; then click the SD12 sheet tab.

The worksheet includes thirty records comprised of data taken from customer surveys the first quarter of 2003.

2. Turn on AutoFilter.

3. Select the *Top 10* option from the drop-down list for the Rental Cost field.

4. Change settings in the Top 10 AutoFilter dialog box, as necessary, to filter for the top 10 percent.

5. Click OK to activate the filter and verify that only 10 percent (three of 30) of the records display.

Make sure that the records displayed are those with the highest values in the Rental Cost field.

6. Save your changes to the *MEC-S1drill* workbook.

Challenge

Challenge exercises expand on or are somewhat related to skills presented in the skill sets. Each exercise provides a brief narrative introduction, followed by instructions, in a numbered-step format, that are not as detailed as those in the Skill Drill section.

Before beginning your Excel Core Skill Set 1 Challenge exercises, complete the following steps:

1. Open the file named *MEC-S106*, and immediately save it as **MEC-S1challenge**.

The workbook contains seven sheets: an overview and six exercise sheets labeled CH1 through CH6.

2. Click the Overview sheet to view the organization and content of the Challenge work-book for Excel Core Skill Set 1.

Each exercise is independent of the others, so you may complete the exercises in any order. Be sure to save the workbook after completing each exercise. If you need a paper copy of one or more completed exercises, enter your name, centered in a header, before printing. Print options have already been set to print compressed to one page and to display the filename, sheet name, and current date in a footer.

Be sure to save your changes and close the workbook if you need more than one work session to complete the desired exercises. Continue working on *MEC-S1challenge* instead of starting over in the original *MEC-S106* file.

1. Copy Cell Contents

As you create a worksheet to summarize volunteer hours, you decide to display data for two years. After setting up worksheet labels for the first year, you can copy those labels to another part of the worksheet and avoid retyping them.

To copy cell contents, follow these steps:

1. If necessary, open the *MEC-S1challenge* workbook; then click the CH1 sheet tab.

The worksheet includes the labels to summarize volunteer hours for the year 2002.

2. Select the range A6:F9.

3. Click the Copy button in the toolbar (or choose <u>E</u>dit, <u>C</u>opy).

4. Click cell A12 to select the first cell in the destination range.

5. Click the Paste button in the toolbar (or choose <u>E</u>dit, <u>P</u>aste).

6. Press Esc to deselect the copied range.

7. Edit cell A12 to read **Year 2003** instead of *Year 2002*.

8. Save your changes to the *MEC-S1challenge* workbook.

2. Use AutoFill to Enter Names of Months

You begin to set up a worksheet to show volunteer hours each month. You know that Excel has an AutoFill feature that you can use to fill in a series of numbers, dates, or other items in a specified range.

A thick black border surrounds the current cell. The ***fill handle***, a small black square, displays in the lower-right corner of that thick border. Dragging the fill handle to adjacent cells produces a data series based on the contents of the current cell or selected range.

To use the AutoFill feature to enter the names of months, follow these steps:

1. If necessary, open the *MEC-S1challenge* workbook; then click the CH2 sheet tab.

The worksheet includes labels for three organizations in Column A.

2. Type **Jan** in cell B6, and press ↵Enter.

3. Click cell B6, and position the cell pointer on the fill handle at the lower-right corner.

4. Click and drag to cell M6, and release the mouse button.

The labels *Jan*, *Feb*, *Mar*, and so on appear in the range B6:M6.

5. Click any cell to deselect the highlighted range, and save your changes to the *MEC-S1challenge* workbook.

3. Calculate Percentage of Change and Format Numbers

You are one of the managers in a small firm and you are responsible for monitoring the following assets: Cash, Accounts Receivable, Inventory, and Supplies. At the moment, you are interested in finding out how the amounts in these accounts at the end of the year compare to the amounts in these accounts at the beginning of the year. You want to show the percentage increase or decrease in each account.

To format numbers, and enter and copy a formula, follow these steps:

1. If necessary, open the *MEC-S1 challenge* workbook; then click the CH3 sheet tab.

The worksheet title *Analysis of Change in Selected Accounts: Year 2003* displays in the range A3:C3.

2. Apply a Currency zero decimal places format to the cells in the range B6:C9.

3. Select cell D6, type =(B6-C6)/C6, and press ↵Enter).

The value *-0.2* displays in cell D6. The decimal 0.2 is equivalent to 20 percent, and the minus sign indicates a decrease. The percentage of change is calculated by finding the difference between the two amounts and dividing the result by the amount at the beginning of the year. Excel performs calculations within parentheses first.

4. Select cell D6, and click the Percent Style button in the toolbar.

The display switches from -0.2 to -20%.

5. Click the Increase Decimal button in the toolbar.

The display switches from -20% to -20.0%.

6. Make sure that cell D6 is the current cell, and position the cell pointer on the fill handle at the lower-right corner.

7. Click and drag to cell D9, release the mouse button, and deselect the range.

The percentages 12.5, -13.6, and 40.0 display in cells D7 through D9. Accounts receivable increased by 12.5 percent, Inventory decreased by 13.6 percent, and Supplies increased by 40 percent. In-depth coverage of copying formulas is provided in Excel Core Skill Set 5, *Creating and Revising Formulas*.

8. Save your changes to the *MEC-S1 challenge* workbook.

4. Calculate a Monthly Rental Fee

You rent a copy machine, for which the rental company charges a fixed amount for the month plus an amount for each copy. Create a worksheet to calculate the amount due for any month. Test your results by changing one or more variables: the rental fee per month, the charge per copy, or the number of copies made in a month.

To calculate a monthly rental fee for a copy machine, follow these steps:

1. If necessary, open the *MEC-S1 challenge* workbook; then click the CH4 sheet tab.

The worksheet title *Calculating the Monthly Charge for a Copy Machine* displays in cell A1.

2. Enter text and numbers, and format the numbers, as shown in Figure 1.76 (do not make an entry in cell B7 yet).

	A	B	C
1	Calculating the Monthly Charge for a Copy Machine		
2			
3	Rental fee per month	$ 200	
4	Charge per copy	0.04	
5	# of copies made during the month	2,000	
6			
7	Total rental fee	??	
8			

Figure 1.76

3. In cell B7, enter the formula to calculate *Total rental fee*. (*Hint:* Multiply the number of copies by the charge per copy, and add the result to the rental fee per month; use cell references instead of numbers in the formula.)

Ensure that *280* displays as the total rental fee in cell B7.

4. Format cell B7 to display Currency two decimal places.

5. In cell B5, change the number of copies to **4000**.

Make sure that *$360.00* displays as the total rental fee in cell B7. Doubling the number of copies increased the total rental fee by 80 dollars. Now, find out how much you would pay if you could negotiate a charge of three cents per copy.

6. In cell B4, change the charge per copy to **0.03**.

Ensure that *$320.00* displays as the total rental fee in cell B7. You save 40 dollars if you pay one cent less on each of 4000 copies.

7. Save your changes to the *MEC-S1challenge* workbook.

5. Calculate a New Rate of Pay per Hour

You put in a request for a raise. Create a worksheet to calculate the new wage rate per hour. Test your results by changing one or both variables—the original wage rate per hour and the percent increase.

To calculate a new rate of pay per hour, follow these steps:

1. If necessary, open the *MEC-S1challenge* workbook; then click the CH5 sheet tab.

The worksheet title *Calculating Your New Rate of Pay per Hour* displays in cell A1.

2. Enter text and numbers, and format the numbers, as shown in Figure 1.77 (do not make an entry in cell B5 yet).

	A	B	C
1	Calculating Your New Rate of Pay per Hour		
2			
3	Original wage rate per hour	$10.00	
4	% increase	10%	
5	New wage rate per hour	??	
6			

Figure 1.77

3. In cell B5, enter the formula to calculate *New wage rate per hour*. (*Hint:* Multiply the original wage rate by the percent of increase, and add the result to the original wage rate; use cell references instead of numbers in the formula.)

Make sure that *$11.00* displays as the new wage rate per hour in cell B5.

4. In cell B3, change the wage rate per hour to **11**.

Ensure that *$12.10* displays as the new wage rate in cell B5.

5. In cell B4, change the percent increase to **5%**.

Make sure that *$11.55* displays as the new wage rate in cell B5.

6. Save your changes to the *MEC-S1challenge* workbook.

6. Use the Auto Fill Options Button and Format Dates

You want to know more about filling a range with data, including use of the Auto Fill Options button. Complete the following steps to enter dates in a variety of sequences:

1. If necessary, open the *MEC-S1challenge* workbook; then click the CH6 sheet tab.

Column headings for six examples display in row 4.

2. Click cell A6, drag its fill handle down to cell A36, and release the mouse button.

Excel fills the range A7:A36 with dates that increment by one (from 1/1/2002 through 1/31/2002).

3. Click cell B6, drag its fill handle down to B28, and release the mouse button.

The Auto Fill Options button displays next to the fill handle of cell B28.

4. Position the pointer on the button; click its down arrow to display the Auto Fill Options drop-down list, and select Fill Weekdays.

The range B6:B28 is filled with dates representing weekdays only. For example, 1/4/2002 (a Friday) displays in cell B9 and 1/7/2002 (a Monday) displays in the next cell, B10.

5. Click cell C6, drag its fill handle down to C29, and use the appropriate Auto Fill Options button to enter a series of dates that increment by one month.

Check that each date in the series is the first day of a month. The series includes monthly dates for the years 2001 and 2002.

6. Repeat the process described in Step 5, and enter a series of dates in the range D6:D29, in which each date is the last day of a month.

7. Click cell E6, drag its fill handle down to E29, and use the appropriate Auto Fill Options button to enter a series of dates that increment by one year.

Check that each date in the series is the first day of a year. The series includes yearly dates for the years 2001 through 2024.

8. Repeat the process described in Step 7, and enter a series of dates in the range F6:F29 in which each date is the last day of a year.

9. Save your changes to the *MEC-S1challenge* workbook.

Managing Workbooks

CHAPTER 2

This skill set includes

Manage workbook files and folders

- Use the Open dialog box to create and rename folders
- Use the Open dialog box to rename, copy, move, and delete workbooks
- Use Search in the Open dialog box to locate files

Create workbooks using templates

Save workbooks using different names and file formats

Skill Set Overview

T hink of managing workbooks in two ways: managing the physical files that you create, and managing the content of your workbooks. Excel provides support from both perspectives.

In this skill set, you learn common file management tasks that include: creating and renaming folders; renaming, copying, moving, and deleting files; and using a Search tool to locate files. A *folder* is a storage location on disk that enables you to store multiple files by type or subject.

You also create a *template*, a workbook (or worksheet) containing standardized content and/or formatting that you can use as the basis for other workbooks (or worksheets). The skill set concludes with opening a workbook and saving it in a different file format.

Skill 2.1: Manage Workbook Files and Folders

Folders provide an organized way to store and retrieve files. You can create a multiple-level file storage system by creating a folder within a folder—sometimes referred to as a *subfolder*.

As a general guideline, folders are created on Zip disks, hard disks, and other storage devices that also have large capacities. You can, however, create folders on smaller-capacity disks, such as a 3-1/2 inch high-density disk. The procedure is the same no matter what disk capacity is involved.

You should always make backup copies of important files, and store the backup copies in a separate physical location. At times, you might want to change the name of a file, delete a file, or move a file from one location to another. Perhaps you want to reorganize files, and place one in a new folder.

Windows Explorer is a utility program that you can use to access programs and documents, as well as create folders and copy, move, delete, and rename files. If you have multiple file-management tasks to perform, you might prefer to use Explorer. However, if you are already working in Excel, you can create a folder and apply any file-management action to a single file through the Open or Save dialog boxes.

In this skill area, you use the Excel dialog box approach to folder and file management.

Use the Open Dialog Box to Create and Rename Folders

In this section, you create two folders using the Open dialog box. The figures illustrate creating the folders on a blank 3-1/2 inch disk formatted to work on a Windows-based computer system. If desired, you can substitute your hard disk, a Zip disk, or a network drive in place of references to the disk drive A.

You also rename one of the folders using the Open dialog box, and create four Excel practice files. You use the practice files to perform file-management tasks in the next section.

Use the Open Dialog Box to Create and Rename Folders

1 **Insert a blank formatted 3-1/2 inch disk in drive A.**
All 3-1/2 inch disks sold in recent years are already formatted. Make sure that the disk you select is formatted for a Windows-based system.

 If you have problems...
If you do not have a blank formatted disk—or if you prefer to practice creating folders on a Zip disk, hard disk, or network drive—omit this step.

Also substitute the drive of your choice in place of all subsequent references to drive A.

You can find information on formatting through the Windows Start menu. Click Start at the left end of the task bar, select *Help and Support*, and enter `format a disk` in the Search text box.

2 **Start Excel; then choose File, Open.**
The Open dialog box opens. Depending on the version of Windows you are using and the files and folders on your system, you can expect slight variations from figures shown in this skill set.

3 **Display the Look in drop-down list, and select 3-1/2 Floppy (A:).**
The drive you selected holds a 3-1/2 inch disk (see Figure 2.1). Remember to select a different drive, such as your hard disk or a Zip disk if you prefer to practice folder and file management on another drive.

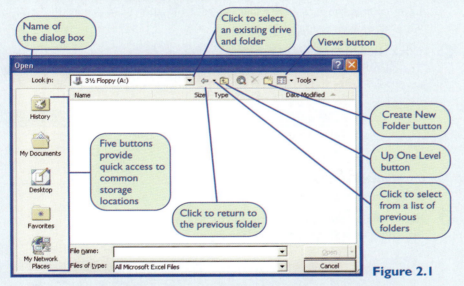

Figure 2.1

 If you have problems...
If columns labeled *Name*, *Size*, *Type*, and *Date Modified* do not display within your Open dialog box, click the down arrow for the Views button (refer to Figure 2.1), and select Details from the Views drop-down list.

4 **Click the Create New Folder button; then enter** `Personal` **in the Name box within the New Folder dialog box (see Figure 2.2).**

Figure 2.2

5 **Click OK.**
Excel creates the new folder and makes it the current folder in the Look in box within the Open dialog box.

continues ▶

Use the Open Dialog Box to Create and Rename Folders (continued)

6   **Click the Up One Level button (refer to Figure 2.1).**

The current folder in the Look in box switches back to *3-1/2 Floppy (A:)* as shown in Figure 2.3. Next you create another subfolder at the same level as the *Personal* subfolder.

Figure 2.3

7   **Click the Create New Folder button, enter `School` in the Name box within the New Folder dialog box, and click OK.**

Excel creates the new folder and makes it the current folder in the Look in box within the Open dialog box.

8   **Click the Up One Level button.**

The current folder in the Look in box switches back to *3-1/2 Floppy (A:)*. You now have two folders and no files on your disk in drive A (see Figure 2.4).

Figure 2.4

9   **Right-click *School*, the name of the second folder.**

Excel displays a short-cut menu (see Figure 2.5).

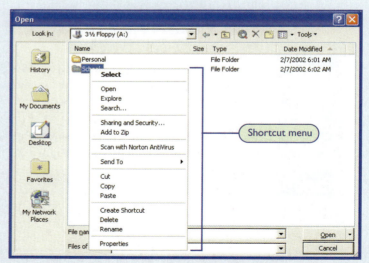

Figure 2.5

10   **Click *Rename* near the end of the shortcut menu options.**

Rename mode is active. A border surrounds the selected folder, and its name is highlighted (see Figure 2.6).

Figure 2.6

11   **Type** Demo Files **and press** (↵Enter).
The name of the folder changes to Demo Files. Changing the name of the folder does not change the date and time it was created (see Figure 2.7).

Figure 2.7

12   **Click the Cancel or Close button in the Open dialog box.**
The Open dialog box closes. You did not intend to open a file. You instead used the Open dialog box to create folders while working in Excel. Now save sample files for use in the next skill area.

13   **Display a new blank workbook in Excel, and enter** This is a practice file **in cell A1.**

14   **Choose** File, Save **A**s; **make sure that 3-1/2 Floppy (A:) displays in the Save** i**n text box.**

15   **Type** File1 Rename **in the File** n**ame text box (see Figure 2.8).**

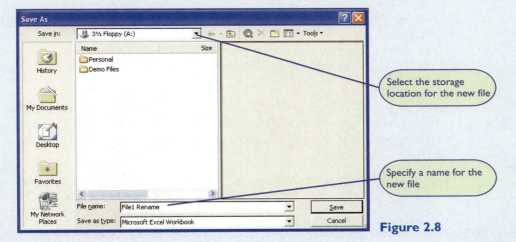

Figure 2.8

16   **Click the** Save **button in the Save As dialog box.**
Excel saves the new file in the root directory of drive A. The **root directory** is the first level of storage on a drive.

17   **Repeat the file save process described in the previous three steps to create three more practice files based on the same worksheet; name the files** File2 Copy, File3 Move, **and** File4 Delete.

18   **Close the** *File4 Delete* **workbook; then choose** File, Open **(or click Open on the toolbar).**

continues ▶

Use the Open Dialog Box to Create and Rename Folders (continued)

Two folders and four files display in the Open dialog box (see Figure 2.9).

Four new files in the root directory of drive A

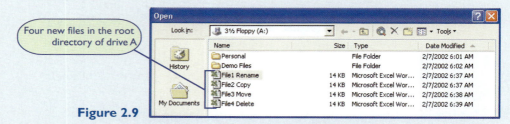

Figure 2.9

19 **Click Cancel to close the Open dialog box.**
Continue with the next skill, or exit Excel.

Use the Open Dialog Box to Rename, Copy, Move, and Delete Workbooks

In the previous section, you changed the name of a folder from within the Open dialog box. A similar process is used to change the name of a file: right-click the filename in the Open dialog box, choose Rename from the shortcut menu, type a new name for the file, and press ⏎Enter).

The process to copy a file or folder from within the Open dialog box consists of four steps: Right-click the name of the file or folder you want to work with; choose Copy from the short-cut menu, display the new location for the duplicate file or folder in the Look in box, and press Ctrl+V. In place of the first two steps, you can click the name of the file or folder, and then press Ctrl+C.

The process to move a file or folder from within the Open dialog box also consists of four steps: Right-click the name of the file or folder you want to work with; choose Move from the shortcut menu, display the new location for the file or folder in the Look in box, and press Ctrl+V. In place of the first two steps, you can click the name of the file or folder, and then press Ctrl+X.

When you are certain that you no longer need a file, it is a good idea to delete it, which makes its storage location available for other files. As long as a file is not in use, you can delete it from within the Open dialog box by right-clicking its name and choosing Delete from the shortcut menu.

In the following steps, you rename, copy, move, and delete files from within the Open dialog box. You work with the practice files you created in the previous section.

To Rename, Copy, Move, and Delete Workbooks Using the Open Dialog Box

1 **Make sure that the 3-1/2 inch disk you used in the previous section is in drive A.**
If you did not create your four practice files on a 3-1/2 disk, omit this step. Also substitute the drive you did use in place of all subsequent references to drive A.

2 **Start Excel, if necessary; then display the Open dialog box.**

3 **Select drive A in the Look in box.**
The two folders and four files created in the previous lesson display (refer to Figure 2.9).

4 **Right-click the file named *File1 Rename*, and choose Rename from the shortcut menu.**

Two features indicate that Rename mode is active. A border surrounds the selected file, and its name is highlighted (see Figure 2.10).

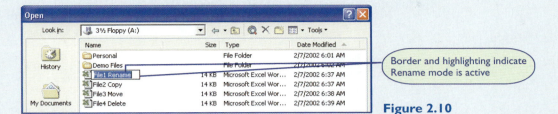

Border and highlighting indicate Rename mode is active

Figure 2.10

5 **Type** New Name **and press** ↵Enter.

The name of the file changes to *New Name*. Changing the name of the file does not change the date and time it was created (see Figure 2.11).

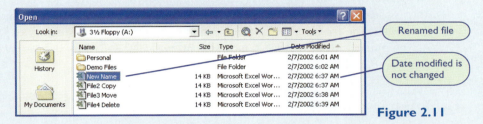

Renamed file

Date modified is not changed

Figure 2.11

6 **Right-click the file named *File2 Copy*, and choose Copy from the shortcut menu.**

7 **Double-click the folder named *Demo Files*.**

A folder icon followed by the folder name *Demo Files* displays in the Look in box.

8 **Press** Ctrl+V.

The original *File2 Copy* workbook remains in the root directory of drive A. A copy of that file is stored in the *Demo Files* folder (see Figure 2.12).

Current storage location

Up One Level button

Copied file

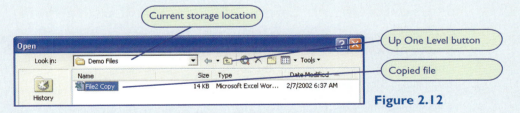

Figure 2.12

9 **Click the Up One Level button in the Open dialog box.**

The current storage location is once again 3-1/2 Floppy (A:). The original file named *File2 Copy* still displays in the root directory of drive A.

10 **Right-click the *File3 Move* workbook, and choose Cut from the shortcut menu.**

11 **Double-click the folder named *Demo Files*.**

A folder icon followed by the folder name *Demo Files* displays in the Look in box.

continues ▶

To Rename, Copy, Move, and Delete Files Using the Open Dialog Box (continued)

⑫ **Press** Ctrl+V.

The original *File3 Move* workbook appears in the *Demo Files* folder (see Figure 2.13). The folder also contains the copied file named *File2 Copy*.

Current storage location

Moved file

Figure 2.13

⑬ **Click the Up One Level button in the Open dialog box.**

The *File3 Move* workbook no longer appears in the root directory of drive A.

⑭ **Right-click the *File4 Delete* workbook, and select Delete from the shortcut menu; choose Yes in the Confirm File Delete dialog box.**

You executed the last of the four basic file-management tasks: rename, copy, move, and delete. The *File4 Delete* workbook is removed from the root directory of drive A. The root directory of drive A includes only two files: *File2 Copy* and *New Name* (see Figure 2.14).

The workbook named *File4 Delete* no longer appears in the root directory of drive A

Figure 2.14

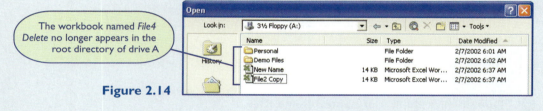

⑮ **Click Cancel to close the Open dialog box.**

Continue with the next skill, or exit Excel.

Use Search in the Open Dialog Box to Locate Files

When you open a file using the Open dialog box, you follow this process: execute a File, Open command; display the Look in drop-down list, and select the folder containing the file; select the name of the file, and click Open. If you do not remember the name and/or the location of the file, Excel provides a Search tool in the Open dialog box.

When you use the Search feature, you specify text as the search condition. Excel searches files, filenames, and file properties for that text. The results are filenames that list one to a line at the bottom of the Search dialog box. Positioning the pointer on a result displays its location. When you double-click a filename in the results list, Excel copies the storage path and filename to the File name box in the Open dialog box.

In the following steps, you use the Search feature to locate all files containing the word *practice* in the filename, in the content of the file, or in the properties for that file. You also select one of the search results and open that file.

To Use Search in the Open Dialog Box to Locate Files

①   **Make sure that the 3-1/2 inch disk you used in the previous section is in drive A.**

If you did not create your four practice files on a 3-1/2 inch disk, omit this step. Also substitute the drive you did use in place of all subsequent references to drive A.

②   **Start Excel, if necessary; then display the Open dialog box.**

③   **Click the My Documents icon at the left side of the dialog box.**

You selected a different folder location than drive A to more easily see that the subsequent search applies to all files and folders on any drives. The folder *My Documents* displays in the Look in box (see Figure 2.15).

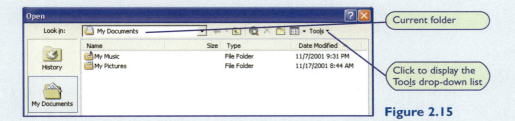

Figure 2.15

④   **Click the down arrow for the Tools button, and select Search (the first option).**

The Search dialog box opens. It includes two tabs—Basic and Advanced.

⑤   **Make sure that Basic is the current tab, and type** practice **in the Search text box (see Figure 2.16).**

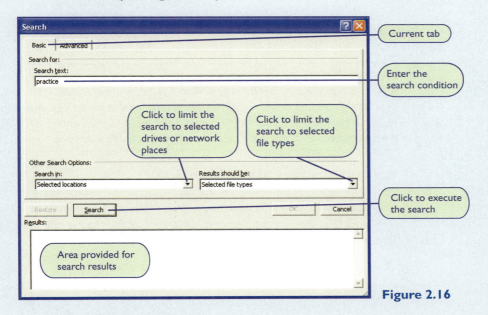

Figure 2.16

You requested a search for the word *practice* in file content, in a filename, or in a file's properties.

continues ▶

To Use Search in the Open Dialog Box to Locate Files (continued)

6 Click the down-arrow to the right of *Selected locations* in the Search in area (refer to Figure 2.16).

Excel displays the locations that you can search. The default setting searches all drives on your computer system (see Figure 2.17). Make no changes at this time.

A check mark indicates a selected location

Click to display a detailed list of drives on the current system

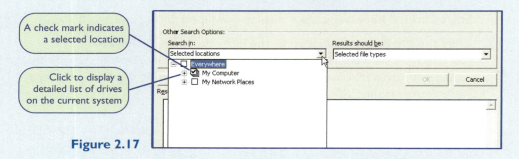

Figure 2.17

7 Click the down-arrow to the right of *Selected file types* in the Results should be area, and deselect all settings except Excel files (see Figure 2.18).

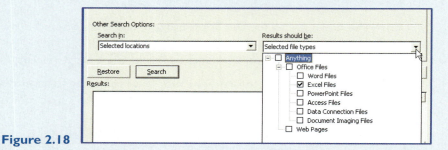

Figure 2.18

> **X** **If you have problems...**
>
> If you do not see a detailed list of Office files (Word, Excel, and so forth), a plus sign displays in front of Office Files instead of the minus sign shown in Figure 2.18. Click the plus sign to expand the list, and then click each box as necessary until a check mark displays only in front of Excel Files.

8 Click the Search button (refer to Figure 2.18).

Excel searches every specified drive on the current system for each occurrence of the word *practice* in a file, in a filename, or in file properties. The search looks only at Excel files. As files meeting the search criteria are found, they list one per line in the Results area (see Figure 2.19).

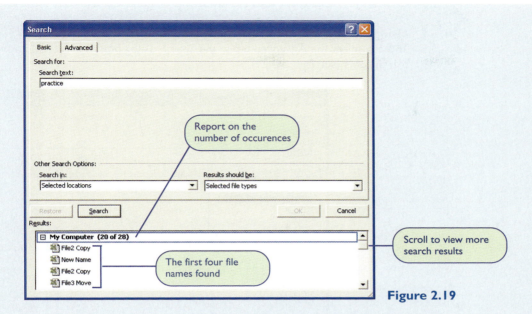

Figure 2.19

While a search is in progress, a <u>S</u>top button displays instead of the <u>S</u>earch button. Click the <u>S</u>top button if you want to interrupt the search, which you might want to do as soon as you recognize the name of the file you want to find.

Excel finds the four files shown in Figure 2.19 plus any others on the current computer system that meet the search criteria. For example, 28 files were found on the system used to produce Figure 2.19. Your results are likely to vary.

⑨ **Position the pointer on the file named *New Name* in the R<u>e</u>sults area.**
A ScreenTip shows the name of the file preceded by its storage location.

⑩ **Double-click the file named *New Name* in the R<u>e</u>sults area.**
The Search dialog box closes, and Excel copies the location and the filename to the File <u>n</u>ame box in the Open dialog box (see Figure 2.20).

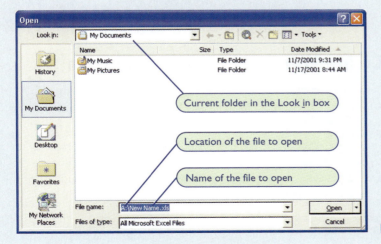

Figure 2.20

⑪ **Click Cancel to close the Open dialog box.**
You completed the steps to locate a file using the Search feature. It was not necessary to actually open the file.

Continue with the next skill, or exit Excel.

In Depth:
Using Advanced Search in the Open Dialog Box

You can select the Advanced tab in the Search dialog box to access additional search tools (see Figure 2.21).

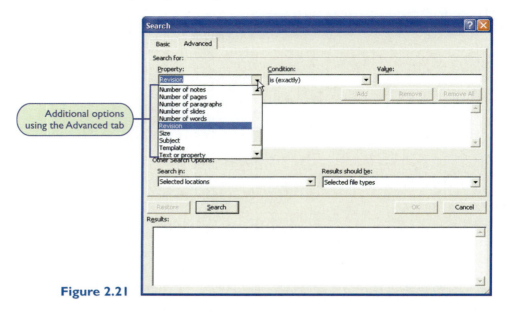

Additional options using the Advanced tab

Figure 2.21

Some of the properties that you can specify are more likely to be set when using PowerPoint or Word than when using Excel—such as searching for files in which the number of slides or number of words match or exceed a specified value. Other options are suitable for Excel, such as searching for files that include a specific revision or that have a file size smaller than a specified value.

For immediate reinforcement, work Skill Drills 1, 2, 3, and 4.

Skill 2.2: Create Workbooks Using Templates

A template is a workbook containing standardized content and/or formatting that you can use as the basis for other workbooks. A template has an .xlt extension, as compared to the .xls extension that indicates a workbook.

A ***custom template*** is a workbook that you create and save with your preferred content and/or formatting in one or more worksheets. A ***built-in template*** is a predefined template provided by Excel that contains content and formatting designed to meet a common business need.

Built-in templates include models for a balance sheet, expense statement, loan amortization schedule, sales invoice, and timecard. To open one of these templates as the basis for a new workbook, select the Spreadsheet Solutions tab in the Templates dialog box, and double-click the built-in template of your choice.

In the following steps, you work with a built-in template that generates an amortization schedule for a loan that requires equal payments at a fixed interest rate. At a minimum, an amortization schedule lists each payment across the life of the loan, shows the distribution of a payment between interest and debt reduction (principal), and displays the amount still owed at any point in time. You open the template, add user instructions, apply a fill color to emphasize the cells that a user can change, and save the file as a workbook. You also use the model by entering and changing loan terms.

To Use a Built-in Template

1 **Choose File, New from the Excel menu bar.**
The New Workbook task pane opens on the right side of the screen.

2 **Click General Templates in the New Workbook task pane.**
The Templates dialog box opens.

3 **Select the Spreadsheet Solutions tab, and click the Loan Amortization option (see Figure 2.22).**

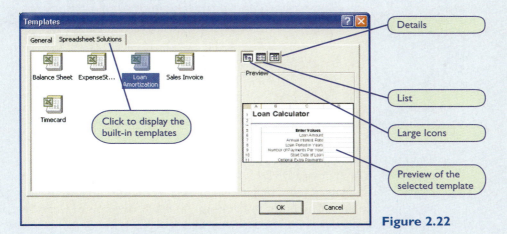

Figure 2.22

Excel displays the built-in templates and shows the selected template in the Preview area. A list might appear instead of the icons shown in Figure 2.22, depending on which view is active—Large Icons, List, or Details.

4 **Click OK.**
A workbook that contains one worksheet named Amortization Table opens. Loan Amortization1—the default name assigned by Excel—displays in the title bar.

5 **Reduce the zoom setting, if necessary, to display columns A through I (see Figure 2.23).**

continues ▶

To Use a Built-in Template (continued)

Descriptions of values used to generate a loan amortization schedule

Types of data in the loan amortization schedule

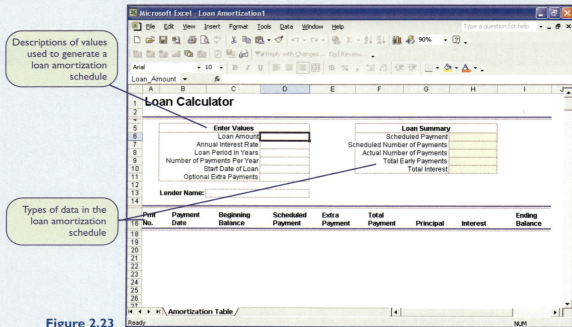

Figure 2.23

The model generates an amortization schedule, beginning in row 18, after a user enters values in the range D6:D11. Worksheet protection is enabled. You can only change the contents of cell C13 and cells in the range D6:D11. Now disable worksheet protection, and add user instructions. (In-depth coverage of worksheet and workbook protection is provided in Excel Expert Skill 9.1, *Modify Passwords, Protections, and Properties*.)

6 **Choose Tools, point to Protection, and click Unprotect Sheet.**
Previously protected cells can now be changed.

7 **Click cell D1, and enter** `To generate the amortization schedule, enter data in the blue cells.`
User instructions are added to the worksheet. Now apply a fill color to the cells a user can change.

8 **Select the range D6:D11; then press and hold down** Ctrl**, click cell C13, and release** Ctrl**.**
Cells C13 and D6 through D11 are selected.

9 **Display the Fill Color drop-down list, select Pale Blue, and click outside the highlighted cells to deselect them.**
Color emphasizes the cells a user can change (see Figure 2.24). Now restore worksheet protection and save the workbook.

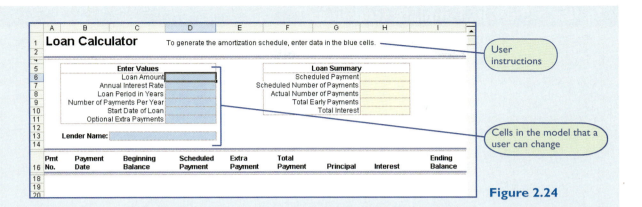

Figure 2.24

10 **Choose Tools, point to Protection, and click Protect Sheet; then click OK to close the Protect Sheet dialog box without specifying a password or changing the user permissions.**

Worksheet protection is restored. A user can change only the cells that have a blue background. Now save your changes to the model before using it to generate a schedule. You can save as a template if you want to modify the loan amortization template provided by Excel. In this lesson, you save as a workbook.

11 **Choose File, Save As; then specify a folder in the Save in drop-down list, and type Loan Schedule in the File name text box.**

12 **Make sure that *Microsoft Excel Workbook* is selected in the Save as type drop-down list, and click the Save button.**

The revised template is saved as an Excel workbook. Now enter values to generate a loan amortization schedule.

13 **Enter the following data in the cells indicated; click cell C13 when you are finished.**

In cell	Enter
D6	150000
D7	6%
D8	30
D9	12
D10	1/1/2002

Excel generates the loan amortization schedule starting with the first payment in row 18 (see Figure 2.25). Summary data displays in the range H6:H10. For a 30-year, 6%, $150,000 loan, the scheduled monthly payment is $899.33, and the total interest on the loan is $173,757.28.

continues ▶

To Use a Built-in Template (continued)

Click and drag down to view the entire amortization schedule

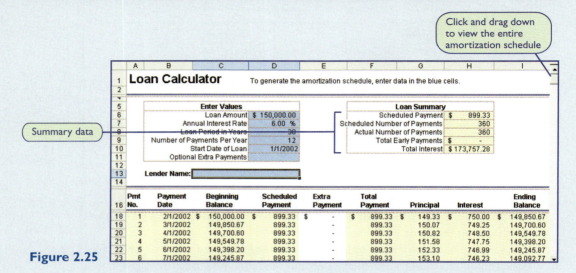

Summary data

Figure 2.25

⑭ **Scroll down to view row 377, the bottom of the amortization schedule.**
The balance remaining in cell I377 is zero.

⑮ **Scroll up and click cell D8; then change the number of years to 15.**
Excel generates a new loan amortization schedule. Cutting the loan time in half raises the monthly payment to $1,265.79, an increase of $366.46 per month; however, the total interest is now only $77,841.34—$95,915.94 less than the interest on a 30-year loan.

⑯ **Click cell D11, and enter 100 as the optional extra payment every month.**
You can see in the Loan Summary area that paying $100 extra each month enables you to eliminate the last 20 payments—only 160 of the 180 scheduled payments are needed to pay off the loan.

⑰ **Generate other loan amortization schedules of your choice by varying the amount borrowed, the annual interest rate, and/or the number of years that payments are due. When you finish, close the workbook without saving your changes.**
In the *Loan Schedule* workbook you saved in Step 12, the cells for loan terms are blank. By closing the file without saving specific loan terms, you have a model stored on disk that you can open and use for any loan specifications.

In Depth:
Creating a Custom Template

A custom template is a workbook that you create and save with your preferred content and/or formatting in one or more worksheets. For example, you might create a personal budget template that includes only the labels and formulas needed to show sources of income and expenses for each of twelve months; the numbers for a specific year would not be present. When you open the template and enter numbers for a specific year, and then attempt to save the changes, Excel automatically displays Microsoft Excel Workbook as the file type. The original template remains unchanged.

To save a workbook as a template, select the Save As option on the File menu, and select Template from the Save as type drop-down list. You create a custom template in the Excel MOUS Expert skill, *Create, Edit, and Apply Templates.*

For immediate reinforcement, work Challenge 1.

Skill 2.3: **Save Workbooks Using Different Names and File Formats**

Clicking the Save button on the toolbar immediately resaves the current workbook under its current name and in its current storage location. If you want to change the name or storage location, or save the workbook as another file type, use the Save As option on the File menu.

By saving under another name, you keep the original file intact. Follow Windows' file-naming rules when you specify a name. You can include spaces as well as upper- and lowercase letters. Excel automatically stores the file in the default Excel file format, adding the XLS (Excel spreadsheet) file extension.

There is a Save as type text box near the bottom of the Save As dialog box. Clicking the arrow at the right end of the box displays predefined file types. For example, you can save as a Web page; save as a template; save as an earlier version of Excel, such as 5.0/95; and save as a (Lotus) 1-2-3, Quattro Pro, or dBASE IV file. A common use for this feature is to save as another file type when you—or someone to whom you send the file— opens and edits a workbook using the version of the software specified in the selected file format.

In Excel Core Skill Set 1, *Working with Cells and Cell Data* you opened student data files and saved them under different names. For example, you opened *MEC-0101*, and saved it using the name Change Cells. In the following steps, you save a workbook in another file format.

To Save a Workbook in Another File Format

1 **Open the *MEC-S201* workbook.**
A worksheet to plan a family reunion opens.

2 **Choose File, Save As.**

3 **From the Save in drop-down list, select the drive and folder in which you are saving your data files for this text.**

4 **In the File name text box, type** Plan Reunion **to replace *MEC-S201*.**

continues ▶

To Save a Workbook in Another File Format (continued)

5 Click the down arrow at the right end of the Save as type box (see Figure 2.26).

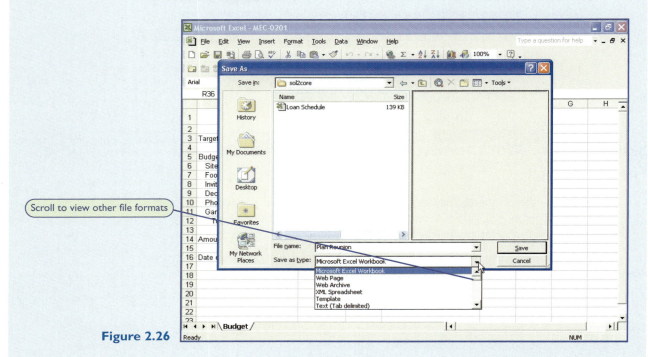

Scroll to view other file formats

Figure 2.26

6 Drag the scroll box down to view other file formats, and click *WK4 (1-2-3)*.

You specified saving the current file as a Lotus 1-2-3 file. *WK4 (1-2-3)* displays in the Save as type box.

7 Click Save.

A Microsoft Excel dialog box opens (see Figure 2.27).

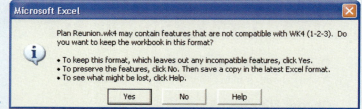

Figure 2.27

8 Select the Help button.

The topic *Formatting and features that are not transferred in Excel file format conversions* displays in the Help window.

9 Select and read the information about converting to Lotus 1-2-3 Release 4 (WK4); then close the Help window.

10 **Click the Yes button in the Microsoft Excel dialog box (refer to Figure 2.27).**

Excel saves the file in the specified format.

11 **Close the workbook.**

Continue with Skill Drill and Challenge exercises, or exit Excel.

For immediate reinforcement, work Challenge 2.

Summary

In the first part of this skill set, you focused on managing existing workbooks, as opposed to developing new ones. Working within the Open dialog box, you created and renamed folders; renamed, copied, moved, and deleted files; and located files using a Search tool. Next you created a workbook using a predefined template. For your final learning experience, you saved a workbook in a different file format.

Skill Drill

Each Skill Drill exercise reinforces the same, or nearly the same, skill presented in the skill set. Detailed instructions are provided in a step-by-step format.

The Skill Drill exercises for this skill set should be worked in the order listed. They use the folders and files stored on a 3-1/2 inch disk as of the end of Skill 2.1, *Manage Workbook Files and Folders*. The root directory includes two folders and two files (see the Name column in Figure 2.28). The Personal folder does not contain any files; the Demo Files folder contains two files named *File2 Copy* and *File3 Move*.

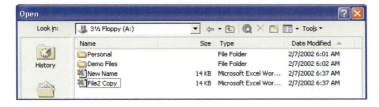

Figure 2.28

If you created your folders and files on a Zip disk, hard disk, or network drive during the skill set, substitute that alternative location in all subsequent references to drive A.

1. Create Folders and Subfolders

You decide to expand the folder structure within the Personal folder. You want to add two folders within Personal: Job Search and Financial Records. Within the Financial Records folder, you want to create two more folders: Taxes and Assets.

To create folders, and subfolders within folders, follow these steps:

1. Insert in drive A the 3-1/2 inch disk that you used for Skill 2.1, *Manage Workbook Files and Folders*.

2. Start Excel, if necessary; then choose File, Open.

3. Display the Look in drop-down list in the Open dialog box, and select 3-1/2 Floppy (A:).

4. Double-click the folder Personal (refer to Figure 2.28); click the Create New Folder button, and enter **Job Search** in the Name box within the New Folder dialog box.

5. Click OK.

   Excel creates the new folder, and makes it the current folder in the Look in box within the Open dialog box.

6. Click the Up One Level button.

   The current folder in the Look in box switches back to *Personal*. Next you create another subfolder at the same level as the *Job Search* subfolder.

7. Click the Create New Folder button, enter **Financial Records** in the Name box within the New Folder dialog box, and click OK.

   Excel creates the new folder, and makes it the current folder in the Look in box. Next you create two subfolders within the *Financial Records* folder.

8. Click the Create New Folder button, enter **Taxes** in the Name box within the New Folder dialog box, and click OK.

   Excel creates the new folder, and makes it the current folder in the Look in box within the Open dialog box.

9. Click the Up One Level button.

   The current folder in the Look in box switches back to *Financial Records*.

10. Click the Create New Folder button, enter **Assets** in the Name box within the New Folder dialog box, and click OK.

    Excel creates the new folder, and makes it the current folder in the Look in box within the Open dialog box.

11. Click the Up One Level button.

    The current folder in the Look in box switches back to *Financial Records*. This folder contains two subfolders: Taxes and Assets.

12. Click the Up One Level button.

    The current folder in the Look in box switches back to *Personal*. This folder contains two subfolders: Job Search and Financial Records.

13. Click the Up One Level button.

    The Look in box displays the root directory for drive A. The original two folders display: Personal and Demo Files.

    Continue with the next exercise, or exit Excel.

2. Copy and Rename a Workbook

You want to copy a workbook and place the copy in a new folder named *Assets*. You also want to rename the copy.

To copy and rename a workbook, follow these steps:

1. If necessary, insert in drive A the 3-1/2 inch disk that you used for Skill 2.1, *Manage Workbook Files and Folders*; then start Excel and choose File, Open.

2. Display the Look in drop-down list in the Open dialog box, and select 3-1/2 Floppy (A:).

3. Click the file named *File2 Copy*, and press Ctrl+C.

4. Double-click the Personal folder; then double-click the Financial Records folder.

   The folder *Financial Records* displays in the Look in box.

5. Double-click the Assets folder; then press `Ctrl`+`V`.

Excel makes a copy of the workbook named *File2 Copy* and places the copy in the Assets folder. The folder name *Assets* displays in the Look in box.

6. Right-click the workbook named *File2 Copy* in the current folder, and select Rename from the shortcut menu.

7. Type **Insurance** and press `⏎Enter`.

The name of the file changes to *Insurance*. Changing the name of the file does not change the date and time it was created.

8. Click the Up One Level button until the root directory 3-1/2 Floppy (A:) displays in the Look in box.

Continue with the next exercise, or exit Excel.

3. Delete a Workbook and Move Another Workbook

You decide you no longer need the workbook named *File2 Copy* stored in the root directory. You also want to move the only other file still in the root directory.

To delete a workbook and move another workbook, follow these steps:

1. If necessary, insert in drive A the 3-1/2 inch disk that you used for Skill 2.1, *Manage Workbook Files and Folders*; then start Excel and choose File, Open.

2. Display the Look in drop-down list in the Open dialog box, and select 3-1/2 Floppy (A:).

3. Click the file named *File2 Copy*; press `Del`, and click Yes in the Confirm File Delete dialog box.

The file named *File2 Copy* no longer appears in the root directory. Clicking `Del` produces the same results as right-clicking a filename and selecting Delete from the shortcut menu.

4. Right-click the file named *New Name*, and select Rename in the shortcut menu.

5. Type **Resume** and press `⏎Enter`.

The name of the file changes to *Resume*. Next move the Resume file to the Job Search folder.

6. Make sure the file named *Resume* is selected, and press `Ctrl`+`X`.

7. Double-click the Personal folder; then double-click the Job Search folder.

The folder *Job Search* displays in the Look in box.

8. Press `Ctrl`+`V`.

Excel pastes the workbook named *Resume* in the Job Search folder.

9. Click the Up One Level button until the root directory 3-1/2 Floppy (A:) displays in the Look in box.

The root directory displays only the folders named Personal and Demo Files.

Continue with the next exercise, or exit Excel.

4. Locating a File from Within the Open Dialog Box

You know that you created a workbook listing insurance information, but you are not sure how you spelled the filename or exactly where on your system you stored the file.

To locate a file from within the Open dialog box, follow these steps:

1. If necessary, insert in drive A the 3-1/2 inch disk that you used for Skill 2.1, *Manage Workbook Files and Folders*; then start Excel and choose File, Open.

2. Click the down arrow to the right of the Tools button; then select Search, and make sure that Basic is the current tab in the Search dialog box.

3. Type `ins*` in the Search text box.

The asterisk (*) is a wild card. You requested a search for a word that begins with *ins* and ends with any other letter(s), whether the word appears in file content, in a file name, or in a file's properties.

4. Click the down-arrow to the right of *Selected locations* in the Search in area; then click the plus sign (+) to the left of My Computer.

5. Uncheck all choices except the A drive and the C drive on your system.

6. Click the down-arrow to the right of *Selected file types* in the Results should be area, and deselect all settings except Excel files.

7. Click the Search button.

Excel searches every specified drive on the current system for each occurrence of the part of a word *ins* in a file, in a filename, or in file properties. The search looks only at Excel files. The results include the *Insurance* file on the disk in drive A.

8. Position the pointer on the filename *Insurance* in the Results area of the Search dialog box.

A:\Personal\Financial Records\Assets\Insurance.xls displays in a ScreenTip. The description is the location and name of the current file.

9. Double-click the file named *Insurance* in the Results area.

The Search dialog box closes, and Excel copies the location and the filename to the File name box in the Open dialog box.

10. Click Cancel to close the Open dialog box.

You completed the steps to locate a file using the Search feature. It was not necessary to actually open the file.

Continue with the Challenge exercises, or exit Excel.

Challenge

Each Challenge exercise provides a brief narrative introduction, followed by instructions, in a numbered-step format, that are not as detailed as those in the Skill Drill section. Exercises in this set might involve application of multiple skills or self-directed learning of related skills.

Each exercise is independent of the other, so you may complete the exercises in any order. If you need a paper copy of the completed exercise, enter your name centered in a header before printing.

1. Create a Workbook from a Predefined Template

You want to create a worksheet that computes the balance in your checking account after each inflow or outflow. You found a predefined template that you think will meet your needs if you make a few changes.

To create a workbook from a predefined template, follow these steps:

1. Choose File, New from the menu bar; then click General Templates in the New Workbook task pane.

2. Select the Spreadsheet Solutions tab in the Templates dialog box; then select Balance Sheet, and click OK.

3. Reduce the zoom setting, if necessary, to display columns A through J (see Figure 2.29).

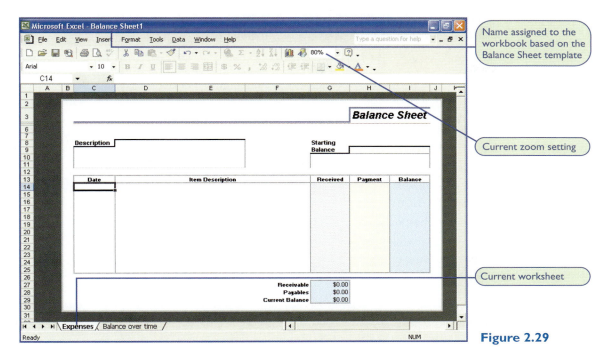

Figure 2.29

4. Choose Tools, point to Protection, and click Unprotect Sheet.

Previously protected cells can now be changed.

5. Change the labels in the following five cells.

Cell	Enter
H3	Check Book
G13	Inflow
H13	Outflow
F27	Total In
F28	Total Out

You modified five cells in the workbook based on a predefined template (see Figure 2.30).

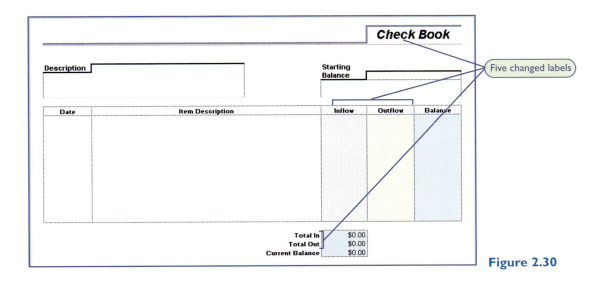

Figure 2.30

6. Choose <u>T</u>ools, point to <u>P</u>rotection, and click <u>P</u>rotect Sheet; then click OK to close the Protect Sheet dialog box without specifying a password or changing the user permissions.

   Worksheet protection is restored.

7. Enter **49.50** as the Starting Balance.

8. In row 14, enter **5/2/2003** in the Date column, enter **Automatic payroll deposit** in the Item Description column, and enter **1780.69** in the Inflow column.

   The amount $1,830.19 displays in the Balance column.

9. In row 15, enter **5/3/2003** in the Date column, enter **Electric bill** in the Item Description column, and enter **72.22** in the Outflow column.

   The amount $1,757.97 displays in the Balance column.

10. Save the workbook using the name **Check Book**, and close the workbook.

    You completed the steps to create a workbook from a predefined template—the objective of this exercise. However, if you were to use the results to maintain your checkbook balance on an ongoing basis, you would likely make additional changes. For example, you might delete the Total In, Total Out, and Current Balance information and modify remaining formulas to handle any number of item descriptions. You might change the worksheet's name to one that is more descriptive of inflows and outflows, and delete the second worksheet that charts the running balance. Subsequent skill sets include in-depth coverage of formulas and working with multiple worksheets.

2. Save a Workbook in a Different File Format

You finished the initial draft of a reunion budget using Excel 2002. You plan to edit the original version after you travel to another city. The friends you plan to visit have Excel installed on their home computer system, but you are not able to find out what version of Excel they have before you leave your home. To make sure you can open and edit the reunion budget, you want to save the file in a format that is compatible with earlier versions.

To save a workbook in another file format, follow these steps:

1. Open the *MEC-S201* workbook.

   A worksheet to plan a family reunion displays.

2. Choose <u>F</u>ile, Save <u>A</u>s; from the Save <u>i</u>n drop-down list, select the drive and folder in which you are saving your solutions for this text.

3. Enter **Reunion Budget1** as the filename.

4. Specify *Microsoft Excel 97-2002 & 5.0/95 Workbook* in the Save as <u>t</u>ype box.

5. Complete the save operation, and close the workbook.

Core Skill Set 3

Formatting and Printing Worksheets

CHAPTER 3

This skill set includes

Apply and modify cell formats
- Align cell contents
- Change font and font size
- Apply bold, italic, and underline
- Add color
- Add borders
- Use Format Painter
- Remove formatting

Modify row and column settings
- Freeze and split the worksheet display
- Hide and unhide rows and columns
- Insert and delete rows and columns

Modify row and column formats
- Adjust row height
- Adjust column width

Apply styles

Use automated tools to format worksheets

Modify Page Setup options for worksheets

Preview and print worksheets and workbooks

Skill Set Overview

substantial portion of this skill set focuses on changing the appearance of cell contents. You change how contents align in cells—left, right, center—and apply or change formats that include font style, font size, bold, italic, underline, color, and border.

You also work with columns and rows—hiding, unhiding, deleting, and inserting them. Your view of a worksheet changes as you freeze selected rows and columns, and view different sections of a worksheet in separate windows. The skill set ends with a comprehensive look at options for previewing and printing all or part of a worksheet.

Skill 3.1: Apply and Modify Cell Formats

After you create a worksheet, you might want to format it so that it is more readable and attractive. When you format a worksheet, you apply attributes to cells that alter the display of cell contents, but not the content itself. For example, you can format a worksheet by italicizing text and displaying a border around a cell or group of cells.

Figure 3.1 shows the worksheet you open in this skill area. Number formats have already been applied (you worked with formatting numbers and formula results in Excel Core Skill 1.2, *Enter and Edit Cell Data Including Text, Numbers, and Formulas*).

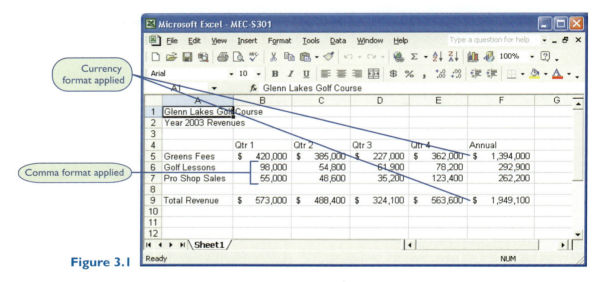

Figure 3.1

In this section, you apply a variety of other cell formats. The results are shown in Figure 3.2.

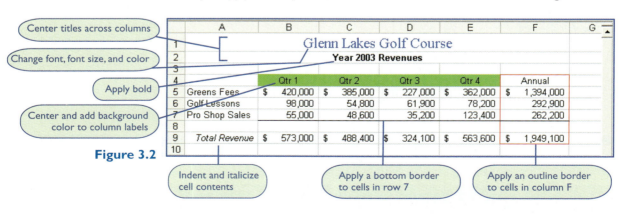

Figure 3.2

Align Cell Contents

When you enter data into a cell, text aligns with the left side of the cell; and numbers, dates, and times automatically align with the right side of the cell. You can change the alignment of cell contents at any time. For instance, you might want to fine-tune the appearance of column headings by centering each heading in its column.

In this section, you use the Merge and Center toolbar button to center the worksheet title and subtitle across six columns. You also use toolbar buttons to center column headings within cells and to indent text in a cell (see Figure 3.3).

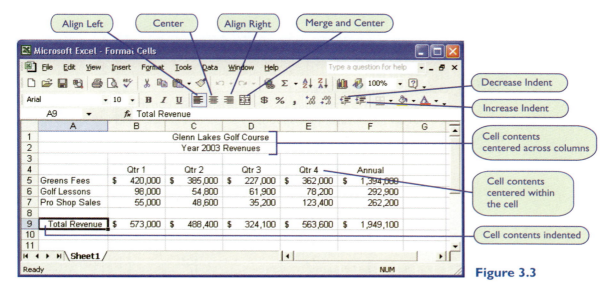

Figure 3.3

To Align Text

① **Open the file *MEC-S301* and save it as** `Format Cells`.

② **Select cells A1 through F1 in Sheet1, and click the Merge and Center button on the Formatting toolbar.**
Excel merges the selected cells into one cell and centers the title *Glenn Lakes Golf Course* across worksheet data in columns A through F (refer to row 1 in Figure 3.3).

Ⓧ *If you have problems...*
If you selected a range other than A1:F1, click the Merge and Center button again to separate the merged cells, and repeat Step 2.

---

③ **Select cells A2 through F2; then click the Merge and Center button.**
Excel merges the selected cells into one cell and centers the subtitle *Year 2003 Revenues* across columns A through F (refer to row 2 in Figure 3.3).

④ **Select cells B4 through F4.**
The range B4 through F4 contains the column headings you want to center.

⑤ **Click the Center button on the toolbar.**
Excel centers the *Qtr* and *Annual* labels (refer to row 4 in Figure 3.3).

⑥ **Click cell A9.**

continues ▶

To Align Text (continued)

The cell containing the label you want to indent is selected.

 7 **Click the Increase Indent button once.**
Excel indents the *Total Revenue* label (refer to cell A9 in Figure 3.3).

8 **Click the Save button in the toolbar.**
Excel saves your changes to the workbook named *Format Cells*. Keep the workbook open for the next skill, or close the workbook and exit Excel.

In Depth:
Other Alignment Options
Toolbar buttons are provided for only the six most common alignment options. You can access all alignment options by selecting Fo͟rmat, C͟ells and choosing the Alignment tab in the Format Cells dialog box (see Figure 3.4).

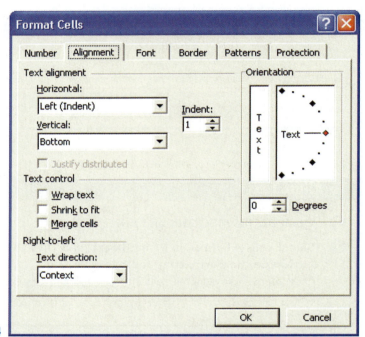

Figure 3.4

Several options in the *Text control* area of the Format Cells dialog box enable you to keep columns narrow and still display longer labels. Choose *W͟rap text* when you want to enter more than one line of text within a cell. As you type, the text automatically wraps to the next line in the cell. Choose *Shrin͟k to fit* if cell contents slightly exceed the current column width and you want to display contents on one line without increasing column width.

Sometimes, a label describing data takes up more space than its associated data. For example, a column heading might be *Days to Ship*, and the data in cells below are comprised of no more than two characters (it assumes no more than 99 days to ship an order). To keep the column narrow, yet display the entire column heading, select settings in the *Orientation* section of the Format Cells dialog box. You can click an option to display each character below the previous one, drag a red marker to change the degrees of orientation, or enter the desired rotation in the _Degrees_ text box.

Excel also supports aligning text vertically within a cell, such as at the top or centered rather than at the bottom.

Change Font and Font Size

You can dramatically improve the appearance of your worksheet by using different fonts. Used as a general term, _font_ refers to the type style, type size, and type attributes that you apply to text and numbers. As a specific command in Excel, font refers to the _typeface_—a style of print, such as Arial, Courier, or Times New Roman. The default font in an Excel worksheet is Arial.

Type size is measured in points. A _point_ is a unit of measurement used in printing and publishing to designate the height of type. There are roughly 72 points in an inch. The default type size in a worksheet is 10 points.

Toolbar buttons let you quickly apply a single formatting characteristic, such as a different font or font size. You can also change typeface, type size, and type attributes using the Font tab of the Format Cells dialog box, which enables you to preview and apply many formatting characteristics at one time.

In this section, you use toolbar buttons to change the font and font size of the worksheet title _Glenn Lakes Golf Course_, as shown in Figure 3.5.

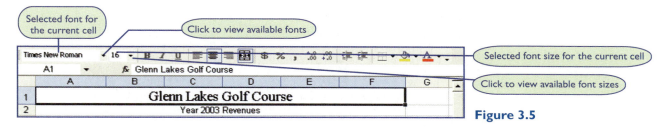

Figure 3.5

To Change Font and Font Size

① **Open the workbook named _Format Cells_, if necessary, and click cell A1 in Sheet1.**
The merged cells containing the title _Glenn Lakes Golf Course_ are selected.

② **Click the down arrow to the right of the current font in the toolbar.**

③ **In the Font drop-down list, select Times New Roman.**
The typeface you want to apply to the active cell is selected. You might have to use the scroll arrows to scroll through the list of fonts to get to Times New Roman.

④ **Click the down arrow to the right of the current font size in the toolbar.**

⑤ **In the Font Size drop-down list, select 16.**
The font size increases to 16 points. Notice that the row height automatically adjusts to accommodate the new font size.

⑥ **Check that the title in your worksheet reflects the changes in font and font size shown in Figure 3.5, and click the Save button in the toolbar.**
Excel saves your changes to the workbook named _Format Cells_. Keep the workbook open for the next skill, or close the workbook and exit Excel.

In Depth:
Selecting Fonts

To open the Format Cells dialog box quickly, right-click the active cell and choose *Format Cells* from the shortcut menu. Click the Font tab to see additional font options. The fonts available in the <u>F</u>ont list vary, depending on the software installed on your computer and the printer(s) you use.

To scroll through the <u>F</u>ont drop-down list quickly, start typing the name of the font you want to apply. Excel locates the fonts alphabetically.

Apply Bold, Italic, and Underline

You can use buttons on the toolbar to apply three common font attributes: **bold**, *italic*, and <u>underline</u>. To change attributes (called font styles in Excel), simply select the cells that you want to format and click the relevant button on the Formatting toolbar. To remove an attribute, click its button again.

In this section, you make the subtitle, *Year 2003 Revenues*, bold and apply italic to the *Total Revenue* label, as shown in Figure 3.6.

Figure 3.6

To Apply Bold and Italic

❶ **Open the workbook named *Format Cells*, if necessary, and click cell A2 in Sheet1.**

The merged cells containing the subtitle *Year 2003 Revenues* are selected.

❷ **Click the Bold button in the toolbar.**

❸ **Click cell A9.**

The cell containing the label *Total Revenue* is selected.

❹ **Click the Italic button in the toolbar.**

❺ **Check that the subtitle in cell A2 and the label in cell A9 reflect the changes in font style shown in Figure 3.6, and click the Save button in the Standard toolbar.**

Excel saves your changes to the workbook named *Format Cells*. Keep the workbook open for the next skill, or close the workbook and exit Excel.

In Depth:

Applying Font Formats

The Font tab in the Format Cells dialog box includes a Bold Italic option. You can also apply color, and select among a variety of underline styles (Single, Double, Single Accounting, and Double Accounting) and special effects (Strikethrough, Superscript, and Subscript).

You can also apply font styles to individual characters within a cell, rather than the entire cell's contents. To do so, double-click the cell, drag to select the characters you want to format, apply the format, and press ⏎Enter.

Add Color

Selective use of color can enhance the appearance of a worksheet. You can apply color to cell contents, to the background of a cell, or to a border surrounding cells. In this section, you display the worksheet title in blue and apply a green background to the column headings for quarters by using the buttons shown in Figure 3.7.

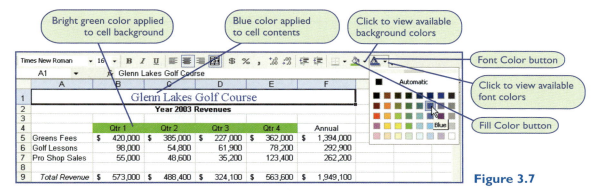

Figure 3.7

To Add Color

1 **Open the workbook named *Format Cells*, if necessary, and click cell A1 in Sheet1.**

The merged cells that contain the title *Glenn Lakes Golf Course* are selected.

2 **Click the down arrow to the right of the Font Color button in the toolbar.**

A palette of 40 colors opens. If you position the mouse pointer on a color square and pause, you see the name assigned to that color.

3 **Click the square named Blue in the Font Color palette (refer to Figure 3.7).**

The title *Glenn Lakes Golf Course* displays in blue.

 If you have problems...

If the background instead of the text displays in blue, you used Fill Color instead of Font Color. Click the Undo button in the toolbar to reverse the incorrect action and repeat steps 2 and 3.

continues ▶

To Add Color (continued)

④ Select cells B4 through E4.
The column headings for quarters 1 through 4 are selected.

⑤ Click the down arrow to the right of the Fill Color button in the toolbar.
A palette of 40 colors opens.

⑥ Click the square named Bright Green in the Fill Color palette.
The backgrounds of cells B4 through E4 display in bright green (refer to Figure 3.7).

 ⑦ Click cell A1 to deselect the range, and click the Save button in the toolbar.
Excel saves your changes to the workbook named *Format Cells*. Keep the workbook open for the next skill, or close the workbook and exit Excel.

 ### In Depth:
Removing Color
You can remove color applied to text by selecting the text, clicking the down arrow next to the Font Color button, and selecting Automatic at the top of the color palette.

You can remove a color background by selecting the cell(s), clicking the down arrow next to the Fill Color button, and selecting No Fill at the top of the color palette.

Applying Patterns
You can draw attention to selected worksheet cells by shading them with a pattern. A *pattern* repeats an effect, such as a horizontal, vertical, or diagonal stripe. To apply a pattern, select the Patterns tab in the Format Cells dialog box and display the Pattern drop-down list. Choose one of 18 predefined settings that include crosshatch and stripe patterns, as well as various percentages of gray. The default pattern color is black, but you can select from a palette of colors.

Color Concerns in Printed Worksheets
You can apply more than one color setting to a cell, such as blue text, yellow background, and red border. However, overuse of color might be distracting. Also, color might be an effective enhancement when viewing a worksheet onscreen, but its use can produce printed output that is hard to read, especially if you are not printing on a color printer. For best results when printing, keep the choices of colors and patterns simple.

Add Borders

A *border* is a solid or dashed line applied to one or more sides of a cell or range of cells. You can use a border as a divider between cell entries. Selective use of borders can also help to focus a user's attention on a specific section of a worksheet.

You can use the Borders button on the toolbar to select among 12 common border styles, or you can draw a border. Additional options—including one to apply color to a border—are available through the Border tab of the Format Cells dialog box.

In this section, you set up two borders (see Figure 3.8)—one using the toolbar and the other using the Format Cells dialog box.

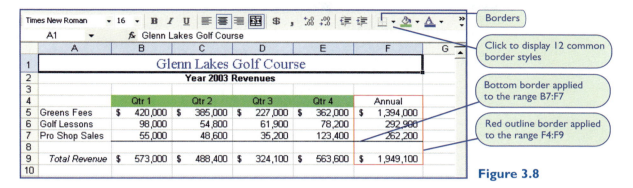

Figure 3.8

To Add Borders

① **Open the workbook named *Format Cells*, if necessary, and select the range B7:F7 in Sheet1.**
The cells containing numbers and a formula related to *Pro Shop Sales* are selected.

② **Click the down arrow to the right of the Borders button in the toolbar.**
A palette of 12 border styles opens. You can also select an option to draw a border.

③ **Position the mouse pointer on the second border style in the first row—the style named Bottom Border (see Figure 3.9).**

Figure 3.9

④ **Click the border style named Bottom Border.**
Excel applies a solid-black single-line border to the bottom edges of the selected cells (refer to row 7 in Figure 3.8).

⑤ **Select cells F4 through F9.**

⑥ **Choose Format, Cells.**
The Format Cells dialog box opens.

⑦ **Click the Border tab.**

⑧ **Click the down arrow to the right of the Color window, and choose Red.**
The selected color appears in the color window (see Figure 3.10).

continues ▶

To Add a Borders (continued)

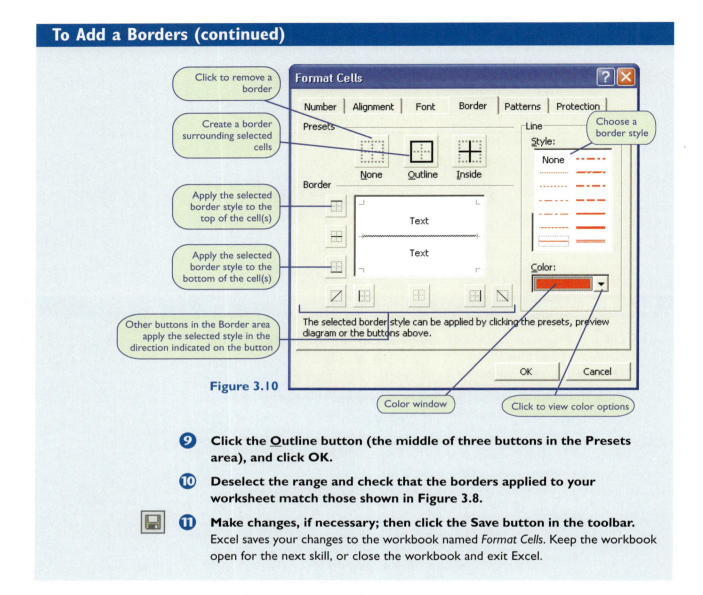

Figure 3.10

⑨ **Click the Underline Outline button (the middle of three buttons in the Presets area), and click OK.**

⑩ **Deselect the range and check that the borders applied to your worksheet match those shown in Figure 3.8.**

  ⑪ **Make changes, if necessary; then click the Save button in the toolbar.**
Excel saves your changes to the workbook named *Format Cells*. Keep the workbook open for the next skill, or close the workbook and exit Excel.

In Depth:
Avoiding Style and Color Problems with Borders
The order in which you select options from the Border tab in the Format Cells dialog box is important. If you select a border style and/or border color after selecting the border's position, Excel ignores the style and color settings.

Drawing and Erasing Borders Quickly
You can click the down arrow by the Borders button on the Formatting toolbar and select the Draw Borders option to draw a new border or erase an existing one. The pointer changes to a pencil, and the Borders toolbar displays with four buttons: Draw Border, Erase Border, Line Style, and Line Color.

To draw an outline border, follow these steps: select a different line style and/or a color on the Borders toolbar if desired, click in the worksheet where you want the upper-left corner of the border to appear, drag right and down to expand the border to include more cells as needed, and click the Close button on the Borders toolbar to turn off drawing. If you prefer a grid effect—showing borders around each cell in the drawn range—over an outline effect, click the down arrow by the Draw Border button on the Borders toolbar, and select Draw Border Grid before you begin drawing.

To erase a border without using the Border tab in the Format Cells dialog box, click the down arrow by the Borders button on the Formatting toolbar, select the Draw Borders option, and click the Erase Border button (the pointer changes to an eraser). Drag the pointer over the borderlines you want to erase, and click the Close button on the Borders toolbar to turn off erasing.

Use Format Painter

Excel provides a Format Painter button on the Standard toolbar that you can use to copy formatting applied to worksheet cells. This feature makes it possible to apply existing formats without opening dialog boxes or making multiple selections from toolbars. Use this feature now to copy the color and alignment settings for the quarterly column headings to the row descriptions of revenue sources (see Figure 3.11).

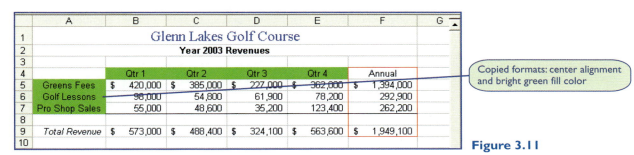

Figure 3.11

To Copy Formats Using Format Painter

1 **Open the *Format Cells* workbook, if necessary, and click cell B4 in Sheet1.**
A cell containing the formats you want to copy is selected.

2 **Click the Format Painter button in the toolbar.**
A flashing dotted line appears around the selected cell (see Figure 3.12).

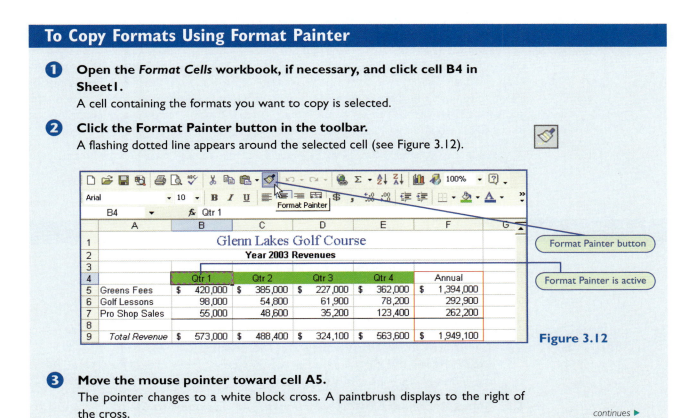

Figure 3.12

3 **Move the mouse pointer toward cell A5.**
The pointer changes to a white block cross. A paintbrush displays to the right of the cross.

continues ▶

To Copy Formats Using Format Painter (continued)

④ Select cells A5 through A7, release the mouse button, and deselect the range.
Excel applies center alignment and a bright green fill color to the specified cells in column A.

 ⑤ Save your changes to the *Format Cells* workbook.
Keep the workbook open for the last skill in this skill area, or close the workbook and exit Excel.

 ### *In Depth:*
Copying Formats to Multiple Locations
If you single-click the Format Painter button to start a copy operation, the feature automatically turns off as soon as you select the target cell or range. If you want to copy formatting to more than one location, double-click the Format Painter button to start the copy. The feature remains active until you click the Format Painter button again.

Copying Column Widths
You can use Format Painter to copy a column width. Select the heading of a column that is already set to the desired width, click the Format Painter button, and then click the heading of the column you want to change.

Remove Formatting

The quickest way to remove all applied formats is to select the cell(s) and choose Edit, Clear, Formats. If you want to remove some, but not all, of the formats applied to a cell, you must remove the effects one at a time. In most cases, you start the process to apply the format and then select an option to restore the default setting (such as Automatic to remove color or None to remove a border). Some effects can be removed by choosing a related button on the toolbar, such as Align Left to remove centering, Decrease Indent to remove indenting, or one of the decimal buttons to adjust number of decimal places.

In this section, you remove one format (a border) and then remove multiple formats with a single command (centering and fill color).

To Remove Formatting

① Open the *Format Cells* workbook, if necessary, and select the range F4:F9 on Sheet1.
The cells surrounded with a red border are selected.

② Choose Format, Cells; then select the Border tab.

③ Click None in the Presets area and then click OK.
Excel removes the single-line red border surrounding the range F4:F9. Now, remove multiple formats with a single command.

④ Select the range A5:A7; then choose Edit, and point to Clear.

Four options display on the Clear menu (see Figure 3.13). The first option removes both contents and formats. Choose the second option to remove only formats.

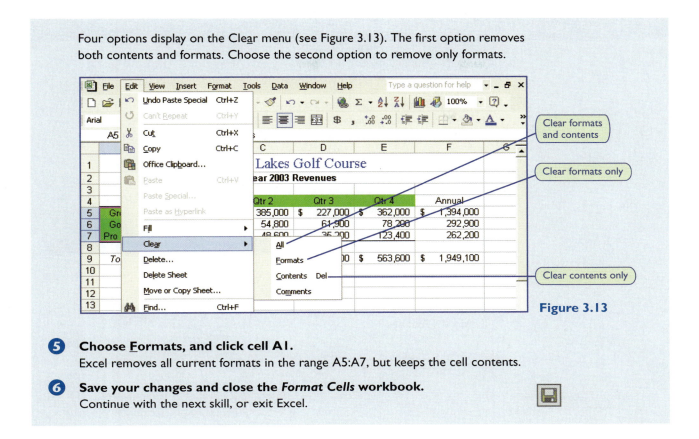

Figure 3.13

5 **Choose Formats, and click cell A1.**
Excel removes all current formats in the range A5:A7, but keeps the cell contents.

6 **Save your changes and close the *Format Cells* workbook.**
Continue with the next skill, or exit Excel.

For immediate reinforcement, work Skill Drills 1 through 3 and Challenges 1 and 2.

Skill 3.2: **Modify Row and Column Settings**

At times the worksheets you create might be quite large. In this section, you learn ways to view more than one area of a worksheet at a time. You also acquire skills to manipulate columns and rows—hiding, unhiding, inserting, and deleting them.

Freeze and Split the Worksheet Display

The combination of screen size, screen resolution, font size, and zoom level determines the amount of a worksheet that you can view on one screen. Font size and zoom level settings are controlled within Excel. As a general guideline, do not alter font sizes just to view a larger area of a worksheet because changes in font size are also reflected on printed output. Changing the zoom level on the toolbar increases or decreases your view of one area of a worksheet without affecting your printed output.

If you want to view different sections of a worksheet at one time, Excel provides two features that you can use alone or in combination. You can split the worksheet window into two or four panes, and scroll to any area of the worksheet in any pane. You can also freeze selected rows and/or columns on the screen. Freezing enables you to keep row and column headings in view as you scroll right and left to view other columns or scroll up and down to view other rows.

In this section, you use both features to view different sections of the Condensed IS worksheet.

To Freeze and Split the Worksheet Display

① **Open the *MEC-S302* workbook, and save it as** `Rows and Columns`.
The workbook includes two worksheets named Condensed IS and Hours.

② **Click cell B5 in the Condensed IS worksheet.**
The current cell determines which rows and columns are affected by a Freeze command. Excel freezes rows above the current cell and columns to the left of the current cell.

③ **Choose <u>W</u>indow, <u>F</u>reeze Panes.**
Horizontal and vertical lines intersect at the upper-left corner of the current cell B5 (see Figure 3.14).

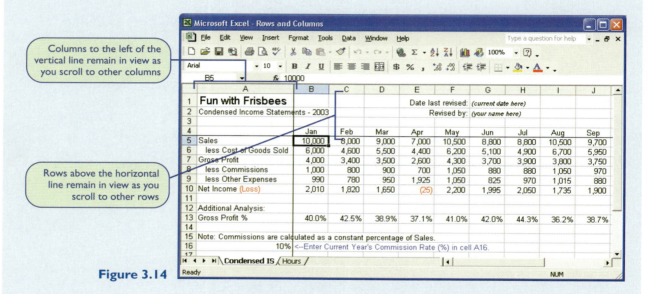

Columns to the left of the vertical line remain in view as you scroll to other columns

Rows above the horizontal line remain in view as you scroll to other rows

Figure 3.14

④ **Scroll right until column G displays next to column A.**
Columns B through F disappear from view, but the row headings in Column A remain on the screen (see Figure 3.15).

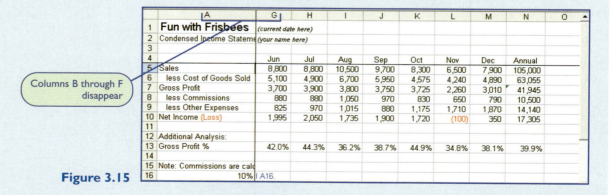

Columns B through F disappear

Figure 3.15

⑤ **Choose <u>W</u>indow, Un<u>f</u>reeze Panes.**

The horizontal and vertical lines disappear, and columns B through F reappear. Panes are no longer frozen onscreen.

6 **Display cell A1 in the upper-left corner of the worksheet window; then click cell E1.**

This makes cell E1 the current cell. Excel splits a worksheet into panes above and to the left of the current cell.

7 **Choose Window, Split.**

Because the current cell is at the top of the worksheet, Excel can split the worksheet only into left and right panes (see Figure 3.16). You can scroll around the worksheet in either pane. You also can drag the gray bar left or right to change the width of the panes.

	A	B	C	D	E	F	G	H	I	J
1	**Fun with Frisbees**				Date last revised:	*(current date here)*				
2	Condensed Income Statements - 2003					Revised by:	*(your name here)*			
3										
4		Jan	Feb	Mar	Apr	May	Jun	Jul	Aug	Sep
5	Sales	10,000	8,000	9,000	7,000	10,500	8,800	8,800	10,500	9,700
6	less Cost of Goods Sold	6,000	4,600	5,500	4,400	6,200	5,100	4,900	6,700	5,950
7	Gross Profit	4,000	3,400	3,500	2,600	4,300	3,700	3,900	3,800	3,750
8	less Commissions	1,000	800	900	700	1,050	880	880	1,050	970
9	less Other Expenses	990	780	950	1,925	1,050	825	970	1,015	880
10	Net Income (Loss)	2,010	1,820	1,650	(25)	2,200	1,995	2,050	1,735	1,900
11										
12	Additional Analysis:									
13	Gross Profit %	40.0%	42.5%	38.9%	37.1%	41.8%	42.0%	44.3%	36.2%	38.7%
14										
15	Note: Commissions are calculated as a constant percentage of Sales.									
16	10%	<--Enter Current Year's Commission Rate (%) in cell A16.								
17										

Condensed IS / Hours /

Use the vertical scrollbar to shift screen display up or down in both panes

Use this horizontal scrollbar to shift worksheet display left or right in the left pane

Use this horizontal scrollbar to shift worksheet display left or right in the right pane

Figure 3.16

8 **Scroll the worksheet display in either pane as desired, and choose Window, Remove Split.**

The split view disappears. You also can drag the gray bar to the left or right edge of the screen to quickly remove the split panes.

9 **Make cell A1 the current cell, and save your changes to the *Rows and Columns* workbook.**

Keep the workbook open for the next skill, or close the workbook and exit Excel.

In Depth:
Editing When Split Panes Are Active
When a worksheet is split into panes, it's possible to see the same section of a worksheet in multiple panes. This effect relates only to the screen display; the command does not create duplicate cells. Therefore, you can edit the contents of a cell in one pane, and the changes immediately appear in any other pane that displays the same cell.

Hide and Unhide Rows and Columns

For privacy or other reasons, there might be rows or columns in a worksheet that you do not want to display at the moment. Perhaps you generally want to keep a column containing employees' salary data hidden, displaying it only when you want to edit an entry. Or you might want to temporarily hide 12 columns that store monthly data, so you can concentrate on re-viewing annual amounts.

When you hide rows or columns in a worksheet, the data in those hidden parts is removed from view but not deleted. If you print the worksheet, the hidden parts do not print.

In this section, you hide 12 columns and three rows, view the results in Print Preview, and then restore display of hidden columns and rows.

To Hide and Unhide Rows and Columns

1 **Open the *Rows and Columns* workbook, if necessary; then set the Zoom level to 75% in the Condensed IS worksheet.**

2 **Click the B column heading in the worksheet frame, and drag right until columns B through M are selected.**

3 **Choose F̲ormat, C̲olumn, H̲ide.**
Excel hides columns B through M (see Figure 3.17). A thick border displays be-tween columns A and N. The border disappears when you move the cell pointer.

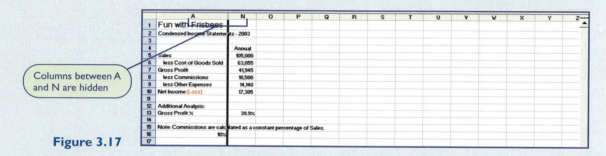

Columns between A and N are hidden

Figure 3.17

4 **Click the row heading 12 in the worksheet frame, and drag down until rows 12 through 14 are selected.**

5 **Choose F̲ormat, R̲ow, H̲ide.**
Excel hides rows 12 through 14. A thick border displays between rows 11 and 15.

6 **Choose F̲ile, Print Pre̲view.**
The hidden columns and rows do not appear in Print Preview mode (see Figure 3.18).

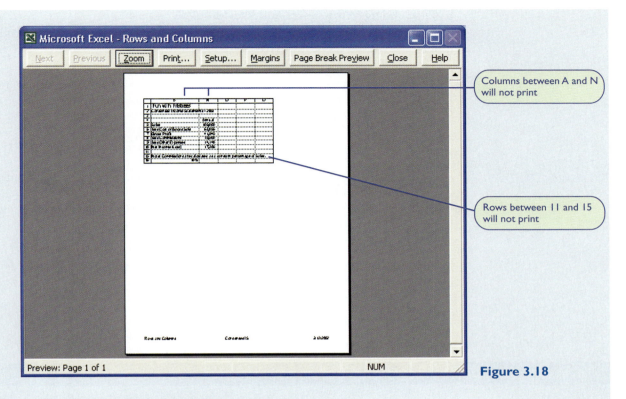

Figure 3.18

Callout: Columns between A and N will not print

Callout: Rows between 11 and 15 will not print

7 Click the **Close** button to exit **Print Preview**.

8 Click the **A** column heading in the worksheet frame, and drag right until column **N** is also selected.

By selecting at least one column heading or cell on each side of the hidden columns, you are also selecting the hidden columns.

9 Choose **Format, Column, Unhide**.

Excel restores the display of columns B through M.

10 Click row **11** in the worksheet frame, and drag down until row **15** is also selected.

By selecting at least one row heading or cell on each side of the hidden rows, you are also selecting the hidden rows.

11 Choose **Format, Row, Unhide**.

Excel restores the display of rows 12 through 14.

12 Click cell **A1** to deselect the restored range, and save the *Rows and Columns* workbook.

Continue with the next skill, or close the workbook and exit Excel.

In Depth:
Unhiding Column A or Row 1

If the first column or row in a worksheet is hidden, you can select it by choosing Edit, Go To and then specifying A1 in the Reference box. After clicking OK to exit the Go To dialog box, point to either Row or Column on the Format menu, and click Unhide.

Hiding Worksheets and Workbooks

You can also hide and unhide workbooks, and worksheets within workbooks. To hide the current worksheet, choose Format, Sheet, Hide. To hide a workbook, open it and then choose Window, Hide.

To unhide a worksheet, choose Format, Sheet, Unhide and select from a list of hidden sheets in the Unhide dialog box. To unhide a workbook, choose Window, Unhide and select from a list of hidden workbooks.

Insert and Delete Rows and Columns

If you decide to add more data within an existing worksheet, you can insert rows and columns. Inserting a row is a two-step process: Select any cell in a row, and then choose Insert, Rows. Inserting a column involves a similar process: Select any cell in a column, and then choose Insert, Columns. Excel always inserts a new row above the row you select, and inserts a new column to the left of the column you select.

Sometimes, you no longer want to include an entire row or column of data. Deleting a row or column can be done in two steps: Select a row heading or a column heading in the worksheet frame and then choose Edit, Delete.

In the following steps, you delete several rows and insert a column.

To Insert and Delete Rows and Columns

1 Open the *Rows and Columns* workbook, if necessary; then set the Zoom level to 100% in the Condensed IS worksheet.

2 Click any cell in column E.

3 Choose Insert, Columns.

The contents of column E and all columns to the right of it shift to the right. A new blank column is inserted as the new column E (see Figure 3.19). Excel automatically changes the letters of the columns to the right of the new column E.

Inserted column

Contents move to the right

Insert Options button

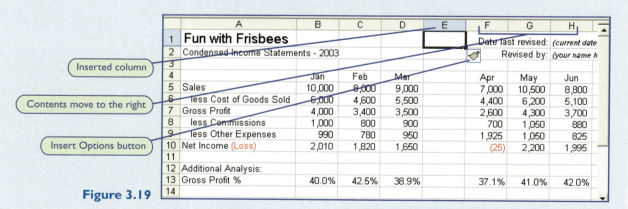

Figure 3.19

 If you have problems...

If you insert the column in the wrong position, you can reverse the action by choosing Edit, Undo Insert Columns.

4 **Position the pointer on the Insert Options button (refer to Figure 3.19), and click its down arrow.**

The button displays if inserted rows or columns are bordered by formatted cells. Three formatting options are available after inserting the column (see Figure 3.20).

	A	B	C	D	E	F	G	H
1	**Fun with Frisbees**					Date last revised:	*(current date h*
2	Condensed Income Statements - 2003					Revised by:	*(your name her*
3						○	
4		Jan	Feb	Mar		● Format Same As Left	
5	Sales	10,000	8,000	9,000		○ Format Same As Right	00
6	less Cost of Goods Sold	6,000	4,600	5,500		○ Clear Formatting	00
7	Gross Profit	4,000	3,400	3,500			00
8	less Commissions	1,000	800	900		700	1,050	880
9	less Other Expenses	990	780	950		1,925	1,050	825
10	Net Income (Loss)	2,010	1,820	1,650		(25)	2,200	1,995
11								
12	Additional Analysis:							
13	Gross Profit %	40.0%	42.5%	38.9%		37.1%	41.0%	42.0%
14								
15	Note: Commissions are calculated as a constant percentage of Sales.							
16		10%	<--Enter Current Year's Commission Rate (%) in cell A16.					

Figure 3.20

5 **Click outside the options list to accept the default setting *Format Same As Left*.**

6 **Enter Qtr 1 in cell E4.**

The label for first quarter data automatically centers in cell E4. It is not necessary at this point to practice entering formulas. Instead, explore several ways to delete rows 12 through 14.

7 **Select the range A12:A14, and choose <u>E</u>dit, <u>D</u>elete.**

The range A12:A14 is selected, and the row numbers 12 through 14 in the worksheet frame display with blue highlighting. The Delete dialog box opens. It includes four options to apply to the selected cells (see Figure 3.21).

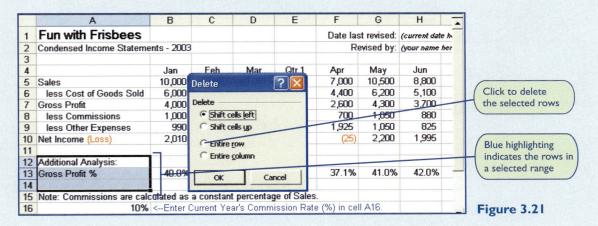

	A	B	C	D	E	F	G	H
1	**Fun with Frisbees**					Date last revised:	*(current date h*
2	Condensed Income Statements - 2003					Revised by:	*(your name her*
3								
4		Jan	Feb	Mar	Qtr 1	Apr	May	Jun
5	Sales	10,000				7,000	10,500	8,800
6	less Cost of Goods Sold	6,000				4,400	6,200	5,100
7	Gross Profit	4,000				2,600	4,300	3,700
8	less Commissions	1,000				700	1,050	880
9	less Other Expenses	990				1,925	1,050	825
10	Net Income (Loss)	2,010				(25)	2,200	1,995
11								
12	Additional Analysis:							
13	Gross Profit %	40.0%				37.1%	41.0%	42.0%
14								
15	Note: Commissions are calculated as a constant percentage of Sales.							
16		10%	<--Enter Current Year's Commission Rate (%) in cell A16.					

Delete dialog box:
Delete
- ● Shift cells left
- ○ Shift cells up
- ○ Entire row
- ○ Entire column

[OK] [Cancel]

> Click to delete the selected rows

> Blue highlighting indicates the rows in a selected range

Figure 3.21

8 **Select Entire <u>r</u>ow, and click OK.**

The selected rows 12 through 14 are removed. The contents of all rows below the deleted rows shift up, and Excel automatically renumbers the rows in the worksheet frame (see Figure 3.22).

continues ▶

To Insert and Delete Rows and Columns (continued)

	A	B	C	D	E	F	G	H	
1	**Fun with Frisbees**					Date last revised:		*(current date h*	
2	Condensed Income Statements - 2003					Revised by:		*(your name her*	
3									
4		Jan	Feb	Mar	Qtr 1	Apr	May	Jun	
5	Sales	10,000	8,000	9,000		7,000	10,500	8,800	
6	less Cost of Goods Sold	6,000	4,600	5,500		4,400	6,200	5,100	
7	Gross Profit	4,000	3,400	3,500		2,600	4,300	3,700	
8	less Commissions	1,000	800	900		700	1,050	880	
9	less Other Expenses	990	780	950		1,925	1,050	825	
10	Net Income (Loss)	2,010	1,820	1,650		(25)	2,200	1,995	
11									
12	Note: Commissions are calculated as a constant percentage of Sales.								
13	10%	<--Enter Current Year's Commission Rate (%) in cell A16.							
14									
15									

Cell contents below the deleted rows shift up

Figure 3.22

⑨ Choose Edit, Undo Delete.

Excel restores the deleted rows. The range A12:A14 is still selected, and the corresponding row numbers in the worksheet frame display with blue highlighting.

⑩ Click row 12 in the worksheet frame, and drag down until row 14 is also selected.

Now entire rows 12 through 14 are selected, and the row numbers 12 through 14 in the worksheet frame display with black highlighting (see Figure 3.23).

	A	B	C	D	E	F	G	H	
1	**Fun with Frisbees**					Date last revised:		*(current date h*	
2	Condensed Income Statements - 2003					Revised by:		*(your name her*	
3									
4		Jan	Feb	Mar	Qtr 1	Apr	May	Jun	
5	Sales	10,000	8,000	9,000		7,000	10,500	8,800	
6	less Cost of Goods Sold	6,000	4,600	5,500		4,400	6,200	5,100	
7	Gross Profit	4,000	3,400	3,500		2,600	4,300	3,700	
8	less Commissions	1,000	800	900		700	1,050	880	
9	less Other Expenses	990	780	950		1,925	1,050	825	
10	Net Income (Loss)	2,010	1,820	1,650		(25)	2,200	1,995	
11									
12	Additional Analysis:								
13	Gross Profit %		40.0%	42.5%	38.9%		37.1%	41.0%	42.0%
14									
15	Note: Commissions are calculated as a constant percentage of Sales.								
16	10%	<--Enter Current Year's Commission Rate (%) in cell A16.							

Black highlighting indicates entire rows are selected

Figure 3.23

⑪ Choose Edit, Delete.

The Delete dialog box does not open. Excel immediately deletes the selected rows. The results are the same as those that were achieved using the Delete dialog box (refer to Figure 3.22).

⑫ Click cell A1, and save your changes to the *Rows and Columns* workbook.

Continue with the next skill, or close the workbook and exit Excel.

Alternate Way:
Inserting and Deleting with a Shortcut Menu

You can use a shortcut menu to insert or delete columns, rows, and cell contents. Follow these steps: Select the column, row, or cell(s); move the mouse pointer to the selected area; right-click the mouse to display the shortcut menu; and choose Insert or Delete.

In Depth:

Inserting Multiple Rows and Columns

If you want to insert more than one row or column at a time, select as many adjacent rows or columns as you need blank rows or columns, and choose Insert, Rows or Insert, Columns. For example, if you want to insert five new rows beginning at row 4, select rows 4 through 8 and choose Insert, Rows.

For immediate reinforcement, work Skill Drills 6 and 7.

Skill 3.3: **Modify Row and Column Formats**

In Skill 1.1, you used the Merge and Center button to center cell contents across selected columns. In Skill 3.3, you adjust row height and column width using a variety of methods.

Adjust Row Height

The height of a row rarely needs to be adjusted. Excel automatically adjusts row height to accommodate the largest font size applied to any cell in the row.

There are several ways that you can change Excel's default row height. Clicking the mouse pointer between two rows in the worksheet frame and then dragging up or down provides a quick and easy way to change the height of the topmost row. You can also choose Row, Height from the Format menu to change the height of selected rows.

In the following steps, you view the automatic changes in row height that occur when you change font size and rotate text. You also manually adjust the height of a row.

To Change Row Height

1 **Open the *Rows and Columns* workbook, if necessary; then click the worksheet tab named *Hours* near the bottom of the worksheet.**

2 **Click cell A1.**
The number *14* displays in the Font Size box (see Figure 3.24).

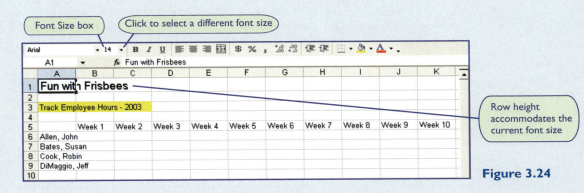

Figure 3.24

3 **Display the Font Size drop-down list and select *10*.**
Excel automatically reduces the height of row 1 to fit the smaller font size (see Figure 3.25).

continues ▶

To Change Row Height (continued)

New font size

Row height adjusts
to the new font size

Figure 3.25

④ **Select the range B5:K5; then choose Format, Cells.**

⑤ **Click the Alignment tab in the Format Cells dialog box, and drag the red diamond in the Orientation box up to a 45 degree setting (see Figure 3.26).**

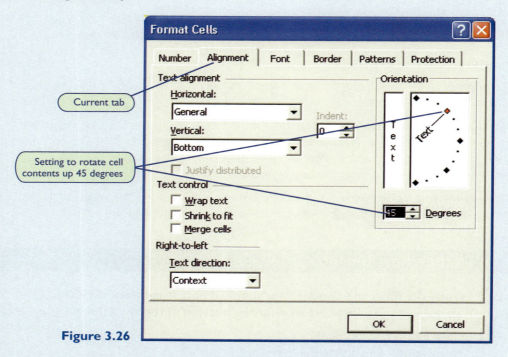

Current tab

Setting to rotate cell
contents up 45 degrees

Figure 3.26

⑥ **Click OK; then click outside row 5 to deselect it.**
Excel automatically increases the height of row 5 to fit the rotated text (see Figure 3.27).

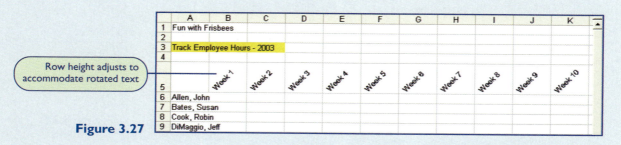

Row height adjusts to
accommodate rotated text

Figure 3.27

⑦ **Position the mouse pointer between row numbers 3 and 4 in the worksheet frame; click and hold down the left mouse button (see Figure 3.28).**

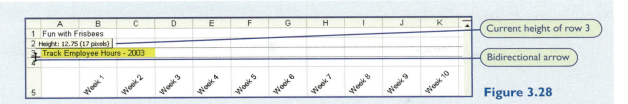

Current height of row 3

Bidirectional arrow

Figure 3.28

The pointer changes to a bidirectional arrow.

8 Drag the pointer down until *21.00* or a value close to 21.00 displays as the row height; then release the mouse button.
You manually increased the height of row 3.

9 Click cell A1, and save your changes to the Rows and Columns workbook.
Continue with the next skill, or close the workbook and exit Excel.

Adjust Column Width

Under selected circumstances, Excel automatically widens a column. For example, if a cell is already formatted as Currency two decimal places, and you enter a number that is larger than the current width of the cell, the column widens automatically to display the cell contents in the applied number format. However, column width does not adjust automatically in other situations, such as when you enter long labels and unformatted numbers.

Clicking the mouse pointer between two columns in the worksheet frame and then dragging left or right provides a quick and easy way to change the width of the leftmost column. Double-clicking between column letters automatically changes the column width to accommodate the longest entry in that column. You can also choose Column from the Format menu, and select options to set a specific width or to automatically change column width to fit cell contents.

In the following steps, you use the click-and-drag method to widen one column. You use the same method to narrow multiple columns at one time.

To Change Column Width

1 Open the *Rows and Columns* workbook and select the *Hours* worksheet, if necessary.

2 Position the mouse pointer between column letters A and B in the worksheet frame; click and hold down the left mouse button (see Figure 3.29).

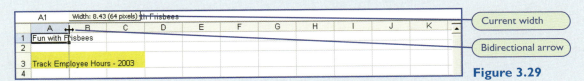

Current width

Bidirectional arrow

Figure 3.29

The pointer changes to a bidirectional arrow. Drag right to increase the width of column A; drag left to reduce the width of column A.

3 Drag the pointer to the right until the column is wide enough to display the *DiMaggio, Jeff* text entry in cell A9; then release the mouse button.
Column A widens to display *DiMaggio, Jeff* within the boundaries of cell A9.

continues ▶

To Change Column Width (continued)

4 Click the column letter **B** in the worksheet frame and drag right until column letter **K** is highlighted; then release the mouse button.
Columns B through K are selected.

5 Position the mouse pointer between column letters **B** and **C** in the worksheet frame; click and hold down the left mouse button (see Figure 3.30).

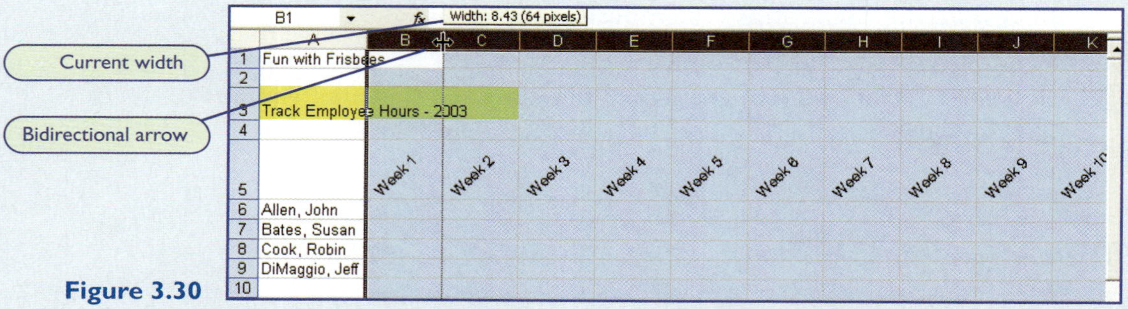

Current width

Bidirectional arrow

Figure 3.30

6 Drag the pointer left until the width displayed is **6.00** or a value close to **6.00**; then release the mouse button, and click cell **A1**.
All selected columns are reduced to the specified width (see Figure 3.31).

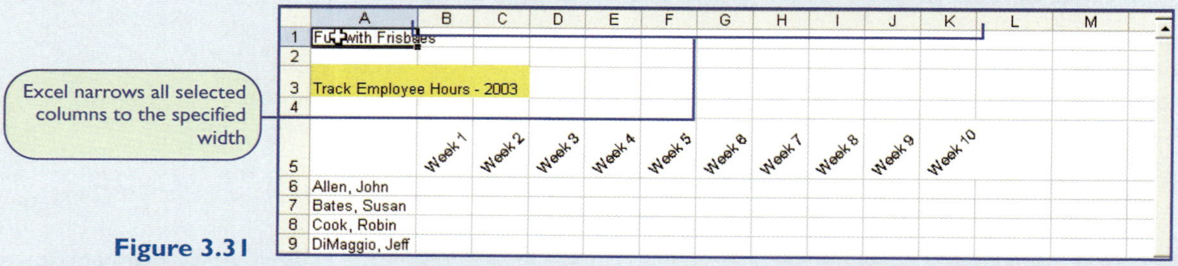

Excel narrows all selected columns to the specified width

Figure 3.31

7 Save your changes to the *Rows and Columns* workbook, and close the workbook.
Continue with the next skill, or exit Excel.

For immediate reinforcement, work Skill Drill 5 and Challenge 1.

Skill 3.4: Apply Styles

A *style* is a means of combining more than one format, such as font type, size, and color, into a single definition that can be applied to one or more cells. Use styles to maintain a consistent look in a worksheet. If you want to change that look, you can change the style once and reapply it, rather than edit individual cell attributes in multiple locations.

You might be surprised to know that you already use styles. When you create a new workbook, each cell is formatted using the Normal style containing Excel's default formats.

The easiest way to define a style is to apply all of the desired formats to a cell; select Format, Style; and give the current style a new name. You can also define a new style in the same manner as you edit a style—by selecting Format, Style; giving the current style a new name; and modifying the current formats as necessary.

Complete four steps to apply a style. First, select the cell range to receive the new style; then select Format, Style, select the appropriate style from the Style name list, and click OK. To remove the effects of applying a style, select the appropriate cell range, and apply a different style or the Normal style.

In this section, you define a style named *comic14gold*. The style includes settings for applying a 14-point bold Comic Sans MS font in a gold color. You create the style, apply it in another location, and remove the style from one location.

To Create and Use Styles

1 **Open the *MEC-S301* workbook and save it as** Styles and AutoFormat. The worksheet includes annual and quarterly Year 2003 revenue data for Glenn Lakes Golf Course. Now, create a style by first applying several formats to cell B4.

2 **Click cell B4, and choose Format, Cells; then select the Font tab in the Format Cells dialog box.**

3 **Specify the Comic Sans MS font, Bold font style, 14-point size, and gold color settings shown in Figure 3.32.**

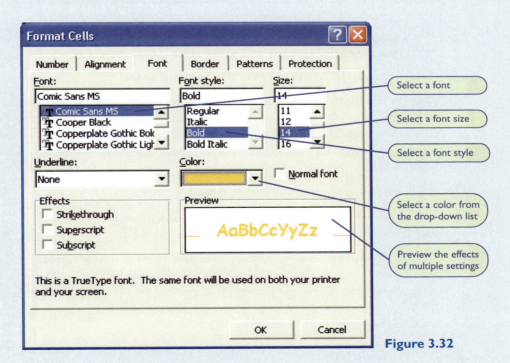

Figure 3.32

You applied to cell B4 all of the settings you want to include in this style, which specifies only font-related attributes. Now create the style.

4 **Click OK.**
Excel applies the four format changes to cell B4.

continues ▶

To Create and Use Styles (continued)

⑤ **Make sure that cell B4 is the current cell, and choose F̲ormat, S̲tyle.**

The Style dialog box opens. *Normal* displays in the S̲tyle name text box. The font assigned to the Normal style—Arial 10—is listed in the *Style includes* section.

⑥ **Type** comic14gold **to replace *Normal* in the S̲tyle name text box.**

Excel automatically displays the newly-applied font settings—Comic Sans MS 14, Bold Color 44—to the right of the F̲ont check box (see Figure 3.33).

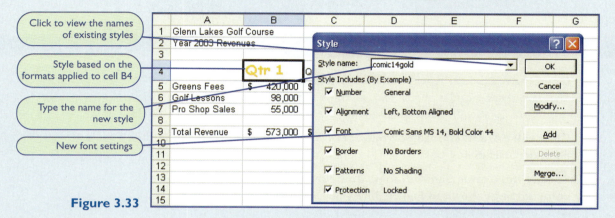

Click to view the names of existing styles

Style based on the formats applied to cell B4

Type the name for the new style

New font settings

Figure 3.33

⑦ **Click the A̲dd button, and click OK.**

Excel adds the comic14gold style to other defined styles. Now apply the new style.

⑧ **Select the range A1:A2, and choose F̲ormat, S̲tyle.**

⑨ **Display the S̲tyle name drop-down list, select the comic14gold style, and click OK.**

The labels in A1:A2 display left-aligned with attributes defined in the selected style—Comic Sans MS bold 14-point font in a gold color. Now remove the style applied to cell B4.

⑩ **Click cell B4, and choose F̲ormat, S̲tyle.**

⑪ **Select *Normal* from the S̲tyle name drop-down list, and click OK.**

Excel removes the elements of the comic14gold style from cell B4.

⑫ **Click cell A1, and save your changes to the *Styles and AutoFormat* workbook.**

Keep the workbook open for the next skill, or close the workbook and exit Excel.

In Depth:
Copying Styles from Another Workbook

You can copy styles from one workbook to another. Open both workbooks. In the workbook you want to copy the styles to, complete the following steps. Choose F̲ormat, S̲tyle and then click the M̲erge button to display the Merge Styles dialog box. In the M̲erge styles from list, double-click the name of the workbook that contains the styles you want to copy. If the two workbooks contain styles with the same names, you must confirm that you want to replace the styles.

For immediate reinforcement, work Challenge 3.

Skill 3.5: **Use Automated Tools to Format Worksheets**

The *AutoFormat* command, located on the Format menu, enables you to apply one of sixteen predefined formats to lists and cell ranges. Each predefined format combines color, line thickness, shading, bold, and/or italics to give a distinctive look to a worksheet. AutoFormats are grouped into five categories: Classic, Accounting, Colorful, List, and 3D Effects. Other choices include Simple and None. Using the Options button, you might decide to apply or reject the AutoFormat's Number, Border, Font, Patterns, Alignment, and Width/Height formats.

In the following steps, you apply the Classic 2 AutoFormat to a worksheet.

To Apply an AutoFormat

1 Open the *Styles and AutoFormat* workbook, if necessary; then select cells **A4:F9 in the** *Sheet1* **worksheet.**

2 Choose Format, AutoFormat; then click the Options button in the **AutoFormat dialog box.**
The AutoFormat dialog box displays (see Figure 3.34).

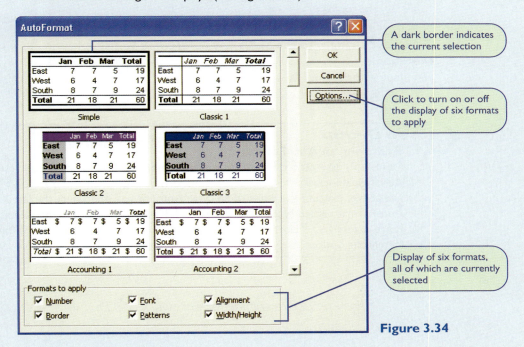

A dark border indicates the current selection

Click to turn on or off the display of six formats to apply

Display of six formats, all of which are currently selected

Figure 3.34

3 Uncheck the Font check box near the bottom of the dialog box.
Deselecting this option retains your current font formatting.

4 Click the Classic 2 format (format descriptions display below the **related format).**

continues ▶

To Apply an AutoFormat (continued)

The dark border surrounding the Classic 2 sample indicates that AutoFormat style has been selected.

5 **Click OK; then click cell A1.**

The Classic 2 AutoFormat is applied to the selected range (see Figure 3.35).

	A	B	C	D	E	F	G
1	Glenn Lakes Golf Course						
2	Year 2003 Revenues						
3							
4		Qtr 1	Qtr 2	Qtr 3	Qtr 4	Annual	
5	Greens Fees	$420,000	$385,000	$227,000	$362,000	$1,394,000	
6	Golf Lessons	98,000	54,800	61,900	78,200	292,900	
7	Pro Shop Sales	55,000	48,600	35,200	123,400	262,200	
8							
9	Total Revenue	$573,000	$488,400	$324,100	$563,600	$1,949,100	
10							

Results of applying the Classic 2 AutoFormat

Figure 3.35

 If you have problems...

If you apply the wrong AutoFormat and want to immediately reverse this action, use the Edit, Undo AutoFormat command or click the Undo button on the toolbar.

6 **Save your changes to the *Styles and AutoFormat* workbook, and close the workbook.**

Continue with the next skill, or exit Excel.

 In Depth:

Removing an AutoFormat

If you apply an AutoFormat and immediately undo the command, Excel restores the original formats. To remove an AutoFormat later when Undo AutoFormat is not active, execute the steps to apply an AutoFormat, and select the last AutoFormat named None. This action removes all formatting in the selected range unless you click the Options button and uncheck one or more of the formatting options.

For immediate reinforcement, work Skill Drill 4.

Skill 3.6: **Modify Page Setup Options for Worksheets**

 To print the current worksheet quickly using the default page setup, click the Print button on the Standard toolbar. The default page setup produces output with the following characteristics: portrait orientation, 100% of normal size, 8-1/2-by-11-inch paper, one-inch top and bottom margins, and 0.75-inch left and right margins. *Portrait orientation* produces a printed page that is longer than it is wide.

You can also change settings to meet your requirements for printed output using the Page Setup dialog box. For example, you can switch to *landscape orientation*, which produces a printed page that is wider than it is long. You can add a header or footer to help identify the contents of the printed page. A *header* displays at the top of each printed page; a *footer* displays at the bottom of each printed page. The contents of a header and footer are not visible in the worksheet.

You can also adjust the page margins, or turn on printing of gridlines and row and column headings. When you save a file, Excel also saves the current page setup specifications.

In the following steps, you use Excel's Page Setup feature to review current settings, create a header, specify that the contents of a column should repeat on every page, and turn on the display of gridlines and row and column headings.

To Set Print Options Using Page Setup

1 **Open the *MEC-S302* workbook and save it as** Print Practice.

2 **Make sure the *Condensed IS* worksheet is selected; then choose File, Page Setup.**
The Page Setup dialog box with four tabs appears. Use this dialog box to adjust the page setup before you print your worksheet.

3 **Click the Page tab, if necessary (see Figure 3.36).**

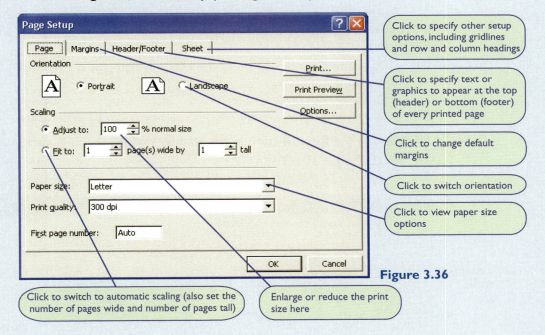

Figure 3.36

4 **Click the Margins tab in the Page Setup dialog box.**
The margin options display. The default top and bottom margins are one inch. The default left and right margins are 0.75 inch. If you want to center the printed output, click the Horizontally check box to center printed output from left to right and/or click the Vertically check box to center the printed output from top to bottom.

5 **Click the Header/Footer tab in the Page Setup dialog box, and click the Custom Header button in the middle of the dialog box.**

continues ▶

To Set Print Options Using Page Setup (continued)

The Header dialog box displays (see Figure 3.37). Directions to enter the contents of the header appear in the upper-left corner of the dialog box. You can type the text of your choice, such as your name, in the Center section. You can also use buttons to insert predefined contents, such as the current date in the Left section and the filename in the Right section.

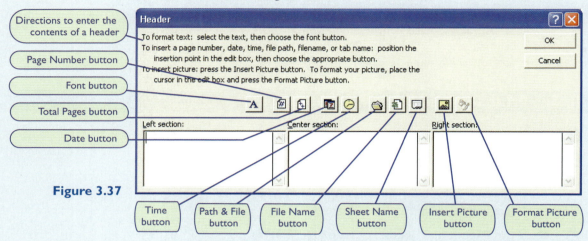

Figure 3.37

⑥ **Click within the Left section of the Header dialog box; then click the Date button (refer to Figure 3.37).**
The code &[Date] displays left-aligned in the Left section.

⑦ **Click within the Center section of the Header dialog box; then type your first and last names.**
Your full name displays in the Center section. Entering your name in a header or footer makes it easy to identify your work if you share a printer with others.

⑧ **Click within the Right section of the Header dialog box; then click the File Name button (refer to Figure 3.37).**
The code &[File] displays right-aligned in the Right section (see Figure 3.38).

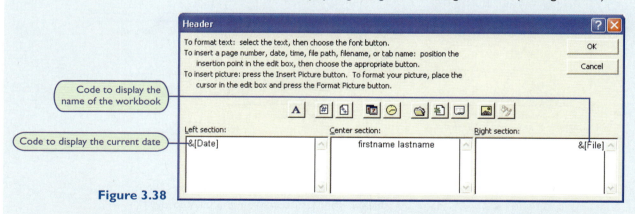

Figure 3.38

⑨ **Click OK.**
The Header dialog box closes. The settings you specified appear in the Header box on the Header/Footer tab. Ignore the fact that some of the same settings are in the Footer box. The Footer settings are standard for all student data files that accompany this text.

10 **Click the Sheet tab in the Page Setup dialog box; then click within the _Columns to repeat at left_ box, and click any cell in column A.**

You set an option to repeat column A on each page of a multiple-page printout (see Figure 3.39). Use this option to repeat descriptive labels on worksheets that are too wide to fit on one page.

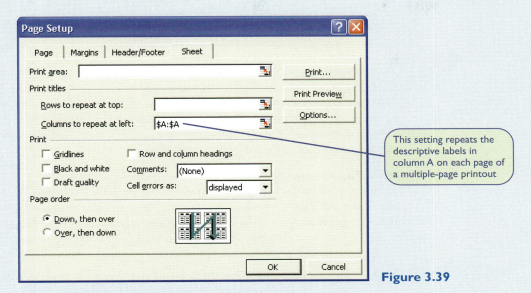

This setting repeats the descriptive labels in column A on each page of a multiple-page printout

Figure 3.39

11 **Click the check box in front of _Gridlines_.**

A check mark appears in the _Gridlines_ box, indicating that the feature is turned on. This setting prints the lines that border cells.

12 **Click the check box in front of Row and column headings.**

A check mark appears in the Row and column headings box, indicating that the feature is turned on (see Figure 3.40). This setting prints the worksheet frame.

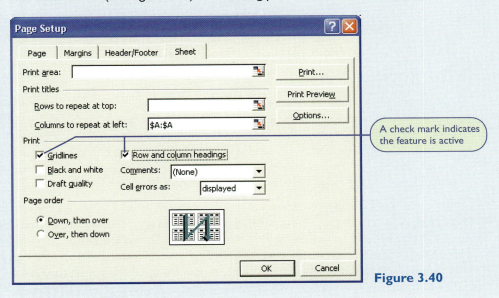

A check mark indicates the feature is active

Figure 3.40

continues ▶

To Set Print Options Using Page Setup (continued)

 Click OK, and save your changes to the *Print Practice* workbook.
You finished setting up the worksheet page for printing. Continue with the next skill, or close the workbook and exit Excel.

 ### *In Depth:*

Other Page Setup Options on the Page Tab

Use the Page tab (refer to Figure 3.36) to specify orientation (portrait or landscape), scaling, paper size, print quality in terms of dpi (density per inch), and the starting page number. Excel provides two scaling options: Adjust to (a user-specified higher or lower percentage of original size) or Fit to (a user-specified number of pages wide by number of pages tall).

Other Page Setup Options on the Sheet Tab

The Sheet tab includes four sections (refer to Figure 3.39): Print area, Print titles, Print, and Page order. You can specify a range to print by entering the upper-left and lower-right cells in the range separated by a colon (for example, B5:H25) in the Print area box. It is helpful to set a print area when there is a specific portion of a large worksheet that you print frequently.

The Print area includes two more check boxes and two drop-down lists. You can print black and white, print draft quality, and print comments attached to cells either as they appear in the worksheet or summarized at the end of the printout. You can also vary how Excel prints error messages in cells by choosing among four options: displayed, <blank>, --, and #N/A.

For immediate reinforcement, work Challenge 4.

Skill 3.7: **Preview and Print Worksheets and Workbooks**

You might want to print all or part of a worksheet for your files or to review while you are away from the computer. Four options on the File menu relate directly to printing: Page Setup, Print Area, Print Preview, and Print. You worked with various Page Setup options in the previous skill. You can set a print area when you frequently print only a smaller portion of a large worksheet. You can set a print area from the File menu or by opening the Page Setup dialog box and entering the range in the first box on the Sheet tab.

 It's a good idea to preview onscreen the way a worksheet will look when it is printed. That way, you can make adjustments to the page setup before you print and save paper. You can access Print Preview mode by clicking the Print Preview button in the toolbar; by selecting File, Print Preview; or by selecting File, Print and clicking the Preview button. Excel automatically sets the page breaks on multiple-page printouts, but you can change those default page breaks in Print Preview mode.

You can print the entire current worksheet at default print settings by clicking the Print button in the toolbar. You can also print currently selected cells or an entire workbook using the Print dialog box. Other options in that dialog box include selecting a different printer and specifying the number of copies.

Be sure to save any changes to a worksheet before you print it. In the following steps, you preview and print an entire worksheet, set a print area, and preview and print nonadjacent sections of a worksheet.

To Preview and Print All or Part of a Worksheet

1 Make sure that the printer is turned on, has paper, and is online.
You can't print if the printer is not turned on, if the printer is out of paper, or if the printer is not online. Printers often have a light that shows whether the printer is online or receiving commands from the computer. If the printer is not online, Excel displays an error message when you attempt to print.

2 Open the *Print Practice* workbook and select the Condensed IS worksheet, if necessary; then choose File, Print from the menu.
The Print dialog box opens, as shown in Figure 3.41. Printer specifications vary depending on the default printer for your system.

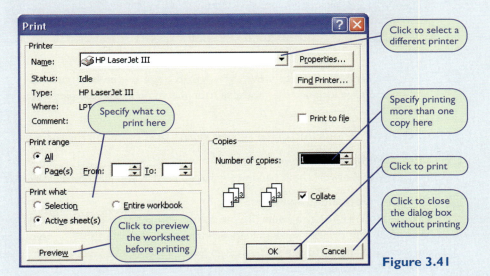

Figure 3.41

3 Click the Preview button in the Print dialog box.
The worksheet now appears in the Print Preview window, which enables you to see how the entire worksheet will look when printed (see the first of two pages in Figure 3.42). In Print Preview, you can see the effects of the changes you made to the page setup, including the header, gridlines, and worksheet frame.

continues ▶

To Preview and Print All or Part of a Worksheet (continued)

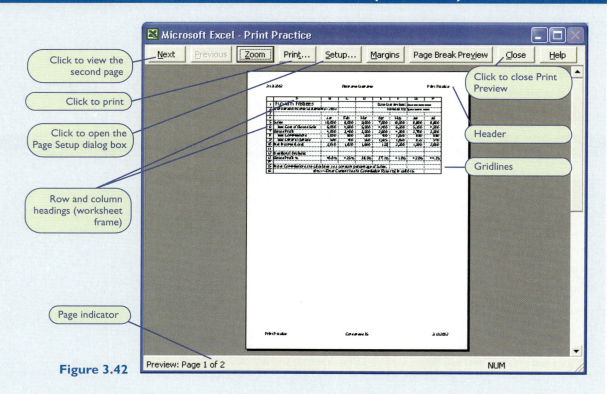

Click to view the second page

Click to print

Click to open the Page Setup dialog box

Row and column headings (worksheet frame)

Page indicator

Click to close Print Preview

Header

Gridlines

Figure 3.42

4 Click the **Next** button to view the second page (refer to Figure 3.42).
The second page includes the repeat of data in column A plus the data in columns I through N.

5 Click the **Previous** button to return to the first page.

6 Click anywhere in the worksheet.
Your view of the worksheet becomes enlarged so that you can more easily read it.

7 Click the worksheet again.
This restores the original view. If you decide you want to make a change in the worksheet data or print settings before you print it, click the **Close** button to close the view and return to the worksheet in Excel, or click the **Setup** button to open the Page Setup dialog box.

8 Click the **Print** button to begin printing the worksheet (or click **Close** to exit Print Preview without printing).
If you click the Print button, Excel sends a copy of your worksheet to the printer and closes the Preview window. Now, view and print nonadjacent sections of the worksheet.

9 Select the range A1:B10; then choose **File, Print Area, Set Print Area**.

 10 Click the **Print Preview** button in the toolbar.
Only the specified print area A1:B10 displays.

⑪ **Click the Page Break Preview button.**

The Welcome to Page Break Preview dialog box opens if that feature has not been turned off (see Figure 3.43). The entire worksheet displays, and the specified print area is enclosed in a yellow border.

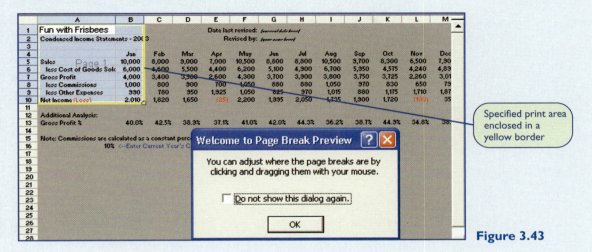

Specified print area enclosed in a yellow border

Figure 3.43

⑫ **Click OK to close the Welcome to Page Break Preview dialog box, if necessary; then select the range N4:N10.**

⑬ **Right-click within the selected range.**

A shortcut menu displays (see Figure 3.44).

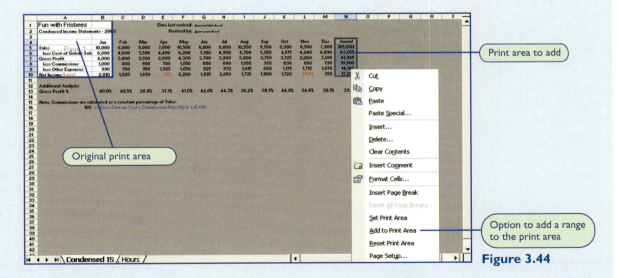

Print area to add

Original print area

Option to add a range to the print area

Figure 3.44

⑭ **Select Add to Print Area from the shortcut menu.**

Excel adds the annual data from column N to the current print area.

⑮ **Choose View, Normal; then click the Print Preview button in the toolbar.**

continues ▶

To Preview and Print All or Part of a Worksheet (continued)

Only the original print area A1:B10 displays on the first page in Print Preview mode.

16 Click the down scroll arrow to display the second page.
Excel repeats column A and shows the additional range N4:N10 on the second page in Print Preview mode. Each addition to a print range is printed on a separate page.

17 Click the Close button to exit Print Preview mode, and click cell A1.
A dotted line displays around the original print area A1:B10 and around the added range (N4:N10).

18 Save your changes to the *Print Practice* workbook, and close the workbook.
Continue with the exercises at the end of this skill set, proceed to another skill set, or exit Excel.

For immediate reinforcement, work Skill Drill 8 and Challenges 5 and 6.

Summary

Most of your efforts in this skill set produced formatting changes—that is, modifications in appearance as opposed to content. You changed the alignment in cells—left, right, and center. You also selected a different font style and font size; applied bold, italic, and underline to text; added color and borders for emphasis; used Format Painter to copy formatting from one cell to others; cleared formats, but not contents; and applied a style and an AutoFormat.

Some of your formatting changes applied to entire rows and columns—hiding, unhiding, deleting, and inserting them. You also adjusted column width and row height. Other formatting changes altered your view of the worksheet. You froze selected rows and columns and viewed different sections of a worksheet in separate windows.

The skill set ended with a comprehensive look at options to preview and print all or part of a worksheet. You learned to set print specifications in the Page Setup dialog box, including orientation, scaling, headers and footers, rows or columns to repeat, gridlines, and row and column headings. You also used Print Preview mode to view a worksheet before printing, Page Break Preview mode to add a nonadjacent range to a print area, and the Print dialog box to print.

Skill Drill

Skill Drill exercises *reinforce* skills. Each skill reinforced is the same, or nearly the same, as a skill presented in the skill set. Detailed instructions are provided in a step-by-step format.

Before beginning your Excel Core Skill Set 3 Skill Drill exercises, complete the following steps:

1. Open the file named *MEC-S303*, and immediately save it as **MEC-S3drill**.

   The workbook contains nine sheets: an overview and eight exercise sheets labeled SD1 through SD8.

2. Click the Overview sheet to view the organization and content of the Skill Drill workbook for Excel Core Skill Set 3.

Each exercise is independent of the others, so you may complete the exercises in any order. Be sure to save the workbook after completing each exercise. If you need a paper copy of one or more completed exercises, enter your name, centered in a header, before printing. Print options have already been set to print compressed to one page and to display the filename, sheet name, and current date in a footer.

Be sure to save your changes and close the workbook if you need more than one work session to complete the desired exercises. Continue working on *MEC-S3drill* instead of starting over in the original *MEC-S303* file.

1. Change Alignment, Font, and Color

Aligning the contents of cells can improve the readability of a worksheet. You decided to right-align the *Qtr* and *Annual* column headings in the Community Volunteer Corps worksheet so they line up with the numeric data below. You also want to indent the *Total Hours* label so it is easier to distinguish it from other row headings.

To draw the reader's attention to the name of the organization, you plan to display the name in a Comic Sans MS 14pt font. You also want to focus a viewer's attention by adding color to your Community Volunteer Corps workbook two ways. You plan to change the color of the organization's name and add background color to column headings.

To make alignment, font, and color changes to your worksheet, follow these steps:

1. If necessary, open the *MEC-S3drill* workbook; then click the sheet tab named SD1.

2. Select the range B8:F8.

3. Click the Align Right button.

4. Select cell A12.

5. Click the Increase Indent button twice.

6. Select cell A4.

7. Click the down arrow to the right of the current font displayed in the toolbar.

8. Scroll through the list of available fonts, and select *Comic Sans MS*.

   If your font options do not include Comic Sans MS, select another font of your choice.

9. Click the down arrow to the right of the current font size displayed in the toolbar, and select *14*.

10. Click the down arrow to the right of the Font Color button on the toolbar.

11. Click Red on the Font Color palette.

12. Select the range B8:F8.

13. Click the down arrow to the right of the Fill Color button on the toolbar.

14. Click Pale Blue on the Fill Color palette.

15. Click cell A1; then save your changes to the *MEC-S3drill* workbook.

2. Add a Border and Apply Bold and Italic

To enhance the appearance of your worksheet by separating data from labels and totals, you decide to add a border around cells containing volunteer hours.

You know that you can emphasize important data such as totals by using Bold and Italic font styles. You decide to italicize all subtotals and make bold the annual total in your Community Volunteer Corps workbook.

To create a border, and apply bold and italic font styles, follow these steps:

 1. If necessary, open the *MEC-S3drill* workbook; then click the sheet tab named SD2.

 2. Select the range B9:E11.

 3. Choose F<u>o</u>rmat, C<u>e</u>lls and select the Border tab in the Format Cells dialog box.

 4. Select the double-line style in the <u>S</u>tyle list.

 5. Display the drop-down palette of colors, and select *Gold*.

 6. Click <u>O</u>utline in the Presets area, and click OK.

 7. Select cells B12:E12, hold down Ctrl, and select cells F9:F11.

 8. Click the Italic button on the toolbar.

 9. Select cell F12, and click the Bold button on the toolbar.

 10. Click cell A1; then save your changes to the *MEC-S3drill* workbook.

3. Use Format Painter and Remove Formatting

You have applied several formats to the Community Volunteer Corps worksheet, and now you want to remove one or more of them. You decide that you don't like the underline effect that you applied to offset data from total hours. You also plan to remove all formatting applied to the names of volunteer organizations after you use Format Painter to copy that formatting to another cell.

To copy and remove formats, follow these steps:

 1. If necessary, open the *MEC-S3drill* workbook; then click the sheet tab named SD3.

 2. Click cell A9; then click the Format Painter button in the toolbar.

 A flashing dotted line appears around the selected cell.

 3. Move the mouse pointer toward cell A4.

 The pointer changes to a white block cross. A paintbrush displays to the right of the cross.

 4. Select the range A4:B4, release the mouse button, and click cell A4.

 Excel applies right alignment, an Arial 12-point font, and Light Green fill color to cell A4.

 5. Click the Align Left button in the toolbar; then select the range B11:F11.

 6. Choose F<u>o</u>rmat, C<u>e</u>lls and select the Font tab in the Format Cells dialog box.

 The current Underline style is *Single Accounting*.

 7. Click the down arrow at the right end of the Underline window; select *None* from the list of <u>U</u>nderline options, and click OK.

 8. Select the range A9:A11, which contains 12-point right-aligned labels with a light green background.

 9. Choose <u>E</u>dit, Cle<u>a</u>r, <u>F</u>ormats; then click cell A1.

 10. Save your changes to the *MEC-S3drill* workbook.

4. Insert a Row, Apply an AutoFormat, and Adjust Column Width

You are modifying a worksheet to summarize volunteer hours, and you want to insert a row for another organization. You also want to apply a predefined AutoFormat to the worksheet, and make any desired changes to the AutoFormat results.

To insert a row and apply the AutoFormat, follow these steps:

 1. If necessary, open the *MEC-S3drill* workbook; then click the SD4 sheet tab.

 2. Click any cell in row 9, such as cell A9.

3. Choose Insert, Rows.

A blank row 9 appears. The *Big Brothers-Big Sisters* row is now row 10.

4. Enter **Literacy League** in cell A9.

5. Enter **670** for Qtr 1 hours in cell B9.

6. Enter **840** for Qtr 2 hours in cell C9.

7. Enter **1130** for Qtr 3 hours in cell D9.

8. Enter **935** for Qtr 4 hours in cell E9.

9. Select the range A4:E10; then choose Format, AutoFormat.

10. Click the Options button in the AutoFormat dialog box; then uncheck the Font check box near the bottom of the dialog box.

11. Select the *Accounting 2* format (format descriptions display below the related format); then click OK.

Excel applies the Accounting 2 AutoFormat to the selected range. The results include widening column A to accommodate the longest entry and right-aligning labels in the range A4:A5.

12. Click between columns A and B in the worksheet frame, and drag left until the width of column A just accommodates the entry *Big Brothers – Big Sisters* in cell A10.

13. Select the range A4:A5; then click the Align Left button in the toolbar.

14. Click cell A1; then save your changes to the *MEC-S3drill* workbook.

5. Delete a Column and Adjust Row Height

Your initial design for summarizing volunteer hours included a column for summing hours after the first and second quarters. Now, you want to present only the annual totals for each organization. You also want to increase the height of a row so that quarter labels are completely visible.

To delete a column and adjust row height, follow these steps:

1. If necessary, open the *MEC-S3drill* workbook; then click the SD5 sheet tab.

2. Click the column letter D in the worksheet frame; then choose Edit, Delete.

Excel deletes the original column D and adjusts remaining column letters to the right of the deleted column. Contents that had been in column E are now in column D.

3. Position the mouse pointer between rows 7 and 8 in the worksheet frame.

4. Click and drag the pointer down until row height is as close as possible to 17.25; then release the mouse button.

You increased row height to display the quarter labels.

5. Click cell A1, and save your changes to the *MEC-S3drill* workbook.

6. Compare the Freeze Panes and Split Commands

You are under consideration for a promotion that would involve a move to another city. While you are waiting for a decision, you continue to collect information through the World Wide Web on homes available in selected areas. Now that the list is getting too long to fit on one screen, you want to view different sections of the worksheet on the screen.

To freeze selected rows and then split the screen into top and bottom panes, follow these steps:

1. Open the *MEC-S3drill* workbook, if necessary; then select the SD6 worksheet tab.

2. Select cell A6.

3. Choose <u>W</u>indow, <u>F</u>reeze Panes.

Cells above and to the left of the current cell remain in view as you scroll through the worksheet.

4. Scroll to the bottom of the worksheet.

Rows 1 through 5 remain onscreen.

5. Choose <u>W</u>indow, Un<u>f</u>reeze Panes.

6. Select cell A13.

7. Choose <u>W</u>indow, <u>S</u>plit.

Excel splits the worksheet view into top and bottom panes.

8. Click any cell in either pane, and use the scrollbar(s) to shift worksheet display.

9. Click cell A1 in the top pane; then save your changes to the *MEC-S3drill* workbook.

7. Hide and Unhide Rows

You maintain a worksheet that tracks sales over a five-year period. You want to hide detail rows, so that only the totals display for the three sources of sales. You also want to unhide two rows that are currently hidden.

To hide and unhide rows, follow these steps:

1. Open the *MEC-S3drill* workbook, if necessary; then select the SD7 worksheet tab.

2. Select the row numbers 10 through 12 in the worksheet frame, hold down (Ctrl), select the row numbers 14 through 17, select the row numbers 19 through 22, and release the mouse button.

Rows 10, 11, 12, 14, 15, 16, 17, 19, 20, 21, and 22 are selected.

3. Choose F<u>o</u>rmat, point to <u>R</u>ow, and click <u>H</u>ide.

4. Position the pointer on the row number 5 in the worksheet frame; then drag down to select row number 8, and release the mouse button.

You selected the row numbers on either side of the hidden rows 6 and 7.

5. Choose F<u>o</u>rmat, point to <u>R</u>ow, and click <u>U</u>nhide.

Excel displays the hidden rows 6 and 7.

6. Click cell A1; then save your changes to the *MEC-S3drill* workbook.

8. Set a Print Area, Preview, and Print

You maintain a large worksheet that includes four sections: a Trial Balance, an Income Statement, a Statement of Retained Earnings, and a Balance Sheet. Each section displays to the right of, and below, the previous one. You want to set a print area limited to the Income Statement, and then preview and print the results.

To set a print area, and then preview and print the results, follow these steps:

1. Open the *MEC-S3drill* workbook, if necessary; then select the SD8 worksheet tab.

2. Select the range D53:F85.

You selected the range containing the Income Statement.

3. Choose <u>F</u>ile, point to Prin<u>t</u> Area, and select <u>S</u>et Print Area.

4. Click any cell to deselect the highlighted range D53:F85; then click Print Preview in the toolbar.

Only the range D53:F85 displays in Print Preview.

5. Click the Prin<u>t</u> button at the top of the Print Preview screen; then click OK (or click <u>C</u> lose at the top of the Print Preview screen if you do not want to print at this time).

6. Press [Ctrl]+[Home] to position the pointer on cell A1; then save your changes to the *MEC-S3drill* workbook.

Challenge

Challenge exercises expand on or are somewhat related to skills presented in the skill set. Each exercise provides a brief narrative introduction, followed by instructions, in a numbered-step format, that are not as detailed as those in the Skill Drill section.

Before beginning your Excel Core Skill Set 3 Challenge exercises, complete the following steps:

1. Open the file named *MEC-S304*, and immediately save it as **MEC-S3challenge**.

   The workbook contains seven sheets: an overview and six exercise sheets labeled CH1 through CH6.

2. Click the Overview sheet to view the organization and content of the Challenge workbook for Excel Core Skill Set 3.

Each exercise is independent of the others, so you may complete the exercises in any order. Be sure to save the workbook after completing each exercise. If you need a paper copy of one or more completed exercises, enter your name, centered in a header, before printing. With the exception of large worksheets CH4, CH5, and CH6, print options have already been set to print compressed to one page. Settings to display the filename, sheet name, and current date in a footer have been set in all worksheets.

Be sure to save your changes and close the workbook if you need more than one work session to complete the desired exercises. Continue working on *MEC-S3challenge* instead of starting over in the original *MEC-S304* file.

1. Change Text Orientation and Adjust Column Width

You maintain a worksheet that tracks sales data for five years, and you want to narrow the width of the sales data columns after you rotate the column headings.

To rotate text, and then narrow columns, follow these steps:

1. Open the *MEC-S3challenge* workbook, if necessary; then select the CH1 worksheet tab.

2. Select the range B8:F8; then display the Format cells dialog box, and click the Alignment tab.

3. Set orientation to 45 degrees.

4. Select columns B through F in the worksheet frame, and drag the pointer to narrow the selected columns as much as possible while still displaying the year labels in row 8.

5. Click cell A1, and save your changes to the *MEC-S3challenge* workbook.

2. Create and Erase Borders Using the Borders Toolbar

You just discovered that buttons on the Borders toolbar enable you to create an outline or grid border and remove borders without opening the Format Cells dialog box. You want to remove a dashed border and create a blue double-line border using that toolbar.

To work with borders using the Borders toolbar, follow these steps:

1. Open the *MEC-S3challenge* workbook, if necessary; then select the CH2 worksheet tab.

   A dashed border surrounds the range A5:D7.

2. Position the pointer on the Borders button in the toolbar.

3. Click the down arrow to the right of the Borders button, and select <u>D</u>raw Borders.

The floating Borders toolbar displays (see Figure 3.45). The mouse pointer changes to a pencil, indicating that Border Draw mode is active.

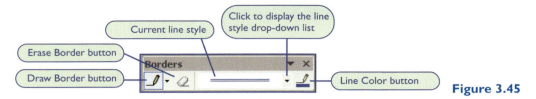

Figure 3.45

4. Drag the toolbar by its title bar to a blank area, if necessary; then click the Erase Border button (refer to Figure 3.45), and move the pointer towards cell A5.

The pointer changes to an eraser, indicating that border erase mode is active.

5. Drag the eraser pointer right across the dashed border in the range A5:D5; then drag the eraser pointer down the dashed border in the range D5:D7, and release the mouse button.

The dashed border disappears.

6. Display the Line Style drop-down list (refer to Figure 3.45), and select the only double line style.

7. Click the Line Color button (refer to Figure 3.45), and select Blue.

8. Make sure that the Draw Border button is active, and move the pointer towards cell B10.

9. Drag the pencil pointer across the top of the range B10:E10; then drag the pencil pointer down the right edge of the range E10:E15, and release the mouse button.

A blue double-line border displays around the range B10:E15.

10. Close the Borders toolbar, and save your changes to the *MEC-S3challenge* workbook.

3. Apply a Style and Compare Number Formats

You set up a worksheet to practice applying number formats. You also want to apply a style to the labels describing the major groupings of number formats.

To apply a style and compare number formats, follow these steps:

1. Open the *MEC-S3challenge* workbook, if necessary; then select the CH3 worksheet tab.

Labels describing a variety of number formats display in column A, with corresponding sample numbers in column B.

2. Click cell A3; then display the Format Cells dialog box, and select the Font tab.

3. Specify Arial, 12-point, and blue color settings; then click OK.

4. Make sure that cell A3 is the current cell, and choose F<u>o</u>rmat, <u>S</u>tyle.

5. Enter `arial12blue` in the <u>S</u>tyle name text box; then click the <u>A</u>dd button, and click OK.

6. Select cells A16 and A22; then display the Style dialog box, apply the *arial12blue* style to the selected cells, and click any cell to deselect.

The labels in cells A3, A16, and A22 display left-aligned in Arial 12-point blue font.

7. Read the format description in cell A4, and apply that format to cell B4 using the appropriate toolbar button.

8. Read the format description in cell A7, and apply that format to cell B7 using the appropriate toolbar buttons.

9. Use the Number tab on the Format Cells dialog box to apply all remaining formats described in column A.

   The descriptive labels in blue (cells A3, A16, and A22) indicate the appropriate category. Display the $ sign drop-down list to view options other than the United States dollar sign.

10. Save your changes to the *MEC-S3challenge* workbook.

4. Modify Page Setup Options

You maintain a worksheet that tracks employee data. Prior to printing it, you want to add or modify selected print settings in the Page Setup dialog box.

To change print settings in the Page Setup dialog box, follow these steps:

1. Open the *MEC-S3challenge* workbook, if necessary; then select the CH4 worksheet tab.

   The worksheet lists data about 111 employees.

2. Display the Page Setup dialog box.

3. Set orientation to portrait.

4. Specify printed output that is one page wide by two pages tall.

5. Create a header with your full name centered and the page number right-aligned.

6. Set rows 3 through 11 to repeat on each page of printed output.

7. Turn off display of gridlines and the worksheet frame on printed output.

8. Use Print Preview to verify your print settings; then close Print Preview.

9. Save your changes to the *MEC-S3challenge* workbook.

5. Add a Range to a Print Area

You maintain a large worksheet with four distinct areas: a Trial Balance, an Income Statement, a Statement of Retained Earnings, and a Balance Sheet. You already set a print area that includes the Income Statement. Now, you want to add the Asset section from the Balance Sheet to the Print area.

To add a range to a print area, follow these steps:

1. Open the *MEC-S3challenge* workbook, if necessary; then select the CH5 worksheet tab.

2. Click Print Preview in the toolbar.

   The range D53:F85, containing the Income Statement, is the defined Print area. Page 1 of 1 displays in the lower-left corner of the Print Preview window.

3. Activate Page Break Preview mode.

4. Select the Asset data in the range I96:L126; then right-click within the range and add it to the print area.

5. Verify in Print Preview mode that the Asset data displays on page 2 of 2; then restore Normal view.

6. Deselect the highlighted range, if necessary; then save your changes to the *MEC-S3challenge* workbook.

6. Set Rows to Repeat and a Manual Page Break

You maintain a worksheet that shows the assets, liabilities, and stockholders' equity of a firm. At current print settings, most of the worksheet prints on the first page of a two-page printout. You want to override the automatic page break set by Excel, so that only the asset-related data displays on the first page. You also want to repeat data on company name, type of statement, and time period on each printed page.

To set rows to repeat and a manual page break, follow these steps:

1. Open the *MEC-S3challenge* workbook, if necessary; then select the CH6 worksheet tab.

2. Display the Page Setup dialog box, and set rows 1 through 5 to print on every page.

3. Activate Page Break Preview mode.

4. Close the Welcome to Page Break Preview dialog box, if necessary; then scroll down to display the bottom of the worksheet.

   The dashed blue line near the bottom of the worksheet indicates Excel's automatic page break.

5. Drag the dashed blue line up to a position between row numbers 33 and 34 in the worksheet frame; then release the mouse button.

   A solid blue line—indicating a manual page break—replaces the dashed blue line. Only the asset data is set to print on page one.

6. Restore Normal view; then save your changes to the *MEC-S3challenge* workbook.

Modifying Workbooks

This skill set includes

Insert and delete worksheets

- Insert a blank worksheet
- Insert a worksheet from another workbook
- Delete a worksheet

Modify worksheet names and positions

Use 3-D references

Skill Set Overview

A substantial portion of this skill set focuses on manipulating worksheets and worksheet tabs. You learn to insert a worksheet—either a blank one, or a worksheet that you move or copy from another workbook. You also delete a worksheet, change the position of a worksheet within a multiple-sheet workbook, and differentiate worksheet tabs by changing their names and applying color.

After you experience handling multiple worksheets, you turn to an important content skill—entering formulas with 3-D references. A **3-D reference** refers to the same cell in multiple worksheets.

Skill 4.1: Insert and Delete Worksheets

The default Excel workbook includes three worksheets named Sheet1, Sheet2, and Sheet3. You can insert, copy, move, and rename worksheets as well as delete them. In this skill area, you insert a blank worksheet, insert a worksheet from another workbook, and delete a worksheet.

Insert a Blank Worksheet

You use the <u>W</u>orksheet option on the <u>I</u>nsert menu to insert a worksheet. Excel places the inserted worksheet to the left of the current worksheet, but you can easily change its position.

In the following steps, you open a workbook containing data on three worksheets for Stores A, B, and D respectively. You insert a blank worksheet in front of the existing worksheets, and enter labels in the new worksheet.

To Insert a Blank Worksheet

1 **Open the file *MEC-S401* and save it as** Modify Workbooks.
The first of three worksheets displays. It contains sales data for Store A over a five-year period.

2 **Click the Sheet2 worksheet tab; then click the Sheet3 worksheet tab.**
Worksheets named Sheet2 and Sheet3 contain data for stores B and D respectively. With one exception—the letter assigned to a store, such as Store A—the content and position of labels and formulas in Sheet2 and Sheet3 match that in Sheet1.

3 **Click the Sheet1 worksheet tab; then choose <u>I</u>nsert, <u>W</u>orksheet.**
Excel inserts a new blank worksheet to the left of Sheet1, and assigns the name Sheet4 to the new worksheet (see Figure 4.1). You learn to reposition worksheets and change the name of a worksheet in the next section.

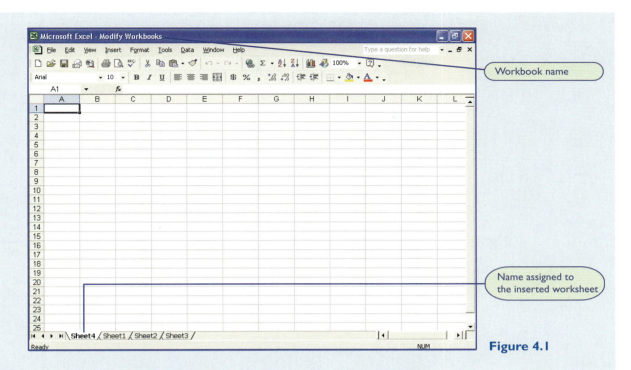

Figure 4.1

4 Copy the range A1:F4 from Sheet1 to the same range in the new blank Sheet4.

5 Edit cell A1 in Sheet4 to read Flowers Your Way: All Stores.

6 Enter Total Sales in cell A5, and widen column A just enough to display the new label within the column (see Figure 4.2).

Figure 4.2

7 Make sure that the contents of Sheet4 match those shown in Figure 4.2; then save your changes to the *Modify Workbooks* file.

Keep the workbook open for the next skill, or close the workbook and exit Excel.

In Depth:
Insert Multiple Blank Worksheets
You can insert more than one blank worksheet at a time. To specify the number of worksheets to add, hold down (◆Shift), and then select the number of existing worksheet tabs that you want to add to the current workbook.

For example, assume that you want to insert three blank worksheets at the beginning of a workbook that currently has five worksheets named Sheet1 through Sheet5. To insert the desired worksheets: click Sheet1, hold down (◆Shift), click Sheet3, and release (◆Shift); then choose Insert, Worksheet.

Change the Number of Default Worksheets
You can change the number of default worksheets by choosing Tools, Options and selecting the General tab. Enter the desired number of worksheets in the *Sheets in new workbook* box.

Insert a Worksheet from Another Workbook

When you need to add another worksheet to a workbook, the content for the new worksheet might be similar or identical to that on an existing worksheet. You can save data entry time by inserting an existing worksheet instead of a blank worksheet and editing the results as necessary.

The Edit menu includes a *Move or Copy Sheet* command. You can use this option to move or copy a worksheet in the same workbook, or to insert a worksheet from another workbook into the current workbook. All workbooks involved in the copy or move process must be open.

In the following steps, you copy a worksheet from another workbook. The copied worksheet contains data on Store C, and you insert the copy between the worksheets containing data for Stores B and D.

To Insert a Worksheet from Another Workbook

1 Open the *Modify Workbooks* file, if necessary.
This workbook will receive the copied worksheet. Currently the workbook includes Sheet4 (to hold data for all stores) and the original worksheets: Sheet1, Sheet2, and Sheet3 (data for Stores A, B, and D respectively).

2 Open the file *MEC-S402*.
This workbook contains the worksheet named Store C that you want to copy.

3 Choose Edit in the menu bar.
The Edit menu includes an option to move or copy a worksheet (see the mouse pointer in Figure 4.3).

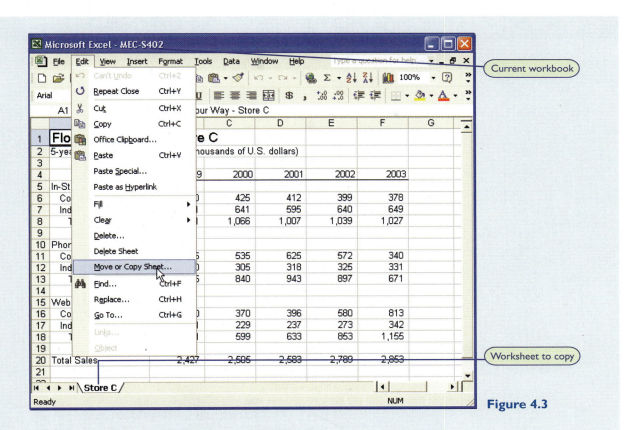

Figure 4.3

4 **Choose Move or Copy Sheet from the Edit menu.**
The Move or Copy dialog box opens (see Figure 4.4).

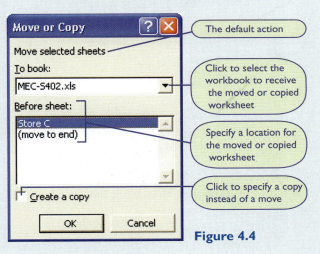

Figure 4.4

continues ▶

To Insert a Worksheet from Another Workbook (continued)

5 Display the *To book* drop-down list (see Figure 4.5).

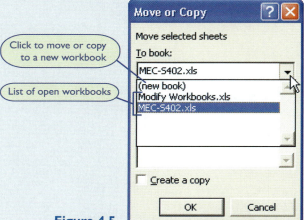

Click to move or copy to a new workbook

List of open workbooks

Figure 4.5

6 Select *Modify Workbooks* in the list of open workbooks.
Excel lists the worksheets in the selected workbook (see Figure 4.6).

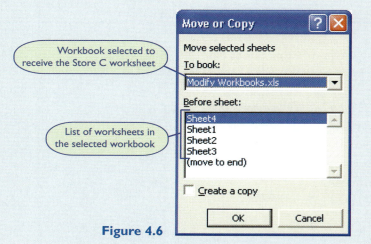

Workbook selected to receive the Store C worksheet

List of worksheets in the selected workbook

Figure 4.6

7 Click *Sheet3* in the list of worksheets; then click the *Create a copy* check box (see Figure 4.7).

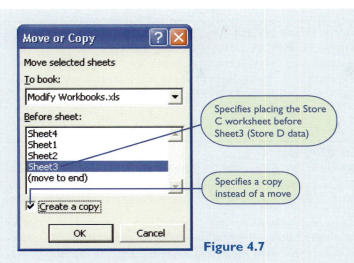

Figure 4.7

8 **Make sure that your settings match those in Figure 4.7; then click OK.**
Excel inserts the copied worksheet in the location specified (see Figure 4.8).

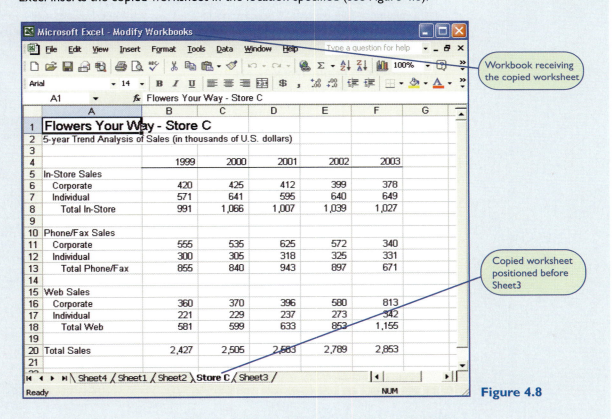

Figure 4.8

9 **Save your changes to the *Modify Workbooks* file.**
Keep the workbook open for the next skill, or close the workbook and exit Excel.

Alternate Way:
Display the Move or Copy Dialog Box
You can use a shortcut menu to display the Move or Copy dialog box. Right-click the worksheet tab of the worksheet you want to copy or move, and select Move or Copy from the shortcut menu.

In Depth:
Reverse the Effects of Moving or Copying a Worksheet
Exercise caution when you use the Move or Copy Sheet command. You cannot use the Edit, Undo command to reverse the effects of moving or copying a worksheet.

If you copy or move a worksheet within a workbook, you can reverse the results by deleting the unwanted copy or repositioning the moved worksheet. You learn to delete and reposition worksheets in the next two sections.

If you intend to copy or move a worksheet between workbooks, save both workbooks before you apply the command. That way you can close either workbook without saving your changes if the desired operation does not go as planned. For example, if you intend to copy a worksheet, but execute a move because you forget to check the Create a copy box, you can recover the moved worksheet by closing the source workbook without saving your changes.

Select Multiple Worksheets
You can select more than one worksheet to move or copy. To select two or more adjacent sheets, click the tab for the first sheet, hold down ⬆Shift), click the tab for the last sheet, and release ⬆Shift). To select two or more nonadjacent sheets, click the tab for the first sheet, hold down Ctrl), click each additional tab, and release Ctrl).

If a worksheet tab is not visible, click the appropriate tab scroll button to display the worksheet you want (see Figure 4.9).

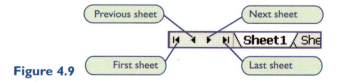

Figure 4.9

Cancel a Selection of Multiple Sheets
If you select the wrong worksheets to move or copy, you can unselect them and start over. Cancel a selection by clicking any unselected sheet, or by right-clicking the tab of a selected sheet and choosing Ungroup Sheets on the shortcut menu.

Delete a Worksheet

You can delete one or more worksheets by using the Delete Sheet command on the Edit menu. Excel provides a warning message that data might exist in the sheet(s) selected for deletion, and you have the opportunity to proceed or cancel.

You cannot use the Undo command to reverse the effects of deleting a worksheet(s). It is a good idea to save a workbook before you apply the command. That way you can close the workbook without saving your changes if the results of the delete operation are not what you want; then reopen the workbook and try again.

You can select more than one worksheet to delete. To select two or more adjacent sheets, click the tab for the first sheet, hold down (▲Shift), click the tab for the last sheet, and release (▲Shift). To select two or more nonadjacent sheets, click the tab for the first sheet, hold down (Ctrl), click each additional tab, and release (Ctrl).

In the following steps, you delete a worksheet containing sales data for Store D—a store that *Flowers Your Way* no longer owns.

To Delete a Worksheet

1 **Open the *Modify Workbooks* file, if necessary; then click the Sheet3 worksheet tab.**
The worksheet contains sales data for Store D.

2 **Choose Edit in the menu bar.**
The Edit menu includes an option to delete a worksheet (see the mouse pointer in Figure 4.10).

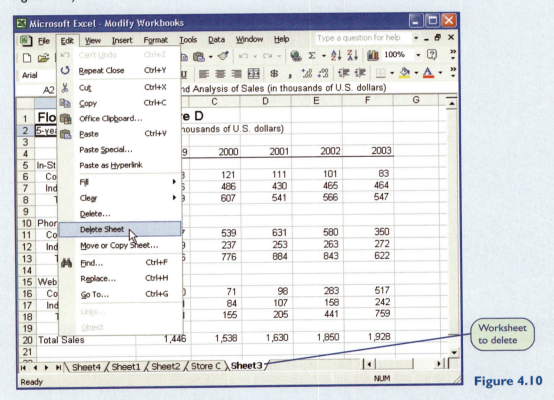

Figure 4.10

3 **Choose Delete Sheet from the Edit menu.**
Excel displays a warning message (see Figure 4.11).

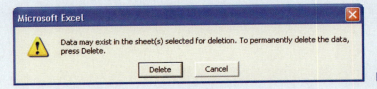

Figure 4.11

continues ▶

To Delete a Worksheet (continued)

4 **Click the Delete button.**
Excel deletes the selected worksheet. The Sheet3 tab no longer appears.

5 **Save your changes to the *Modify Workbooks* file.**
Keep the workbook open for the next skill, or close the workbook and exit Excel.

Alternate Way:
Using a Shortcut Menu to Delete a Worksheet
You can use a shortcut menu to delete a worksheet. Right-click the worksheet tab of the worksheet you want to remove, and select Delete from the shortcut menu; then click the Delete button when Excel displays a warning message.

For immediate reinforcement, work Skill Drill 1.

Skill 4.2: Modify Worksheet Names and Positions

Excel assigns names to worksheets—Sheet1, Sheet2, and so forth. Changing the default names of worksheets in a multiple-sheet workbook makes it easier to understand the purpose of each sheet.

To further differentiate multiple worksheets within a workbook, you can apply a color to the sheet tab. The color fills the background of an unselected sheet tab and displays as a thin color bar below the name of a selected worksheet.

You can easily change the position of a worksheet by clicking its sheet tab and dragging left or right. In the following steps, you rename worksheet tabs, add color to worksheet tabs, and move a worksheet to another position within the workbook.

To Rename Tabs, Add Color to Tabs, and Reposition a Worksheet

1 **Open the *Modify Workbooks* file, if necessary.**
The workbook includes four worksheets: Sheet4 (to hold data about all stores), Sheet1 (Store A), Sheet2 (Store B), and Store C.

2 **Double-click the Sheet4 worksheet tab (or right-click the Sheet4 tab and choose Rename from the shortcut menu).**
Sheet4 displays with a black background, indicating that Rename mode is active (see Figure 4.12).

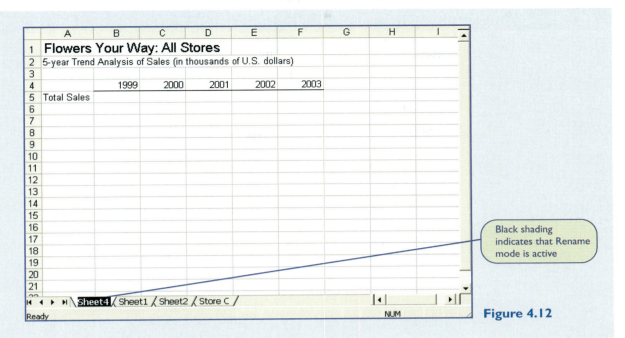

Figure 4.12

(callout) Black shading indicates that Rename mode is active

3 **Type** All Stores **and press** ⏎Enter).
The black shading disappears. The sheet is renamed and the worksheet tab displays *All Stores* instead of *Sheet4*.

4 **Use the process described in Steps 2 and 3 to change the name of** *Sheet1* **to** Store A.

5 **Use the process described in Steps 2 and 3 to change the name of** *Sheet2* **to** Store B.
The workbook includes four worksheets: All Stores, Store A, Store B, and Store C (see Figure 4.13).

(callout) Renamed worksheets

Figure 4.13

6 **Right-click the** *All Stores* **sheet tab, and choose** <u>T</u>ab **Color from the shortcut menu.**
The Format Tab Color dialog box opens (see Figure 4.14).

continues ▶

To Rename Tabs, Add Color to Tabs, and Reposition a Worksheet (continued)

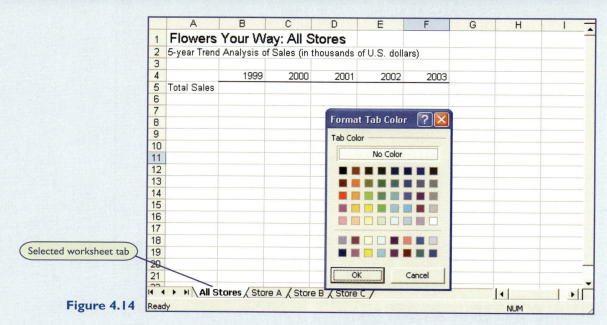

Selected worksheet tab

Figure 4.14

7 **Click the Red color square, and click OK.**
A red color bar displays below the worksheet name in the sheet tab (see Figure 4.15).

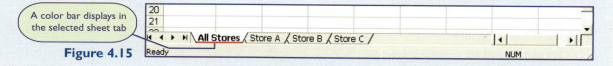

A color bar displays in the selected sheet tab

Figure 4.15

8 **Click the Store A sheet tab.**
The sheet name *All Stores* displays in white letters against a red background. A sheet tab color fills the background of an unselected sheet tab.

9 **Click and drag the All Stores sheet tab to the right of the Store C sheet tab, and release the mouse button.**
The All Stores sheet is now the last sheet instead of the first sheet (see Figure 4.16).

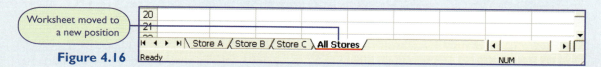

Worksheet moved to a new position

Figure 4.16

10 **Save your changes to the *Modify Workbooks* file.**
Keep the workbook open for the next skill, or close the workbook and exit Excel.

In Depth:

Modify or Remove Sheet Tab Color

To change the color assigned to a sheet tab, right-click it, and choose <u>T</u>ab Color from the shortcut menu. Click a different color square, and click OK.

To remove the color assigned to a sheet tab, right-click it and choose <u>T</u>ab Color from the shortcut menu. Choose *No Color* above the color squares, and click OK.

For immediate reinforcement, work Skill Drill 2.

Skill 4.3: **Use 3-D References**

Up to this point in the skill set, you worked with multiple sheets without changing their content. You applied color to sheet tabs, and you learned to insert, delete, move, copy, and rename worksheets.

Now it is time to make a content change involving multiple worksheets. If you want to refer to data in the same cell or range of cells on multiple sheets within a workbook, include a 3-D reference in a formula.

A 3-D reference includes the cell or range reference preceded by a range of worksheet names. For example, the reference to cell B20 in the formula =SUM('Store A:Store C'!B20) is a 3-D reference. The formula tells Excel to add the contents of each cell B20 in the range of worksheets that starts with the sheet named Store A and ends with the sheet named Store C.

In the following steps, you enter the formula described in the previous paragraph. The formula adds the 1999 sales for Stores A, B, and C, and places the result in the All Stores worksheet. The entire Excel Core Skill Set 5 provides additional coverage on creating and revising formulas.

To Use a 3-D Reference in a Formula

1 **Open the *Modify Workbooks* file, if necessary.**
The workbook includes four worksheets: Store A, Store B, Store C, and All Stores.

2 **Click the first three sheet tabs, and note the amount of 1999 total sales in cell B20.**
Cell B20 in each of the first three worksheets contains a formula that calculates total sales in thousands for the associated store—1,172 for Store A, 2,014 for Store B, and 2,427 for Store C.

3 **Select the *All Stores* sheet tab.**

4 **Type =SUM('Store A:Store C'!B20) in cell B5, and press** Enter ;
then click cell B5.
The formula containing a 3-D reference displays in the formula bar, and the formula result displays in cell B5 (see Figure 4.17).

continues ▶

To Use a 3-D Reference in a Formula (continued)

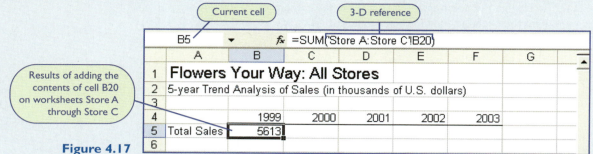

Current cell

3-D reference

Results of adding the contents of cell B20 on worksheets Store A through Store C

Figure 4.17

 If you have problems...
If Excel displays an error message or your results do not match those in Figure 4.17, check each part of the formula you entered. Make sure that an apostrophe (') precedes *Store A* and follows *Store C*. Also check that a colon separates Store A and Store C and an exclamation point precedes the B20 cell reference.

5 Apply a **Comma style zero decimal places** format to cell **B5** in the *All Stores* worksheet.

You entered one formula containing a 3-D cell reference and formatted the results. You learn to copy a formula in Core Skill Set 5. Do not complete the All Stores worksheet at this time.

6 Save your changes to the *Modify Workbooks* file, and close the workbook.

Work one or more of the exercises at the end of this skill set, start another skill set, or exit Excel.

 In Depth:
Get Help on 3-D Reference
Onscreen Help provides substantial information on 3-D references. Enter 3 - D reference in Excel's Ask a Question box, select the topic *About cell and range references*, and click the Show All button. Read the information on functions that allow a 3-D reference, including the AVERAGE, COUNT, MAX, and MIN functions you use in Core Skill Set 5. Another subtopic explains how 3-D references change when you move, copy, insert, or delete worksheets.

For immediate reinforcement, work Challenges 1 and 2.

Summary

In this skill set, you manipulated worksheets and worksheet tabs. You learned two ways to add a worksheet to an open workbook: inserting a blank worksheet, and copying a worksheet from an open workbook. You also added color to a sheet tab and deleted, renamed, and moved worksheets. You completed your experiences with multiple worksheets by entering a formula containing a 3-D reference.

Skill Drill

Skill Drill exercises *reinforce* skills. Each skill reinforced is the same, or nearly the same, as a skill presented in the skill set. Detailed instructions are provided in a step-by-step format.

You work with a different multiple-sheet file for each exercise. The exercises are independent, so you may complete them in any order. Be sure to save the workbook after completing each exercise. If you need a paper copy of one or more completed exercises, enter your name, centered in a header, before printing. Print options have already been set to print compressed to one page and to display the filename, sheet name, and current date in a footer.

1. Insert and Delete Worksheets

You are developing a workbook to summarize operating expenses for selected Indiana state parks. Currently the workbook includes worksheets for state parks in the north and central regions. You need to add a worksheet for another park in the north region, and delete all of the worksheets for parks in the central region.

To insert and delete sheets as you finalize the workbook, follow these steps:

1. Open the *MEC-S403* workbook and save it as **MEC-S4drill#1**.

   The workbook includes eleven worksheets—sheets named N1 through N6 with data on state parks located in the north region, and sheets named C1 through C5 with data on state parks located in the central region.

2. Click the C1 sheet tab , and choose Insert, Worksheet.

   A new blank worksheet named Sheet1 displays between sheet N6 and sheet C1. Now, you realize that you would have far less data entry to do if you created the new worksheet by copying an existing one.

3. Right-click the sheet tab of the new worksheet, and choose Delete from the shortcut menu.

   Excel removes the newly inserted worksheet named Sheet1.

4. Click the sheet tab named N6, and choose Edit, Move or Copy Sheet.

5. Make sure that *MEC-S4drill#1.xls* displays in the *To book* box in the Move or Copy dialog box.

6. Scroll down in the *Before sheet* box, and click C1.

7. Click the *Create a copy* check box, and click OK.

   Excels inserts a copy of the N6 worksheet before sheet C1, and assigns the name N6(2).

8. Double-click the N6(2) sheet tab, type **N7**, and press ↵Enter.

   You renamed the new worksheet.

9. Edit cell A4 in the N7 worksheet to read **Pokagen State Park** instead of *Chain O'Lakes State Park*.

10. Click the C1 sheet tab, hold down ⬆Shift, click the C5 sheet tab, and release ⬆Shift.

    Sheets C1 through C5 display with white backgrounds, indicating they are selected.

11. Right-click any of the selected sheets C1 through C5, and select Delete from the shortcut menu; then click the Delete button in response to the warning message.

    Excel deletes the five selected worksheets. The workbook now contains seven worksheets named N1 through N7.

12. Click cell A1 in the N1 worksheet; then save your changes to the *MEC-S4drill#1* workbook.

2. Move and Rename Worksheets

You are developing a workbook to summarize operating expenses for selected Indiana state parks. Currently the workbook includes worksheets for state parks in the central region. You want to rename the worksheets, and then reorder them alphabetically.

To rename and move worksheets, follow these steps:

1. Open the *MEC-S404* workbook and save it as MEC-S4drill#2.

   The workbook includes five worksheets—sheets named C1 through C5 with data on state parks located in the central region.

2. Double-click the C1 sheet tab, type **Mounds**, and press ⏎Enter.

3. Double-click the C2 sheet tab, type **Shades**, and press ⏎Enter.

4. Double-click the C3 sheet tab, type **Turkey Run**, and press ⏎Enter.

5. Double-click the C4 sheet tab, type **Fort Harrison**, and press ⏎Enter.

6. Double-click the C5 sheet tab, type **Summit Lake**, and press ⏎Enter.

7. Drag the sheet tab named *Fort Harrison* to the beginning of the sheet tabs, and release the mouse button.

8. Drag the sheet tab named *Turkey Run* to the end of the sheet tabs, and release the mouse button.

   You renamed the five worksheets and positioned them in alphabetical order based on sheet name.

9. Click cell A1 in the Fort Harrison worksheet; then save your changes to the *MEC-S4drill#2* workbook.

Challenge

Challenge exercises expand on or are somewhat related to skills presented in the skill set. Each exercise provides a brief narrative introduction, followed by instructions, in a numbered-step format, that are not as detailed as those in the Skill Drill section.

You work with a different multiple-sheet file for each exercise. The exercises are independent, so you may complete them in any order. Be sure to save the workbook after completing each exercise. If you need a paper copy of one or more completed exercises, enter your name, centered in a header, before printing. Print options have already been set to print compressed to one page and to display the filename, sheet name, and current date in a footer.

1. Enter a Formula with a 3-D Reference, Rename and Reorder Worksheets, and Apply Color to Sheet Tabs: Case 1

You maintain a workbook that tracks selected basketball statistics each week for thirteen teams. Currently the workbook includes four worksheets—three with data for weeks 1 through 3, and a summary sheet for calculating averages. You want to calculate an average for all three weeks by using a 3-D reference in a formula. You also plan to rename the worksheets containing weekly data, add color to the Summary sheet tab, and move the Summary sheet to the end.

To make the desired changes, follow these steps:

1. Open the *MEC-S405* workbook and save it as **MEC-S4challenge#1**.

   The workbook maintains data on basketball statistics. It contains a Summary sheet and three worksheets named Sheet1, Sheet2, and Sheet3.

2. View the content and organization of each worksheet by clicking each sheet tab sequentially.

All of the worksheets use the same organization for data—separate columns for points, assists, and rebounds respectively; team names in alphabetical order, one per row.

3. Click cell B4 in the Summary worksheet, and enter the formula
`=AVERAGE(Sheet1:Sheet3!B4).`

The formula includes the 3-D reference *Sheet1:Sheet3!B4*. If you use default sheet names to specify the range of worksheets in a 3-D reference, you do not have to include an apostrophe before the starting sheet and after the ending sheet.

Excel computes the average points per game scored by the Bucks based on the results of three games. The value *92* displays in cell B4 of the Summary worksheet.

4. Apply a blue color to the Summary sheet tab.

5. Make the Summary sheet the last sheet instead of the first sheet.

6. Rename the Sheet1, Sheet2, and Sheet3 worksheets. Change the names to **Week 1**, **Week 2**, and **Week 3**, respectively.

7. Click cell B4 in the Summary worksheet.

The formula *=AVERAGE('Week 1:Week 3'!B4)* displays in the formula bar. Excel automatically updates the 3-D reference in the formula to reflect the changes in sheet names. The revision includes the insertion of apostrophes at either end of the worksheet range.

8. Save your changes to the *MEC-S4challenge#1* workbook.

2. Enter a Formula with a 3-D Reference, Rename and Reorder Worksheets, and Apply Color to Sheet Tabs: Case 2

You maintain a workbook that tracks the number of volunteers assisting three organizations for four schools. Currently, the workbook includes five worksheets: four with data for individual schools, and a summary sheet for calculating totals. In the Summary worksheet, you want to calculate the total number of Into the Streets volunteers by using a 3-D reference in a formula. You also plan to rename and reorder the remaining worksheets, add color to all sheet tabs.

To make the desired changes, follow these steps:

1. Open the *MEC-S406* workbook and save it as **MEC-S4challenge#2**.

The workbook maintains data on volunteers for three organizations. It contains a Summary sheet and four worksheets named Sheet1 through Sheet4.

2. View the content and organization of each worksheet by clicking each sheet tab sequentially.

All of the worksheets use the same organization for data—column B for the number of volunteer hours; and three organizations, one per row, in column A. The contents of cell A1 include the name of the school.

3. Apply your choice of color to the Summary sheet tab, and select one other color to apply to the remaining sheet tabs.

4. Rename the Sheet1, Sheet2, Sheet3, and Sheet4 worksheets. Change each name to a word that describes the school. For example, change *Sheet1* to **Butler**, *Sheet2* to **IUPUI**, and so forth.

5. Keep the Summary sheet as the first worksheet, and rearrange the other sheets in alphabetical order based on sheet name.

6. In cell B6 of the Summary worksheet, enter a formula to sum the number of volunteers for Into the Streets from all four schools.

If you entered the correct =SUM formula containing a 3-D reference, Excel displays the value *354* in cell B6 of the Summary worksheet.

If you have problems...

If Excel displays an error message or your formula produces a different result, check for mistakes in the formula. Make sure that you include an exclamation point before the cell reference, and two apostrophes in the worksheet range—one before the starting sheet, and one after the ending sheet. Also, check that the cell reference in the formula is B4, not B6.

7. Make corrections as necessary, and save your changes to the *MEC-S4challenge#2* workbook.

CHAPTER 5

Creating and Revising Formulas

This skill set includes

Create and revise formulas

- ▌ Work with operators and order of precedence
- ▌ Enter and edit formulas
- ▌ Compare absolute and relative cell references
- ▌ Create and copy formulas with absolute or relative cell references
- ▌ Display formulas instead of formula results

Use statistical, date and time, financial, and logical functions in formulas

- ▌ Analyze data with AVERAGE, MAX, and MIN
- ▌ Calculate a loan payment with PMT
- ▌ Create a loan payment table
- ▌ Evaluate investment plans with FV
- ▌ Use IF to display messages
- ▌ Use IF to calculate
- ▌ Use NOW to display the current date
- ▌ Use dates in calculations

Skill Set Overview

This entire skill set focuses on calculations. The first of two parts covers formulas in general. You begin by learning the basics of effective worksheet design. After you view samples of operators and learn the order in which Excel performs calculations, you use a variety of methods to enter, edit, and copy formulas. You also display formulas instead of formula results.

The second of two parts provides multiple opportunities to use functions—predefined formulas. Your experiences include finding the average, highest, and lowest amounts in a range of values. You also determine a monthly loan payment; evaluate investment plans; use a function to display messages and perform calculations that vary, according to whether a test condition is met; and use a date-and-time function as the only entry in a cell and as part of a formula that calculates based on dates.

Skill 5.1: Create and Revise Formulas

You should plan the layout of each worksheet in a workbook before you begin to enter constants and formulas. Good worksheet design includes explanations about purpose and revisions, separate cells for data subject to change, and instructions to users.

In this skill area, you create the worksheet shown in Figure 5.1. The worksheet contains monthly and annual data.

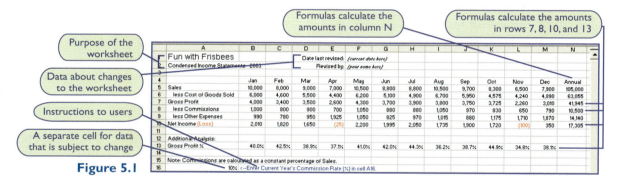

Figure 5.1

Work with Operators and Order of Precedence

Let's review what you know about calculations from Excel Core Skill Set 1, *Working with Cells and Cell Data*. The terms *formula* and *arithmetic operator* were introduced, and you used the arithmetic operator (*) in a formula to multiply the contents of two cells. The terms *AutoSum* and *function* were also introduced, and you used AutoSum to enter the function =SUM(B6:B11). The colon (:) connected the first and last cells of the range to sum. The colon is an example of a **reference operator,** which is used to combine cell references in calculations.

Excel provides two other types of operators: comparison and concatenation. A **comparison operator** is used to test the relationship between two items. For example a comparison operator can help you find out whether the items are equal, or whether one is greater than the other. A **concatenation operator** joins one or more text entries to form a single entry.

The following steps provide an in-depth look at operators and the order in which Excel performs calculations—sometimes referred to as the **order of precedence**. For example, you learn that multiplication and division take place before addition and subtraction. If you understand the order of precedence, and how to modify that order by using parentheses, you have the minimum skills required to create and edit formulas and functions.

To Work with Operators and Order of Precedence

1 **Open the file *MEC-S501*, and save it as** frisbees.
The workbook includes five worksheets: Condensed IS, Operators, Precedence, Abs1, and Abs2.

2 **Click the Operators sheet tab.**
The Operators worksheet displays four categories of operators in blue: arithmetic, comparison, text concatenation, and reference (see Figure 5.2). The symbol to type for each operator appears in red.

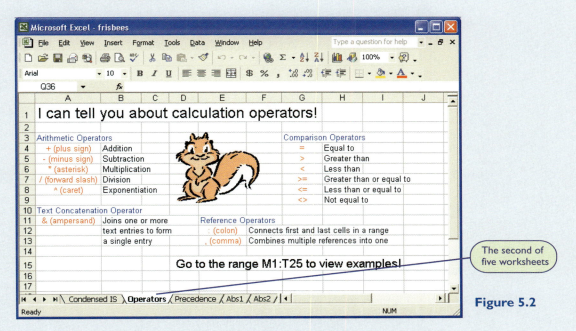

Figure 5.2

3 **After studying the categories of operators, display columns M through T on the screen, starting with row 1.**
This area of the worksheet contains one example for each operator category (see Figure 5.3). An arrow points to each cell that contains an operator in the formula.

continues ▶

To Work with Operators and Order of Precedence (continued)

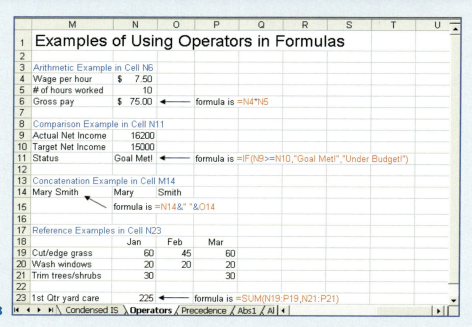

Figure 5.3

4 Click cell N6.

A formula that contains the arithmetic operator for multiplication (*) appears in the formula bar.

5 Click cell N11.

An IF function that contains the comparison operator for greater than or equal to (>=) appears in the formula bar. The operator tests whether the contents of cell N9 (*Actual Net Income*) are greater than or equal to the contents of cell N10 (*Target Net Income*) and displays one of two messages, depending on whether the comparison is true or false.

6 Click cell M14.

A formula that contains the concatenate operator (&) appears in the formula bar. The formula joins the contents of cells N14 and O14 and adds a space between the first and last names. Quotation marks surround literal text in a formula. Literal text is text that does not change—in this case, the blank space.

7 Click cell N23.

A formula that contains the reference operators colon (:) and comma (,) appears in the formula bar. The colon marks the beginning and ending cells in a range; the comma separates the ranges in the formula.

8 Click the Precedence sheet tab.

A text box, which contains the question *What is 5 plus 3 times 2?* appears near the top of the worksheet. How would you answer the question?

9 Click cell D8.

The formula *=5+3*2* appears in the formula bar; the formula result displays in cell D8. Excel first multiplies 3*2 and then adds the result (6) to the number 5.

10 Click cell D12.

The formula =(5+3)*2 appears in the formula bar; the formula result displays in cell D12. Operations within parentheses take precedence over those not encased in parentheses. In this case, Excel first adds the numbers 5 and 3; then multiplies the result (8) by 2.

⑪ After studying the two examples, display columns M through R on the screen, starting with row 1.

This area of the worksheet lists the order of Excel operations in formulas (see Figure 5.4). Keep this order in mind as you construct your own formulas.

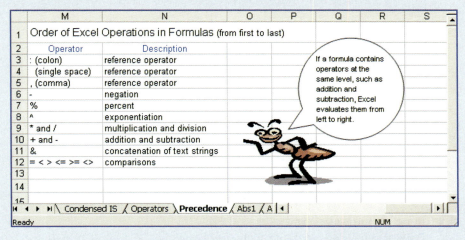

Figure 5.4

This concludes the overview of operators and order of calculations. Now that you have a better understanding of operators and order of calculations, you are ready to enter the five formulas needed to complete the condensed income statements for Fun with Frisbees. Keep the *frisbees* workbook open for the next skill, or close the workbook and exit Excel.

Enter and Edit Formulas

You can complete the design of the Condensed IS worksheet for Fun with Frisbees by entering five formulas and copying them to related cells. One of the formulas involves addition—computing annual sales as the sum of sales for each month. Calculations performed by the other formulas include subtraction, multiplication, and division.

You can easily create a simple formula by typing the entire equation into a cell. You can also enter a formula using the type-and-point method, in which you type operators and use the mouse to point to a cell or range of cells. Pointing to a cell or range of cells using the mouse simplifies the process of creating a formula and helps to ensure that you enter the correct cell addresses.

In the following steps, you enter four formulas to complete the January column in the Condensed Income Statements for Fun with Frisbees. Your efforts include making two mistakes and editing the formulas to produce correct results.

To Enter and Edit Formulas

❶ Open the *frisbees* workbook, if necessary, and click the Condensed IS sheet tab.

❷ Click cell B7, and type the equal sign (see Figure 5.5).

continues ▶

To Enter and Edit Formulas (continued)

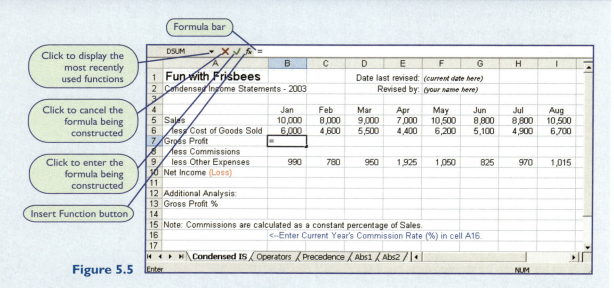

Figure 5.5

- Click to display the most recently used functions
- Click to cancel the formula being constructed
- Click to enter the formula being constructed
- Insert Function button
- Formula bar

③ **Click cell B5.**

=B5 appears in the formula bar and in cell B7.

④ **Type a minus sign, and click cell B6.**

Excel enters −B6 into the formula (see Figure 5.6). A flashing dotted line appears around cell B6 to remind you that it is the cell you most recently selected for the formula.

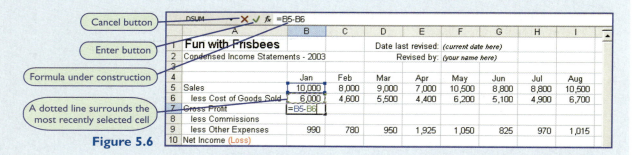

Figure 5.6

- Cancel button
- Enter button
- Formula under construction
- A dotted line surrounds the most recently selected cell

⑤ **Click the Enter button on the formula bar (a green check mark).**

Excel enters the formula to calculate January's Gross Profit in cell B7, and cell B7 is the active cell (see Figure 5.7). You could also press ↵Enter in place of Step 5. If you did, the active cell would be cell B8.

Figure 5.7

- Gross Profit formula
- Formula results

6 **Click cell B8; then type =B5*.1 and press ⏎Enter.**
You entered a formula to calculate commissions as 10 percent of January sales. The value *1,000* displays in cell B8.

You realize, however, that typing a raw number in a formula reflects poor worksheet skills if that number is subject to change. The results are accurate, but each time the commission rate changes, you must revise the formula.

7 **Click cell A16 in the Condensed IS worksheet.**
This selects a separate cell in which to enter the current year's commission rate.

8 **Type 10% and press ⏎Enter.**

9 **Double-click cell B8.**
The flashing cursor within cell B8 indicates that in-cell edit mode is active. Excel color-codes the cell reference in the formula and borders the referenced cell in the same color (see Figure 5.8).

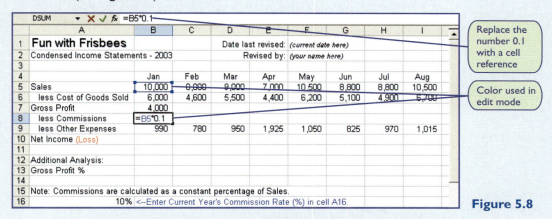

Figure 5.8

10 **Change =B5*0.1 to =B5*A16; then press ⏎Enter and click cell B8.**
The formula multiplies January Sales in cell B5 by the current commission rate in cell A16. The formula *=B5*A16* displays in the formula bar, and the value *1,000* displays in cell B8 (see Figure 5.9).

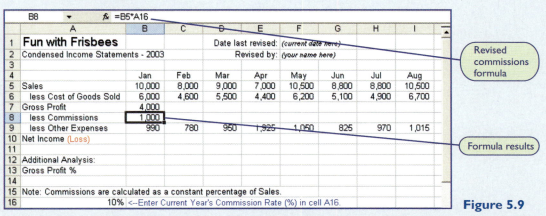

Figure 5.9

The formula in cell B8 correctly calculates the commissions for January. However, it will not produce the correct results for February through December when copied across row 8. You learn what the problem is, and how to correct it, in the next section. For now, proceed to enter the next formula.

continues ▶

To Enter and Edit Formulas (continued)

11 **Click cell B10, and enter** =B7 - B8 - B9 **by typing the entire formula or by using the type-and-point technique.**

The formula =*B7-B8-B9* in cell B10 calculates the 2,010 January Net Income by subtracting the contents of cells B8 (Commissions) and B9 (Other Expenses) from the amount in cell B7 (Gross Profit).

12 **Click cell B13, and enter** =B10/B5 **by typing the entire formula or by using the type-and-point technique.**

You planned to enter a formula to calculate January Gross Profit—Gross Profit divided by Sales. However, you realize you used the Net Income amount in cell B10 instead of the correct Gross Profit amount in cell B7.

13 **Make sure that cell B13 is the current cell, and click the formula in the formula bar.**

The flashing cursor in the formula bar indicates that edit mode is active. Excel color-codes each cell reference in the formula and borders the referenced cells in the same color (see Figure 5.10).

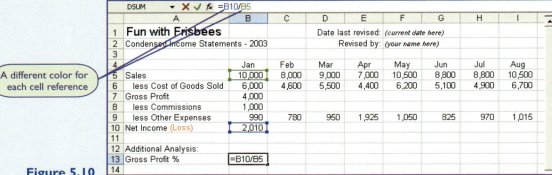

A different color for each cell reference

Figure 5.10

14 **Edit the formula in the formula bar to read** =B7/B5 **and press** ⏎Enter.

The formula =*B7/B5* in cell B13 calculates the 40.0 percent January Gross Profit percent by dividing the contents of cell B7 (Gross Profit) by the amount in cell B5 (Sales).

 15 **Save your changes to the** *frisbees* **workbook.**

You entered four formulas to compute January values. Before you copy those formulas to compute February through December values, you need to know the difference between relative and absolute cell references. Keep the *frisbees* workbook open for the next skill, or close the workbook and exit Excel.

Compare Absolute and Relative Cell References

Each reference to a cell in a formula is a *relative cell reference* if the row and/or column cell references change as a formula is copied. A reference to a cell in a formula is an *absolute cell reference* if the row and/or column cell references do not change as a formula is copied.

If you don't want Excel to adjust a reference to a cell when you copy a formula, use an absolute reference to that cell in the formula. You can specify an absolute cell reference by placing a dollar sign ($) in front of the column letter and/or row number. For example, A4 is a relative cell reference and $A$4 is an absolute cell reference.

You may find it easier to understand the concept of relative and absolute cell references if you compare the effects of copying with and without absolute cell references. In the following steps, you view results of copying a formula that is similar to the one needed for the Fun with Frisbees workbook. In the first example, copying a formula with only relative cell references produces errors. In the second example, changing one cell reference to absolute—by placing a dollar sign ($) in front of both the column letter and row number—produces correct results.

To Compare Absolute and Relative Cell References

❶ Open the *frisbees* workbook, if necessary; select the Abs1 sheet tab, and click cell B9.

Case 1 displays, showing errors after copying the Commissions formula *=B8*A4* from B9 to C9:E9 (see Figure 5.11).

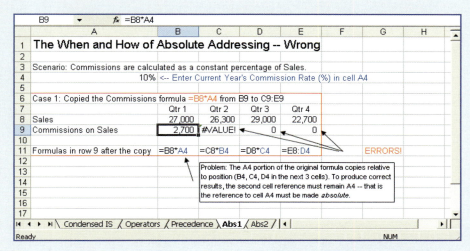

Figure 5.11

❷ Click cell C9.

#VALUE! displays in cell C9, indicating an error in the formula *=C8*B4*. The formula tells Excel to multiply Qtr 2 Sales by the contents of cell B4. Excel cannot multiply an amount by a label.

❸ Click cell D9.

The number zero displays in cell D9, indicating an error in the formula *=D8*C4*. The formula tells Excel to multiply Qtr 3 Sales by the contents of cell C4. Cell C4 is blank; the text that displays in cell C4 is part of the label entered in cell B4. Multiplying a value by zero produces zero as the result.

❹ Read the analysis provided in the Problem text box; then select the Abs2 sheet tab, and click cell B9.

Case 2 displays, showing the correct results after copying the Commissions formula *=B8*$A$4* from B9 to C9:E9 (see Figure 5.12).

continues ▶

To Compare Absolute and Relative Cell References (continued)

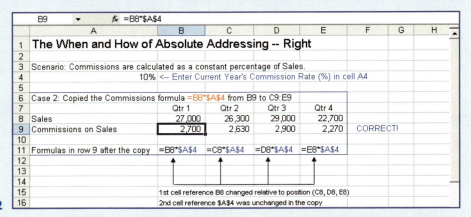

B9	▾	*fx*	=B8*$A$4					
	A	B	C	D	E	F	G	H
1	The When and How of Absolute Addressing -- Right							
2								
3	Scenario: Commissions are calculated as a constant percentage of Sales.							
4	10%	<-- Enter Current Year's Commission Rate (%) in cell A4						
5								
6	Case 2: Copied the Commissions formula =B8*$A$4 from B9 to C9:E9							
7		Qtr 1	Qtr 2	Qtr 3	Qtr 4			
8	Sales	27,000	26,300	29,000	22,700			
9	Commissions on Sales	2,700	2,630	2,900	2,270	CORRECT!		
10								
11	Formulas in row 9 after the copy	=B8*$A$4	=C8*$A$4	=D8*$A$4	=E8*$A$4			
12								
13								
14								
15		1st cell reference B8 changed relative to position (C8, D8, E8)						
16		2nd cell reference $A$4 was unchanged in the copy						

Figure 5.12

⑤ Click cells C9, D9, and E9, one after the other. After selecting each cell, look at the associated formula in the formula bar.

Formula results are consistent with the explanation provided in rows 11 through 16. Keep the workbook open for the next skill, or close the workbook and exit Excel.

Alternate Way:

Using F4 to Make Cell References Absolute

Excel can enter the dollar sign(s) to make one or more parts of a cell reference absolute. While you create or edit a formula, click within a cell reference and press F4 until you get the desired result (such as =$B$8, =B$8, =$B8 or =B8).

In Depth:

Using Mixed Cell References

You already know that you can mix relative and absolute cell references in a formula. For example, the previous Case 2 showed the effects of copying the formula =B8*$A$4. In that formula, the reference to cell B8 is relative and the reference to cell A4 is absolute. You can also mix relative and absolute settings within a single cell reference, if needed, to produce the desired copy results.

Create and Copy Formulas with Absolute or Relative Cell References

Now that you have a better understanding of the effects on copying with absolute references in formulas, you can copy the existing formulas in the Condensed IS worksheet of the *frisbees* workbook. You also complete the worksheet by entering a function that calculates annual sales and copying that function to generate other annual data.

To Create and Copy Formulas with Absolute or Relative Cell References

1 **Open the *frisbees* workbook and select the condensed IS worksheet, if necessary.**

2 **If columns A through M are not in view on your screen, display the drop-down list of predefined Zoom percentages, and select 75%.**

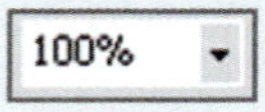

`100%  ▾`

3 **Click cell B7 in the Condensed IS worksheet.**
This selects the cell containing a formula that calculates January Gross Profit. A thick black border surrounds the selected cell. The small, solid black square in the lower-right corner of the selected cell is the fill handle.

4 **Position the mouse pointer on the fill handle in the lower-right corner of cell B7.**
The pointer changes to a thin black cross (see Figure 5.13).

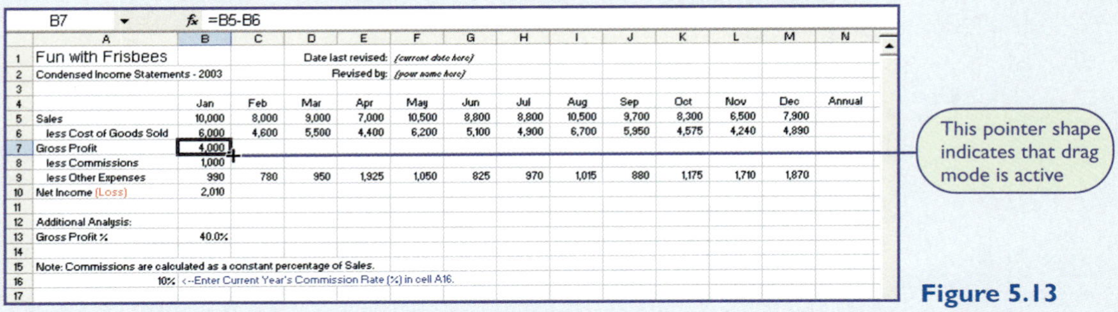

This pointer shape indicates that drag mode is active

Figure 5.13

5 **Press the left mouse button, drag the fill handle right to cell M7, and release the mouse button.**
The Auto Fill Options button displays (see Figure 5.14), and Excel fills the range C7:M7 with formulas that are relative to their locations: =C5-C6 in column C, =D5-D6 in column D, =E5-E6 in column E, and so forth. The copied formulas subtract Cost of Goods Sold from Sales for each month February through December.

Copied formulas in row 7

Auto Fill Options smart tag

Figure 5.14

6 **Position the pointer on the smart tag (refer to Figure 5.14), and click its down arrow.**
You can take one of three actions related to copy results: accept the default option Copy Cells, which retains the formatting assigned to cell B8; or choose either Fill Formatting Only or Fill Without Formatting.

7 **Click any cell to exit the Auto Fill Options drop-down list and deselect the highlighted range; then check that your results match those in Figure 5.14.**

continues ▶

To Create and Copy Formulas with Absolute or Relative Cell References (continued)

8   **Click cell B8; then click within the cell reference A16 in the formula bar.**

9   **Press F4 once.**

The reference to cell A16 changes to *$A$16* in the formula bar and in cell B8 (see Figure 5.15). Neither the column reference (A) nor the row reference (16) changes when you copy the formula.

Absolute reference to column A and row 16

Dollar signs indicate an absolute cell reference

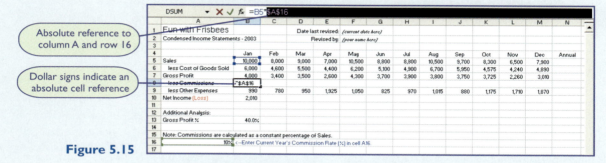

Figure 5.15

Alternate Way:
Manually Specify Absolute Addressing
As an alternative to F4, you can manually type dollar signs to indicate absolute addressing.

10   **Press F4 repeatedly.**

Each time you press F4, Excel assigns one of four combinations of relative, absolute, or mixed cell references—A$16, $A16, A16, and $A$16.

11   **Press F4 until $A$16 displays in the formula (refer to Figure 5.15), and press ↵Enter.**

The formula that multiplies January Sales in cell B5 by the current commission rate in cell A16 will now produce correct results for February through December when copied across row 8.

12   **Drag the formula in cell B8 to fill the range C8:M8, and release the mouse button.**

The copied formulas multiply February sales through December sales by the commission rate in A16 (see Figure 5.16).

Copied formula

Formula results in row 8

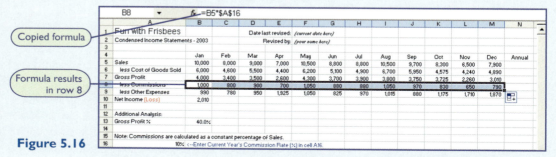

Figure 5.16

13   **Click any cell to deselect the highlighted range; then check that your results match those in Figure 5.16.**

If you have problems...

If your calculated results in row 8 do not match those shown in Figure 5.16, you may have an incorrect or missing percentage in cell A16, there may be an error in the formula in cell B8, or you may have had trouble copying the formula. Check your work, correct any mistakes, and try the copy operation again.

14 **Copy the formula in cell B10 to the range C10:M10; then copy the formula in cell B13 to the range C13:M13, and deselect the highlighted range.**

The Net Income (Loss) and Gross Profit percent values for February through December are added to the worksheet (see Figure 5.17). The negative amounts in cells E10 and L10 indicate a Net Loss instead of Net Income. The cells in row 10 were previously formatted to display negative numbers in red within parentheses.

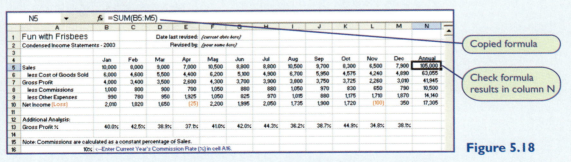

Check formula results in rows 10 and 13

Figure 5.17

15 **Click cell N5 and click AutoSum in the toolbar.**

The formula =SUM(B5:M5) appears in the formula bar.

16 **Press ⏎Enter to accept the suggested range of cells to sum.**

Excel adds the contents of cells B5 through M5, and displays *105,000* as annual sales.

17 **Copy the formula in cell N5 to the range N6:N10; then click cell N5.**

Annual totals for other line items in the condensed income statement display in column N (see Figure 5.18).

N5			f_x =SUM(B5:M5)											
	A	B	C	D	E	F	G	H	I	J	K	L	M	N
1	Fun with Frisbees			Date last revised: {current date here}										
2	Condensed Income Statements - 2003			Revised by: {your name here}										
3														
4		Jan	Feb	Mar	Apr	May	Jun	Jul	Aug	Sep	Oct	Nov	Dec	Annual
5	Sales	10,000	8,000	9,000	7,000	10,500	8,800	8,800	10,500	9,700	8,300	6,500	7,900	105,000
6	less Cost of Goods Sold	6,000	4,600	5,500	4,400	6,200	5,100	4,900	6,700	5,950	4,575	4,240	4,890	63,055
7	Gross Profit	4,000	3,400	3,500	2,600	4,300	3,700	3,900	3,800	3,750	3,725	2,260	3,010	41,945
8	less Commissions	1,000	800	900	700	1,050	880	880	1,050	970	830	650	790	10,500
9	less Other Expenses	990	780	950	1,925	1,050	825	970	1,015	880	1,175	1,710	1,870	14,140
10	Net Income (Loss)	2,010	1,820	1,650	(25)	2,200	1,995	2,050	1,735	1,900	1,720	(100)	350	17,305
11														
12	Additional Analysis:													
13	Gross Profit %	40.0%	42.5%	38.9%	37.1%	41.0%	42.0%	44.3%	36.2%	38.7%	44.9%	34.8%	38.1%	
14														
15	Note: Commissions are calculated as a constant percentage of Sales.													
16		10%	<--Enter Current Year's Commission Rate (%) in cell A16.											

Copied formula

Check formula results in column N

Figure 5.18

18 **Restore the zoom level to 100%, if necessary; then save your changes to the *frisbees* workbook.**

The Condensed IS worksheet is complete. Keep the workbook open for the next skill, or close the workbook and exit Excel.

Display Formulas Instead of Formula Results

As you create larger, more complex worksheets, you may find it useful to check your work by displaying formulas instead of formula results. Viewing or printing a worksheet in this display mode can help you understand the calculations the worksheet performs. Printed copy can also be a valuable resource if disk versions are damaged or missing and you have to reconstruct the worksheet.

In the following steps, you set the worksheet display to show the formulas in the Condensed IS worksheet, and then you turn off the setting.

To Display Formulas Instead of Formula Results

1 Open the *frisbees* workbook and click the **Condensed IS** sheet tab, if necessary.

2 Choose **Tools, Options**.
The Options dialog box opens with 13 tabs: View, Calculation, Edit, General, Transition, Custom Lists, Chart, Color, International, Save, Error Checking, Spelling, and Security.

3 Click the View tab if it is not the active tab.

4 In the Window options section, click the check box to the left of **Formulas (see Figure 5.19).**

The active tab

Click to accept the current settings and close the dialog box

Check to display formulas instead of formula results

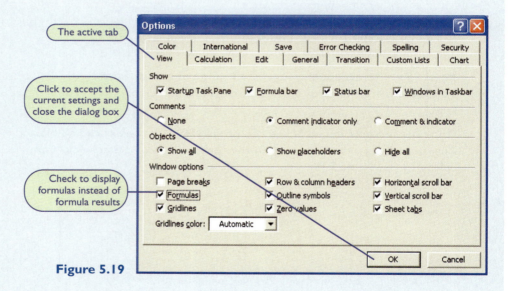

Figure 5.19

5 Click OK.
Excel displays the Formula Auditing toolbar, doubles the width of each column, and displays what is stored in each cell (see Figure 5.20).

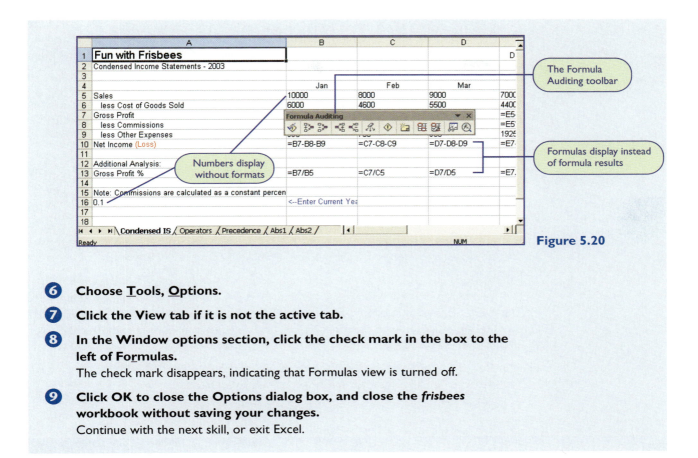

Figure 5.20

⑥ **Choose Tools, Options.**

⑦ **Click the View tab if it is not the active tab.**

⑧ **In the Window options section, click the check mark in the box to the left of Formulas.**

The check mark disappears, indicating that Formulas view is turned off.

⑨ **Click OK to close the Options dialog box, and close the** *frisbees* **workbook without saving your changes.**

Continue with the next skill, or exit Excel.

Alternate Way:
Switch View Between Formula Results and Formulas
You can use the keyboard to switch between viewing formula results and viewing formulas. Press the two-key combination Ctrl+~ to activate formula view. Press Ctrl+~ again to restore formula results.

For immediate reinforcement on formulas, work Skill Drills 1 and 2;
also Challenges 1 through 4.

Skill 5.2: **Use Statistical, Date and Time, Financial, and Logical Functions in Formulas**

Excel provides hundreds of functions to help you with tasks, such as adding a list of values and determining loan payments. Functions are organized in categories that include: Financial, Date & Time, Math & Trig, Statistical, Lookup & Reference, Database, Text, Logical, and Information. In this skill area, you glimpse the power of functions by working with one or more functions from four categories: Statistical, Financial, Logical, and Date & Time.

You start this skill area by using the statistical functions AVERAGE, MAX, and MIN to find the average, highest, and lowest monthly sales, respectively. Next, you use a single financial function PMT to determine a monthly loan payment, create a table of PMT functions, and use the financial function FV to evaluate investment plans. Two of the remaining skills focus on using the logical function IF to display messages and perform calculations that vary, according to whether a test condition is met. To complete the skill area, you use the date-and-time function NOW in two ways: as the only entry in a cell and as part of a formula that calculates based on dates.

Analyze Data with AVERAGE, MAX, and MIN

A function is a predefined formula that calculates by using arguments in a specific order. An *argument* is a specific value in a function, such as a range of cells. For example, the function =AVERAGE(B5:M5) has one argument—the range of cells from B5 through M5.

You can enter functions in more than one way. If you know the name and structure of the function you want to use, you can type it into the cell in which you want the results to appear or you can type it into the formula bar. You can also use the Insert Function dialog box to select from a list of functions.

Excel provides a substantial number of statistical functions, including AVERAGE, MAX, and MIN. The *AVERAGE function* calculates the average of specified values. Use the *MAX function* to display the largest value among specified values. The *MIN function* calculates the smallest value among specified values.

In the following steps, you use the three statistical functions AVERAGE, MAX, and MIN to analyze sales. Each function has the same structure—equal sign, function name, and a range of cells within parentheses.

To Analyze Data with AVERAGE, MAX, and MIN

1 **Open the *MEC-S502* workbook, and save the file as** Statistical functions.
The workbook contains one sheet named Condensed IS.

2 **Click cell B16 and type** =AVERAGE(B5:M5.
The nearly complete function appears in the formula bar and in cell B16 (see Figure 5.21).

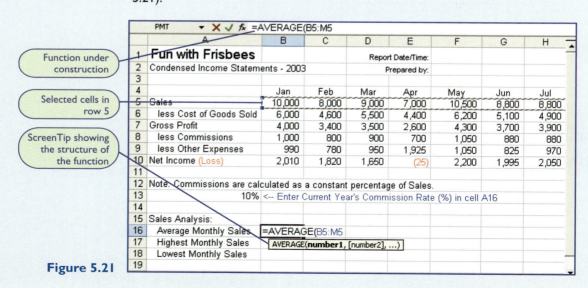

Figure 5.21

3 **Click the green check mark in the formula bar.**
Excel automatically adds the closing parenthesis. The function =AVERAGE(B5:M5) appears in the formula bar. The function result *$8,750* displays in cell B16.

 If you have problems...
If you press ⏎Enter instead of the green check mark in the formula bar, the cell below cell B16 is the current cell. Click cell B16 to see the AVERAGE function in the formula bar.

4 **Enter =MAX(B5:M5) in cell B17, and make cell B17 the current cell.**
The function =MAX(B5:M5) appears in the formula bar. The function result *$10,500* displays in cell B17.

5 **Enter =MIN(B5:M5) in cell B18, and make cell B18 the current cell.**
The function =MIN(B5:M5) appears in the formula bar. The function result *$6,500* displays in cell B18 (see Figure 5.22).

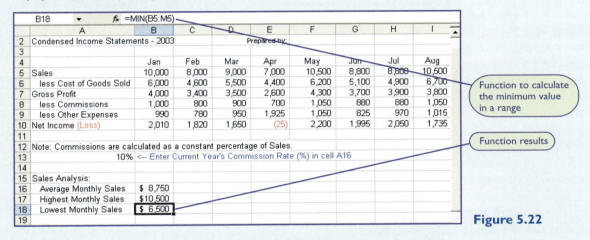

	A	B	C	D	E	F	G	H	I
	B18 ▼	*fx* =MIN(B5:M5)							
2	Condensed Income Statements - 2003			Prepared by:					
3									
4		Jan	Feb	Mar	Apr	May	Jun	Jul	Aug
5	Sales	10,000	8,000	9,000	7,000	10,500	8,800	8,800	10,500
6	less Cost of Goods Sold	6,000	4,600	5,500	4,400	6,200	5,100	4,900	6,700
7	Gross Profit	4,000	3,400	3,500	2,600	4,300	3,700	3,900	3,800
8	less Commissions	1,000	800	900	700	1,050	880	880	1,050
9	less Other Expenses	990	780	950	1,925	1,050	825	970	1,015
10	Net Income (Loss)	2,010	1,820	1,650	(25)	2,200	1,995	2,050	1,735
11									
12	Note: Commissions are calculated as a constant percentage of Sales.								
13		10%	<-- Enter Current Year's Commission Rate (%) in cell A16						
14									
15	Sales Analysis:								
16	Average Monthly Sales	$ 8,750							
17	Highest Monthly Sales	$10,500							
18	Lowest Monthly Sales	$ 6,500							
19									

Function to calculate the minimum value in a range

Function results

Figure 5.22

6 **Make sure that the results are accurate. (You might have to scroll right or change the zoom level to view columns A through M.)**
The highest monthly sales ($10,500) occurred in May and August; the lowest monthly sales ($6,500) occurred in November.

7 **Save your changes to the *Statistical functions* workbook, and close the workbook.**
Continue with the next skill, or exit Excel.

In Depth:
Other Functions to Analyze a Set of Values

Other statistical functions to analyze a set of values include MODE, MEDIAN, COUNT, COUNTA, and COUNTBLANK. The MODE function returns the value that appears most frequently in a specified set of values. If no duplicate data points exist, the error value *#N/A* displays. The MEDIAN function displays the middle value in the data set.

Use one of the COUNT functions to count selected cells within a specified range. The COUNT function returns a count of the cells that contain numbers or the results of formulas. The COUNTA function—think of the "A" as meaning "All"—counts all cells in the specified range that are not blank. The COUNTBLANK function counts all cells in the specified range that are blank.

Calculate a Loan Payment with PMT

The *PMT function* calculates the payment due on a loan, assuming equal payments and a fixed interest rate. In this skill, you use the Insert Function dialog box to enter a PMT function that calculates the monthly payment on a loan. You set up the worksheet as a model. A *worksheet model* generally contains labels and formulas, but the cells that hold variable data are blank. *Variable data* are amounts that are subject to change, such as the interest rate or the amount borrowed in a loan situation.

The PMT function requires that you specify three arguments in order: the annual interest rate adjusted for the number of payments within a year, the total number of payments, and the amount borrowed.

If a minus sign (–) precedes the amount borrowed, the function result is a positive number. If a minus sign does not precede the amount borrowed, the function result is a negative number. You determine the display you want; either way, the dollar amount is the same.

In the following steps, you work with the first three worksheets in a four-sheet workbook. On the first worksheet, you look at the questions that can be answered by using a PMT function. On the second worksheet, you vary the results of an existing PMT function by changing data in cells that are referenced by the function. In the third worksheet, you enter and test a PMT function.

To Calculate a Loan Payment with PMT

1 **Open the *MEC-S503* workbook, and save it as** PMT function.
The workbook includes four worksheets: Intro PMT, Single PMT, Create PMT, and Multiple PMT.

2 **Click the Intro PMT sheet tab, and read its contents to learn about uses for the PMT function.**

3 **Select the Single PMT worksheet, and click cell B10.**
The function *=PMT(B6/B7,B8,-B5)* appears in the formula bar. The function result displays in cell B10 (see Figure 5.23). The monthly payment on an 8.5 percent, 4-year, $8,000 loan is *$197.19*.

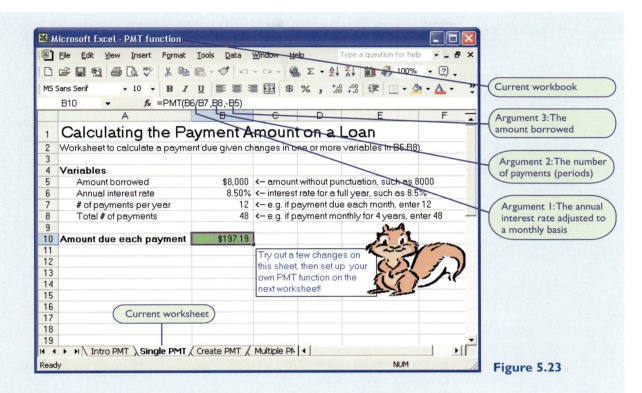

Figure 5.23

④ **Scroll down to view the syntax explanation in the range A31:F44; then scroll up to view the top of the worksheet.**

⑤ **Click cell B8, and enter** 36 **instead of** *48* **as the total number of payments.**
The function recalculates by using the revised number of payments. Reducing the loan term to 36 months raises the monthly payment on an 8.5 percent, $8,000 loan to *$252.54*. You now enter a PMT function by using the Function Arguments dialog box.

⑥ **Select the Create PMT worksheet.**
A worksheet similar to the Single PMT worksheet displays. Because the worksheet is set up as a model for any combination of loan terms, a note about an error message has been set up in a text box.

⑦ **Click cell B12 and click the Insert Function button in the formula bar.**
The Insert Function dialog box opens (see Figure 5.24). The most recently used function category appears selected. (This may vary from the selection on your screen.)

continues ▶

To Calculate a Loan Payment with PMT (continued)

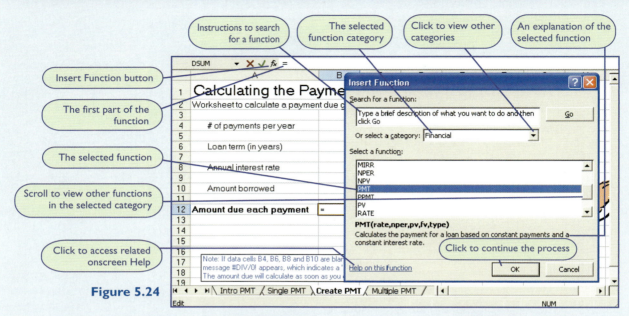

Figure 5.24

8 **Select the Financial function category and the PMT function, as shown in Figure 5.24, and click OK.**

The Function Arguments dialog box for PMT opens. If the dialog box covers the cells in column B, click the title bar of the dialog box and drag it to the right. The dialog box includes text boxes to define up to five arguments. If equal payments are made at the end of each time period, as opposed to the beginning, you specify only the first three arguments.

9 **Click in the Rate text box, and click cell B8.**

Excel displays *B8* in the Rate text box, and displays *=PMT(B8)* in cell B12 and the formula bar.

10 **Type / (the symbol for division), and click cell B4.**

The specification of the first argument, the annual interest rate adjusted to a monthly basis, is complete. Excel displays *B8/B4* as the first argument in the dialog box, and displays *=PMT(B8/B4)* in cell B12 and the formula bar (see Figure 5.25).

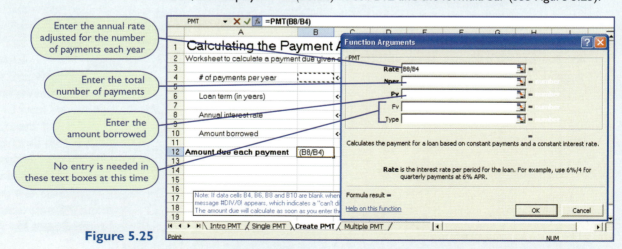

Figure 5.25

11   **Click in the Nper (number of periods) text box of the Function Arguments dialog box.**

12   **Click cell B6, type an asterisk (*), and click cell B4.**

The specification of the second argument, the number of payments, is complete. This argument calculates the total payments as the number of years for the loan multiplied by the number of payments each year. Excel displays *B6*B4* in the Nper text box, and displays *=PMT(B8/B4,B6*B4)* in cell B12 and the formula bar.

13   **Click in the Pv (present value) text box of the Function Arguments dialog box, and click cell B10.**

The specification of the third argument, the amount borrowed, is complete. Make sure that the display in your formula bar matches that shown in Figure 5.26, and make changes in the PMT Function Arguments dialog box as necessary.

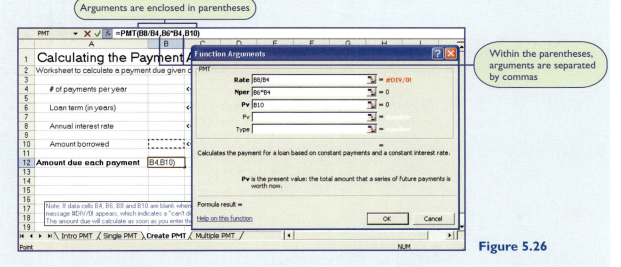

Figure 5.26

14   **Click OK, and position the pointer on the Trace Error button (see Figure 5.27).**

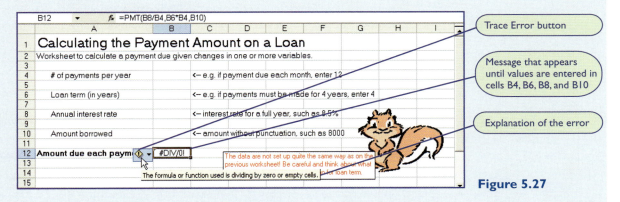

Figure 5.27

15   **Save your changes to the *PMT function* workbook.**

You saved the worksheet as a model that you can use for any combination of loan terms. Cells B4, B6, B8, and B10 are blank.

continues ▶

To Calculate a Loan Payment with PMT (continued)

 Use the model by entering the data to compute the loan payment on a 4-year, 8.5 percent, $8,000 loan assuming monthly payments—12 in cell B4, 4 in cell B6, 8.5% in cell B8, and 8000 in cell B10.

The payment amount *($197.19)* displays in cell B12 (see Figure 5.28). The parentheses indicate a negative number. If you prefer that the result be expressed as a positive number, precede the third argument in the PMT function with a minus sign.

Monthly payment based on loan terms in cells B4, B6, B8, and B10

	A	B	C	D	E	F	G	H	I
1	Calculating the Payment Amount on a Loan								
2	Worksheet to calculate a payment due given changes in one or more variables.								
3									
4	# of payments per year	12	←– e.g. if payment due each month, enter 12						
5									
6	Loan term (in years)	4	←– e.g. if payments must be made for 4 years, enter 4						
7									
8	Annual interest rate	8.50%	←– interest rate for a full year, such as 8.5%						
9									
10	Amount borrowed	$8,000	←– amount without punctuation, such as 8000						
11									
12	Amount due each payment	($197.19)	The data are not set up quite the same way as on the previous worksheet! Be careful and think about what you need to put in the PMT function for loan term.						
13									
14									
15									

Figure 5.28

 Try other combinations of the four variables; then close the workbook without saving your changes to the data.

You saved the labels and the PMT function in Step 15. By closing without saving your changes to cells containing loan-specific data, the model is ready to use with another set of loan terms. You can now exit Excel, or continue with the next skill.

In Depth:
Other Financial Functions

Excel provides a variety of financial functions for business and personal use. Some relate to the time value of money, such as FV (future value) and NPV (net present value). Others provide investment information, such as IRR (internal rate of return). Some functions even calculate depreciation under a variety of methods, including SLN (straight line), DDB (double-declining balance), and SYD (Sum-of-the-Years Digits).

Create a Loan Payment Table

Calculating loan payment due, based on one set of loan terms, has limited use. You understand how to set up and copy formulas containing absolute and relative cell references, so you decide to create a table of payments at varying interest rates, loan terms, or amounts borrowed.

In the following steps, you create a table that shows payments due on loans of varying length. You also set up two additional columns for summary information over the life of the loan—one for total payments and the other for total interest.

To Create a Loan Payment Table

① **Open the *PMT function* workbook, and select the worksheet named Multiple PMT.**

The partially completed Multiple PMT worksheet is designed to provide three types of information about multiple loan terms: the amount of a payment on a loan (column C), the total payments on a loan (column D), and the total interest on a loan (column E). Loan terms in half-year increments are listed in column A, and formulas in column B calculate the corresponding number of months. After you enter the appropriate formulas in columns C through E, you can quickly generate information by varying the interest rate in cell B7 or the amount borrowed in cell D7.

② **Click cell C11, and click the Insert Function button in the formula bar.**

This action starts the process of entering a PMT function in the first cell below the *Amount of Each Payment* column heading.

③ **Select the Financial function category, select the PMT function, and click OK.**

The PMT Function Arguments dialog box opens. If the dialog box covers row 7 or cell C11, drag the dialog box to the right.

④ **Enter the three arguments shown in Figure 5.29.**

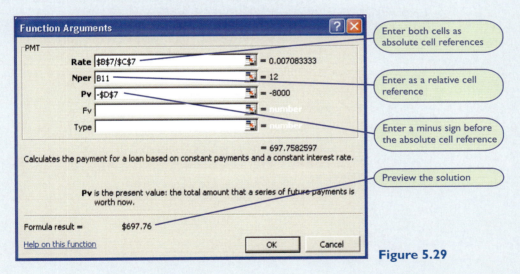

Figure 5.29

You can type each argument in its text box: $B$7 / $C$7 in the Rate text box, B11 in the Nper text box, and -$D$7 in the Pv text box. You can also use a combination of typing the arithmetic operators and pointing to (clicking) the cell references, followed by changing all but one cell reference to an absolute reference. To convert a relative cell reference to absolute, click it in the PMT dialog box, and press F4.

⑤ **Click OK.**

The function =PMT($B$7/$C$7,B11,-$D$7) appears in the formula bar. The function result $697.76 displays in cell C11 (see Figure 5.30).

continues ▶

To Create a Loan Payment Table (continued)

Function to calculate a loan payment

Function results

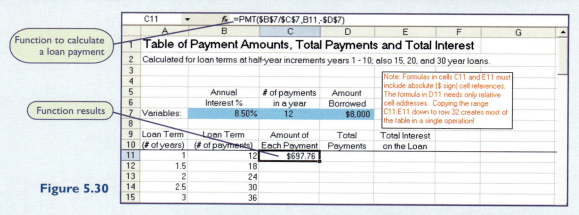

Figure 5.30

Now, enter formulas to calculate total payments and total interest for the first loan term of 12 months.

6 **Click cell D11, and enter the formula =B11*C11.**

The value *$8,373.10* displays in cell D11. The formula calculates the total payments as the number of payments multiplied by the amount of each payment. If you copy the function down the column, Excel correctly calculates total payments for other loan terms, because both cell references are relative.

7 **Click cell E11, and enter the formula =D11 - $D$7 (see Figure 5.31).**

Relative cell reference

Absolute cell reference

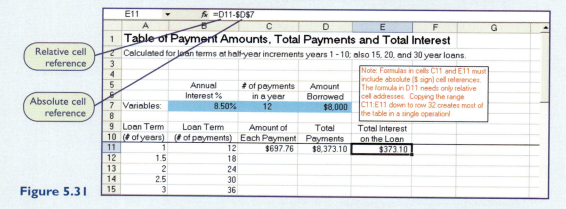

Figure 5.31

This formula calculates the total interest on the loan as the total of the payments minus the original amount borrowed. If you copy the function down the column, Excel correctly calculates total interest for other loan terms because the reference to the amount borrowed is absolute. Now, create the rest of the table with a single copy operation.

8 **Select the range C11:E11 and position the mouse pointer on the lower-right corner of cell E11.**

9 **Press and hold down the left mouse button, drag the fill handle down to include row 32, and release the mouse button.**

10 **Scroll down to view the end of the table, and click cell E32 (see Figure 5.32).**

E32	▼	*fx* =D32-$D$7				
	A	B	C	D	E	F	G

1 Table of Payment Amounts, Total Payments and Total Interest

2 Calculated for loan terms at half-year increments years 1 - 10; also 15, 20, and 30 year loans.

	A	B	C	D	E
3					
4					Note: Formulas in cells C11 and E11 must include absolute ($ sign) cell references.
5		Annual	# of payments	Amount	The formula in D11 needs only relative
6		Interest %	in a year	Borrowed	cell addresses. Copying the range C11:E11 down to row 32 creates most of
7	Variables:	8.50%	12	$8,000	the table in a single operation!
8					
9	Loan Term	Loan Term	Amount of	Total	Total Interest
10	(# of years)	(# of payments)	Each Payment	Payments	on the Loan
25	8	96	$115.14	$11,053.15	$3,053.15
26	8.5	102	$110.41	$11,262.12	$3,262.12
27	9	108	$106.23	$11,473.36	$3,473.36
28	9.5	114	$102.52	$11,686.87	$3,686.87
29	10	120	$99.19	$11,902.63	$3,902.63
30	15	180	$78.78	$14,180.25	$6,180.25
31	20	240	$69.43	$16,662.21	$8,662.21
32	30	360	$61.51	$22,144.71	$14,144.71

Figure 5.32

Excel fills the range C12:E32 with the formula heading each column, and displays the results of the formulas in each cell.

11 **Save your changes to the *PMT function* workbook.**

Now, you can use the Multiple PMT worksheet to perform a what-if analysis, such as calculating the monthly payment for a home mortgage.

12 **Change the amount borrowed to 150000 in cell D7.**

The monthly payment on a $150,000, 8.5 percent loan for 30 years is approximately $1,153 (see the formula results in row 32). Over the life of the loan, you would pay $415,213 to retire a $150,000 loan. The monthly payment on a $150,000, 8.5 percent loan for 15 years is approximately $1,477 (see the formula results in row 30). Over the life of the loan, you would pay about $265,880 to retire a $150,000 loan—approximately $149,334 less than for the 30-year loan.

13 **Try other combinations of interest rates and amounts borrowed, as desired.**

14 **Close the *PMT function* workbook without saving your changes to the loan terms in Steps 12 and 13.**

Continue with the next skill, or exit Excel.

Evaluate Investment Plans with FV

The *FV function* calculates the future value of an investment based on fixed payments (deposits) that earn a fixed rate of interest across equal time periods. Excel refers to such fixed payments at equal intervals as an *annuity*, a term used in explanations of the function's arguments.

The FV function requires that you specify three arguments in order: the annual interest rate adjusted for the number of payments within a year, the total number of payments, and the amount of each periodic payment. If a minus sign (−) precedes the amount of the periodic payment, the function result is a positive number.

In the following steps, you enter and copy a FV function that calculates future value based on a variety of interest rates. Let's begin with an introduction to future value.

To Evaluate Investment Plans with FV

① **Open the *MEC-S504* workbook, and save it as** `FV function`**; then select the Intro FV worksheet.**

The Intro FV worksheet shows two ways to calculate the future value of a 10-year investment plan: computing interest earned each year (the range A9:E19) and a FV function (cell G8).

② **Click a variety of cells within the range B10:E19 to learn how formulas in that area calculate future value (principal plus interest), one year at a time.**

③ **Click cell G8.**

The function *=FV(D4,D5,-D6)* appears in the formula bar. The function result displays in cell G8 (see Figure 5.33). The future value of a series of equal deposits earning 8 percent interest is *$14,486.56* at year's end.

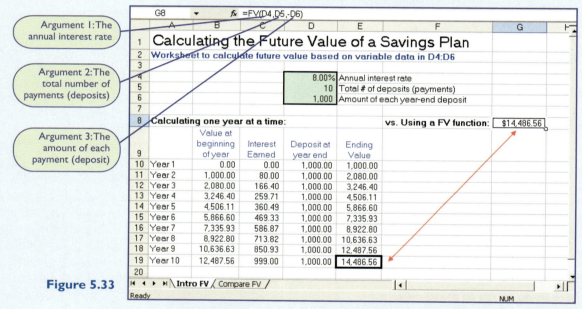

Figure 5.33

④ **Click cell D4, and enter** 9% **instead of 8% as the annual interest rate.**

The function recalculates by using the revised interest rate. An increase of 1 percent in the interest rate increases the future value to *$15,192.93*. Now, it's your turn to enter a FV function.

⑤ **Select the Compare FV worksheet.**

This worksheet is designed to calculate future value at various interest rate levels. If you use the correct combination of absolute and relative addressing when you enter a FV function in cell B9, you can compute future value at other interest rates by copying the function across row 9.

⑥ **Click cell B9, and click the Insert Function button in the formula bar; then select the FV function in the Financial category, and click OK.**

The FV Function Arguments dialog box opens. If the dialog box covers the cells in column B, drag the dialog box to the right.

⑦ **Enter the FV arguments shown in Figure 5.34 (B8 in the Rate text box, $B$6 in the Nper text box, and –$B$5 in the Pmt text box).**

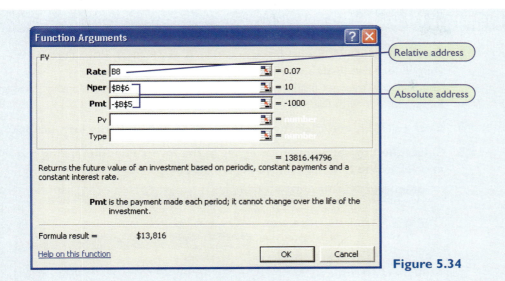

Figure 5.34

8 **Click OK.**

The function *=FV(B8,$B$6,-$B$5)* appears in the formula bar. The function result displays in cell B9. The future value of end-of-year deposits of $1,000 for ten years, using a 7 percent interest rate, is *$13,816.*

9 **Copy the function to the range C9:G9, and click cell G9.**

Excel calculates future values at other interest rates (see Figure 5.35).

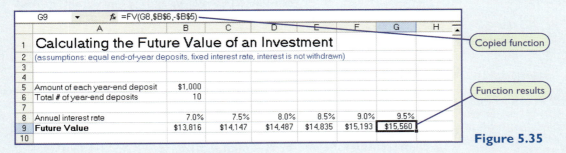

Figure 5.35

10 **Enter 2000 in cell B5.**

Values in row 9 reflect doubling the deposit amount. For example, the future value of investing $2,000, earning 9 percent, at the end of each year for 10 years is *$30,386.*

11 **Close the *FV function* workbook, saving your changes.**

Continue with the next skill, or exit Excel.

Use IF to Display Messages

You have heard that you can use a logical function named IF to implement different actions, depending on whether a condition is true or false. If the condition is true, Excel displays one result; if the condition is false, Excel displays a different result. The **IF function** requires that you specify three arguments in order: the logical test, the value if true, and the value if false.

In the following steps, you use the IF function to display a *Met Goal!* message if an individual's sales for the month meet or exceed the target sales. Otherwise, you don't want any message to display.

To Use IF to Display a Message

❶ Open the *MEC-S505* workbook and save it as IF and Now functions; **then select the IF-duo worksheet.**

The IF-duo worksheet displays a partially completed Sales Force Monthly Earnings Report for Fun with Frisbees.

❷ Click cell C11, and click the Insert Function button in the formula bar.

❸ Select the Logical function category in the Insert Function dialog box, and select the IF function (see Figure 5.36).

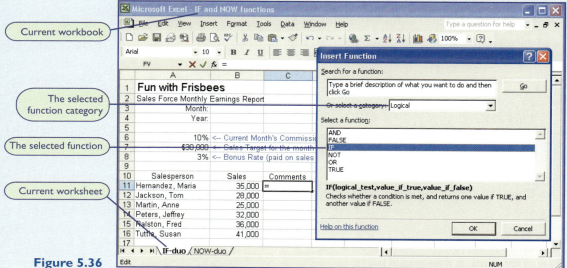

Current workbook

The selected function category

The selected function

Current worksheet

Figure 5.36

❹ Click OK.

The Function Arguments dialog box for the IF function opens. If columns A through C are not visible, drag the dialog box to the right.

❺ Click in the Logical_test text box, click cell B11, and type >= (a greater-than symbol followed by an equal sign).

❻ Click cell A7, and press F4 **to make the reference absolute.**

The first argument in the IF function, which tests whether sales for the first sales-person are greater than or equal to the sales target for the month, is entered (see Figure 5.37). Excel displays *B11$=$A$7* in the Logical_test text box and displays *=IF(B11$=$A$7)* in the formula bar.

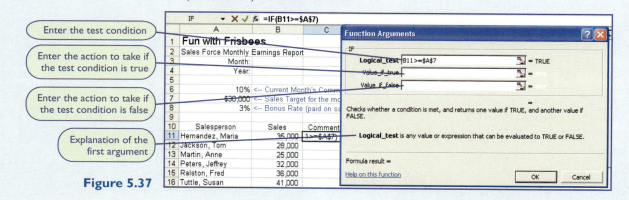

Enter the test condition

Enter the action to take if the test condition is true

Enter the action to take if the test condition is false

Explanation of the first argument

Figure 5.37

7   **Click in the Value_if_true text box, type** Met Goal!**, and click in the Value_if_false text box.**

Excel automatically adds quotations around the text you entered in the Value_if_true text box.

8   **Type " " in the Value_if_false text box (that is, hold down ⬆Shift) and press the quotation mark key twice).**

Make sure that your specifications for the three arguments match those shown in Figure 5.38.

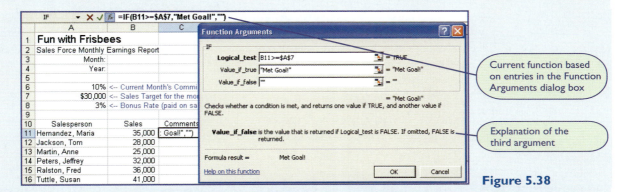

Figure 5.38

If you do not enter a second argument, Excel displays the word *TRUE* if the test condition is met. If you do not enter a third argument, Excel displays the word *FALSE* if the test condition is not met. Typing two quotation marks with nothing in between ensures that a cell remains blank if the test condition is not met.

9   **Click OK.**

The phrase *Met Goal!* displays in cell C11. The sales amount in cell B11 (*35,000*) exceeds the target sales amount in cell A7 (*$30,000*).

10   **Click cell C11, drag the cell's fill handle down to copy the IF function to the range C12:C16; then deselect the range.**

The phrase *Met Goal!* displays in three more cells: C14, C15, and C16 (see Figure 5.39). No message appears in cells C12 and C13, because the corresponding sales amounts in column B are less than the target sales in cell A7.

	A	B	C	D	E	F	G	H
1	**Fun with Frisbees**							
2	Sales Force Monthly Earnings Report							
3	Month:							
4	Year:							
5								
6	10%	<-- Current Month's Commission Rate (%)						
7	$30,000	<-- Sales Target for the month						
8	3%	<-- Bonus Rate (paid on sales in excess of sales target)						
9							Total	
10	Salesperson	Sales	Comments		Commission	Bonus	Earnings	
11	Hernandez, Maria	35,000	Met Goal!					
12	Jackson, Tom	28,000						
13	Martin, Anne	25,000						
14	Peters, Jeffrey	32,000	Met Goal!					
15	Ralston, Fred	36,000	Met Goal!					
16	Tuttle, Susan	41,000	Met Goal!					

Figure 5.39

continues ▶

To Use IF to Display a Message (continued)

⑪ Save your changes to the *If and Now functions* workbook.
Now that you know how to display text based on whether a condition is met, you can work with more complex IF functions that perform calculations. Keep the workbook open for the next skill, or close the workbook and exit Excel.

Use IF to Calculate

As you continue to develop the Sales Force Monthly Earnings Report for Fun with Frisbees, you realize that you can use an IF function to calculate bonuses. Only those members of the sales staff whose sales exceed the sales target for the month earn a bonus, currently calculated as 3 percent of sales in excess of target sales. If sales are equal to or below the target sales, the bonus is zero.

In the following steps, you enter and copy two formulas and one logical function. The first formula calculates each salesperson's commission on sales at the current rate of 10 percent. The IF function calculates a bonus, if applicable. The second formula computes total earnings by adding commission and bonus.

To Use IF to Calculate

① Open the *If and NOW functions* workbook, if necessary; then click cell E11 in the IF-duo sheet.

② Type =B11*$A$6, press ⏎Enter, and click cell E11.
The formula =B11*$A$6 displays in the formula bar, and *3,500* displays as the commission amount in cell E11.

③ Drag the fill handle for cell E11 down to copy the formula to the range E12:E16; then click cell E16 to deselect the range.
Ensure that the commissions for the other members of the sales force compute correctly at 10 percent of sales. For example, Tom Jackson's commission is *2,800*; Susan Tuttle's commission is *4,100* (see Figure 5.40).

	E16	▼	*fx*	=B16*$A$6				
	A	B	C	D	E	F	G	H
1	**Fun with Frisbees**							
2	Sales Force Monthly Earnings Report							
3	Month:							
4	Year:							
5								
6	10%	<-- Current Month's Commission Rate (%)						
7	$30,000	<-- Sales Target for the month						
8	3%	<-- Bonus Rate (paid on sales in excess of sales target)						
9							Total	
10	Salesperson	Sales	Comments		Commission	Bonus	Earnings	
11	Hernandez, Maria	35,000	Met Goal!		3,500			
12	Jackson, Tom	28,000			2,800			
13	Martin, Anne	25,000			2,500			
14	Peters, Jeffrey	32,000	Met Goal!		3,200			
15	Ralston, Fred	36,000	Met Goal!		3,600			
16	Tuttle, Susan	41,000	Met Goal!		4,100			

Figure 5.40

If you have problems...

If your results are not consistent with those in Figure 5.40, make sure that the reference to cell A6 is absolute in the commission formula (a dollar sign should precede both the column letter A and the row number 6).

4 **Click cell F11, and click the Insert Function button in the formula bar.**

5 **Select the Logical function category, select the IF function, and click OK.**

The Function Arguments dialog box for the IF function displays. If cell contents in rows 1 through 11 are not visible, drag the dialog box below row 11.

6 **Click in the Logical_test text box, click cell B11, and type > (a greater-than symbol).**

7 **Click cell A7, and press F4 to make the reference absolute.**

The first argument in the IF function, which tests whether sales for the first salesperson are greater than the sales target for the month, is entered.

8 **In the Value_if_true text box, enter (B11-$A$7)*$A$8.**

The second argument in the IF function, which subtracts target sales from actual sales and then multiplies the difference by the current bonus percentage, is entered.

9 **In the Value_if_false text box, enter 0 (zero).**

The third argument in the IF function is entered. In this case, you decide to enter a zero if no bonus is earned, instead of leaving the cell blank. Make sure that your specifications for the three arguments match those shown in Figure 5.41.

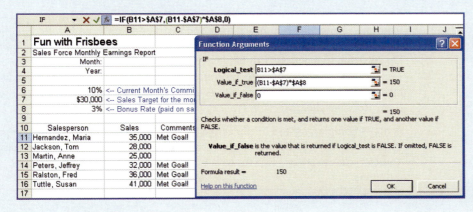

Figure 5.41

10 **Click OK and copy the function in cell F11 down to the range F12:F16; then click cell F16 to deselect the highlighted range.**

Four members of the sales force earn bonuses and two do not (see Figure 5.42).

continues ▶

To Use IF to Calculate (continued)

Figure 5.42

⑪ **Click cell G11 and enter the formula =E11+F11.**

⑫ **Copy the formula in cell G11 to the range G12:G16.**

⑬ **Enter the current month and year in cells B3 and B4, respectively; and save your changes to the *If and NOW functions* workbook.**
Keep the workbook open for the next skill, or close the workbook and exit Excel.

In Depth:
Nested IF Functions

You can, in effect, set up more than one test condition in an IF function by including additional IF functions as Value_if_true and Value_if_false arguments. Up to seven IF functions can be nested in one IF statement. For example, you can create a nested IF to display *Overbooked* if reservations exceed capacity, *Full* if reservations match capacity, and *Available* if reservations are less than capacity (refer to Challenge exercise 7).

A more complex nested IF can assign an A, B, C, D, or F grade after comparing the earned score to the associated grade levels of >=90, >=80, and so forth. You can use onscreen Help to learn more about nesting functions within functions.

Use NOW to Display the Current Date

Excel stores dates as sequential (also called serial) numbers. For example, a 1900 date system assigns the number 1 to January 1, 1900 and the number 2 to January 2, 1900. For each succeeding day, the assigned number increments by one. Under this system, the numbers 37257 and 37622 are assigned to January 1, 2002 and January 1, 2003, respectively.

A variety of Date & Time functions are available, including DATE, NOW, and TODAY. For example, the **NOW function** enters the serial number of the current date and time—numbers to the left of a decimal point represent the date, and numbers to the right of the decimal point represent the time. Before or after you enter a NOW function, you can apply a variety of date and/or time formats to the cell.

In the following steps, you enter a NOW function and change its format to display only the current date.

To Use NOW to Display the Current Date

1 **Open the *IF and NOW functions* workbook, if necessary; then select the NOW-duo worksheet, and click cell D1.**

2 **Type** =NOW( ) **and press** ⏎Enter.
The current date and time displays in cell D1. Now, change the format of cell D1 to display only the date.

3 **Click cell D1 and choose F<u>o</u>rmat, C<u>e</u>lls.**
The Format Cells dialog box opens.

4 **Choose the Number tab, select Date in the <u>C</u>ategory window, and select the setting in the <u>T</u>ype window that displays only a date in the form 03/14/01.**
Check that your selections match those displayed in Figure 5.43, and make changes as necessary.

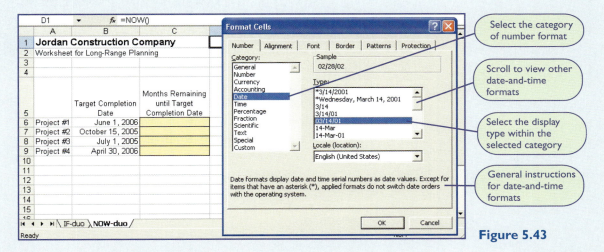

Select the category of number format

Scroll to view other date-and-time formats

Select the display type within the selected category

General instructions for date-and-time formats

Figure 5.43

5 **Click OK.**
The current date displays in cell D1 in the form *mm/dd/yy*.

6 **Save your changes to the *IF and NOW functions* workbook.**
Keep the workbook open for the last skill, or close the workbook and exit Excel.

In Depth:
Entering a Date that Doesn't Change
If you do not want the date to update each time you open a workbook, type the date without using a function. If you type the date in a common format, such as *12/31/02*, you can still use the Format Cells dialog box to apply a different date style.

Use Dates in Calculations

There are many uses for calculations involving date-and-time data. For example, you can calculate the time it takes to complete a job by finding the difference between the start and end times. You can also find the days, weeks, months, or years until some future event.

In the following steps, you enter and copy a formula that calculates the months remaining until the target completion date for a long-term construction project. The formula includes a reference to a cell containing a NOW function, so that the months remaining update each day.

To Use Dates in Calculations

① **Open the *IF and NOW functions* workbook, if necessary; and select the NOW-duo worksheet.**

② **Enter** `# of days in a month` **in cell E3.**

③ **Enter** `30` **in cell D3.**

You use the contents of cell D3 to convert days to months. Using 30 as the average days in a month is an accepted business practice. Putting the number 30 in a separate cell instead of entering the number 30 in a formula makes it easy to view and change the basis for the days-to-months conversion.

④ **Click cell C6 and type** `=(B6-$D$1)/$D$3`. **(Do not press** ⏎Enter **yet.)**

The formula under construction displays in the formula bar and in cell C6 (see Figure 5.44). The formula subtracts the current date (produced by the NOW function in cell D1) from the first target completion date (cell B6), and divides the result by the number of days in a month (cell D3).

Figure 5.44

⑤ **Press** ⏎Enter.

The months remaining until the first project completion date displays in cell C6. A different result displays each day, because the current date changes daily. Check that your answer is reasonable. For example, if the difference between the first target completion date and the current date is just over two years, the result should be 24+ months.

⑥ **Format the range C6:C9 to Comma, one decimal place.**

⑦ **Copy the formula in cell C6 to the range C7:C9; then click cell A1.**

⑧ **Save your changes to the *IF and NOW functions* workbook, and close the workbook.**

You can continue with Skill Drill and Challenge exercises, start another skill set, or exit Excel.

For immediate reinforcement on functions, work Skill Drills 3 through 6 and Challenges 5 through 8.

Summary

This entire skill set focused on entering formulas and functions in well-designed worksheets. Throughout the skill set, you used separate cells for data subject to change, rather than type raw numbers in formulas or functions. After you viewed samples of operators and learned the order in which Excel performs calculations, you used a variety of methods to enter, edit, and copy formulas. You also displayed formulas instead of formula results.

The remaining sections in the skill set presented a small sample of the hundreds of predefined formulas that Excel provides. By working with AVERAGE, MAX, and MIN, you added to your knowledge of statistical functions. (SUM was introduced in Skill Set 1.) You had an in-depth experience with one financial function—first by using PMT to calculate a single monthly payment and then by constructing a table of monthly payments and other data. The FV scenario provided you with the opportunity to see the effects of varied interest rates on the future value of a savings plan.

You glimpsed the power of an electronic worksheet over a calculator when you used the logical IF function to vary results, depending on whether a test condition was met. After you learned how Excel stores dates, you used the date-and-time function NOW to enter a date that automatically updated to the current system date. The project ended with a calculation that used the results of a NOW function.

Skill Drill

Skill Drill exercises *reinforce* skills. Each skill reinforced is the same, or nearly the same, as a skill presented in the skill set. Detailed instructions are provided in a step-by-step format.

Before beginning your Excel Core Skill Set 5 Skill Drill exercises, complete the following steps:

1. Open the file named *MEC-S506*, and immediately save it as **MEC-S5drill**.

   The workbook contains seven sheets: an overview and six exercise sheets labeled SD1 through SD6.

2. Click the Overview sheet to view the organization and content of the Skill Drill workbook for Excel Core Skill Set 5.

Each exercise is independent of the others, so you may complete the exercises in any order. Be sure to save the workbook after completing each exercise. If you need a paper copy of one or more completed exercises, enter your name, centered in a header, before printing. Print options have already been set to print compressed to one page and to display the filename, sheet name, and the current date in a footer.

Be sure to save your changes and close the workbook if you need more than one work session to complete the desired exercises. Continue working on *MEC-S5drill* instead of starting over in the original *MEC-S506* file.

1. Create and Copy a Formula with an Absolute Cell Reference

You are in charge of putting price tags on 10 products, all of which are to be marked up by the same percentage on cost. You are nearly finished with a worksheet that will do the necessary calculations. The final step involves entering a formula to compute the selling price of the first item and copying it to calculate selling price for the other products. The formula must include an absolute reference to the cell containing the current markup on cost percentage.

To create and copy the formula, follow these steps:

1. Open the *MEC-S5drill* workbook, if necessary; then select the SD1 worksheet.

2. Click cell C6 and type an equal sign (=).

   This starts the formula to calculate the selling price for Product A.

3. Click cell B6; then type an asterisk (*).

4. Click cell D4.

   The partially completed formula =B6*D4 appears in the formula bar. The flashing cursor displays at the end of =B6*D4 in cell C6.

5. Press F4.

   The formula =B6*$D$4 appears in the formula bar.

6. Type a plus sign (+), and click cell B6.

   The formula =B6*$D$4+B6 appears in the formula bar.

7. Click the Enter button in the formula bar, or press ↵Enter.

   The formula =B6*$D$4+B6 results in *10* as the Selling Price (marked up 25 percent over its eight dollar cost). Excel performs the multiplication first—B6*$D$4 computes the increase of two dollars over cost—and then adds the increase to the cost.

8. Click cell C6, drag its fill handle down to copy the formula to the other cells in the range C7:C15; then click any cell to deselect the range.

   Make sure that your results are accurate. For example, the selling price of Product J is *125* dollars at a 25 percent markup over its *100* dollar cost.

9. Test the model by entering other markup percentages in cell D4.

10. Click cell A1 and save your changes to the *MEC-S5drill* workbook.

2. Display Formulas Instead of Formula Results

A friend of yours just gave you a copy of a worksheet on disk, which keeps track of workout time in hours. You plan to modify the worksheet to fit your own exercise plan. Before you begin, you want to turn on the display of formulas to get a better understanding of what the current worksheet does.

To turn on the display of formulas, follow these steps:

1. Open the *MEC-S5drill* workbook, if necessary; then select the SD2 worksheet.

   The worksheet tracks hours spent jogging, working with weights, and doing aerobics during January, February, and March of the year 2003.

2. Choose Tools, Options.

3. Click the View tab if it is not the active tab.

4. In the Window options section, click the check box to the left of Formulas, and click OK.

   Excel doubles the width of each column and displays formulas in rows 12 through 15.

5. Save your changes to the *MEC-S5drill* workbook.

3. Analyze Data with SUM, AVERAGE, MAX, and MIN

You manage a sales force of 10, and it's time to analyze last month's data on commissions earned. To perform simple statistical analyses, follow these steps:

1. Open the *MEC-S5drill* workbook, if necessary; then select the SD3 worksheet.

2. Click cell E11 and enter the function =SUM(C11:C20).

   The total 22,032.75 displays in cell E11.

3. Click cell E12 and enter the function =AVERAGE(C11:C20).

The average 2,203.28 displays in cell E12.

4. Click cell E13 and enter the function =MAX(C11:C20).

The highest value 2,987.00 displays in cell E13.

5. Click cell E14 and enter the function =MIN(C11:C20).

The lowest value 1,247.00 displays in cell E14.

6. Click cell A1, and save your changes to the *MEC-S5drill* workbook.

4. Use IF to Display a Message

Your firm's monthly sales meeting is next month, and you are in charge of identifying those members of the sales force who will receive the Super Star Award. You already have a worksheet that lists names alphabetically, along with the amount of sales and commissions earned. Now, you want to add a column in which the phrase *Super Star* appears for those whose sales meet or exceed the minimum sales for the award. You also decide to display the phrase *Keep Trying* for those who did not reach the award minimum.

To use an IF function to produce the desired results, follow these steps:

1. Open the *MEC-S5drill* workbook, if necessary; then select the SD4 worksheet.

2. Click cell D10 and click the Insert Function button in the formula bar.

3. Select the IF function in the Logical category, and click OK.

The Function Arguments dialog box for the IF function opens. If the cells in rows 1 through 10 are not visible, drag the dialog box below row 10.

4. Click within the Logical_test text box, click cell B10, and type >= (a greater-than symbol followed by an equal sign).

5. Click cell D5 and press F4.

You entered B10>=$D$5 as the first argument in the IF function, which tests whether sales for the first salesperson are greater than or equal to the sales needed for the award.

6. Click within the Value_if_true text box, and type **Super Star**.

7. Click within the Value_if_false text box, and type **Keep Trying**.

8. Click OK and check that the phrase *Keep Trying* displays in cell D10.

9. Click cell D10, drag the cell's fill handle down to copy the IF function to the range D11:D19; then click any cell to deselect the range.

The phrase *Super Star* displays for Jessica Keller, Shea Lewis, and Sarah Tyler if you entered and copied the function correctly. The phrase *Keep Trying* displays for the remaining individuals.

10. Save your changes to the *MEC-S5drill* workbook.

5. Use IF to Calculate a Bonus

Recently, your company set up a bonus program as part of its marketing plan to attract new customers. Currently, the bonus is 100 dollars for each new customer over the quarterly quota of 50, but either value is subject to change. To calculate the bonus using an IF function, follow these steps:

1. Open the *MEC-S5drill* workbook, if necessary; then select the SD5 worksheet.

2. Click cell C9, and click the Insert Function button in the formula bar.

3. Select the IF function in the Logical category, and click OK.

The Function Arguments dialog box for the IF function opens. If the cell contents in rows 1 through 9 are not visible, drag the dialog box below row 9.

4. Click within the Logical_test text box, click cell B9, and type **>** (greater-than symbol).

5. Click cell A3, and press F4.

You entered B9>$A$3 as the first argument in the IF function, which tests whether the number of new customers for the first salesperson is greater than the quarterly quota for new customers.

6. Enter **(B9-$A$3)*$A$4** in the Value_if_true text box.

You entered the second argument in the IF function, which subtracts the quarterly quota for new customers from the actual number of new customers and then multiplies the difference by the current bonus.

7. Click in the Value_if_false text box; then type a quotation mark followed by a second quotation mark.

8. Click OK.

Make sure that *200.00* displays in cell C9. The number of new customers for Jordan Fields (52) exceeds the current quota (50) by 2. For each customer over 50, a salesperson earns 100 dollars.

9. Click cell C9 and drag its fill handle down to copy the function to the range C10:C18; then click any cell to deselect the range.

Jessica Keller also earned a bonus if you entered and copied the function correctly. The cells in column C appear blank for the other names.

10. Click cell A1 and save your changes to the *MEC-S5drill* workbook.

6. Use NOW to Determine the Number of Years as an Employee

You created a worksheet to calculate the number of years of service of the employees under your supervision. All that remains to complete the worksheet is to calculate the difference between the current date and the date of hire. To set up the calculation so that it always displays results as of the current system date, follow these steps:

1. Open the *MEC-S5drill* workbook, if necessary; then select the SD6 worksheet.

2. Enter the function **=NOW()** in cell A3, and enter the number **365** in cell A4.

3. In cell C8, enter the formula **=($A$3-B8)/$A$4**.

Subtracting the date of hire (B8 for the first salesperson) from the current date (A3) calculates the number of *days* of service. Dividing by the contents of cell A4 converts days to years. The formula to calculate number of years of service must contain absolute references to cells A3 and A4 before you copy the formula.

4. Copy the formula in cell C8 to the range C9:C17.

The results vary according to the current date. Make sure that the results are reasonable.

5. Click cell A1, and save your changes to the *MEC-S5drill* workbook.

Challenge

Challenge exercises expand on or are somewhat related to skills presented in the skill set. Each exercise provides a brief narrative introduction, followed by instructions in a numbered-step format that are not as detailed as those in the Skill Drill section.

Before beginning your Excel Core Skill Set 5 Challenge exercises, complete the following steps:

1. Open the file named *MEC-S507*, and immediately save it as **MEC-S5challenge**.

   The workbook contains nine sheets: an overview and eight exercise sheets labeled CH1 through CH8.

2. Click the Overview sheet to view the organization and content of the Challenge workbook for Excel Core Skill Set 5.

Each exercise is independent of the others, so you may complete the exercises in any order. Be sure to save the workbook after completing each exercise. If you need a paper copy of one or more completed exercises, enter your name, centered in a header, before printing. Print options have already been set to print compressed to one page. Settings to display the filename, sheet name, and the current date in a footer have been set in all worksheets.

Be sure to save your changes and close the workbook if you need more than one work session to complete the desired exercises. Continue working on *MEC-S5challenge* instead of starting over in the original *MEC-S507* file.

1. Enter and Test a Formula to Compute Adjusted Selling Price

Even if you have only been using Excel for a short time, you realize that its power lies in performing calculations. You are interested in developing your ability to set up formulas so that the worksheet can still be used if the data changes. You are currently developing a simple worksheet to calculate the amount due if an item is on sale at a reduced percent. For example, if an item with an original cost of $30.00 is now on sale at 25% percent off, the pretax sale price is $22.50.

The labels are already in place. To enter and test a formula to compute adjusted selling price, follow these steps:

1. Open the *MEC-S5challenge* workbook, if necessary; then select the CH1 worksheet.

2. Enter a sample original price, **30**, in cell B5.

3. Enter a sample percentage discount, **25%**, in cell B6.

4. Enter a formula in cell B7 to compute the pretax sale price.

   If the formula in cell B7 is correct, **22.5** is the pretax sale price that displays in cell B7. Make sure that your formulas contain only cell references and math operators.

5. Correct the formula, if necessary, and test the formula again by changing the sample numbers to **100** in cell B5 and **10%** in cell B6.

   If the formula in cell B7 is correct, **90** is the pretax sale price that displays in cell B7.

6. Make changes as necessary, and save the *MEC-S5challenge* workbook.

2. Enter and Test a Formula to Compute Years of Service

You are a member of a committee that is planning an employee recognition program to be held next month, and you need to know the number of years each employee has worked for the company. You have already entered descriptive labels and data for four employees in a worksheet. Before you enter data for more than 100 other employees, you want to enter the formula to compute years of service and test the results on your small sample.

To enter and test a formula to compute years of service, follow these steps:

1. Open the *MEC-S5challenge* workbook, if necessary; then select the CH2 worksheet.

2. Select cell C8 and think through the calculation needed in that cell.

   Assume that the current date is March 15, 2003. If you calculate the difference between that current date (in cell E8) and the date of hire for the first employee (in cell B8), you will know the number of *days* that John Byrd worked for the company. You also have to include a way to change days into years in the formula.

3. Enter a formula in cell C8 to calculate the years of service for the first employee. (Make sure that you use absolute cell references as appropriate so that the formula can be copied to compute years of service for the other three employees.)

   Check that the formula result is reasonable, and make changes as necessary. Assuming a current date of 3/15/2003, John Byrd worked for the firm eight years.

4. Copy the formula to compute years of service for the other three employees.

5. Check that the formula results are reasonable, and make changes as necessary.

   Assuming a current date of 3/15/2003, Jill Langley worked for the firm for 42.3 years.

 If you have problems...
If the initial formula produces correct results, but errors are evident in the copied formulas, check that the appropriate cell references are absolute in the first formula.

---

6. Save your changes to the *MEC-S5challenge* workbook.

3. Design a Worksheet to Calculate Rental Fees

You must make a decision soon about whether to buy or rent a copy machine. As part of the decision process, you are evaluating three pricing structures from firms that rent copy machines. All have a two-part rental plan—a monthly charge plus an amount per copy. You spent a few minutes yesterday setting up a worksheet to evaluate the rental options. Now, you need to finish the design and test the model with various assumptions about the numbers of copies made in a month.

To design a worksheet to calculate rental fees, follow these steps:

1. Open the *MEC-S5challenge* workbook, and select the CH3 worksheet.

2. Think about the elements that affect total rental fee—two are set by the rental companies (monthly fee and charge per copy,) and the other is related to actual usage (number of copies).

3. Enter appropriate labels in cells A9 and A10 to describe the monthly fee and the charge per copy.

4. For the rows described as monthly fee and charge per copy, enter the appropriate numbers related to the three rental options in columns B, C, and D:

   Option A   Monthly Fee $500, Charge per Copy $0.03
   Option B   Monthly Fee $200, Charge per Copy $0.04
   Option C   Monthly Fee $800, Charge per Copy $0.015

5. Click the cell containing the charge per copy for option C, and format it to display to three decimal places.

6. Enter **10,000** in cell A6 as the initial number of copies.

7. Enter a formula in cell B12 to compute the total rental fee, and copy the formula to cells C12 and D12.

8. Check the accuracy of your results, and make changes in formulas as necessary.

   At the 10,000-copy level, the total rental fees are as follows: Option A: $800.00; Option B: $600.00; Option C: $950.00. Assuming that service arrangements are comparable, you would probably select Option B as the most attractive pricing structure.

9. Change the number of copies to **20,000**.

10. Below row 12, type a note in the worksheet summarizing the best option if copies per month are likely to average 20,000.

11. Change the number of copies to **30,000**.

12. Below your previous note, type another note that summarizes the best option if copies per month are likely to average 30,000.

13. Save your changes to the *MEC-S5challenge* workbook.

4. Design a Worksheet to Calculate Gross Pay

You started a full-time job recently, and, for the first time, you work for a firm that pays overtime (the usual rate of 1.5 times your regular pay rate per hour, which is applied to every hour worked over 40 hours). You want to be sure that your pay is computed correctly each week, so you are designing a worksheet to calculate your weekly pay before any deductions for taxes and benefits.

To design a worksheet to calculate gross pay, follow these steps:

1. Open the *MEC-S5challenge* workbook, if necessary; then select the CH4 worksheet.

2. To avoid using a number instead of a cell reference in a formula, enter the label **Overtime Premium Rate** in cell A8 and the number **1.5** in cell B8.

3. Select cell B15, and enter a formula to compute the total gross pay for the week.

   The formula you enter should reflect the fact that your pay has two components: regular hours at regular pay (a maximum of 40 hours) and overtime hours (those in excess of 40) at 1.5 times your regular pay. Remember to use cell references instead of numbers in your formula.

4. Test the formula by entering sample numbers in the input cells: **40** in B11, **1** in B12, and **10** in B13.

   If the formula in B15 is correct, the total gross pay for the week is **$415**—40 hours at $10 an hour (or $400), plus $15 for the one overtime hour.

5. Test that the formula computes correctly if there are no overtime hours: Enter **38** in B11, **0** in B12, and **12** in B13.

   If the formula in B15 is correct, total gross pay for the week is **$456**: 38 hours at $12 an hour.

6. Test the overtime calculation again, assuming that the total hours worked are **45** and pay per hour does not change.

   The total gross pay for the week is **$570**: 40 hours at $12 an hour, plus 5 hours at $18 an hour.

7. Save your changes to the *MEC-S5challenge* workbook.

5. Use Functions to Create New Data

You enjoy tracking daily average temperatures each month. For the current month, you want to calculate the average temperature for the month, and to find the highest and lowest temperatures in the month. You also want to display the message *Below Freezing* each day that the average temperature was less than 32 degrees Fahrenheit.

To use functions to create the new data, follow these steps:

1. Open the *MEC-S5challenge* workbook, if necessary; then select the CH5 worksheet.
2. In cell F9, enter a function to display the highest temperature stored in column B.
3. In cell F10, enter a function to display the lowest temperature stored in column B.
4. In cell F11, enter a function to calculate the average of the temperatures stored in column B.
5. In cell C6, enter a function to display the message *Below Freezing* if the average temperature for the first day of the month is less than the freezing temperature stored in cell E5. Cell C6 should appear blank if the average temperature for Day 1 is at or above the freezing temperature.

   Use good worksheet design techniques. Do not use raw numbers in formulas! Enter the formula in such a way that you can copy it.
6. Copy the function down column C to all cells adjacent to the temperatures for days 1 through 31.
7. Ensure that the results are accurate, and make changes as necessary.
8. Click cell A1, and save your changes to the *MEC-S5challenge* workbook.

6. Use IF to Calculate Gross Pay Including Overtime

You want to calculate gross pay, including overtime, by using the minimum number of columns for data and formulas. At the present time, your firm follows a common policy of paying one-and-a-half times the base wage rate for each hour worked over 40. The overtime premium and number of hours to work are subject to change, and you want to set up a worksheet model that still works if there are changes in policy. Your worksheet model to calculate weekly gross pay is almost finished.

To use an IF function to calculate gross pay including overtime, follow these steps:

1. Open the *MEC-S5challenge* workbook, if necessary; then select the CH6 worksheet.
2. Select cell D10, click the Insert Function button in the formula bar, and display the Function Arguments dialog box for the IF function.
3. Enter appropriate arguments in the Function Arguments dialog box for the IF function.

   Remember to use cell references, not numbers, in formulas; and check whether a cell reference needs to be absolute before copying.
4. Make sure that the function in cell D10 correctly computes the *550* weekly gross pay for Jordan Fields, and make corrections to the function, as needed.
5. Copy the function to compute weekly gross pay for the other employees, and verify that your results are accurate.

   It is a good idea to verify that the IF function operates as intended by checking for hours worked greater than, equal to, and less than 40. If you entered and copied the function correctly, you see the following results: Linda Fraley, *237.5*; Jessica Keller, *400*; and Jose Mendoza, *570*.
6. Format the range D10:D19 to Comma, 2 decimal places; and save your changes to the *MEC-S5challenge* workbook.

7. Use a Nested IF to Monitor Capacity

Your job responsibilities include monitoring seat availability on airplane flights. For each scheduled flight, you want to compare the plane's capacity to the number of seats sold and to display one of three messages: *overbooked*, *full*, or *available*.

To produce the desired results using a nested IF statement, follow these steps:

1. Open the *MEC-S5challenge* workbook, if necessary; then select the CH7 worksheet.

2. Click cell D5, click the Insert Function button on the formula bar, and display the Function Arguments dialog box for the IF function.

3. Specify **C5>B5** in the Logical_test text box.

4. Click within the Value_if_true text box, and type **overbooked**.

5. Click within the Value_if_false text box, and click the large IF button at the left end of the formula bar.

   A new Function Arguments dialog box for the IF function opens. Now, begin to enter the specifications for a nested IF.

6. Type **C5<B5** in the new Logical_test text box.

7. Type **available** in the new Value_if_true text box.

8. Type **full** in the new Value_if_false text box.

9. Click OK to accept the current specifications for the nested IF function.

   If the nested IF was entered correctly, the message *overbooked* displays in cell D5, and the function =IF(C5>B5,"overbooked",IF(C5<B5,"available","full")) displays in the formula bar.

10. Correct the function, if necessary, and copy it to the range D6:D9.

    The message *overbooked* displays in cells D5 and D7 because the number of seats sold exceeded the capacity. The message *available* displays in cells D8 and D9, because the number of seats sold is less than the capacity. The message *full* displays in cell D6 because the number of seats sold was neither more than nor less than the capacity. Therefore, seats sold must be equal to capacity.

11. Save your changes to the *MEC-S5challenge* workbook.

8. Create a PMT Table with Multiple Interest Rates

You have a PMT table that displays loan payments at varying loan terms. Now, you want to have a PMT table that displays loan payments at varying interest rates. Rather than create the entire table from a blank worksheet, you decide to modify the existing one.

To create a PMT table with multiple interest rates, follow these steps:

1. Open the *MEC-S5challenge* workbook, if necessary; then select the CH8 worksheet.

2. Think about how to rearrange the data and determine the changes needed in titles and formulas, including the PMT function.

   For example, you can keep the area for variables in rows 5 through 7, but interest percentage should be replaced with loan terms in that area. You like the idea of a schedule filling rows 11 through 32, but interest rates should display in column A instead of loan terms. The data in column B on the number of payments is not needed for a PMT table that varies interest rates.

3. Format cell B7 to Comma, zero decimal places; then make the following changes in the cells indicated.

Enter **Loan Term** in cell B5.

Enter **(in years)** in cell B6.

Enter **5** in cell B7.

Enter **Annual** in cell A9.

Enter **Interest** in cell A10.

Enter **5%** in cell A11.

Enter **5.5%** in cell A12.

4. Select the range A11:A12; then drag the fill handle for cell A12 down to fill the range A13:A32 with percents incrementing by one-half percent.

Percents fill the range A11:A32 (5%, 5.5%, 6%, 6.5%, and so forth).

5. Select the range B9:B32 and choose Edit, Delete. Select Shift cells left in the Delete dialog box, and click OK.

As data shifts left from columns C through E, the error message #REF! fills cells in columns B through D. The message tells you that you deleted a cell referenced in the formula.

6. Scroll up the worksheet; then starting in row 12, delete the contents of the range B12:D32.

7. Click cell B11; then press the Insert Function button in the formula bar.

The current PMT settings display in the Function Arguments dialog box.

8. Revise the function argument as needed to reflect the new organization of the worksheet, and click OK.

If you correctly revised the PMT function, $150.97 displays as the monthly payment on a five-year 5 percent, $8,000 loan.

9. Revise the formula in cell C11 as needed to reflect the new organization of the worksheet. (The formula in cell D11 produces accurate results as soon as you complete the edit of cells B11 and C11.)

If you correctly revise the formula in cell C11, Excel computes *9,058.19* as the total payments on a 5-year 5 percent, $8,000 loan. Total interest of $1,058.19 displays in cell D11.

10. Make corrections to formulas and/or the PMT function, as necessary, including absolute cell references; then use a single drag process to copy the formulas in cells B11 through D11 down their respective columns to row 32.

11. Check your results, and make changes as necessary.

If you entered and copied formulas and the PMT function correctly, the following values display in row 21 for a 5-year, 10 percent $8,000 loan: monthly payment, $169.98; total payments, $10,198.58; and total interest on the loan, $2,198.58.

12. Click cell A1, and save your changes to the *MEC-S5challenge* workbook.

Creating and Modifying Graphics

CHAPTER 6

This skill set includes

Create, modify, position and print charts

- Identify common chart types and features
- Use Chart Wizard to create an embedded pie chart
- Use Chart Wizard to create an embedded column chart
- Change the chart type
- Chart nonadjacent data series
- Modify chart formats
- Add, reorder, and delete a data series
- Create and print a combination chart

Create, modify, and position graphics

- Create WordArt
- Insert and rotate an AutoShape
- Create a text box
- Group objects
- Add emphasis with lines and arrows
- Add emphasis with callouts
- Insert clips

Skill Set Overview

This skill set focuses on adding eye-catching elements to your worksheets. It includes in-depth coverage of charts and an assortment of graphics.

You begin by transforming data in the worksheet into a ***chart***, a graphical representation of data that makes it easy for users to see trends and make comparisons. After you view common chart types and features, you create several types of charts and modify chart formats. Your efforts include charting nonadjacent data, changing the chart type, changing the order of multiple data series, and printing a chart.

Excel also provides a variety of special effects tools to help make worksheets look professional, yet be easy to use. These effects include lines, arrows, basic shapes, callouts, text boxes, word art, images, and predefined diagrams. In this skill set, you create, resize, and reposition most of these special effects.

Skill 6.1: Create, Modify, Position and Print Charts

In this skill area, you create an ***embedded chart***, a graphical representation of data created within the worksheet instead of as a separate worksheet. You create several types of charts based on revenue data for four quarters. You also learn to modify chart features, change the order of charted data, and print charts. Before you begin creating charts, take some time to learn basic chart types and elements.

Identify Common Chart Types and Features

You can create a variety of chart types by using Excel. Chart features include titles and labels that explain the graphed data; and enhancements, such as gridlines and color, which improve readability or add visual appeal.

In the following steps, you view examples of common chart types and features. You apply this knowledge in subsequent skills as you create and modify charts similar to those shown in the examples.

To Identify Common Chart Types and Features

1 **Open the file *MEC-S601* and save it as** Sample Charts.
The workbook includes seven sheets, the first of which is named Charts. The remaining sheets illustrate three common types of charts: pie (sheets Pie1 and Pie2), line (sheets Line1 and Line2), and column (sheets Column1 and Column2).

2 **Select the worksheet named Pie1.**
The sample embedded pie chart shown in Figure 6.1 appears. A ***pie chart*** is a circular chart, in which each piece (wedge) shows a data segment and its relationship to the whole. The sample pie chart displays the percentage of Greens Fees earned in each quarter, based on the amounts in row 5. The corresponding text entries in row 4 (*Qtr 1*, *Qtr 2*, and so on) appear as data labels for the pie slices.

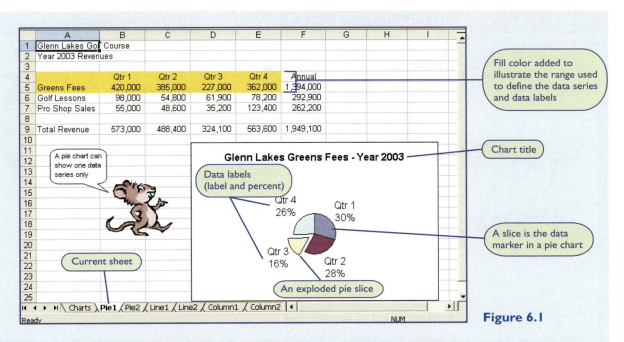

Figure 6.1

A pie chart is limited to one *data series*, which is a set of related values entered in a row or column of the worksheet. Excel uses data markers to represent a data series in a chart. A *data marker* is a slice, bar, dot, area, or other symbol that represents a value that originates from a worksheet cell.

❸ Click the Pie2 sheet tab.

The chart embedded in the Pie2 worksheet displays the percentage contribution that each revenue source made toward the total revenues for the year (see Figure 6.2).

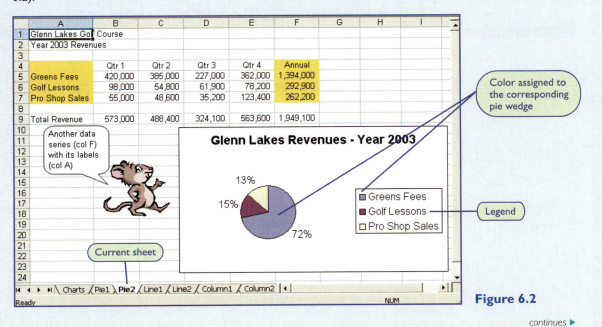

Figure 6.2

continues ▶

To Identify Common Chart Types and Features (continued)

The data series for this chart is a set of values entered in a column instead of a row. In this sample pie chart, a legend appears to the right of the pie. A *legend* displays the colors, patterns, or symbols that identify data categories.

4 **Click the Line1 sheet tab.**

A *line chart* plots one or more data series as connected points along an axis, as shown in Figure 6.3.

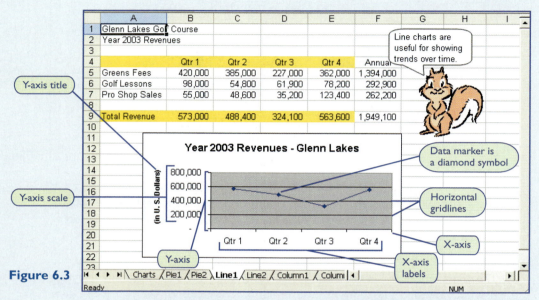

Figure 6.3

The chart in Figure 6.3 illustrates total revenue for each quarter in the year 2003. Data markers for each quarter are arranged above the **X-axis**, the horizontal axis of a chart that generally appears at the bottom edge. Each quarterly amount is reflected in the height of its data marker in relation to the scale shown on the **Y-axis**, a vertical axis of a chart that usually appears at the left edge.

5 **Click the Line2 sheet tab.**

The sample line chart embedded in sheet Line2 includes three data series: Greens Fees, Golf Lessons, and Pro Shop Sales. Excel assigns a different color and data marker to each series (see Figure 6.4). The legend displays the symbols and colors that identify each data series.

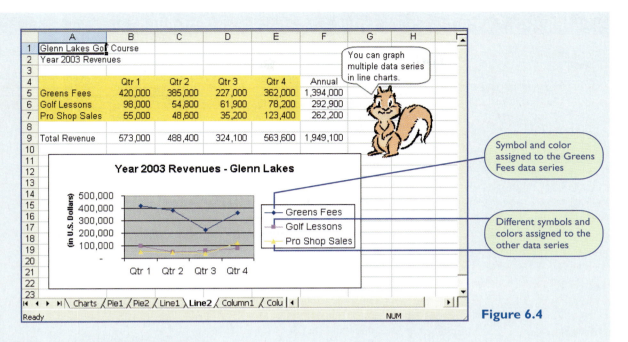

Figure 6.4

6 Click the Column1 sheet tab.

The sample embedded column chart shown in Figure 6.5 appears. In a *column chart*, each data point is reflected in the height of its column in relation to the scale shown on the Y-axis. In this chart, columns are grouped along the X-axis by quarter—a result achieved by specifying that data series are organized in rows.

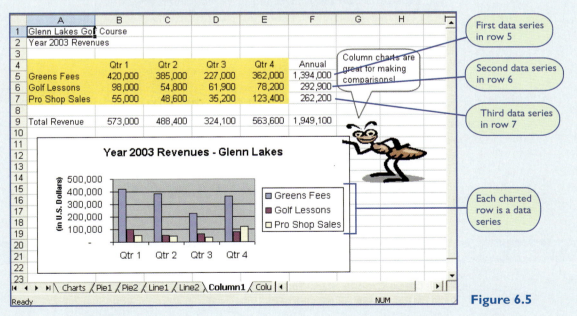

Figure 6.5

7 Click the Column2 sheet tab.

Yellow highlighting indicates the range used to define the column chart, which is the same range used to produce the chart in the Column1 sheet. In this chart, however, columns are grouped along the X-axis by type of revenue—a result achieved by specifying that data series are organized in columns (see Figure 6.6).

continues ▶

To Identify Common Chart Types and Features (continued)

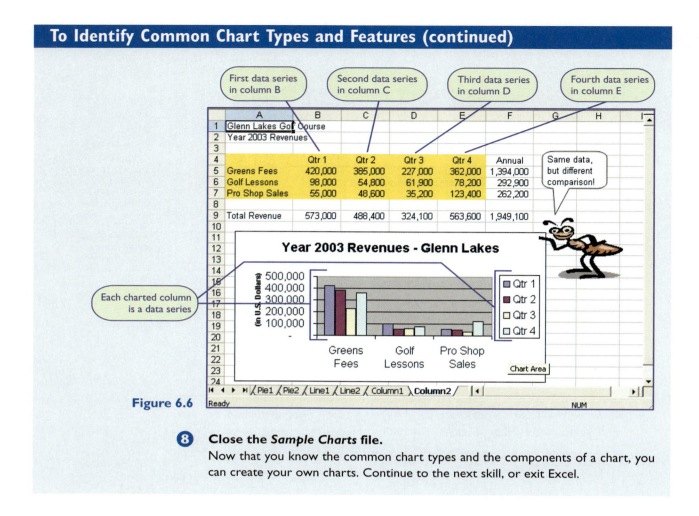

Figure 6.6

8 **Close the *Sample Charts* file.**
Now that you know the common chart types and the components of a chart, you can create your own charts. Continue to the next skill, or exit Excel.

Use Chart Wizard to Create an Embedded Pie Chart

To create a chart, you select the data you want to use in the chart; then choose Insert, Chart or click the Chart Wizard button on the Standard toolbar. The Chart Wizard provides step-by-step assistance through a series of dialog boxes for choosing a chart type and specifying chart options. It automatically creates the chart from the selected data and places it in a box (frame). You can then move, size, change, or enhance the chart. Now, try creating an embedded pie chart that shows the percentage of Year 2003 Greens Fees earned in each quarter.

To Create an Embedded Pie Chart

1 **Open the file *MEC-S602* and save it as** My Charts.
A workbook opens with seven sheets, the first of which is named Pie.

2 **Select the range A4:E5 in the Pie worksheet, and click the Chart Wizard button in the toolbar.**
The Chart Type dialog box opens (Chart Wizard – Step 1 of 4), as shown in Figure 6.7.

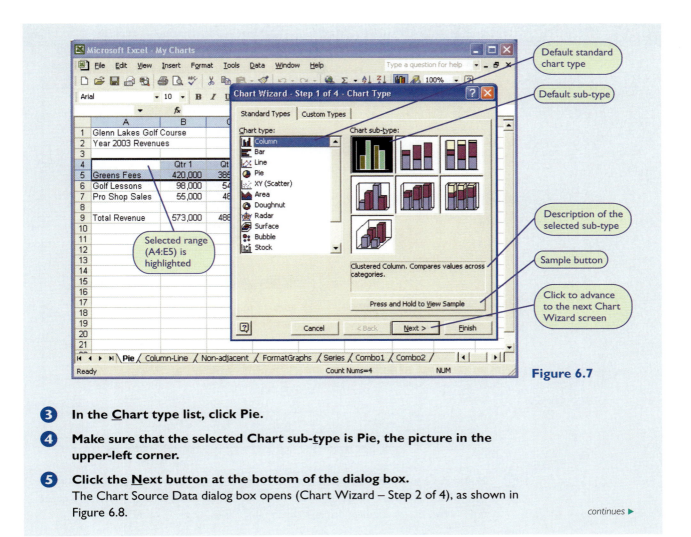

Figure 6.7

In the image, the following callouts appear:
- Default standard chart type
- Default sub-type
- Description of the selected sub-type
- Sample button
- Click to advance to the next Chart Wizard screen
- Selected range (A4:E5) is highlighted

3 In the **C**hart type list, click **Pie.**

4 Make sure that the selected Chart sub-**t**ype is Pie, the picture in the upper-left corner.

5 Click the **N**ext button at the bottom of the dialog box.
The Chart Source Data dialog box opens (Chart Wizard – Step 2 of 4), as shown in Figure 6.8.

continues ▶

To Create an Embedded Pie Chart (continued)

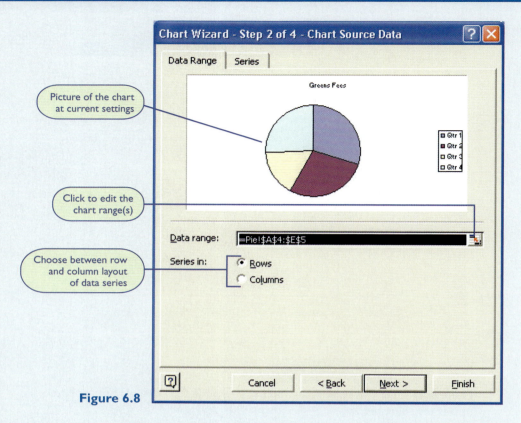

Figure 6.8

6   **Make sure that the direction of the data series is Rows, and click Next.**
The Chart Options dialog box opens (Chart Wizard – Step 3 of 4). When the chart
type is Pie, the dialog box displays three tabs: Titles, Legend, and Data Labels.

7   **Click the Titles tab, if necessary, to display the dialog box shown in
Figure 6.9.**

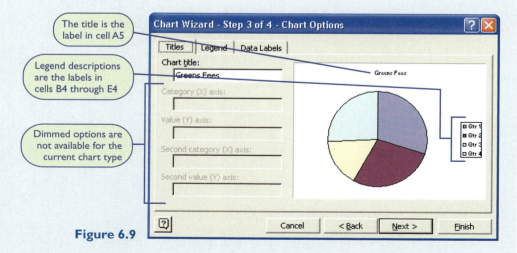

Figure 6.9

8   **Click within the Chart title text box, and edit the title to read** Year
2003 - Greens Fees.

After a short delay, the revised title automatically appears in the sample chart that fills the right half of the Chart Options dialog box.

 If you have problems…

If you press ⏎Enter after editing the title, the Chart Location dialog box opens (Chart Wizard – Step 4 of 4). Click the Back button to return to the Chart Options dialog box.

9 **Click the Legend tab in the Chart Options dialog box, and click the Show legend text box to remove the check mark.**

The legend no longer appears on the pie chart.

10 **Click the Data Labels tab in the Chart Options dialog box, and click the Category name and Percentage options.**

Quarter labels and associated percents appear by their respective pie slices (see Figure 6.10).

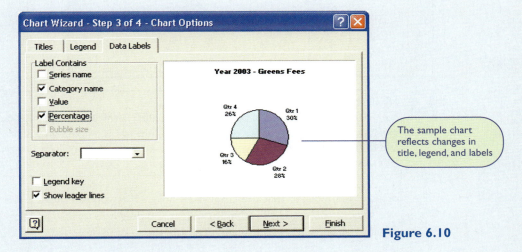

Figure 6.10

11 **Click Next.**

The Chart Location dialog box opens (Chart Wizard – Step 4 of 4). Select the default option, *As object in*, if you want to see the chart displayed next to its source data (see Figure 6.11). Select the option *As new sheet* if you prefer to work with the chart separately on its own sheet.

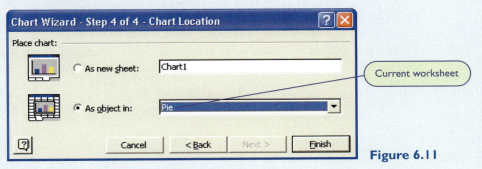

Figure 6.11

continues ▶

To Create an Embedded Pie Chart (continued)

⑫ **Make sure that the current setting is to place the chart as an object in the current worksheet Pie, and click Finish.**

Excel creates the chart and displays it with eight black squares called *sizing handles* at the corners and midpoints of the border surrounding the chart box (see Figure 6.12).

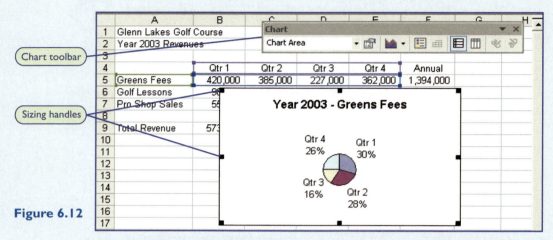

Figure 6.12

X *If you have problems...*

Your screen might display a floating Chart toolbar after you click Finish to exit the Chart Wizard (refer to Figure 6.12). If there is a floating toolbar and it displays on the chart you are about to move, click the Close button (the X in the upper-right corner of the toolbar).

The sizing handles indicate that the chart is an object that you can move and size. To move a selected object, click within the object and drag it to its new location. To size a selected object, click a handle and drag it in the desired direction.

⑬ **Click inside the chart area (in any blank area); then drag the chart so that the upper-left corner is positioned near the middle of cell A11, and release the mouse button.**

As you drag the chart, the pointer changes to a four-headed arrow.

⑭ **Click outside the chart to deselect it.**

The content and layout of the pie chart in your worksheet should resemble the one shown in Figure 6.13. If there are slight differences in chart height, width, or location, you can size or move the chart as desired. There might also be differences in the font size of titles and labels in the charts you create due to differences in computer systems.

	A	B	C	D	E	F	G	H
1	Glenn Lakes Golf Course							
2	Year 2003 Revenues							
3								
4		Qtr 1	Qtr 2	Qtr 3	Qtr 4	Annual		
5	Greens Fees	420,000	385,000	227,000	362,000	1,394,000		
6	Golf Lessons	98,000	54,800	61,900	78,200	292,900		
7	Pro Shop Sales	55,000	48,600	35,200	123,400	262,200		
8								
9	Total Revenue	573,000	488,400	324,100	563,600	1,949,100		
10								
11								
12								

Year 2003 - Greens Fees

Qtr 4 26% Qtr 1 30% Qtr 3 16% Qtr 2 28%

Figure 6.13

  15 **Save your changes to the *My Charts* workbook.**
The embedded pie chart is saved in the Pie worksheet, which is the first sheet within the *My Charts* workbook. Keep the workbook open for the next skill, or close the workbook and exit Excel.

Alternate Way:
Access the Chart Wizard
You can access the Chart Wizard by using menu options instead of a toolbar button. Select the range you want to chart; then click Insert on the menu bar, and select Chart.

In Depth:
Resizing and Deleting Charts
When you resize a chart by dragging a handle on the middle of one side of the box, you change the size horizontally or vertically. When you drag a corner handle, you change the vertical and horizontal dimensions at the same time. If you hold down ◆Shift while dragging a corner handle, you maintain the original proportions of the chart.

To delete a chart, click within a blank area of the chart to select it; then press Del.

Use Chart Wizard to Create an Embedded Column Chart

A pie chart is limited to one data series, and the data charted must be components of a whole. Excel provides a variety of other types, including a column chart, suitable for charting multiple data series. You can use the Chart Wizard to construct all chart types. Now, try creating an embedded column chart that compares Year 2003 quarterly revenues from three sources: Greens Fees, Golf Lessons, and Pro Shop Sales.

To Create an Embedded Column Chart

1 **Open the *My Charts* file, if necessary, and select the Column-Line worksheet.**

The Column-Line sheet, like the previous sheet named Pie, contains the Year 2003 revenue data for Glenn Lakes Golf Course.

2 **Select the range A4:E7, and click the Chart Wizard button in the Standard toolbar.**

The Chart Type dialog box opens (Chart Wizard – Step 1 of 4).

3 **Click *Column* in the Chart type list, if it isn't already selected.**

4 **Make sure that the Clustered Column sub-type from the Chart sub-type list is selected.**

5 **Point to the *Press and Hold to View Sample* button, and click and hold down the left mouse button.**

A sample of the chart is displayed in the Sample box, as shown in Figure 6.14.

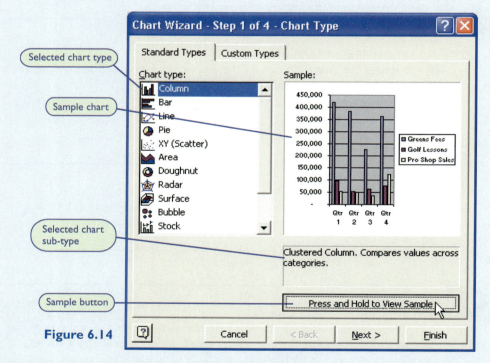

Figure 6.14

6 **Release the mouse button, and click Next.**

The Chart Source Data dialog box opens (Chart Wizard – Step 2 of 4).

7 **Make sure that the data range is $A$4:$E$7 in the Column-Line worksheet and the data series is in Rows, and click Next.**

The Chart Options dialog box opens (Chart Wizard – Step 3 of 4). When the chart type is Column, the dialog box displays six tabs: Titles, Axes, Gridlines, Legend, Data Labels, and Data Table.

8 **Click the Titles tab, if necessary, and enter the chart title and X-axis title shown in Figure 6.15.**

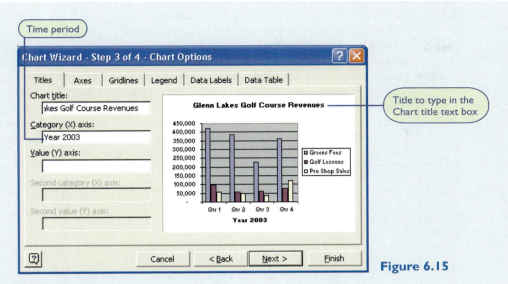

Figure 6.15

9 **Click Finish.**

Clicking Finish bypasses the Chart Location dialog box (Chart Wizard – Step 4 of 4). Excel automatically creates an embedded chart, as opposed to a chart on a separate sheet, unless you specify otherwise.

10 **Click inside the chart area (in any blank area), and drag the chart below the worksheet data.**

11 **Drag one or more sizing handles until your column chart resembles the one shown in Figure 6.16; then click outside the chart to deselect it.**

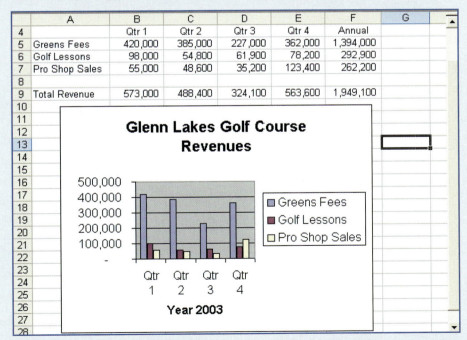

Figure 6.16

12 **Click cell A1, and save your changes to the *My Charts* workbook.**

The embedded column chart is saved in the Column-Line worksheet, which is the second sheet in the *My Charts* workbook. Keep the workbook open for the next lesson, or close the workbook and exit Excel.

> ### *In Depth:*
> **Comparing Clustered and Stacked Column Charts**
> A *clustered column chart* sub-type presents multiple data series as side-by-side columns (refer to Figure 6.16). If you select the *stacked column chart* sub-type, multiple data series appear as stacked components of a single column instead of as side-by-side columns. The stacked column sub-type is appropriate if the multiple data series total to a meaningful number. For example, stacking three revenue amounts—greens fees, golf lessons, and pro shop sales—in a single column for each quarter is meaningful, because it shows the contribution of each revenue source to the total revenue for the quarter.

Change the Chart Type

It is important to select a chart type that can help you display the data in the most dramatic, appropriate, and meaningful manner possible. For example, you can usually spot trends more easily with a line chart; whereas a pie chart is best for showing parts of a whole.

After you create a chart, you might decide that you do not like the type of chart that you selected, or you might want to compare different chart types using the same data series. Excel enables you to change the chart type without re-creating the entire chart.

Now, make a copy of the embedded column chart and change the type of the copied chart to Line.

To Change the Chart Type

1 **Open the *My Charts* file, if necessary, and select the Column-Line worksheet.**
The Column-Line sheet includes the embedded column chart that you created in the previous skill.

 2 **Click inside the chart area (in any blank area) to select the entire chart, and click the Copy button.**
A moving dashed line appears just inside the chart border. The chart is copied to the Windows Clipboard.

 3 **Select a cell below the lower-left corner of the original column chart, and click the Paste button.**
Two identical column charts appear in the Column-Line worksheet, one below the other.

4 **Scroll down to display the second chart, and right-click in any blank area of the second column chart.**
A shortcut menu with chart options appears, as shown in Figure 6.17.

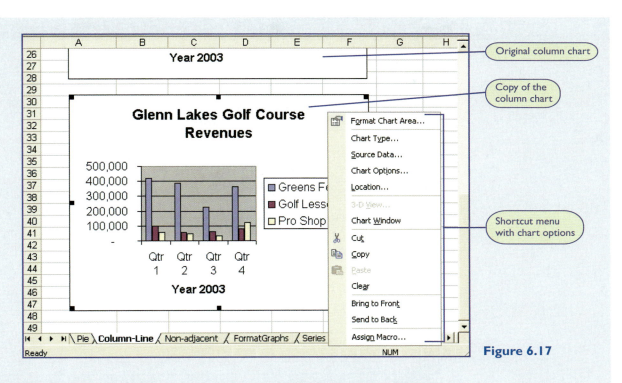

Figure 6.17

5 **Choose Chart Type on the shortcut menu, and choose Line in the Chart type list.**

The default line chart is *Line with markers displayed at each data value*, as shown in Figure 6.18.

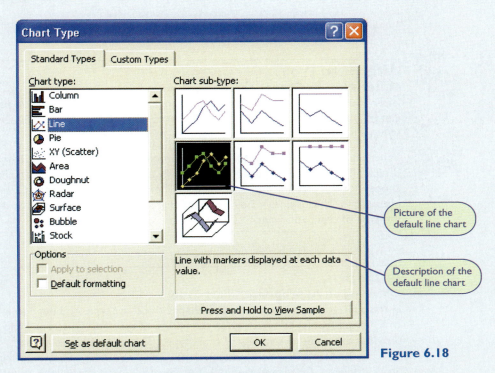

Figure 6.18

6 **Click the OK button in the Chart Type dialog box, and click outside the line chart to deselect it.**

continues ▶

To Change the Chart Type (continued)

Data series are presented in lines instead of columns, as shown in Figure 6.19.

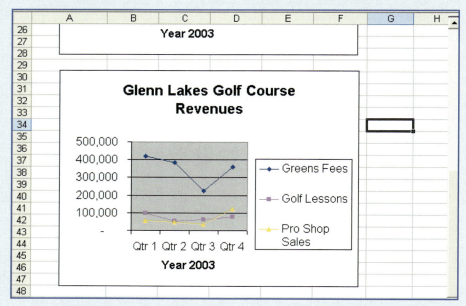

Figure 6.19

 7 **Click cell A1, and save your changes to the *My Charts* workbook.**
The embedded column and line charts are saved in the Column-Line worksheet, the second sheet within the *My Charts* workbook. Keep the workbook open for the next skill, or close the workbook and exit Excel.

Alternate Way:
Other Ways to Change the Chart Type
After you select the chart you want to change, there are other ways to display a Chart Type dialog box. You can choose Chart, Chart Type, or click the Chart Wizard button.

 You can also change a chart to one of 18 predefined types using the Chart toolbar. If this toolbar does not automatically appear when you select a chart, choose View, Toolbars, and select Chart. The drop-down list for the Chart Type button on this toolbar is a 3x6 display of chart icons. Click the icon that depicts the type of chart you want.

In Depth:
Choosing an Appropriate Chart Type
In this skill, you learned the steps to change the chart type. You need to know which chart type(s) to select, given the nature of the data. Onscreen Help provides examples of a variety of chart types. The standard built-in charts are Column, Bar, Line, Pie, XY (Scatter), Area, Doughnut, Radar, Surface, Bubble, Stock, Cylinder, Cone, and Pyramid. You can also select among built-in custom chart types—Area Blocks, Column – Area, Columns with Depth, Cones, Floating Bars, Line – Column on 2 Axes, and so forth—or create user-defined chart types.

Chart Nonadjacent Data Series

You can select nonadjacent sets of numbers to be charted by holding down Ctrl while dragging over cells in the various areas of the worksheet. Make sure that the sets of numbers selected represent the same data series.

Now, try creating an embedded column chart that compares Year 2003 Greens Fees (the data series in row 5) to Total Revenue (the data series in row 9).

To Chart Nonadjacent Data Series

1 **Open the *My Charts* file, if necessary, and select the Non-adjacent worksheet.**
The Non-adjacent worksheet contains a copy of the data used in the previous sheets: Pie and Column-Line.

2 **Select the range A4:E5, and press and hold down Ctrl.**

3 **Select the range A9:E9, and release Ctrl.**
Only the ranges A4:E5 and A9:E9 are highlighted.

 If you have problems...
Only the first five cells in rows 4, 5, and 9 should be highlighted. If any other cells are selected, click outside the selected areas to deselect them, and repeat Steps 2 and 3.

4 **Click the Chart Wizard button, and make sure that the Standard Types tab is selected in the Chart Type dialog box.**

5 **Select Column as the chart type and Clustered Column as the chart sub-type, and click Next.**
The Chart Source Data dialog box (Chart Wizard – Step 2 of 4) opens, as shown in Figure 6.20.

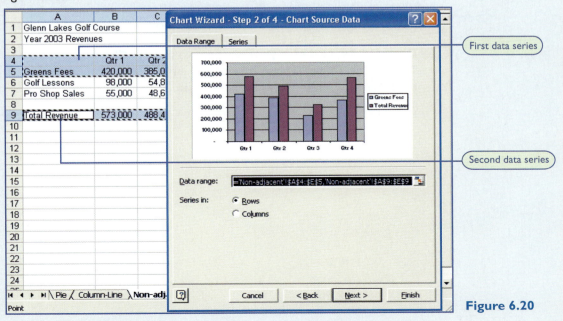

Figure 6.20

continues ▶

To Chart Nonadjacent Data Series (continued)

6 Make sure that the *Series in* setting is **R**ows, and click **N**ext.
The Chart Options dialog box opens (Chart Wizard – Step 3 of 4).

7 On the **Titles tab, type** Impact of Greens Fees on Revenue **in the Chart title text box.**

8 **Type** Glenn Lakes Golf Course – Year 2003 **in the Category (X) axis text box, and click F**inish.

9 Move the newly created chart below its associated worksheet data.

10 Drag one or more sizing handles until your column chart resembles the one shown in Figure 6.21; then click outside the chart to deselect it.

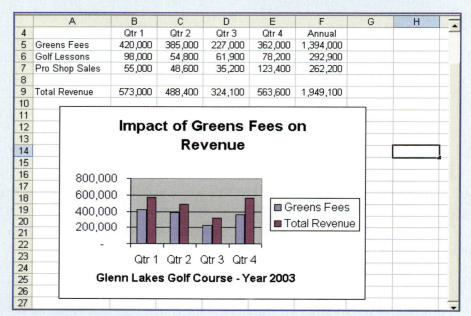

Figure 6.21

11 Click cell A1, and save your changes to the *My Charts* workbook.
The embedded column chart is saved in the Non-adjacent worksheet, which is the third sheet in the *My Charts* workbook. Keep the workbook open for the next skill, or close the workbook and exit Excel.

Modify Chart Formats

After you create a chart, you can make changes that improve readability or enhance visual appeal. For example, you can display dollar signs in front of the numbers in a Y-axis scale, italicize a title, add a textured background, and change the color of a data series. The chart in Figure 6.22 reflects these enhancements. You can make these changes yourself now.

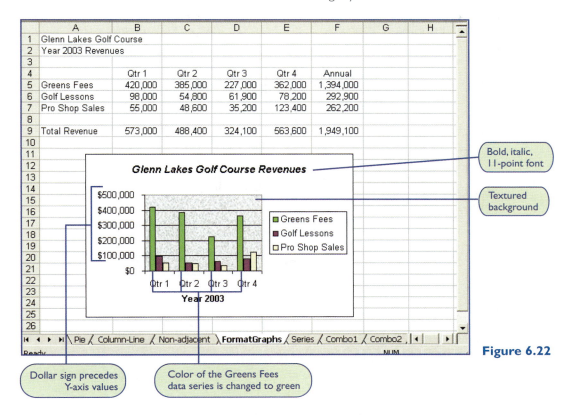

Bold, italic, 11-point font

Textured background

Dollar sign precedes Y-axis values

Color of the Greens Fees data series is changed to green

Figure 6.22

To Modify Chart Formats

1 **Open the *My Charts* file, if necessary, and select the FormatGraphs worksheet.**
The FormatGraphs worksheet contains an embedded column chart below the worksheet data.

2 **Position the pointer on any value in the Y-axis scale, and right-click.**
A pop-up menu appears with two options: Format Axis and Clear. Two small square sizing handles at the top and bottom of the Y-axis indicate that the Y-axis is selected.

3 **Choose Format Axis.**
The Format Axis dialog box opens.

4 **Click the Number tab and click Currency in the Category list (see Figure 6.23).**

continues ▶

To Modify Chart Formats (continued)

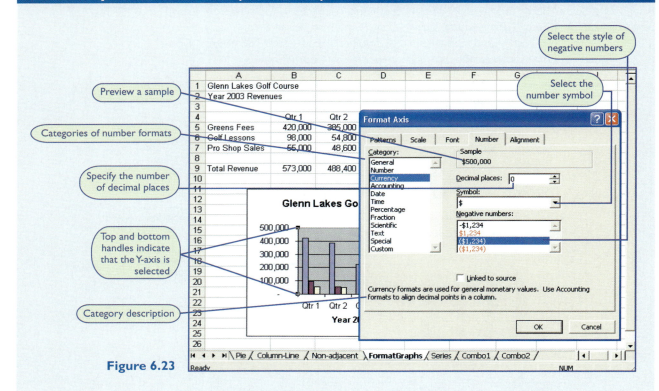

Figure 6.23

Labels pointing to the figure:
- Preview a sample
- Categories of number formats
- Specify the number of decimal places
- Top and bottom handles indicate that the Y-axis is selected
- Category description
- Select the style of negative numbers
- Select the number symbol

5 Specify the settings for **D**ecimal places, **S**ymbol, and **N**egative numbers that display in **Figure 6.23**, and click **OK**.

The Format Axis dialog box closes, and dollar signs appear in front of the Y-axis numbers. The Y-axis remains selected.

6 Position the pointer anywhere on the chart title, and right-click.

A shortcut menu appears with two options: F**o**rmat Chart Title and Cle**a**r. Sizing handles at the corners and midpoints of the border surrounding the title indicate that the title is selected. The sizing handles on the Y-axis disappear, indicating that a selected area of a chart is deselected as soon as another area is selected.

7 Choose F**o**rmat Chart Title, and click the Font tab in the Format Chart Title dialog box.

8 Select Bold Italic in the F**o**nt style list, and select 11 in the **S**ize list (see **Figure 6.24**).

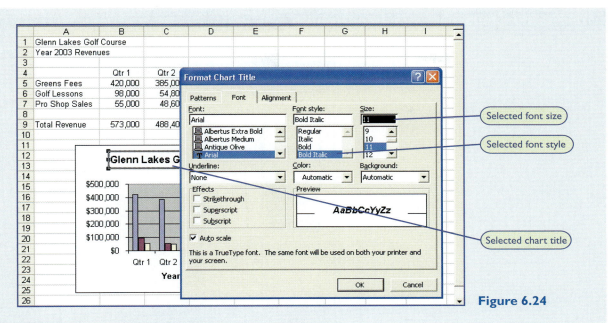

Figure 6.24

9 **Click OK.**

The Format Chart Title dialog box closes, and the 11-point chart title displays in boldface and italic. The title remains selected.

10 **Position the pointer on a blank area between gridlines in the chart, and right-click.**

A shortcut menu appears with multiple options, the first and last of which are Format Plot Area and Clear. Sizing handles at the corners and midpoints of the gray shaded area indicate the plot area is selected.

11 **Choose Format Plot Area.**

The Format Plot Area dialog box opens.

12 **Click the Fill Effects button, and click the Texture tab in the Fill Effects dialog box (see Figure 6.25).**

continues ▶

To Modify Chart Formats (continued)

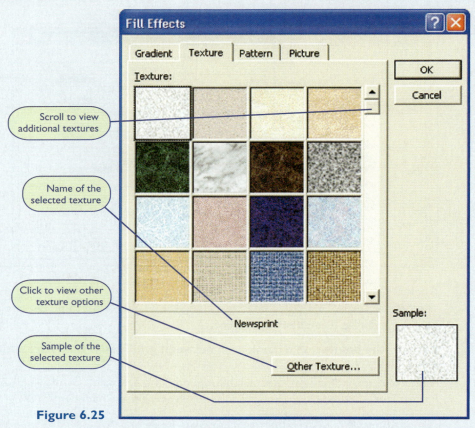

Scroll to view additional textures

Name of the selected texture

Click to view other texture options

Sample of the selected texture

Figure 6.25

⓭ **Click the first style in the upper-left corner of the display to select the texture named Newsprint, and click OK twice to close, in sequence, the Fill Effects and Format Plot Area dialog boxes.**

A textured background (fill) replaces the solid gray background in the plot area. The plot area remains selected.

⓮ **Position the pointer on any of the blue columns that represent quarterly Greens Fees, and right-click.**

A shortcut menu appears with the options shown in Figure 6.26. The small black square in each blue column indicates that you selected the Greens Fees data series.

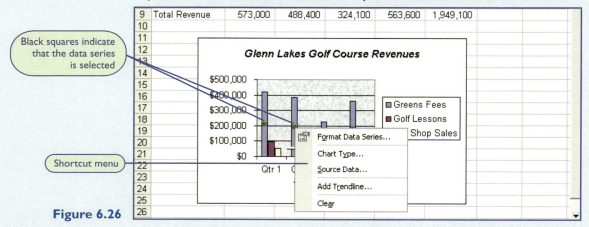

Black squares indicate that the data series is selected

Shortcut menu

Figure 6.26

15 **Choose F̲ormat Data Series and click the Patterns tab in the Format Data Series dialog box.**

The Patterns tab includes three sections: Border and Sample on the left, and Area on the right (see Figure 6.27).

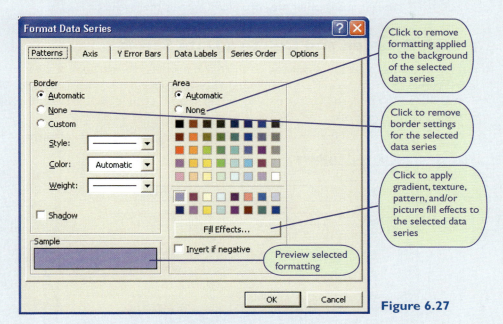

Click to remove formatting applied to the background of the selected data series

Click to remove border settings for the selected data series

Click to apply gradient, texture, pattern, and/or picture fill effects to the selected data series

Preview selected formatting

Figure 6.27

16 **Click the bright green square (the fourth color square in the fourth row) in the Area section, and click OK.**

The color of the Greens Fees data series changes from blue to bright green. The data series remains selected.

17 **Click cell A1 to deselect the data series, and save your changes to the *My Charts* workbook.**

The modified column chart is saved in the FormatGraphs worksheet, which is the fourth sheet within the *My Charts* workbook. Keep the workbook open for the next skill, or close the workbook and exit Excel.

Alternate Way:

Alternatives to Shortcut Menus

Right-clicking a chart area displays a context-sensitive shortcut menu that enables you to clear or modify the selected area. You can access chart dialog boxes and modify settings in other ways as well. Double-clicking a chart area opens the dialog box for formatting that area. You can also access C̲hart options from the menu bar after you select a chart area or the entire chart.

Ways to View a Chart

Instead of scrolling through the worksheet to view an embedded chart, you can view the chart in its own window. Select the chart, and choose V̲iew, Chart W̲indow. You can edit the chart while it is open in the window.

If you select an embedded chart before clicking the Print Preview button, Excel displays only the chart instead of the worksheet data and the chart. You can view but not change a chart displayed in the Print Preview mode.

In Depth:

Changing Other Chart Elements

In this skill, you made changes to four areas in a chart: Y-axis, chart title, background, and a data series. You started the change process by positioning the pointer on the area and right-clicking. You can use the same steps to initiate changes in any other area of a chart, such as the legend or X-axis.

Add, Reorder, and Delete a Data Series

Even a relatively small set of data can be charted in a variety of ways. Look at the range A4:E7 in Figure 6.28. In that example, a data series can be a column of data, such as the sales for each year from 2000 through 2003. A data series can also be a row of data, such as the four-year sales pattern for each city.

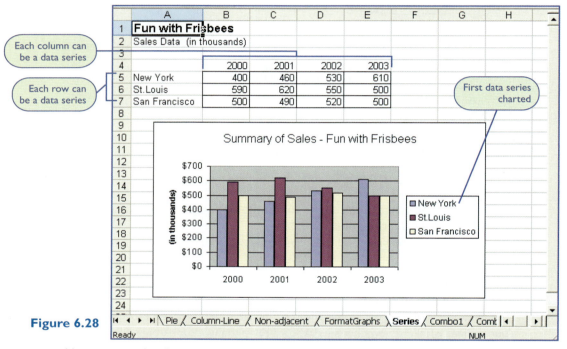

Figure 6.28

You can vary the data presented in a chart by adding a data series, rearranging the order of data series, and deleting a data series. In this skill, you learn to use all three methods to manipulate data series on an existing chart.

To Add, Reorder, and Delete a Data Series

❶ Open the *My Charts* file, if necessary, and select the Series worksheet.
This worksheet contains a column chart showing sales for the New York office of Fun with Frisbees over a period of four years. Dollar amounts are displayed along the vertical axis to the left of the plot area, and a legend to the right of the plot area displays the color assigned to the single data series.

❷ Position the mouse pointer on one of the four columns in the chart.
A ScreenTip shows the data series (New York), the year, and the value (in thousands) for that year. Next, add the data for St. Louis and San Francisco to the chart. Although there is more than one way to accomplish this, the easiest way is to use the drag-and-drop method.

3 **Select cells A6:E7, click the border of the selected cells and drag them within the chart, release the mouse button, and deselect the chart.**
The chart displays data for all three cities, as shown in Figure 6.28. Next, exchange the positions of St. Louis and San Francisco, so the cities are in alphabetical order.

4 **Right-click any column in the chart, and select Format Data Series.**

5 **Select the Series Order tab in the Format Data Series dialog box, and select San Francisco in the Series order list box (see Figure 6.29).**

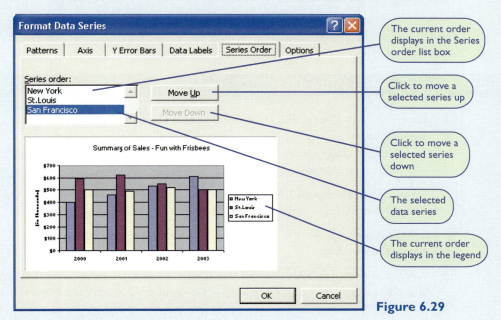

Figure 6.29

6 **Click the Move Up button and click OK; then click outside the chart to deselect the data series.**
The order of the data series changes in both the legend and the plot area. Within the set of columns for each year, San Francisco is now the middle column. The re-ordering does not affect the order of the source data in the worksheet. Now, re-move the St. Louis data from the chart.

7 **Click any column that represents St. Louis data, and press Del.**
Any reference to St. Louis data disappears from the plot area and the legend.

8 **Click cell A1, and save your changes to the *My Charts* workbook.**
The modified column chart is saved in the Series worksheet, which is the fifth sheet within the *My Charts* workbook. Keep the workbook open for the next skill, or close the workbook and exit Excel.

Alternate Way:
Alternative Ways to Add or Delete Data Series
The methods used to add and delete data series illustrated in this skill are the simplest ways to make those changes to an existing chart. Add by dragging a selected series and dropping it into the chart; remove by selecting the charted data series and pressing Del. You can also make both changes from the Series

tab of the Source Data dialog box. Select the chart; choose Chart, Source Data; and select the Series tab. To add a data series, click the Add button and specify the location of the series. To delete a data series, select its name in the Series list, and click the Remove button.

Create and Print a Combination Chart

A *combination chart* includes two or more chart types, such as showing one data series as a column and another as a line. Create a combination chart if the values in the data series vary widely or if you want to emphasize differences in the data.

The reasons for creating a combination chart do not apply to the Glenn Lakes Golf Course data charted in previous lessons. In this lesson, you chart two data series with widely varying values: the total miles walked and the average miles per walk.

To Create and Print a Combination Chart

❶ Open the *My Charts* file, if necessary, and select the Combo1 worksheet.
The Combo1 sheet illustrates the problem encountered when you chart data series with values that vary widely.

❷ Read the Problem and Solution text, and click the Combo2 sheet tab.
The sheet contains only the Year 2003 summary of walking data.

❸ Select the range A3:E5, and click the Chart Wizard button in the Standard toolbar.

❹ Click the Custom Types tab in the Chart Type dialog box, scroll down the Chart type list, and click Line – Column on 2 Axes (see Figure 6.30).

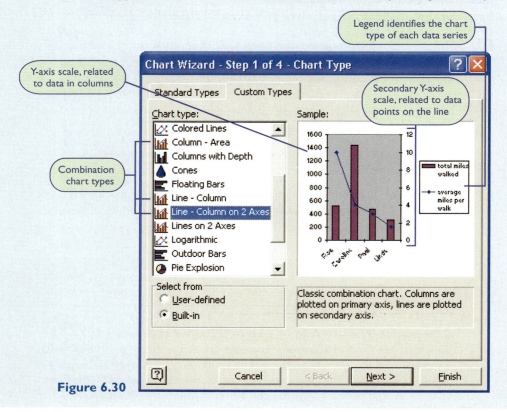

Figure 6.30

5 Click **Next** two times to advance to the **Chart Options** dialog box (**Chart Wizard – Step 3 of 4**), and click the **Titles** tab.

6 Enter the titles for the chart, as shown in **Figure 6.31**.

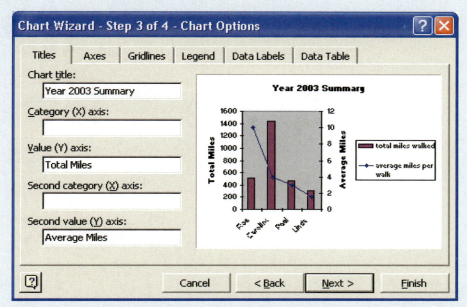

Figure 6.31

7 Click **Finish**; then drag the embedded combination chart below the associated data.

8 Drag one or more sizing handles until your column chart resembles the one shown in **Figure 6.32**; then click outside the chart to deselect it.

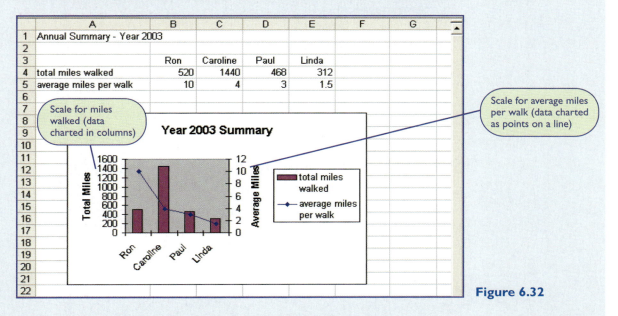

Figure 6.32

9 Click cell A1 and save your changes to the *My Charts* workbook.

continues ▶

To Create and Print a Combination Chart (continued)

The embedded combination chart is saved in the Combo2 worksheet, which is the seventh sheet in the *My Charts* workbook. Get in the habit of saving changes before you print to protect against data loss if your system freezes and requires a reboot.

10 Click any blank area inside the chart to select it, and choose **File, Print.**

11 Make sure that the **Selected Chart** option is selected in the *Print what* area (see **Figure 6.33**).

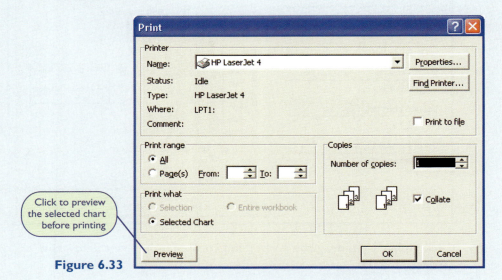

Click to preview the selected chart before printing

Figure 6.33

12 Click **OK, or click Cancel if you do not want to print at this time; then close the workbook.**

Continue with the next skill, or exit Excel.

For immediate reinforcement, work Skill Drills 1 through 4 and Challenge 1.

Skill 6.2: Create, Modify, and Position Graphics

Excel's toolbox of special effects includes AutoShapes—such as lines, arrows, basic shapes, and callouts—and text boxes, WordArt, pictures, clip art, and predefined diagrams. You can glimpse the power of Excel's special effects tools by viewing Figure 6.34.

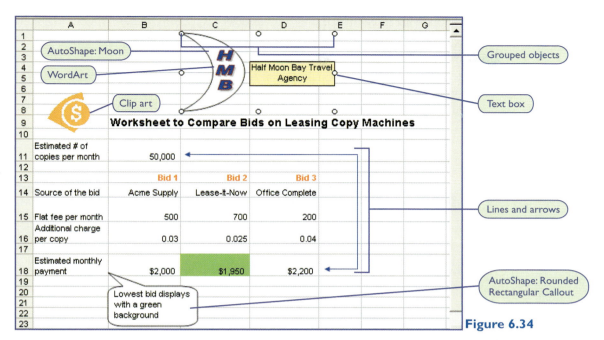

Figure 6.34

In this skill area, you add the special effects shown in Figure 6.34 to a worksheet for the Half Moon Bay Travel Agency. The worksheet computes the expected cost per month of leasing a copy machine—a cost that varies with the expected number of copies made. Consistent with company policy, three bids are being evaluated, each with a different fixed monthly fee and charge per copy.

Create WordArt

WordArt displays user-specified text in one of 30 predefined styles (refer to the WordArt Gallery in Figure 6.35). The styles include curved, slanted, and vertical text. Each style has a predefined color scheme.

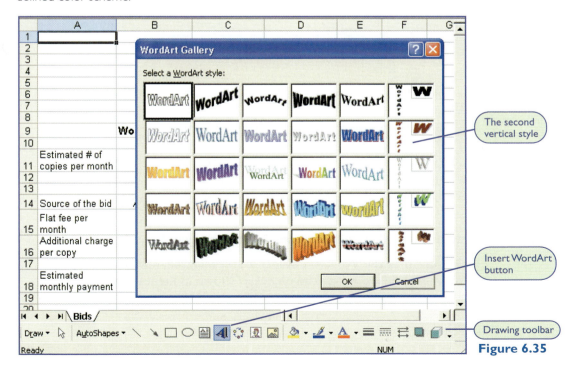

Figure 6.35

WordArt is not entered in a cell. It is a separate object that can be moved, sized, and edited. For example, you can select a WordArt object and change its color scheme, apply a Shadow or 3-D effect, and edit its text.

In this skill, you create the Half Moon Bay Travel Agency initials HMB using WordArt. You select a vertical WordArt style and size it appropriately. The result is part of a three-object logo displayed at the top of the Half Moon Bay Travel Agency's worksheet model to analyze copy machine bids (refer to Figure 6.34). You assemble the logo over the course of four sets of hands-on instruction.

To Create WordArt

1 **Open the *MEC-S603* file, and save it as** Lease Options.
The file contains a single worksheet named Bids.

2 **If the Drawing toolbar does not appear on your screen, select** **V**iew, **T**oolbars and click Drawing.

 3 **Click the Insert WordArt button on the Drawing toolbar.**

4 **Click the second vertical style (refer to Figure 6.35), and click OK.**
The Edit WordArt Text dialog box opens.

5 **Replace *Your Text Here* by typing HMB (see Figure 6.36).**

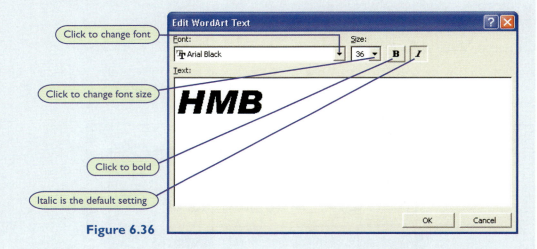

Figure 6.36

6 **Click OK.**
The initials *HMB* display in the selected WordArt style in the middle of the screen. The round sizing handles at the midpoints and corners indicate that the object is selected. The WordArt toolbar displays.

7 **Drag the WordArt object to column B, above row 9.**

8 **Make sure that the WordArt object is still selected, and then drag one or more handles to resize the object as shown in Figure 6.37.**

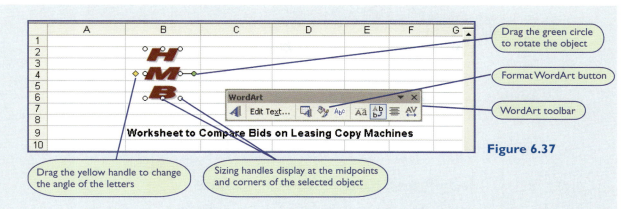

Figure 6.37

This is a temporary adjustment. In a subsequent skill, you resize the object to fit within a moon shape.

9 Make sure that the WordArt object is still selected; then click the Format WordArt button on the WordArt toolbar, and click the Colors and Lines tab in the Format WordArt dialog box.

10 Display the <u>C</u>olor drop-down list in the Fill section near the top of the dialog box, and apply the Blue fill color to the WordArt object; then click OK, and click outside the object to deselect it.

The selected color fills the background of the WordArt object (see Figure 6.38).

Figure 6.38

11 Save your changes to the *Lease Options* workbook.

Keep the *Lease Options* workbook open for the next skill, or close the workbook and exit Excel.

In Depth:

Deleting an Object

To delete WordArt or any other object, click within the object to select it, and press Del.

Formatting WordArt

Use the Format WordArt dialog box to format a shape. You can display this dialog box by right-clicking the WordArt object and selecting Format W<u>o</u>rdArt from the shortcut menu. You can then work with one or more of the following five tabs.

Colors and Lines	Specify settings in three areas: Fill, Line, and Arrows
Size	Set height, width, rotation, and scale
Protection	Lock or unlock the object before setting protection
Properties	Specify if an object is to move or resize when the cells under the object change, and enable or disable printing of the object when the worksheet is printed
Web	Add alternative text to an object that appears when the worksheet is loading as a Web page or the object is missing from the Web page

Insert and Rotate an AutoShape

An *AutoShape* is a predefined shape that you create using the Autoshapes menu from the Drawing toolbar (see Figure 6.39). Categories of AutoShapes include Lines, Connectors, Basic Shapes, Block Arrows, Flowchart, Stars and Banners, and Callouts.

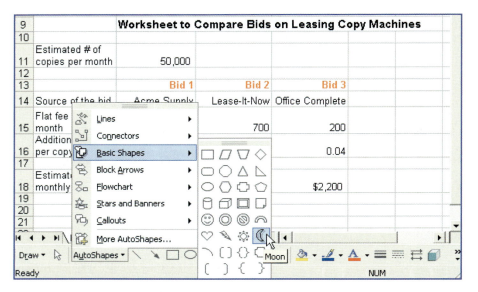

Figure 6.39

To create a shape, select it from the AutoShapes menu, and draw it on the worksheet with the mouse; alternatively, you can click a cell and let Excel draw it for you. You can then move, size, rotate, or flip the shape, and then apply a variety of formats.

If you select a shape with some open space inside of it—a banner, circle, star, block arrow, and so forth—you can insert text in that open space. Lines and connectors show relationships and do not allow messages to be attached.

In this skill, you create Half Moon Bay's corporate symbol, a half-moon. You select a basic shape and flip it.

To Insert and Rotate an AutoShape

1 **Open the *Lease Options* workbook, and display the Drawing toolbar, if necessary.**

2 **Click the AutoShapes button on the Drawing toolbar, and position the mouse pointer on Basic Shapes.**
A display of shapes, four in each row, appears to the right of the AutoShapes menu (refer to Figure 6.39).

3 **Click the Moon shape (the last option in the sixth row).**

The shape is a crescent moon curved in the direction of the letter C, or a left parenthesis. The mouse pointer changes to a thin black cross.

4 **Click cell A1.**

Excel inserts the shape and displays it with sizing handles, indicating the shape is selected.

5 **Click the Draw button at the left end of the Drawing toolbar, and position the mouse pointer on Rotate or Flip.**

Excel displays the draw options that can be applied to the selected object (see Figure 6.40).

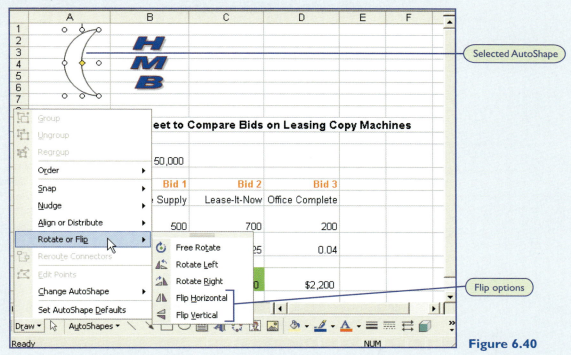

Figure 6.40

6 **Click Flip Horizontal.**

The crescent moon flips to the opposite direction—that is, it curves similar to a right parenthesis (see Figure 6.41).

Figure 6.41

7 **Click outside the object to deselect it, and save your changes to the** *Lease Options* **workbook.**

Keep the *Lease Options* workbook open for the next skill, or close the workbook and exit Excel.

In Depth:
Formatting AutoShapes

Use the Format AutoShape dialog box to format a shape. You can display this dialog box by right-clicking a shape and then selecting Format Aut<u>o</u>Shape from the shortcut menu.

Adding Text to an AutoShape

To add text to an AutoShape, right-click the object and then select Add Te<u>x</u>t from the shortcut menu. Type the text and then select the text. Change the font style, or size and apply other enhancements such as color, and click outside the object to deselect it. If some of the text does not display, select the object and increase its size.

Adding a Fill Color to an AutoShape

You can add a fill (background) color to an AutoShape without using the Format AutoShape dialog box. Select the shape, click the down arrow attached to the Fill Color button in the Formatting or Drawing toolbar, click the desired color, and click outside the object to deselect it.

If a flashing cursor displays when you select an AutoShape, the object includes text, and text edit mode is active. Before you can apply a fill color, you must exit text edit mode by clicking the border of the selected object.

Replacing One AutoShape with Another

You can easily change an AutoShape from one style to another. Click the AutoShape to select it and then click D<u>r</u>aw on the Drawing toolbar. Select <u>C</u>hange AutoShape, pick a general category, and click the desired style.

Create a Text Box

A *text box* is an object, usually shaped like a square or rectangle, that contains words. Text automatically wraps to fit within the boundaries of the box, and you can make the box larger or smaller by dragging a sizing handle. If you create a text box by dragging the mouse pointer, it displays with a solid border; if you click the worksheet to add the box and then resize it or begin typing, the text does not have a border.

You can edit the words in a text box in the same way you would edit text in a word-processing document—select the text to be changed and then type the correction. Some formatting can be done using the Fill Color, Line Color, Font Color, and Line Style toolbar buttons. For other formatting, you can choose F<u>o</u>rmat, Text B<u>o</u>x, and make selections within the Format Text Box dialog box.

In this skill, you create a text box containing the name of the Half Moon Bay Travel Agency. You draw the box using the mouse, enter the text using the default font, and apply a light yellow fill (background) to the box.

To Create a Text Box

❶ **Open the *Lease Options* workbook, if necessary.**

 ❷ **Click the Text Box button on the Drawing toolbar.**

❸ **Drag open the text box beginning in cell D4 (similar in size and position to the box shown in Figure 6.42).**

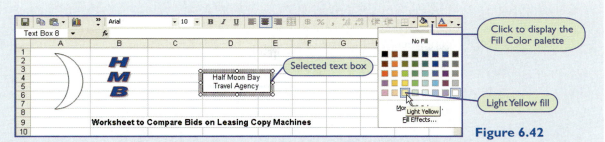

Figure 6.42

The text box is selected. A flashing cursor displays in the upper-left corner of the text box.

④ **Click the Center button on the Standard toolbar, and then type** Half Moon Bay Travel Agency **in the text box.**

⑤ **Click the text box border.**

⑥ **Click the down arrow to the right of the Fill Color button on the Formatting toolbar or the Drawing toolbar. (Figure 6.42 illustrates use of the Formatting toolbar.)**
The Fill Color palette displays.

☒ **_If you have problems …_**
If the Fill Color palette is dim, you have not selected the text box border. Text boxes have two selection modes, both of which cause sizing handles to display. A flashing cursor, which indicates text-editing mode, displays if you click within a text box. Clicking the border of a text box enables you to edit the text box properties, including fill, border color, and line style.

---

⑦ **Select Light Yellow from the Fill Color palette.**

⑧ **Click outside the text box to deselect it, and save your changes to the _Lease Options_ workbook.**
Keep the _Lease Options_ workbook open for the next skill, or close the workbook and exit Excel.

 In Depth:
Formatting a Text Box
Use the Format Text Box dialog box to format a text box. You can display this dialog box by clicking within the text box, right-clicking a border of the box, and then selecting Format Text Box from the shortcut menu.

Readability
As you add text color and background fill, be mindful of a reader's ability to see the text. Strive for sharp color contrast. For example, yellow text on a white background is nearly impossible to read, and red on green is a problem for people who are color blind.

Linking to Cell Contents
If the text you want to enter in a text box or AutoShape already exists in a cell, you can set a link to that cell instead of typing the text. Click within the text box or shape, click the formula bar, type an equal sign, click the cell containing the desired text, and then press ↵Enter.

Group Objects

Grouped objects consist of two or more objects that can be manipulated as a single object. Prior to grouping, each object has its own set of sizing handles (see Figure 6.43). After grouping, a single set of sizing handles surrounds the objects.

Figure 6.43

When objects are grouped, any action applied to the group impacts each object in the group. You can, for example, resize all the objects in a group, rotate and flip them, drag them to a different location, and apply attributes such as text, fill, and line color. If you want to change only one object in the group, you can ungroup the objects, make the change, and then regroup the objects.

Stacked objects, such as the moon and the WordArt shown in Figure 6.43, display in layers. You can change the order in which objects display by using an Order option accessed through the Drawing toolbar, or by right-clicking any object in the group and selecting Order from the shortcut menu. Four options are available on the Order menu. Send to Back or Bring to Front places the selected object at the bottom or top of the stack, respectively. If there are three or more layers, use the Bring Forward and Send Backward options to move an object one layer at a time.

In this skill, you group the moon and the *HMB* WordArt as one object and then add a third object to the group—the text box containing the company name. You start by adjusting size and order of the individual objects—the WordArt initials must fit within the moon shape, and the initials must display on top of the moon.

To Group Objects

① **Open the *Lease Options* workbook, if necessary.**

② **Drag the WordArt object on top of the moon.**
The moon obscures the WordArt object. Now reverse the two objects to get the effect of text inside the moon.

③ **Right-click the moon shape, position the mouse pointer on O<u>r</u>der, and select Send to Ba<u>c</u>k.**

④ **Resize the moon so that it extends from cell A1 to cell A8 (refer to Figure 6.43).**

⑤ **Click within the WordArt object, and resize it so that the initials *HMB* fit inside the moon.**

⑥ **Hold down ⬆Shift, and select both the moon and the WordArt objects.**
Each object displays its own set of sizing handles (refer to Figure 6.43).

7 **Right-click the selected objects and position the mouse pointer on Grouping (see Figure 6.44).**

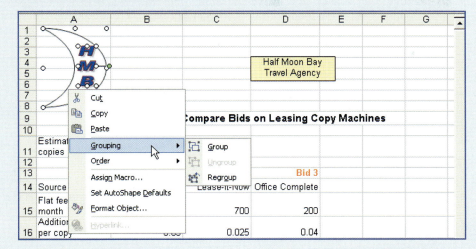

Figure 6.44

8 **Select Group.**
Now only one set of sizing handles appears because grouped objects take on the characteristics of a single object.

9 **Move the grouped objects from column A to column C.**

10 **Repeat the procedures described in steps 6 through 8 to include the text box in a grouping of three objects (see Figure 6.45).**

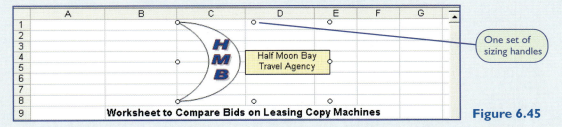

Figure 6.45

11 **Click outside the grouped objects, and save your changes to the *Lease Options* workbook.**
Keep the *Lease Options* workbook open for the next skill, or close the workbook and exit Excel.

In Depth:
Changing the Order of Stacked Objects
Sometimes an object in a stack is hidden by another object. You can select an object and then press Tab↹ or ⬆Shift+Tab↹ to move forward or backward through the objects on a worksheet.

Ungrouping and Regrouping Drawing Objects
To ungroup drawing objects, click within any object in the group, display the Draw menu on the Drawing toolbar, and select Ungroup.

To regroup drawing objects, select any one of the objects previously grouped, display the Draw menu on the Drawing toolbar, and select Regroup.

Limitations of Grouping Objects

Grouping works best on drawing objects. Including other objects, such as text boxes, in the group limits what you can do with the group. You can rotate and flip an AutoShape, for example, but the same actions cannot be applied to a text box. Therefore, if one of the objects in a group is a text box, the group cannot be flipped and rotated. When this happens, the affected menu items or buttons appear dimmed.

Add Emphasis with Lines and Arrows

Use arrows to point to a specific location in a worksheet, or to show a connection between two or more related areas or objects on the worksheet. Lines can be used to frame an area, connect or separate areas and objects, or show relationships.

To create an arrow or line, select the object from the Drawing toolbar and then drag the line or arrow in the worksheet using the mouse. You can then apply line styles, such as color, thickness, pattern, and arrow. Figure 6.46 illustrates many of the tools for drawing lines and arrows.

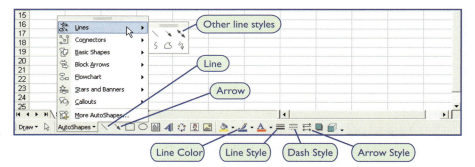

Figure 6.46

Lines and arrows are objects that can be moved, copied, resized, and rotated. Clicking anywhere on a line or arrow selects it and displays sizing handles at each end. To move the object to a new location, position the mouse pointer over it until you see the drag-and-drop symbol— a four-headed arrow—and drag the line to its new location. To change the length, click a sizing handle, and drag the object longer or shorter, or pivot its angle.

In this skill, you create objects to show a relationship in the Bids worksheet between the estimated number of copies per month and the estimated monthly payments. You create two left arrows connected with a vertical line.

To Add Emphasis with Lines and Arrows

1 Open the *Lease Options* workbook, if necessary.

2 Scroll down to display row 18, if necessary, and click the **Arrow** button on the Drawing toolbar.

3 Click toward the right end of cell E18, and drag left to create a short arrow pointing left (refer to the higher of the two arrows in Figure 6.47).

Figure 6.47

 If you have problems...

If you can't make the arrow straight, press and hold down ⬆Shift before releasing the mouse button. If the object is still not drawn as you want it, you can select it and press Del to start over, or you can move and size it as necessary.

---

4 **Make sure that sizing handles display on the arrow, and click the Copy button.**

5 **Click the Paste button.**

Excel creates a copy of the original arrow (refer to Figure 6.47).

6 **Drag the copy of the arrow to cell E11; then lengthen the copied arrow by dragging its arrowhead end to cell C11, and deselect it.**

The worksheet includes two arrows pointing left (see Figure 6.48).

Figure 6.48

7 **Click the Line button on the Drawing toolbar.**

8 **Drag the line so it connects the right ends of the arrows in cells E11 and E18 (see Figure 6.49).**

continues ▶

To Add Emphasis with Lines and Arrows (continued)

Line connecting two arrows

Figure 6.49

✖ *If you have problems...*

You may find it difficult to drag an object the exact distance you need by using the mouse. You can move a selected object in small increments by holding down Ctrl and clicking an arrow key that points to the direction you want to move the object—left, right, up, or down.

---

9 Hold down ⬆Shift and click each of the three lines you just created.
Sizing handles indicate that all three lines are selected.

 10 Click the down arrow to the right of the Line Color button on the Drawing toolbar, select Blue, and deselect the drawn objects.

11 Check your results with Figure 6.50, and make changes as necessary.

Figure 6.50

Three line and arrow objects show the relationship between the input variable for the model (cell B11) and the calculated results (cells B18 through D18).

12 Save your changes to the *Lease Options* workbook.
Keep the *Lease Options* workbook open for the next skill, or close the workbook and exit Excel.

In Depth:
Creating Arrows and Lines

An arrow is a line with an arrowhead symbol attached to either or both ends. You can use buttons and menu items to apply styles to lines and arrows (refer to Figure 6.46).

Use the Line Style button to specify the thickness of a solid line or arrow. Use the Dash Style button to change lines and arrows from solid to different patterns of lines.

Use the Arrow Style button to add or change the style of arrowhead attached to a line or arrow. You can also specify a diamond or circular shape at one or both ends instead of an arrowhead.

Use the Lines menu on the AutoShapes menu to select advanced line drawing tools, such as curve, scribble, and freeform lines. Use the Connectors menu on the AutoShapes menu to select a line style that connects two shapes and keeps them connected. After you select a connector style, blue connector sites appear on objects as you move the mouse pointer over them. The blue points indicate where you can attach a connector line.

Add Emphasis with Callouts

A *callout* is a text-filled object that points to other text or another object. Perhaps you have seen a callout as the balloon or cloud over a cartoon character's head showing what the character is thinking or saying.

You can select among predefined callout styles on the AutoShapes, Callouts menu (see Figure 6.51). Positioning the mouse pointer on a callout displays its name.

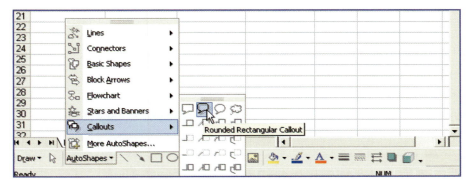

Figure 6.51

To create a callout, select the style you want to use, begin drawing the callout or click a cell on the worksheet where you want to insert the object, type the text that appears inside the callout, and size the object appropriately. Each predefined callout has an **adjustment handle**, a yellow diamond-shaped handle used to adjust the appearance, but not the size, of most Auto-Shapes. To change the area a callout points to, drag the yellow adjustment handle (see Figure 6.52).

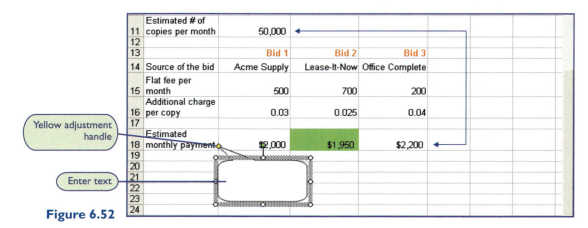

Figure 6.52

In this skill, you create a rounded rectangular callout on the Bids worksheet. You select the callout style, draw it on the worksheet, type the appropriate message in the callout, and resize and position the callout.

To Add Emphasis with a Callout

1 Open the *Lease Options* workbook, if necessary.

2 Select <u>C</u>allouts from the A<u>u</u>toShapes menu on the Drawing toolbar (refer to Figure 6.51).

3 Choose Rounded Rectangle Callout (the second option in the first row).

4 Click cell B21 and drag sizing handles to increase the size of the callout. You can resize the callout again later.

5 Click the yellow adjustment handle, and drag to point the callout toward cell A18.

6 With the callout selected, type Lowest bid displays with a green background.

7 Make final adjustments to the size and position of the callout similar to that shown in Figure 6.53.

Figure 6.53

8 Click outside the callout, and then save your changes to the *Lease Options* workbook.

Keep the *Lease Options* workbook open for the next skill, or close the workbook and exit Excel.

In Depth:

Applying Shadows and 3-D Effects to Shapes

You can add a shadow or a 3-D effect to most AutoShapes, including callouts. To add a shadow effect, select the shape, click the Shadow Style button in the Drawing toolbar, and click the desired style. Follow a similar process to apply a 3-D effect, substituting the 3-D Style button in place of the Shadow Style button.

Inserting Predefined Diagrams

Excel provides another form of graphics—diagrams. A *diagram* is a drawing that generally illustrates relationships. Choose Insert, Diagram; then use the Diagram Gallery dialog box to insert one of six predefined diagram types—Organization Chart, Cycle, Radial, Pyramid, Venn, and Target. You can enter text in a diagram, format the entire diagram with a preset style, or make formatting changes to selected portions of the diagram. You can modify the original structure of a diagram. For example, you can remove a layer from a pyramid diagram or add several circles to a target diagram.

An organization chart makes it easy to see the levels of responsibility in an organization. Use a Cycle diagram to show a continuous cycle. A Radial diagram enables you to show relationships between elements and a core element. A Pyramid diagram makes it easy to show relationships that build on a foundation. Use a Venn diagram to show areas of overlap between and among elements. The Target diagram is commonly used to show the steps toward a goal.

Insert Clips

When you add WordArt, a line, a callout, or another AutoShape in an Excel worksheet, you add a graphic that is available through buttons or menu selections. You can also insert a *clip*—a drawing, photograph, or other media type, such as sound, animation, or movies.

In this skill, you perform a keyword search of Microsoft Office clips, which include drawings—sometimes referred to as *clip art*—as well as photographs and sound files. You select an image among the search results, and insert the image in the Bids worksheet of the *Lease Options* workbook (see Figure 6.54). You also change the size and position of the inserted image.

Figure 6.54

To Insert Clip Art

1 **Open the *Lease Options* file, if necessary, and click cell A3.**
You specified the location for inserting clip art. The upper-left corner of the current cell becomes the upper-left corner of inserted clip art.

2 **Click the Insert Clip Art button on the Drawing toolbar.**

3 **If the Add Clips to Organizer dialog box displays, click the Later button to close it.**
The Insert Clip Art task pane displays at the right side of the screen.

4 **Type money in the Search text box, as shown in Figure 6.55.**

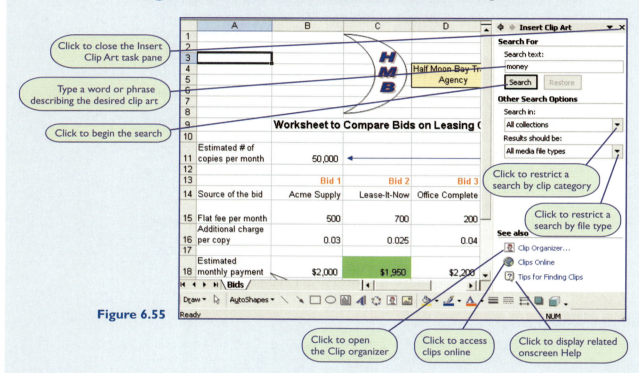

Figure 6.55

5 **Click the Search button in the Insert Clip Art task pane.**
Several thumbnails of money-related clips display in the Insert Clip Art task pane. A *thumbnail* is a miniature representation of an image.

6 **Position the pointer in the middle of the first picture.**
A ScreenTip displays that includes related keywords, the height and width of the clip in pixels, the file size, and the file type.

7 **Click the down arrow at the right side of the first clip.**
A drop-down menu displays (see Figure 6.56).

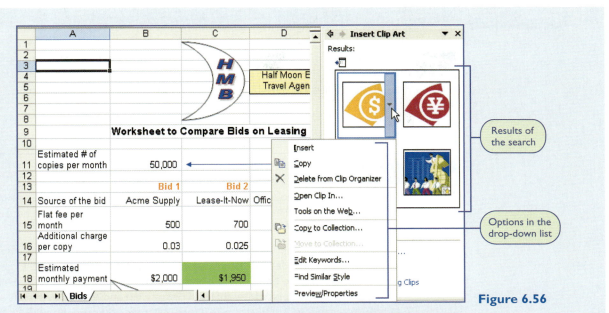

Figure 6.56

8 **Click Insert in the drop-down list; then close the Picture toolbar and the Insert Clip Art task pane.**

Excel inserts the selected image. The upper-left corner of the image is in cell A3, and sizing handles display at the corners and midpoints. Now reduce the size of the image and reposition it.

9 **Press and hold down** Ctrl **and** Shift **, and drag the lower-right sizing handle diagonally toward the center of the image.**

The image is reduced in size, but its center does not move.

10 **Adjust the image in column A to the approximate size and location shown in Figure 6.57, and deselect it.**

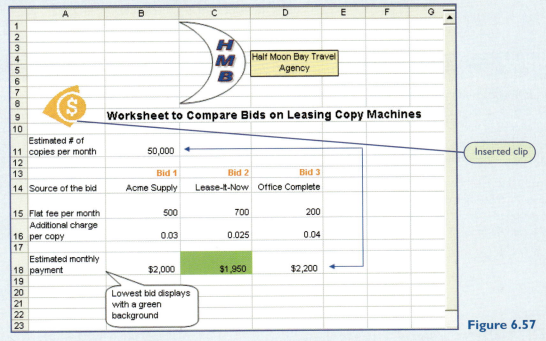

Figure 6.57

continues ▶

To Insert Clip Art (continued)

 Save your changes to the *Lease Options* workbook, and close the workbook.

Continue with Skill Drill and Challenge exercises, start another skill set, or exit Excel.

 ### *In Depth:*
Graphics File Types Accepted by Excel

You are not limited to using media files provided by Microsoft. Other sources of files include clip art that you can purchase, and images scanned from hardcopy or copied from the Web.

There are several graphics file types you can insert directly into a worksheet. These file types include: Enhanced Metafile (.emf), Joint Photographic Experts Group (.jpg), Portable Network Graphics (.png), Microsoft Windows Bitmap (.bmp, .rle, .dib), Graphics Interchange Format (.gif) and Windows Metafile (.wmf). You can also install graphics filters to insert other graphics file formats. The onscreen Help topic *Graphics file types Excel can use* provides a complete list.

Inserting a Graphics File
To insert a graphics file, click Insert in the menu bar, point to Picture, and select From File. An Insert Picture dialog box that is similar in layout to the Open dialog box opens. Display the folder containing the file in the Look in text box; then select the file you want, and click Insert. Move and size the inserted object as desired.

---

*For immediate reinforcement, work Skill Drills 5 and 6
and Challenges 1, 3, and 4.*

Summary

In this skill set, you learned the tasks essential to creating, editing, saving, and printing embedded charts. You used the Chart Wizard to create embedded pie, column, line, and combination charts. You also modified some of the individual elements in a chart: the number format of Y-axis values, font style and size in the chart title, fill effect applied to the plot area, color assigned to a data series, the number of data series, and the order of data series.

In the second section of the skill set, you applied a variety of special effects to a worksheet. As an alternative to entering text in cells, you learned how to create WordArt, callouts, and text boxes. You grouped objects that you wanted to manipulate as a unit. You also focused attention on specific areas of the worksheet using lines and arrows, and added clip art.

Skill Drill

Skill Drill exercises *reinforce* project skills. Each skill reinforced is the same, or nearly the same, as a skill presented in the skill set. Detailed instructions are provided in a step-by-step format.

Before beginning your Excel Core Skill Set 6 Skill Drill exercises, complete the following steps:

1. Open the file named *MEC-S604*, and immediately save it as **MEC-S6drill**.

    The workbook contains seven sheets: an overview and six exercise sheets labeled SD1 through SD6.

2. Click the Overview sheet to view the organization and content of the Skill Drill workbook for Excel Core Skill Set 6.

Each exercise is independent of the others, so you may complete the exercises in any order. Be sure to save the workbook after completing each exercise. If you need a paper copy of one or more completed exercises, enter your name, centered in a header, before printing. Print options have already been set to print compressed to one page and to display the filename, sheet name, and current date in a footer.

Be sure to save your changes and close the workbook if you need more than one work session to complete the desired exercises. Continue working on *MEC-S6drill* instead of starting over in the original *MEC-S604* file.

1. Create an Embedded 3-D Pie Chart

You have used Excel to create a number of pie charts in the past. For the upcoming Community Volunteer Corps event, however, you want to present data in a three-dimensional pie chart.

To create an embedded 3-D pie chart, follow these steps:

1. Open the *MEC-S6drill* workbook, if necessary, and select the SD1 worksheet.

    You plan to create a pie chart based on the labels and data shown in light yellow. (The label range A6:A9 and the data range F6:F9 are nonadjacent.)

2. Select the range A6:A9.

3. Press and hold down Ctrl.

4. Select the range F6:F9 and release Ctrl.

5. Click the Chart Wizard button to display the Chart Type dialog box.

6. Select Pie as the chart type, and select *Pie with a 3-D Visual Effect* as the chart sub-type.

7. Click Next to display the Chart Source Data dialog box, and ensure that the series is in Columns.

8. Click Next to display the Chart Options dialog box.

9. Type **Allocation of 11,340 Volunteer Hours** in the Chart title text box on the Titles tab.

10. Deselect Show legend on the Legend tab, and select the Category name and Percentage options on the Data Labels tab.

11. Click Finish to accept the default embedded chart and exit Chart Wizard.

12. Move the chart below the data, size as appropriate, and click outside the chart to deselect it.

13. Save your changes to the *MEC-S6drill* workbook.

2. Create an Embedded Stacked Column Chart

You are looking for a variety of ways to present data on volunteer hours at the upcoming Community Volunteer Corps event. As you look through the sub-types of a column chart, you discover that a stacked column chart compares the contribution of each value to a total across all categories. You decide to illustrate the proportion of volunteer hours associated with each volunteer organization in a stacked-column format.

To create a stacked column chart, follow these steps:

1. Open the *MEC-S6drill* workbook, if necessary, and select the SD2 worksheet.

   You plan to create a stacked column chart based on the labels and data shown in light yellow (the range A6:E9).

2. Select the range A6:E9, and click the Chart Wizard button.

3. In the Chart Type dialog box, select Column as the chart type, and select Stacked Column as the sub-type. Click Next.

4. In the Chart Source Data dialog box, make sure that Series is in Rows. Click Next.

5. In the Chart Options dialog box, specify the following titles, and then click Finish: **Community Volunteer Corps** (chart title), **Year Just Ended** (X-axis title), and **Volunteer Hours** (Y-axis title).

6. Click Finish to accept the default embedded chart, and exit Chart Wizard.

7. Move the chart below the data, size as appropriate, and deselect the chart.

8. Save your changes to the *MEC-S6drill* workbook.

3. Change Chart Type, Font Style, and Number Format

As you explore creating a variety of charts for presenting volunteer data, you decide to create a line chart by modifying the chart type of an existing column chart. You also decide to change the font style and size in the title of a chart and display commas as the thousands separator in numbers on the Y-axis scale of the chart.

To change the chart type, font style, and number format, follow these steps:

1. Open the *MEC-S6drill* workbook, if necessary, and select the SD3 worksheet.

   The sheet contains a column chart based on data in the range A6:E9.

2. Right-click in a blank area of the chart, and select Chart Type from the shortcut menu.

3. Select Line as the chart type, and select *Line with markers displayed at each data value* as the sub-type.

4. Click OK, and click outside the line chart to deselect it.

5. Click once within the chart title, and select (highlight) all the text in the title.

6. Click the Italic button in the Formatting toolbar.

7. Click the Font Size down arrow in the Formatting toolbar, and select 14 as the point size.

8. Position the mouse pointer on any number in the Y-axis scale to the left of the chart's plot area.

9. Right-click and select Format Axis on the shortcut menu.

10. Click the Number tab in the Format Axis dialog box, and click Number in the Category window.

11. Change the number of decimal places to zero, and click the <u>U</u>se *1000 Separator (,)* option.

12. Click OK to apply your changes and close the dialog box.

13. Deselect the chart, and save your changes to the *MEC-S6drill* workbook.

4. Add a Data Series and Reorder Data Series

You charted two data series in a column chart. Now, you want to add a third series (Literacy League) and change the position of the first series (Habitat for Humanity).

To add a data series and reorder the data series, follow these steps:

1. Open the *MEC-S6drill* workbook, if necessary, and select the SD4 worksheet.

2. Select the *Literacy League* label and data in the range A8:E8.

3. Click the border of the selected cells, drag them within the chart, release the mouse button, and deselect the chart.

   Excel adds the Literacy League data to the chart and updates the legend to include a third data series.

4. Right-click any column in the chart, choose F<u>o</u>rmat Data Series, and select the Series Order tab.

5. Make sure that Habitat for Humanity is the selected series in the <u>S</u>eries order list, and click the Move <u>D</u>own button twice.

   The sample chart in the Format Data Series dialog box shows that the Habitat for Humanity data series is now the third data series instead of the first data series.

6. Click OK, deselect the chart, and save your changes to the *MEC-S6drill* workbook.

5. Create a Banner

You decide to put the company name *Glenn Lakes Blue Ribbon Lawn Care* on a worksheet. To convey the name graphically, you decide to use one of the ribbons on the A<u>u</u>toShapes menu, type the name in the ribbon, and add a blue fill color to the ribbon. Also, you improve readability by making the text in the ribbon bold and centering it horizontally and vertically.

To add a banner to a worksheet, follow these steps:

1. Open the *MEC-S6drill* workbook, if necessary, and select the SD5 sheet.

2. Display the Drawing toolbar, if necessary; then select the Curved Up Ribbon style from the A<u>u</u>toShapes, <u>S</u>tars and Banners menu.

3. Click cell A3, and drag the lower-right sizing handle to cell C7.

4. Right-click the ribbon object and select Add Te<u>x</u>t.

5. Click the Bold button and type `Glenn Lakes Blue Ribbon Lawn Care`.

6. Center the text vertically and horizontally using the Alignment tab in the Format AutoShape dialog box.

   To access the Format AutoShape dialog box containing the Alignment tab, you must first click the border around the object. A shadow border made up of dots appears when the object is correctly selected.

7. While the ribbon object is selected, turn on a sky blue fill color.

8. Resize as necessary to display text on two lines within the ribbon, deselect the object, and save your changes to the *MEC-S6drill* workbook.

6. Create WordArt and a Text Box

You need a title on a worksheet indicating what its purpose is, and you decide to use WordArt. The worksheet's title will be *Loan Payment Analysis*, typed into one of the colorful WordArt styles and rotated slightly to give it an upward slant from left to right. You also decide to add a text box to the worksheet reminding users that they should only change the loan information in blue cells.

To add WordArt and a text box to a worksheet, follow these steps:

1. Open the *MEC-S6drill* workbook, if necessary, and select the SD6 sheet.
2. Select the Insert WordArt button on the Drawing toolbar.
3. Select the WordArt style in the fourth column, third row, and click OK.
4. Type **Loan Payment Analysis** in the Edit WordArt Text dialog box, and click OK.
5. Move, size, and rotate the WordArt so that it displays above the data in row 10, from column A through column D, with its right end higher than the left.

   You can drag the green circle above the WordArt object, and rotate the right end up about two rows higher than the left end.
6. Make any final adjustments to size and position, and deselect the object.
7. Select the Text Box button on the Drawing toolbar.
8. Drag open the text box over cells F12 to H14.

   Remember, if you click the location where you want to position the text box and then drag it open, the box appears without a border. Dragging it open immediately creates an object with a border.
9. Click the text area and type **To use the model, change data only in the blue cells.**
10. Make final adjustments as necessary to the position and size of the text box so that the text just fits on two lines within the box.
11. Save your changes to the *MEC-S6drill* workbook.

Challenge

Challenge exercises expand on or are somewhat related to skills presented in the skill set. Each exercise provides a brief narrative introduction, followed by instructions in a numbered-step format that are not as detailed as those in the Skill Drill section.

Before beginning your Excel Core Skill Set 6 Challenge exercises, complete the following steps:

1. Open the file named *MEC-S605*, and immediately save it as **MEC-S6challenge**.

   The workbook contains five sheets: an overview and four exercise sheets labeled CH1 through CH4.
2. Click the Overview sheet to view the organization and content of the Challenge workbook for Excel Core Skill Set 6.

Each exercise is independent of the others, so you may complete the exercises in any order. Be sure to save the workbook after completing each exercise. If you need a paper copy of one or more completed exercises, enter your name, centered in a header, before printing. Print options have already been set to print compressed to one page. Settings to display the filename, sheet name, and current date in a footer have been set in all worksheets.

Be sure to save your changes and close the workbook if you need more than one work session to complete the desired exercises. Continue working on *MEC-S6challenge* instead of starting over in the original *MEC-S605* file.

1. Explode (Cut) a Pie Slice and Add Clip Art

You already created a suitable pie chart that shows the allocation of hours among the three volunteer groups comprising the Community Volunteer Corps. Now, you want to modify the chart to draw attention to the volunteer activity with the least number of hours (Literacy League). You can do this by pulling that pie slice away from the rest of the pie. You also decide to add clip art showing a clock to the worksheet that summarizes volunteer hours.

To explode (pull out) a piece of a pie, and add clip art, follow these steps:

1. Open the *MEC-S6challenge* workbook, if necessary, and select the CH1 worksheet.
2. Select only the pie slice representing the Literacy League.

 If you have problems...
Clicking a pie slice the first time selects the entire pie; clicking it again enables you to select the pie slice.

Sizing handles appear at only the corners and midpoints of the Literacy League pie slice.

3. Drag the Literacy League pie slice out a short distance from the rest of the pie.
4. If necessary, increase the size of the chart to restore the display of all labels; then click outside the chart to deselect it.
5. Display the Insert Clip Art task pane.
6. Search for clips that include a clock.
7. Insert the clock clip art of your choice; then move and size the object so that it is centered within the range D3:E6.
8. Close the Insert Clip Art task pane, and save your changes to the *MEC-S6challenge* workbook.

2. Move a Legend, Enlarge a Plot Area, and Change Scale Increment

Long text descriptions may result in a legend that is quite large in comparison with the plot area of its associated chart. This effect appears in many of the charts based on volunteer data. You decide to move the legend to the bottom of the chart, reduce the font size in the legend, and enlarge the plot area.

You know that Excel automatically assigns an increment to the numbers displayed on the Y-axis scale. However, you want to change the Y-axis scale to display in increments of 300 (0, 300, 600, and so on) instead of increments of 500 (0, 500, 1,000, and so on).

To reposition a legend, enlarge a plot area, and change scale increment, follow these steps:

1. Open the *MEC-S6challenge* workbook, if necessary, and select the CH2 worksheet.
2. Double-click a blank area within the legend, click the Placement tab on the Format Legend dialog box, and click <u>B</u>ottom.

3. Click the Font tab on the Format Legend dialog box, and select the smallest point size; then close the dialog box, accepting your new settings.

4. Click the gray background within the plot area, and increase the width and height of the plot area as much as possible to fit within the outside chart border. (Be sure that the changes in height are proportional to the changes in width.)

5. Double-click any number on the Y-axis scale, and click the Scale tab on the Format Axis dialog box.

6. Change the Major Unit to **300** instead of *500;* then close the dialog box, accepting your new setting.

7. Increase the width of the chart in proportion to its height until sufficient spacing exists between scale increments; then deselect the chart, and save your changes to the *MEC-S6challenge* workbook.

3. Add Text to a Shape and Draw an Oval Shape

You added a 16-point star to the worksheet showing budgeted revenues for the year 2004. Now you decide to enlarge the blank space in the center of the star and add text stating that the year 2004 is expected to be the best year yet. You also want to emphasize the Total Revenue in cell F17 by drawing a circle around it. The shape you draw covers the value, so you need to select the object and turn off the fill color.

To add text to a star shape, and draw an oval, follow these steps:

1. Open the *MEC-S6challenge* workbook, if necessary, and select the CH3 sheet.

2. Click the star until you see the yellow adjustment handle.

3. Drag the yellow handle outward to enlarge the white space in the center. (The space should hold the words *Best Year Yet!* one word to a line.)

4. Center the phrase *Best Year Yet!* within the star.

5. Resize and reposition the object as desired.

6. Select the Oval button on the Drawing toolbar, and drag it over cell F17.

   The shape covers the value in cell F17 so you can't see it. This happens because the fill color is white.

7. Change the fill color to No Fill.

8. Change the size and position of the oval as necessary so that it surrounds the value 1,949,100 in cell F17.

9. Save your changes to the *MEC-S6challenge* workbook.

4. Ungroup, Edit, and Regroup Objects

You created an eye-catching grouped object that includes clip art and a callout. You realize that some of the text in the callout does not display, and that an uppercase letter in the callout should be made lowercase. To make the changes, ungroup the objects, select only the callout, edit and resize as necessary, and then regroup the objects.

To ungroup, edit, and regroup objects, follow these steps:

1. Open the *MEC-S6challenge* workbook, if necessary, and select the CH4 sheet.

2. Access onscreen Help; then search for and read information about ungrouping and regrouping objects.

3. Exit onscreen Help and ungroup the cloud callout and clip art.

4. Increase the size of only the cloud callout, so that all text displays.

5. Change the uppercase C in *Can't* to a lowercase c.

6. Regroup the two objects.

7. Save your changes to the *MEC-S6challenge* workbook.

Workgroup Collaboration

C H A P T E R 7

This skill set includes

Convert worksheets into Web pages	
Create hyperlinks	▌ Create a hyperlink between worksheets in an Excel workbook
	▌ Create a hyperlink between a Word document and an Excel worksheet
View and edit comments	▌ Add, edit, and delete comments attached to worksheet cells
	▌ Work with discussion comments

Skill Set Overview

In this skill set, you explore a variety of features that support working with multiple applications and collaborating with others on end products. You begin by saving Excel data as a Web page, and using your browser software to preview how the data will look on a Web site. Refer to Chapter 8 (Excel Expert Skill Set 1) Skill 1.3, "Publish Worksheets and Workbooks to the Web," for more in-depth coverage.

You also learn to create links among worksheets, and between a worksheet and another application. Remaining experiences focus on viewing and editing comments—those that you attach to worksheet cells, and discussion comments created by multiple users.

Skill 7.1: Convert Worksheets into Web Pages

You can save a workbook, worksheet, range of cells, or other worksheet item, such as an embedded chart, as a Web page. You can then make the saved element available for others to use on an HTTP site, an FTP site, a Web server, or a network server.

When you publish a workbook, worksheet, or portion of a worksheet, you can do so with or without interactivity. When you **publish with interactivity**, users can modify as well as view the content and formatting of the element from within a Web browser. They can also enter, analyze, sort, and filter data on the Web page. When you **publish without interactivity**, users can view only the content and formatting of the published element from within a Web browser.

Before you publish a page for others to use on the Web, you should save it as a Web page to a local system and view it in a Web browser. When you save an entire workbook as a Web page without interactivity, you can preview the page without publishing by selecting the Web Page Preview option on the File menu.

In the following steps, you save a worksheet with chart as a Web page without interactivity and preview the saved Web page. You save the Web page on your own computer system (sometimes referred to as a local system). Saving to a local system enables you to use a browser, such as Netscape Navigator or Microsoft Internet Explorer, to view the Web page before publishing it to a Web site.

To Save a Workbook as a Web Page and Preview in a Browser

1 **Open the *MEC-S701* file, and save it as** Reunion on Web.
The single worksheet in the workbook includes budget data for a reunion and a related pie chart.

2 **Click File in the menu bar.**
Two options relate to saving as a Web page (see Figure 7.1).

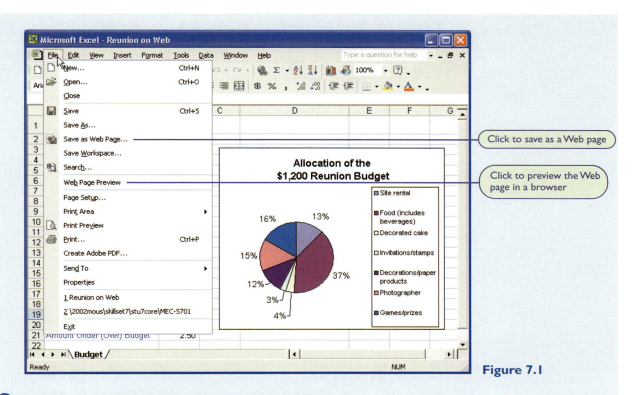

Figure 7.1

③ Click Save as Web Page on the list of File options.
The Save As dialog box opens. It includes Web-related options and settings (see Figure 7.2).

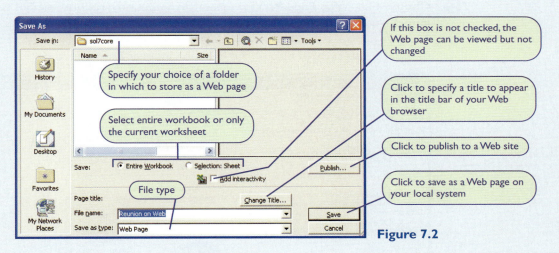

Figure 7.2

④ Display the Save in drop-down list, and specify the folder where you want to store the current worksheet as a Web page.
Unless you prefer another location, store the page in the same folder as the other files you have been saving.

⑤ Click the Change Title button in the Save As dialog box.
The Set Page Title dialog box opens.

⑥ In the Page title text box, type `Last revised by your name xx/xx/xx`**, making the substitutions shown in Figure 7.3.**

continues ▶

To Save a Workbook as a Web Page and Preview in a Browser (continued)

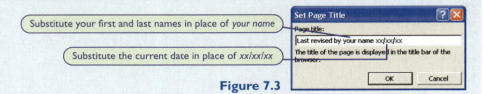

Substitute your first and last names in place of *your name*

Substitute the current date in place of *xx/xx/xx*

Figure 7.3

7 **Click the OK button.**

The Set Page Title dialog box closes. The title you specified displays in the Page title area near the bottom of the Save As dialog box (see Figure 7.4). The Web page title you specified is not entered in the Budget worksheet.

Title for the Web page

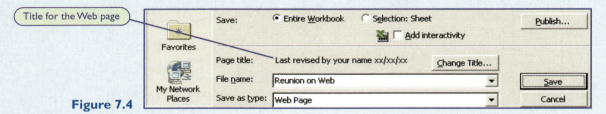

Figure 7.4

8 **Click the Save button in the lower-right corner of the Save As dialog box.**

Excel saves the workbook as a Web page. If you do not have access to a Web browser, close the *Reunion on Web* file and skip the remaining steps.

9 **Choose File, Web Page Preview; then complete any actions needed to launch your Web browser if it doesn't launch automatically.**

The page displays as it will appear when published to a Web site. Figure 7.5 shows the Budget sheet viewed through the Microsoft Internet Explorer browser.

Web page title

Name of browser

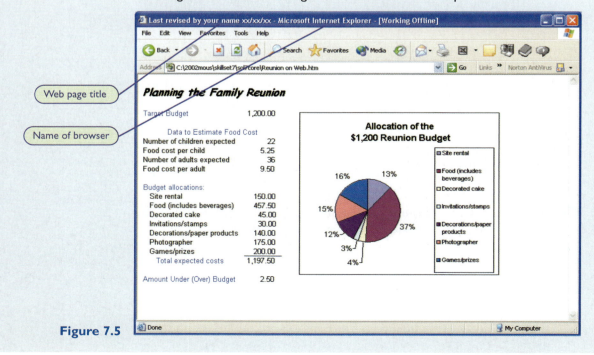

Figure 7.5

Alternate Way:
Previewing a Web Page
You can also use your browser's File, Open feature to see how the worksheet data and chart would display on a Web page.

10 **Close your browser and close the *Reunion on Web* file.**
You can continue with the next skill, or exit Excel.

In Depth:
Using the Publish as Web Page Dialog Box
If you have already selected the element you want to publish, such as a chart, or you want to publish an entire workbook without interactivity, you can complete a save as Web page operation by pressing the Save button (refer to Figure 7.2). If you did not already select the element you want to publish, or you want to publish an entire workbook with interactivity, click the Publish button (refer to Figure 7.2). This action opens the Publish as Web Page dialog box (see Figure 7.6).

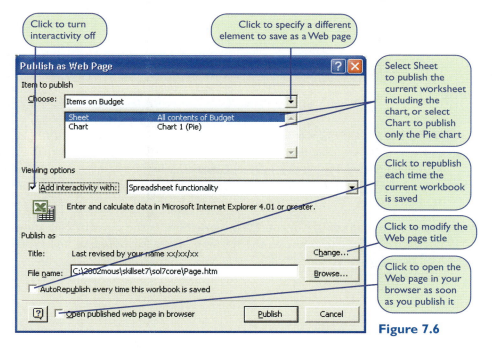

Figure 7.6

After you select the desired settings in the Publish as Web Page dialog box, you can press the Publish button in that dialog box to complete the process of saving as a Web page. Refer to Chapter 8 (Excel Expert Skill Set 1) Skill 1.3, "Publish Worksheets and Workbooks to the Web," for more in-depth coverage.

For immediate reinforcement, work Challenge 1.

Skill 7.2: **Create Hyperlinks**

While working with multiple applications and collaborating with others on end products, you are likely to encounter a *hyperlink*—a link from a document that you can click to jump to another location, open another file, or start a process—such as send an e-mail or transfer a file. Hyperlinks in Web pages enable you to link to other locations in the current Web site and to other Web sites. You can create your own hyperlinks in Microsoft Office applications that refer to other application files, other locations within the current file, or Internet links.

In this skill area, you create and use two hyperlinks—a link to another worksheet in the current Excel workbook, and a link from a Word document to an Excel worksheet.

Create a Hyperlink Between Worksheets in an Excel Workbook

A hyperlink can be text, which generally displays blue and underlined, or a picture. When you position the pointer on a hyperlink, the pointer changes to a hand, which indicates that the text or picture is an item you can click.

You can set up a hyperlink to provide a quick means to move from one location to another by clicking the link. If the hyperlink is set up in an Excel worksheet, the connection can be to a position within the same worksheet, to another worksheet in the same workbook, to another workbook, to another application, or to a place within a Web site.

In the following steps, you open a workbook containing a preliminary design for a company's annual report. You set up hyperlinks between two worksheets.

To Create a Hyperlink Between Worksheets

1 **Open the *MEC-S702* workbook, and save it as** XYZ Annual Report.
The workbook contains the beginnings of a layout for an annual report. The first worksheet named TOC is the Table of Contents. Now create a hyperlink to jump to the start of the Balance Sheet and another link to jump back to the top of the TOC worksheet.

2 **Make sure that cell A1 in the TOC worksheet is the current cell; then click within the name box at the left end of the formula bar, and type** TOC **(see Figure 7.7).**

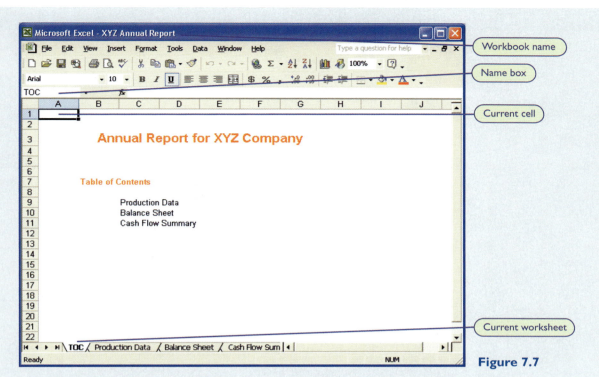

Workbook name

Name box

Current cell

Current worksheet

Figure 7.7

Although you can jump to specific cells, it is easier and less confusing to jump to named cells.

3 **Press** ⏎Enter.
You can now refer to cell A1 by its name *TOC*.

4 **Click cell A3 in the Balance Sheet worksheet; then click within the Name box, type** BalSheet, **and press** ⏎Enter.

5 **Save your changes to the** *XYZ Annual Report* **workbook.**

6 **Click cell C10 in the TOC worksheet, and select Insert, Hyperlink.**
The Insert Hyperlink dialog box opens.

7 **In the Link to area—a column along the left side of the dialog box—click Place in This Document.**
An outline of cell references and defined names displays in the Insert Hyperlink dialog box (see Figure 7.8).

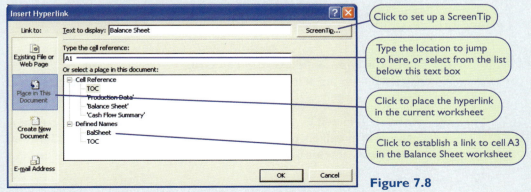

Click to set up a ScreenTip

Type the location to jump to here, or select from the list below this text box

Click to place the hyperlink in the current worksheet

Click to establish a link to cell A3 in the Balance Sheet worksheet

Figure 7.8

continues ▶

To Create a Hyperlink Between Worksheets (continued)

8   Click **BalSheet**, the first name listed under **Defined Names**.

 If you have problems...
If you do not see BalSheet, you may need to expand the Defined Names outline by clicking the plus (+) outline symbol next to it.

9   Click the **ScreenTip** button in the upper-right corner of the dialog box, and type `Click to view the Balance Sheet` in the Screen**Tip** text box (see **Figure 7.9**).

Figure 7.9

10   Click **OK** to close the **Set Hyperlink ScreenTip** dialog box, and then click **OK** to close the **Insert Hyperlink** dialog box.
Balance Sheet in cell C10 displays blue and underlined, indicating it is a hyperlink.

11   Position the pointer on the blue underlined text in cell **C10**.
The pointer changes to a hand, and the ScreenTip *Click to view the Balance Sheet* displays (see Figure 7.10).

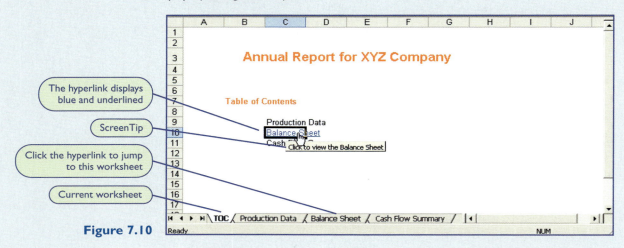

Figure 7.10

12   Click the hyperlinked text in cell **C10**.
Excel jumps to the destination for the hyperlink, cell A3 in the Balance Sheet worksheet.

13   Enter `TOC` in cell **E1** in the **Balance Sheet** worksheet; then create a hyperlink in cell **E1** to the cell named **TOC** in the **Table of Contents** worksheet. (Include the **ScreenTip** `Click to view the Table of Contents`.)
The steps to complete this step are similar to those described in steps 6 through 10.

14 **Click the new hyperlink.**
If the TOC hyperlink is set up properly, cell A1 in the TOC worksheet becomes the active cell.

15 **Save your changes to the *XYZ Annual Report* workbook, and close the workbook.**
Continue with the next skill, or exit Excel.

In Depth:

Editing a Hyperlink
To edit a hyperlink, right-click the cell containing the hyperlink, and select Edit Hyperlink on the shortcut menu. Make changes as necessary in the Edit Hyperlink dialog box, and click OK.

Deactivating or Deleting Hyperlink
To deactivate a hyperlink, right-click the cell containing the hyperlink and select Remove Hyperlink on the shortcut menu. If you deactivate a hyperlink in error, you can immediately choose Edit, Undo Remove Hyperlink to restore the link.

To delete a hyperlink and the associated text or graphic, right-click the cell containing the hyperlink, and select Clear Contents on the shortcut menu.

Copying or Moving a Hyperlink
Follow a four-step process to copy a hyperlink: right-click the hyperlink, click Copy on the shortcut menu, right-click the destination cell for the copied hyperlink, and click Paste on the shortcut menu. Follow a similar process to move a hyperlink, except click Cut instead of Copy in the second step.

Create a Hyperlink Between a Word Document and an Excel Worksheet

You can easily set up hyperlinks between Microsoft Office applications. For example, you can create a hyperlink in an Excel worksheet that jumps to a specific location in a Word document. You can also create a hyperlink in a Word document that jumps to an Excel worksheet.

Assume you are writing a sales report in Microsoft Word, and you want its readers to be able to quickly see data in an Excel worksheet that supports statements made in the report. If the report is a formal one, to be distributed widely throughout the organization, you would probably copy or link the worksheet data to the Word document. Then, its readers could view the worksheet data as they read the report online or in hardcopy format. However, if the report is not yet final, or is intended strictly for internal use among a few readers, you might prefer to shorten the word-processed report by including hyperlinks to worksheet data instead of the actual worksheet data. If you choose the hyperlink approach, the workbook referenced in the hyperlink must continue to be stored in the location captured in the hyperlink.

In the following steps, you open a Word document containing the initial lines in a sales report and create a hyperlink in that report to supporting data stored in an Excel workbook. You then test the hyperlink.

To Create a Hyperlink Between a Word Document and an Excel Worksheet

① **Launch Microsoft Word; then open the Word document *MEC-S703* and save it as** `wordlink`.

② **Select the phrase *(Click to view the Excel data)* in the *wordlink* document.**

③ **Choose Insert, Hyperlink.**

④ **In the *Link to* area on the left side of the dialog box, click Existing File or Web Page.**

⑤ **Select the Excel workbook *MEC-S704* from the location in which you are storing the student files that accompany this text.**

⑥ **Click the ScreenTip button, type** `Click to view the associated Excel file`, **and click OK.**

⑦ **Click OK to close the Insert Hyperlink dialog box.**
The hyperlinked text *(Click to view the Excel data)* displays blue and underlined. Now test the hyperlink.

⑧ **Position the pointer on the hyperlink.**
The ScreenTip *Click to view the associated Excel file* displays (see Figure 7.11). You also see the message *CTRL + click to follow link* in bold.

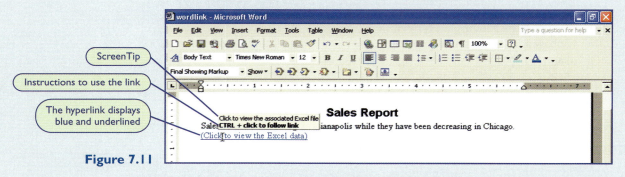

ScreenTip

Instructions to use the link

The hyperlink displays blue and underlined

Figure 7.11

⑨ **Press and hold** ⟨Ctrl⟩ **and click the hyperlink in the Word document.**
The Data worksheet displays (see Figure 7.12). When Excel is accessed through a hyperlink, the Web toolbar displays automatically.

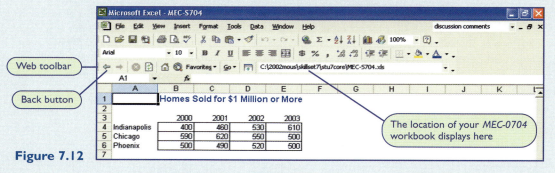

Web toolbar

Back button

The location of your *MEC-0704* workbook displays here

Figure 7.12

⑩ **Click the Back button in the Web toolbar.**
The word-processed report displays.

⑪ **Save and close the *wordlink* document, and exit Word.**
The Excel workbook displays.

⓬ **Choose View, position the pointer on Toolbars, and click Web.**
You closed the Web toolbar.

⓭ **Close the *MEC-S704* workbook without saving it.**
Continue with the next skill, or exit Excel.

In Depth:

Setting a Hyperlink to Excel Data
When you set a hyperlink to an Excel worksheet from another Office
application, the link accesses the first worksheet of the workbook. Make sure
that the Excel data you want to display is in the first worksheet or store it in its
own workbook.

Changing the Appearance of Hyperlinks
Hyperlinks initially display blue and underlined, which tends to be a standard for
links on Web sites, links within e-mail, and so forth. However, the appearance of
a hyperlink you create is entirely under your control, and you can apply any
formatting—font, color, size, shading, and so on—to it. To change the formatting
of a hyperlink, right-click it, and choose Format Cells from the shortcut menu.
Make your desired selections from the Format Cells dialog box, and click OK.

---

*For immediate reinforcement, work Skill Drills 1 through 3
and Challenges 2 through 4.*

Skill 7.3: **View and Edit Comments**

Comments enable you to attach information to a worksheet that you do not want to type in a
cell. A *comment* is an annotation attached to a cell that displays within a box whenever the
mouse pointer rests on the cell. You can attach comments for your own use, or insert comments to be read by others.

You can also create, edit, and delete discussion comments associated with a workbook that is
stored on a discussion server, and you can reply to the discussion comments written by others.
These features support a dynamic collaborative process that promotes working smarter by
sharing ideas and information.

Add, Edit, and Delete Comments Attached to Worksheet Cells

You can easily attach a comment to any cell in an Excel worksheet. If a comment has been attached, you see the *comment indicator*—a small red triangle—in the cell's upper-right corner.
Use the comment feature when you want supplementary information available, but not visible
all the time.

When you attach or edit a comment, you can alter the size of the comment box by dragging
the handles on its sides and corners. You can also move or delete a comment, change its text
font or color, and hide or display comments and their indicators. The Page Setup dialog box includes options to print comments below the worksheet or where they are displayed on the
worksheet.

In the following steps, you set a View option to display only comment indicators. You then create and view three comments, one for each vendor providing a bid for leasing copy machines.

To Attach Comments to a Cell

1 **Open the *MEC-S705* workbook, and save it as** Comments.

2 **Choose Tools, Options.**
The Options dialog box opens.

3 **Select the View tab.**
The View tab includes four sections: Show, Comments, Objects, and Window options.

4 **Make sure that *Comment indicator only* is selected in the Comments section, and click OK.**

5 **Click cell B9.**
The cell containing *Acme Supply* is selected. Acme is the provider of the first bid.

6 **Select Insert, Comment.**
Excel displays a comment box. An arrow extends from the upper-left corner of the box to the comment indicator in cell B9.

7 **Delete existing text in the box, if any, and type the following comment:**
Bid valid for 60 days. Guaranteed service within 24 hours.

8 **Click outside the box to deselect it; then position the mouse pointer on cell B9.**
The newly created comment displays (see Figure 7.13).

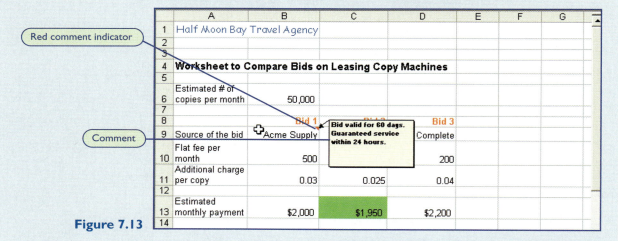

Figure 7.13

9 **Click cell C9, and repeat the previous steps to create the following comment:**
Started business 6 months ago. Bid valid for 30 days. Same-day service if call before noon.

10 **Click cell D9, and repeat the previous steps to create the following comment. (If necessary, drag a sizing handle to enlarge the box.)**
Bid valid for 30 days. Promises service within 4 hours but has not been reliable in the past.

11 **Click outside the comment box, and select View, Comments.**
The three comments and the Reviewing toolbar display (see Figure 7.14).

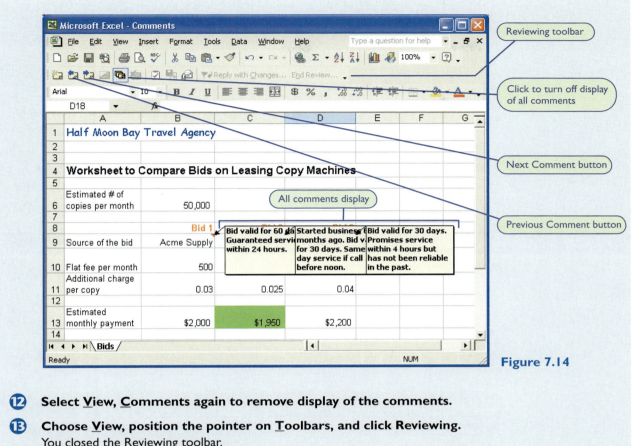

Figure 7.14

⑫   **Select View, Comments again to remove display of the comments.**

⑬   **Choose View, position the pointer on Toolbars, and click Reviewing.**
You closed the Reviewing toolbar.

⑭   **Save your changes to the *Comments* workbook, and close the workbook.**
Continue with the next skill, or exit Excel.

In Depth:

Editing and Deleting Comments
Right-clicking a cell with an attached comment displays a shortcut menu. Select Edit Comment to revise the text in a comment. Select Delete Comment to remove the comment entirely.

If you want to remove all comments, select Go To on the Edit menu, click the Special button, click Comments, and click OK. This highlights all cells with attached comments. Then select Edit, Clear, Comments.

Printing Comments
You can apply settings to print comments by selecting File, Page Setup and accessing the Sheet tab. Select the Comments drop-down list, and select *At end of sheet* or *As displayed on sheet*. Click OK.

Work with Discussion Comments

Microsoft Office also supports collaborative efforts through its discussion comments feature. A *discussion comment* is a remark associated with a Web page or Office application file that is stored on a discussion server. When you are a participant in a discussion, you can reply to comments made by others. You can also create, edit, and delete your own comments.

The comments are stored separately from the Web page or application document under discussion. Moving or renaming a document breaks the links between the document and the discussion comments.

To use discussion comments, you must have access to a discussion server and permission to participate in the discussion. A server administrator sets up a subscription process and sets permissions to read and create discussion comments. The server may be on the Internet or an organization's intranet.

The requirement to have an organization-specific discussion server limits the hands-on component for this topic. In the following steps, you turn on the Web Discussions toolbar and view related buttons and dialog boxes.

To Use Discussion Comments

1 **Launch Excel, if necessary.**

2 **Select Tools, Online Collaboration, Web Discussions.**
The Web Discussions toolbar displays at the bottom of the screen (see Figure 7.15). The callouts to buttons show the ScreenTips that display when you position the pointer on the toolbar buttons.

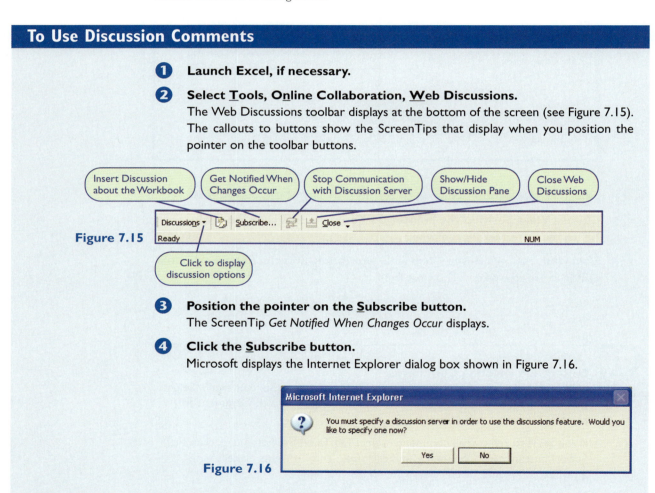

Figure 7.15

3 **Position the pointer on the Subscribe button.**
The ScreenTip *Get Notified When Changes Occur* displays.

4 **Click the Subscribe button.**
Microsoft displays the Internet Explorer dialog box shown in Figure 7.16.

Figure 7.16

5 **Click No to close the dialog box.**

6 **Click the small arrow at the right end of the Discussions button on the Web Discussions toolbar.**
A pop-up menu with five options displays. The options to refresh, filter, and print discussions are not available unless you are connected to a discussion.

7 **Choose Discussion Options from the pop-up menu.**
The Discussion Options dialog box displays (see Figure 7.17).

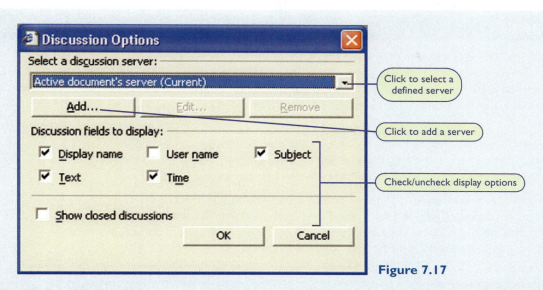

Figure 7.17

8 **Click the Add button.**

The Add or Edit Discussion Servers dialog box opens (see Figure 7.18).

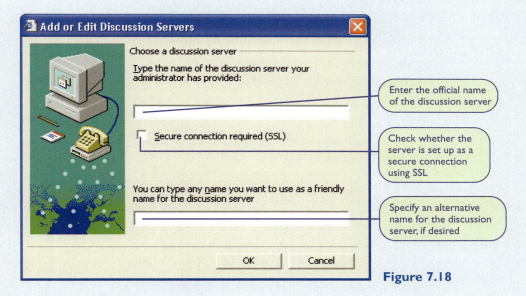

Figure 7.18

9 **Click Cancel to close the Add or Edit Discussion Servers dialog box, and click Cancel to close the Discussion Options dialog box.**

10 **Click the Close button on the Web Discussions toolbar.**

You can continue with end-of-skill-set exercises, start another skill set, or exit Excel.

For immediate reinforcement, work Skill Drills 4 and 5 and Challenge 5.

Summary

In this skill set, you explored a variety of features that support working with multiple applications and collaborating with others on end products. You first learned to save Excel data as a Web page, and you used a browser to view how the page will look on a Web site. Coverage on actually publishing worksheets and workbooks to the Web is provided in Chapter 8 (Excel Expert Skill Set 1).

You worked with hyperlinks, creating one hyperlink between two worksheets, and another hyperlink between a Word document and a worksheet. You also attached comments to three cells in a worksheet and learned to view all comments or only one comment at a time.

The skill set ended with an overview of discussion comments. The requirement to have an organization-specific discussion server limited the hands-on component for this topic. You viewed the toolbar and assorted screens associated with setting up and using a discussion server to add your own comments as well as reply to those of others.

Skill Drill

Skill Drill exercises *reinforce* project skills. Each skill reinforced is the same, or nearly the same, as a skill presented in the skill set. Detailed instructions are provided in a step-by-step format.

Before beginning your Excel Core Skill Set 7 Skill Drill exercises, complete the following steps:

1. Open the file named *MEC-S706*, and immediately save it as **MEC-S7drill**.

   The workbook contains five sheets: an overview and four exercise sheets labeled SD1 through SD4.

2. Click the Overview sheet to view the organization and content of the Skill Drill workbook for Excel Core Skill Set 7.

Each exercise is independent of the others, so you may complete the exercises in any order. Be sure to save the workbook after completing each exercise. If you need a paper copy of one or more completed exercises, enter your name, centered in a header, before printing. Print options have already been set to print compressed to one page and to display the filename, sheet name, and current date in a footer.

Be sure to save your changes and close the workbook if you need more than one work session to complete the desired exercises. Continue working on *MEC-S7drill* instead of starting over in the original *MEC-S706* file.

1. Create a Hyperlink

You work for Real Estate for Tomorrow, Inc., and you manage a listing of residential real estate for sale. You want to create a hyperlink within the worksheet to the mailing address for the firm. To create and test the hyperlink, follow these steps:

1. Open the *MEC-S7drill* workbook, if necessary, and select the SD1 worksheet.

2. Enter **Mailing Address** in cell A6.

3. Click cell M3, and click within the Name box at the left end of the formula bar; then type **address**, and press ⏎Enter.

4. Save the workbook; then click cell A6, and select Insert, Hyperlink.

5. In the Link to area—a column along the left side of the dialog box—click Place in This Document.

   An outline of cell references and defined names displays in the Insert Hyperlink dialog box.

6. Click *address* under Defined Names.

7. Click the ScreenTi<u>p</u> button in the upper-right corner of the dialog box, and enter `Click to view the firm's mailing address` in the ScreenT<u>i</u>p text box.

8. Click OK to close the Set Hyperlink ScreenTip dialog box, and then click OK to close the Insert Hyperlink dialog box.

   Mailing Address in cell A6 displays blue and underlined, indicating it is a hyperlink.

9. Position the pointer on the blue underlined text in cell A6.

   The pointer changes to a hand, and the ScreenTip *Click to view the firm's mailing address* displays.

10. Click the hyperlinked text in cell A6.

    Excel jumps to cell M3, the destination for the hyperlink.

11. Save your changes to the *MEC-S7drill* workbook.

2. Edit a Hyperlink

You work for Real Estate for Tomorrow, Inc., and you manage a listing of residential real estate for sale. You want to improve the display of data by changing the destination cell in a hyperlink. To edit a hyperlink, follow these steps:

1. Open the *MEC-S7drill* workbook, if necessary, and select the SD2 worksheet.

2. Click the *Contact us!* hyperlink in cell A5.

   Excel jumps to cell M3. Depending on your display settings, you may not be able to see the complete phone and fax numbers.

3. Right-click the *Contact us!* hyperlink in cell A5, and select Edit <u>H</u>yperlink from the short-cut menu.

4. In the *Type the c<u>e</u>ll reference* text box, change *M3* to **O3** (be sure to type the letter *O* instead of a zero).

5. Click OK, and then click the edited link in cell A5.

   Excel jumps to cell O3. You see the complete phone and fax numbers.

6. Save your changes to the *MEC-S7drill* workbook.

3. Remove a Hyperlink

You work for Real Estate for Tomorrow, Inc., and you manage a listing of residential real estate for sale. You want to delete data about real estate agents from the worksheet. To remove a hyperlink to agent names, and delete the associated data, follow these steps:

1. Open the *MEC-S7drill* workbook, if necessary, and select the SD3 worksheet.

2. Right-click the *Agent List* hyperlink in cell A5, and select <u>R</u>emove Hyperlink from the shortcut menu.

   The hyperlink is removed. The text *Agent List* no longer displays blue and underlined.

3. Delete the contents of cell A5 and the range M3:M7.

4. Save your changes to the *MEC-S7drill* workbook.

4. Add, Edit, and Delete Comments

You decide to modify documentation for a budget worksheet by adding, editing, and deleting comments. Follow these steps:

1. If necessary, open the *MEC-S7drill* workbook.

2. Select the SD4 worksheet.

3. Click cell B10 and select Insert, Comment.

4. Delete any existing text in the comment box, type **Net of seasonal discounts**, and click outside the comment box.

5. Right-click cell E12 and select Edit Comment from the shortcut menu.

6. Change *Christmas sales* to **Holiday sales** in the comment box, and click outside the box.

7. Right-click cell A16 and select Delete Comment from the shortcut menu.

8. Save your changes to the *MEC-S7drill* workbook.

5. Get Help on Discussion Comments

You work for Real Estate for Tomorrow, Inc., and you manage a listing of residential real estate for sale. You want to learn more about discussion comments. To view information about discussion comments in onscreen Help, follow these steps:

1. Launch Excel, if necessary, and enter **discussion comments** in the Ask a Question box.

2. Select the topic *About Web Discussions*, and read the related information.

3. Display the Contents, Answer Wizard, and Index tabs, if necessary.

4. Click the Index tab, type **discussion** in the Type keywords text box, and click the Search button.

   Excel finds and lists 17 topics related to discussions.

5. Read the topics of your choice.

   Make sure that you are connected to the Internet before you select any Help topic that begins with WEB.

6. Close the Microsoft Excel Help window.

Challenge

Challenge exercises expand on or are somewhat related to skills presented in the lessons. Each exercise provides a brief narrative introduction, followed by instructions in a numbered-step format that are not as detailed as those in the Skill Drill section.

Before beginning your Excel Core Skill Set 7 Challenge exercises, complete the following steps:

1. Open the file named *MEC-S707*, and immediately save it as **MEC-S7challenge**.

   The workbook contains six sheets: an overview and five exercise sheets labeled CH1 through CH5.

2. Click the Overview sheet to view the organization and content of the Challenge workbook for Excel Core Skill Set 7.

Each exercise is independent of the others, so you may complete the exercises in any order. Be sure to save the workbook after completing each exercise. If you need a paper copy of one or more completed exercises, enter your name, centered in a header, before printing. With the exception of the large worksheet CH2, print options have already been set to print compressed to one page. Settings to display the filename, sheet name, and current date in a footer have been set in all worksheets.

Be sure to save your changes and close the workbook if you need more than one work session to complete the desired exercises. Continue working on *MEC-S7challenge* instead of starting over in the original *MEC-S707* file.

1. Create a Chart Sheet and Save It as a Web Page

You are developing a multiple-sheet workbook to track real estate listings and sales. You want to present summary data in chart form on your company's intranet. Before you make the chart available for general viewing, save it to your own computer system for viewing with a Web browser. You can edit it later, as necessary, and then publish it to the intranet.

To create and save the chart, follow these steps:

1. Open your *MEC-S7challenge* workbook, if necessary, and select the CH1 worksheet.
2. Select the nonadjacent ranges A6:E6 and A11:E11.
3. Activate Chart Wizard, and create a pie chart showing values as data labels.
4. Specify the title `Individual Sales Summary - Year Just Ended`.
5. Finish the chart creation process by embedding it as an object in the CH1 worksheet.
6. Move and size the chart as desired.
7. Edit the chart title so that *Year Just Ended* displays on a second line.

    You can press ⬆Shift+⮐Enter just before the word *Year* to move remaining text to the next line.
8. Click within a blank area of the chart to select the entire chart; then save only the chart as a noninteractive Web page using the filename `sales-pie`.
9. Deselect the chart and save your changes to the *MEC-S7challenge* workbook.
10. View the chart using the browser of your choice; then close the browser.

2. Create Hyperlinks in a Large Worksheet

You are managing an employee database in an Excel worksheet. You want to set up hyperlinks to various areas within the worksheet. To create and test the links, follow these steps:

1. Open the *MEC-S7challenge* workbook, if necessary, and select the CH2 worksheet.
2. Set up four hyperlinks in the worksheet using the following cells and cell references:

    Criteria in cell F3, jumping to cell C12
    Database in cell F4, jumping to cell C21
    Drop-down lists in cell F5, jumping to cell T1
    Extract in cell F6, jumping to cell K134
3. Enter `List of hyperlinks` in cell A133, and set a hyperlink jumping to cell F3.
4. Copy the hyperlink in cell A133 to cells K136 and R1.
5. Make sure that each link in the range F3:F6 jumps to the appropriate area in the worksheet, and that each *List of hyperlinks* link jumps to cell F3.
6. Save your changes to the *MEC-S7challenge* workbook.

3. Create a Hyperlink to a Web Site

You developed a worksheet to track annual revenues for three cities over a four-year period. Now you want to create a hyperlink to a Web site for the first city. To create the hyperlink to a Web site, follow these steps:

1. Open the *MEC-S7challenge* workbook, if necessary, and select the CH3 worksheet.
2. Click cell A13 and start the process to insert a hyperlink.
3. Select the Existing File or Web Page option in the Insert Hyperlink dialog box.
4. Type `www.indy.org` in the Address text box, and click OK.

5. Save your changes to the *MEC-S7challenge* workbook.

6. Connect to the Internet, if necessary, and click the link to the Indianapolis Web site.

7. Use the Back button in your browser to return to Excel.

4. Create a Hyperlink to an E-mail Address

You are the Indianapolis Sales Director, and you developed a worksheet to track annual revenues for three cities over a four-year period. Now you want to create a hyperlink to your e-mail address. To create the hyperlink, follow these steps:

1. Open the *MEC-S7challenge* workbook, if necessary, and select the CH4 worksheet.

2. Click cell A13 and start the process to insert a hyperlink in the current document.

3. Select the E-mail Address option in the Insert Hyperlink dialog box.

4. Enter your personal e-mail address in the E-mail address text box, and click OK.

5. Save your changes to the *MEC-S7challenge* workbook.

5. Find and Edit a Comment

You remember attaching a comment that includes the phrase "Expected loss." You decide this is not a comment you want users of the worksheet to see. To find and edit a comment, follow these steps:

1. Open the *MEC-S7challenge* workbook, if necessary, and select the worksheet named CH5.

2. Change a View setting so that you can see all comments and indicators instead of only the comment indicators.

3. Select the cell that includes the phrase *Expected loss* in its attached comment.

4. Edit that comment to remove the phrase *Expected loss*.

5. Restore the original display so that only the comment indicators appear (that is, a comment should not display unless you position the mouse pointer on a cell with an attached comment).

6. Close the Reviewing toolbar.

7. Save your changes to the *MEC-S7challenge* workbook.

Importing and Exporting Data

CHAPTER 8

This skill set includes

Import data to Excel

- Import data from a text file
- Import data from an Access database

Export data from Excel

- Link Excel data to a Word document
- Embed Excel data in a Word document
- Link an Excel range and chart to PowerPoint slides

Publish worksheets and workbooks to the Web

Skill Set Overview

Excel provides a variety of ways to import and export data. When you *import* data into a worksheet, you add data that originates outside of Excel. Import activities in this skill set include adding data from a text file (.txt extension) and an Access database. You learn ways to get data from the Web in Chapter 14, (Expert Skill Set 7, "Summarizing Data.")

When you *export* data, you prepare Excel data for use in another program or data source. Your initial export activities in this skill set include copying Excel data to a Word document and a PowerPoint slide show. You also publish a worksheet as a Web page in a manner that enables users to modify it from within a browser.

Skill 1.1: Import Data to Excel

When you import data, you avoid retyping data that already exists in another source. Each time data changes in the original source, you can also automatically update any analysis you performed in Excel on the imported data.

You can import most data using the Import External Data option on the Data menu. In this skill area, you import data from a text file and from an Access database.

Import Data from a Text File

Data in text form appears as a string of characters. Spaces or commas separate (delimit) fields, although other characters are sometimes used to delimit fields in a string. Excel's Text Import Wizard is available to guide you through the process of importing text data into the columns and rows of a worksheet.

In the following steps, you use the Text Import Wizard to import data in a text file concerning donations to the Save the Manatee fund.

To Import Data from a Text File

1 Open a new workbook in Excel.

2 Choose **Data** in the menu bar, and point to Import External **Data** (see Figure 8.1).

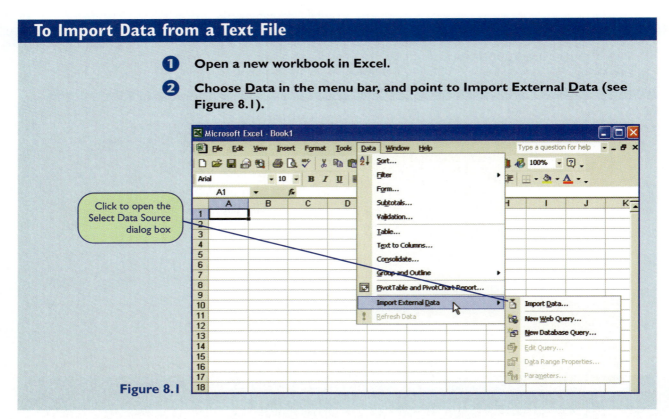

Click to open the Select Data Source dialog box

Figure 8.1

❸ Click Import Data.
The Select Data Source dialog box opens.

❹ Choose *Text Files* in the Files of type drop-down list.

❺ Locate the folder containing the student data files that accompany this text, and open the text file named *MEE-S101*.
The first Text Import Wizard dialog box opens (see Figure 8.2). Records display in the Preview area across the bottom of the dialog box. Data fields in each record are separated by commas (name, address, city, and so on).

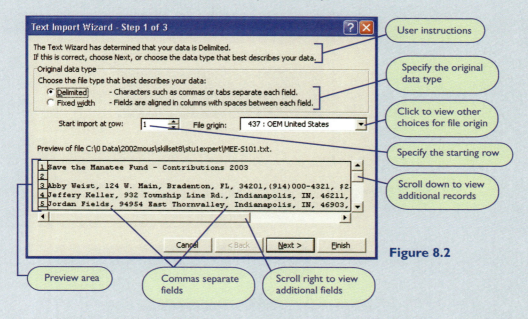

Figure 8.2

❻ Select Delimited as the original data type, and click Next.
The Text Import Wizard – Step 2 of 3 dialog box opens. An explanation of the screen appears at the top of the dialog box.

❼ In the Delimiters area, uncheck Tab and check Comma (see Figure 8.3).

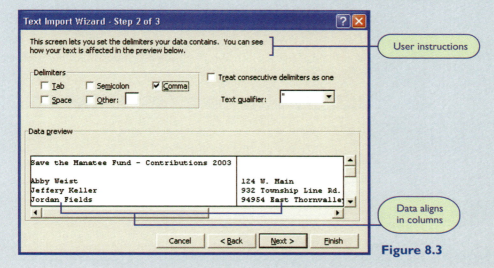

Figure 8.3

continues ▶

To Import Data from a Text File (continued)

8   **Click Next.**

The Text Import Wizard – Step 3 of 3 dialog box opens (see Figure 8.4).

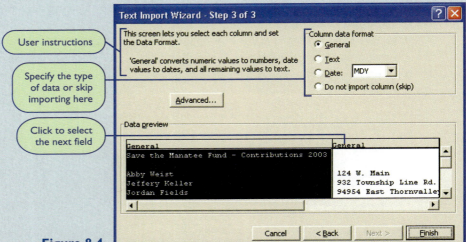

Figure 8.4

9   **Click Finish to accept the current settings.**

The Import Data dialog box opens (see Figure 8.5).

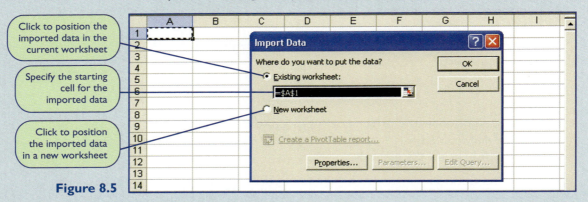

Figure 8.5

10   **Click OK to accept cell A1 as the starting position for imported data.**

The Import Data dialog box closes. Excel imports the data and arranges it in rows (records) and columns (fields) as shown in Figure 8.6. Now, make adjustments to column width and content.

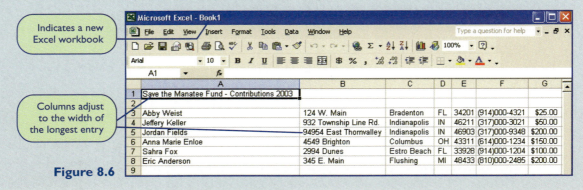

Figure 8.6

⑪ **Narrow column A to a width that accommodates *Anna Marie Enloe* in cell A6.**

⑫ **Change *Jeffery* to `Jeffrey` in cell A4; then change *Sahra* to `Sarah` in cell A7.**

⑬ **Save the imported data as an Excel workbook named `Save the Manatee`; then close the workbook.**

Continue with the next skill, or exit Excel.

Alternate Way:

Using File, Open to Import a Text File

In this skill set, you displayed a blank worksheet and selected Data, Import External Data, Import Data to import a text file using the Text Import Wizard. Excel provides an alternative way to start the Text Import Wizard without opening a blank worksheet. Select Open from the File menu; specify Text Files as the file type, and select the text file to open.

The alternative way produces similar, but not identical, results. The three Text Import Wizard screens are the same, but you do not have an opportunity to specify where you want to put the data. Instead, Excel automatically displays the imported data starting in cell A1. The name of the imported text file displays in the title bar instead of Book1, and column widths do not adjust to fit incoming data (see Figure 8.7).

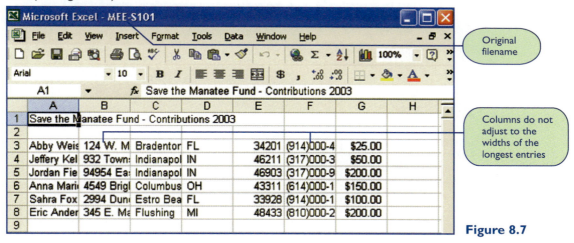

Figure 8.7

The remaining difference involves file type. Excel retains Text Files as the file type when you use File, Open to import a text file. If you want to save the imported data as an Excel file, select File, Save As and change the file type to Excel workbook.

Import Data from an Access Database

When data becomes too voluminous and complex, you are likely to maintain it in a relational database program, such as Microsoft Access, rather than as a list in Excel. Yet for some information needs—such as producing a chart—Excel might be the better program to use. Excel's Import External Data feature enables you to reach from Excel into an Access database.

If you want to import all records (rows) and fields (columns) from one table in an Access database, use the Import Data command after you select Import External Data. If you want to sort or filter data before importing it to Excel, use the New Database Query command after you select Import External Data.

In this skill, you work with an Access database that lists properties for sale. You import data from all records and fields using the Import Data command. You learn to filter data prior to importing it in Chapter 14, "Summarizing Data," Skill 7.5 *Retrieve External Data and Create Queries*.

The coverage focuses only on the mechanics of getting data from an Access database into an Excel worksheet and does not include using the results. The sample Access database has only one table—most databases have multiple tables—which is sufficient to illustrate the process of creating a query prior to extracting data to an Excel worksheet.

To Import Data from an Access Database

① **Open the Excel workbook named *MEE-S102*, and save it as** All Clients**.**

② **Choose Data; point to Import External Data, and select Import Data.**
The Select Data Source dialog box opens.

③ **Display the Files of type list (see Figure 8.8).**

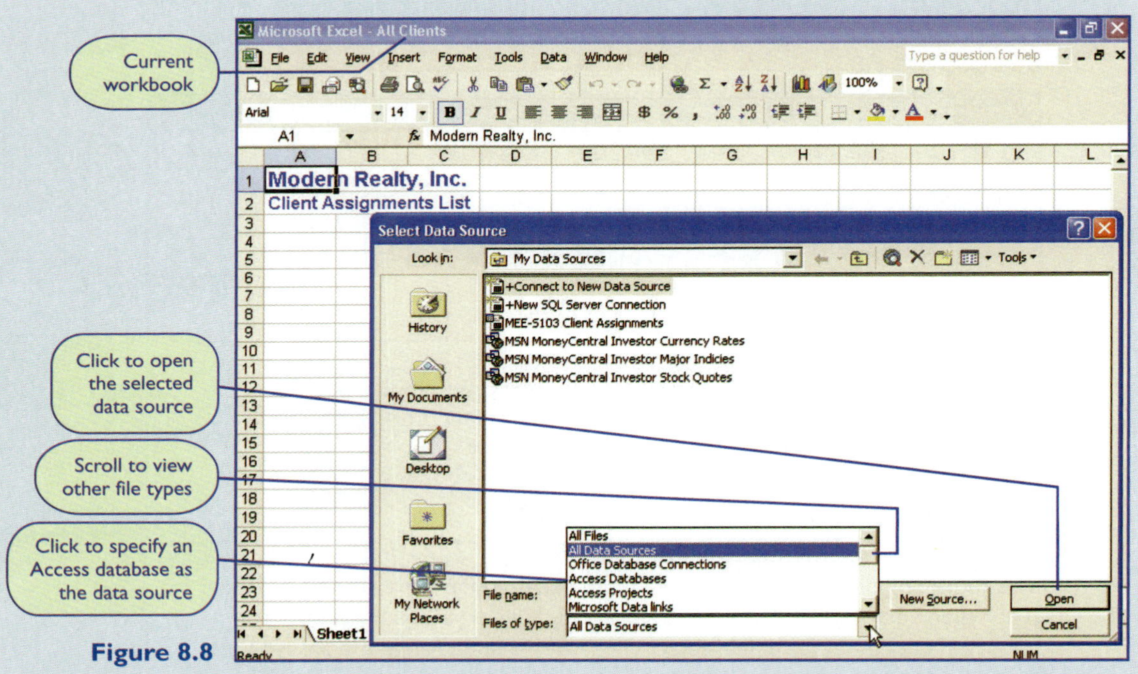

Figure 8.8

④ **Select Access Databases.**

⑤ **In the Look in text box, locate the folder containing the student data files that accompany this text, and select *MEE-S103*.**

⑥ **Click the Open button (refer to Figure 8.8).**
The Import Data dialog box opens.

7 **Click cell A5.**

You specified cell A5 as the location for imported data in the existing worksheet (see Figure 8.9).

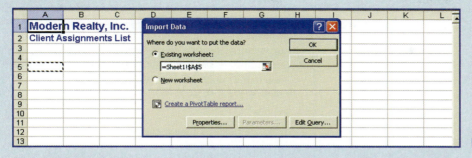

Figure 8.9

8 **Click OK.**

Excel imports all records and fields from the selected Access database. Column widths automatically adjust to accommodate the incoming data (see Figure 8.10).

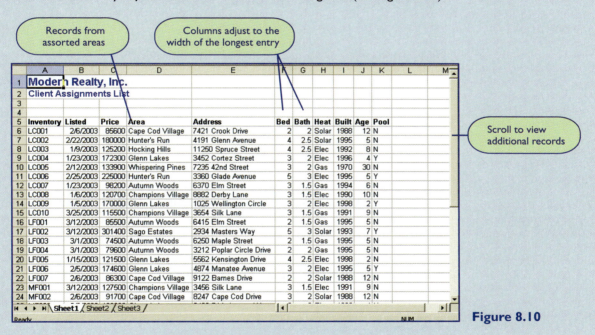

Records from assorted areas

Columns adjust to the width of the longest entry

Scroll to view additional records

Figure 8.10

9 **Save your changes to the *All Clients* workbook, and close the workbook.**

In Depth:

Copying Data from Other Microsoft Office Applications

In the previous hands-on steps, you imported data from an Access database. You can also use copy commands to place text, tables, charts, and images from other Office applications in an Excel worksheet. For example, you can copy a Word table or an image on a PowerPoint slide to an Excel worksheet. For guidance on this skill, refer to the Excel Help topic *Move or copy information between programs*.

Importing Data from a Web Page

To import data from a Web page, choose <u>D</u>ata, point to Import External <u>D</u>ata, and select New <u>W</u>eb Query. You work with Web queries in Chapter 14,

"Summarizing Data," Skill 7.5 *Retrieve External Data and Create Queries*, and Skill 7.6 *Create Extensible Markup Language (XML) Web Queries*.

Importing Data from Other Sources

The Select Data Source dialog box includes a New Source button if the external data source you want to use is not available in the dialog box. Clicking that button activates the Data Connection Wizard (see Figure 8.11).

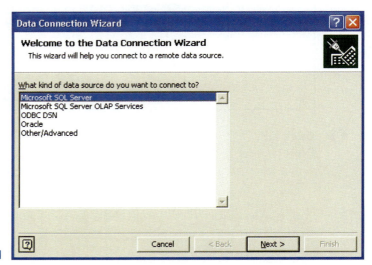

Figure 8.11

The wizard guides you through the process to connect to a remote data source. You may need to have a password or permissions set before you can use the data source.

For immediate reinforcement, work Skill Drill 1 and Challenge 2.

Skill 1.2: **Export Data from Excel**

You can export data from Excel as well as import data to Excel. The most likely destinations for exported Excel data are other Microsoft Office applications. For example, you might create a budget in Excel and insert it in a Word document to your supervisor. You might create a chart showing a sales trend in Excel and insert it in a PowerPoint slide presentation. As your information needs increase in complexity, you may switch Excel data to an Access database.

In this skill area, you sample the powerful integrating opportunities available when using Excel. You complete two operations that place a worksheet range in a Word document. The first one results in a Word table that updates for any subsequent change in the Excel worksheet range. The second one produces a Word table that does not update for changes in the related worksheet. You also place an Excel chart on a PowerPoint slide.

Link Excel Data to a Word Document

Object Linking and Embedding (OLE) is a method of sharing data that is supported by many different programs, including all Office XP applications. An *object* in this context has properties and can be referenced and used by another program. In Excel, an object can be as large as an entire workbook, or as small as a worksheet cell. Charts, clip art, and WordArt in an Excel worksheet are also examples of objects.

You can link or embed an object from a source file to a destination file. The file that contains linked or embedded data is called the **destination file**. The file providing the data to link or embed is the **source file**. For example, if you copy a section of an Excel worksheet to a Word document, the source file is the Excel workbook and the destination file is the Word document.

A **linked object** is an object in a destination file that updates whenever the data in the source file changes. If files are linked, a change in the source file results in the same change in the destination file.

An **embedded object** is an object in a destination file that does not update when the data in the source file changes. Changing data in the source file does not change the same data in the destination file.

In the following steps, you link a range of cells containing annual sales data to a sales report in Word. After creating the link, you test it by changing data in the worksheet.

To Link Excel Data to a Word Document

1 **Open the Excel workbook *MEE-S104*, and save it as** SalesData01.
The file contains worksheet data and a chart. Now copy a range of data to a Word document.

2 **Select cells A3:E6 and choose Edit, Copy or click the Copy button.**

3 **Start Microsoft Word; then open the Word document *MEE-S105*, and save it as** SalesReport01.
The document consists of a title and the opening sentence in a sales report.

4 **Place the insertion point below the single sentence in the document, and choose Edit, Paste Special.**
The Paste Special dialog box opens.

5 **Click the Paste link option, and click Microsoft Excel Worksheet Object in the As list box (see Figure 8.12).**

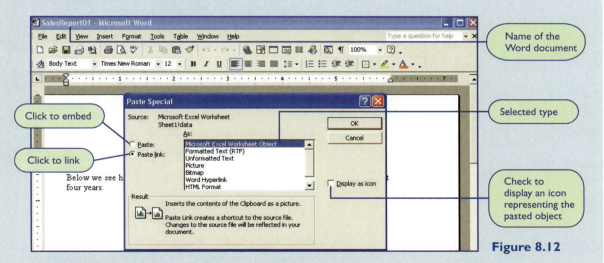

Figure 8.12

6 **Leave the Display as icon option unchecked, and click OK.**
The results of the Paste Special operation display in the sales report (see Figure 8.13).

continues ▶

To Link Excel Data to a Word Document (continued)

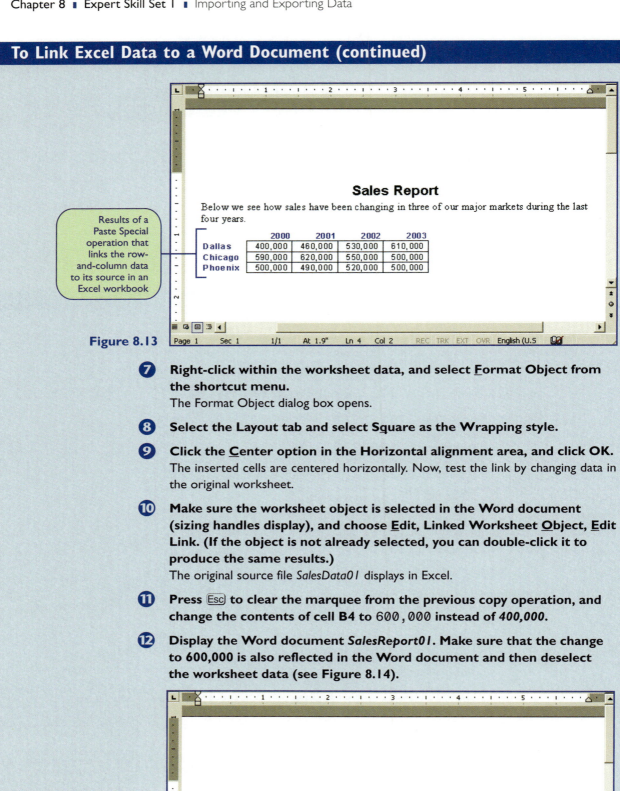

Results of a Paste Special operation that links the row-and-column data to its source in an Excel workbook

Figure 8.13

⑦ **Right-click within the worksheet data, and select Format Object from the shortcut menu.**
The Format Object dialog box opens.

⑧ **Select the Layout tab and select Square as the Wrapping style.**

⑨ **Click the Center option in the Horizontal alignment area, and click OK.**
The inserted cells are centered horizontally. Now, test the link by changing data in the original worksheet.

⑩ **Make sure the worksheet object is selected in the Word document (sizing handles display), and choose Edit, Linked Worksheet Object, Edit Link. (If the object is not already selected, you can double-click it to produce the same results.)**
The original source file *SalesData01* displays in Excel.

⑪ **Press Esc to clear the marquee from the previous copy operation, and change the contents of cell B4 to** 600,000 **instead of** *400,000.*

⑫ **Display the Word document *SalesReport01*. Make sure that the change to 600,000 is also reflected in the Word document and then deselect the worksheet data (see Figure 8.14).**

Results of changing data in the source file

Figure 8.14

13 **Save and close both the Word document *SalesReport01* and the Excel workbook *SalesData01*.**

Continue with the next skill, or exit Excel.

In Depth:

Getting Data from Excel into Access

You can use a copy-and-paste technique to place Excel data—or an object in an Excel worksheet, such as a chart—within a Word document or a PowerPoint slide. Getting data from Excel into an Access database, however, involves a different process.

First make sure that the Excel data is in a list format—each column has a label in the first row and holds similar data, each row contains related data items, and there are no blank rows or columns within the list. Also make sure that the Excel workbook is closed.

To create a new Access database, open the Excel workbook in Access, and follow the directions in the Link Spreadsheet Wizard. To add Excel data to an existing Access database, open the Access database into which you want to copy the Excel data. On the Access File menu, select Get External Data and click Import. Locate and select the workbook you want to import; then click Import and follow directions in the Import Spreadsheet Wizard. Refer to onscreen Help in Access for more information.

Embed Excel Data in a Word Document

Embedded data actually becomes a part of the destination file. Initially the results of an embed operation appear to be the same as if a link operation was executed. One major difference, however, is that if the source data in the worksheet changes, the change is not reflected in the destination file. Because embedded data does not have links, you do not have to be concerned about breaking links if a source file gets moved or renamed. This is especially important if you send the file(s) to someone else.

In the following steps, you execute the same copy operation you performed in the previous hands-on steps, except that you embed—rather than link—the annual sales data from a worksheet into the sales report. You then access Excel features from within Word, change a value, and verify that the change is not reflected in the linked worksheet.

To Embed Excel Data in a Word Document

1 **Open the Excel file named *MEE-S104*, and save it as** `SalesData02`**.**

2 **Select cells A3:E6 and choose Edit, Copy.**

3 **In Microsoft Word, open the *MEE-S105* file and save it as** `SalesReport02`**.**

4 **Place the insertion point below the single sentence, and choose Edit, Paste Special.**

5 **In the Paste Special dialog box, click the Paste option (not the Paste link option).**

6 **Click Microsoft Excel Worksheet Object in the As list, and leave the Display as icon option unchecked (see Figure 8.15).**

continues ▶

To Embed Excel Data in a Word Document (continued)

Click to embed, instead of link

Selected type

Explanation of the result

Figure 8.15

7 **Click OK.**

The copied data displays in a table aligned with the left margin.

8 **Right-click within the worksheet data in the Word document, and select Format Object from the shortcut menu.**

9 **Select the Layout tab in the Format Object dialog box, and select Square as the Wrapping style.**

10 **Click the Center option in the Horizontal alignment area; then click OK and deselect the data.**

The inserted cells are centered horizontally (see Figure 8.16). Now make sure that links do not exist between the source file and the destination file. Start by accessing Excel features from within the Word document.

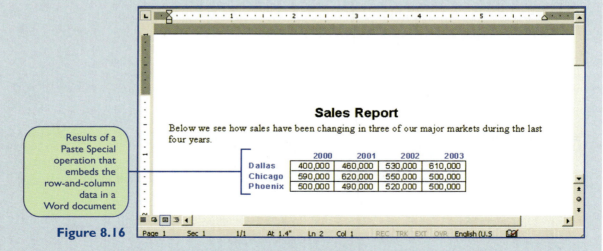

Results of a Paste Special operation that embeds the row-and-column data in a Word document

Figure 8.16

11 **Right-click within the embedded worksheet in the *SalesReport02* document; then select Worksheet Object from the shortcut menu, and select Edit.**

A miniature Excel worksheet displays, and Word's horizontal menu and toolbars are temporarily replaced with Excel's horizontal menu and toolbars (see Figure 8.17).

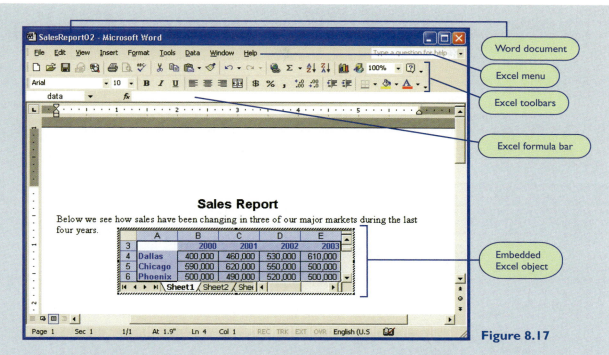

Figure 8.17

12 In the Excel window, change the contents of cell **B4** to 500,000 instead of *400,000.*

13 Click an area in the Word document that is outside the Excel window.
The object is deselected, and Word's menu and toolbars reappear.

14 Save your changes to the Word document *SalesReport02* and then switch to the *SalesData02* workbook.
Making a change to an embedded worksheet in a Word document does not change the corresponding data in the Excel source file. The original value of *400,000* still displays in cell B4 of the *SalesData02* workbook. Now make a change in the source file.

15 Change the contents of cell **B4** in *SalesData02* to 600,000 instead of *400,000,* and check the associated cell in the Word document.
The edited value of *500,000* in *SalesReport02* does not change. The two files are not linked in either direction.

16 Save and close both the Word document *SalesReport02* and the Excel workbook *SalesData02.*
Continue with the next skill, or exit Excel.

In Depth:
Comparing File Size: Embedded and Linked Objects
A destination file containing an embedded object is much larger than a destination file in which the same object is linked to its source. Embedding inserts a copy of the object. Think of linking as inserting a picture of the object with a shortcut (that is, link) between the destination file and the source of the data. There are size-of-file benefits to this approach. The destination file is only a few bytes larger than it would have been without the link to data in another application. The primary disadvantage of this approach is that the link is broken if the destination file is not stored in the same location as the source file.

Link an Excel Range and Chart to PowerPoint Slides

When creating a PowerPoint presentation, you may want to include row-and-column data or a chart that already exists in an Excel worksheet. The two methods you used to place selected contents of an Excel worksheet in a Word document—linking and embedding—are available when integrating between Excel and any Microsoft Office application. The procedures are quite similar.

In the following steps, you link a section of an Excel worksheet to the first of two slides in a PowerPoint presentation. Then you link an Excel chart of annual sales to the second slide. You also test the links by varying the data in the Excel source file.

To Link an Excel Range and Chart to PowerPoint Slides

1 **Open the Excel file _MEE-S104,_ and save it as** SalesData03.

2 **Select cells A3:E6 and choose <u>E</u>dit, <u>C</u>opy.**

3 **Start Microsoft PowerPoint; then open the PowerPoint presentation named _MEE-S106,_ and save it as** SalesReport03.
This file contains two slides that are the start of a sales report presentation.

4 **Make sure that the first slide is selected; then choose <u>E</u>dit, Paste Special.**

5 **Click Paste link and specify Microsoft Excel Worksheet Object in the As list box (see Figure 8.18).**

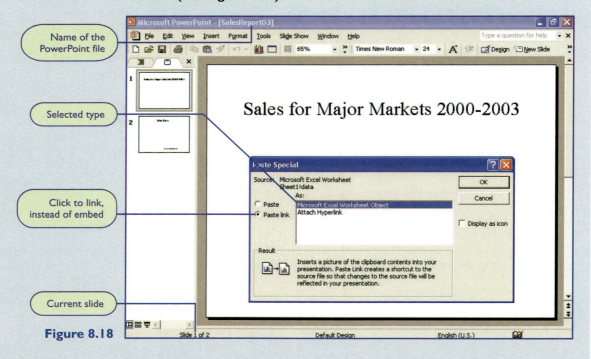

Figure 8.18

6 **Click OK.**
The copied cells display on Slide 1, but the cells are too small to read easily.

7 **Resize and move the object as shown in Figure 8.19.**

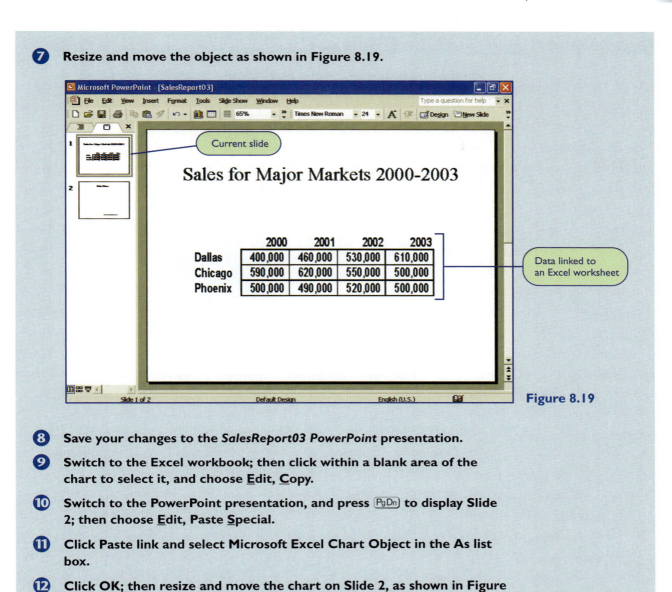

Figure 8.19

8 **Save your changes to the *SalesReport03* PowerPoint presentation.**

9 **Switch to the Excel workbook; then click within a blank area of the chart to select it, and choose Edit, Copy.**

10 **Switch to the PowerPoint presentation, and press PgDn to display Slide 2; then choose Edit, Paste Special.**

11 **Click Paste link and select Microsoft Excel Chart Object in the As list box.**

12 **Click OK; then resize and move the chart on Slide 2, as shown in Figure 8.20.**

continues ▶

To Link an Excel Range and Chart to PowerPoint Slides (continued)

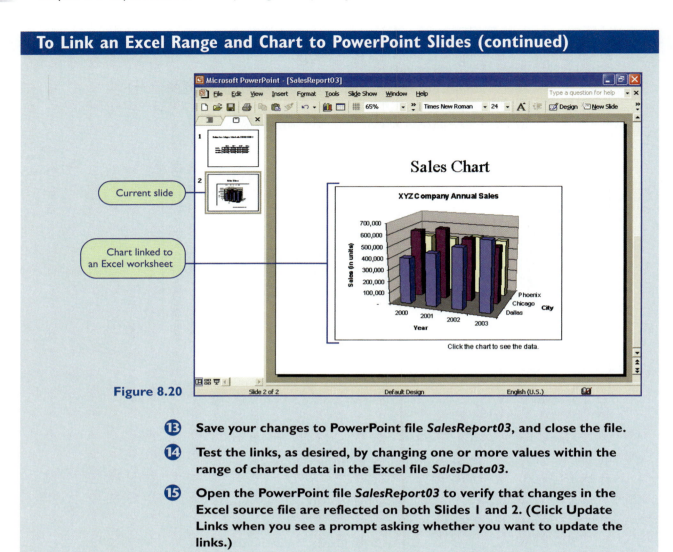

Current slide

Chart linked to an Excel worksheet

Figure 8.20

13 Save your changes to PowerPoint file *SalesReport03*, and close the file.

14 Test the links, as desired, by changing one or more values within the range of charted data in the Excel file *SalesData03*.

15 Open the PowerPoint file *SalesReport03* to verify that changes in the Excel source file are reflected on both Slides 1 and 2. (Click Update Links when you see a prompt asking whether you want to update the links.)

16 Close the PowerPoint file *SalesReport03* and the Excel file *SalesData03* without saving changes made to verify the links.
Continue with the next skill, or exit Excel.

In Depth:
Exchanging Data Between Excel and Outlook
You can export names and addresses in a Microsoft Excel workbook to Microsoft Outlook. You can also import Outlook contacts into Excel. Both processes begin by selecting Import and Export from the File menu in Outlook. For more information, enter `export to Outlook` in Excel's Ask a Question box, and select the topic *Share contact data between Excel and Outlook*.

For immediate reinforcement, work Skill Drills 2 and 4 and Challenges 1, 3, and 4.

Skill 1.3: **Publish Worksheets and Workbooks to the Web**

You know from Skill 7.1 *Convert Worksheets into Web Pages* in Chapter 7, "Workgroup Collaboration," that you can save a workbook, worksheet, range of cells, or other worksheet item, such as an embedded chart, as a Web page. Doing so makes the saved element available for others to use on an HTTP site, FTP site, Web server, or network server.

You also know that you can publish a workbook, worksheet, or portion of a worksheet with or without interactivity. When you publish with interactivity, users can modify as well as view the content and formatting of the element you publish by using the Web browser *Internet Explorer 4.01* or later. They can also enter, analyze, sort, and filter data on the Web page. *Dynamic Web page* is an alternative term for an interactive Web page.

When you publish without interactivity, users can only view the content and formatting of the published element from within a Web browser, such as Internet Explorer or Netscape Navigator. *Static Web page* is an alternative term for a noninteractive Web page.

Choosing File, Save as Web Page starts the publishing process. If you select the element you want to publish before executing the initial command sequence, or you want to publish an entire workbook without interactivity, you can complete a save as Web page operation by pressing the Save button in the Save As dialog box. If you have not yet selected the element you want to publish, or you want to publish an entire workbook with interactivity, click the Publish button in the Save As dialog box.

If you use Excel to save or publish *noninteractive* data on a Web page, you can open the resulting HTML file in Excel and make changes. If you use Excel to save or publish *interactive* data on a Web page, you can modify the Web page while you have it open in a browser, but the changes are not saved when you exit the browser. To make permanent changes, modify the original Excel workbook file and republish.

In the following steps, you publish a reunion budget worksheet as an interactive Web page. If you have access to Internet Explorer 4.01 or later, you make a temporary change to the Web page from within a browser and view features applied through the Commands and Options dialog box.

To Publish an Interactive Workbook as a Web Page and Make Temporary Changes

1 **Open the *MEE-S107* file, and save it as the Excel workbook named** Budget Review.
The Sheet1 worksheet in the workbook includes budget data for a reunion.

2 **Choose File, Save as Web Page.**
The Save As dialog box opens. It includes Web-related options and settings (see Figure 8.21).

continues ▶

To Publish an Interactive Workbook as a Web Page and Make Temporary Changes (continued)

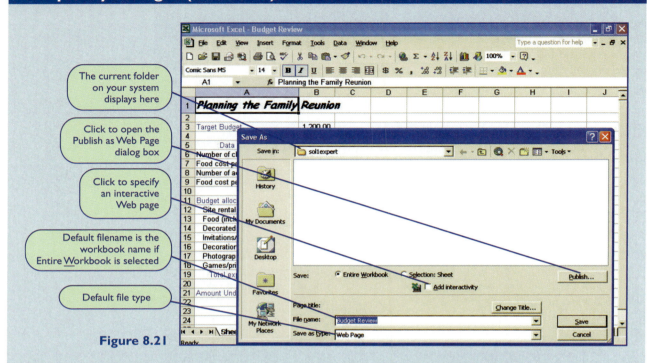

- The current folder on your system displays here
- Click to open the Publish as Web Page dialog box
- Click to specify an interactive Web page
- Default filename is the workbook name if Entire Workbook is selected
- Default file type

Figure 8.21

❸ **Display the Save in drop-down list, and specify the folder on your local system where you want to store the current worksheet as a Web page.** You are storing your Web page on a local system. Doing so enables you to preview the Web page before publishing it to a Web site. Unless you prefer another location, store the page in the same folder as the other files you have been saving.

❹ **Change the filename to** Budget Review on Web.htm.

❺ **Click Selection: Sheet instead of Entire Workbook, and click the Add interactivity check box (see Figure 8.22).**

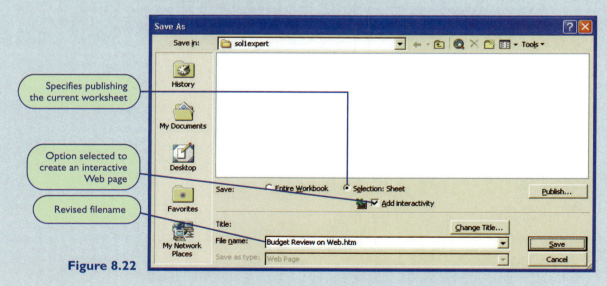

- Specifies publishing the current worksheet
- Option selected to create an interactive Web page
- Revised filename

Figure 8.22

6 **Click the Publish button.**

The Publish as Web Page dialog box opens.

7 **Click both check boxes at the bottom of the Publish as Web Page dialog box.**

You turned on the *AutoRepublish every time this workbook is saved* and *Open published web page in browser* options (see Figure 8.23).

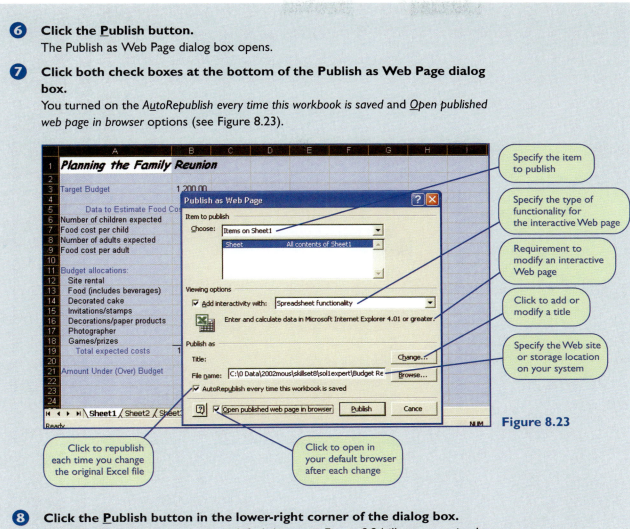

Figure 8.23

8 **Click the Publish button in the lower-right corner of the dialog box.**

The new Web page opens in your default browser. Figure 8.24 illustrates using Internet Explorer.

continues ▶

To Publish an Interactive Workbook as a Web Page and Make Temporary Changes (continued)

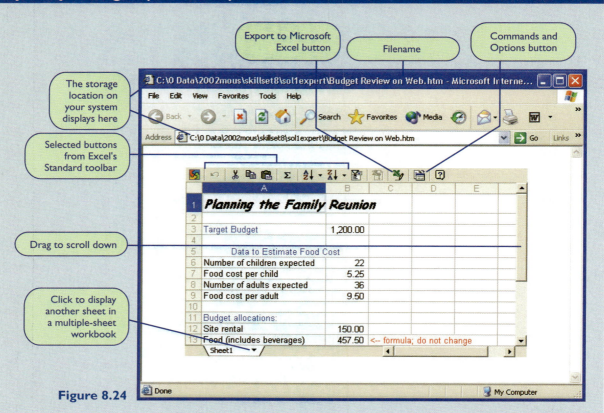

The storage location on your system displays here

Export to Microsoft Excel button

Filename

Commands and Options button

Selected buttons from Excel's Standard toolbar

Drag to scroll down

Click to display another sheet in a multiple-sheet workbook

Figure 8.24

❌ *If you have problems...*

If you use Netscape Navigator as your default Web browser, you may have to use Windows Explorer to open the *Budget Review on Web.htm* file. Right-click the Start button on the Windows taskbar and select Explore; select the folder containing the new Web page file, and double-click the filename.

---

9 **Scroll to the bottom of the worksheet.**
Food cost per adult in cell B9 is 9.50, and the amount under budget in cell B21 is 2.50.

10 **Change the contents of cell B9 from *9.50* to 10.50, and click cell B21.**
You changed the contents of a cell on an interactive Web page. The amount over budget in cell B21 is (33.50). Now view, but do not change, other items that you can modify in an interactive Web page.

11 **Click the Commands and Options button on the toolbar (refer to Figure 8.24), and make sure that Format is the current tab.**
Formatting options display in the Commands and Options dialog box (see Figure 8.25).

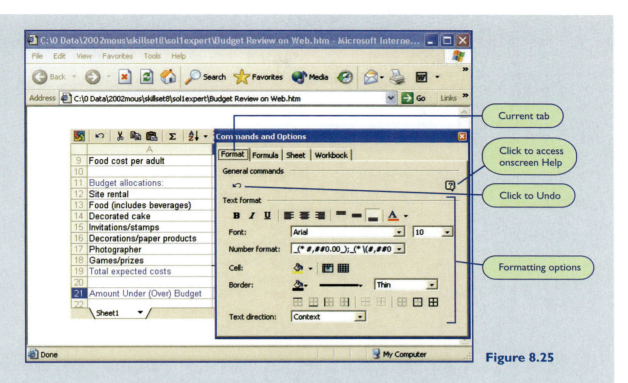

Figure 8.25

12 **Click the Formula tab in the Commands and Options dialog box.**

Excel displays information about the current formula (see Figure 8.26).

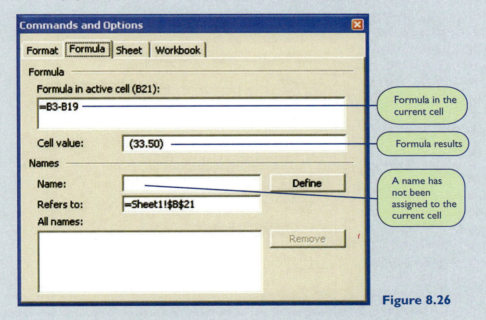

Figure 8.26

13 **Click the Sheet tab in the Commands and Options dialog box.**

Excel displays search and display options for the current worksheet (see Figure 8.27).

continues ▶

To Publish an Interactive Workbook as a Web Page and Make Temporary Changes (continued)

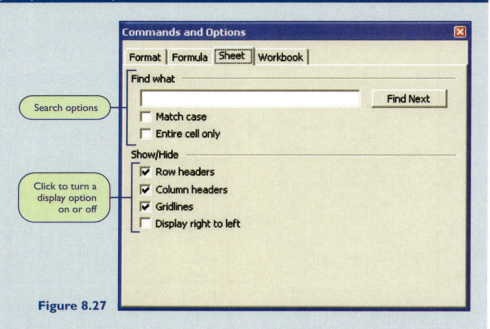

Search options

Click to turn a display option on or off

Figure 8.27

🔵 14 **Click the Workbook tab in the Commands and Options dialog box.**
Excel displays options related to the workbook (see Figure 8.28).

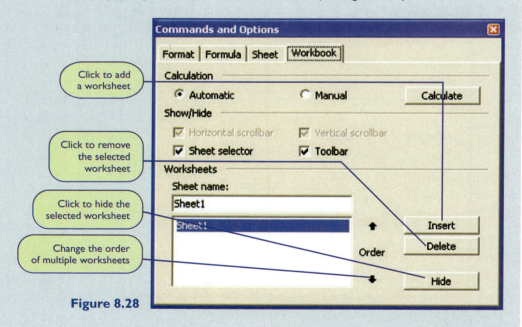

Click to add a worksheet

Click to remove the selected worksheet

Click to hide the selected worksheet

Change the order of multiple worksheets

Figure 8.28

🔵 15 **Close the Commands and Options dialog box; close your browser, and close the *Budget Review on Web* file.**
You can continue with the Skill Drill and Challenge exercises, start another skill set, or exit Excel.

In Depth:

Publishing a Web Page on a Web Site or Intranet

In this book, you publish Excel data on a Web page that is stored on your local system. Doing so enables you to verify that the Web page operates as intended. When you are ready to publish on an actual Web site, you must arrange for an Internet service provider (ISP) to host your page or get instructions from the system administrator about publishing to a company or school intranet.

Putting a Chart on a Web Page

You can publish a chart with or without interactivity. When you publish, an image of the chart is saved as a .gif file, and the image appears on the Web page. When you publish a chart to a Web page with interactivity, Excel automatically includes the source data for the chart. If you change the source data, the corresponding chart updates automatically.

Making Temporary Changes to an Interactive Web Page Permanent

Recall that changes you make to Excel data or features on an interactive Web page are only temporary; they are not saved when you close your browser. To make a change to a number, label, or formula permanent, edit the original Excel workbook and republish. If you do not have access to the original Excel workbook, you can use the Export to Microsoft Excel button (refer to Figure 8.24) to create an Excel file in which to make your changes.

You can also open a Web page with Excel data in a design program and make other types of changes. For example, you can use Microsoft FrontPage 2002 to rearrange items on a Web page and customize the interactive functionality for spreadsheets and charts. Refer to the Excel Help topic *About changing data on a Web page* for more information.

For immediate reinforcement, work Skill Drill 3.

Summary

In this skill set, you sampled a variety of ways to exchange data with other applications and programs. You imported data from two sources that originated outside of Excel—a text file, and an Access database. You exported Excel data to a Word document and a PowerPoint slide presentation. You also published a worksheet as an interactive Web page.

Skill Drill

Skill Drill exercises *reinforce* skills. Each skill reinforced is the same, or nearly the same, as a skill presented in the skill set. Detailed instructions are provided in a step-by-step format.

Before beginning your Excel Expert Skill Set 1 Skill Drill exercises, complete the following steps:

1. Open the file named *MEE-S108*, and immediately save it as **MEE-S1drill**.

   The workbook contains four sheets: an overview and three exercise sheets labeled SD1 through SD3.

2. Click the Overview sheet to view the organization and content of the Skill Drill workbook for Excel Expert Skill Set 1.

Each exercise is independent of the others, so you may complete the exercises in any order. Be sure to save the workbook after completing each exercise. If you need a paper copy of one or more completed exercises, enter your name, centered in a header, before printing. Print options have already been set to print compressed to one page and to display the filename, sheet name, and current date in a footer.

Be sure to save your changes and close the workbook if you need more than one work session to complete the desired exercises. Continue working on *MEE-S1drill* instead of starting over in the original *MEE-S108* file.

1. Import Data to an Existing Worksheet from a Text File

You are keeping a record of the business miles you drive using Notepad, which creates a text file. Now you want to import that text file into Excel as the starting point for a worksheet that computes business expenses.

To import data to an existing worksheet from a text file:

1. Open the *MEE-S1drill* workbook, if necessary; then select the SD1 worksheet.
2. Click cell A4.
3. Choose Data, Import External Data, and select Import Data.

   The Select Data Source dialog box opens.
4. Display the Look in drop-down list, and select the folder containing the student data files.
5. Select the *MEE-S109* text file, and click Open.
6. Check that Delimited is selected in the Text Import Wizard – Step 1 of 3 dialog box, and click Next.
7. Make sure that a check mark displays in the Tab check box in the Text Import Wizard – Step 2 of 3 dialog box, and click Finish.
8. Make sure that *Existing worksheet* and =$A$4 are the settings for the location of imported data, and click OK.

   Excel imports the text data, starting in cell A4.
9. Save your changes to the *MEE-S1drill* workbook.

2. Create a Link and View Information About Links

You maintain data in an Excel worksheet on homes available for sale. You created a memo in Word to convey information about properties available in the Glenn Lakes subdivision. Now you want to link the data in the worksheet to the Word memo so that each time you open the Word document, the linked data updates automatically. You also want to view information about links in the memo.

To create a link, and view information about links:

1. Open the *MEE-S1drill* workbook in Excel, if necessary, and select the SD2 worksheet.
2. Open the *MEE-S110* document in Word, and save it as **Glenn Lakes Memo**.
3. Switch to the SD2 worksheet; then select the list range A8:I16, and click the Copy button.
4. Switch to the *Glenn Lakes Memo* document, and position the insertion point below the last sentence.
5. Choose Edit, Paste Special.
6. Select Paste link, specify pasting as a Microsoft Excel Worksheet Object, and click OK.

   The range of data from an Excel worksheet is linked within the Word document.

7. Choose <u>E</u>dit, Lin<u>k</u>s.

The Links dialog box opens and lists one link. The description of Item #1 near the bottom of the dialog box indicates that the link is a Microsoft Excel Worksheet.

8. Click OK to close the dialog box.

9. Save your changes to the *Glenn Lakes Memo* document, and exit Word.

10. Deselect the list range in the SD2 worksheet, and press (Esc) to remove the marquee from the copy operation.

3. Save an Excel Chart as an Interactive Web Page

You developed a worksheet and associated chart estimating quarterly sales for Glenn Lakes Golf Course. Eventually you want to publish the chart on a Web page for others to view and modify. For now, save the chart as a Web page on your local system and make sure that the desired results are achieved in your browser.

1. Open the *MEE-S1drill* workbook, if necessary, and select the SD3 worksheet.

2. Click within a blank area of the chart to select it.

3. Choose <u>F</u>ile, Save as Web Page.

4. Display the Save <u>i</u>n drop-down list, and specify the folder on your local system where you want to store the current worksheet as a Web page.

You are storing your Web page on a local system. Doing so enables you to preview the Web page before publishing it to a Web site. Unless you prefer another location, store the page in the same folder as the other files you have been saving.

5. Click Se<u>l</u>ection: Chart instead of Entire <u>W</u>orkbook, and click the <u>A</u>dd interactivity check box.

6. Click the Change Title button; then type `Year 2004 Revenues Budget Review` as the title in the Set Title dialog box, and click OK.

7. In the File <u>n</u>ame text box, type `Year 2004 Budget.htm` as the file name; then click the <u>P</u>ublish button.

The Publish as Web Page dialog box opens.

8. Make sure that both check boxes at the bottom of the Publish as Web Page dialog box are checked.

You turned on the A<u>u</u>toRepublish *every time this workbook is saved* and <u>O</u>pen published *web page in browser* options.

9. Make sure that other settings in the dialog box include publishing interactively with chart functionality; then click the <u>P</u>ublish button.

The chart displays in your default browser at the top of the new Web page. Fourth-quarter budgeted Greens Fees are less than $400,000.

 If you have problems...
If you use Netscape Navigator as your default Web browser, you may have to use Windows Explorer to open the *Year 2004 Budget.htm* file. Right-click the Start button on the Windows taskbar and select Explore; select the folder containing the new Web page file, and double-click the filename.

10. Scroll to view the related worksheet data below the chart.

11. Change the contents of cell E2 from *362,000* to `405,000`; then scroll up if necessary to view the chart.

You changed the contents of a cell on an interactive Web page. The increase in expected fourth quarter Greens Fees is reflected in the chart.

12. Close your browser; then click cell A1 to deselect the chart on the SD3 worksheet.

4. Get Help on Linking and Embedding

You know how to embed and link objects, but you want to know more about when to use which method. Onscreen Help can provide the information you desire.

To access related onscreen Help, follow these steps:

1. Open a blank Excel workbook, and enter `about linking` in the Ask a Question box.

2. Select the topic *About linking to another workbook or program.*

3. Click the topic *The difference between linking and embedding other programs in Excel* in the right pane.

4. Study the diagram showing an embedded object, a linked object, and a source file.

5. Read the next two sections: *When to use linked objects* and *When to use embedded objects.*

6. Read other topics of your choice listed in the Contents tab.

7. Close onscreen Help, and close the blank workbook without saving it.

Challenge

Challenge exercises expand on or are somewhat related to skills presented in the skill set. Each exercise provides a brief narrative introduction, followed by instructions in a numbered-step format that are not as detailed as those in the Skill Drill section.

Before beginning your Excel Expert Skill Set I Challenge exercises, complete the following steps:

1. Open the file named *MEE-S1 I I*, and immediately save it as **MEE-S1challenge**.

   The workbook contains three sheets: an overview and two sheets labeled CH1 and CH2.

2. Click the Overview sheet to view the organization and content of the Challenge workbook for Excel Expert Skill Set I.

Each exercise is independent of the others, so you may complete the exercises in any order. Be sure to save the workbook after completing each exercise. If you need a paper copy of one or more completed exercises, enter your name, centered in a header, before printing. Print options have already been set to print compressed to one page. Settings to display the filename, sheet name, and current date in a footer have been set in all worksheets.

Be sure to save your changes and close the workbook if you need more than one work session to complete the desired exercises. Continue working on *MEE-S1challenge* instead of starting over in the original *MEE-S1 I I* file.

I. Embed Excel Data in a Word Document

You prepared a memo to the Accounting department, asking for a review of your monthly expenses. Embed in the memo a copy of those expenses, which are available in an Excel worksheet.

To embed Excel data in a Word document, follow these steps:

1. Open the Word document *MEE-S1 I 2*, and save it as a document named **Expense Review**.

2. Open the *MEE-S1challenge* workbook, if necessary, and select the CH1 worksheet.

3. Turn off display of gridlines and row and column headings on printed output.

4. Copy the range A7:E21 and switch to the *Expense Review* document.

5. Paste the copied Excel data after the last sentence, making sure that you embed (not link) the data as a Microsoft Excel worksheet object.

6. View an option on the <u>E</u>dit menu to verify that there is no link to the CH1 worksheet in the document.

7. Save your changes to the *Expense Review* document; then close the document and exit Word.

8. Deselect ranges as necessary in the CH1 worksheet.

2. Import Access Data into an Excel Worksheet

Expense data is currently stored in an Access database, and you want to import selected data into an Excel worksheet. To import all records with fields in the same order as stored in the Access database, you would choose <u>D</u>ata, Import External <u>D</u>ata, and select Import <u>D</u>ata. You want, however, to extract only the Office and Other category expenses (category 1 or 4 expenses), and you want the columns in a slightly different order. Use Excel's Import External Data feature, and select <u>N</u>ew Database Query instead of Import <u>D</u>ata, to produce the desired result.

To import Access data into an Excel worksheet, follow these steps:

1. Open the *MEE-S1 challenge* workbook, if necessary, and select the CH2 worksheet; then click cell A9.

2. Choose <u>D</u>ata, Import External <u>D</u>ata, and select <u>N</u>ew Database Query.

3. Choose MS Access Database as the data source, and specify that you want to use the Query Wizard.

4. In the Select Database dialog box, find and open the *MEE-S113* Access database.

5. Click the + sign to display fields (columns) in the Expense List table; then choose columns ID, Category, Expense, Date, Amount, and Client (select them in the order given).

6. Filter the data so only category 1 or 4 records are imported.

   To do this, you must use two filter lines and specify the OR button between the two specifications.

7. Sort the data by the Expense field in Ascending order.

8. Select <u>R</u>eturn Data to Microsoft Excel, and click Finish. Make sure that cell A9 in the existing worksheet is the location for imported data, and click OK.

   Imported data displays starting in cell A9 of the CH2 worksheet. The Client column is blank because Category 1 and 4 type expenses do not have clients.

9. Reformat as needed, including changing column widths and formatting entries in the Date column to show the date only. Save your changes to the *MEE-S1 challenge* workbook.

3. Break a Link

You want to break the links in a PowerPoint slide to data and a chart in an Excel worksheet. You know that when you break a link to a source, the action cannot be undone.

To break links, follow these steps:

1. Open the PowerPoint file *MEE-S114*; click Cancel to bypass updating links, and save the file as **No Links**.

   The data and chart on Slide 2 are linked to an Excel worksheet.

   2. Choose Edit, Links.

      The Links dialog box opens.

   3. Select the two links listed; then click Break Link and close the Links dialog box.

   4. Choose Edit.

      The Links option on the Edit menu is dim, indicating that there are no links in the file.

   5. Close the Edit menu; save your changes to *No Links*, and exit PowerPoint.

4. Compare Sizes of Linked Versus Embedded Files

In this skill set, you created *SalesReport01.doc*, in which you linked a worksheet range and you created *SalesReport02.doc*, in which you embedded the same range. You want to compare the sizes of the two files.

To compare file sizes by using Windows Explorer:

   1. Open Windows Explorer, and display the contents of the folder in which you stored the solutions to this project.

   2. Note that the file size of *SalesReport01.doc* (containing only a link to data in an Excel worksheet) is smaller than the file size of *SalesReport02.doc* (containing embedded Excel data).

   3. Close Windows Explorer.

CHAPTER 9

Expert Skill Set 2

Managing Workbooks

This skill set includes

Create, edit, and apply templates

Create workspaces

Use Data Consolidation

Skill Set Overview

ou begin this skill set by creating, editing, and applying a template that you define. This activity builds on your experiences with predefined templates in Chapter 2 (Core Skill Set 2, "Managing Workbooks.")

The second topic focuses on an efficient way to work with the same workbooks repeatedly. You create a file that enables you to open workbooks as a group and display those workbooks in a predefined arrangement.

The final topic expands your ability to combine the values from multiple ranges of data on different worksheets. In Chapter 4 (Core Skill Set 4, "Modifying Workbooks,"), you used 3-D references in formulas to consolidate data. In this skill set, you use the Data, Consolidate command.

Skill 2.1: Create, Edit, and Apply Templates

In Chapter 2, you learned that a template is a workbook containing standardized content and/or formatting that you can use as the basis for other workbooks. A template has an .xlt extension, as compared to the .xls extension that indicates a workbook.

You can modify and use predefined templates—known as built-in templates—as you did in Chapter 2. You can also create and save custom templates—templates based on worksheets with your preferred content and/or formatting.

The steps to save a workbook as a custom template are the same as those used to save modifications to a predefined template. Select the Save As option on the File menu, and select Template from the Save as type drop-down list. Excel automatically selects the Templates folder as the storage location, but you can specify another location.

To use a template as the basis for a new workbook, choose File, Open from the menu bar. Find the folder containing the desired template and open it; then modify data as needed and save the file as a workbook.

In the following steps, you complete and test a worksheet that prepares and prints a quote for computer training. After making sure that the worksheet produces the intended results, you remove sample data, set a print area, and save the workbook as a custom template. In a second set of steps, you modify the template and use it to create a worksheet for a specific training quote.

To Create a Custom Template

❶ Open the *MEE-S201* workbook and save it as test training quote.

❷ Scroll to view the contents of the worksheet.
The worksheet calculates total cost and cost per person of training, based on data provided by those requesting and preparing the quote (see Figure 9.1).

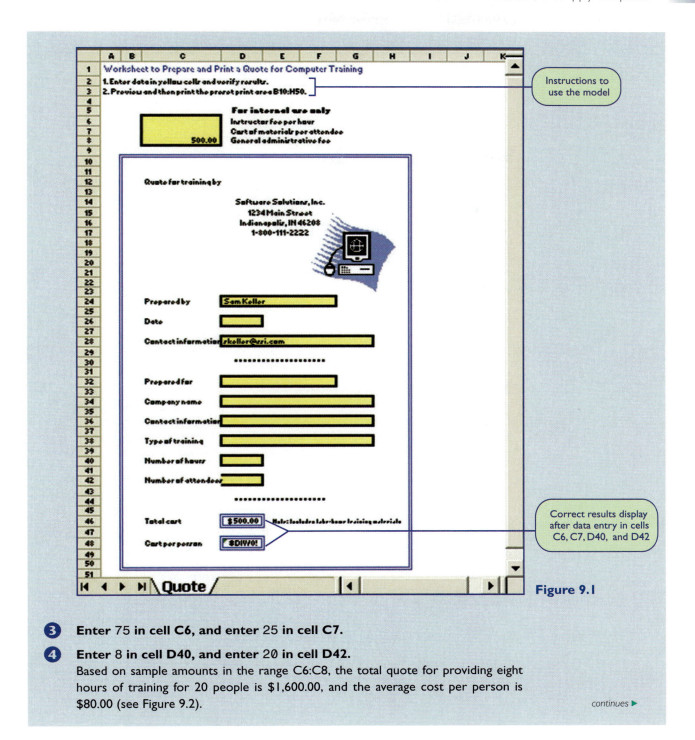

Instructions to use the model

Correct results display after data entry in cells C6, C7, D40, and D42

Figure 9.1

③ **Enter** 75 **in cell C6, and enter** 25 **in cell C7.**

④ **Enter** 8 **in cell D40, and enter** 20 **in cell D42.**

Based on sample amounts in the range C6:C8, the total quote for providing eight hours of training for 20 people is $1,600.00, and the average cost per person is $80.00 (see Figure 9.2).

continues ▶

To Create a Custom Template (continued)

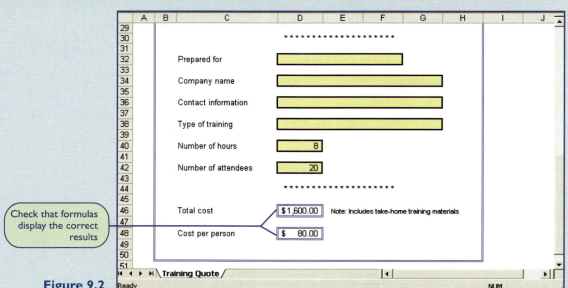

Check that formulas display the correct results

Figure 9.2

5 Delete the contents of cells C6, C7, D40, and D42.

You removed the data subject to change each time you prepare a new quote. You did not remove the amount for an administrative fee in cell C8, because that number stays constant for extended periods. You also retained the name and contact information for the person who usually prepares all training quotes.

6 Select the range B10:H50; then choose **F**ile, Prin**t** Area, **S**et Print Area.

You specified the portion of the worksheet to print and send to the person requesting a training quote. The print range excludes the instructions on using the worksheet and the data for internal use only.

7 Click cell A1 to deselect the range.

8 Choose **F**ile, Save **A**s; then select Template from the Save as **t**ype drop-down list.

The settings in the Save As dialog box resemble those shown in Figure 9.3.

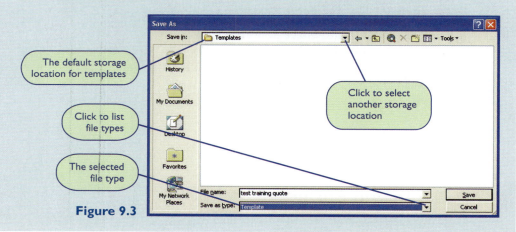

The default storage location for templates

Click to select another storage location

Click to list file types

The selected file type

Figure 9.3

⑨ **If you are working in a lab environment that doesn't permit saving to the Microsoft Templates folder, specify your own folder location in the Save in drop-down list.**

⑩ **Change the name in the File name text box to** `Training Quote`**; then click Save.**
You completed the process to save a custom template.

⑪ **Choose File, Close.**

You saved a template to prepare and print a training quote. Now modify the template, and use it to create a new workbook.

To Modify and Apply a Custom Template

① **Choose File, Open; then make sure that Templates is specified in the Files of type box.**

② **In the Look in box, specify the folder in which you stored the Training Quote template; then select Training Quote and click the Open button.**
The template for preparing a training quote opens (refer to Figure 9.1).

③ **Enter** `Note: Quote valid for 30 days` **in cell E26.**

④ **Choose File, Save As; then make sure that Template displays in the Save as type text box, and click Save.**
A warning message displays (see Figure 9.4).

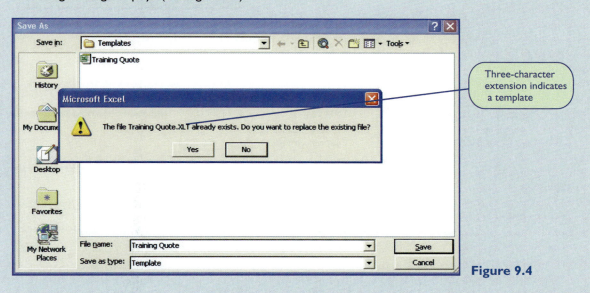

Three-character extension indicates a template

Figure 9.4

⑤ **Click Yes.**
You modified the template. Now use the template currently open to create a specific training quote. You begin by saving the template as a workbook, so that the template itself is not changed.

continues ▶

To Modify and Apply a Custom Template (continued)

6 Choose **File, Save As**; then use the **Save in** drop-down list to select the folder in which you are storing solutions for this text.

7 Enter Acme3-12-03 in the File **name** text box.

8 Select *Microsoft Excel Workbook* from the Save as **type** drop-down list; then click the **Save** button.

You specified that the current document is a workbook, not a template. Now complete, preview, and print a specific quote for Acme Supply Company.

9 Enter 60 in cell **C6**, and enter 20 in cell **C7**.

10 Enter the remaining data in the yellow cells, as shown in Figure 9.5.

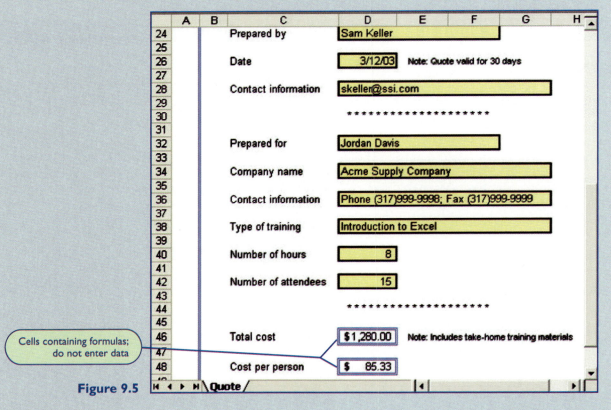

Figure 9.5

11 Click cell **A1**, and save your changes to the Acme3-12-03 workbook.

12 Click **Print Preview** in the toolbar to view the training quote; then close **Print Preview**.

13 Print the current worksheet, if desired; then close the workbook.

Continue with the next skill, or exit Excel.

Alternate Way:
Creating a Workbook from a Template

In this skill, you used File, Open to display a template, and then you saved the open template as a Microsoft Excel workbook. If a template is not already open, you can choose File, New from the menu bar and choose a template source in the New Workbook task pane (see Figure 9.6).

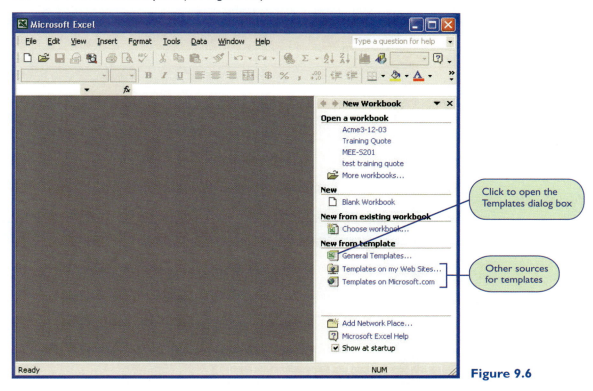

Figure 9.6

For immediate reinforcement, work Challenge 1.

Skill 2.2: **Create Workspaces**

If you frequently display more than one workbook on the screen, and specify approximately the same window sizes and screen positions for those multiple workbooks, Excel's workspace feature can save the startup time needed to open and arrange multiple workbooks. A *workspace* file saves information about all open workbooks, including filenames, screen positions, and window sizes. It does not contain the workbooks themselves.

When you are ready to open the group of files defined in the workspace, you execute a File, Open command and select the associated workspace file from a list of files that have .xlw extensions. The "w" at the end of the extension indicates a workspace file.

In the following steps, you open two workbooks, display one below the other, and save that grouping as a workspace. You then close the two original files, and test that the workspace file functions as intended.

To Create a Workspace

1 **Open the *MEE-S202* workbook, and save it as** Region1.
The workbook includes a single worksheet named East.

2 **Open the *MEE-S203* workbook, and save it as** Region2.
The workbook includes a single worksheet named West.

3 **Choose <u>W</u>indow, <u>A</u>rrange; then select H<u>o</u>rizontal and click OK (see Figure 9.7).**

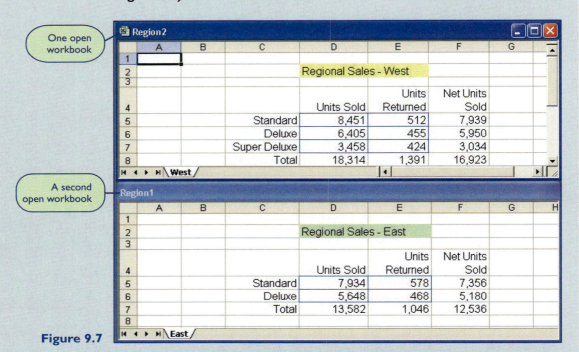

One open workbook

A second open workbook

Figure 9.7

4 **Choose <u>F</u>ile, Save <u>W</u>orkspace.**
The Save Workspace dialog box opens. The Save as <u>t</u>ype text box at the bottom displays *Workspaces*.

5 **In the Save <u>i</u>n drop-down list, select the folder in which you are storing solution files.**

6 **Enter** EastWest **as the filename (see Figure 9.8).**

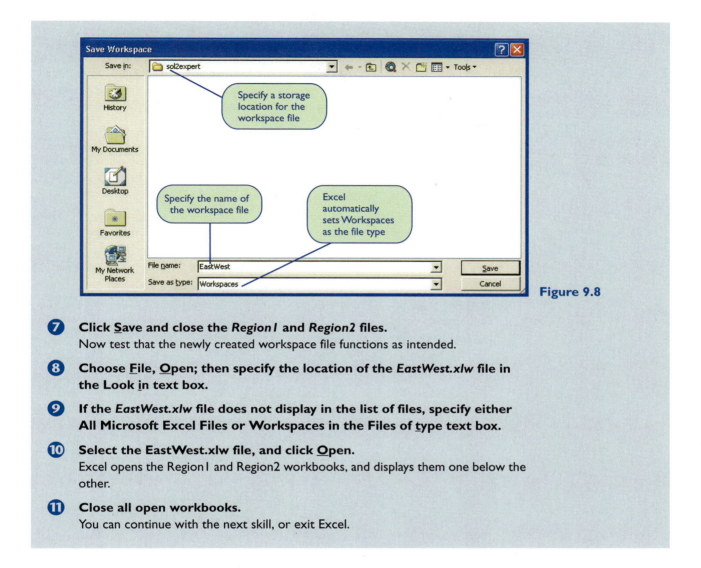

Figure 9.8

7 **Click Save and close the *Region1* and *Region2* files.**
Now test that the newly created workspace file functions as intended.

8 **Choose File, Open; then specify the location of the *EastWest.xlw* file in the Look in text box.**

9 **If the *EastWest.xlw* file does not display in the list of files, specify either All Microsoft Excel Files or Workspaces in the Files of type text box.**

10 **Select the EastWest.xlw file, and click Open.**
Excel opens the Region1 and Region2 workbooks, and displays them one below the other.

11 **Close all open workbooks.**
You can continue with the next skill, or exit Excel.

For immediate reinforcement, work Skill Drill 1.

Skill 2.3: **Use Data Consolidation**

Excel workbooks are often used to record data for different time periods, for different products, for different departments, and for different locations. When this is the case, it is often necessary to consolidate data stored in multiple worksheets into a single worksheet. In Excel, the term **consolidate** refers to combining the values from multiple cells or ranges. Math operations commonly performed in a data consolidation include sum, count, or average.

The most flexible way to consolidate data is to create a *3-D formula*—a formula that refers to cells in multiple worksheets. If you use this method, you enter a formula in the consolidation worksheet that includes references to the source cells on each worksheet containing the data you want to consolidate. Chapter 4 Skill 4.3, *Use 3-D References,* illustrates this method. For example, the formula =SUM('Store A:Store C'!B20) in that chapter adds the contents of cell B20 in the range of worksheets beginning with Store A and ending with Store C in the current workbook. The formula =AVERAGE(Sheet1:Sheet3!B4) in the Chapter 4 Challenge Exercise 1 averages the contents of cell B4 on Sheets 1 through 3.

You can also use the Consolidate option on the Data menu to consolidate data. This command enables you to consolidate by position or category if you set up the data properly. For example, each range to be consolidated must be organized in a list format—a label for each column, the same type of data in each column, and no blank rows or columns within the list. Other requirements include a name defined for each range involved in the consolidation, each range located on a separate worksheet, and a different worksheet for the consolidated data. (You learn to define named ranges in Chapter 11, "Working with Ranges.")

If you consolidate by position, each range must have the same layout. If you consolidate by category, the labels for columns or rows that guide the consolidation must be identical in spelling and capitalization. Any label that does not match labels in the other ranges to consolidate displays in a separate row or column in the consolidation.

The worksheets you consolidate can be in a single workbook or multiple workbooks. Often, different workbooks hold the data to consolidate. For example, an organization might maintain sales data at different regional headquarters. Periodically, each region forwards a copy of its workbook for consolidation with others at a central location, such as a corporate headquarters or accounting center.

In the following steps, you use the Consolidate option on the Data menu to combine data about two sales regions—East and West—in a new workbook. You consolidate the two data ranges by category, based on identical row and column labels (see Figure 9.9).

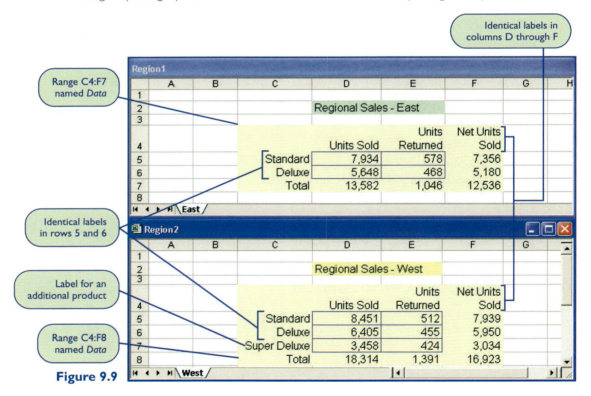

Figure 9.9

To Consolidate Data from Multiple Workbooks

① **Open the Region1 and Region2 workbooks.**

These are the two workbooks to consolidate in a new workbook. Each includes a single named range called *Data*, defined as the range C4:F7 in the Region1 workbook and C4:F8 in the Region2 workbook (refer to Figure 9.9). Note that the named ranges contain the same row and column labels; however, the West region includes the Super Deluxe product that is not sold in the East region.

② **Open a new workbook, and save it as** `Total Sales` **in the same folder as the Region1 and Region2 files.**

Three workbooks—Region1, Region2, and Total Sales—are now open.

③ **Select cell B3 in the Total Sales workbook, and choose Data, Consolidate.**

The Consolidate dialog box opens (see Figure 9.10). The Sum function displays in the Function text box, but other functions are available to use in a consolidation.

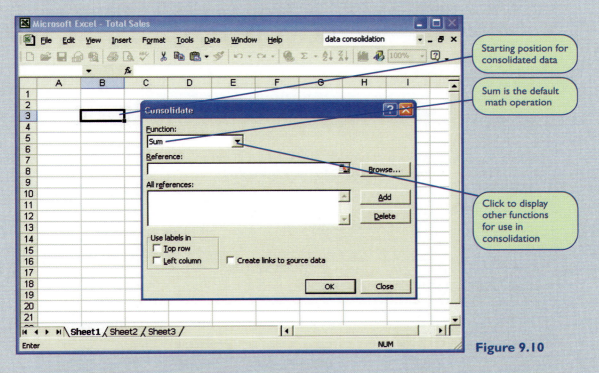

Figure 9.10

④ **In the Reference text box, type** `Region?.xls!Data`.

The question mark (?) after Region is a wildcard character indicating that you want to use files in the current folder that contain a single character after Region—in this case, Region1 and Region2. The exclamation mark (!) character indicates the end of the filename. It is followed by the name of the data range, which must be the same in every file if you want to execute the consolidation using a single reference.

continues ▶

To Consolidate Data from Multiple Workbooks (continued)

5 Select the three check boxes at the bottom of the dialog box (see Figure 9.11).

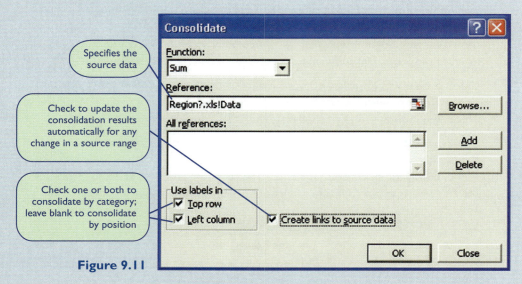

Specifies the source data

Check to update the consolidation results automatically for any change in a source range

Check one or both to consolidate by category; leave blank to consolidate by position

Figure 9.11

6 Click OK, and deselect the highlighted range.

Excel adds data from rows and columns with identical labels in all ranges named *Data*, and creates a consolidation table in the new workbook.

7 Widen column B and set text to wrap and center in the range D3:F3; then click cell D6 (see Figure 9.12).

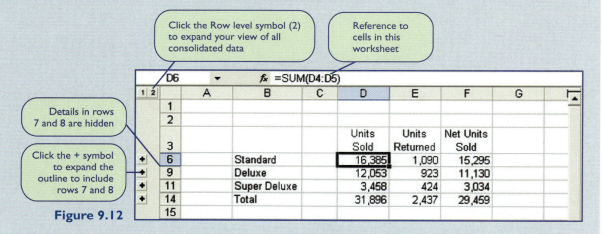

Click the Row level symbol (2) to expand your view of all consolidated data

Reference to cells in this worksheet

Details in rows 7 and 8 are hidden

Click the + symbol to expand the outline to include rows 7 and 8

Figure 9.12

8 Click the Row level symbol, the 2 button near the upper-left corner of the worksheet frame; then click cell D5.

Rows hidden in the collapsed view expand to reveal data (see Figure 9.13).

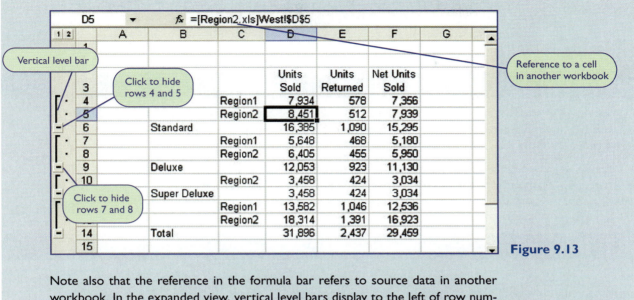

Figure 9.13

D5   *fx* =[Region2.xls]West!$D$5

Note also that the reference in the formula bar refers to source data in another workbook. In the expanded view, vertical level bars display to the left of row numbers and horizontal level bars might also display above the column letters. The level bars span groups of data. A plus (+) or minus (–) symbol displays at an end of each level bar. Clicking the – symbol collapses the view.

9 **Save and close the *TotalSales* workbook.**

10 **Close the *Region1* and *Region2* workbooks.**

Alternate Way:
Specifying the Reference in a Consolidation
In this illustration, the data files to consolidate were in the same folder, each filename began with the word *Region*, and the name *Data* defined each range to consolidate. If the files have different names, different locations, or different named ranges, you can still perform a consolidation, but you must enter each complete reference individually, clicking the Add button in the Consolidate dialog box after each entry.

In Depth:
Changing a Data Consolidation
If you select the *Create links to source data* check box in the Consolidate dialog box, you cannot add, edit, or delete any of the source ranges. If you do not select the *Create links to source data* check box, you can add, edit, or delete any source range.

To start the change process, click the upper-left cell in the consolidated data and choose Data, Consolidate. To add another source range, click within the Reference box, and click the sheet tab of the new range to consolidate; then type the name you gave the range or select it, and click the Add button. To edit an existing range, click the range you want to change in the All references list; then edit the selected reference in the Reference box, and click the Add button. To delete a source range, click the range you want to remove in the All references list, and click the Delete button.

For immediate reinforcement, work Skill Drills 2 and 3, and Challenges 2 and 3.

Summary

This skill set focused on ways to manage multiple workbooks. In the first of three topic areas, you worked with a user-defined template. You saved an existing workbook as a template, revised the template, and then used the template to create a new workbook.

You also created a workspace—a file that enables you to open workbooks as a group and display those workbooks in a predefined arrangement. The final topic provided a glimpse of the powerful Data, Consolidate command. You used it to add values by category from two workbooks.

Skill Drill

Skill Drill exercises *reinforce* skills. Each skill reinforced is the same, or nearly the same, as a skill presented in the skill set. Detailed instructions are provided in a step-by-step format.

Before beginning your Excel Expert Skill Set 2 Skill Drill exercises, complete the following steps:

1. Open the file named *MEE-S204*, and immediately save it as **MEE-S2drill**.

   The workbook contains six sheets: Overview, SD2, Data1, Data2, Data3, and SD3.

2. Click the Overview sheet to view the organization and content of the Skill Drill workbook for Excel Expert Skill Set 2.

Each exercise is independent of the others, so you may complete the exercises in any order. Be sure to save the workbook after completing each exercise. If you need a paper copy of one or more completed exercises, enter your name, centered in a header, before printing. Print options have already been set to print compressed to one page and to display the filename, sheet name, and current date in a footer.

Be sure to save your changes and close the workbook if you need more than one work session to complete the desired exercises. Continue working on *MEE-S2drill* instead of starting over in the original *MEE-S204* file.

1. Create a Workspace

You want to create a workspace that automatically opens three files and displays them in a tiled layout.

1. Open the *MEE-S205*, *MEE-S206*, and *MEE-S207* workbooks, and save them as **Person1**, **Person2**, and **Person3**, respectively, in the folder in which you are storing your solution files.

2. Make sure that only the Person1, Person2, and Person 3 workbooks are open.

3. Choose Window, Arrange; then select Tiled and click OK.

4. Choose File, Save Workspace.

   The Save Workspace dialog box opens. The Save as type text box at the bottom displays *Workspaces*.

5. In the Save in drop-down list, select the folder in which you are storing your solution files.

6. Enter **salesdata** as the filename; then click Save, and close all files.

   Now check that the workspace file functions as intended.

7. Choose File, Open; then specify the location of the *salesdata.xlw* file in the Look in text box.

8. If the *salesdata.xlw* file does not display in the list of files, specify either All Microsoft Excel Files or Workspaces in the Files of type text box.

9. Select the *salesdata.xlw* file, and click Open.

   Excel opens the *Person1*, *Person2*, and *Person3* workbooks, and displays them in a tiled layout.

10. Close all open workbooks.

2. Consolidate Data Using a 3-D Formula

Worksheets Data1, Data2, and Data3 contain sales data for three salespersons. You want to sum the data in these sheets and place the results in the SD2 worksheet using a 3-D formula.

1. Open the *MEE-S2drill* workbook, if necessary, and examine worksheets Data1, Data2, and Data3.

2. Select the SD2 worksheet.

3. In cell D8, type **=SUM(**

4. Click the Data1 worksheet tab.

5. Press and hold down ⬆Shift.

6. Click the Data3 worksheet tab, and release ⬆Shift.

7. Click cell C6, and type the closing right parenthesis.

   The formula =SUM(Data1:Data3!C6) displays in the formula bar.

8. Press ⏎Enter.

   Pressing Enter returns you to the SD2 worksheet. Notice that the consolidated value of 899 (model AR353) from the three worksheets appears in cell D8.

9. Copy the formula in cell D8 to the range D9:D10.

   The consolidated values of 363 (model WB-23) and 1109 (model SPR/34-2) display in cells D9 and D10, respectively.

10. Click cell D10.

    The formula =SUM(Data1:Data3!C8) displays in the formula bar.

11. Save your changes to the *MEE-S2drill* workbook.

3. Use the Data, Consolidate Command

This exercise uses the same data as the second Skill Drill exercise, except the data for the three salespersons are in three separate workbooks. Steps 1 through 3 show you the data involved in the consolidation. Step 4 begins the process to implement the consolidation.

1. Open the Person1, Person2, and Person3 workbooks. (If you did not complete Exercise 1, open the *MEE-S205*, *MEE-S206*, and *MEE-S207* workbooks, and save them as **Person1**, **Person2**, and **Person3**, respectively, in the folder in which you are storing your solution files.)

2. For each of the files, click the Name box drop-down arrow at the left end of the formula bar, and click the named range *Sold*.

   Each range named Sold defines an eight-cell range that includes labels and sales data for the same three products.

3. Close all three files when you are finished.

4. Open the *MEE-S2drill* workbook, if necessary.

5. Select the SD3 worksheet and click cell B4.

6. Choose Data, Consolidate.

   The Consolidate dialog box opens.

7. Type `Person?.xls!Sold` in the Reference text box.

8. Select the check boxes for Use labels in *Left column* and *Create links to source data*.

9. Click OK and widen the columns as necessary.

10. Click the outlining buttons and note how they expand the consolidation cells.

11. Click cell A1 and save your changes to the *MEE-S2drill* workbook.

Challenge

Challenge exercises expand on or are somewhat related to skills presented in the skill set. Each exercise provides a brief narrative introduction, followed by instructions in a numbered-step format that are not as detailed as those in the Skill Drill section.

Before beginning your Excel Expert Skill Set 2 Challenge exercises, complete the following steps:

1. Open the file named *MEE-S208*, and immediately save it as **MEE-S2challenge**.

   The workbook contains three sheets: an overview and two sheets labeled CH1 and CH2-3.

2. Click the Overview sheet to view the organization and content of the Challenge workbook for Excel Expert Skill Set 2.

Exercise 1 is independent of the others. Work Exercise 2 before working Exercise 3. Be sure to save the workbook after completing each exercise. If you need a paper copy of one or more completed exercises, enter your name, centered in a header, before printing. Print options have already been set to print compressed to one page. Settings to display the filename, sheet name, and current date in a footer have been set in all worksheets.

Be sure to save your changes and close the workbook if you need more than one work session to complete the desired exercises. Continue working on *MEE-S2challenge* instead of starting over in the original *MEE-S208* file.

1. Create a Weekly Payroll Template

You created and tested a worksheet to compute weekly gross pay. Now you want to save the worksheet as a template for use in generating weekly payroll reports in subsequent weeks.

1. Open the *MEE-S2challenge* workbook, if necessary; then select the CH1 worksheet.

2. Copy the CH1 worksheet to a blank workbook; then apply subsequent changes to the new workbook.

3. Delete rows 1 and 2; then apply a Classic 2 AutoFormat to the range A9:D19.

4. Delete the Hours Worked data in C10:C19, and delete the date in cell B7.

5. Save the worksheet as a template named **Weekly Gross Pay** in the same location as your other student solution files; then close the file.

2. Consolidate Different Source Files

When consolidating data from multiple files, it is good practice to use a consistent file naming convention with the same named range in each file (as illustrated within the text and Skill Drill exercises). However, as this exercise demonstrates, you can have different filenames and different named ranges. It is important that the named ranges have the same row or column labels within the ranges because the labels set up the consolidation. The ranges do not need all the same labels, but the areas you want to consolidate must have exactly the same labels.

1. Open the *MEE-S209* and *MEE-S210* workbooks, and save them as **Standard** and **Deluxe**, respectively, in the folder in which you are storing your solution files.

2. Examine the files, making note of the named ranges.

The named range is *Sales* in the Deluxe workbook and *Data* in the Standard workbook. Because the names are different, you must specify each range separately in the data consolidation.

3. Close the Standard and Deluxe workbooks.

4. Open the *MEE-S2challenge* workbook, if necessary, and select the CH2-3 worksheet.

5. Click cell B4, and choose Data, Consolidate.

6. Type **Deluxe.xls!Sales** in the Reference text box, and click Add.

7. Type **Standard.xls!Data** as the next Reference and click Add.

8. Check all three check boxes at the bottom of the Consolidate dialog box, and then click OK.

9. Expand the outline and format the table by aligning column headings and adjusting column widths.

10. Save your changes to the *MEE-S2challenge* workbook.

3. Test Consolidation Links

When you ran the consolidation challenge in Exercise 2, you specified that you wanted to create links to the source data. This enables the consolidated data to be updated automatically if changes are made in either of the source files. Now you want to verify the links.

1. Open the *MEE-S2challenge* workbook, if necessary, and select the CH2-3 worksheet.

2. Open the *Deluxe* and *Standard* workbooks.

Only three files should be open: *Deluxe*, *Standard*, and *MEE-S2challenge*.

3. Choose Window, Arrange; then select Tiled, and click OK.

4. Size the windows and use the scrollbars to view the data areas of all three workbooks.

5. Expand the outlined data in the CH2-3 worksheet in the *MEE-S2challenge* workbook, if necessary.

6. Select cell C8 within the *Standard* workbook, and change the Q1 value for the East region from *232* to **274**.

The change in Q1 data for the East region impacts the CH2-3 worksheet. The values *274* and *400* display in cells D6 and D7, respectively.

7. Save your changes and close the workbooks.

Formatting Numbers

CHAPTER 10

This skill set includes

Create and apply custom number formats

Use conditional formats

Skill Set Overview

Excel provides a variety of features to promote consistency in worksheet content and formatting with a minimum of effort. To format numbers and formula results, you generally apply predefined number formats. Core Skill 1.2 *Enter and Edit Cell Data Including Text, Numbers, and Formulas* introduced predefined number formats, such as Currency and Comma.

In this skill set, you explore two alternative methods to format numbers and formula results. You apply a number format that you create and set up formatting that varies depending on whether or not the value in the cell meets a specified condition.

Skill 3.1: Create and Apply Custom Number Formats

Formats are masks that, when applied to a cell, change the display of the content without changing the value in the cell. For a unique situation in which a predefined number format does not meet your needs, you can create a **custom number format** that Excel saves with the current workbook. The process includes displaying the Number tab in the Format Cells dialog box, selecting the Custom category, and typing the appropriate codes in the Type text box.

You can enter a variety of codes including ones for currency, percentage, scientific notation, days, months, years, hours, minutes, seconds, text, repeating characters, spaces, thousands separators, decimal places, colors, and conditions. Table 10.1 shows several custom number format examples found in Excel's onscreen Help.

Table 10.1 Selected Custom Number Formats	
Custom Number Format	**Description**
#.000	Displays 8.9 as 8.900
#,	Displays 12000 as 12
???.???	Displays 44.398, 102.65, and 2.8 with aligned decimals
[Red][<=100];[Blue][>100]	Displays numbers less than or equal to 100 in a red font and numbers greater than 100 in a blue font
$0.00" Surplus";$0.00" Shortage"	Displays the value in a currency format with two decimal places; the word *Surplus* follows a positive number and the word *Shortage* follows a negative number

In the following steps, you create and apply a custom number format similar to the one in the last row of the preceding table. You create the custom format using the Format Cells dialog box.

To Create a Custom Number Format

1 **Open the *MEE-S301* workbook, and save it as** Custom Format.
The single worksheet named Budget provides a budget analysis for a family reunion.

2 **Click cell A16, and change the label to** Budget Status **instead of *Amount Under (Over) Budget*.**

3 **Click cell B16.**

The formula =B5-B14 displays in the formula bar. You are going to change the display of formula results, not the formula itself.

4 **Choose F̲ormat, C̲ells; then select the Number tab.**

5 **Click Custom in the C̲ategory list.**

Excel displays the dialog box shown in Figure 10.1.

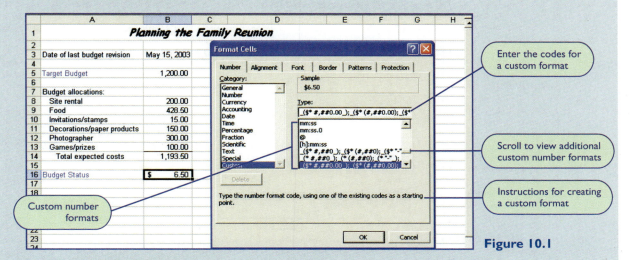

Figure 10.1

6 **Delete the contents currently in the T̲ype text box.**

7 **Type $0.00" Surplus";$0.00" Shortage" in the T̲ype text box (see Figure 10.2).**

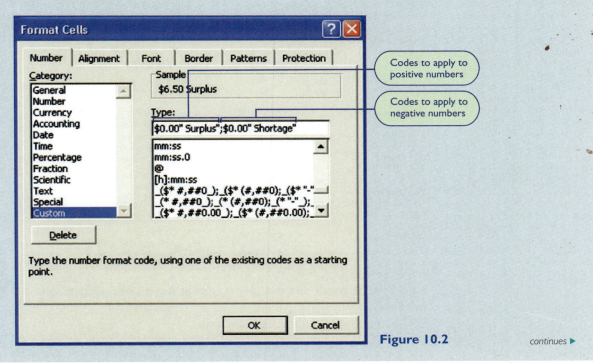

Figure 10.2

continues ▶

To Create a Custom Number Format (continued)

You use quotation marks to encase text, and a semicolon to separate instructions for positive and negative numbers. Make sure that you include a space between the quotation mark and Surplus, and a space between the quotation mark and Shortage.

8   Click OK.

Excel saves your custom format in the current workbook, and applies it to the current cell B16 (see Figure 10.3).

The word *Surplus* displays when the formula result is a positive number

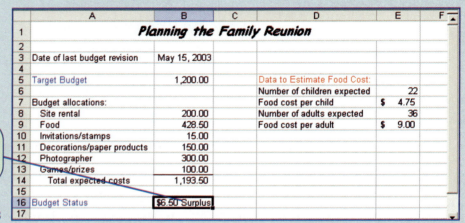

Figure 10.3

9   In cell E8, change the number of adults expected to 40; then double-click between columns B and C in the worksheet frame to widen column B.

Expected costs exceed the target budget. The text displayed in cell B16 changes (see Figure 10.4).

The word *Shortage* displays when the formula result is a negative number

	A	B	C	D	E
1		*Planning the Family Reunion*			
2					
3	Date of last budget revision	May 15, 2003			
4					
5	Target Budget	1,200.00		Data to Estimate Food Cost:	
6				Number of children expected	22
7	Budget allocations:			Food cost per child	$ 4.75
8	Site rental	200.00		Number of adults expected	40
9	Food	464.50		Food cost per adult	$ 9.00
10	Invitations/stamps	15.00			
11	Decorations/paper products	150.00			
12	Photographer	300.00			
13	Games/prizes	100.00			
14	Total expected costs	1,229.50			
15					
16	Budget Status	$29.50 Shortage			
17					

Figure 10.4

10   Save your changes to the *Custom Format* workbook, and close the workbook.

Continue with the next skill, or exit Excel.

In Depth:

Deleting a Custom Number Format

You can easily delete a custom number format stored in a workbook. Choose Format, Cells; then click the Number tab, and select Custom in the Category list. Scroll to the bottom of the list in the Type box; then click the custom format you want to remove, and click the Delete button.

Using Color and Conditions in Custom Number Formats

You can create a custom number format for use only if a number meets a condition you specify. Simply enclose the condition in square brackets. You can also specify one of eight colors—black, cyan, magenta, white, blue, green, red, and yellow—to apply to a section of a custom number format. Type the name of the color within square brackets, and make sure that the color code is the first item in the section. For example, if you create and apply the custom number format [red][<=70], Excel applies a red color to the value in the cell if that value is less than or equal to 70.

Using a Custom Number Format to Hide Cell Contents

You can hide the contents of selected cells that use a custom number format. If you want to apply the format to any cell(s) in the workbook at any time, begin by clicking a blank unused cell in the workbook. Choose Format, Cells; then click the Number tab, and select Custom in the Category list. Delete the current contents in the Type box; then type ; ; ; (three semicolons), and click OK.

To apply the format, select the cell(s) whose contents you want to hide; then click the Number tab in the Format Cells dialog box, and click Custom in the Category list. Scroll to the bottom of the Type list; select the custom format ;;; and click OK.

To redisplay cell contents hidden with the ;;; custom number format, apply an appropriate predefined number format using toolbar buttons or the Number tab in the Format Cells dialog box. For example, if you select cells with hidden contents that are dates, use the following process to redisplay the dates: Click the Number tab in the Format Cells dialog box, and select Date in the Category list; then click the desired date format, and click OK.

For immediate reinforcement, work Skill Drills 1, 3, 5 and Challenge 1.

Skill 3.2: **Use Conditional Formats**

Using formats to emphasize cells in a worksheet can call attention to specific data. If you want to accent a cell, depending on the value of the cell, you can use *conditional formatting*. Conditional formats return a result based on whether the value in the cell meets a specified condition. Formatting options include specifying font style, font color, shading, patterns, borders, bold, italic, and underline.

You apply conditional formatting using the Conditional Formatting dialog box. You can specify up to three conditions, with varying formats for each condition.

In the following steps, you apply conditional formatting based on one condition—whether an individual's monthly sales meet or exceed the target sales for that month. You also copy the format to cells containing sales data for other employees.

To Apply and Copy a Conditional Format

1 **Open the *MEE-S302* workbook, and save it as** Conditional Format.
The workbook includes one worksheet that generates a Sales Force Monthly Earnings report.

2 **Click cell B11, and choose F<u>o</u>rmat, Con<u>d</u>itional Formatting.**
The Conditional Formatting dialog box opens (see Figure 10.5).

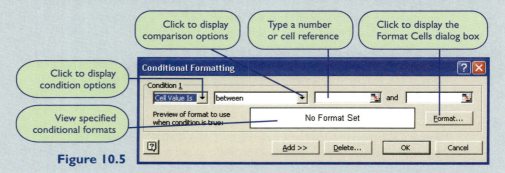

Figure 10.5

3 **Display the comparison options drop-down list (see Figure 10.6).**

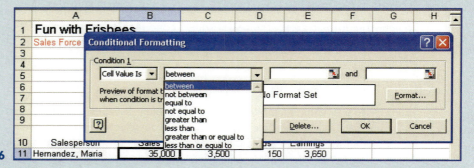

Figure 10.6

4 **Select *greater than or equal* to from the comparison options drop-down list.**

5 **In the text box to the right of the comparison option, type =$A$7 (see Figure 10.7).**

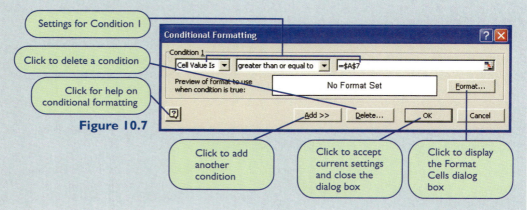

Figure 10.7

You set a condition for cell B11 with a cell value greater than or equal to the contents of cell A7. Now, specify the format of cell B11 if the condition is true—that is, if the monthly sales of Maria Hernandez meet or exceed the sales target for the month.

6 **Click the Eormat button in the Conditional Formatting dialog box (refer to Figure 10.7), and select the Font tab in the Format Cells dialog box.**

7 **Select Bold in the Font style list box.**

8 **Display the Color drop-down list, and select gold.**
You specified the settings for the conditional format (see Figure 10.8).

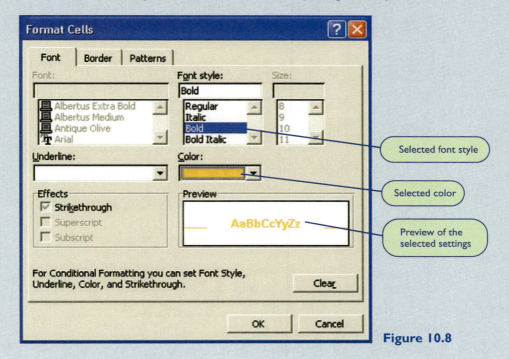

Figure 10.8

9 **Click OK.**
The Format Cells dialog box closes. The preview area displays AaBbCcYyZz in the selected bold and gold formats.

10 **Click OK.**
The Conditional Formatting dialog box closes. The amount in cell B11 displays in bold and gold because it exceeds the target sales in cell A7.

11 **Make sure that cell B11 is the current cell, and click the Copy button on the toolbar.**

12 **Select the range B12:B16; then choose Edit, Paste Special.**
The Paste Special dialog box opens.

continues ▶

To Apply and Copy a Conditional Format (continued)

13 Click **Forma<u>t</u>s** in the **Paste** area (see Figure 10.9).

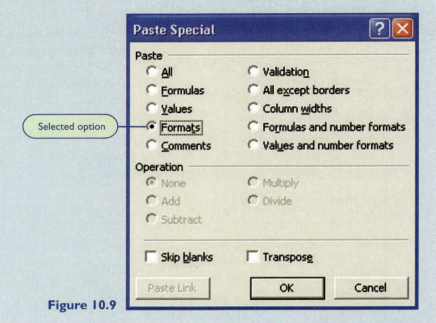

Figure 10.9

14 Click **OK**; then click cell **A1** to deselect the range, and press Esc to remove the marquee around cell **B11**.

You copied the conditional formatting to cells containing sales data for other employees. The sales amounts for Maria Hernandez, Jeffrey Peters, Fred Ralston, and Susan Tuttle display in bold and gold because these amounts meet or exceed the current $30,000 sales target (see Figure 10.10).

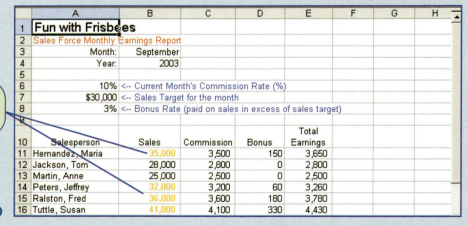

Figure 10.10

15 **Save your changes to the *Conditional Format* workbook, and close the workbook.**

In Depth:

Removing Conditional Formatting

You can remove conditional formatting along with other formats by using an option on the Edit menu. Select the formatted cell(s), and choose Edit, Clear, Formats.

To remove conditional formatting but retain other formatting, select the formatted cell(s) and choose Format, Conditional Formatting. Click the Delete button to display the Delete Conditional Formatting dialog box; then check the Condition 1, Condition 2, and/or Condition 3 check boxes, and click OK.

*For immediate reinforcement, work Skill Drills 2 and 4,
and Challenges 2 and 3.*

Summary

In this skill set, you expanded your ability to format numbers and formula results. You created and applied a custom number format that included text. You also used the Conditional Formatting dialog box to set up formatting that varied depending on whether the value in the cell met a specified condition.

Skill Drill

Skill Drill exercises *reinforce* skills. Each skill reinforced is the same, or nearly the same, as a skill presented in the skill set. Detailed instructions are provided in a step-by-step format.

Before beginning your Excel Expert Skill Set 3 Skill Drill exercises, complete the following steps:

1. Open the file named *MEE-S303*, and immediately save it as **MEE-S3drill**.

   The workbook contains five sheets: An Overview sheet, and sheets SD1 through SD4.

2. Click the Overview sheet to view the organization and content of the Skill Drill workbook for Excel Expert Skill Set 3.

Each exercise is independent of the others, so you may complete the exercises in any order. Be sure to save the workbook after completing each exercise. If you need a paper copy of one or more completed exercises, enter your name, centered in a header, before printing. Print options have already been set to print compressed to one page and to display the filename, sheet name, and current date in a footer.

Be sure to save your changes and close the workbook if you need more than one work session to complete the desired exercises. Continue working on *MEE-S3drill* instead of starting over in the original *MEE-S303* file.

1. Apply a Custom Number Format

You are constructing a worksheet to display decimal and fraction equivalents for values between zero and one. The decimal values are already in place. You want to copy the decimal values to a second column, and apply a custom format to change the display in the second column to fractions.

To make the changes, including a custom format to display fractions, follow these steps:

1. Open the *MEE-S3drill* workbook, if necessary, and click the SD1 worksheet.
2. Copy the contents of A6:A25 to B6:B25.
3. Select the range B6:B25, and choose Format, Cells.
4. Select the Number tab, and click Custom at the bottom of the Category list.
5. Scroll down to view other options in the Type list; then select the custom format # ??/??, and click OK.

    Check that 1/20, 1/10, 3/20, and so forth displays in the fraction column B.
6. Right-align the labels in A5:B5, and deselect the range.
7. Adjust column widths to eliminate unnecessary white space.
8. Click cell A1, and save your changes to the *MEE-S3drill* workbook.

2. Apply Conditional Formatting (One Condition)

You are developing a multiple-sheet workbook to keep track of residential real estate listings and sales. You want to use Excel's conditional formatting feature to display annual sales of one million or more with a blue border around the cell.

To set up the conditional formatting, follow these steps:

1. Open the *MEE-S3drill* workbook, if necessary, and select the SD2 worksheet.
2. Click cell B12.

    You selected the cell containing annual sales for Jessica Blair.
3. Choose Format, Conditional Formatting.

    The Conditional Formatting dialog box opens.
4. In the first of three boxes for condition 1, specify *Cell Value Is*.
5. In the second of three boxes for condition 1, specify *greater than or equal to*.
6. In the third of three boxes for condition 1, type **1000000**.
7. Click the Format button in the Conditional Formatting dialog box.
8. Select the Border tab in the Format Cells dialog box, and select a bright blue color from the Color drop-down list.
9. Choose the Outline preset, and click OK to close the Format Cells dialog box.
10. Click OK to close the Conditional Formatting dialog box, and click a cell other than cell B12.

    Cell B12 displays with a blue border because formula results are greater than or equal to one million dollars.
11. Save your changes to the *MEE-S3drill* workbook.

3. Assign Color Using a Custom Number Format

You are developing a worksheet that tracks grades on exams. You want to display grades in red that are less than 70 and display grades in blue that are 70 or greater. Such formatting makes it easy to distinguish between grades equal to or higher than a C (blue) and those lower than a C (red).

To achieve the desired effects using a custom number format, follow these steps:

1. Open the *MEE-S3drill* workbook, if necessary; then select the SD3 worksheet.

2. Select the range B5:B12.

3. Choose F**o**rmat, C**e**lls; then select the Number tab.

4. Click Custom in the **C**ategory list.

5. Delete the contents currently in the **T**ype text box.

6. Type **[red][<70];[blue][>=70]** in the **T**ype text box; then click OK, and deselect the range in column B.

   Excel saves your custom format in the workbook and applies it to the range B5:B12. The Exam 1 grades for Abbott, Cook, Dawson, Farmer, and Gibbons display in blue. The Exam 1 grades for Baker, Evans, and Hunter display in red.

7. Enter **Ingalls, Josh** in cell A13; then enter **86** in cell B13 and make sure that cell B13 is the current cell.

   The Exam 1 grade for Ingalls displays in blue. Excel automatically assigns the format from the cell above.

8. Save your changes to the *MEE-S3drill* workbook.

4. Assign Color Using the Conditional Formatting Dialog Box

You are developing a worksheet that tracks grades on exams. You want to display grades in red that are less than 70 and grades in blue that are 70 or greater. Such formatting makes it easy to distinguish between grades equal to or higher than a C (blue) and those lower than a C (red).

To achieve the desired effects using the Conditional Formatting dialog box, follow these steps:

1. Open the *MEE-S3drill* workbook, if necessary; then select the SD4 worksheet.

2. Select the range B5:B12 and choose F**o**rmat, Con**d**itional Formatting.

   The Conditional Formatting dialog box opens.

3. In the first of three boxes for condition 1, specify *Cell Value Is*.

4. In the second of three boxes for condition 1, specify *greater than or equal to*.

5. In the third of three boxes for condition 1, type **70**.

6. Click the **F**ormat button and select the Font tab in the Format Cells dialog box.

7. Display the **C**olor drop-down list; then select a blue color and click OK.

8. Click the **A**dd button in the Conditional Formatting dialog box.

9. Make sure that *Cell Value Is* displays in the first of three boxes for condition 2.

10. In the second of three boxes for condition 2, specify *less than*.

11. In the third of three boxes for condition 2, type **70**.

12. Click the **F**ormat button and select the Font tab in the Format Cells dialog box.

13. Display the **C**olor drop-down list; then select a red color and click OK.

14. Click OK to close the Conditional Formatting dialog box, and deselect the highlighted range.

    Excel applies the conditional formatting to the range B5:B12. The Exam 1 grades for Abbott, Cook, Dawson, Farmer, and Gibbons display in blue. The Exam 1 grades for Baker, Evans, and Hunter display in red.

15. Enter `Ingalls, Josh` in cell A13; then enter `86` in cell B13.

The Exam 1 grade for Ingalls displays in blue. Excel automatically assigns the format from the cell above.

16. Save your changes to the *MEE-S3drill* workbook.

5. Get Help with Custom Number Formats

You know that there are numerous custom number formats in addition to those presented in Table 10.1 and the hands-on exercises, and you want to explore the substantial onscreen Help related to the topic.

To get onscreen Help on custom number formats, follow these steps:

1. Display a blank Excel workbook.

2. Enter `custom number formats` in the Ask a question box.

3. Select the Help topic *Number format codes*, and click Show All.

4. Read information in the *Text and spacing* section.

5. Read information in the *Decimal places, spaces, colors, and conditions* section.

6. Read information in the *Currency, percentages, and scientific notation* section.

7. Read information in the *Dates and times* section.

8. Close onscreen Help.

Challenge

Challenge exercises expand on or are somewhat related to skills presented in the skill set. Each exercise provides a brief narrative introduction, followed by instructions in a numbered-step format that are not as detailed as those in the Skill Drill section.

Before beginning your Excel Expert Skill Set 3 Challenge exercises, complete the following steps:

1. Open the file named *MEE-S304*, and immediately save it as **MEE-S3challenge**.

The workbook contains four sheets: an overview and sheets labeled CH1 through CH3.

2. Click the Overview sheet to view the organization and content of the Challenge workbook for Excel Expert Skill Set 3.

Each exercise is independent of the others. Be sure to save the workbook after completing each exercise. If you need a paper copy of one or more completed exercises, enter your name, centered in a header, before printing. Print options have already been set to print compressed to one page. Settings to display the filename, sheet name, and current date in a footer have been set in all worksheets.

Be sure to save your changes and close the workbook if you need more than one work session to complete the desired exercises. Continue working on *MEE-S3challenge* instead of starting over in the original *MEE-S304* file.

1. Hide Values Using a Custom Number Format

You are developing a workbook to track selected data on students. You want to hide data in the grade point average (GPA) column. You plan to keep that data hidden except during update sessions.

To hide the values using a custom number format, and redisplay the hidden values, follow these steps:

1. Review the In Depth note titled, *Using a Custom Number Format to Hide Cell Contents* at the end of Skill 3.1, *Create and Apply Custom Number Formats*.
2. Open your *MEE-S3challenge* workbook, if necessary, and select the CH1 worksheet.
3. Select the cells containing GPA data in column C.
4. Open the Format Cells dialog box; display the Number tab, and select Custom in the Category list.
5. Delete existing codes in the Type text box; then enter the custom number format to hide values in cells, and click OK.

   GPA data no longer displays. You created the custom number format that hides values in cells, and Excel applied it to the selected cells.
6. Click cell C5.

   The value *3.402* displays in the formula bar, but does not display in cell C5.
7. Select the cells containing hidden GPA data, and apply a Comma, three decimal places format.

   GPA data redisplay in column C, each value shown to three decimal places.
8. Select the cells containing GPA data, and apply a General format using the Number page in the Format Cells dialog box.

   GPA data display with the original number of decimal places.
9. Reapply the custom number format to hide values, and save your changes to the *MEE-S3challenge* workbook.

2. Apply Conditional Formatting (Two Conditions)

You are developing a workbook to keep track of residential real estate listings and sales. You want to use Excel's Conditional Formatting feature to draw attention to quarterly sales greater than or equal to $250,000 or quarterly sales less than $150,000.

To set up the desired conditional formatting, follow these steps:

1. Open your *MEE-S3challenge* workbook, if necessary, and select the worksheet named CH2.
2. Select the range B10:E13. (Do not include the totals in row 14.) Choose Format, Conditional Formatting.
3. Specify condition 1 as cell value greater than or equal to **250000**.
4. Click the Format button and specify gold shading (not gold text).
5. Redisplay the Conditional Formatting dialog box, and click the Add button.
6. Specify condition 2 as cell value less than **150000**, and set up red text as the format.
7. Make sure that the conditional formats display as intended, and make changes as necessary.

   Cells in the ranges D10:E10 and B12:E12 should display with gold backgrounds. Cell contents should display red in cells B11, B13, D11, and D13.
8. Save your changes to the *MEE-S3challenge* workbook.

3. Apply Conditional Formatting (Three Conditions)

You are developing a workbook to keep track of bookings on selected flights. You want to use Excel's Conditional Formatting feature to draw attention to flights that are overbooked, at capacity, and available.

To set up the desired conditional formatting, follow these steps:

1. Open your *MEE-S3challenge* workbook, if necessary, and select the CH3 worksheet.

2. Select cell C5 and choose Format, Conditional Formatting.

3. Specify condition 1 as cell value greater than **=B5**.

   Make sure that you do *not* include dollar signs in the reference to cell B5. The relative cell reference enables you to copy the custom formatting to other cells in a subsequent step.

4. Click the Format button and specify a red outline border.

5. Redisplay the Conditional Formatting dialog box, and click the Add button.

6. Specify condition 2 as cell value less than **=B5**, and set a bright green font color as the format.

7. Redisplay the Conditional Formatting dialog box, and click the Add button.

8. Specify condition 3 as cell value equal to **=B5**, and set a bold font style as the format.

9. Copy only the formatting in cell C5 to the range C6:C9. (*Hint:* Remember to use Paste Special, and specify Formats as shown in Figure 10.9.)

10. Make sure that the conditional formats display as intended, and make changes in the Conditional Formatting dialog box as necessary.

    Cells C5 and C7 should display with red borders. The contents of cells C8 and C9 should display in a bright green color. The contents of cell C6 should display bold.

11. Save your changes to the *MEE-S3challenge* workbook.

Working with Ranges

This skill set includes

Use named ranges in formulas	▌ Create and use range names ▌ View ranges defined by range names
Use Lookup and Reference functions	▌ Create data using the VLOOKUP function ▌ Create data using the HLOOKUP function

Skill Set Overview

You continually work with ranges as you create and maintain Excel workbooks—entering and editing data, formatting multiple cells, copying or moving content from one location to another, setting a print area, and so forth. In this skill set, you expand your knowledge of ranges in two areas. You learn to create meaningful names to represent ranges. You also work with selected functions in the Lookup and Reference category.

Skill 4.1: Use Named Ranges in Formulas

A *range name* is a word or string of characters that refers to a cell or range of cells. The contents of the named cells can be labels, numbers, and/or formulas.

The most common use for a range name is to make a formula easier to read and understand. For example, the formula =SUM(JanDecSales) conveys more information than =SUM(B5:M5). You can also move the cell pointer to another section of a large worksheet, or print a section of a worksheet, by specifying the name assigned to that section instead of a cell reference.

In this skill, you specify two range names: one to use in a formula and the other to identify a section of the worksheet. You also create a list of range names and the cell or range of cells that each represents.

Create and Use Range Names

A range name must start with a letter or an underscore. The rest of the name can include numbers and letters up to a maximum of 255 characters. Spaces are not allowed, but you can use underscore characters and periods to separate words.

You can use uppercase and lowercase letters in range names, but range names in a workbook cannot differ only in case. For example, you cannot use the names *Data* and *DATA* to represent different ranges in the same workbook.

Range names use absolute cell addresses. When you define a name in one worksheet, it is available to other worksheets in the workbook. Therefore, a range name cannot refer to one cell or range of cells in one worksheet, and a different cell or range of cells in another worksheet within the same workbook.

You can define a name that refers to cells in another workbook. You can also link to a defined name in another workbook. For example, you specify *Region?.xls!Data* in a data consolidation in Expert Skill 2.3. The results sum the contents of each range named *Data* in the Region1.xls and Region2.xls workbooks.

In the following steps, you specify two range names: one to use in a formula and the other to identify a section of the worksheet. You then include one defined name in a formula and use the other to go to the named location in the worksheet.

To Create and Use Range Names

1 **Open the *MEE-S401* file, and save it as** Range Names.
The workbook contains a single worksheet named *Copy Bids*.

2 **Click cell B6, and click the Name box at the left end of the formula bar (see Figure 11.1).**

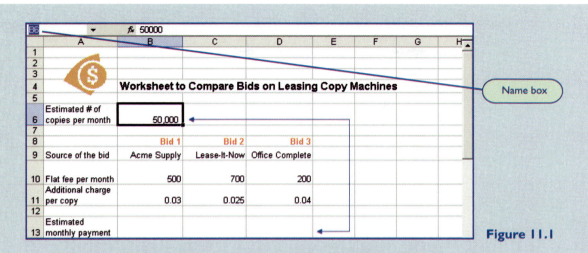

Figure 11.1

3 Type num.of.copies **in the Name box, and press** Enter.
You assigned the name *num.of.copies* to cell B6 (see Figure 11.2).

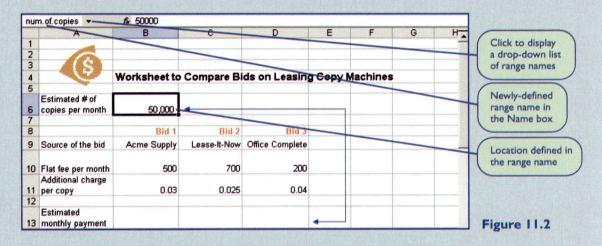

Figure 11.2

4 **Select the range A20:A34 and click the Name box at the left end of the formula bar.**

5 Type ContactVendor **in the Name box, and press** Enter.
You assigned the name *ContactVendor* to the range A20:A34. Now use the type-and-point method to enter a formula in cell B13.

6 **Click cell B13; then type = to start a formula.**

7 **Click cell B10; type + (a plus sign), and click cell B6.**
The partially completed formula *=B10+num.of.copies* displays in the formula bar (see Figure 11.3). When you click a cell reference instead of typing it as you create a formula, Excel displays its associated range name instead of the row-and-column reference (see the range name *num.of.copies* representing cell B6 in Figure 11.3).

continues ▶

To Create and Use Range Names (continued)

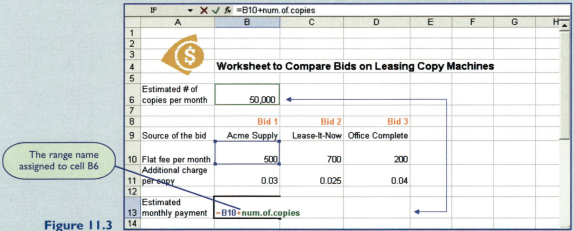

The range name assigned to cell B6

Figure 11.3

8 **Type * (an asterisk) and click cell B11; then press ⏎Enter and make cell B13 the active cell.**

The formula *=B10+num.of.copies*B11* displays in the formula bar, and the formula result *$2,000* displays in cell B13 (see Figure 11.4). The formula *=B10+B6*B11* would display if you typed the entire formula instead of typing the math operators and clicking the cell references.

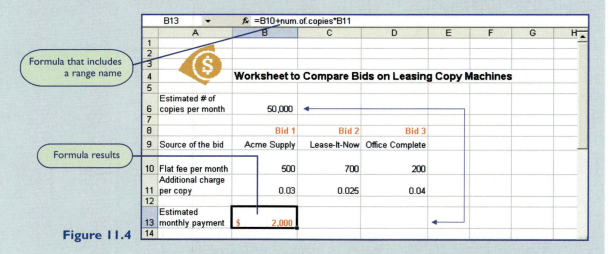

Formula that includes a range name

Formula results

Figure 11.4

9 **Copy the formula in cell B13 to the range C13:D13.**

The monthly payments for Bid 2 and Bid 3 are $1,950 and $2,200, respectively. The formula copies correctly because a range name uses absolute cell references.

10 **Choose Edit, Go To (or press F5).**

The Go To dialog box opens (see Figure 11.5).

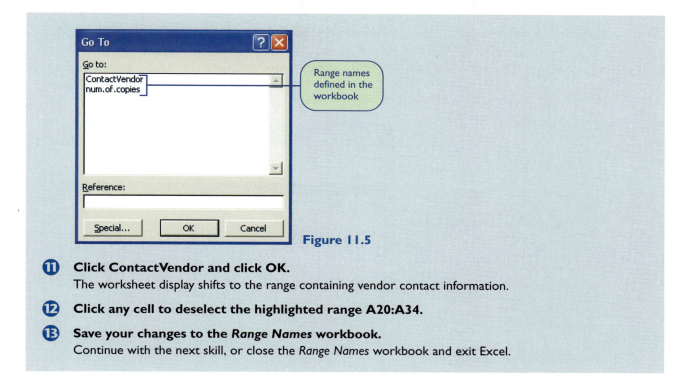

Range names defined in the workbook

Figure 11.5

⑪ **Click ContactVendor and click OK.**
The worksheet display shifts to the range containing vendor contact information.

⑫ **Click any cell to deselect the highlighted range A20:A34.**

⑬ **Save your changes to the *Range Names* workbook.**
Continue with the next skill, or close the *Range Names* workbook and exit Excel.

Alternate Way:
Defining a Range Name

You know that you can define a range name by selecting a range and then entering the range name in the Name box at the left end of the formula bar. You can also use a menu approach to define a range name. Choose Insert, Name, Define to open the Define Name dialog box. Enter the range name in the Names in workbook box; specify the worksheet location in the Refers to box, and click OK.

View Ranges Defined by Range Names

If you want to find out what a range name refers to without moving the cell pointer to the defined location, you can select the command sequence Insert, Name, Define, and select the name. Its associated range displays in the Refers to box within the Define Name dialog box.

You can also create a two-column list of range names and associated ranges in the worksheet. The process involves selecting a cell to be the upper-left cell in a blank area large enough to hold the list and executing an Insert, Name, Paste command.

In the following steps, you execute a command sequence to learn the range defined by a selected range name. You also create a list of range names in a worksheet.

To View Ranges Defined by Range Names

❶ **Open the *Range Names* workbook, if necessary.**
The workbook contains a single worksheet named *Copy Bids*.

❷ **Choose Insert, Name, Define.**
The Define Name dialog box opens.

continues ▶

To View Ranges Defined by Range Names (continued)

3 **Click ContactVendor in the _Names in workbook_ list (see Figure 11.6).**
Information about the selected range name displays in the <u>R</u>efers to box near the bottom of the dialog box (see Figure 11.6).

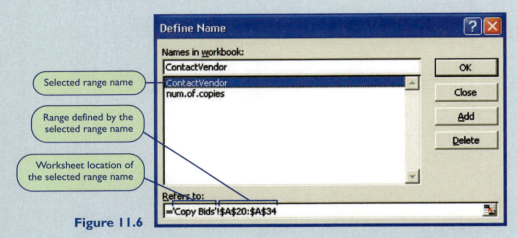

Selected range name

Range defined by the selected range name

Worksheet location of the selected range name

Figure 11.6

4 **Click the Close button; the click cell D20.**
You closed the Define Name dialog box and selected the starting position for a list of range names.

5 **Choose <u>I</u>nsert, <u>N</u>ame, <u>P</u>aste.**
The Paste Name dialog box opens (see Figure 11.7).

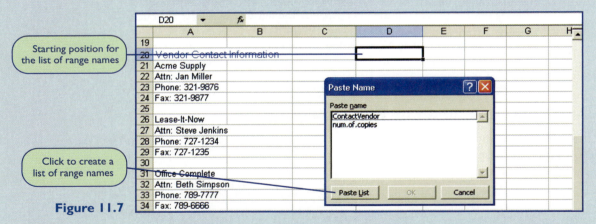

Starting position for the list of range names

Click to create a list of range names

Figure 11.7

6 **Click Paste <u>L</u>ist, and click any cell to deselect the list.**
Information about the names defined in the _Range Names_ workbook displays in D20:E21 (see Figure 11.8).

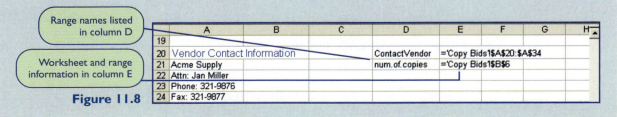

Range names listed in column D

Worksheet and range information in column E

Figure 11.8

7 **Enter** `List of Range Names` **in cell D19; then apply an Arial 12-pt bright blue font to cell D19.**

8 **Click cell A1; then save your changes to the *Range Names* workbook, and close the workbook.**
Continue with the next skill, or exit Excel.

In Depth:
Deleting a Range Name
You can delete a range name using a three-step process. Select the command sequence Insert, Name, Define; then select the name to delete from the list that appears in the Define Name dialog box, and click the Delete button (refer to Figure 11.6).

For immediate reinforcement, work Skill Drills 1 and 2.

Skill 4.2: **Use Lookup and Reference Functions**

The lookup functions find values in worksheet ranges, and the reference functions generally pertain to worksheet addresses. Table 11.1 describes the functions in this category as explained in onscreen Help.

Table 11.1	Lookup and Reference Functions
Function	**Description**
ADDRESS	Returns a reference as text to a single cell in a worksheet
AREAS	Returns the number of areas in a reference
CHOOSE	Chooses a value from a list of values
COLUMN	Returns the column number of a reference
COLUMNS	Returns the number of columns in a reference
HLOOKUP	Looks in the top row of an array and returns the value of the indicated cell
HYPERLINK	Creates a shortcut or jump that opens a document stored on a network server, an intranet, or the Internet
INDEX	Uses an index to choose a value from a reference or array
INDIRECT	Returns a reference indicated by a text value
LOOKUP	Looks up values in a vector or array
MATCH	Looks up values in a reference or array
OFFSET	Returns a reference offset from a given reference
ROW	Returns the row number of a reference
ROWS	Returns the number of rows in a reference
RTD	Retrieves real-time data from a program that supports COM automation
TRANSPOSE	Returns the transpose of an array
VLOOKUP	Looks in the first column of an array and moves across the row to return the value of a cell

Some of the descriptions in the table include the word *array*. An **array** is a set of items operated on as a group or individually. Excel supports one- and two-dimensional arrays. A one-dimensional array can be stored in a range that consists of one row (a horizontal array) or one column (a vertical array). A two-dimensional array can be stored in a rectangular range of cells.

This skill introduces two lookup functions—VLOOKUP and HLOOKUP. These two functions are among the most commonly used lookup and reference functions.

Create Data Using the VLOOKUP Function

If the data you want to look up is stored vertically in a table—that is, in columns—then use the VLOOKUP function. The **VLOOKUP function** looks for a specified value in the leftmost column of a table array. When that value is found in a cell within the table, the function displays the contents of another cell in that same row from the column you specify.

Looking at an example helps to clarify the purpose of this function. Figure 11.9 illustrates using the VLOOKUP function to convert an abbreviation for a major to the full name of the major. For example, the VLOOKUP function in cell D13 returns the description *Finance* when it encounters the abbreviation *FN*.

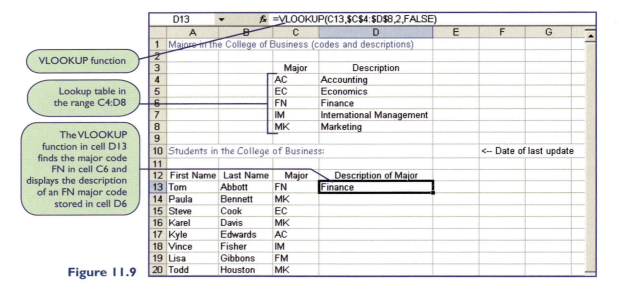

Figure 11.9

You can specify exact or approximate matches when using the VLOOKUP function. Approximate matches enable you to work with values within a specified range.

In this skill area, you complete two sets of hands-on steps. In the first set, you view the syntax (structure) of the VLOOKUP function and then use it to create text descriptions for major codes based on exact matches to entries in the lookup table (refer to Figure 11.9). In the second set, you use the VLOOKUP function to create descriptions of donor level based on approximate matches. For example, VLOOKUP finds the donor level *Chairman Circle* for any donation between $1,000 and $2,499.

To Create Data Using the VLOOKUP Function (Exact Match)

1 Open the *MEE-S402* workbook, and save it as VLOOKUP.

2 Select the **VLOOKUP** syntax worksheet; then study the function syntax and explanations in rows 2 through 8 (see Figure 11.10).

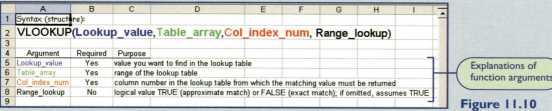

Figure 11.10

The syntax (structure) of the VLOOKUP function displays in Row 2. The illustration shows each argument in a different color. The function includes three required arguments and one optional argument. If you want to find exact matches, specify FALSE as the fourth argument. Otherwise, you can omit the fourth argument.

3 Click cell D19; then study the example in rows 11 through 19 (see Figure 11.11).

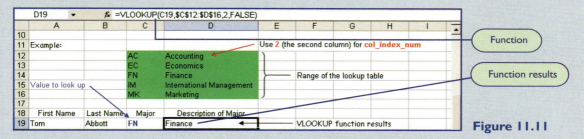

Figure 11.11

A bracket and colored arrows point to arguments used in the VLOOKUP function. Blue indicates the value to look up; green indicates the range of the lookup table, and red indicates how to specify the column from which to select the matching value.

4 Select the **VLOOKUP (exact)** worksheet.
The lookup table containing major codes and descriptions displays in the range C4:D8. You plan to enter a VLOOKUP function in cell D13 and copy it to the range D14:D20.

5 Select cell D13; then click the **Insert Function** button in the formula bar.

6 Select the *Lookup & Reference* category in the Insert Function dialog box; then select **VLOOKUP** as the function name, and click **OK**.
The Function Arguments dialog box for the VLOOKUP function opens.

7 Enter C13 in the **Lookup_value** text box.

8 Enter $C$4:$D$8 in the **Table_array** text box.
In this case, the range C4:D8 is an *array constant*, which means it is a group of constants arranged in a special way and is used as an argument in a formula. Specifying dollar signs makes the reference to the table absolute. This is necessary because you are going to copy the VLOOKUP function.

9 Enter 2 in the **Col_index_num** text box.

continues ▶

To Create Data Using the **VLOOKUP** Function (Exact Match) (continued)

⑩   **Enter FALSE in the Range_lookup text box (see Figure 11.12).**

The VLOOKUP function displays in the formula bar

Data to find in the table

Range of the lookup table

Result of the VLOOKUP function to be entered in cell D13

Figure 11.12

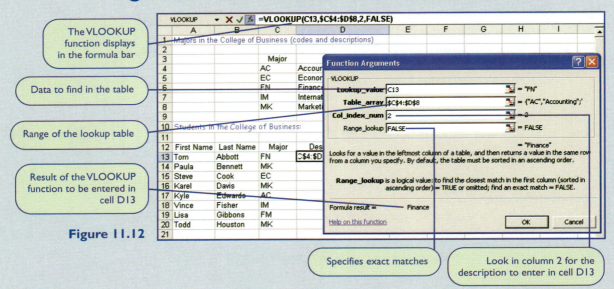

Specifies exact matches

Look in column 2 for the description to enter in cell D13

⑪   **Make sure that your settings match those shown in Figure 11.12, and click OK to close the dialog box.**

Finance displays in cell D13 as the description for major code FN.

 If you have problems...
When cell D13 is selected, =VLOOKUP(C13,$C$4:$D$8,2,FALSE) should display in the formula bar. Edit the formula as needed. Be sure to include the dollar signs that make the reference to the range C4:D8 absolute before you copy the function in the next step.

⑫   **Copy the function in cell D13 to the range D14:D20, and deselect the range.**

The correct major descriptions display in column D except for cell D19, which holds the error value #N/A (see Figure 11.13). The lookup table does not contain an exact match for major code *FM* in cell C19.

Indicates an error

Value does not match an entry in the left-most column of the lookup table

Figure 11.13

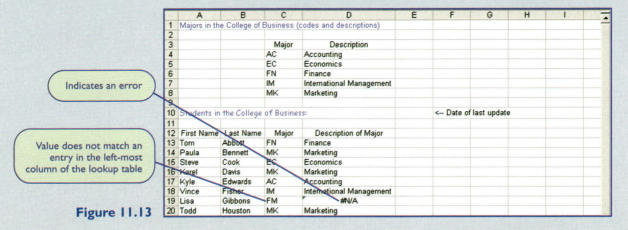

13   **Change the entry in cell C19 to FN instead of FM.**
The description *Finance* displays in cell D19.

14   **Save your changes to the VLOOKUP workbook.**
Keep the *VLOOKUP* workbook open for the next set of hands-on steps, or close the workbook and exit Excel.

In the previous hands-on steps, you specified FALSE as the optional Range_lookup argument in the VLOOKUP function. When you specify FALSE as the Range_lookup, only exact matches satisfy the lookup. If the Range_lookup is FALSE, you do not have to organize the values in ascending order in the first column of the lookup table.

Specify the logical value TRUE for the Range_lookup argument, or omit it, if the data you want to look up is not an exact match to an entry in the lookup table. The function finds the next largest value in the lookup table that is less than the lookup value. If the Range_lookup setting is TRUE or omitted, the values in the first column of the lookup table must be in ascending order to ensure correct results.

In the following hands-on steps, you use the VLOOKUP function to create descriptions of donor levels that depend on the amount donated. Omitting the Range_lookup argument enables the function to assign the donor level description based on a range of values.

To Create Data Using the VLOOKUP Function (Approximate Match)

1   **Open the VLOOKUP workbook, if necessary; then select the VLOOKUP (approx) worksheet.**
The worksheet tracks donations to the Sun City Zoological Society. The contributions needed to achieve a variety of donation levels form the lookup table in the range F2:G11 (see Figure 11.14).

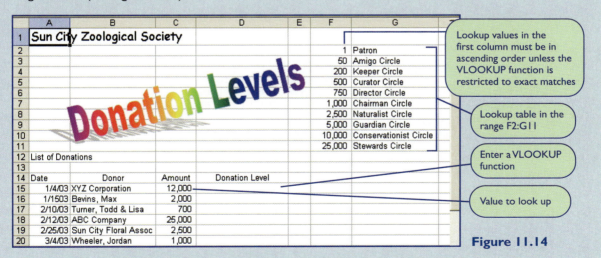

Figure 11.14

2   **Select cell D15; then click the Insert Function button in the formula bar.**

3   **Select the Lookup & Reference category in the Insert Function dialog box; then select VLOOKUP as the function name, and click OK.**
The Function Arguments dialog box for the VLOOKUP function opens.

continues ▶

To Create Data Using the VLOOKUP Function (Approximate Match) (continued)

④ **Enter** C15 **in the Lookup_value text box.**

⑤ **Enter** $F$2:$G$11 **in the Table_array text box.**
Make sure that you enter the dollar signs that make the reference to the table absolute. This is necessary because you are going to copy the VLOOKUP function.

⑥ **Enter 2 in the Col_index_num text box (see Figure 11.15).**

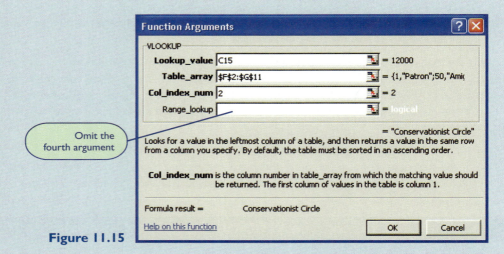

Omit the fourth argument

Figure 11.15

⑦ **Make sure that your settings match those shown in Figure 11.15, and click OK to close the dialog box.**
Conservationist Circle displays in cell D15 as the description for the donation level associated with contributing $12,000.

 If you have problems...
When cell D15 is selected, =VLOOKUP(C15,$F$2:$G$11,2) should display in the formula bar. Edit the formula as needed. Be sure to include the dollar signs that make the reference to the range F2:G22 absolute before you copy the function in the next step.

⑧ **Copy the function in cell D15 to the range D16:D20, and deselect the range.**
Donation levels associated with the values in C16:C20 display in the range D16:D20 (see Figure 11.16).

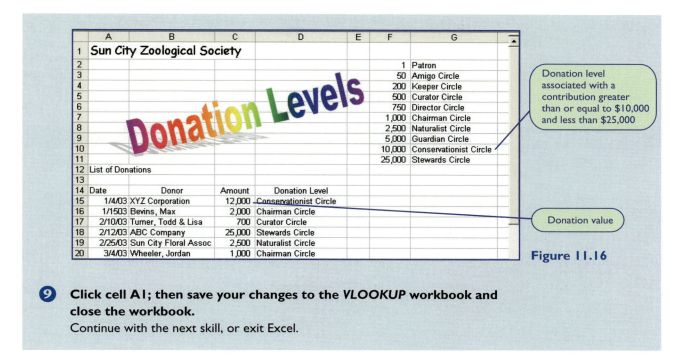

Figure 11.16

Donation level associated with a contribution greater than or equal to $10,000 and less than $25,000

Donation value

9 **Click cell A1; then save your changes to the _VLOOKUP_ workbook and close the workbook.**
Continue with the next skill, or exit Excel.

Create Data Using the HLOOKUP Function

Recall that the VLOOKUP function looks for a specified value in the leftmost column of a table array. When that value is found in a cell within the table, the function displays the contents of another cell in that same row from the column you specify.

Another function serves a similar purpose. The **HLOOKUP function** looks for a specified value in the topmost row of a table array. When that value is found in a cell within the table, the function displays the contents of another cell in that same column from the row you specify.

Looking at an example helps to clarify the purpose of this function. Figure 11.17 illustrates using the HLOOKUP function to convert the name of an organization to a number code 1 through 7. You might make a text-to-number conversion like this if you plan to use Excel's FREQUENCY function to summarize occurrences.

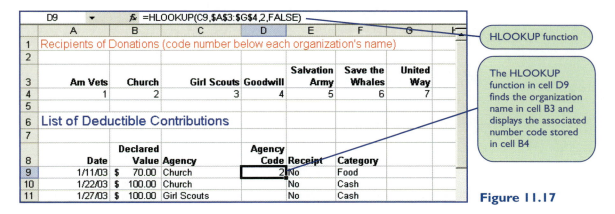

Figure 11.17

HLOOKUP function

The HLOOKUP function in cell D9 finds the organization name in cell B3 and displays the associated number code stored in cell B4

If the data you want to look up is stored vertically in a table—that is, in columns—use the VLOOKUP function. The V stands for _vertical_. If the data you want to look up is stored horizontally in a table—that is, in rows—then use the HLOOKUP function. The H stands for _horizontal_.

You can specify exact or approximate matches when using the VLOOKUP or HLOOKUP functions. Approximate matches enable you to work with values within a specified range.

In the following steps, you view the syntax (structure) of the HLOOKUP function and then use it to create number codes for organization names based on exact matches to entries in the lookup table.

To Create Data Using the HLOOKUP Function (Exact Match)

1 **Open the *MEE-S403* workbook, and save it as** HLOOKUP.

2 **Select the HLOOKUP syntax worksheet; then study the function syntax and explanations in rows 2 through 8 (see Figure 11.18).**

The only difference in arguments between a VLOOKUP function and an HLOOKUP function

Figure 11.18

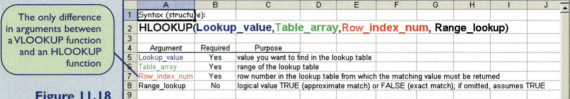

The syntax of the HLOOKUP function displays in row 2. The illustration shows each argument in a different color. The function includes three required arguments and one optional argument. If you want to find exact matches, specify FALSE as the fourth argument. Otherwise, you can omit the fourth argument.

3 **Click cell D18; then study the example starting with row 11 (see Figure 11.19).**

Function

Function results

Figure 11.19

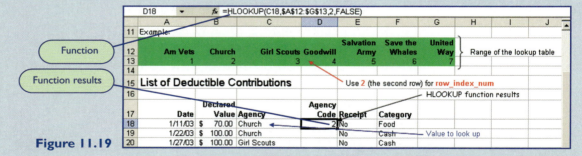

A bracket and colored arrows point to arguments used in the HLOOKUP function. Blue indicates the value to look up; green indicates the range of the lookup table, and red indicates how to specify the row from which to select the matching value.

4 **Select the HLOOKUP (exact) worksheet.**

The lookup table containing organization names and associated code numbers displays in the range A3:G4. You plan to enter an HLOOKUP function in cell D9 and copy it to the range D10:D40.

5 **Select cell D9; then click the Insert Function button in the formula bar.**

⑥ Select the Lookup & Reference category in the Insert Function dialog box; then select HLOOKUP as the function name, and click OK.
The Function Arguments dialog box for the HLOOKUP function displays.

⑦ Enter C9 in the Lookup_value text box.

⑧ Enter $A$3:$G$4 in the Table_array text box.
Specifying dollar signs makes the reference to the table absolute. This is necessary because you are going to copy the HLOOKUP function.

⑨ Enter 2 in the Row_index_num text box.

⑩ Enter FALSE in the Range_lookup text box (see Figure 11.20).

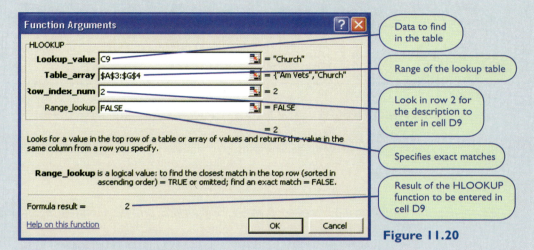

Figure 11.20

⑪ Make sure that your settings match those shown in Figure 11.20, and click OK to close the dialog box.
The number 2 displays in cell D9 as the number code for Church.

 If you have problems...
When cell D9 is selected, =HLOOKUP(C9,$A$3:$G$4,2,FALSE) should display in the formula bar. Edit the formula as needed. Be sure to include the dollar signs that make the reference to the range A3:G4 absolute before you copy the function in the next step.

⑫ Copy the function in cell D9 to the range D10:D40, and deselect the range.
The correct number codes display in column D (see Figure 11.21).

continues ▶

To Create Data Using the HLOOKUP Function (Exact Match) (continued)

	A	B	C	D	E	F	G	H
1	Recipients of Donations (code number below each organization's name)							
2								
3	**Am Vets**	**Church**	**Girl Scouts**	**Goodwill**	**Salvation Army**	**Save the Whales**	**United Way**	
4	1	2	3	4	5	6	7	
5								
6	**List of Deductible Contributions**							
7								
8	**Date**	**Declared Value**	**Agency**	**Agency Code**	**Receipt**	**Category**		
9	1/11/03	$ 70.00	Church	2	No	Food		
10	1/22/03	$ 100.00	Church	2	No	Cash		
11	1/27/03	$ 100.00	Girl Scouts	3	No	Cash		
12	1/30/03	$ 80.00	Church	2	Yes	Cash		
13	2/21/03	$ 50.00	Am Vets	1	No	Furniture		
14	2/28/03	$ 80.00	Church	2	Yes	Cash		
15	3/9/03	$ 25.00	Goodwill	4	Yes	Television		
16	3/14/03	$2,300.00	Goodwill	4	Yes	Car		
17	3/23/03	$ 140.00	Goodwill	4	No	Appliances		
18	3/30/03	$ 80.00	Church	2	Yes	Cash		

Data created using the HLOOKUP function

Figure 11.21

⓭ **Save your changes to the *HLOOKUP* workbook, and close the workbook.**

You can continue with the exercises, start another skill set, or exit Excel.

For immediate reinforcement, work Skill Drill 3 and Challenges 1, 2, and 3.

Summary

This skill set introduced two topics: creating and using range names, and using selected lookup and reference functions. You began by setting up two range names—one that you used in a formula and the other that you used to navigate to a different section of the worksheet. You also created a list of range names in a blank area of the worksheet.

Table 11.1 introduced the functions in the Lookup and Reference category. You used VLOOKUP and HLOOKUP functions to create data by looking up values in a table based on exact and approximate matches.

Skill Drill

Skill Drill exercises *reinforce* skills. Each skill reinforced is the same, or nearly the same, as a skill presented in the skill set. Detailed instructions are provided in a step-by-step format.

Before beginning your Excel Expert Skill Set 4 Skill Drill exercises, complete the following steps:

1. Open the file named *MEE-S404*, and immediately save it as **MEE-S4drill**.

   The workbook contains four sheets: An overview, and sheets SD1 through SD3.

2. Click the Overview sheet to view the organization and content of the Skill Drill workbook for Excel Expert Skill Set 4.

Each exercise is independent of the others, so you may complete the exercises in any order. Be sure to save the workbook after completing each exercise. If you need a paper copy of one or more completed exercises, enter your name, centered in a header, before printing. Print options have already been set to print compressed to one page and to display the filename, sheet name, and current date in a footer.

Be sure to save your changes and close the workbook if you need more than one work session to complete the desired exercises. Continue working on *MEE-S4drill* instead of starting over in the original *MEE-S404* file.

1. Create a Range Name and Use It in a Formula

One formula must still be entered in a worksheet that budgets quarterly revenue for the year 2004. The formula calculates the average quarterly revenue expected in a best-case scenario. You decide to assign a name to the range of cells to average, and use the range name in the formula.

To create a range name and use it in a formula, follow these steps:

1. If necessary, open the *MEE-S4drill* workbook; then select the SD1 worksheet.
2. Select the range B14:E14 and click the Name box at the left end of the formula bar.
3. Type **QtrRev** and press (←Enter).

   The name *QtrRev* is assigned to the range B14:E14.
4. Enter **=average(QtrRev)** in cell A16, and make cell A16 the current cell.

   The amount *487275* displays in cell A16, and *=AVERAGE(QtrRev)* displays in the formula bar.
5. Format cell A16 to Comma, zero decimal places.
6. Save your changes to the *MEE-S4drill* workbook.

2. Display a List of Range Names

You would like to create a list of range names and their definitions in the current worksheet. Follow these steps:

1. Open the *MEE-S4drill* workbook, if necessary; then select the SD2 worksheet.
2. Enter **List of Range Names** in cell A20.
3. Click cell A21; then choose Insert, Name, Paste.

   The Paste Name dialog box opens.
4. Click Paste List.

   If you already worked Skill Drill 1, your list of range names includes QtrRev defined in sheet SD1 along with five range names previously defined in sheet SD2: AnnualData, CommissionRate, Dec, Nov, and Oct.
5. Deselect the range name list, and save your changes to the *MEE-S4drill* workbook.

3. Use VLOOKUP to Create Data

You decide to analyze data on the type of heat for homes in your residential real estate list. Some time in the future, you intend to create a frequency distribution on type of heat. To prepare for that now, you want to convert the data in the Heat column to corresponding number codes in the adjacent column. You can do this by using the VLOOKUP function.

To use a VLOOKUP function to create data, follow these steps:

1. Open the *MEE-S4drill* workbook, if necessary; then select the SD3 worksheet.

   Lookup table values display in the range G4:H7. For every occurrence of Solar in the Heat column G, you want the number 1 assigned in the Hcode (heat code) column H.

For every occurrence of Oil in the Heat column G, you want the number 2 assigned in the Hcode (heat code) column H. The values in the first column of the lookup table do not have to be in ascending order because you are looking for exact matches.

2. Click cell H12; then click the Insert Function button on the formula bar.

3. Select the Lookup & Reference category; select the VLOOKUP function, and click OK.

4. Enter **G12** in the Lookup_value text box.

5. Enter **$G$4:$H$7** in the Table_array text box.

   Make sure that you include the dollar signs making cell references absolute, as you are going to copy the VLOOKUP function to remaining cells in the Hcode column.

6. Enter **2** in the Col_index_num box.

7. Enter **FALSE** in the Range_lookup text box; then click OK to execute the function.

   Make sure that VLOOKUP returns the number 1 in cell H12. Compare that result to your lookup table to see that the number 1 is the number used to represent Solar heat.

8. Copy the contents of cell H12 to the range H13:H46; then deselect the range.

   Visually scan your results. If you see errors, make sure that your cell references are correct and that the reference to the lookup table is absolute. If necessary, rework the exercise steps to generate accurate results.

9. Save your changes to the *MEE-S4drill* workbook.

Challenge

Challenge exercises expand on or are somewhat related to skills presented in the skill set. Each exercise provides a brief narrative introduction, followed by instructions in a numbered-step format that are not as detailed as those in the Skill Drill section.

Before beginning your Excel Expert Skill Set 4 Challenge exercises, complete the following steps:

1. Open the file named *MEE-S405*, and immediately save it as **MEE-S4challenge**.

   The workbook contains three sheets: an overview and two sheets labeled CH1-2 and CH3.

2. Click the Overview sheet to view the organization and content of the Challenge workbook for Excel Expert Skill Set 4.

Each exercise is independent of the others. Be sure to save the workbook after completing each exercise. If you need a paper copy of one or more completed exercises, enter your name, centered in a header, before printing. Print options have already been set to print compressed to one page. Settings to display the filename, sheet name, and current date in a footer have been set in all worksheets.

Be sure to save your changes and close the workbook if you need more than one work session to complete the desired exercises. Continue working on *MEE-S4challenge* instead of starting over in the original *MEE-S405* file.

1. Use VLOOKUP to Display Descriptions of Coded Data

You are analyzing survey data completed by customers who recently rented vehicles from Indy 500 Motor Works. When you print a report showing satisfaction ratings, you want descriptions to appear next to the numeric codes 1 through 5.

To use VLOOKUP to create labels from numbers, follow these steps:

1. Open the *MEE-S4challenge* workbook, if necessary; then select the CH1-2 worksheet.

2. Select cell K20, and display the Insert Function dialog box.

3. Select VLOOKUP as the function name, and click OK.

4. Enter **J20** in the Lookup_value text box.

5. Enter **$C$11:$D$15** in the Table_array text box.

6. Enter the appropriate column number in the Col_index_num text box.

7. Enter **FALSE** in the Range_lookup text box; then click OK to close the dialog box.

   Below Average displays in cell K20 as the description for rating code 4.

 If you have problems...

When cell K20 is selected, =VLOOKUP(J20,$C$11:$D$15,2,FALSE) should display in the formula bar. Edit the formula as needed.

---

8. Copy the function in cell K20 to the range K21:K49.

9. Verify that the results are accurate; then widen column K as needed, and save your changes to the *MEE-S4challenge* workbook.

2. Use VLOOKUP with Two Exact Matches

Indy 500 Motor Works offers three discount plans to its customers. The discount under each plan varies with the type of payment—credit card (cc), corporate account (acct), and cash. Now you want to use VLOOKUP to enter the applicable discount for the first rental record and copy the formula to create the discount data for the remaining records. You can use VLOOKUP to create data based on two conditions—in this case, looking up the discount percent for a combination of payment type and discount plan.

To use VLOOKUP with multiple values, follow these steps:

1. Open the *MEE-S4challenge* workbook, if necessary; then select the CH1-2 worksheet and scroll to display cell A4 in the upper-left corner.

2. Select cell J16, and choose <u>W</u>indow, <u>F</u>reeze Panes.

   This action enables you to continue displaying data in columns A through I as you scroll to view remaining columns.

3. Scroll to display data in columns L and M (see Figure 11.22).

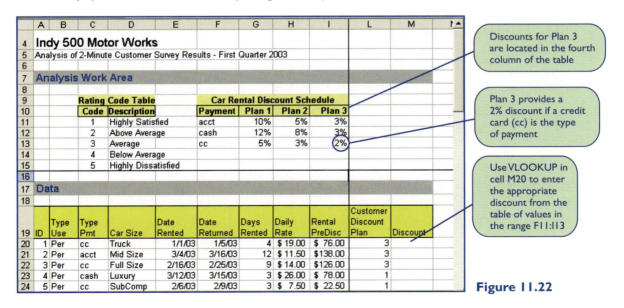

Figure 11.22

4. Select cell M20 and display the Insert Function dialog box; select the VLOOKUP function, and click OK.

5. Enter **C20** in the Lookup_value text box.

6. Enter **$F$11:$I$13** in the Table_array text box.

7. Enter **L20+1** in the Col_index_num text box.

The value in L20 is 3. Adding 1 to 3 tells Excel to use the value in the fourth column of the table.

8. Enter **FALSE** in the Range_lookup text box; then click OK to close the dialog box.

The value *0.02* displays in cell M20.

 If you have problems...
The function =VLOOKUP(C20,$F$11:$I$13,L20+1,FALSE) should display in the formula bar when you select cell M20. Edit the formula as needed.

9. Format cell M20 to Percent, zero decimal places.

The value *2%* displays in cell M20.

10. Copy the function in cell M20 to the range M21:M49, and then click cell M23 (see Figure 11.23).

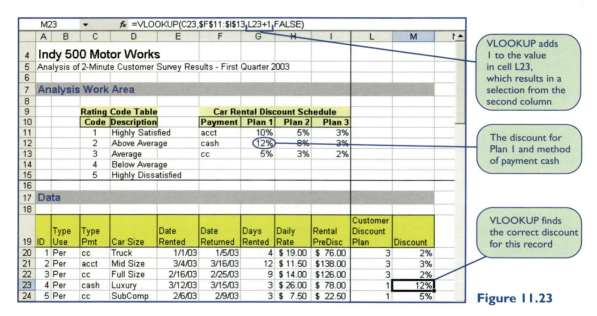

Figure 11.23

11. Verify that results are accurate; then choose Window, Unfreeze Panes.

12. Save your changes to the *MEE-S4challenge* workbook.

3. Use HLOOKUP to Find Approximate Matches

You are designing a worksheet to show total credit hours earned and class standing for selected students. You want to use HLOOKUP to look up the class standing based on the total credit hours earned to date.

To use HLOOKUP to create labels based on ranges of values, follow these steps:

1. Open the *MEE-S4challenge* workbook, if necessary; then select the CH3 worksheet.

2. Select cell D7 and display the Insert Function dialog box.

3. Select HLOOKUP as the function name, and click OK.

4. Enter **C7** in the Lookup_value text box.

5. Enter the appropriate lookup table range in the Table_array text box.

Make sure that cell references are absolute in the Table_array text box. You copy the HLOOKUP function in a subsequent step.

6. Enter the appropriate row number in the Row_index_num text box.

7. Decide what to enter, if anything, in the Range_lookup text box.

8. Complete entry of the HLOOKUP function.

Junior should display in cell D7 as the correct year in school for an individual who has earned 77 credit hours to date.

9. Copy the function in cell D7 to the range D8:D14, and verify that results are accurate.

Class standings should be as follows: *Freshman* for Davis and Fisher; *Sophomore* for Edwards; *Junior* for Abbott, Bennett, and Gibbons; *Senior* for Cook and Houston.

10. Correct your HLOOKUP function and recopy, if necessary; then save your changes to the *MEE-S4challenge* workbook.

Customizing Excel

CHAPTER 12

This skill set includes

Customize toolbars and menus
- Add buttons to a toolbar
- Remove buttons and attach a toolbar to a workbook
- Customize a menu

Create, edit, and run macros
- Record a macro
- Play a macro
- Edit a macro using the Visual Basic Editor
- Create a macro button in a worksheet

Skill Set Overview

ou use many Excel toolbars and menus as you design, create, test, and maintain your worksheets. In this skill set, you learn to create and change toolbars and menus to fit your specialized needs.

You also learn to create and run macros. A *macro* enables you to combine multiple commands and keystrokes, and then execute them as a single command.

Skill 5.1: Customize Toolbars and Menus

You can make some changes to Excel's built-in toolbars and menus. You can also create your own toolbars and menus. In this skill area, you create a custom toolbar, remove buttons from the toolbar, and attach the custom toolbar to a workbook.

Add Buttons to a Toolbar

Clicking a button on a toolbar produces the associated result more quickly than you can open a menu and select the desired command(s). The changes you can make depend on the type of toolbar—built-in or custom.

A *built-in toolbar* is a toolbar provided by Microsoft Office programs that includes buttons to perform common tasks. The Standard toolbar and the Formatting toolbar are examples of built-in toolbars. You cannot delete a built-in toolbar, but you can remove a button on a built-in toolbar, add and remove other menu items and buttons, and reset a built-in toolbar to its default buttons, menus, and submenus.

A *custom toolbar* is a toolbar created by the user. You can delete a custom toolbar, and add or remove the menu items, commands, and buttons of your choice. You can also create a macro and assign it to a toolbar button.

In this skill, you create a custom toolbar with seven buttons from three categories of commands. In the next skill, you use the buttons, remove two buttons, and attach the toolbar to a workbook. Plan to work through both skills in a single session on the computer.

If you are working on a networked system that prevents creating a custom toolbar, you can learn the process by reading the hands-on steps and reviewing the associated figures.

To Add Buttons to a Toolbar

1 Display a blank Excel workbook and select **T**ools, **C**ustomize.

2 Select the Tool**b**ars tab, and click **N**ew.

3 Type Special Effects in the **T**oolbar name text box (see Figure 12.1).

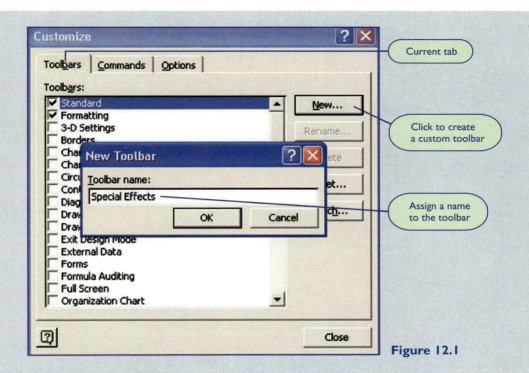

Figure 12.1

4 **Click OK.**
The Customize dialog box remains open and *Special Effects* is added to the list of toolbars. Excel displays an empty toolbar (see Figure 12.2).

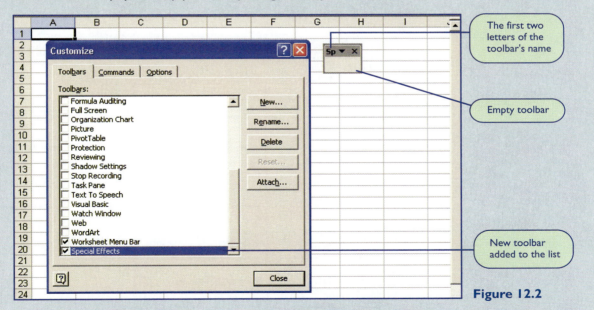

Figure 12.2

5 **Click the Commands tab in the Customize dialog box, and click Format in the Categories list at the left side of the dialog box.**

6 **Scroll down and select Cycle Font Color in the Commands list at the right side of the dialog box (see Figure 12.3).**

continues ▶

To Add Buttons to a Toolbar (continued)

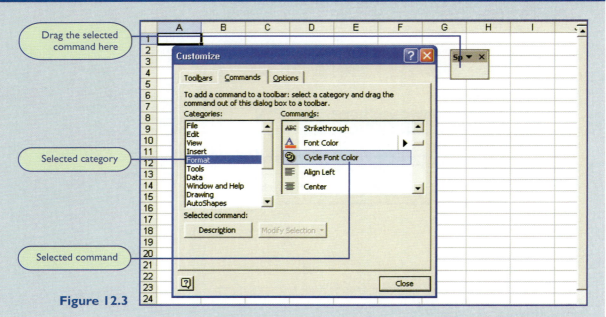

Drag the selected command here

Selected category

Selected command

Figure 12.3

7 **Click and drag Cycle Font Color to the empty toolbar, and release the mouse button.**

Excel adds the Cycle Font Color button to the Special Effects toolbar (see Figure 12.4). Now add two more formatting buttons to the right of the Cycle Font Color button.

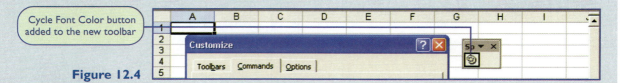

Cycle Font Color button added to the new toolbar

Figure 12.4

8 **Scroll about half-way down the list of commands, and drag the Angle Clockwise and Angle Counterclockwise commands to the new toolbar (see Figure 12.5).**

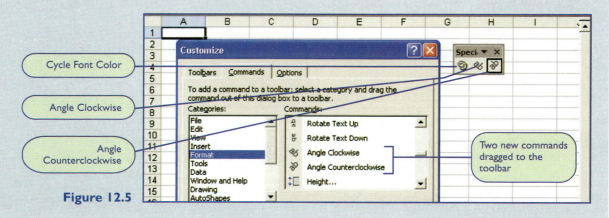

Cycle Font Color

Angle Clockwise

Angle Counterclockwise

Two new commands dragged to the toolbar

Figure 12.5

If you have problems...
The order of buttons in a custom toolbar is a matter of personal preference. If you drop a button in a different position than that shown in a figure, you can drag it left or right to the desired location within the toolbar or leave it in its current location.

9 **Scroll about three-fourths of the way down the list of formatting commands, and drag the Pattern command just to the left of the Cycle Font Color button (see Figure 12.6).**

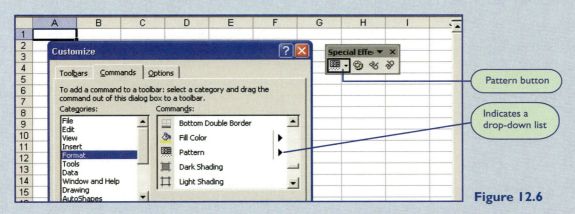

Pattern button

Indicates a drop-down list

Figure 12.6

10 **Click Drawing in the Categories list; then drag the Shadow On/Off button and the Lighting command to the right end of the Special Effects toolbar (see Figure 12.7).**

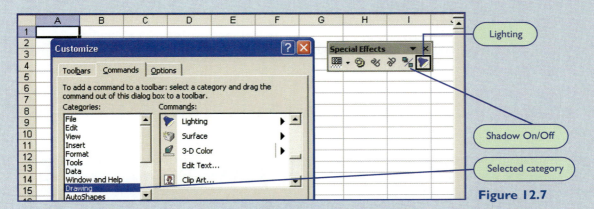

Lighting

Shadow On/Off

Selected category

Figure 12.7

11 **Click Edit in the Categories list; then drag the Clear Formatting command to the right end of the Special Effects toolbar.**

12 **Close the Customize dialog box, and position the pointer on the Lighting button (refer to Figure 12.7).**
The custom toolbar is complete. If the ScreenTip feature is active, Excel displays a button's name when you position the pointer on a button in a custom toolbar (see Figure 12.8).

continues ▶

To Add Buttons to a Toolbar (continued)

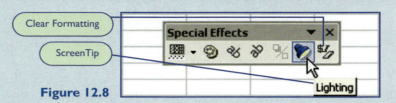

Figure 12.8

⑬ **Continue with the next skill.**

> ### In Depth:
> **Renaming a Toolbar**
> You cannot rename a built-in toolbar, but you can rename a custom toolbar. Display the Customize dialog box, click the Toolbars tab, and click the custom toolbar you want to rename. Click the Rename button and type a new name in the Toolbar name text box; then click OK and close the Customize dialog box.

Remove Buttons and Attach a Toolbar to a Workbook

You can remove a button from a built-in toolbar or a custom toolbar. On a built-in toolbar, click its Toolbar Options button—a small button with an arrowhead pointing down—and point to Add or Remove Buttons. Point to the toolbar name and clear the check box next to the button you want to remove; then click outside the menu to close it.

If the toolbar is a custom toolbar, display the custom toolbar and open the Customize dialog box. Make sure that the Customize dialog box does not cover the custom toolbar. On the custom toolbar, right-click the button you want to delete, click Delete, and close the Customize dialog box.

If you know that you will edit or use a workbook on another computer system, you can attach a custom toolbar to the workbook. Opening the file on another system opens the workbook and makes the custom toolbar available on that system.

In this skill, you make sure that the buttons on the Special Effects toolbar work as intended. You also remove two buttons and attach the toolbar to a workbook.

To Remove Buttons and Attach a Toolbar to a Workbook

① **Open the *MEE-S501* workbook, and save it as** Customize.

② **Display the *Special Effects* toolbar, if necessary.**
Now make sure that several buttons on the Special Effects toolbar work as intended.

③ **Click cell B20 and click the Cycle Font Color button at least ten times.**
Excel applies a different font color each time you click the Cycle Font Color button.

4 **Click the Clear Formatting button on the Special Effects toolbar.**
Excel restores the default font color.

5 **Click within the Fun with Frisbees WordArt; click the Lighting button, and position the pointer on the third option in the second row (see Figure 12.9).**

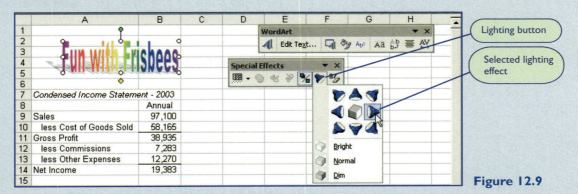

Figure 12.9

6 **Click the selected option.**
Excel applies the selected lighting effect (see Figure 12.10).

Figure 12.10

7 **Click the Shadow On/Off button until the lighting and shadow effects disappear, and deselect the WordArt.**

8 **Click cell B8 and click the Angle Counterclockwise button.**
The text in cell B8 rotates so that the left end is lower than the right end.

9 **Click cell B17; use the Pattern button to apply a bright green color, and again to apply the thin diagonal crosshatch pattern.**
Next, you remove the Angle Clockwise and Angle Counterclockwise buttons from the Special Effects custom toolbar.

10 **Select Tools, Customize.**
The Customize dialog box opens. The dialog box must be open to make changes to a custom toolbar, but you do not use the dialog box to remove a toolbar button.

11 **Make sure that the Customize dialog box does not cover the custom toolbar, and then right-click the Angle Clockwise button.**
A shortcut menu opens (see Figure 12.11).

continues ▶

To Remove Buttons and Attach a Toolbar to a Workbook (continued)

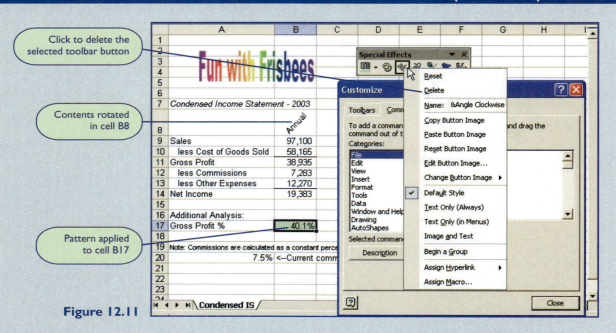

Figure 12.11

⓬ **Click <u>D</u>elete on the shortcut menu.**

⓭ **Right-click the Angle Counterclockwise button, and click <u>D</u>elete.**
The Special Effects toolbar contains five buttons instead of seven buttons. Now attach the toolbar to the active workbook.

⓮ **Select the Tool<u>b</u>ars tab, if necessary; then click the Attac<u>h</u> button near the right side of the Customize dialog box.**
The Attach Toolbars dialog box opens.

⓯ **Click Special Effects in the C<u>u</u>stom toolbars list (see Figure 12.12).**

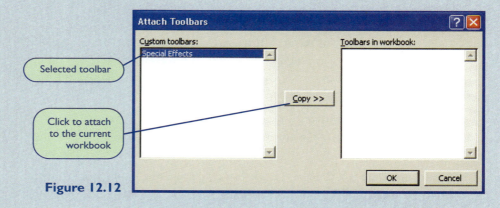

Figure 12.12

⓰ **Click the <u>C</u>opy button and click OK.**
You attached the Special Effects toolbar to the *Customize* workbook.

⑰ **Close the Special Effects toolbar and the Customize dialog box; then save your changes to the *Customize* workbook, and close the workbook.**

⑱ **If desired, delete the custom toolbar. (Instructions are provided in the "In Depth" section at the end of this skill.)**
Continue with the next skill, or exit Excel.

In Depth:

Deleting a Toolbar
You cannot delete a built-in toolbar, but you can delete a custom toolbar. Choose View, Toolbars, Customize to display the Customize dialog box. Click the Toolbars tab; click the custom toolbar you want to delete, and click Delete. Click OK to confirm the deletion of the toolbar, and close the Customize dialog box.

Moving or Copying a Toolbar Button
To move or copy a toolbar button, first display the toolbar(s) you want to change. To move a toolbar button, hold down Alt and drag the button to its new location. To copy a toolbar button, hold down Alt+Ctrl and drag the button to its duplicate location.

Customize a Menu

In the two previous skills, you created and modified a custom toolbar. You can also customize menus. A ***custom menu*** includes one or more user-specified menu options that you can select to perform a designated task. You can place a new menu on the built-in menu bar, or you can add a menu or command to a toolbar.

Generally, you customize menus to include frequently used commands. Imagine that you frequently place AutoShapes in worksheets and do not want the remaining buttons on the Drawing toolbar to take up space while you are working. In this skill, you add the AutoShapes menu to the menu bar. You make sure that you can draw shapes from the new menu on the menu bar. You conclude the skill by removing the new menu so that the menu bar displays only the original built-in menus.

To Customize a Menu

1 **Display a blank Excel workbook, and select Tools, Customize.**
The Customize dialog box opens.

2 **Click the Commands tab; scroll down to the bottom of the Categories list, and click New Menu (see Figure 12.13).**

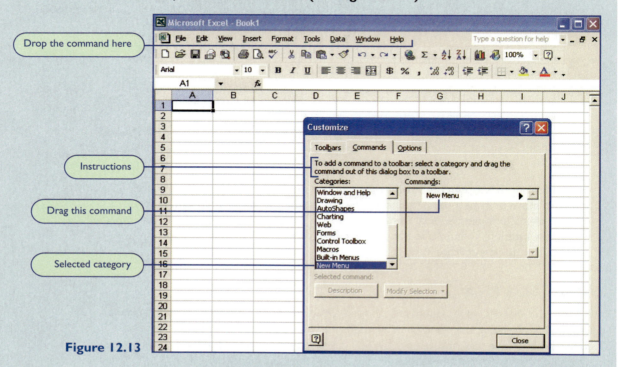

Drop the command here

Instructions

Drag this command

Selected category

Figure 12.13

3 **Drag New Menu in the Commands list up to the menu bar, and drop it just to the right of the Help menu.**

4 **Click New Menu on the menu bar.**
Excel displays an empty drop-down list (see Figure 12.14).

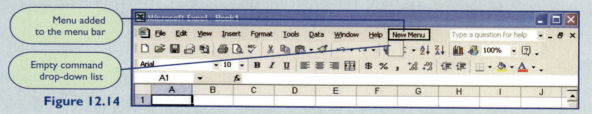

Menu added to the menu bar

Empty command drop-down list

Figure 12.14

5 **Right-click New Menu in the menu bar, and click the Name text box. Delete the existing text, and type Shapes (see Figure 12.15).**

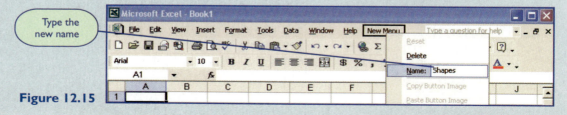

Type the new name

Figure 12.15

6 Press ↵Enter to complete changing the name.

7 Click AutoShapes in the Categories list in the Customize dialog box, and select AutoShapes in the Commands list.

8 Drag AutoShapes in the Commands list to the empty drop-down list below Shapes in the menu bar (see Figure 12.16).

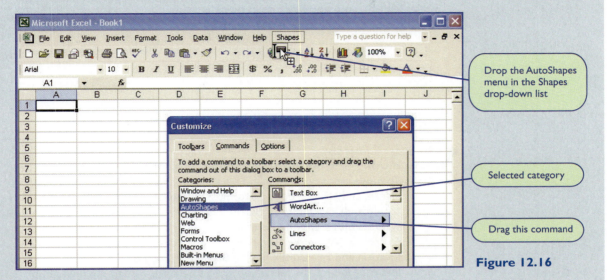

Drop the AutoShapes menu in the Shapes drop-down list

Selected category

Drag this command

Figure 12.16

9 Drop the dragged command and close the Customize dialog box.
Excel adds the complete AutoShapes menu and submenus to the menu bar. Now check that you can draw AutoShapes by using a menu on the menu bar instead of the Drawing toolbar.

10 Click Shapes at the right end of the menu bar, point to AutoShapes, and point to Basic Shapes (see Figure 12.17).

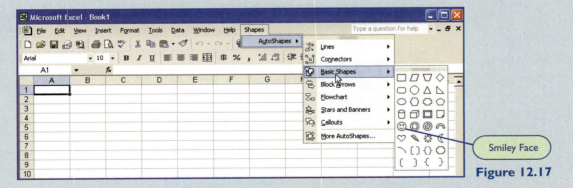

Smiley Face

Figure 12.17

11 Click Smiley Face in the list of basic shapes; then draw a smiley face object near the upper-left corner of the worksheet, and deselect the object.
Now, restore the original menu bar by removing the Shapes menu.

continues ▶

To Customize a Menu (continued)

⑫ Select Tools, Customize.
The Customize dialog box opens. The dialog box must be open to make changes to the custom menu, but you do not use the dialog box to remove the menu.

⑬ Drag the Shapes menu off the menu bar to a blank area of the worksheet, and release the mouse button.
You removed the recently added custom menu.

⑭ Close the Customize dialog box, and close the workbook without saving your changes.
Continue with the next skill, or exit Excel.

In Depth:

Moving or Copying a Command on a Menu

To move or copy a command on a menu, make sure that the destination menu is visible, and select Tools, Customize. In the Customize dialog box, click the Commands tab and then click the category that contains the command you want to move or copy. To move the command, drag it over the menu you want to change. When the menu displays a list of commands, point to your desired location and release the mouse button. To copy the command, hold down Ctrl and drag it over the menu you want to change. When the menu displays a list of commands, point to your desired location and release the mouse button.

Moving or Copying a Menu to a Toolbar

To move or copy a menu, make sure that the destination toolbar is visible and select Tools, Customize. To move the menu, drag it from the menu bar to its new location on the toolbar. To copy the menu, hold down Ctrl and drag it to the duplicate location.

For immediate reinforcement, work Skill Drill 1 and Challenges 1 through 3.

Skill 5.2: **Create, Edit, and Run Macros**

A macro enables you to combine multiple commands and keystrokes and then execute them as a single command. If you execute a particular action frequently, using a macro to perform that function with a single keystroke or a button can be a real timesaver and help you produce consistent results. A macro can be simple, such as one that types a lengthy company name or prints selected sections of a large worksheet. A macro can also produce more complex results, such as creating a chart or calculating and printing a price quote for a customer.

When a macro you recorded is played back, it is as if an invisible typist is rapidly entering keystrokes. Some early macro recorders literally did just that—recorded keystrokes and played them back on command. However, Excel handles macros differently. Because all Microsoft Office programs are object-oriented, the macro recorder does not look at your keystrokes, but instead looks at the results of your keystrokes. It then creates a subroutine in a language known as *Visual Basic for Applications (VBA)*, which produces the same results as your keystrokes.

You can view and edit macros using the *Visual Basic Editor*. Use this editor to edit existing macro code or delete lines that resulted from incorrect keystrokes. Working in Visual Basic Editor, you can also create new code by typing it. This is how many add-in programs, such as data analysis tools, are created.

In this skill area, you create and run a macro that impacts only the associated workbook. You also edit a macro and add a *macro button* to a worksheet. Clicking a macro button activates the macro assigned to the button.

Record a Macro

Before you can record a macro, you need to decide what to name the macro and where to store it. A macro name must start with a letter and can contain letters, numbers, and the underscore character. Spaces are not allowed. You may store your macro in the current workbook or a new workbook. You can also store it in the Personal Macro Workbook so that it is available for use in any existing or future workbook.

In this skill, you record a macro that copies the contents of a row to the next available blank row in another worksheet before deleting the selected row in the original worksheet. This macro makes it easy to move data from a work order in progress to a database of completed work orders. You store the macro in the current workbook.

The steps you want to record are copying the contents of the selected row in the Current Projects worksheet, pasting the data to the first available blank row in the Completed Projects worksheet, and deleting the selected row from the Current Projects worksheet.

To Record a Macro

1 **Open the *MEE-S502* workbook, and save it as** Project List.
This workbook contains two worksheets named Current Projects and Completed Projects.

2 **Type** 4/8/2003 **in cell F4 of the Current Projects worksheet, and press** ↵Enter.
The entry indicates that the project described in row 4 has been completed.

3 **Select row 4 by clicking its row heading.**
This action specifies which row's contents to copy before recording the macro. You cannot specify a specific row to transfer within the macro, because projects might not be completed in order.

4 **Select Tools, Macro, Record New Macro.**
The Record Macro dialog box opens (see Figure 12.18).   *continues* ▶

To Record a Macro (continued)

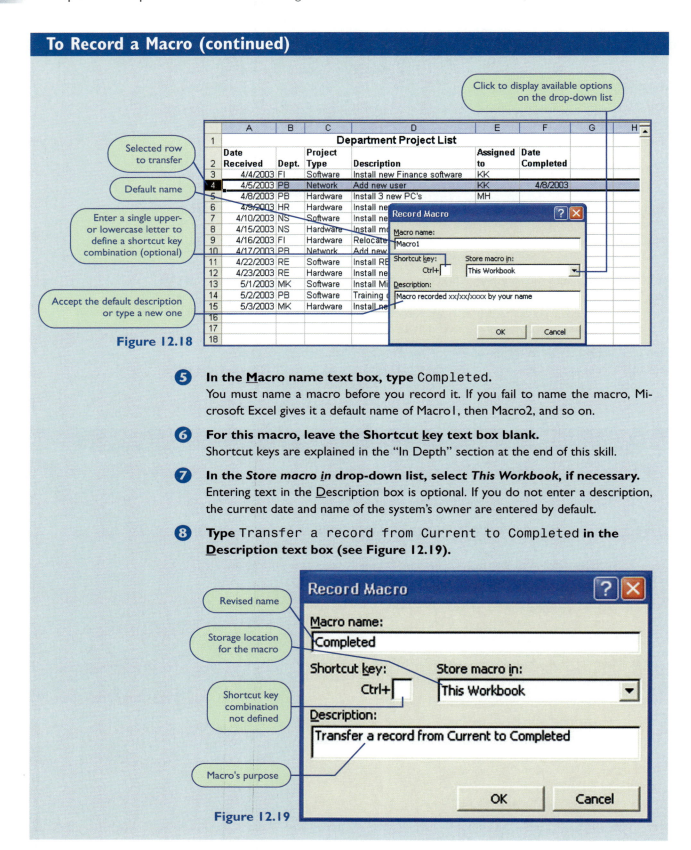

Figure 12.18

Figure 12.19

5 In the **Macro name text box, type** `Completed`.
You must name a macro before you record it. If you fail to name the macro, Microsoft Excel gives it a default name of Macro1, then Macro2, and so on.

6 **For this macro, leave the Shortcut key text box blank.**
Shortcut keys are explained in the "In Depth" section at the end of this skill.

7 **In the *Store macro in* drop-down list, select *This Workbook*, if necessary.**
Entering text in the Description box is optional. If you do not enter a description, the current date and name of the system's owner are entered by default.

8 **Type** `Transfer a record from Current to Completed` **in the Description text box (see Figure 12.19).**

9 **Make sure that your entries match those shown in Figure 12.19, and click OK.**

The macro recorder is now on. You should see a Stop Recording toolbar and the *Recording* message at the bottom of the screen (see Figure 12.20).

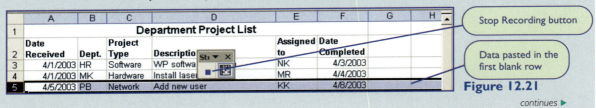

	A	B	C	D	E	F	G	H
1				**Department Project List**				
2	**Date Received**	**Dept.**	**Project Type**	**Description**	**Assigned to**	**Date Completed**		
3	4/4/2003	FI	Software	Install new Finance software	KK			
4	4/5/2003	PB	Network	Add new u	KK	4/8/2003		
5	4/8/2003	PB	Hardware	Install 3 ne	MH			
6	4/9/2003	HR	Hardware	Install new laser printer	GB			
7	4/10/2003	NS	Software	Install new archive software	JB			
8	4/15/2003	NS	Hardware	Install modems	GB			
9	4/16/2003	FI	Hardware	Relocate department	JB			
10	4/17/2003	PB	Network	Add new user	KK			
11	4/22/2003	RE	Software	Install RE software	KK			
12	4/23/2003	RE	Hardware	Install new PC	MH			
13	5/1/2003	MK	Software	Install Microsoft Office - 3 PC's	KK			
14	5/2/2003	PB	Software	Training on Report Software	MH			
15	5/3/2003	MK	Hardware	Install new PC	GB			
16								
17								
18								
19								
20								
21								
22								

Current Projects / Completed Projects /

Ready   Recording   Count Nums=2   NUM

Stop Recording button

Relative Reference button

Indicates that recording mode is active

Figure 12.20

10 **Click the Relative Reference button on the Stop Recording toolbar (refer to Figure 12.20).**

Make sure that the Relative Reference button is surrounded by a blue border that indicates it is selected. Click again, if necessary, until you see the blue border. Recording a macro when the Relative Reference button is active enables you to play the macro anywhere on the worksheet. An absolute reference ties the macro to specific locations.

11 **Click the Copy button on the toolbar.**

The contents of row 4 are copied to the Clipboard. A marquee appears around row 4.

12 **Click the Completed Projects sheet tab.**

Completed Projects is now the active sheet.

13 **Press Ctrl + Home.**

This keystroke combination makes cell A1 the active cell.

14 **Press End and then press ↓ twice.**

The active cell is now cell A5, the first cell in the first blank row below the data.

15 **Click the Paste button on the toolbar.**

The selected data from row 4 of the Current Projects worksheet is pasted in the first blank row of the Completed Projects worksheet (see Figure 12.21).

	A	B	C	D	E	F	G	H
1				**Department Project List**				
2	**Date Received**	**Dept.**	**Project Type**	**Descriptio**	**Assigned to**	**Date Completed**		
3	4/1/2003	HR	Software	WP softwa	NK	4/3/2003		
4	4/1/2003	MK	Hardware	Install laser	MR	4/4/2003		
5	4/5/2003	PB	Network	Add new user	KK	4/8/2003		

Stop Recording button

Data pasted in the first blank row

Figure 12.21

continues ▶

To Record a Macro (continued)

16 **Press ⬇, and click the Current Projects sheet tab.**
This action deselects the pasted row and returns the active cell to the Current Projects worksheet. Row 4 should still be selected.

17 **Choose Edit, Delete.**
Row 4 is deleted from the Current Projects worksheet—the last step in transferring a record from the Current Projects worksheet to the Completed Projects worksheet.

18 **Click elsewhere on the worksheet, such as cell A1, to deselect row 4.**

19 **Click the Stop Recording button (refer to Figure 12.21).**
The word *Recording* no longer displays in the status bar.

20 **Save your changes to the *Project List* workbook.**
You can close the workbook and exit Excel, or continue with the next skill.

In Depth:
Assigning a Shortcut Key to a Macro
You can assign a shortcut key to your macro that can be an upper- or lowercase letter. To do so, type a letter in the Shortcut key text box within the Record Macro dialog box. To run a macro using this shortcut key, press and hold Ctrl and then press the letter you assigned to the macro. If your shortcut key is an uppercase letter, press and hold both Ctrl and ⬆Shift with the appropriate key.

Levels of Macro Security
You can select one of three levels of macro security: Low, Medium, and High. If you open a workbook that contains a macro when the security level is Low, Excel opens the workbook and enables the macros. If you open a workbook that contains a macro when the security level is High, Excel automatically disables the macros.

If you open a workbook that contains a macro when the security level is Medium, you can choose to enable or disable macros. As a general guideline, click the option Enable Macros only if the workbook is from a trusted source.

To change the level of macro security, choose Tools, Options and click the Security tab. Click the Macro Security button in the lower-right corner of the Options dialog box; click the Security Level tab in the Security dialog box, and select the desired security level—High, Medium, or Low.

Play a Macro

After you record a macro you can play (or run) it at any time. You can play a macro by using the Tools, Macro command. You can also activate a shortcut key, if you assigned one to the macro. If you want to stop a macro that is currently running, press Esc and then click End in the Microsoft Visual Basic dialog box.

In the following steps, you use the Tools, Macro command to play a macro that updates a project list.

To Play a Macro

1 **Display the Current Projects worksheet in the *Project List* workbook; then type** 4/11/2003 **in cell F5, and press** ↵Enter**.**
You updated the Current Projects worksheet to show that the project in row 5 was completed on 4/11/2003.

2 **Select row 5.**

3 **Select Tools, Macro, Macros.**
The Macro dialog box opens.

4 **Select *This Workbook* from the Macros in drop-down list.**
This lists all macros defined for the current workbook, named Project List. The name of one macro, the newly created *Completed*, displays in the Macro name list (see Figure 12.22).

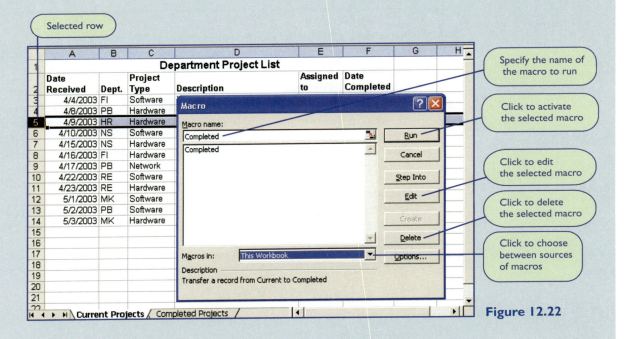

Figure 12.22

5 **Make sure that *Completed* displays in the Macro name text box, and click Run.**
More quickly than the eye can follow, each action captured in the macro executes. Excel copies the contents of row 5 in the Current Projects sheet to the first blank row in the Completed Projects sheet and then deletes row 5 in the Current Projects sheet.

6 **Click the Completed Projects sheet tab.**
Four records display, including the new one in row 6 with a completion date of 4/11/2003 (see Figure 12.23).

continues ▶

To Play a Macro (continued)

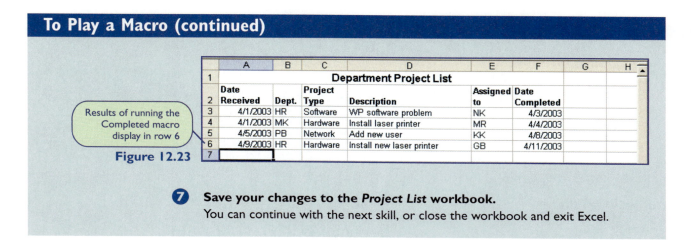

Results of running the Completed macro display in row 6

Figure 12.23

	A	B	C	D	E	F	G	H
1	Department Project List							
2	Date Received	Dept.	Project Type	Description	Assigned to	Date Completed		
3	4/1/2003	HR	Software	WP software problem	NK	4/3/2003		
4	4/1/2003	MK	Hardware	Install laser printer	MR	4/4/2003		
5	4/5/2003	PB	Network	Add new user	KK	4/8/2003		
6	4/9/2003	HR	Hardware	Install new laser printer	GB	4/11/2003		
7								

7 Save your changes to the *Project List* workbook.
You can continue with the next skill, or close the workbook and exit Excel.

In Depth:

Recording a Macro in the Personal Macro Workbook

In this skill, you created the macro named *Completed* for use with one specific workbook, and you saved it in that workbook. You can also create a macro for use in any workbook.

A ***Personal Macro Workbook*** is a Microsoft Excel file named *Personal.xls* that contains macros that are available to all workbooks. To create a macro for use in more than one workbook, select *Personal Macro Workbook* instead of *This Workbook* when you choose a storage location for the macro. Excel adds the macro to the *Personal.xls* workbook.

Deleting a Macro

To delete a macro, select the macro from the list in the Macro dialog box, and click the <u>D</u>elete button (refer to Figure 12.22). If the macro you want to delete is stored in the *Personal.xls* workbook and that workbook is hidden, you can display it by choosing <u>W</u>indows, <u>U</u>nhide.

Edit a Macro Using the Visual Basic Editor

Microsoft's *Visual Basic Editor* is an editing program that you can use to view and edit Excel macros. Lines of code, such as those shown in Figure 12.24 for a macro that creates a header, display when the editor is active.

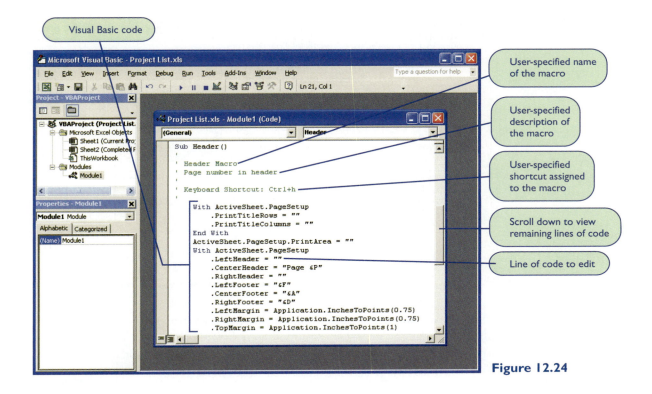

Figure 12.24

In this skill, you work through two sets of hands-on steps. In the first set, you create the macro shown in Figure 12.24 and assign a shortcut key to execute it. The macro inserts the page number code in a header for the current worksheet. In the second set of steps, you access the Visual Basic Editor and edit one line of code in the macro.

The action performed by the macro is one that is useful for any workbook, and normally you would store it in the Personal Macro Workbook. However, some networked environments do not permit you to alter the *personal.xls* file, so for this illustration you continue to work with macros stored in the current workbook.

To Record a Header Macro

1 **Display the Current Projects worksheet in the *Project List* workbook.**

2 **Select _Tools, _Macro, _Record New Macro.**
The Record Macro dialog box opens.

3 **Type Header in the Macro name text box.**

4 **Type the lowercase letter h in the Shortcut _key text box.**

5 **Select *This Workbook* in the *Store macro _in* drop-down list.**

6 **Type Page number in header in the _Description text box (see Figure 12.25).**

continues ▶

To Record a Header Macro (continued)

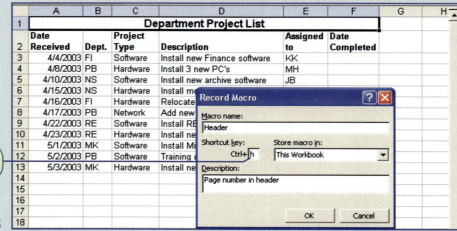

	A	B	C	D	E	F	G	H
1				Department Project List				
2	Date Received	Dept.	Project Type	Description	Assigned to	Date Completed		
3	4/4/2003	FI	Software	Install new Finance software	KK			
4	4/8/2003	PB	Hardware	Install 3 new PC's	MH			
5	4/10/2003	NS	Software	Install new archive software	JB			
6	4/15/2003	NS	Hardware	Install m				
7	4/16/2003	FI	Hardware	Relocate				
8	4/17/2003	PB	Network	Add new				
9	4/22/2003	RE	Software	Install RE				
10	4/23/2003	RE	Hardware	Install ne				
11	5/1/2003	MK	Software	Install Mi				
12	5/2/2003	PB	Software	Training				
13	5/3/2003	MK	Hardware	Install ne				
14								
15								
16								
17								
18								

Shortcut key assigned to the macro

Record Macro

Macro name:
Header

Shortcut key: Store macro in:
Ctrl+ h   This Workbook

Description:
Page number in header

OK   Cancel

Figure 12.25

7 **Make sure that your settings match those shown in Figure 12.25, and click OK.**

The Record Macro dialog box closes, and the word *Recording* displays in the status bar.

X *If you have problems...*

If the name of the macro or the letter assigned to the shortcut key is already in use, Excel displays a message that explains the problem and provides instructions to correct it. For example, a message that there is already a macro assigned to the key displays if the upper- or lowercase letter you specify is assigned to another shortcut.

8 **Select File, Page Setup; then click the Header/Footer tab in the Page Setup dialog box.**

9 **Click the Header drop-down arrow (see Figure 12.26).**

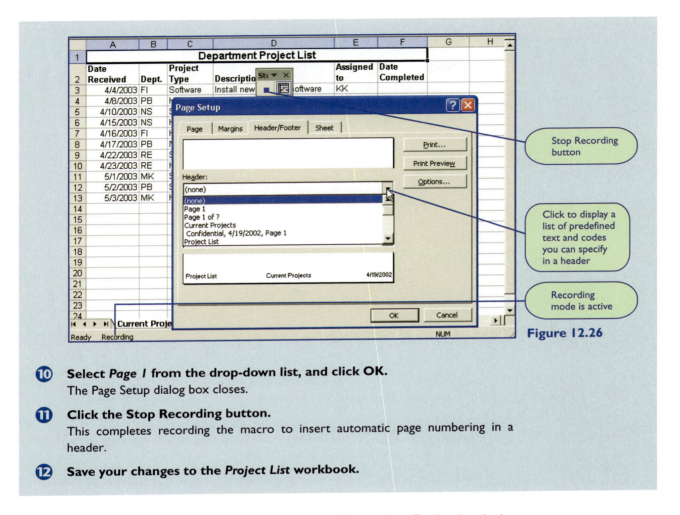

Figure 12.26

Labels in figure:
- Stop Recording button
- Click to display a list of predefined text and codes you can specify in a header
- Recording mode is active

🔟 **Select *Page 1* from the drop-down list, and click OK.**
The Page Setup dialog box closes.

⑪ **Click the Stop Recording button.**
This completes recording the macro to insert automatic page numbering in a header.

⑫ **Save your changes to the *Project List* workbook.**

You created a macro that you can execute using the assigned shortcut key. Excel writes the instructions in its programming language Visual Basic for Applications (VBA). Now use the Visual Basic Editor to modify the macro, and make sure that it works as intended.

To Edit a Macro

① **Make sure that the *Project List* workbook is open; then select <u>T</u>ools, Macro, <u>M</u>acros.**
The Macro dialog box lists the names of the macros in the *Project List* workbook.

② **Select Header in the <u>M</u>acro name list, and click <u>E</u>dit.**
The Visual Basic window opens and displays the Visual Basic code for the macro (refer to Figure 12.24).

③ **Locate the line of code .*LeftHeader* = " "**
Edit this line to add preparer information at the left edge of the header.

④ **Click between the " " (double quotation marks) symbols and then type Prepared by: XXX (substitute your initials for XXX).**
The revised line of code displays as shown in Figure 12.27.

continues ▶

To Edit a Macro (continued)

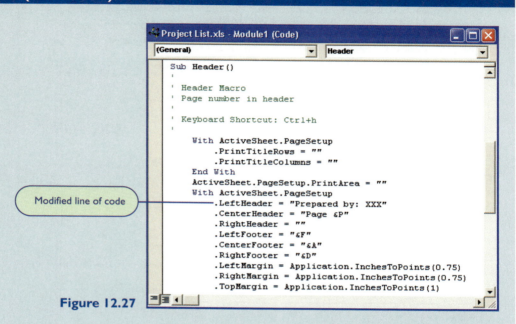

Modified line of code

```
Project List.xls - Module1 (Code)
(General)                                    Header

Sub Header()
'
' Header Macro
' Page number in header
'
' Keyboard Shortcut: Ctrl+h
'
        With ActiveSheet.PageSetup
            .PrintTitleRows = ""
            .PrintTitleColumns = ""
        End With
        ActiveSheet.PageSetup.PrintArea = ""
        With ActiveSheet.PageSetup
            .LeftHeader = "Prepared by: XXX"
            .CenterHeader = "Page &P"
            .RightHeader = ""
            .LeftFooter = "&F"
            .CenterFooter = "&A"
            .RightFooter = "&D"
            .LeftMargin = Application.InchesToPoints(0.75)
            .RightMargin = Application.InchesToPoints(0.75)
            .TopMargin = Application.InchesToPoints(1)
```

Figure 12.27

5 **Select File, Save Project List.xls.**
The changes to the Header macro code are saved in the *Project List* workbook.

6 **Select File, Close and Return to Microsoft Excel.**
The Visual Basic Editor closes. Now check that the revised macro operates as intended.

7 **Select the Completed Projects worksheet, and click Print Preview in the Standard toolbar.**
A header has not been set up for the Completed Projects worksheet.

8 **Close Print Preview; then press Ctrl+h to execute the macro.**

9 **Click the Print Preview button.**
The phrase *Prepared by: XXX* displays at the left edge of the header (your initials should display in place of "XXX"). The page number displays at the center of the header.

10 **Click the Close button and save your changes to the *Project List* workbook.**
You can continue with the next skill, or close the workbook and exit Excel.

In Depth:
Stepping Through a Macro
If a macro does not perform as intended, and you cannot figure out the problem by looking at the lines of code in the Visual Basic Editor, you can run the macro step-by-step. To do this, select the Step Into button in the Macro dialog box, and then press F8 to see each line as it executes.

Create a Macro Button in a Worksheet

Excel provides multiple methods to run a macro that include choosing a menu sequence, entering the assigned shortcut keystrokes, clicking a macro button embedded in a worksheet, and clicking a macro button added to a new or existing toolbar.

If you embed a macro button in a worksheet, the macro assigned to that button can only be applied to that worksheet. You can also create a macro button on a new or existing toolbar that can be applied to any workbook. In the following steps, you create a macro button in a worksheet.

To Create a Macro Button in a Worksheet

① **Open the *Project List* workbook, if necessary; then select the Current Projects worksheet.**

② **Click cell G2.**
Now create a macro button located in cell G2.

③ **Select View, Toolbars and then click Forms.**
The Forms toolbar displays (see Figure 12.28).

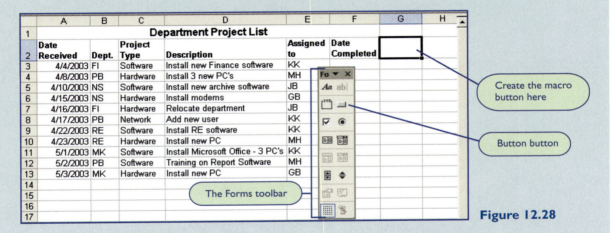

Figure 12.28

④ **Click the Button button on the Forms toolbar.**
The message *Drag in document to create a button* displays in the status bar, and the mouse pointer changes to a thin black cross.

⑤ **Click the upper-left corner of cell G2, and drag the mouse pointer down and to the right; release the mouse button when the drawn box fills cell G2.**
The Assign Macro dialog box opens, and *Button I* displays in cell G2, as shown in Figure 12.29.

continues ▶

To Create a Macro Button in a Worksheet (continued)

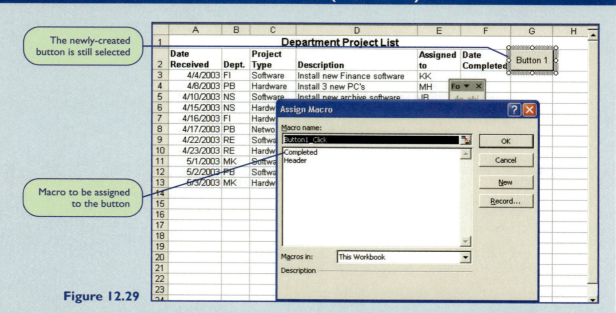

The newly-created button is still selected

Macro to be assigned to the button

Figure 12.29

6 **Click** *Completed* **in the** <u>M</u>**acro name list, and click OK.**
The Completed macro is assigned to the button in cell G2. Now change the name of the button.

7 **Replace the phrase** *Button 1* **with the word** Transfer**, and then deselect the button.**
Now check that the Transfer macro button in the Current Projects worksheet works as intended.

8 **Close the Forms toolbar and click cell F7.**

9 **Enter** 5/3/2003 **in cell F7 and select row 7.**
The button and selected row display as shown in Figure 12.30.

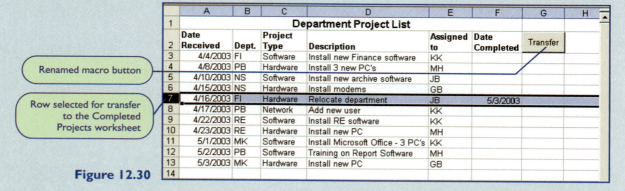

Renamed macro button

Row selected for transfer to the Completed Projects worksheet

Figure 12.30

10 **Click the Transfer button.**
Data about the project completed 05/03/2003 is copied to the next available blank row in the Completed Projects worksheet and removed from the Current Projects worksheet.

⑪ Click the Completed Projects worksheet tab.

There are now five records in the Completed Projects list (see Figure 12.31).

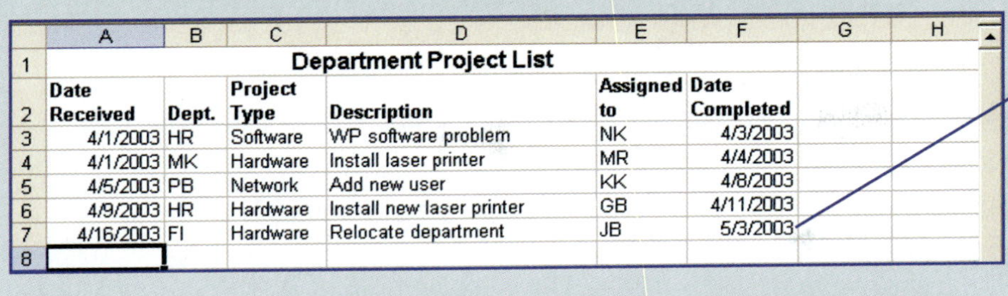

	A	B	C	D	E	F	G	H
1				**Department Project List**				
2	**Date Received**	**Dept.**	**Project Type**	**Description**	**Assigned to**	**Date Completed**		
3	4/1/2003	HR	Software	WP software problem	NK	4/3/2003		
4	4/1/2003	MK	Hardware	Install laser printer	MR	4/4/2003		
5	4/5/2003	PB	Network	Add new user	KK	4/8/2003		
6	4/9/2003	HR	Hardware	Install new laser printer	GB	4/11/2003		
7	4/16/2003	FI	Hardware	Relocate department	JB	5/3/2003		
8								

Row transferred to the Completed Projects worksheet

Figure 12.31

⑫ Select the Current Projects worksheet, and click cell A1; then save your changes and close the *Project List* workbook.

Continue with the exercises, start another skill set, or exit Excel.

In Depth:
Modifying, Moving, and Deleting a Macro Button

If a macro button in a worksheet is too small to contain the descriptive word you specify as its name, you can resize the button by using the handles. If the handles are not in view, press Ctrl while left-clicking the button. This activates the handles.

You can change characteristics, such as the font, of a macro button by right-clicking the button and selecting Format Control from the shortcut menu.

A macro button can be relocated anywhere on the worksheet by right-clicking the button and dragging it by its shaded border to the new location.

To remove a macro button in the worksheet, right-click it and select Cut from the shortcut menu.

For immediate reinforcement, work Skill Drills 2 through 6 and Challenges 3 through 5.

Summary

This skill set began with a focus on customizing toolbars and menus. You added buttons to a new custom toolbar, removed buttons, and attached your custom toolbar to a workbook. You also created, used, and removed a custom menu on Excel's menu bar.

The rest of the skill set provided an introduction to macros. You created and played two macros—one to transfer data from a worksheet, and the other to insert a header. In the process, you learned three ways to run a macro: selecting a menu sequence, using a shortcut key combination, and clicking a macro button embedded in a worksheet. Your experiences also included a brief introduction to editing a macro by using the Visual Basic Editor.

Skill Drill

Skill Drill exercises *reinforce* skills. Each skill reinforced is the same, or nearly the same, as a skill presented in the skill set. Detailed instructions are provided in a step-by-step format.

Before beginning your Excel Expert Skill Set 5 Skill Drill exercises, complete the following steps:

1. Open the file named *MEE-S503*, and click <u>E</u>nable Macros, if prompted; then immediately save the file as `MEE-S5drill`.

> The workbook contains five sheets: an overview and four exercise sheets labeled SD2-3, SD4, SD5, and SD6. It also contains the macro RedBold.

 If you have problems...

If the macro security level for your system is High, Excel disables the macro stored in the workbook and displays a message. Click OK to proceed with exercises that are not dependent on preexisting macros.

2. Click the Overview sheet to view the organization and content of the Skill Drill workbook for Excel Expert Skill Set 5.

Each exercise is independent of the others, so you may complete the exercises in any order. Be sure to save the workbook after completing each exercise. If you need a paper copy of one or more completed exercises, enter your name, centered in a header, before printing. Print options have already been set to print compressed to one page and to display the filename, sheet name, and current date in a footer.

Be sure to save your changes and close the workbook if you need more than one work session to complete the desired exercises. Continue working on *MEE-S5drill* instead of starting over in the original *MEE-S503* file.

1. Create a Custom Toolbar Attached to a Workbook

You frequently enter symbols, and you want to put the symbols that you use most often on a toolbar. To create a custom toolbar for selected symbols and attach it to a workbook, complete the following steps. If you are working on a networked system that prevents the creation of a custom toolbar, you can review the process by reading the hands-on steps.

1. Open the *MEE-S5drill* workbook, if necessary. (Also click <u>E</u>nable Macros, if prompted.)

2. Scroll to a blank area in the Overview sheet.

> You can create the toolbar in any part of any sheet, but a blank area makes it easier to see the dialog boxes.

3. Select <u>T</u>ools, <u>C</u>ustomize and select the Tool<u>b</u>ars tab in the Customize dialog box.

4. Click the <u>N</u>ew button, type `AsstSymbols` in the <u>T</u>oolbar name text box, and click OK.

5. Click the Commands tab in the Customize dialog box, and click Insert in the Categories list at the left side of the dialog box.

6. Scroll down, and select Symbol in the Comman<u>d</u>s list at the right side of the dialog box.

7. Drag Symbol to the empty toolbar, and release the mouse button.

8. Drag five arithmetic operators from the Comman<u>d</u>s list to the AsstSymbols toolbar in the following order: Equal Sign, Plus Sign, Minus Sign, Multiplication Sign, and Division Sign.

9. Drag four more items used in formulas from the Commands list to the AsstSymbols toolbar in the following order: Left Parenthesis, Right Parenthesis, Colon, and Comma.

10. Click the Toolbars tab in the Customize dialog box. Make sure that AsstSymbols is the selected toolbar, and click the Attach button.

   The Attach Toolbars dialog box opens.

11. Click AsstSymbols in the Custom toolbars list; click the Copy button, and click OK.

12. Close the Customize dialog box, and close the AsstSymbols toolbar.

13. Click cell A1 and save your changes to the *MEE-S5drill* workbook.

2. Create and Play a Macro that Enters an Address

You work for Everglo Corporation, and you want to create a macro that enters the complete address of the firm on three lines. Normally you would create such a macro in the Personal Macro Workbook so that it is available for use in all workbooks. For this exercise, however, create the macro in the *MEE-S5drill* workbook.

To create and play a macro to enter a three-line address, follow these steps:

1. Open the *MEE-S5drill* workbook, if necessary. (Also click Enable Macros, if prompted.)

2. Select the SD2-3 worksheet.

3. Click cell A3, and select Tools, Macro, Record New Macro.

   The Record Macro dialog box opens.

4. In the Macro name text box, type `EvergloAddress`.

5. In the *Store macro in* drop-down list, select *This Workbook*, if necessary.

6. Type `Enter the Everglo mailing address` in the Description text box, and click OK.

   The macro recorder is now on. The message *Recording* displays at the bottom of the screen, and a two-button Stop Recording toolbar displays within the screen.

7. Click the Relative Reference button on the Stop Recording toolbar until a blue border surrounds the button.

8. Type the following address in cells A3:A5.

   ```
   Everglo Corporation
   9999 Smith Valley Road
   Indianapolis, IN 46250
   ```

9. Select the range A3:A5, and apply a Comic Sans MS 12pt font to the range. (Substitute a different font style if Comic Sans MS is not available on your system.)

10. Press ↑ to deselect the range A3:A5, and click the Stop Recording button.

11. Select the range A3:A5, and select Edit, Clear, All.

   The content and formats applied to cells A3:A5 are removed. Rows 3 through 5 revert to the default row height.

12. Click cell A3 and select Tools, Macro, Macros.

   The Macro dialog box opens.

13. Select *This Workbook* in the Macros in drop-down list.

   The macro named *EvergloAddress* displays in the Macro name list.

14. Select *EvergloAddress* in the Macro name list box, and click Run.

   Excel automatically enters the three-line Everglo address in the range A3:A5. Now test that the macro works in another location.

15. Click cell F4 and run the EvergloAddress macro. (Refer to steps 12 through 14.)

Excel enters the three-line Everglo address in the range F4:F6.

16. Save your changes to the *MEE-S5drill* workbook.

3. Create and Play a Macro that Enters Column Labels

You frequently enter the names of months across a row, and you want to create a macro to automate that task. Normally, you would create such a macro in the Personal Macro Workbook so that it is available for use in all workbooks. For this exercise, however, create the macro in the *MEE-S5drill* workbook.

To create and play a macro that enters the names of months across a row, follow these steps:

1. Open the *MEE-S5drill* workbook, if necessary. (Also click Enable Macros, if prompted.)

2. Select the SD2-3 worksheet.

3. Click cell A8 and select Tools, Macro, Record New Macro.

The Record Macro dialog box opens.

4. Click in the Macro name text box and type **JanDecRight**.

5. In the *Store macro in* drop-down list, select *This Workbook*, if necessary.

6. Type **Enter Jan through Dec across a row** in the Description text box, and click OK.

The macro recorder is now on. The message *Recording* displays at the bottom of the screen, and a two-button Stop Recording toolbar displays within the screen.

7. Make sure that the Relative Reference button on the Stop Recording toolbar is selected—that is, a blue border surrounds the button. If necessary, click the button to select it.

8. Make sure that cell A8 is the current cell; click the Center button on the Formatting toolbar, and enter **Jan** in cell A8.

9. Click the cell A8 fill handle; drag right to fill the range A8:L8, and release the mouse button.

10. Press ⬇ to deselect the range A8:L8.

11. Click the Stop Recording button.

Make sure that the macro operates correctly from any starting position.

12. Select the range A8:L8, and select Edit, Clear, All.

13. Click cell A10 and select Tools, Macro, Macros.

14. Select *This Workbook* in the Macros in drop-down list; select *JanDecRight* in the Macro name list box, and click Run.

Excel automatically enters the abbreviated monthly labels in the range A10:L10.

15. Save your changes to the *MEE-S5drill* workbook.

4. Create and Play a Macro that Applies Font and Border Color

Your responsibilities include reviewing a list of delinquent accounts. You determined which accounts should be referred to an attorney at this time. You will be giving the list to another staff member with instructions to call the firm's current attorney, and you want the relevant accounts to be easy to identify. You decide to create a macro that applies a red font and border to a user-specified cell.

1. Open the *MEE-S5drill* workbook, if necessary. (Also click Enable Macros, if prompted.)

2. Select the SD4 worksheet.

3. Click cell B14 and select <u>T</u>ools, <u>M</u>acro, <u>R</u>ecord New Macro.

4. Name the macro **RedInOut** and select *This Workbook* in the *Store macro i<u>n</u>* drop-down list, if necessary.

5. Enter **Apply red font and border** in the <u>D</u>escription text box, and click OK.

   The Stop Recording toolbar opens, and the word *Recording* displays in the status bar. Now start the keystrokes to set up the desired effects.

6. Make sure that Relative Reference is selected in the Stop Recording toolbar.

7. Select F<u>o</u>rmat, C<u>e</u>lls and click the Font tab.

8. Select Red in the <u>C</u>olor drop-down list.

9. Select the Border tab; select Red in the <u>C</u>olor drop-down list; click the <u>O</u>utline preset, and click OK.

10. Click the Stop Recording button, and click any cell to deselect cell B14.

   The contents of cell B14 display red, and a red border displays around the cell. Now test the macro.

11. Click cell B18 and select <u>T</u>ools, <u>M</u>acro, <u>M</u>acros.

12. Select the RedInOut macro; click <u>R</u>un, and click any cell to deselect B18.

   The contents of cell B18 display red, and a red border displays around the cell.

13. Save your changes to the *MEE-S5drill* workbook.

5. Create and Play a Macro Assigned to a Shortcut Key

Your responsibilities include reviewing a list of delinquent accounts. You want an easy way to enter and format the current date before printing the report. You decide to create a macro activated by a shortcut key that enters the TODAY function in a user-specified cell, followed by formatting the results to display in the form dd-mmm-yyyy (such as 14-Feb-2003).

1. Open the *MEE-S5drill* workbook, if necessary. (Also click <u>E</u>nable Macros, if prompted.)

2. Select the SD5 worksheet.

3. Click cell B5 and select <u>T</u>ools, <u>M</u>acro, <u>R</u>ecord New Macro.

4. Name the macro **Today** and select *This Workbook* in the *Store macro i<u>n</u>* drop-down list, if necessary.

5. Type the lowercase letter **t** in the Shortcut <u>k</u>ey text box.

6. Type **Enter the system date; show as dd-mmm-yyyy** in the <u>D</u>escription text box, and click OK.

   The Stop Recording toolbar opens, and the word *Recording* displays in the status bar. Now start the keystrokes to enter and format the desired function.

 If you have problems...
   If a message displays that there is already a macro assigned to Ctrl+t, specify another letter.

7. Type **=today()** and click the green checkmark in the formula bar.

8. Choose F<u>o</u>rmat, C<u>e</u>lls and click the Number tab.

9. Select *Date* in the <u>C</u>ategory list; then scroll down and select **14-Mar-2001** in the <u>T</u>ype list.

10. Click OK and click the Stop Recording button.

Now test that the macro works as intended.

11. Click cell B5 and select Edit, Clear, All.

12. Press Ctrl+t.

The current date displays in cell B5 in the form dd-mmm-yyyy. The function =TODAY() displays in the formula bar.

13. Save your changes to the *MEE-S5drill* workbook.

6. Create and Use a Macro Button

You have been playing a macro by selecting from menu options and lists. Now you decide to set the macro up as a button on the worksheet, because someone who is not as familiar with Excel as you are is going to take over management of the file.

1. Open the *MEE-S5drill* workbook, if necessary. (Also click Enable Macros, if prompted.)

2. Select the SD6 worksheet.

3. Display the Forms toolbar and click the Button button.

4. Click the upper-left corner of cell F2, and drag the mouse pointer down and to the right. Release the mouse when the drawn box fills the range F2:F3.

The Assign Macro dialog box opens, and *Button 1* displays in cells F2:F3.

5. Click *RedBold* in the Macro name list, and click OK.

The RedBold macro is assigned to the button in cells F2:F3. Now change the name of the button.

6. Delete the *Button 1* text and replace it with **RedBold**.

7. Close the Forms toolbar and deselect the RedBold button by clicking outside the button's shadow border.

8. Right-click the macro button; then select Format Control and click the Properties tab.

9. Make sure that a check mark appears in the Print object check box, and click OK.

10. Deselect the RedBold button.

Now test that the macro button works as intended.

11. Click cell B10 and click the RedBold macro button.

The contents in cell B10 display in bold, and a red background fills cell B10.

12. Save your changes to the *MEE-S5drill* workbook.

Challenge

Challenge exercises expand on or are somewhat related to skills presented in the skill sets. Each exercise provides a brief narrative introduction, followed by instructions in a numbered-step format that are not as detailed as those in the Skill Drill section.

Before beginning your Excel Expert Skill Set 5 Challenge exercises, complete the following steps:

1. Open the file named *MEE-S504* and click Enable Macros, if prompted; then immediately save the file as **MEE-S5challenge**.

The workbook contains four sheets: an overview and three exercise sheets labeled CH3 through CH5. It also contains the macros *Heading* and *Supervisor*.

If you have problems...

If the macro security level for your system is High, Excel disables the macros stored in the workbook and displays a message. Click OK to proceed with exercises that are not dependent on preexisting macros.

2. Click the Overview sheet to view the organization and content of the Challenge workbook for Excel Expert Skill Set 5.

Each exercise is independent of the others, so you may complete the exercises in any order. Be sure to save the workbook after completing each exercise. If you need a paper copy of one or more completed exercises, enter your name, centered in a header, before printing. Print options have already been set to print compressed to one page. Settings to display the filename, sheet name, and current date in a footer have been set in all worksheets.

Be sure to save your changes and close the workbook if you need more than one work session to complete the desired exercises. Continue working on *MEE-S5challenge* instead of starting over in the original *MEE-S504* file.

1. Add Text to a Toolbar Button

A custom toolbar named AsstShapes is attached to a workbook. Now you want to open that workbook and add text that describes the image on one of the toolbar buttons.

To add text to a toolbar button, follow these steps:

1. Open the *MEE-S5challenge* workbook, if necessary. (Also click <u>E</u>nable Macros, if prompted.)
2. Scroll to a blank area on any worksheet in the workbook.
3. Display the Customize dialog box, and display the AsstShapes custom toolbar attached to the workbook.
4. Click the Cloud Callout button on the AsstShapes toolbar, and click the <u>C</u>ommands tab in the Customize dialog box; then click the <u>M</u>odify Selection button in the dialog box.
5. Select Image <u>a</u>nd Text from the shortcut menu, and close the Customize dialog box.

   <u>C</u>loud Callout displays after the cloud image in the toolbar.
6. Close the AsstShapes custom toolbar, and save your changes to the *MEE-S5challenge* workbook.

2. Group Related Buttons on a Toolbar

You created a custom toolbar with assorted symbols and attached it to a workbook. Now you want to add separator bars so that related buttons display as a group. To group the buttons, follow these steps:

1. Open the *MEE-S5challenge* workbook, if necessary. (Also click <u>E</u>nable Macros, if prompted.)
2. Scroll to a blank area on any worksheet in the workbook.
3. Display the Customize dialog box, and display the AsstSymbols custom toolbar.
4. Right-click the Plus Sign button on the toolbar, and click Begin a <u>G</u>roup on the shortcut menu.

   A separator bar displays between the Equal Sign button and the Plus Sign button. You can remove a separator bar between two buttons by dragging one button closer to the other.

5. Right-click the Left Parenthesis button on the toolbar, and click Begin a <u>G</u>roup on the shortcut menu.

A separator bar displays between the Division Sign button and the Left Parenthesis button.

6. Close the Customize dialog box; close the AsstSymbols custom toolbar, and save your changes to the *MEE-S5challenge* workbook.

3. Create a Macro Button on a Custom Toolbar

Assume that you use a macro named *Supervisor* to enter your supervisor's name—Jordan Fields—in a worksheet cell. You understand that if you embed a macro button in a worksheet and assign the Supervisor macro to that button, that the macro can only be applied to that worksheet. You decide to create a macro button on a custom toolbar and assign the Supervisor macro to that macro button, so that you can use the macro in other worksheets.

You find out that three actions are required if you do not want to put a custom button on an existing Excel toolbar: create a new blank toolbar, create a button on the new toolbar, and assign a macro to the new button.

If you are working in an environment that does not permit you to create a custom toolbar, you will not be able to work through this exercise.

1. Open the *MEE-S5challenge* workbook, if necessary. (Also click <u>E</u>nable Macros, if prompted.)

2. Select the CH3 worksheet.

3. Choose <u>V</u>iew, <u>T</u>oolbars and click <u>C</u>ustomize.

4. Select the Tool<u>b</u>ars tab; click the <u>N</u>ew button; change the name of the new toolbar to **MyTools**, and click OK.

The New Toolbar dialog box closes, but the Customize dialog box remains open. A new floating toolbar displays. It is quite small at this point, containing room for one button. Now create a button on the new toolbar.

5. Select the <u>C</u>ommands tab in the Customize dialog box, and select Macros in the Categories list box.

6. Drag the yellow smiley face in the Comman<u>d</u>s section to your new MyTools toolbar.

A copy of the yellow smiley face displays on the new toolbar. A thick black border surrounds it, indicating the new button is selected. Now assign a macro.

7. Right-click the yellow smiley face button on the new toolbar.

A shortcut menu displays with many options, including Assign <u>M</u>acro near the bottom.

8. Click Assign <u>M</u>acro in the shortcut menu, and assign the *Supervisor* macro to the button.

9. Display the shortcut menu again, and change the name *&Custom Button* to **JF**.

10. Check the <u>T</u>ext Only (Always) option in the shortcut menu, and close the Customize dialog box.

Now test that the new macro button on a custom toolbar operates as intended.

11. Select cell F4, and click the JF button on your custom toolbar.

Check that the name *Jordan Fields* displays in red in cell F4.

12. Close the new custom toolbar, and save your changes to the *MEE-S5challenge* workbook.

13. Delete the custom toolbar, if desired. (Onscreen Help provides an explanation of the process.)

4. Create a Macro that Transposes a Range

You want to create a macro that automates the process of transposing data previously entered in a row. For example, the desired macro could be used to convert monthly headings entered in a row to monthly headings entered in a column.

To create and use a macro that transposes a user-specified range, follow these steps:

1. Open the *MEE-S5challenge* workbook, if necessary. (Also click Enable Macros, if prompted.)

2. Select the CH4 worksheet, and select the range A4:L4.

3. Select Tools, Macro, Record New Macro, and name the macro **RowToColumn**.

4. Specify that you want to store the macro in the current workbook; enter the description **Transpose data from row to column**, and click OK.

   The message *Recording* displays at the bottom of the screen and a two-button Stop Recording toolbar displays within the screen. Now capture the commands to transpose the selected range.

5. Make sure that the Relative Reference button on the Stop Recording toolbar is selected—that is, a blue border surrounds the button. If necessary, click the button to select it.

6. Click the Copy button; press ⬇, and select Edit, Paste Special.

7. Click the Transpose check box in the Paste Special dialog box, and click OK.

8. Click ⬆ and click the current row's header number in the worksheet frame.

9. Select Edit, Delete and press ⬆ to deselect the transposed range.

10. Click the Stop Recording button.

   Now make sure that the macro operates correctly by using it to transpose quarter labels.

11. Select the quarter labels in the range G17:J17.

12. Select Tools, Macro, Macros and then run the *RowToColumn* macro.

   Excel automatically enters the abbreviated quarter labels down column G and deletes the row containing the original label data.

13. Save your changes to the *MEE-S5challenge* workbook.

5. Edit a Macro

If you want to make changes in a macro, you can modify it using the Visual Basic Editor. The editor takes a little practice but is often faster and easier than rerecording the macro. In this exercise, you edit a macro that enters the name and address of your company in a worksheet. You use the Visual Basic Editor to make the change.

1. Open the *MEE-S5challenge* workbook, if necessary. (Also click Enable Macros, if prompted.)

2. Select the CH5 worksheet.

3. Display the Macro dialog box; select the Heading macro, and click Edit.

4. Change the text *5151 Smith Road* to reflect the new street address **10 North Sunset Lane**.

   Make sure that quotation marks still surround the street address.

5. Save the change and exit the Visual Basic window.

6. Select cell D5 and run the macro.

7. Examine the difference between the two addresses to make sure that the address change you made in the macro is reflected in the worksheet after running the macro.

8. Save your changes to the *MEE-S5challenge* workbook.

Auditing Worksheets

This skill set includes

Audit formulas
- Use the Formula Watch Window
- Trace Precedents

Locate and resolve errors
- Get help on correcting errors in formulas
- Correct errors using the Formula Auditing toolbar

Identify dependencies in formulas

Skill Set Overview

Worksheets generally contain multiple formulas, and decisions are made based on formula results. If calculations are wrong, decisions based on that data are likely to be wrong—often with costly results.

In this skill set, you learn a variety of methods to find and fix common errors in formulas. You begin by displaying a window to watch selected formulas that are out of view. You also examine the relationships of other cells to a formula—cells that are used in the formula, and cells that use the formula's results. After viewing related onscreen Help topics about correcting errors in formulas, you evaluate errors on an income statement worksheet. Your efforts include using the Error Checking dialog box.

Keep in mind, however, that Excel does not catch every error. It is your responsibility to make sure that the worksheets you design and use produce accurate results.

Skill 6.1: **Audit Formulas**

Excel provides several methods to check the accuracy of formula results. In this skill area, you learn about the Formula Watch Window and tracing precedents. The *Formula Watch Window* enables you to view cells containing formulas even when the cells are out of view. *Trace Precedents* shows what cells provide data to the current cell.

Use the Formula Watch Window

You can select the cells you want to watch in the Formula Watch Window. You can also add or delete cells under watch as desired.

In the following steps, you select two named cells to watch—a cell displaying the amount of the monthly payment on a 15-year loan, and a cell displaying the amount of the monthly payment on a 30-year loan. The cells are named *yrs15* and *yrs30*, respectively. You make changes to loan terms and view the effects of the changes on monthly payments in the Formula Watch Window.

To Use the Formula Watch Window

① Open the *MEE-S601* workbook, and save it as Watch Demo.
The workbook contains a single worksheet named Multiple PMT.

② Scroll down to view the loan data at the end of the table (row 32), if necessary.

③ Click cell C30, hold down Ctrl**, and click cell C32.**
You selected the cells calculating the monthly payment for 15-year and 30-year loans, respectively.

④ Select Tools, Formula Auditing, Show Watch Window.
Data about the selected cells display in the Watch Window (see Figure 13.1).

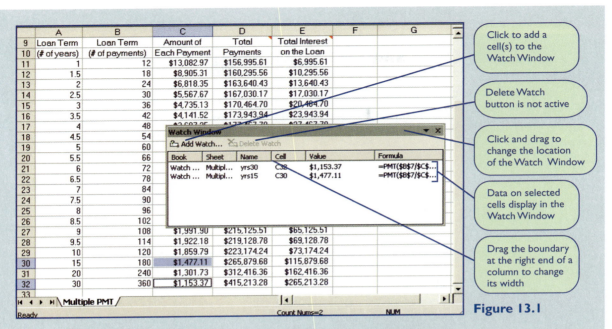

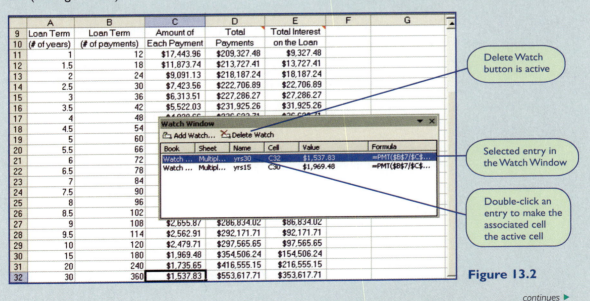

Figure 13.1

The monthly payment on a 15-year 8.5 percent $150,000 loan is $1,477.11. The monthly payment on a 30-year 8.5 percent $150,000 loan is $1,153.37.

⑤ Enter 200000 in cell D7.

Cells C30 and C32 may be out of view in the worksheet, but you see the effects of the change in the Watch Window. The monthly payment on a 15-year 8.5 percent $200,000 loan is $1,969.48. The monthly payment on a 30-year 8.5 percent $200,000 loan is $1,537.83.

⑥ Double-click any data item in the first row within the Watch Window, such as *yrs30* in the Name column.

Excel displays the cell that the data item refers to—in this case, cell C32. The first row in the Watch Window is selected, and the Delete Watch button is no longer dim (see Figure 13.2).

Figure 13.2

continues ▶

To Use the Formula Watch Window (continued)

7 **Click the Delete Watch button in the Watch Window.**
The data about cell C32 no longer display in the Watch Window.

8 **Close the Watch Window; then save your changes to the *Watch Demo* workbook and close the workbook.**
Continue with the next skill, or exit Excel.

In Depth:
Watching Cells That Link to Another Workbook
To watch cells that have links to another workbook, you must open the other workbook.

Trace Precedents

Trace Precedents and Trace Dependents are auditing tools that enable you to review your worksheets for errors or to help you understand how a worksheet performs its calculations. Trace Precedents shows which cells provide data to the current cell, and *Trace Dependents* shows which cells use the results of the current cell. You trace dependencies in formulas in Skill 6.3 in this skill set.

A *tracer arrow* shows the relationship between the current cell and its related cells. Tracer arrows are blue when pointing from a cell that provides data to another cell and red if a cell contains an error.

In the following steps, you trace precedents in an error-free worksheet. You display precedents at two levels and then remove the tracer arrows.

To Trace Precedents

1 **Open the *MEE-S601* workbook, and save it as** Audit1.

2 **Choose Tools, Formula Auditing, Show Formula Auditing Toolbar.**
The worksheet and Formula Auditing toolbar display (see Figure 13.3).

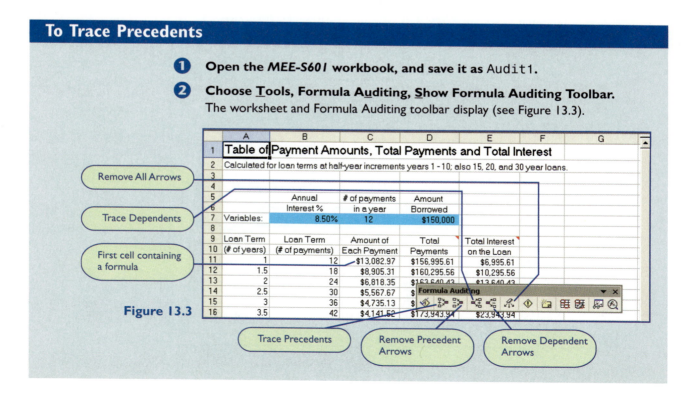

Figure 13.3

③ Click cell C11 and click the Trace Precedents button on the Formula Auditing toolbar.

Excel draws four blue tracer arrows from the four precedent cells—B7, C7, D7, and B11—that provide data to the current cell C11 (see Figure 13.4).

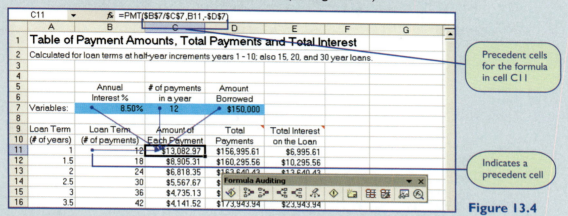

Precedent cells for the formula in cell C11

Indicates a precedent cell

Figure 13.4

④ Click the Trace Precedents button again.

Two additional tracer arrows illustrate the next level of cells that provided data to the current cell (see Figure 13.5).

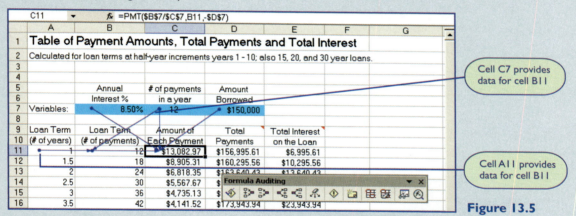

Cell C7 provides data for cell B11

Cell A11 provides data for cell B11

Figure 13.5

⑤ Click the Trace Precedents button again.

Additional tracer arrows do not display. The next level of precedent cells does not exist.

⑥ Click the Remove Precedent Arrows button on the Formula Auditing toolbar.

The tracer arrows from cells A11 and C7 disappear.

⑦ Click the Remove Precedent Arrows button again.

The remaining tracer arrows disappear. You could also remove all tracer arrows at the same time by clicking the Remove All Arrows button on the Formula Auditing toolbar.

⑧ Click cell C20 and click the Trace Precedents button on the Formula Auditing toolbar.

Blue tracer arrows from cells B7, C7, D7, and B20 point to the current cell C20 (see Figure 13.6).

continues ▶

To Trace Precedents (continued)

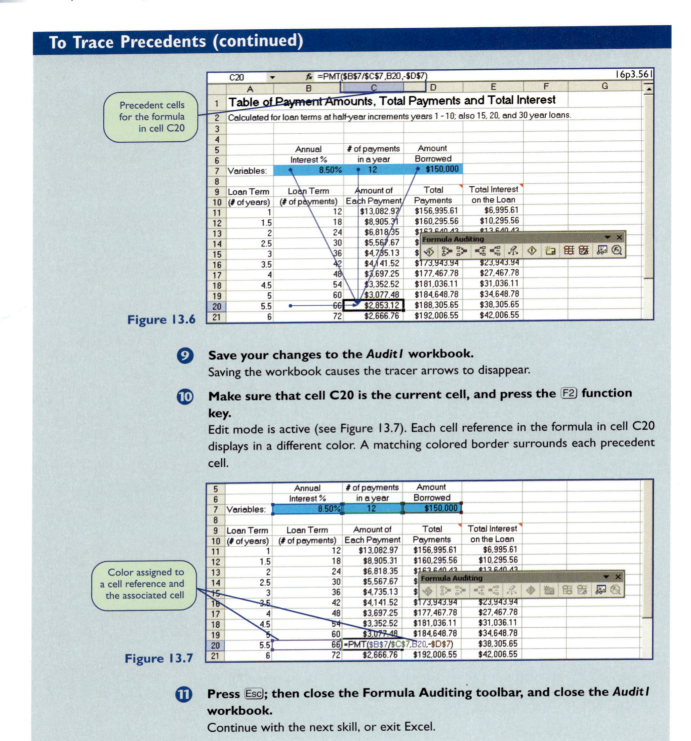

Figure 13.6

9 **Save your changes to the *Audit1* workbook.**
Saving the workbook causes the tracer arrows to disappear.

10 **Make sure that cell C20 is the current cell, and press the [F2] function key.**
Edit mode is active (see Figure 13.7). Each cell reference in the formula in cell C20 displays in a different color. A matching colored border surrounds each precedent cell.

Figure 13.7

11 **Press [Esc]; then close the Formula Auditing toolbar, and close the *Audit1* workbook.**
Continue with the next skill, or exit Excel.

In Depth:
Tracing Precedents in Another Worksheet or Workbook
If a selected cell has precedent cells in another worksheet or workbook, make sure that you open the other workbook before clicking the Trace Precedents button on the Formula Auditing toolbar. If the current cell has precedents in another worksheet or workbook, a black dashed arrow points from a

worksheet icon to the current cell. To jump to the precedent cell of your choice, you can double-click the arrow to display a Go To dialog box and then double-click your choice of references listed in that dialog box.

For immediate reinforcement, work Skill Drills 1 and 3 and Challenge 2.

Skill 6.2: **Locate and Resolve Errors**

You begin this skill area by viewing some of the extensive onscreen Help about finding and fixing errors in formulas. You also use the Error Checking and Trace Error buttons on the Formula Auditing toolbar to view errors found by Excel's *Formula error checker*—a feature that uses rules to check for errors in formulas. You can select Tools, Options and turn the rules on or off individually by using the Error Checking tab in the Options dialog box.

Get Help on Correcting Errors in Formulas

Knowing how to correct errors in formulas is an essential skill when you develop and maintain worksheets. In the following steps, you explore some of the extensive onscreen Help on locating and evaluating such errors.

To Get Help on Correcting Errors in Formulas

1 **Open the *MEE-S602* workbook, and save it as** Audit2.
The workbook contains one worksheet named Condensed IS. The worksheet includes monthly and annual data for the year 2003 in a condensed Income Statement format. Small triangles, indicating possible errors in formulas, display in the upper-left corner of several cells (see Figure 13.8).

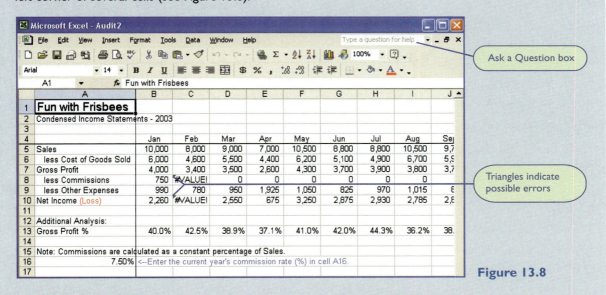

Figure 13.8

 If you have problems...
If the triangles do not display in the upper-left corner of several cells, including cells C8 and C10, select Tools, Options. Select the Error Checking tab in the Options dialog box; click the *Enable background error checking* check box, and click OK.

continues ▶

To Get Help on Correcting Errors in Formulas (continued)

2 Type errors in formulas **in the Ask a question box, and press** ⏎Enter.

3 **Select the topic** *About correcting formulas* **in the Help topics drop-down list.**
Four subtopics display: *Watch Window, Formula error checker, Formula Auditing toolbar,* and *Evaluate Formula* (see Figure 13.9).

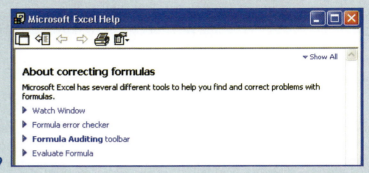

Figure 13.9

4 **Widen the Help pane, if desired, and click the topic** *Formula error checker.*

5 **Read the information provided in the section titled "The rules and what they check for."**

6 **Scroll to the top of the Help window, if necessary, and click Show All in the upper-right corner.**

7 **Explore the expanded Help topics as desired, and close the Help window.**

8 **Enter** errors in formulas **in the Ask a question box, and select the topic** *Find and correct errors in formulas* **in the Help topics drop-down list.**
Five subtopics display: *Correct an error value, such as #NAME?; Watch a formula and result of a cell; Calculate a nested formula one step at a time; Trace the relationships between formulas and cells;* and *Correct common problems in formulas.*

9 **Click the topic** *Correct an error value, such as #NAME?.*
Error value subtopics display (see Figure 13.10). An **error value** is a message that Excel displays in a cell to indicate a specific type of error.

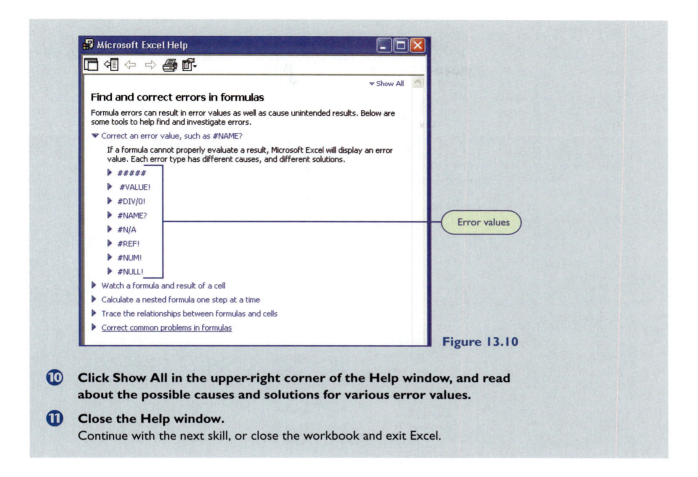

Figure 13.10

 Click Show All in the upper-right corner of the Help window, and read about the possible causes and solutions for various error values.

 Close the Help window.
Continue with the next skill, or close the workbook and exit Excel.

In Depth:
Error-Checking Rules

Excel uses rules to check for common mistakes in formulas. A triangle appears in the top-left corner of a cell that contains an error according to the active error-checking rules. You can turn these rules on or off individually using the Error Checking tab in the Options dialog box (see Figure 13.11).

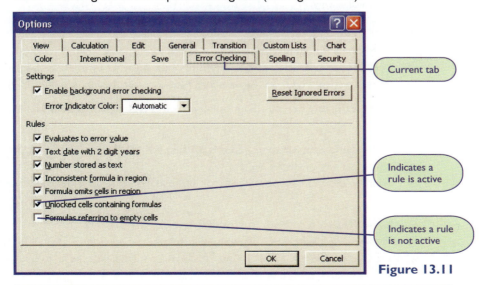

Figure 13.11

Correct Errors Using the Formula Auditing Toolbar

In the previous skill, you explored some of the extensive onscreen Help on errors in formulas. In this skill, you apply what you learned as you evaluate problem areas in a condensed income statement worksheet. You review possible errors one at a time after activating Excel's Formula error checker, and make corrections as needed.

To Use the Error Checking Button on the Formula Auditing Toolbar

1 **Open the *Audit2* workbook, if necessary.**

2 **Display the Formula Auditing toolbar, and click the Error Checking button at the left end of the toolbar.**

Excel makes cell N6 active—the first cell displaying an error indicator—and opens the Error Checking dialog box. (see Figure 13.12).

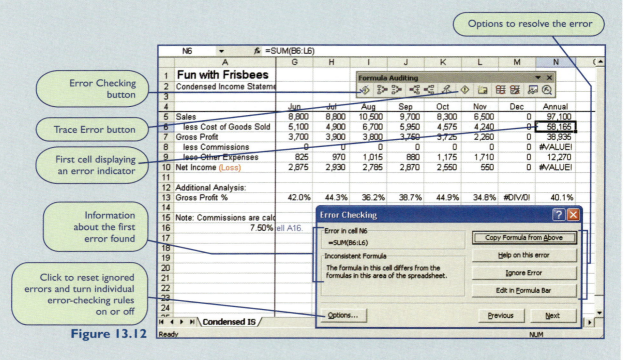

Figure 13.12

The range B6:L6 is not consistent with the range in the cell N5 formula above or below, in the cell N7 formula. The end point in both of the adjacent formulas is column M (for December), not column L (for November). Now correct the formula in cell N6.

3 **Click the Edit in Formula Bar button in the dialog box (refer to Figure 13.12).**

4 **In the formula bar, change =SUM(B6:L6) to =SUM(B6:M6), and press ↵Enter.**

The triangle indicating a possible error disappears from the upper-left corner of cell N6.

5 **Click the Resume button in the dialog box.**

Excel makes cell C8 active—the next cell displaying an error indicator. The message *#VALUE!* displays when Excel cannot evaluate a formula because it contains the wrong type of argument or operand. An **operand** is an item on either side of an operator in a formula.

6   Click cell D8.

The formula =D5*C16 displays in the formula bar, and zero displays in the cell (see Figure 13.13). There is an error in the formula that is not recognized by the error check rules. The same problem exists with the formulas in cells E8 through M8.

	A	C	D	E	F	G	H	I	J	K
1	Fun with Frisbees									
2	Condensed Income Statement									
3										
4		Feb	Mar	Apr	May	Jun	Jul	Aug	Sep	Oc
5	Sales	8,000	9,000	7,000	10,500	8,800	8,800	10,500	9,700	8,3
6	less Cost of Goods Sold	4,600	5,500	4,400	6,200	5,100	4,900	6,700	5,950	4,5
7	Gross Profit	3,400	3,500	2,600	4,300	3,700	3,900	3,800	3,750	3,7
8	less Commissions	#VALUE!	0	0	0	0	0	0	0	
9	less Other Expenses	780	950	1,925	1,050	825	970	1,015	880	1,1
10	Net Income (Loss)	#VALUE!	2,550	675	3,250	2,875	2,930	2,785	2,870	2,5

D8   fx =D5*C16   Formula

Formula Auditing

Formula results

Figure 13.13

7   Click cell C10.

The formula =C7-C8-C9 displays in the formula bar, and *#VALUE!* displays in cell C10. In this case, the formula is correct, but it includes a reference to the problem cell C8. When the problem in cell C8 is resolved, #VALUE! disappears from cells C8, C10, N8, and N10.

8   Close the Error Checking dialog box, and scroll column B into view if necessary.

9   Click cell C8 and click the Trace Error button on the Formula Auditing toolbar.

Two blue tracer arrows display (see Figure 13.14). The arrows indicate that cells B16 and C5 are the precedent cells for the formula in cell C8.

	A	B	C	D	E	F	G	H	I	J
1	Fun with Frisbees									
2	Condensed Income Statements - 2003									
3										
4		Jan	Feb	Mar	Apr	May	Jun	Jul	Aug	Sep
5	Sales	10,000	8,000	9,000	7,000	10,500	8,800	8,800	10,500	9,7
6	less Cost of Goods Sold	6,000	4,600	5,500	4,400	6,200	5,100	4,900	6,700	5,9
7	Gross Profit	4,000	3,400	3,500	2,600	4,300	3,700	3,900	3,800	3,7
8	less Commissions	0	#VALUE!	0	0	0	0	0	0	
9	less Other Expenses	990	780	950	1,925	1,050	825	970	1,015	8
10	Net Income (Loss)	2,260	#VALUE!	2,550	675	3,250	2,875	2,930	2,785	2,8
11										
12	Additional Analysis:									
13	Gross Profit %	40.0%	42.5%	38.9%	37.1%	41.0%	42.0%	44.3%	36.2%	38.
14										
15	Note: Commissions are calculated as a constant percentage of Sales.									
16		7.50%	Enter the current year's commission rate (%) in cell A16.							
17										

C8   fx =C5*B16

Formula Auditing

The formula multiplies a number by text

A number in cell C5

Text in cell B16

Figure 13.14

Excel cannot evaluate the formula because it multiplies a number in cell C5 by text in cell B16. The error occurred because the formula in cell B8 was copied to C8:M8 without making the reference to cell A16 absolute. Now fix the errors in row 8.

10   Change the formula in cell B8 from =B5*A16 to =B5*$A$16.

11   Copy the formula in cell B8 to the range C8:M8.

The blue tracer arrows and the #VALUE! error values disappear.

continues ▶

To Use the Error Checking Button on the Formula Auditing Toolbar (continued)

⑫ Click the Error Checking button on the Formula Auditing toolbar.
Excel makes cell M13 active—the next cell displaying an error indicator (see Figure 13.15).

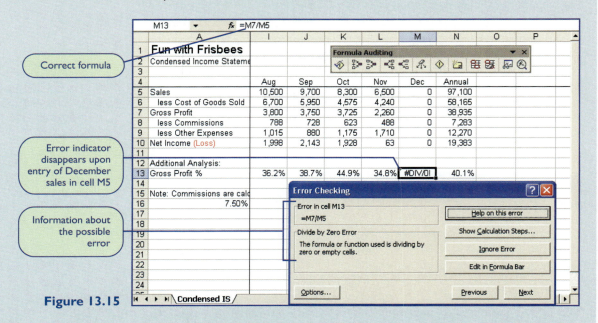

Correct formula

Error indicator disappears upon entry of December sales in cell M5

Information about the possible error

Figure 13.15

The formula =M7/M5 displays in the formula bar, and #DIV/0! displays in the cell. The formula evaluates to zero because the December data is not available yet. The formula itself is correct.

⑬ Click the Ignore Error button in the Error Checking dialog box.
A message displays that the error check is complete for the entire sheet.

⑭ Click OK to close the message box, and close the Formula Auditing toolbar.

⑮ Save your changes and close the *Audit2* workbook.
Continue with the next skill, or exit Excel.

In Depth:
Avoiding the Display of #DIV/0
In this skill, the formula =M7/M5 produced a #DIV/0 message because cell M5 did not contain a value (refer to Figure 13.15). You can change a formula to a conditional statement that gives a blank result if the divisor is zero. For example, entering the formula =IF(M5<>0,M7/M5,"") in cell M13 leaves cell M13 blank unless cell M5 contains a value other than zero.

For immediate reinforcement, work Skill Drill 4 and Challenges 1 through 3.

Skill 6.3: **Identify Dependencies in Formulas**

In Skill 6.1 within this skill set, you traced precedent cells—the cells that are referred to by a formula in the current cell. In this skill, you trace dependent cells—the cells that use the results of the current cell.

In the following steps, you open the Audit1 workbook that you used to trace precedent cells. You display dependencies at multiple levels, and then remove the tracer arrows.

To Trace Dependents

1 **Open the *Audit1* workbook and display the Formula Auditing toolbar.**

2 **Click cell B11 and click the Trace Dependents button on the Formula Auditing toolbar.**

Excel draws two blue tracer arrows pointing to the two dependent cells—C11 and D11—that use the contents of the current cell B11 (see Figure 13.16).

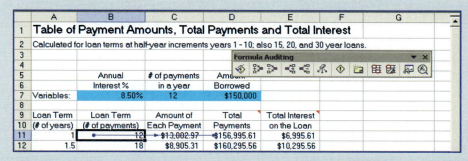

	A	B	C	D	E	F	G
1	Table of Payment Amounts, Total Payments and Total Interest						
2	Calculated for loan terms at half-year increments years 1 - 10; also 15, 20, and 30 year loans.						
3					Formula Auditing		
4							
5		Annual	# of payments	Am			
6		Interest %	in a year	Borrowed			
7	Variables:	8.50%	12	$150,000			
8							
9	Loan Term	Loan Term	Amount of	Total	Total Interest		
10	(# of years)	(# of payments)	Each Payment	Payments	on the Loan		
11	1	12	$13,002.97	$156,995.61	$6,995.61		
12	1.5	18	$8,905.31	$160,295.56	$10,295.56		

Figure 13.16

The PMT function in cell C11 uses the number of payments in cell B11 to calculate the monthly payment. The formula in cell D11 calculates the total payments by multiplying the payment amount by the number of payments in cell B11.

3 **Click the Trace Dependents button again.**

A third tracer arrow points to cell E11, the next level of dependency. The result in cell E11 depends on the values in cells C11 and D11.

4 **Click cell A18 and click the Trace Dependents button.**

A blue tracer arrow points from cell A18 to cell B18 (see Figure 13.17). The total number of loan payments in cell B18 is dependent on the number of years for the loan in cell A18.

9	Loan Term	Loan Term	Amount of	Total	Total Interest		
10	(# of years)	(# of payments)	Each Payment	Payments	on the Loan		
11	1	12	$13,002.97	$156,995.61	$6,995.61		
12	1.5	18	$8,905.31	$160,295.56	$10,295.56		
13	2	24	$6,818.35	$163,640.43	$13,640.43		
14	2.5	30	$5,567.67	$167,030.17	$17,030.17		
15	3	36	$4,735.13	$170,464.70	$20,464.70		
16	3.5	42	$4,141.52	$173,943.94	$23,943.94		
17	4	48	$3,697.25	$177,467.78	$27,467.78		
18	4.5	54	$3,352.52	$181,036.11	$31,036.11		
19	5	60	$3,077.48	$184,648.78	$34,648.78		

Figure 13.17

continues ▶

To Trace Dependents (continued)

⑤ Click the Trace Dependents button two more times.
Excel displays the next level of dependency each time you click the Trace Dependents button.

⑥ Click cell A1 and save your changes to the *Audit1* workbook.
Saving the workbook removes all tracer arrows.

⑦ Close the Formula Auditing toolbar, and close the *Audit1* workbook.
Continue with the skill set exercises, start another skill set, or exit Excel.

For immediate reinforcement, work Skill Drill 2.

Summary

In this skill set, you learned a variety of ways to view formulas and to locate and correct errors. You used the Formula Watch Window to view changes in formula results taking place in a distant part of a worksheet. You displayed tracer arrows, which track precedents and dependents, to show the relationships of other cells to formula cells. After viewing extensive Help screens on correcting errors in formulas, you used Excel's Formula error checker to correct or ignore the cells marked with error indicators.

Skill Drill

Skill Drill exercises *reinforce* skills. Each skill reinforced is the same, or nearly the same, as a skill presented in the skill set. Detailed instructions are provided in a step-by-step format.

Before beginning your Excel Expert Skill Set 6 Skill Drill exercises, complete the following steps:

1. Open the file named *MEE-S603*, and immediately save it as **MEE-S6drill**.

The workbook contains four sheets: an overview and three exercise sheets labeled SD1-2, SD3, and SD4.

2. Click the Overview sheet to view the organization and content of the Skill Drill workbook for Excel Expert Skill Set 6.

Each exercise is independent of the others, so you may complete the exercises in any order. Be sure to save the workbook after completing each exercise. If you need a paper copy of one or more completed exercises, enter your name, centered in a header, before printing. Print options have already been set to print compressed to one page and to display the filename, sheet name, and current date in a footer.

Be sure to save your changes and close the workbook if you need more than one work session to complete the desired exercises. Continue working on *MEE-S6drill* instead of starting over in the original *MEE-S603* file.

1. Trace Precedents

You just received a large worksheet that generates three financial statements based on amounts entered in columns B and C. You want to display tracer arrows that show which cells are used in producing formula results. To display tracer arrows showing the relationship between a formula and its precedent cells, follow these steps:

1. Open the *MEE-S6drill* workbook, if necessary, and select the SD1-2 worksheet.

2. Choose Tools, Formula Auditing, Show Formula Auditing Toolbar.

3. Press F5; click IS in the Go to list, and click OK.

4. Scroll down the highlighted Income Statement; click cell F87, and click the Trace Precedents button on the Formula Auditing toolbar.

   Cells F85 and F86 are the first-level precedent cells that impact the Net Income formula in cell F87.

5. Click the Trace Precedents button again.

   Blue tracer arrows for the next level of precedent cells are added to the display. The new arrows show that cells E84 and F79 are referred to in the *Income before Income Taxes* formula in cell F85, and cell B45 is referred to in the *Income Tax Expense* formula in cell F86.

6. With cell F87 still selected, click the Trace Precedents button two more times.

   Blue tracer arrows for the third and fourth levels of precedent cells are added to the display. Many of the new tracer arrows show that cells in columns B and C are referred to in Income Statement cells.

7. Click the Remove Precedent Arrows button once.

   The fourth-level blue tracer arrows disappear.

8. Click the Remove All Arrows button.

   The remaining blue tracer arrows disappear.

9. Press F5; click BS in the Go to list, and click OK.

10. Scroll down the highlighted Balance Sheet; click cell L111, and click the Trace Precedents button on the Formula Auditing toolbar.

    A blue border surrounds the range K104:K110, and a single blue tracer arrow from within that border points to the Total Current Assets cell L111. The blue border indicates the range referred to in the formula in cell L111.

11. Click the Trace Precedents button again.

12. Continue to display and remove the arrows that show precedent relationships for the formulas of your choice.

13. Save the *MEE-S6drill* workbook.

    Saving the workbook removes all tracer arrows. Closing a workbook without saving your changes also removes all tracer arrows.

2. Trace Dependents

You just received a large worksheet that generates three financial statements based on amounts entered in columns B and C. You want to display tracer arrows that show which cells use the results of a formula. To display tracer arrows that show the relationships between a formula and its dependent cells, follow these steps:

1. Open the *MEE-S6drill* workbook and display the Formula Auditing toolbar, if necessary.

2. Select the SD1-2 worksheet.

3. Press F5; click IS in the Go to list, and click OK.

4. Scroll down the highlighted Income Statement; click cell F87, and click the Trace Dependents button on the Formula Auditing toolbar.

Cell H95 in the Statement of Retained Earnings is the first cell to use the results of the Net Income formula in cell F87.

5. Click the Trace Dependents button again.

Cell H97 is the next cell to use the results of the Net Income formula in cell F87.

6. Click the Trace Dependents button again, and scroll right and down to view the new blue tracer arrow that points to cell K147.

7. Click the Remove All Arrows button.

8. Click cell L111, and click the Trace Dependents button.

The formula in cell L128 uses the results of the formula in cell L111.

9. Continue to display and remove the arrows that show dependent relationships for the formulas of your choice.

10. Save the *MEE-S6drill* workbook.

Saving the workbook removes all tracer arrows. Closing a workbook without saving your changes also removes all tracer arrows.

11. Close the Formula Auditing toolbar.

3. Use the Formula Watch Window

You just received a large worksheet that generates three financial statements based on amounts entered in columns B and C. You need to make some changes to amounts in columns B and C, and you want to monitor the effect of those changes on the financial statements. To watch selected cells containing formulas in Excel's Watch Window, follow these steps:

1. Open the *MEE-S6drill* workbook, if necessary, and select the SD3 worksheet.

2. Create three new range names: `NetIncome` for cell F87, `TotalAssets` for cell L128, and `TotalLiab` for cell L142.

Range names make it easier to know the purpose of cells in a Formula Watch Window. Make sure that you type the range names without spaces.

3. Click cell F87; while holding down Ctrl, click cell L128, and click cell L142; then release Ctrl.

You selected the cells with formulas to calculate Net Income, Total Assets, and Total Liabilities, respectively.

4. Select Tools, Formula Auditing, Show Watch Window.

A blank Watch Window dialog box opens.

5. Click the Add Watch button near the upper-left corner of the Watch Window dialog box.

The three cells you selected in the SD3 worksheet display in the Add Watch dialog box.

6. Click Add.

Data about the selected cells display in the Watch Window.

7. Widen the Name column and narrow the Value column in the Watch Window.

8. Scroll the worksheet to display cell A1 in the upper-left corner, and position the Watch Window between rows 10 and 20 starting in column D.

Next, you change data to reflect a $200 credit sale that was overlooked, and view the effects on the cells under watch.

9. Change Accounts Receivable in cell B13 from 23,100 to **23,300**, and change Sales in cell C35 from 524,900 to **525,100**.

In the Watch Window, Total Assets increase by $200 to 242,700. Net Income increases by $200 to 32,230. Now change data to correct for the omission of a $1,000 short-term loan.

10. Change Cash in cell B10 from 19,400 to **20,400**, and change Notes Payable (short term) in cell C26 from 12,000 to **13,000**.

In the Watch Window, Total Assets increase by $1,000 to 243,700. Total Liabilities increase by $1,000 to 105,420. Net Income stays the same at 32,230.

11. Close the Watch Window and save your changes to the *MEE-S6drill* workbook.

4. Locate and Correct Errors in Formulas

You just received a large worksheet that generates three financial statements based on amounts entered in columns B and C. You know that Excel's Formula error checker can find common errors according to selected rules. To use the Formula error checker, follow these steps:

1. Open the *MEE-S6drill* workbook, if necessary, and select the SD4 worksheet.

2. Display the Formula Auditing toolbar, and click the Error Checking button.

Excel makes cell F62 active—the first cell displaying an error indicator—and opens the Error Checking dialog box. The formula in cell F62 is not consistent with nearby formulas, but it is correct.

3. Click the Ignore Error button.

Excel makes cell H97 active—the next cell displaying an error indicator. The message *#VALUE!* Displays, because one of the cell references in the Ending Retained Earnings formula refers to a cell containing text. Now correct the formula in cell H97.

4. Click the Edit in Formula Bar button in the dialog box.

5. Change *=H94+H95-G96* to **=H94+H95 - H96**, and press ↵Enter).

6. Click the Resume button in the dialog box.

Excel makes cell J121 active. The formula in cell J121 is not consistent with nearby formulas, but it is correct.

7. Click the Ignore Error button.

Excel makes cell J122 active. The formula in cell J122 is not consistent with nearby formulas, but it is correct.

8. Click the Ignore Error button.

A message box indicates that the error check is complete.

9. Click OK to close the message box.

You used one means to verify the accuracy of formulas. But Excel's error-checking feature might not find all errors. Now fix an error that was not found.

10. Click cell L128 and note the 240,520 amount for Total Assets.

11. Click cell L149 and note the 242,500 amount for Total Liabilities & Stockholders' Equity.

The amount for Total Assets should equal the amount for Total Liabilities & Stockholders' Equity. There is no feature in Excel that can tell you whether either amount is correct or the location and nature of the error(s) in this case. The remaining steps show you how to fix the error, but in your own worksheets, you must carefully review every formula.

12. Click the Total Current Assets cell L111, and click the Trace Precedents button on the Formula Auditing toolbar.

The amount for Prepaid Expenses in cell K110 should be included in the calculation of Total Current Assets, but the cell does not fall within the blue border that shows the cells referenced by the formula in cell L111. Now correct the formula.

13. Change =*SUM(K104:K109)* in cell L111 to **=SUM(K104:K110)**.

Total Current Assets in cell L111 increase by 1,980 to 77,500. Total Assets of 242,500 in cell L128 equal Total Liabilities & Stockholders' Equity in cell L149.

14. Close the Formula Auditing toolbar; then click cell A1, and save your changes to the *MEE-S6drill* workbook.

Challenge

Challenge exercises expand on or are somewhat related to skills presented in the skill set. Each exercise provides a brief narrative introduction, followed by instructions in a numbered-step format that are not as detailed as those in the Skill Drill section.

Before beginning your Excel Expert Skill Set 6 Challenge exercises, complete the following steps:

1. Open the file named *MEE-S604*, and immediately save it as **MEE-S6challenge**.

The workbook contains four sheets: an overview and three exercise sheets labeled CH1 through CH3.

2. Click the Overview sheet to view the organization and content of the Challenge workbook for Excel Expert Skill Set 6.

Each exercise is independent of the others, so you may complete the exercises in any order. Be sure to save the workbook after completing each exercise. If you need a paper copy of one or more completed exercises, enter your name, centered in a header, before printing. Print options have already been set to print compressed to one page. Settings to display the filename, sheet name, and current date in a footer have been set in all worksheets.

Be sure to save your changes and close the workbook if you need more than one work session to complete the desired exercises. Continue working on *MEE-S6challenge* instead of starting over in the original *MEE-S604* file.

1. Use the Evaluate Formula Feature

Your assistant has asked you to review a worksheet being developed to calculate overtime pay. You want to step through the complex IF function using Excel's Evaluate Formula feature. To evaluate a formula, follow these steps:

1. Open the *MEE-S6challenge* workbook, if necessary, and select the CH1 worksheet.

2. Click cell D10; display the Formula Auditing toolbar, and click the Evaluate Formula button. The Evaluate Formula dialog box opens.

3. Click the Evaluate button in the dialog box.

Excel converts the first cell reference to the actual number used in the calculation.

4. Continue to click the Evaluate button to review the rest of the formula. Also click Step In and Step Out periodically when those buttons are not dim.

At the end of the review, only the final result *550.00* displays, and a Restart button appears.

5. Close the Evaluate Formula dialog box.

2. Resolve an Error Marked with a Red Tracer Arrow

You are developing a worksheet to calculate weekly pay, including overtime. You entered and tested a formula computing the first employee's pay, and that formula is correct. When you copied that formula to compute pay for other employees, error messages displayed. Now you want to display tracer arrows and resolve the problem(s).

1. Open the *MEE-S6challenge* workbook, if necessary, and select the CH2 worksheet.

2. Click cell D21 and click the Trace Precedents button on the Formula Auditing toolbar.

A red tracer arrow extends from cell D10 to cell D21, but the error(s) is not yet obvious.

3. Click the Trace Precedents again.

Numerous blue tracer arrows display, including ones that start from consecutive cells in column A. The multiple arrows that start from cell A4 spread out to consecutive cells in column D. It appears that an absolute reference to cell A4 was used in a copied formula, thus producing accurate results for that part of the formula. The other arrows in column A that start from blank cells and text cells reflect errors. It appears that a reference to cell A5 in a copied formula is relative when it should be absolute.

4. Remove the tracer arrows, and edit the formula in cell D10 so that the reference to cell A5 is absolute—that is, $A$5 instead of A5.

5. Copy the revised formula in cell D10 to the range D11:D19.

All error values disappear.

6. Close the Formula Auditing toolbar; then click cell A1, and save your changes to the *MEE-S6challenge* workbook.

3. Turn Off an Error-Checking Rule

An error value displays throughout a row in a worksheet that calculates net income at various combinations of unit sales and selling price. The formulas in that row are accurate. You want to turn off the error-checking rule that produces the error values.

To turn off an error-checking rule, follow these steps:

1. Open the *MEE-S6challenge* workbook, if necessary, and select the CH3 worksheet.

Triangles that indicate possible errors display in the upper-left corner of cells in row 13.

2. Click cell B13.

The formula =$B$5 displays in the formula bar and *540,000* displays in cell B13. The formula is correct, and the same formula calculates the other fixed cost amounts in row 13.

3. Choose Tools, Options; then select the Error Checking tab in the Options dialog box.

4. Read each of the error-checking rules, and decide which one produces the error indicators in row 13. (If necessary, review the Help topic, "The rules and what they check for," that you viewed while working through Skill 6.2.)

5. Uncheck the error-checking rule that produces the error indicators in row 13, and click OK.

The triangles that indicate possible errors disappear.

6. Save your changes to the *MEE-S6challenge* workbook.

Summarizing Data

CHAPTER 14

This skill set includes

Use subtotals with lists and ranges

- Sort data
- Subtotal sorted data

Define and apply filters

- Use Custom AutoFilter with OR criteria
- Use Custom AutoFilter with AND criteria

Add group and outline criteria to ranges

Use data validation

- Attach an input message to a cell
- Restrict cell entries to data from a list
- Restrict cell entries to whole numbers within specified limits
- Create a user-specified error alert message
- Copy data restrictions and messages to other cells

Retrieve external data and create queries

- Use Microsoft Query to import data from an Access database
- Create Web queries

Create Extensible Markup Language (XML) Web queries

Skill Set Overview

This skill set includes a variety of topics in three areas: viewing existing data, ensuring the accuracy of data entry, and acquiring data from external sources. First you create subtotals that sum and count similar data. You also extend your knowledge of custom filters and learn to outline worksheet data. After you experience setting rules that validate data entry, you learn more ways to get data from Web sources.

Skill 7.1: **Use Subtotals with Lists and Ranges**

You can automatically create subtotals and a grand total based on any column in a list that contains numbers. First sort the data so that the rows you want to subtotal are grouped together, and then apply a Data, Subtotals command. Figure 14.1 illustrates a subtotal that finds the average price of homes for sale.

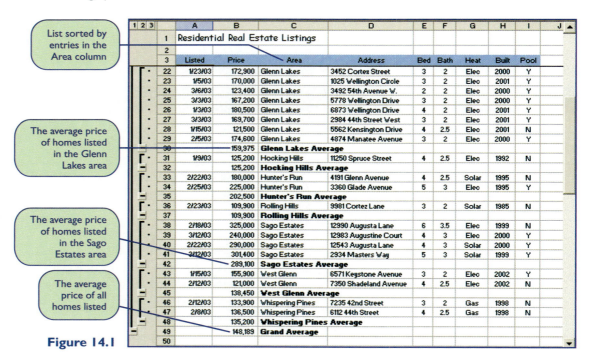

List sorted by entries in the Area column

The average price of homes listed in the Glenn Lakes area

The average price of homes listed in the Sago Estates area

The average price of all homes listed

Figure 14.1

In this skill area, you first learn to sort data. You also create the average subtotals shown in Figure 14.1 as well as subtotals that sum and count.

Sort Data

To *sort* a list means to rearrange the records in the list, based on the contents of one or more fields. Figure 14.1 illustrates sorting a list based on data in the Area column. Other sorts are possible. You might sort records according to price, from lowest to highest. Or you might sort by the date listed—the most recent first.

Executing a sort involves two selections. First, you must specify the column you want Excel to use in sorting, known as the *sort field* (sometimes called a *sort key*). You can also choose the order you want Excel to follow when sorting records: *ascending order* (A to Z, lowest to highest value, earliest to most recent date, and so on) or *descending order* (Z to A, highest to lowest value, most recent to earliest date, and so on).

You can carry out a meaningful sort on two or more fields in a list if there is a relationship or order of importance between the fields. For example, you might organize records first by area and then by price within area. Sorting the records in this way enables you to see the price range of homes in various areas quickly.

In the following steps, you sort the residential real estate records on a single sort field by using the Sort Ascending and Sort Descending buttons on the Standard toolbar. You also sort on the contents of two fields by using Excel's Sort dialog box.

To Sort Records

1 **Open the *MEE-S701* workbook and save it as** Sort.

2 **Click any cell within column B between row 3 (the field name row) and row 38 (the last record in the list).**
Clicking a cell in column B within the top and bottom boundaries of the list tells Excel that you want to sort on the contents of the Price field.

3 **Click the Sort Ascending button in the Standard toolbar.**
Records appear in order of price, from lowest to highest (see Figure 14.2). Because there are no blank columns or rows in the database area A3:I38, Excel automatically treats the area as a list and sorts entire records instead of sorting only the contents in column B.

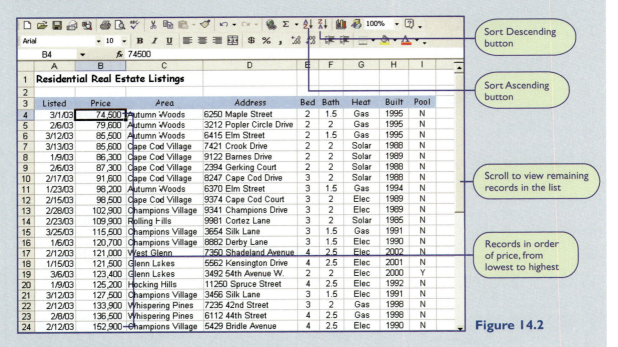

Figure 14.2

4 **Choose Edit, Undo Sort.**
Excel restores the original order of records. The list remains selected (see Figure 14.3).

continues ▶

To Sort Records (continued)

Field name row is not selected

All records in the list are selected

Figure 14.3

5 **Click any cell within column E, between row 3 and row 38.**

Clicking a cell in column E within the top and bottom boundaries of the list tells Excel that you want to sort on the contents of the Bed (number of bedrooms) field.

6 **Click the Sort Descending button in the Standard toolbar.**

Records appear in order according to the number of bedrooms, starting with one six-bedroom listing in *Sago Estates* and followed by two five-bedroom listings—one in *Hunter's Run* and the other in *Sago Estates*.

7 **Choose Data, Sort.**

The Sort dialog box opens, with settings from the most recent sort (see Figure 14.4).

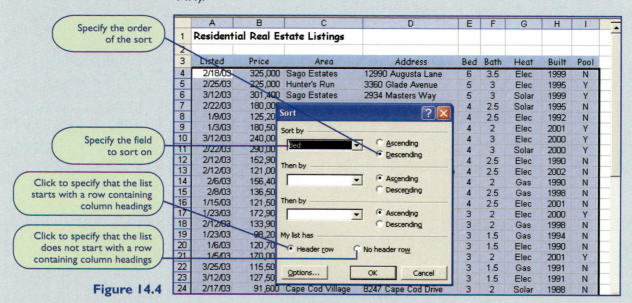

Specify the order of the sort

Specify the field to sort on

Click to specify that the list starts with a row containing column headings

Click to specify that the list does not start with a row containing column headings

Figure 14.4

8 **Click the drop-down arrow at the right end of the *Sort by* text box.**

A scrollable drop-down list appears that includes all field names in the list (see Figure 14.5).

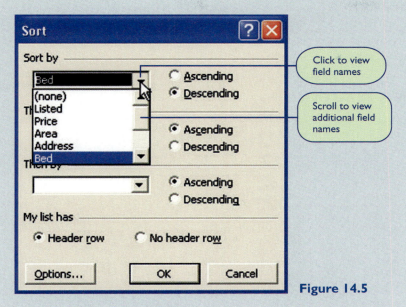

Figure 14.5

⑨ **Click *Area* in the drop-down list, and select *Ascending*.**
You have specified that Excel should initially sort records in ascending order, based on the contents of the Area column.

⑩ **Click the drop-down arrow at the right end of the first *Then by* text box, and select *Price*.**

⑪ **Select *Descending* as the sort order.**
You specified that Excel should execute a second sort after sorting on Area. Within each area, records are sorted in descending order on the contents of the Price field (see Figure 14.6).

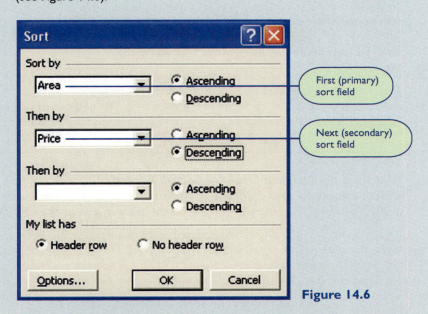

Figure 14.6

continues ▶

To Sort Records (continued)

⑫ **Click OK.**

Excel closes the Sort dialog box and sorts the records (see Figure 14.7). Within each group of homes in the same area, the records are arranged by price in descending order.

Within Autumn Woods, sorted descending on price

Within Cape Cod Village, sorted descending on price

	A	B	C	D	E	F	G	H	I
1	Residential Real Estate Listings								
2									
3	Listed	Price	Area	Address	Bed	Bath	Heat	Built	Pool
4	1/23/03	98,200	Autumn Woods	6370 Elm Street	3	1.5	Gas	1994	N
5	3/12/03	85,500	Autumn Woods	6415 Elm Street	2	1.5	Gas	1995	N
6	2/6/03	79,600	Autumn Woods	3212 Popler Circle Drive	2	2	Gas	1995	N
7	3/1/03	74,500	Autumn Woods	6250 Maple Street	2	1.5	Gas	1995	N
8	2/15/03	98,500	Cape Cod Village	9374 Cape Cod Court	3	2	Elec	1989	N
9	2/17/03	91,600	Cape Cod Village	8247 Cape Cod Drive	3	2	Solar	1988	N
10	2/6/03	87,300	Cape Cod Village	2394 Gerking Court	2	2	Solar	1988	N
11	1/9/03	86,300	Cape Cod Village	9122 Barnes Drive	2	2	Solar	1989	N
12	3/13/03	85,600	Cape Cod Village	7421 Crook Drive	2	2	Solar	1988	N
13	2/6/03	156,400	Champions Village	2398 Sulky Court	4	2	Gas	1990	N
14	2/12/03	152,900	Champions Village	5429 Bridle Avenue	4	2.5	Elec	1990	N
15	3/12/03	127,500	Champions Village	3456 Silk Lane	3	1.5	Elec	1991	N
16	1/6/03	120,700	Champions Village	8882 Derby Lane	3	1.5	Elec	1990	N
17	3/25/03	115,500	Champions Village	3654 Silk Lane	3	1.5	Gas	1991	N
18	2/28/03	102,900	Champions Village	9341 Champions Drive	3	2	Elec	1989	N
19	1/3/03	180,500	Glenn Lakes	6873 Wellington Drive	4	2	Elec	2001	Y
20	2/5/03	174,600	Glenn Lakes	4874 Manatee Avenue	3	2	Elec	2000	Y
21	1/23/03	172,900	Glenn Lakes	3452 Cortex Street	3	2	Elec	2000	Y

Figure 14.7

⑬ **Save your changes, and close the *Sort* workbook.**

Continue to the next skill, or exit Excel.

Alternate Way:

Sorting on Multiple Fields Using Toolbar Buttons

You can also sort on more than one field by using the Sort Ascending and Sort Descending toolbar buttons. If you choose this method, you are not limited to sorting on three fields. However, you must perform successive sorts, starting with a sort on the least important field first, which is the opposite of the order in which you specify sort fields in the Sort dialog box.

For example, to sort records first by area and then by price within area by using sort buttons, you execute two sorts. The first sort arranges records in descending order on the contents of the Price field. The second sort then arranges the records in ascending order on the content of the Area field.

In Depth:

Restoring the Original Order of Sorted Records

Usually, there is no need to restore records to their original order. You can quickly rearrange records in any order you choose and view or print the results.

If you do want the ability to display records in their original order after one or more sorts, design the layout of the list to include an initial column of sequential numbers. For example, specify a column heading of Rec# (for record number), and fill subsequent rows in the column with numbers incrementing by one—1, 2, 3, 4, and so forth. After sorting on one or more other columns, you can then restore the original order through an ascending sort on the Rec# column.

Subtotal Sorted Data

Excel uses a summary function, such as Sum or Average, to generate subtotal and grand total values. Those values recalculate automatically whenever you change the detail data.

Grand total values are based on detail data, not subtotal data. For example, when you use the Average summary function, the grand total value finds the average based on all detail rows instead of averaging the subtotals.

Excel automatically outlines a subtotaled list by grouping detail rows with each related subtotal row and by grouping subtotal rows with the grand total row. You learn to view various levels of detail and create manual outlines in Skill 7.3 within this skill set.

In the following steps, you complete the two-step process to automatically subtotal and total data in a list: sort the list on the subtotal field (column), and apply the <u>D</u>ata, Su<u>b</u>totals command. You create subtotals using the summary functions Average, Sum, and Count.

To Subtotal Data

1 Open the *MEE-S701* workbook and save it as Subtotal.

2 Click any cell in the Area column within the list, such as cell C4.

3 Click the Sort Ascending button on the toolbar.
The list of homes for sale sorts by area in ascending order.

4 Make sure that the current cell is within the range A4:I38 and choose <u>D</u>ata, Su<u>b</u>totals.
The Subtotal dialog box opens (see Figure 14.8).

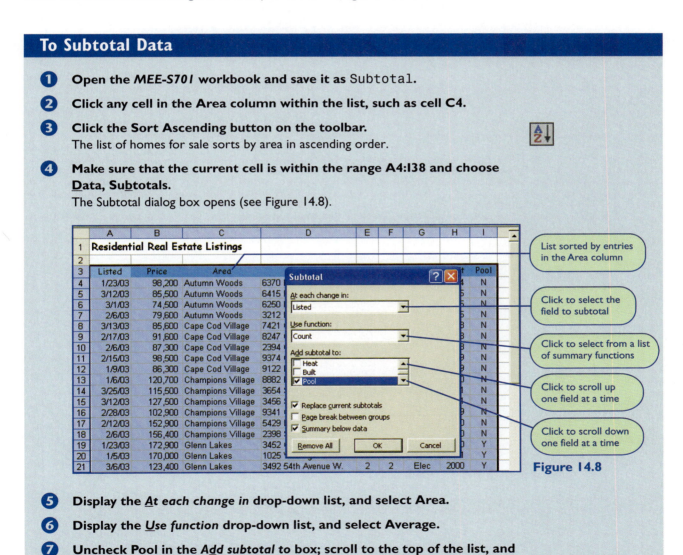

- List sorted by entries in the Area column
- Click to select the field to subtotal
- Click to select from a list of summary functions
- Click to scroll up one field at a time
- Click to scroll down one field at a time

Figure 14.8

5 Display the <u>A</u>t each change in drop-down list, and select Area.

6 Display the <u>U</u>se function drop-down list, and select Average.

7 Uncheck Pool in the A<u>d</u>d subtotal to box; scroll to the top of the list, and check Price.

continues ▶

To Subtotal Data (continued)

8 Make sure that the settings in your Subtotal dialog box, including the check boxes at the bottom, match those shown in Figure 14.9.

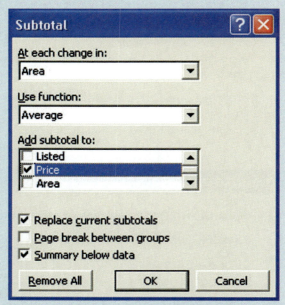

Figure 14.9

9 Click OK.

Average subtotals display after each change in area (see Figure 14.10). Excel automatically outlines subtotaled data and creates outline buttons.

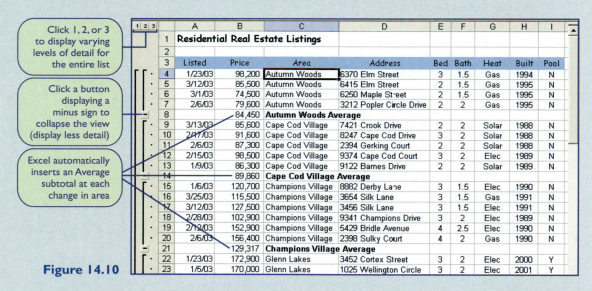

Click 1, 2, or 3 to display varying levels of detail for the entire list

Click a button displaying a minus sign to collapse the view (display less detail)

Excel automatically inserts an Average subtotal at each change in area

Figure 14.10

	Listed	Price	Area	Address	Bed	Bath	Heat	Built	Pool
1	**Residential Real Estate Listings**								
2									
3	Listed	Price	Area	Address	Bed	Bath	Heat	Built	Pool
4	1/23/03	98,200	Autumn Woods	6370 Elm Street	3	1.5	Gas	1994	N
5	3/12/03	85,500	Autumn Woods	6415 Elm Street	2	1.5	Gas	1995	N
6	3/1/03	74,500	Autumn Woods	6250 Maple Street	2	1.5	Gas	1995	N
7	2/6/03	79,600	Autumn Woods	3212 Popler Circle Drive	2	2	Gas	1995	N
8		84,450	**Autumn Woods Average**						
9	3/13/03	85,600	Cape Cod Village	7421 Crook Drive	2	2	Solar	1988	N
10	2/17/03	91,600	Cape Cod Village	8247 Cape Cod Drive	3	2	Solar	1988	N
11	2/6/03	87,300	Cape Cod Village	2394 Gerking Court	2	2	Solar	1988	N
12	2/15/03	98,500	Cape Cod Village	9374 Cape Cod Court	3	2	Elec	1989	N
13	1/9/03	86,300	Cape Cod Village	9122 Barnes Drive	2	2	Solar	1989	N
14		89,860	**Cape Cod Village Average**						
15	1/6/03	120,700	Champions Village	8882 Derby Lane	3	1.5	Elec	1990	N
16	3/25/03	115,500	Champions Village	3654 Silk Lane	3	1.5	Gas	1991	N
17	3/12/03	127,500	Champions Village	3456 Silk Lane	3	1.5	Elec	1991	N
18	2/28/03	102,900	Champions Village	9341 Champions Drive	3	2	Elec	1989	N
19	2/12/03	152,900	Champions Village	5429 Bridle Avenue	4	2.5	Elec	1990	N
20	2/6/03	156,400	Champions Village	2398 Sulky Court	4	2	Gas	1990	N
21		129,317	**Champions Village Average**						
22	1/23/03	172,900	Glenn Lakes	3452 Cortex Street	3	2	Elec	2000	Y
23	1/5/03	170,000	Glenn Lakes	1025 Wellington Circle	3	2	Elec	2001	Y

10 Scroll down to view the remaining subtotals by area and the grand average *148,189* in row 49.

11 Make sure that the current cell is within the range A4:I38, and choose **D**ata, Su**b**totals.

⑫ **Specify settings in the Subtotal dialog box as shown in Figure 14.11.**

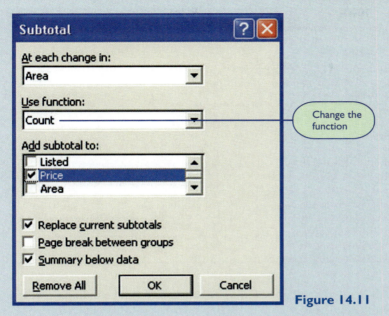

Change the function

Figure 14.11

⑬ **Click OK.**

Excel provides counts of homes for sale in each area (see Figure 14.12).

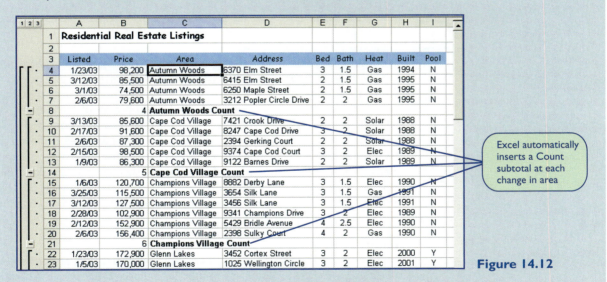

Excel automatically inserts a Count subtotal at each change in area

Figure 14.12

⑭ **Repeat the process described in steps 11 through 13, except specify *Sum* as the function.**

Excel provides the total price of homes for sale in each area (see Figure 14.13), but the results are not meaningful unless you want to buy all of the houses for sale in an area. Make sure that you select a math function that results in meaningful data—such as finding the average cost of the homes for sale in each area or the number of homes for sale in each area.

continues ▶

To Subtotal Data (continued)

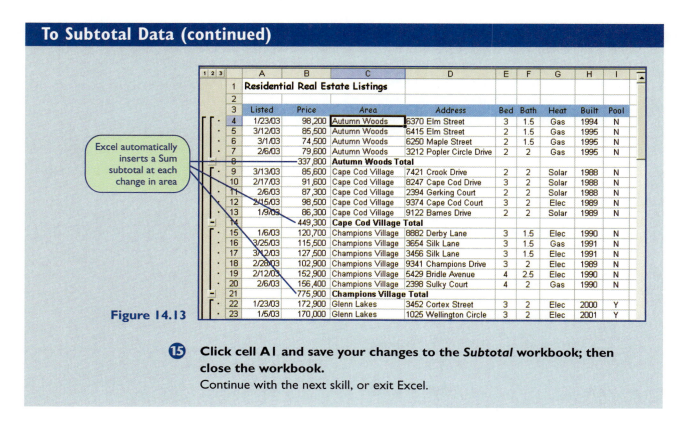

Excel automatically inserts a Sum subtotal at each change in area

Figure 14.13

		A	B	C	D	E	F	G	H	I
	1	Residential Real Estate Listings								
	2									
	3	Listed	Price	Area	Address	Bed	Bath	Heat	Built	Pool
	4	1/23/03	98,200	Autumn Woods	6370 Elm Street	3	1.5	Gas	1994	N
	5	3/12/03	85,500	Autumn Woods	6415 Elm Street	2	1.5	Gas	1995	N
	6	3/1/03	74,500	Autumn Woods	6250 Maple Street	2	1.5	Gas	1995	N
	7	2/6/03	79,600	Autumn Woods	3212 Popler Circle Drive	2	2	Gas	1995	N
	8		337,800	Autumn Woods Total						
	9	3/13/03	85,600	Cape Cod Village	7421 Crook Drive	2	2	Solar	1988	N
	10	2/17/03	91,600	Cape Cod Village	8247 Cape Cod Drive	3	2	Solar	1988	N
	11	2/6/03	87,300	Cape Cod Village	2394 Gerking Court	2	2	Solar	1988	N
	12	2/15/03	98,500	Cape Cod Village	9374 Cape Cod Court	3	2	Elec	1989	N
	13	1/9/03	86,300	Cape Cod Village	9122 Barnes Drive	2	2	Solar	1989	N
	14		449,300	Cape Cod Village Total						
	15	1/6/03	120,700	Champions Village	8882 Derby Lane	3	1.5	Elec	1990	N
	16	3/25/03	115,500	Champions Village	3654 Silk Lane	3	1.5	Gas	1991	N
	17	3/12/03	127,500	Champions Village	3456 Silk Lane	3	1.5	Elec	1991	N
	18	2/28/03	102,900	Champions Village	9341 Champions Drive	3	2	Elec	1989	N
	19	2/12/03	152,900	Champions Village	5429 Bridle Avenue	4	2.5	Elec	1990	N
	20	2/6/03	156,400	Champions Village	2398 Sulky Court	4	2	Gas	1990	N
	21		775,900	Champions Village Total						
	22	1/23/03	172,900	Glenn Lakes	3452 Cortex Street	3	2	Elec	2000	Y
	23	1/5/03	170,000	Glenn Lakes	1025 Wellington Circle	3	2	Elec	2001	Y

15 Click cell A1 and save your changes to the *Subtotal* workbook; then close the workbook.

Continue with the next skill, or exit Excel.

In Depth:

Creating Nested Subtotals

If you want to create subtotals within subtotals—that is, *nested subtotals*— sort the data on two fields before you start the subtotal process. For example, suppose you want to create subtotals of the average price of homes in each area. Within each area, you also want to create subtotals of the average price depending on the number of bedrooms—4-bedroom, 3-bedroom, and so forth. Sort the data on two fields: first on the column containing area data, and then by the column containing number-of-bedrooms data. After completing the sort, execute a subtotal command based on area, and then execute a second subtotal command based on number of bedrooms. Make sure that you clear the Replace current subtotals check box in the Subtotal dialog box before executing the nested subtotal command.

Removing Subtotals

You can remove subtotals by using a two-step process. Select any cell within the subtotaled list; then choose Data, Subtotals, and click the Remove All button.

For immediate reinforcement, work Skill Drill 1 and Challenges 1 and 2.

Skill 7.2: Define and Apply Filters

Users of large databases with hundreds or thousands of records generally do not want to view all of the records. Filtering data enables you to work with a more manageable set of records. When you filter a list, you hide all the rows except those that meet specified criteria. A filter produces a temporary view. Canceling the filter operation redisplays all of the records.

Excel provides two filtering commands: AutoFilter and Advanced Filter. You can use AutoFilter to limit the display based on simple search conditions. Advanced Filter enables you to specify more complex criteria and to copy filtered records to another location.

Skill 1.5 within Core Skill Set 1, "Working with Cells and Cell Data," introduced filters. Your experiences included using AutoFilter to set filters for exact matches. You also worked with the Top 10 and Blanks/NonBlanks options on the AutoFilter menu.

This skill area focuses primarily on using the Custom option on the AutoFilter menu. In addition, selected Challenge exercises explore filters that you can set using Advanced Filter.

Use Custom AutoFilter with OR Criteria

Retrieving the information you need from a database quite often requires filtering records based on multiple criteria. In Core Skill Set 1, for example, you set two filters to display only records of four-bedroom homes for sale in the Glenn Lakes area. Each filter required an exact match to data in one field—Glenn Lakes in the Area field and 4 in the Bed field. Both conditions had to be met for a record to display.

Using the Custom filter option within AutoFilter, you can specify two search conditions based on the contents of one field. If you specify that *either* condition must be met, you are using **OR search criteria**. For example, to display only the records of homes for sale in Glenn Lakes or West Glenn, filter for Area equal to Glenn Lakes *or* Area equal to West Glenn. You tell AutoFilter to examine the Area field of each record and display the record if it contains either Glenn Lakes or West Glenn. You set this filter in the following steps.

To Use Custom AutoFilter with OR Search Criteria

1 **Open the *MEE-S701* workbook and save it as** Custom AutoFilter.
The workbook contains a single worksheet that lists homes for sale.

2 **Click any cell in the list range A3:I38.**

3 **Choose Data, point to Filter, and click AutoFilter.**
Filter arrows display next to each field name.

4 **Click the filter arrow for the Area field in cell C3, and select *(Custom)*.**
The Custom AutoFilter dialog box opens (see Figure 14.14). You use the default comparison option for the first search condition (*equals*) in the current filter operation.

continues ▶

To Use Custom AutoFilter with OR Search Criteria (continued)

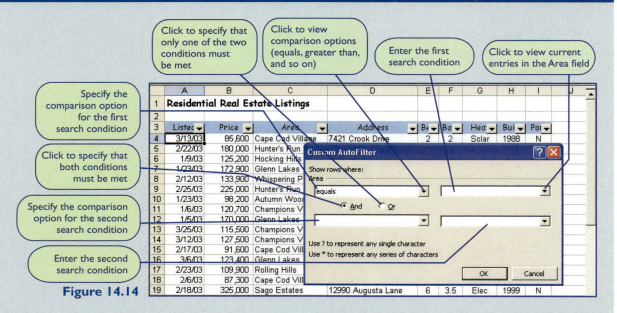

Click to specify that only one of the two conditions must be met

Click to view comparison options (equals, greater than, and so on)

Enter the first search condition

Click to view current entries in the Area field

Specify the comparison option for the first search condition

Click to specify that both conditions must be met

Specify the comparison option for the second search condition

Enter the second search condition

Figure 14.14

5 **In the upper-right section of the dialog box, click the arrow to view current entries in the Area field and select *Glenn Lakes*.**

The search condition *Glenn Lakes* appears in the dialog box (see Figure 14.15).

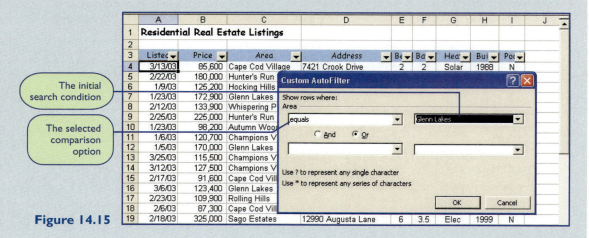

The initial search condition

The selected comparison option

Figure 14.15

6 **Select _Or_ instead of _And_ in the Custom AutoFilter dialog box.**

7 **Click the arrow for viewing comparison options in the middle-left section of the dialog box.**

Ten comparison options display in the drop-down list (see Figure 14.16).

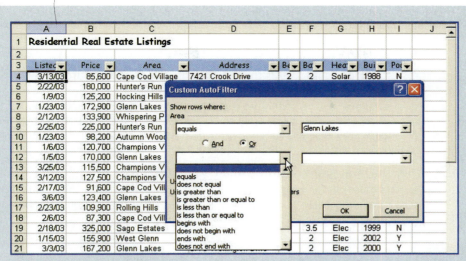

Figure 14.16

8 Select *equals* from the drop-down list.

9 In the middle-right section of the dialog box, click the arrow to view current entries in the Area field; scroll down, and select *West Glenn*.
Specifications are complete for limiting the display of records to those meeting either one of two conditions, both of which apply to the same field.

10 Check that your criteria match those shown in Figure 14.17, and edit the dialog box as necessary.

Figure 14.17

11 Click OK in the Custom AutoFilter dialog box.
The current filter limits the display to homes in either Glenn Lakes or West Glenn (see Figure 14.18).

	A	B	C	D	E	F	G	H	I	J
1	Residential Real Estate Listings									
2										
3	Listed	Price	Area	Address	Be	Ba	Hea	Bui	Po	
7	1/23/03	172,900	Glenn Lakes	3452 Cortex Street	3	2	Elec	2000	Y	
12	1/5/03	170,000	Glenn Lakes	1025 Wellington Circle	3	2	Elec	2001	Y	
16	3/6/03	123,400	Glenn Lakes	3492 54th Avenue W.	2	2	Elec	2000	Y	
20	1/15/03	155,900	West Glenn	6571 Keystone Avenue	3	2	Elec	2002	Y	
21	3/3/03	167,200	Glenn Lakes	5778 Wellington Drive	3	2	Elec	2000	Y	
22	1/3/03	180,500	Glenn Lakes	6873 Wellington Drive	4	2	Elec	2001	Y	
27	3/3/03	169,700	Glenn Lakes	2984 44th Street West	3	2	Elec	2001	Y	
33	2/12/03	121,000	West Glenn	7350 Shadeland Avenue	4	2.5	Elec	2002	N	
36	1/15/03	121,500	Glenn Lakes	5562 Kensington Drive	4	2.5	Elec	2001	N	
37	2/5/03	174,600	Glenn Lakes	4874 Manatee Avenue	3	2	Elec	2000	Y	
39										

Figure 14.18

continues ▶

To Use Custom AutoFilter with OR Search Criteria (continued)

 If you have problems...

It is important to verify that your results are correct. Ensure that all displayed records meet your criteria and that records are not missing that you know are stored in the database. If there is a problem, be sure that you selected the <u>O</u>r logical operator in the Custom AutoFilter dialog box. Also, make sure that you selected the *equals* comparison option for both criteria.

⑫ **Choose <u>D</u>ata, point to <u>F</u>ilter, and click Auto<u>F</u>ilter.**
All records display, and the arrow at the end of each field name disappears; this indicates that AutoFilter is no longer active. Close the *Custom AutoFilter* workbook now, or leave it open and continue to the next skill. It is not necessary to save the workbook because no changes have been made.

 In Depth:

Using Wildcards in Search Criteria
You can use two kinds of wildcards in the Custom AutoFilter dialog box: the asterisk character (*) in place of any sequence of characters and the question-mark character (?) in place of any one character (refer to the lower-left corner of the dialog box in Figure 14.17). For example, a filter for the single search condition **Glenn** in the Area field of the Listings database finds records of homes in Glenn Lakes or West Glenn. The first asterisk indicates that any sequence of characters can precede the word *Glenn*—for example, West Glenn. The second asterisk indicates that any sequence of characters can follow the word Glenn—for example, Glenn Lakes.

Use Custom AutoFilter with AND Criteria

If you specify two search conditions in a filter, and both conditions must be met, you are using *AND search criteria*. When you use Custom AutoFilter to apply AND search criteria to a single field, Excel displays records that fall within a range. For example, to display the records of homes selling only in the $150,000 to $175,000 range, filter for entries in the Price field that are less than or equal to $175,000 *and* greater than or equal to $150,000. To display the records of homes listed only in January 2003, filter for entries in the Listed field that are greater than 12/31/2002 *and* less than 2/1/2003.

In the following steps, you filter using AND search criteria applied to a single field. You set a filter to find homes for sale in the $150,000 to $175,000 range.

To Use Custom AutoFilter with AND Search Criteria

❶ **Open the *Custom AutoFilter* workbook, if necessary, and click any cell within the list range A3:I38.**

❷ **Choose <u>D</u>ata, point to <u>F</u>ilter, and click Auto<u>F</u>ilter.**

❸ **Click the filter arrow for the Price field, and select *(Custom)* from the drop-down list.**

4 **Specify the five settings shown in Figure 14.19. (Select the two comparison options from drop-down lists, click <u>A</u>nd, and type the numbers** 150000 **and** 175000 **.)**

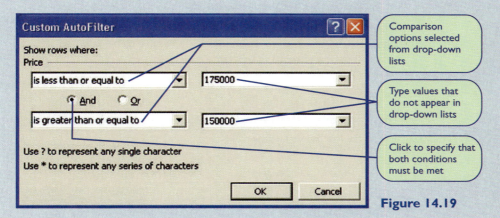

Comparison options selected from drop-down lists

Type values that do not appear in drop-down lists

Click to specify that both conditions must be met

Figure 14.19

5 **Click OK to close the Custom AutoFilter dialog box and execute the filter.**

The current filter limits the display to the eight homes priced between $150,000 and $175,000 (see Figure 14.20).

	A	B	C	D	E	F	G	H	I	J
1	Residential Real Estate Listings									
2										
3	Listec	Price	Area	Address	Be	Ba	Hea	Bui	Po	
7	1/23/03	172,900	Glenn Lakes	3452 Cortex Street	3	2	Elec	2000	Y	
12	1/5/03	170,000	Glenn Lakes	1025 Wellington Circle	3	2	Elec	2001	Y	
20	1/15/03	155,900	West Glenn	6571 Keystone Avenue	3	2	Elec	2002	Y	
21	3/3/03	167,200	Glenn Lakes	5778 Wellington Drive	3	2	Elec	2000	Y	
27	3/3/03	169,700	Glenn Lakes	2984 44th Street West	3	2	Elec	2001	Y	
32	2/12/03	152,900	Champions Village	5429 Bridle Avenue	4	2.5	Elec	1990	N	
34	2/6/03	156,400	Champions Village	2398 Sulky Court	4	2	Gas	1990	N	
37	2/5/03	174,600	Glenn Lakes	4874 Manatee Avenue	3	2	Elec	2000	Y	
39										

Figure 14.20

 If you have problems...

It is important to verify that your results are correct. Check that all displayed records meet your criteria. If there is a problem, be sure you selected the <u>A</u>nd button in the Custom AutoFilter dialog box. Also ensure that you selected the appropriate comparison options and typed the upper and lower values correctly.

6 **Save your changes to the *Custom AutoFilter* workbook, and close the workbook.**

You saved the display of records meeting AND criteria in a filter on one field. When you save and close a workbook that displays filtered records, the filter is still active when you open the workbook again.

In Depth:
Using Advanced Filter

There is a two-condition limit when using AutoFilter's Custom option. You can set three or more conditions for a filter by setting up a separate criteria range and activating Excel's Advanced Filter option.

Figure 14.21 illustrates setting a filter in place for records that meet three conditions, all of which must be met for a record to be selected. These AND criteria must be entered in the same row.

Figure 14.21

Figure 14.22 illustrates setting a filter in place on one field for records that meet any one of three conditions. These OR criteria must be entered in different rows, and the criteria range must be expanded to include the extra rows.

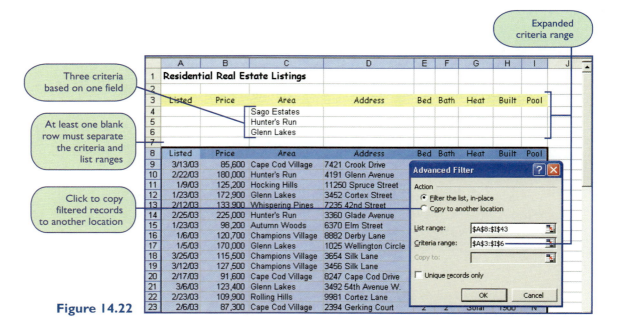

Figure 14.22

If you prefer to copy filtered rows to another location rather than filter in place, you can click the *Copy to another location* option button (refer to Figure 14.21). Refer to the onscreen Help topic *Filter by using advanced criteria* for more information.

For immediate reinforcement, work Skill Drills 2 through 4 and Challenges 3 and 4.

Skill 7.3: **Add Group and Outline Criteria to Ranges**

If you create an outline for your worksheet data, you can show or hide levels of detail. Outlining can be automatic or manual. In Skill 7.1 in this skill set, you learned that Excel automatically outlines a subtotaled list by grouping detail rows with each related subtotal row, and by grouping subtotal rows with the grand total row. In Skill 2.3 in Expert Skill Set 2, "Managing Workbooks," you learned that Excel automatically outlines data created with the Data, Consolidate command. In this skill set, you create your own outlines using the Data, Group and Outline command.

To outline data automatically using the Auto Outline option, the data must meet certain structural requirements. Generally, the data should be in a list format. In a list, each column has a label in the first row, and there are no blank rows or columns within the list. If a worksheet contains blank rows or columns, you can still create an automatic outline if rows or columns of summary functions, such as Average or Sum functions, are adjacent to the detail data. If the Auto Outline command does not produce the results you want, you can manually group and outline the data.

An outline can have up to eight levels of detail. You can display an outlined list at several levels of detail using small buttons labeled 1, 2, 3, and so forth. Clicking the 1 button displays the least amount of data, such as a grand total row. The higher the number on the button, the more detail displays.

You can also collapse or expand outlined data by clicking minus (-) or plus (+) buttons, respectively. At the greatest level of detail, only minus (-) buttons display next to outlined data. At the least level of detail, only plus (+) buttons display next to outlined data.

In the following steps, you automatically outline a worksheet that contains monthly, quarterly, and annual data. You also display various levels of detail, clear the original outline, and create another outline with fewer groupings.

To Insert a Blank Worksheet

1 **Open the *MEE-S702* workbook and save it as** Auto Outline.

The one-sheet workbook contains the Year 2003 Condensed Income Statements for Fun with Frisbees (see Figure 14.23).

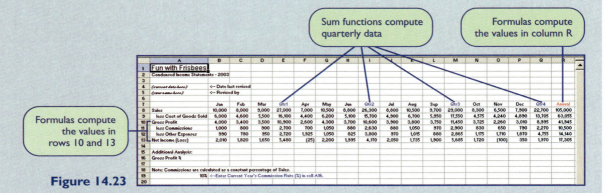

Figure 14.23

2 **Choose Data, Group and Outline, Auto Outline.**

Excel looks at the structure of the data in the worksheet and automatically creates an outline in which the summary rows and columns are the ones that contain formulas or functions (see Figure 14.24).

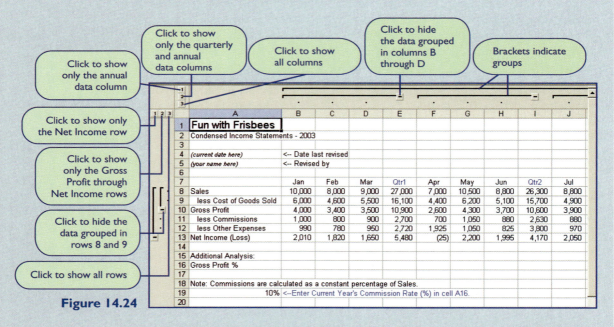

Figure 14.24

3 **Click the minus (-) symbol above column E.**

Excel hides the January, February, and March data in columns B through D—the detail data in the first quarter data group (see Figure 14.25).

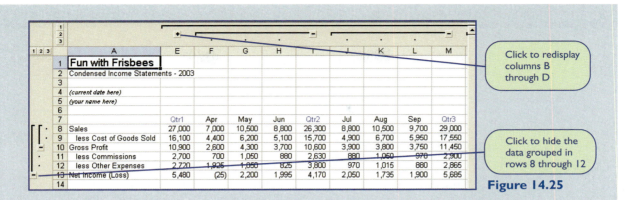

Figure 14.25

4 **Click the minus (-) symbol to the left of row 13 (refer to Figure 14.25).**
Excel hides the detail data in rows 8 through 12 (see Figure 14.26).

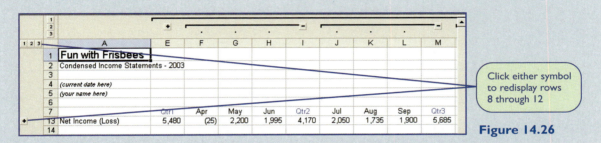

Figure 14.26

5 **Click the plus (+) sign to the left of row 13, and click the small button labeled 2 above the worksheet frame. (Do not click the small button labeled 2 that displays left of the worksheet frame.)**
All the hidden rows redisplay, and Excel hides all the monthly detail columns (see Figure 14.27).

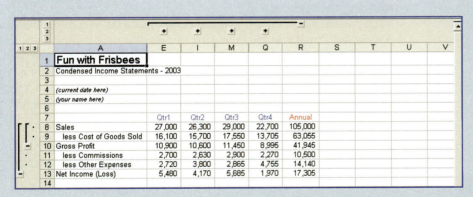

Figure 14.27

6 **Choose Data, Group and Outline, Clear Outline.**
The outlining symbols disappear. Now, outline only columns instead of rows and columns.

7 **Select columns B through R in the worksheet frame.**
You selected a range of columns for inclusion in an automatic outline. This action eliminates row groupings from the outline.

continues ▶

To Insert a Blank Worksheet (continued)

8 Choose **D**ata, **G**roup and Outline, **A**uto Outline; then click cell A1 to deselect the range.

Excel creates an outline with column groupings only (see Figure 14.28).

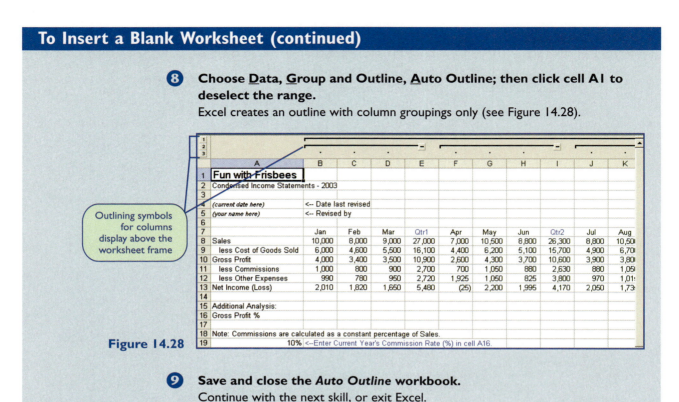

Outlining symbols for columns display above the worksheet frame

Figure 14.28

9 Save and close the *Auto Outline* workbook.

Continue with the next skill, or exit Excel.

In Depth:

Printing Outlined Data

You can expand or collapse outlined data to vary printed output. Rows and columns that are hidden from view in a collapsed outline do not print.

Outlining Data Manually

If Auto Outline does not produce the results you want, you can outline the data manually. Select the first group of rows or columns; then choose **D**ata, **G**roup and Outline, **G**roup. Repeat the process for each additional group of rows or columns that you want to outline. The grouping brackets and outline symbols display beside each group that you create manually. To ungroup data, select the rows or columns in the group, and choose **D**ata, **G**roup and Outline, **U**ngroup.

For immediate reinforcement, work Skill Drill 5 and Challenge 5.

Skill 7.4: **Use Data Validation**

You can introduce errors in a worksheet by entering the wrong data. Excel provides a variety of data validation options to guide data entry and prevent common data entry errors. *Data validation* options enable you to set up data entry instructions, drop-down lists of allowable entries, and error messages.

To apply a validation method to a worksheet, select a cell and then open the Data Validation dialog box containing three tabs (see Figure 14.29). These tabs can be used individually or in combination to set up messages and apply a variety of restrictions to a cell.

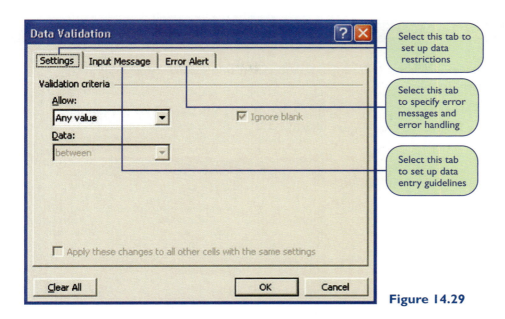

Figure 14.29

In this skill, you use lists and limits to validate data entry, attach input messages to cells, and specify error messages. Other topics include copying, editing, and deleting validation features. To make it easier to focus on individual validation techniques, the data for each technique is set up on a separate worksheet. You begin by setting up a message that displays whenever a cell is selected.

Attach an Input Message to a Cell

An *input message* is a convenient way to display instructions to users when they access a specific cell in a worksheet. The display can have two parts—the heading (optional) and the message itself. Clicking a cell formatted with an input message causes the predefined text to display in a box near the lower-right corner of the cell (or in the Office Assistant balloon, if that Help feature is active).

In the following steps, you are developing a worksheet to hold survey data provided by customers who recently rented vehicles from Indy 500 Motor Works. Staff members enter the data from the surveys, and you want to give them as much guidance as possible. You decide to include data validation features in the worksheet design.

You begin by providing instructions to enter one of two Type Use codes—*Per* and *Bus*. These codes denote that a rental was for *Personal* or *Business* use.

To Attach an Input Message to a Cell

1 **Open the *MEE-S703* workbook and save it as** `Validation`.
The workbook contains five worksheets: Message, List, Limits, Error Alert, and Copy.

2 **Select the Message worksheet and click cell B18.**
Cell B18 is the first cell in the Type Use column of the data area in the Message worksheet.

3 **Select <u>D</u>ata, Va<u>l</u>idation.**
The Data Validation dialog box opens (refer to Figure 14.29).

continues ▶

To Attach an Input Message to a Cell (continued)

④ **Select the Input Message tab, and type** `Codes for Type Use` **in the** **<u>T</u>itle text box.**

⑤ **Type** `Enter Per (personal) or Bus (business)` **in the <u>I</u>nput message area (see Figure 14.30).**

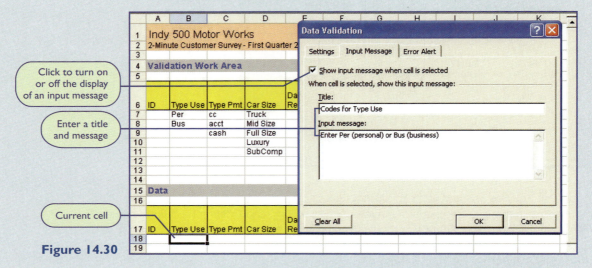

Click to turn on or off the display of an input message

Enter a title and message

Current cell

Figure 14.30

⑥ **Make sure that the <u>*Show input message when cell is selected*</u> check box is selected, and click OK.**

The specified message displays near the lower-right corner of cell B18 if the Office Assistant is not active (see Figure 14.31). The message displays in the Office Assistant's balloon if that feature is active.

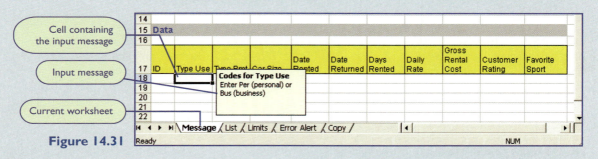

Cell containing the input message

Input message

Current worksheet

Figure 14.31

⑦ **Save your changes to the *Validation* workbook.**

Keep the *Validation* workbook open for the next skill, or close the workbook and exit Excel.

In Depth:
Positioning an Input Message

If the Office Assistant is active, an input message displays in its balloon rather than as a box near the cell. If desired, you can drag the Assistant closer to the cells where you are entering data.

Restrict Cell Entries to Data from a List

Options on the Settings page of the Data Validation dialog box enable you to restrict the type of data that you can enter in a cell. Choices range from allowing any value to allowing only whole numbers, decimals, dates, times, values between two numbers, or values in a list.

The last option—values in a list—is the focus of this skill. Selecting from a list instead of typing is likely to improve both the speed and the accuracy of data entry. You decide to use this feature to set up a list of car sizes. Figure 14.32 shows the options for restricting data entry to values in a list.

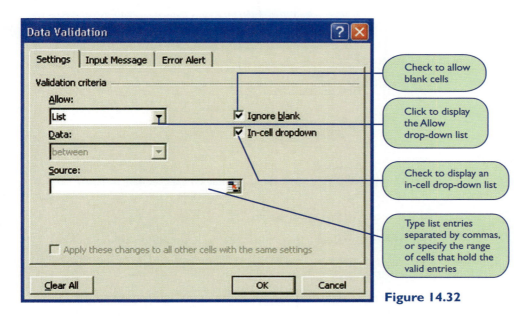

Figure 14.32

You can create a list directly in the Source text box by typing allowable entries separated by commas. You might find it easier to type the allowable entries in another area of the worksheet and then refer to that range in the Source text box.

In this lesson, you apply a validation list to the first cell in the Car Size field. Users of the worksheet can then select among Truck, Mid Size, Full Size, Luxury, and SubComp instead of typing each entry. Those allowable entries are already set up for you in a separate area of the worksheet.

To Restrict Cell Entries to Data from a List

1 **Open the *Validation* workbook, if necessary; then select the List worksheet and click cell D18.**
You selected the first cell below Car Size in the Data area of the List worksheet.

2 **Choose *Data, Validation, and select the Settings tab.***

3 **Display the *Allow* drop-down list (see Figure 14.33).**   *continues* ▶

To Restrict Cell Entries to Data from a List (continued)

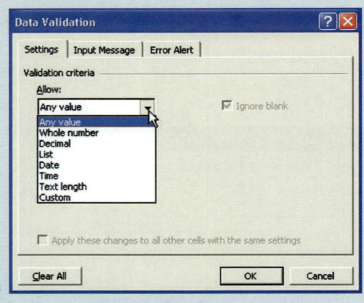

Figure 14.33

4 **Select** *List* **from the** A**llow drop-down list.**

5 **Click within the Source text box; then use the mouse to select the range D7:D11.**
Notice that the entry starts with an equal (=) sign.

6 **Check that your specifications match those shown in Figure 14.34, including the check mark in the** I**n-cell drop-down check box and the dollar signs that make the reference to range D7:D11 absolute.**

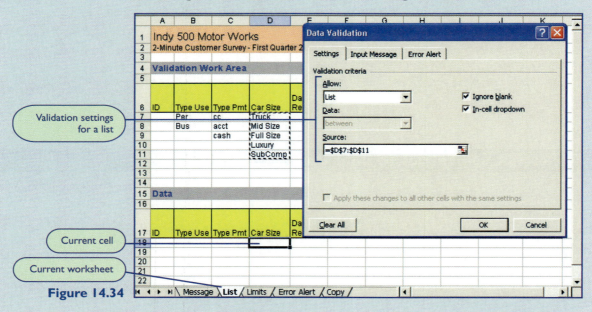

Figure 14.34

7 **Click OK.**
Excel applies the specified validation to cell D18.

8 Display the drop-down list in cell **D18** (that is, click the small arrowhead at the right end of cell **D18**).

9 Select *Luxury* from the drop-down list.
The word *Luxury* displays in cell D18.

10 Save your changes to the *Validation* workbook.
Keep the *Validation* workbook open for the next skill, or close the workbook and exit Excel.

Restrict Cell Entries to Whole Numbers Within Specified Limits

Controlling data entry through a drop-down list is suitable for selecting among relatively few exact-match entries. Some data, such as whole numbers, decimals, dates, and times, normally would not be validated using a list. For example, to allow any date in the year 2003 using a drop-down list, you would have to set up 365 dates. Selecting from such a list would take longer than typing the date.

As an alternative, you can specify that data must fit specified criteria, and that any attempt to enter invalid data produce an **error alert message** in one of three styles—Stop, Warning, or Information. For example, you can require that data be above or below a stated value, within a range of values, or outside a range of values. While this form of validation is not as accurate as restricting entries to a list, it still prevents some errors.

As you continue working with Indy 500 Motor Works survey data, you decide to set up a validation that limits data entry for customer rating to a whole number between 1 and 5. Further, you decide to skip using an input message because you know that validation automatically generates an error message if an invalid entry is attempted.

To Restrict Cell Entries to Whole Numbers Within Specified Limits

1 Open the *Validation* workbook, if necessary; then select the Limits worksheet and click cell J18.

2 Choose **D**ata, Va**l**idation.

3 Select the Settings tab in the Data Validation dialog box, and select *Whole number* from the **A**llow drop-down list.
The phrase *Whole number* displays in the **A**llow text box, and the word *between* displays in the **D**ata text box.

4 Type 1 in the **M**inimum text box and 5 in the Ma**x**imum text box.

5 Check that your specifications match those in Figure 14.35, and make changes as necessary.

continues ▶

To Restrict Cell Entries to Whole Numbers Within Specified Limits (continued)

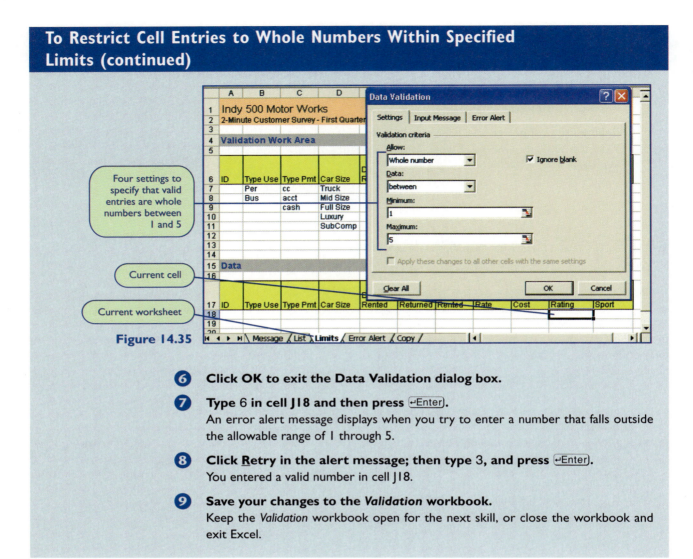

Figure 14.35

6 Click **OK** to exit the Data Validation dialog box.

7 Type 6 in cell J18 and then press ⏎Enter.
An error alert message displays when you try to enter a number that falls outside the allowable range of 1 through 5.

8 Click Retry in the alert message; then type 3, and press ⏎Enter.
You entered a valid number in cell J18.

9 Save your changes to the *Validation* workbook.
Keep the *Validation* workbook open for the next skill, or close the workbook and exit Excel.

Create a User-Specified Error Alert Message

When validation settings are active, Excel displays an error alert message when you try to enter invalid data in a cell. The message is a general one that does not explain how to correct the problem. You can specify an error alert message that replaces the one generated by Excel.

You can choose from three different levels of error alerts: Information, Warning, and Stop. Each style of error message offers different levels of protection. Information messages enable you to accept the invalid data or cancel the entry. Warnings enable you to accept the invalid data, change your data, or cancel the entry. Stop messages prevent the entry of invalid data.

Figure 14.36 illustrates the Error Alert page of the Data Validation dialog box. Creating a message involves a three-step process. Select the style of error alert you want to use; then compose your message, and check the option to display your message.

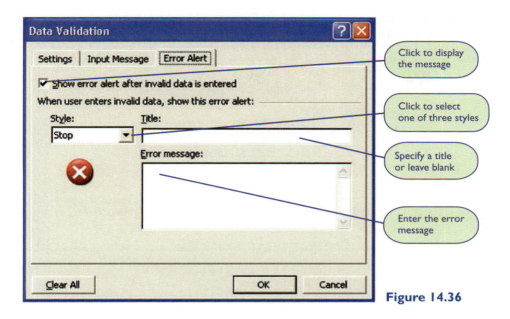

Figure 14.36

In the following steps, you use validation techniques to ensure the entry of the correct customer rating code. You already applied the validation technique to cell J18; however, the Excel-generated error message does not give the user enough information about what the correct data should be. You decide to use the Stop style and display your own message.

To Create a User-Specified Error Alert Message

1 **Open the** *Validation* **workbook, if necessary; then select the Error Alert worksheet and click cell J18.**

2 **Choose Data, Validation.**

3 **Select the Error Alert tab.**
Stop displays in the Style text box. The Title and Error message text boxes are blank.

4 **Type** Customer rating **in the Title text box.**

5 **Type** Please enter a value between 1 and 5 **in the Error message text box.**

6 **Click OK to exit the Data Validation dialog box; type 6 in cell J18, and press ⏎Enter.**
Excel displays the error message you specified (see Figure 14.37). The error message is more helpful this time.

continues ▶

To Create a User-Specified Error Alert Message (continued)

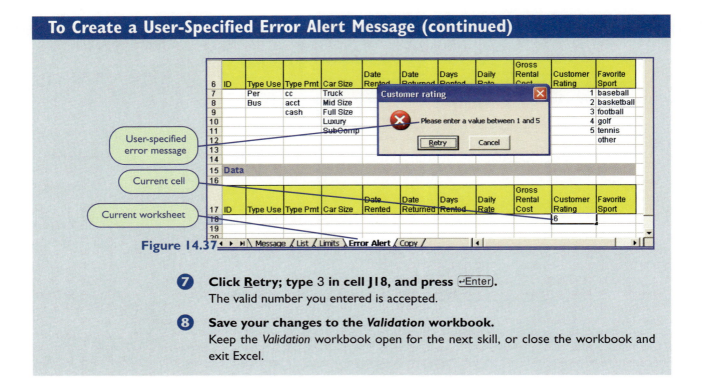

Figure 14.37

7 **Click Retry; type 3 in cell J18, and press ⏎Enter.**
The valid number you entered is accepted.

8 **Save your changes to the *Validation* workbook.**
Keep the *Validation* workbook open for the next skill, or close the workbook and exit Excel.

Copy Data Restrictions and Messages to Other Cells

You can apply validation settings and messages to a single cell or an entire range of cells. If you are designing a worksheet and have not yet entered data, you can apply one or more validation settings to the first blank cell of a range and then copy the specifications to the rest of the range. To do this, copy the cell containing the validation restrictions using Copy and Paste commands or by dragging the fill handle.

You can also apply validation specifications to existing data by using Paste Special instead of Paste. Paste Special enables you to select from a variety of paste options, one of which is Validation.

The Favorite Sport column in the survey results for Indy 500 Motor Works already contains data and a drop-down list validation setting applied to the first data cell in that column. Now you want to copy the validation setting to other cells in the column and check the accuracy of records already entered.

To Copy Data Restrictions and Messages to Other Cells

1 **Open the *Validation* workbook, if necessary; then select the Copy worksheet and click cell K18.**
A small arrow indicating a drop-down list displays at the right end of the cell.

2 **Click several other cells in column K below cell K18.**
A drop-down list has not been applied to remaining cells in the column.

3 **Click cell K18 and click the Copy button in the toolbar.**

④ **Select the range K19:K47.**

⑤ **Right-click within the highlighted range K19:K47, and select Paste Special.**

The Paste Special dialog box opens.

 If you have problems...

If *golf* displays in all cells, you selected Paste instead of Paste Special. Choose Edit, Undo Paste to reverse the paste results and start again with Step 5.

⑥ **Select Validation (see Figure 14.38).**

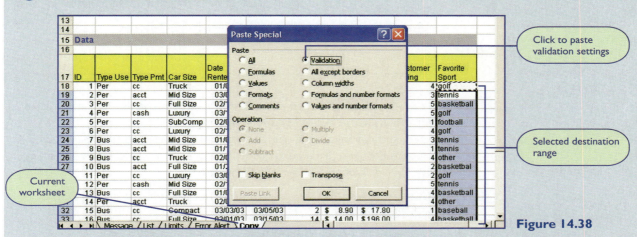

Figure 14.38

⑦ **Click OK and press Esc.**

You pasted the validation drop-down list for Favorite Sport to all remaining cells in the column that contain data. Pressing Esc removes the marquee from cell K18.

⑧ **Click cell K19 and display its drop-down list.**

Options on the pasted drop-down list include *basketball* and *golf* (see Figure 14.39).

	ID	Type Use	Type Pmt	Car Size	Date Rented	Date Returned	Days Rented	Daily Rate	Gross Rental Cost	Customer Rating	Favorite Sport
18	1	Per	cc	Truck	01/01/03	01/05/03	4	$ 19.00	$ 76.00	4	golf
19	2	Per	acct	Mid Size	03/04/03	03/16/03	12	$ 11.50	$138.00	3	tennis
20	3	Per	cc	Full Size	02/16/03	02/25/03	9	$ 14.00	$126.00	5	baseball
21	4	Per	cash	Luxury	03/12/03	03/15/03	3	$ 26.00	$ 78.00	5	basketball
22	5	Per	cc	SubComp	02/06/03	02/09/03	3	$ 7.50	$ 22.50	1	football
23	6	Per	cc	Luxury	02/19/03	02/22/03	3	$ 26.00	$ 78.00	4	golf
24	7	Bus	acct	Mid Size	01/01/03	01/05/03	4	$ 11.50	$ 46.00	3	tennis
25	8	Bus	acct	Mid Size	01/12/03	01/13/03	1	$ 11.50	$ 11.50	1	other

Drop-down list pasted to cell K19

Figure 14.39

⑨ **Choose Tools, Formula Auditing, Show Formula Auditing Toolbar.**

⑩ **Click the Circle Invalid Data button in the Formula Auditing toolbar, and scroll to view records in rows 18 through 47.**

All invalid data according to validation settings display circled in red (see Figure 14.40). Data already entered in column K include two errors in spelling—*basketbal* in cell K27 and *gulf* in cell K35.

continues ▶

To Copy Data Restrictions and Messages to Other Cells (continued)

	ID	Type Use	Type Pmt	Car Size	Date Rented	Date Returned	Days Rented	Daily Rate	Gross Rental Cost	Customer Rating	Favorite Sport
18	1	Per	cc	Truck	01/01/03	01/05/03	4	$ 19.00	$ 76.00	4	golf
19	2	Per	acct	Mid Size	03/04/03	03/16/03	12	$ 11.50	$138.00	3	tennis
20	3	Per	cc	Full Size	02/16/03	02/25/03	9	$ 14.00	$126.00	5	basketball
21	4	Per	cash	Luxury	03/12/03	03/15/03	3	$ 26.00	$ 78.00	5	golf
22	5	Per	cc	SubComp	02/06/03	02/09/03	3	$ 7.50	$ 22.50	1	football
23	6	Per	cc	Luxury	02/19/03	02/22/03	3	$ 26.00	$ 78.00	4	golf
24	7	Bus	acct	Mid Size	01/01/03	01/05/03	4	$ 11.50	$ 46.00	3	tennis
25	8	Bus	acct	Mid Size	01/12/03	01/13/03	1	$ 11.50	$ 11.50	1	tennis
26	9	Bus	cc	Truck	02/01/03	02/07/03	6	$ 19.00	$114.00	4	other
27	10	Bus	acct	Full Size	01/23/03	01/27/03	4	$ 14.00	$ 56.00	2	basketbal
28	11	Per	cc	Luxury	03/02/03	03/09/03	7	$ 26.00	$182.00	2	golf
29	12	Per	cash	Mid Size	02/13/03	02/14/03	1	$ 11.50	$ 11.50	5	tennis
30	13	Bus	cc	Full Size	01/09/03	01/12/03	3	$ 14.00	$ 42.00	4	basketball
31	14	Per	acct	Truck	02/06/03	02/21/03	15	$ 19.00	$285.00	4	other
32	15	Bus	cc	Compact	03/03/03	03/05/03	2	$ 8.90	$ 17.80	1	baseball
33	16	Bus	cc	Full Size	03/01/03	03/15/03	14	$ 14.00	$196.00	4	basketball
34	17	Bus	cc	Truck	02/25/03	02/27/03	2	$ 19.00	$ 38.00	5	other
35	18	Per	acct	Luxury	01/15/03	01/30/03	15	$ 26.00	$390.00	1	gulf
36	19	Bus	acct	Compact	03/14/03	03/16/03	2	$ 8.90	$ 17.80	4	baseball

Circle Invalid Data button

Spelling errors

Figure 14.40

⓫ **Display the drop-down list in cell K27, and select** *basketball*; **then display the drop-down list in cell K35, and select** *golf*.

You corrected the errors in the worksheet. Note, however, that the red circles did not disappear after you made corrections from drop-down lists. You must reapply the Circle Invalid Data option to recheck for errors.

⓬ **Click the Circle Invalid Data button on the Formula Auditing toolbar.**

There should be no cells circled in red.

⓭ **Close the Formula Auditing toolbar; then save and close the** *Validation* **workbook.**

Continue with the next skill, or exit Excel.

In Depth:
Finding Cells That Have Validation Settings

You may not know whether the worksheet you are using contains data validation restrictions and messages. This is especially true if you are using a worksheet that someone else has designed. You can use the Go To Special dialog box to highlight cells that contain validation restrictions and messages.

Choose Edit, Go To; then click the Special button, and click the Data validation option in the lower-right corner of the Go To Special dialog box. Select one of two data validation options: All, to highlight all cells containing data validation restrictions; or Same, to highlight cells with data validation specifications that match those in the current cell. Click OK.

For immediate reinforcement, work Skill Drills 6 and 7, and Challenges 6, and 7.

Skill 7.5: **Retrieve External Data and Create Queries**

You can easily copy and link data between Excel workbooks and other Microsoft Office XP applications. For other information needs, you may need to rely on external data sources. *External data* is data stored outside the current application software. If the external data you want to use is not stored on your local computer system, you may need to pay a fee, acquire a password, have permissions set, and so forth to access the data.

A *query* is a tool for extracting and displaying data that meets the condition(s) you specify. In Excel, you can create queries to import data from external sources.

In Expert Skill Set I (Chapter 8), "Importing and Exporting Data," you selected the Import Data option after choosing Data, Import External Data. You used the command to import data from a text file and to import data from all fields for all records in an Access database. In this skill, you work with two other options for importing external data: New Database Query and New Web Query. You begin by importing selected data from an Access database.

Use Microsoft Query to Import Data from an Access Database

Selecting the New Database Query command activates *Microsoft Query*, an optional feature accessible from within Excel that enables you to perform specialized query tasks. In the following steps, you use this feature to restrict the data to selected records in an Access database before you import it to an Excel worksheet.

To Import Selected Records from an Access Database

① **Open the Excel *MEE-S704* workbook and save it as** Access Query**.**

② **Choose Data, Import External Data, New Database Query. If a message displays that Microsoft Query is not installed, click Yes to begin the installation.**
The *Choose Data Source* dialog box opens (see Figure 14.41). If the Office Assistant asks whether you want help, click *No, don't provide help now.*

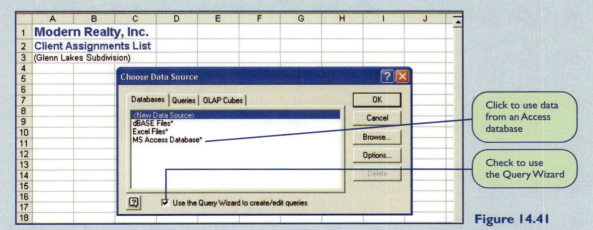

Figure 14.41

 If you have problems...
If Microsoft Query is not available on your system, close any open dialog boxes and close the workbook. You can read the steps and view the figures before continuing with the next skill area.

③ **On the Databases page, select MS Access Database; then make sure a check mark displays in the Use the Query Wizard to create/edit queries check box, and click OK.**

continues ▶

To Import Selected Records from an Access Database (continued)

The Select Database dialog box opens. Use this dialog box to select the Access file that contains the data you want to import into Excel (see Figure 14.42).

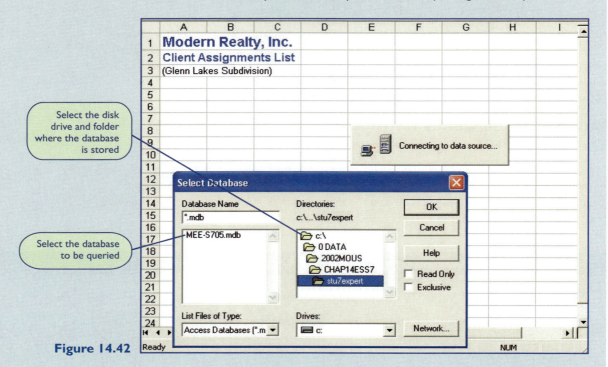

Figure 14.42

4   **Select the folder containing the student data files; then select the Access database named *MEE-S705*, and click OK.**

The Query Wizard—Choose Columns dialog box opens (see Figure 14.43). A single table named Client Assignments appears in the *Available tables and columns* list.

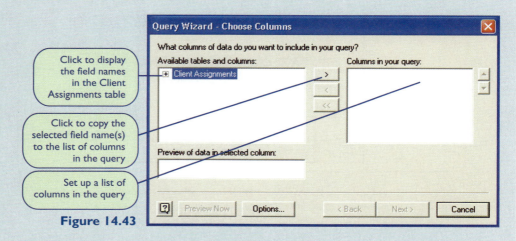

Figure 14.43

5   **Click the + indicator next to the Client Assignments table name in the *Available tables and columns* list box.**

6 Select the Client Assignments table name, and then click the > button.
When you highlight a table name and click the > button, all fields in the table are transferred to the *Columns in your query* list box (see Figure 14.44). To specify fewer fields, select individual field names instead of selecting the table name. The order in which you select the fields is the order in which they appear in your worksheet.

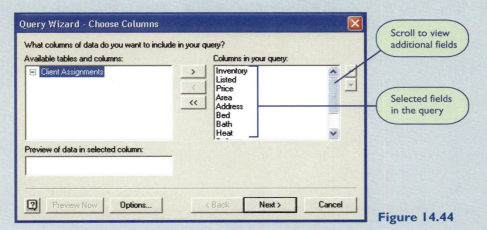

Figure 14.44

7 Click Next.
The Query Wizard—Filter Data dialog box opens.

8 Select Area in the *Column to filter* list box.

9 Select *equals* from the drop-down list in the first of two active text boxes in the *Only include rows where* section for Area (see Figure 14.45).

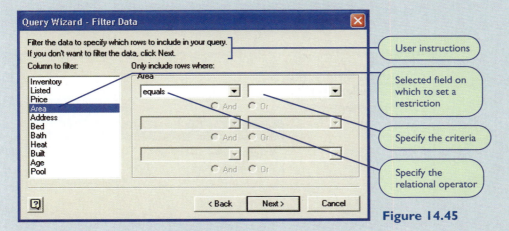

Figure 14.45

10 Click the drop-down list in the blank text box to the right of the one in which you specified a relational operator, and select *Glenn Lakes*.
You set a filter to select only those records from the Access database in which the entry in the Area field equals Glenn Lakes.

11 Click Next.
The Query Wizard—Sort Order dialog box opens.

continues ▶

To Import Selected Records from an Access Database (continued)

⑫ **Click the Sort by drop-down list; then select Inventory, and click Ascending.**

Check that your settings match those shown in Figure 14.46.

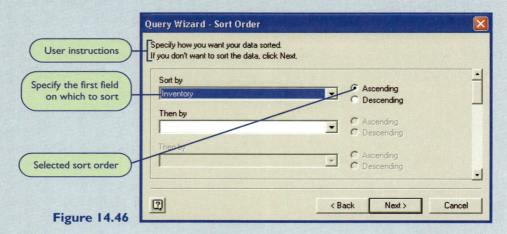

Figure 14.46

⑬ **Click Next.**

The Query Wizard—Finish dialog box opens.

⑭ **Select *Return Data to Microsoft Excel*, and then click Finish.**

The Import Data dialog box opens, asking where you want to put the data.

⑮ **Select *Existing worksheet*, if necessary; then click cell A5 in the worksheet.**

Check that the settings in your Import Data dialog box match those shown in Figure 14.47.

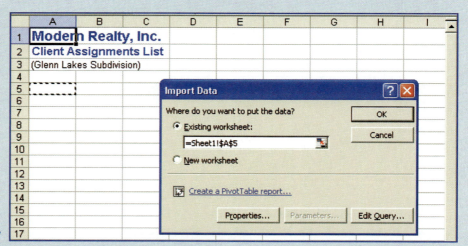

Figure 14.47

⑯ **Click OK.**

This completes your Import External Data operation. Excel copies the records shown in Figure 14.48 from the Access database and places them in Excel's list format beginning in cell A5.

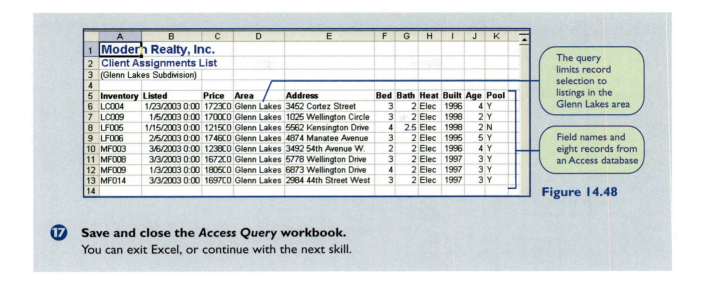

Figure 14.48

The query limits record selection to listings in the Glenn Lakes area

Field names and eight records from an Access database

⑰ Save and close the *Access Query* workbook.
You can exit Excel, or continue with the next skill.

Create Web Queries

You can create Web queries that enable you to retrieve tables of data or entire Web pages into Excel for analysis. A ***Web query*** retrieves data stored on the Internet or your company's intranet or extranet. Keep in mind that it is your responsibility to comply with any conditions for the use of the data as determined by the creator of the site from which you retrieve data.

In the following steps, you focus on getting external data from the Web. You use a pre-defined query to import MSN MoneyCentral Investors data on world currency rates into an Excel worksheet. The data can be refreshed on demand or at predetermined intervals. When you refresh data, all calculations using that data are updated.

You also create a new Web query that accesses the Microsoft Corporation Web site and imports data from an annual report to stockholders.

You must have an Internet connection to perform the steps in this skill. If you are in an academic or business environment, or have an "always on" connection, such as cable or DSL, you may already be connected. Figures reflect using Microsoft's Internet Explorer browser software.

To Create Web Queries

1 **Connect to the Internet and display the first worksheet in a new workbook.**

2 **Choose Data, Import External Data, Import Data.**
The Select Data Source dialog box opens (see Figure 14.49).

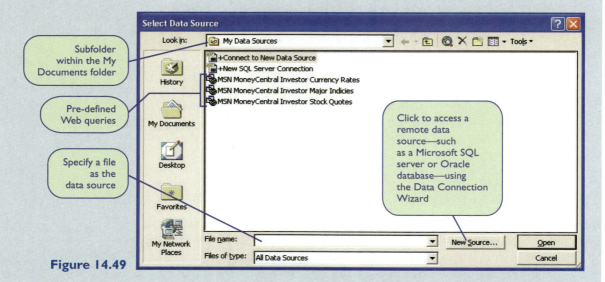

Subfolder within the My Documents folder

Pre-defined Web queries

Specify a file as the data source

Click to access a remote data source—such as a Microsoft SQL server or Oracle database—using the Data Connection Wizard

Figure 14.49

3 **Select MSN MoneyCentral Investor Currency Rates, and click Open.**
The Import Data dialog box opens.

4 **Click Existing worksheet; select cell A4 as the location, and click OK.**
After a brief delay, Excel imports the most recent data on world currency rates in a layout similar to that shown in Figure 14.50. These rates change frequently, and the values in your worksheet are likely to vary from those in the sample figure.

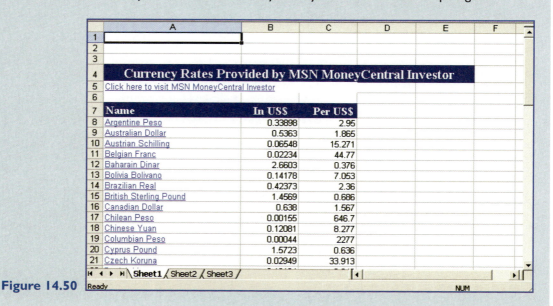

Figure 14.50

⑤ **Enter your name in cell A1, and today's date in cell A2.**

⑥ **Rename the worksheet** World Rates, **and save the workbook as** Web Queries.

Now use an import external data command that enables you to specify the Web site of your choice.

⑦ **Display the second worksheet in the *Web Queries* workbook, and rename it** MS Data.

⑧ **Choose Data, Import External Data, New Web Query.**

The New Web Query window opens.

⑨ **Enter** http://www.microsoft.com **in the Address text box, and click Go.**

The homepage for Microsoft Corporation displays (see Figure 14.51). The current look and content is likely to vary from that shown in the figure as Microsoft updates its Web site. On a Web site, each yellow square containing a right arrow indicates a data table that you can select. If the yellow squares do not display, click Show Icons at the top of the dialog box.

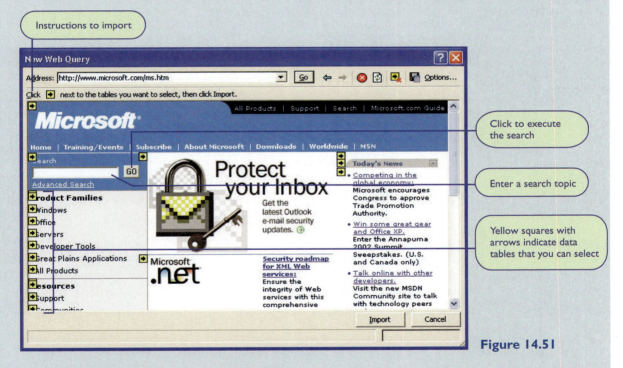

Figure 14.51

⑩ **Enter** Income Statement **or** Earnings **in the Search text box, and click the GO button at the right end of the box.**

⑪ **Scroll down and browse through search results until you find a link to a recent Income Statement or other earnings data; then follow links as necessary to find a yellow square next to income-related data, and click the yellow square.**

The yellow square containing an arrow switches to a green square containing a check mark, which indicates that the associated data is selected (see the sample in Figure 14.52).

continues ▶

To Create Web Queries (continued)

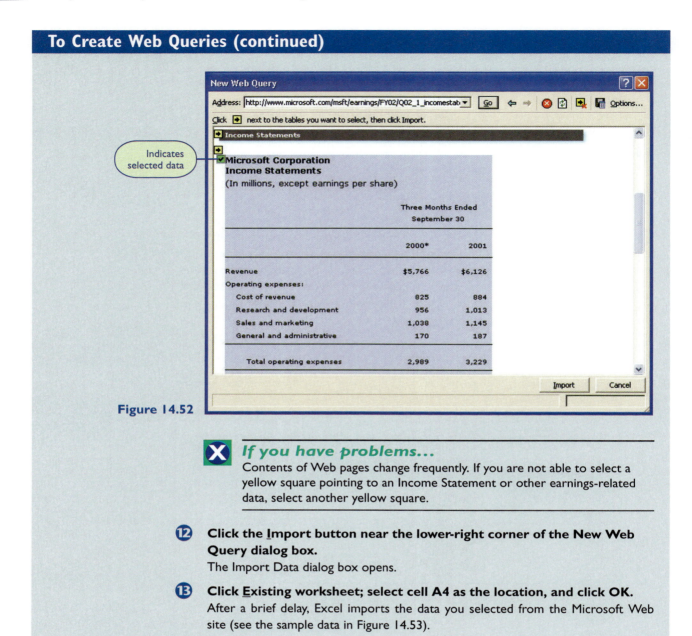

Figure 14.52

❎ *If you have problems...*
Contents of Web pages change frequently. If you are not able to select a yellow square pointing to an Income Statement or other earnings-related data, select another yellow square.

⓬ Click the Import button near the lower-right corner of the New Web Query dialog box.
The Import Data dialog box opens.

⓭ Click Existing worksheet; select cell A4 as the location, and click OK.
After a brief delay, Excel imports the data you selected from the Microsoft Web site (see the sample data in Figure 14.53).

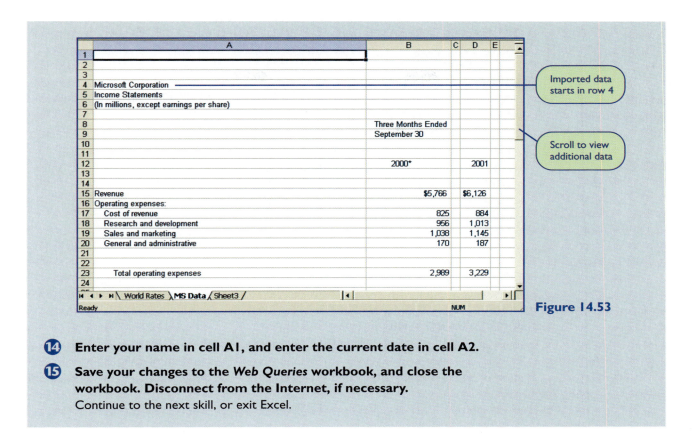

Figure 14.53

14 Enter your name in cell A1, and enter the current date in cell A2.

15 Save your changes to the *Web Queries* workbook, and close the workbook. Disconnect from the Internet, if necessary.
Continue to the next skill, or exit Excel.

In Depth:

Starting a Web Query in a Browser
In this skill, you started a Web query from within Excel. You can also browse to a Web page and start a query. For example, using Internet Explorer, you can click the arrow on the Edit button, and select *Edit with Microsoft Excel*.

Saving a Web Query
When you import data using a Web query, Excel automatically saves the Web query with your workbook. If you want to save the query so you can run it with other workbooks, click the Save Query button in the New Web Query dialog box. The query is saved in a text file with an .iqy extension. To run a saved query, choose Data, Import External Data, Import Data, and locate the folder where the query file is stored. Select the Web query you want to run; click Open; select Existing worksheet or New worksheet, and click OK.

Other Ways to Get Data from a Web Page
You can use copy and paste commands to bring selected data from a Web page into an Excel worksheet. Select the Web page content; execute your browser's copy process; switch to the desired location in the worksheet, and click Excel's Paste button.

For immediate reinforcement, work Skill Drill 8 and Challenge 8.

Skill 7.6: **Create Extensible Markup Language (XML) Web Queries**

Exchanging data across intranets and the Internet can be a challenging task due to differences in data formats, application programs, and computer systems. HTML, and more recently XML, are technologies designed to facilitate the desired access to data.

As stated in Excel's onscreen Help, **HTML (Hypertext Markup Language)** is the standard language for creating and displaying Web pages, and **XML (Extensible Markup Language)** is the standard language for describing and delivering data on the Web. Both are text-based technologies comprised of attributes, elements, and tags. HTML communicates the way your Web browser should display a document. XML enables you to define and structure the data within a document so that it displays in the format of your choice. For example, you might display an XML document as an Adobe .pdf file or as text in the body of an e-mail.

Excel supports the creation of XML files as well as HTML files. Use a File, Save As command to save an Excel workbook, and select HTML or XML as the desired format in the Save as type drop-down list within the Save As dialog box. You can also open an HTML or XML file in Excel using the File, Open command sequence. Select HTML or XML in the Files of type drop-down list within the Open dialog box.

This skill focuses on creating a query that imports data stored in an XML format on the Web. In the following steps, you simulate creating such a query. You use an XML file included with your student data files, rather than rely on a specific Web site being active at the time you work through this skill.

To Create an XML Web Query

1 **Display a new blank workbook, and make sure that Sheet1 is the current worksheet.**

2 **Choose Data, Import External Data, New Web Query.**
The New Web query dialog box opens. You do not have to connect to the Internet or an intranet for this simulation. When you create your own XML Web Queries, you would connect to the Internet or an intranet.

3 **In the Address text box, type** MEE-S706.xml **preceded by the storage location for your student data files.**
The sample in Figure 14.54 illustrates storage on drive A. Make sure that you type the storage path on your local system before you type the filename. When you create your own XML Web Queries, you type the Web site's URL or your firm's intranet location in the Address text box.

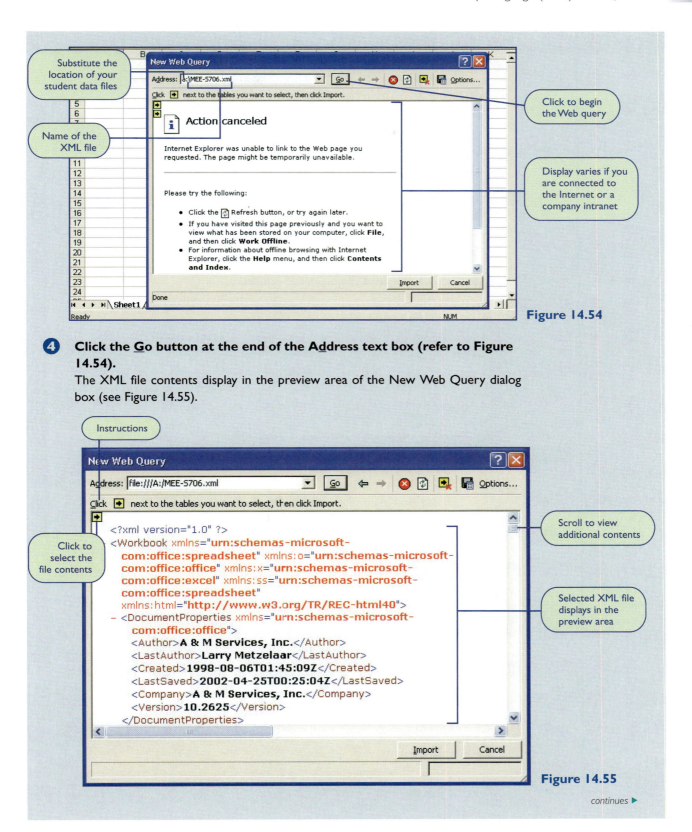

Figure 14.54

❹ Click the Go button at the end of the Address text box (refer to Figure 14.54).

The XML file contents display in the preview area of the New Web Query dialog box (see Figure 14.55).

Figure 14.55

continues ▶

To Create an XML Web Query (continued)

⑤ Scroll to view the attributes, elements, and tags in the XML document; then click the yellow square in the top-left corner of the preview area.
File contents display highlighted, which indicates that you selected the contents of the XML document.

⑥ Click Import in the lower-right corner of the dialog box.
The Import Data dialog box opens.

⑦ Make sure that Existing worksheet is selected as the location for the data; then click cell A3, and click OK.
Excel imports the data stored in XML format and automatically adjusts column widths to the longest entry in a column (see Figure 14.56).

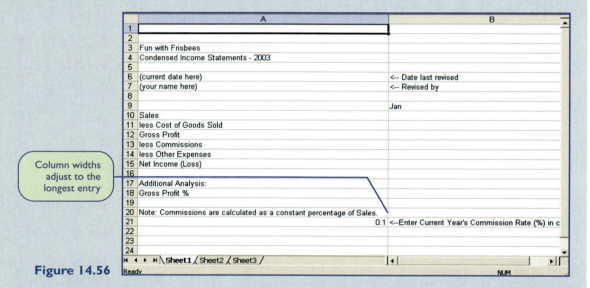

Figure 14.56

⑧ Close the External Data toolbar if it displays; then enter `Import XML (Adjust column width property turned on)` **in cell A1.**
Now repeat the process to create an XML Web query with one change.

⑨ Select the Sheet2 worksheet, and repeat steps 2 through 6.
The Import Data dialog box opens.

⑩ Click the Properties button at the bottom of the Import Data dialog box.
The External Data Range Properties dialog box opens.

⑪ Clear the Adjust column width check box (see Figure 14.57).

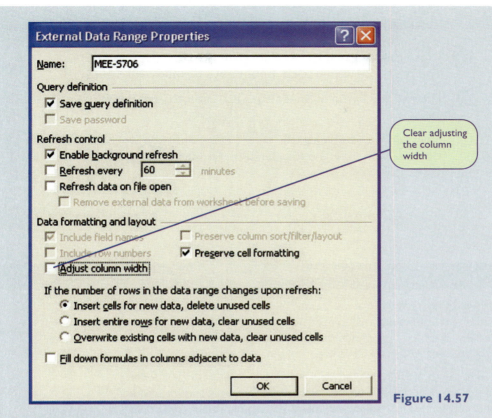

Figure 14.57

12 **Click OK.**

You turned off the property that adjusts column width. The Import Data dialog box reopens.

13 **Make sure that Existing worksheet is selected as the location for the data; then click cell A3, and click OK.**

Excel again imports the data stored in XML format, but retains the default column width of the destination worksheet instead of adjusting widths to the longest entry (see Figure 14.58).

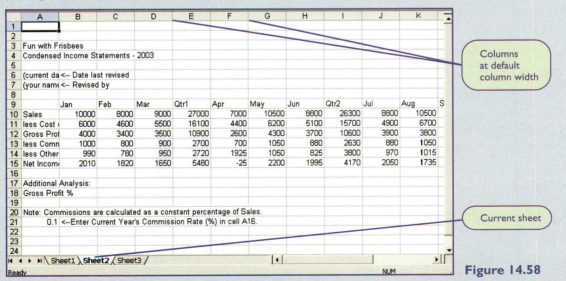

Figure 14.58

continues ▶

To Create an XML Web Query (continued)

14 **Close the External Data toolbar if it displays; then enter** `Import XML` `(Adjust column width property turned off)` **in cell A1.**

15 **Change the name of Sheet1 to** `XML1`**, and change the name of Sheet2 to** `XML2`**.**

16 **Save the workbook as** `XML Query`**, and close the workbook.**
Continue with the end-of-chapter exercises, start another skill set, or exit Excel.

For immediate reinforcement, work Skill Drills 9 and 10.

Summary

This skill set included a variety of topics in three areas: viewing existing data, ensuring the accuracy of data entry, and acquiring data from external sources. Your work in the first area included sorting on one or more fields in a list and creating subtotals that average, count, and sum similar data. You also set custom filters using AND and OR criteria and outlined worksheet data.

Data validation activities were varied. You attached an input message to a cell, restricted cell entries to data from a list, restricted cell entries to whole numbers within specified limits, created an error alert message, and copied data restrictions and messages to other cells.

You glimpsed the power of Web queries at the end of the skill set. You used a predefined Web query to import data on currency exchange rates. You also selected and imported data from a specified Web site—in this case, earnings-related data from Microsoft's site—and simulated creating an XML Web query by importing data stored in an XML format.

Skill Drill

Skill Drill exercises *reinforce* skills. Each skill reinforced is the same, or nearly the same, as a skill presented in the skill set. Detailed instructions are provided in a step-by-step format.

Before beginning your Excel Expert Skill Set 7 Skill Drill exercises, complete the following steps:

1. Open the file named *MEE-S707*, and immediately save it as **MEE-S7drill**.

The workbook contains eleven sheets: an overview and ten exercise sheets labeled SD1 through SD10.

2. Click the Overview sheet to view the organization and content of the Skill Drill workbook for Excel Expert Skill Set 7.

Each exercise is independent of the others, so you may complete the exercises in any order. Be sure to save the workbook after completing each exercise. If you need a paper copy of one or more completed exercises, enter your name, centered in a header, before printing. Print options have already been set to print compressed to one page and to display the filename, sheet name, and current date in a footer.

Be sure to save your changes and close the workbook if you need more than one work session to complete the desired exercises. Continue working on *MEE-S7drill* instead of starting over in the original *MEE-S707* file.

1. Sort on One, Two, or Three Fields

You know that you can use the Sort Ascending or Sort Descending button on the toolbar to sort on one field and the Sort dialog box to sort on up to three fields. Now you want to arrange survey records in a variety of ways. For the first sort, you want to show records in ascending order based on the contents of the Type Use field. Next, you want to organize records on the Car Size field (Compact, Full Size, and so on), and then within each car size, by days rented (highest to lowest). Finally, you want to sort on three fields, beginning with ascending order on the contents of the Type Use field. Within each type, you want to sort records by Car Size (ascending order). Finally, within Car Size, you want to organize records by Customer Rating in descending order.

To sort using buttons and the Sort dialog box, follow these steps:

1. Open the *MEE-S7drill* workbook, if necessary, and select the SD1 worksheet.
2. Click any cell containing data in the Type Use column.
3. Click the Sort Ascending button on the toolbar.
   Check that *Bus* (business) records display before *Per* (personal) records. Now, sort on the contents of two fields.
4. Click any cell in the list range A6:K36.
5. Choose Data, Sort.
6. Display the drop-down list for Sort by, and select the Car Size field.
7. Ensure that Ascending is the selected order for the Car Size field.
8. Display the drop-down list for the first of two *Then by* text boxes, and select the *Days Rented* field.
9. Specify Descending as the sort order.
10. Click OK.
    Make sure that records are organized first within groups (Compact, Full Size, and so on), and then within each group by days rented (highest to lowest). Now, sort on the contents of three fields.
11. Click any cell within the list, and display the Sort dialog box.
12. For the *Sort by* settings, select the Type Use field and specify ascending order.
13. For the first of two *Then by* settings, select the Car Size field and specify ascending order.
14. For the second of two *Then by* settings, select the Customer Rating field and specify descending order.
15. Execute the sort, and verify that records appear in the desired order.
16. Save your changes to the *MEE-S7drill* workbook.

2. Filter Using OR Criteria

As you review car rental data, you decide to analyze the records for customer ratings 1 and 5—the lowest and highest customer ratings.

To filter with two search conditions on one field, limiting the display to records with Customer Rating 1 or Customer Rating 5, follow these steps:

1. Open the *MEE-S7drill* workbook, if necessary, and select the SD2 worksheet.
2. Click any cell within the list, and choose Data, Filter, AutoFilter.
3. Click the filter arrow for the field Customer Rating.
4. Select *(Custom)* from the drop-down list.
5. Click the upper-right text box and type **1** (or select *1* from the drop-down list).

6. Click the <u>O</u>r option (as opposed to *And*) in the Custom AutoFilter dialog box.

7. Click the filter arrow for the lower-left text box and select *equals*.

8. Click the lower-right text box and type **5**.

9. Click OK.

   Ensure that the record display is limited to those with a Customer Rating of 1 or 5.

10. Save your changes to the *MEE-S7drill* workbook.

3. Filter Using AND Criteria

As you look at car rental data, you decide to focus on records of cars rented for periods of between six and 10 days, inclusive (that is, including 6 and 10 within the range).

To filter for records within a range—days rented more than five and fewer than 11—follow these steps:

1. Open the *MEE-S7drill* workbook, if necessary, and select the SD3 worksheet.

2. Click within any cell in the list, and choose <u>D</u>ata, <u>F</u>ilter, Auto<u>F</u>ilter.

3. Click the filter arrow next to the field name *Days Rented*.

4. From the drop-down list, select *(Custom)*.

5. Click the drop-down arrow next to the upper-left text box, and select *is greater than*.

6. Click the upper-right text box and type **5**.

7. Click the <u>A</u>nd option (as opposed to *Or*) in the Custom AutoFilter dialog box.

8. Click the drop-down arrow next to the lower-left text box, and select *is less than*.

9. Click the lower-right text box, and type **11**.

10. Click OK.

    Make sure that the display of records is limited to those showing days rented between 6 and 10.

11. Save your changes to the *MEE-S7drill* workbook.

4. Use a Wildcard in Filter Criteria

The Custom AutoFilter dialog box displays instructions to use a question mark (?) to represent any single character and an asterisk (*) to represent any series of characters. You want to use the asterisk wildcard character to filter for records that contain *news* in the Favorite Magazine field.

To filter for records using a wildcard character, follow these steps:

1. Open the *MEE-S7drill* workbook, if necessary, and select the SD4 worksheet.

2. Click within any cell in the list, and choose <u>D</u>ata, <u>F</u>ilter, Auto<u>F</u>ilter.

3. Click the filter arrow next to the field name *Favorite Magazine*.

4. From the drop-down list, select *(Custom)*.

5. Make sure that *equals* displays in the upper-left text box.

6. Type ***news*** in the upper-right text box.

7. Click OK.

   Make sure that the display of records is limited to those with *U.S. News* or *Newsweek* in the Favorite Magazine field.

8. Save your changes to the *MEE-S7drill* workbook.

5. Use Outlining with a Chart

You maintain a worksheet that tracks sales by type of order—In-Store, PhoneFax, and Web. You wonder whether you can use Excel's outline capability to alter the amount of detail shown in a chart. You decide to set up data groupings by type of order and use outline buttons to vary the amount of detail shown.

To group data and vary the amount of detail displayed in a worksheet and embedded chart, follow these steps:

1. Open the *MEE-S7drill* workbook, if necessary, and select the SD5 worksheet.
2. Select rows 7 through 10 in the worksheet frame, and choose <u>D</u>ata, <u>G</u>roup and Outline, <u>G</u>roup.
3. Select rows 12 through 15 in the worksheet frame, and choose <u>D</u>ata, <u>G</u>roup and Outline, <u>G</u>roup.
4. Select rows 17 through 20 in the worksheet frame, and choose <u>D</u>ata, <u>G</u>roup and Outline, <u>G</u>roup; then click any cell to deselect the highlighted range.
5. Scroll down to display the column chart.

    Three data series display in the column chart—Total In-Store sales, Total Phone/Fax sales, and Total Web sales.
6. Click the minus sign button to the left of row 11 in the worksheet frame.

    The In-Store Sales data series disappears from the column chart, and Excel hides rows 7 through 10.
7. Click the minus sign button to the left of row 16 in the worksheet frame.

    The Phone/Fax Sales data series disappears from the column chart, and Excel hides rows 12 through 15.
8. Click the plus sign button to the left of row 11 in the worksheet frame.

    The In-Store Sales data series reappears in the column chart, and Excel unhides rows 7 through 10.
9. Deselect the highlighted range, and save your changes to the *MEE-S7drill* workbook.

6. Create an Input Message and Restrict Data Entry

You are concerned that your tax data related to contributions is accurate, particularly that the date of a contribution is correct. Last year, you kept typing in the correct month and day, but the wrong year. To include a reminder in the worksheet, you decide to add a message to the first date cell reminding you to type the correct year. You also decide to control data entry in the Receipt field and copy both validation techniques to additional rows.

To create an input message, restrict data entry to a list of values, and copy the validation settings to other rows, follow these steps:

1. Open the *MEE-S7drill* workbook, if necessary, and select the SD6 worksheet.
2. Select cell A19 and choose <u>D</u>ata, Va<u>l</u>idation.
3. Select the Input Message tab, and type **Contribution Date** in the <u>T</u>itle text box.
4. Type **Check that the date you enter is for the year 2003** in the <u>I</u>nput message text box, and click OK.

    Check cell A19 to see that your message is attached and is correct.
5. Select cell D19 and choose <u>D</u>ata, Va<u>l</u>idation.
6. Click the Settings tab and select List from the <u>A</u>llow drop-down list.

7. Enter `=$D$5:$D$7` in the Source text box, and click OK.

8. Type **Lost** in cell D19, and press ⏎Enter.

An Excel Stop Error message appears advising you that the entry you just made is in-valid.

9. Click Cancel to close the message box.

10. Select the range A19:D19, and choose Edit, Copy.

11. Select the range A20:A50; then choose Edit, Paste Special.

12. Select the Validation button, and click OK.

You copied the first validation setting to the range A20:A50 and the second validation setting to the range D20:D50.

13. Press Esc and click any cell in the range A20:A50.

The input message about contribution date displays.

14. Click any cell in the range D20:D50.

An arrow indicating a drop-down list displays.

15. Save your changes to the *MEE-S7drill* workbook.

7. Apply a Warning Error Alert Message

You are concerned that the dates of your contributions fall in the year 2003. You want to apply the data validation setting to the Date column that restricts contribution dates to the year 2003. To do this, you must refer to the first and last days in the year 2003.

To limit data to a range of dates and set up a related error alert message, follow these steps:

1. Open the *MEE-S7drill* workbook, if necessary, and select the SD7 worksheet.

2. Select cell A19 and choose Data, Validation.

3. Click the Settings tab and select Date from the Allow drop-down list.

4. Type **01/01/2003** in the Start date text box, and **12/31/2003** in the End date text box.

5. Click the Error Alert tab and select Warning from the Style drop-down list.

6. Type **Contribution Date** in the Title text box.

7. Type **Please enter a date between January 1, 2003 and December 31, 2003** in the Error message text box.

8. Click OK to exit the Data Validation dialog box.

9. Click cell A19; type **July 4, 3003**, and press ⏎Enter.

Excel displays your message guiding data entry, followed by *Continue?* You can choose one of three buttons: Yes, No, and Cancel. Clicking Yes enters the invalid date. You can also click No to correct the entry, or click Cancel to stop the data entry attempt.

10. Select Cancel; type **July 4, 2003**, and press ⏎Enter.

Excel accepts the entry this time because the date falls within the allowable range of dates.

11. Save your changes to the *MEE-S7drill* workbook.

8. Get Data Using a Pre-Defined Web Query

In this skill set you executed a pre-defined Web query to import world currency rates from the MSN MoneyCentral Investor Web site. Now you want to execute a pre-defined Web query that generates stock information.

1. Connect to the Internet.

2. Open the *MEE-S7drill* workbook, if necessary, and select the SD8 worksheet.

3. Choose Data, Import External Data, Import Data.

   The Select Data Source dialog box opens.

4. Select MSN MoneyCentral Investor Stock Quotes in the Select Data Source dialog box, and click Open.

5. Enter cell A4 in the current worksheet as the location for the imported data, and click OK.

6. Enter **MSFT** as the parameter value.

   MSFT is the stock market symbol for Microsoft Corporation.

7. Click OK.

   Excel imports the most recent stock market data for Microsoft Corporation.

8. Save your changes to the *MEE-S7drill* workbook.

9. Learn More About How Microsoft Excel Uses XML

This skill set provided a brief introduction to XML. You want to get more information about how Excel uses XML.

To get information on XML using Excel's onscreen Help, follow these steps:

1. Open the *MEE-S7drill* workbook, if necessary, and select the SD9 worksheet.

2. Enter **XML** in the Ask a Question box.

3. Click the topic *About XML and Excel.*

   Two topics display in the Help pane: *What is XML?* and *How does Microsoft Excel use XML?.*

4. Read the paragraphs in the *What is XML?* section, and then select the title and content of the second topic area.

5. Drag the selected second Help topic to the SD9 worksheet beginning in cell A4.

   You copied information about how Microsoft Excel uses XML from the Help screen to the SD9 worksheet.

6. Click cell A1 to deselect the pasted data, and close the Help pane.

7. Save your changes to the *MEE-S7drill* workbook.

10. Explore the Limitations of XML Spreadsheet Format

Outlining is lost when you save a workbook as an XML file. You want to know what other features are not retained when saving in an XML format. The information you need is part of Excel's Web-based Help system. You must have Web access to complete this exercise.

1. Use your browser software, such as Netscape Navigator or Internet Explorer, to connect to the Web.

2. Open the *MEE-S7drill* workbook, if necessary, and right-click any one of the four navigation arrows to the left of the worksheet names.

   A pop-up list of worksheets displays.

3. Select SD10.

4. Enter `limitations of XML` in the Ask a Question box.

5. Click the topic *WEB: Features and limitations of XML Spreadsheet format.*

6. Scroll through the Web-based Help table that lists features retained and not retained when saving an Excel workbook as an XML file.

7. Starting in cell A4 of the SD10 worksheet, list at least six features—one per row—not retained when saving an Excel workbook as an XML file.

You can select and drag a listed item instead of retyping it.

8. Close the Web-based Help; disconnect from the Internet, and save your changes to the *MEE-S7drill* workbook.

Challenge

Challenge exercises expand on or are somewhat related to skills presented in the skill sets. Each exercise provides a brief narrative introduction, followed by instructions in a numbered-step format that are not as detailed as those in the Skill Drill section.

Before beginning your Excel Expert Skill Set 7 Challenge exercises, complete the following steps:

1. Open the file named *MEE-S708*, and immediately save it as **MEE-S7challenge**.

The workbook contains nine sheets: an overview and eight exercise sheets labeled CH1 through CH8.

2. Click the Overview sheet to view the organization and content of the Challenge workbook for Excel Expert Skill Set 7.

Each exercise is independent of the others, so you may complete the exercises in any order. Be sure to save the workbook after completing each exercise. If you need a paper copy of one or more completed exercises, enter your name, centered in a header, before printing. Sheets CH6 and CH7 have been set to print compressed on two pages; the others are set to print compressed on one page. Settings to display the filename, sheet name, and current date in a footer have been set in all worksheets.

Be sure to save your changes and close the workbook if you need more than one work session to complete the desired exercises. Continue working on *MEE-S7challenge* instead of starting over in the original *MEE-S708* file.

1. Subtotal on Two Fields

In this skill set, you created subtotals by applying a single function to one field. For example, you created subtotals that averaged the price of homes for sale in each area. Now you want to create subtotals in survey results about car rentals. For each car size, you want to display subtotals showing the average number of days rented and the total rental cost.

To subtotal using two functions, each applied to a different field, follow these steps:

1. Open the *MEE-S7challenge* workbook, if necessary, and select the CH1 worksheet.

2. Click any cell within the range D7:D36, and click the Sort Ascending button in the Standard toolbar.

3. Display the Subtotal dialog box and specify the following settings:

A̲t each change in   Car Size
U̲se function   Average
Ad̲d subtotal to   Days Rented

4. Make sure that you uncheck any other selected boxes in the A̲dd subtotal to area; then click OK.

At each change in car size, Excel inserts a subtotal showing the average number of days rented. For example, 6.875 is the average number of days rented for full-size cars.

5. Make sure that a cell within the list is the current cell; then display the Subtotal dialog box, and specify the following settings:

    At each change in   Car Size
    Use function   Sum
    Add subtotal to   Rental Cost

6. Make sure that you uncheck any other selected boxes in the *Add subtotal to* area.

7. Uncheck the Replace current subtotals setting, and click OK. Widen the Rental Cost column, if necessary, to view the subtotals.

    At each change in car size, Excel inserts another subtotal row showing the total rental cost. For example, $770.00 is the total rental cost for full-size cars during the first quarter 2003.

8. Save your changes to the *MEE-S7challenge* workbook.

2. Create Nested Subtotals

In this skill set, you created subtotals by applying a single function to one field. For example, you created subtotals that averaged the price of homes for sale in each area. Now you want to create subtotals in survey results about car rentals. For each type use—business or personal—you want to display subtotals showing the total rental cost. Within each type use, you also want to display total rental cost for each car size.

To create nested subtotals, follow these steps:

1. Open the *MEE-S7challenge* workbook, if necessary, and select the CH2 worksheet.

2. Sort the list of survey results by the Type Use field in ascending order, and then by the Car Size field in ascending order.

3. Display the Subtotal dialog box, and specify the following settings:

    At each change in   Type Use
    Use function   Sum
    Add subtotal to   Rental Cost

4. Make sure that you clear any other selected boxes in the *Add subtotal to* area; then click OK. Widen the Rental Cost column, if necessary, to view the subtotals.

    At each change in type of use, Excel inserts a subtotal showing the total rental cost. For example, $1,013.60 is the total rental cost for business use.

5. Make sure that a cell within the list is the current cell; then display the Subtotal dialog box, and specify the following settings:

    At each change in   Car Size
    Use function   Sum
    Add subtotal to   Rental Cost

6. Uncheck the Replace current subtotals setting, and click OK.

    At each change in car size, Excel inserts another subtotal row showing the total rental cost. For example, $504.00 is the total rental cost for full-size cars rented for business use during the first quarter 2003.

7. Scroll to view rows 27 and 28.

    Total rental cost of trucks rented for business use displays in cell I27. Total rental cost of all rentals for business use displays in cell I28.

8. Save your changes to the *MEE-S7challenge* workbook.

3. Filter on Three Criteria (One Field)

You use an Excel list to track results about vehicle rentals. You want to display only those records in which the car type is Mid Size, Full Size, or Luxury; but you realize there is a two-condition limit when using AutoFilter's Custom option. You wonder whether you can produce the desired results using the Advanced Filter option that appears when you choose Data, Filter.

To get help on advanced filter options, and filter on three criteria applied to one field, follow these steps:

1. Open the *MEE-S7challenge* workbook, if necessary, and select the CH3 worksheet.

2. Use onscreen Help to learn about the Advanced Filter option, focusing on examples that use a separate criteria range; then close Help.

3. Study the organization of the CH3 worksheet.

   The worksheet includes the field names for a criteria range in row 6. All fields are included, but you are going to enter criteria below only the Car Size field.

4. Enter criteria in the cells indicated: **Mid Size** in cell D7, **Full Size** in cell D8, and **Luxury** in cell D9.

5. Click any cell within the list; then choose Data, Filter, Advanced Filter.

   The Advanced Filter dialog box opens.

6. Make sure that *Filter the list, in-place* is selected, and that the list range setting is $A$11:$J$41.

7. Select A6:J9 as the criteria range.

   You can also select D6:D9 as the criteria range. The range A6:J9 works because Excel ignores any blank cells in the specified criteria range.

8. Click OK, and verify that you set a filter to display only those records that contain Mid Size, Full Size, or Luxury in the Car Size field.

9. Save your changes to the *MEE-S7challenge* workbook.

4. Filter on Three Criteria (Three Fields)

You are excited about the capabilities that the Advanced Filter option provides for viewing data. Now, you want to view only the records of full-size car rentals for business use with a rental period exceeding five days.

To set three criteria on three fields using Advanced Filter and specify that all three criteria must be met, follow these steps:

1. Open the *MEE-S7challenge* workbook, if necessary, and select the CH4 worksheet.

2. Enter criteria in the cells indicated: **Full Size** in cell D7, **Bus** in cell B7, and **>5** in cell G7.

3. Click any cell within the list; then choose Data, Filter, Advanced Filter.

   The Advanced Filter dialog box opens.

4. Make sure that *Filter the list, in-place* is selected, and that the list range setting is $A$11:$J$41.

5. Specify A6:J7 as the criteria range.

   You can also specify B6:G7 as the criteria range. The range A6:J7 works because Excel ignores any blank cells in the specified criteria range.

6. Click OK, and verify that the results are limited to rental records for business use of full-size cars for more than five days.

Three records meet all three criteria.

7. Save your changes to the *MEE-S7challenge* workbook.

5. Create a Manual Outline

You maintain a list of survey results related to car rentals. You want to use Excel's manual outline feature to hide and redisplay several columns in the list.

To accomplish the desired results with manual outlining, follow these steps:

1. Open the *MEE-S7challenge* workbook, if necessary, and select the CH5 worksheet.

2. Sort the list by the Type Use field and then by the Type Pmt field, both in ascending order.

3. Select the range E6:F6 (Date Rented and Date Returned); then choose Data, Group and Outline, Group.

   The Group dialog box opens.

4. Select Columns and click OK.

5. Follow the process described in steps 3 and 4 to establish cell J6 as a group.

   Outline brackets and buttons display above the worksheet frame.

6. Hide columns E and F by clicking the minus sign button above the column letter G in the worksheet frame.

7. Use the appropriate outline button to hide column J.

8. Use an outline button(s) to restore display of all hidden columns, and save your changes to the *MEE-S7challenge* workbook.

6. Create Drop-Down Lists and Input Messages

You have been experiencing keyboard errors entering data in the Position and Department fields of an employee list. You decide to apply a drop-down list to these fields. The lists already exist in the Database Work area. Apply drop-down lists and input messages to both fields. The input message should advise the user to select an entry from the drop-down list attached to the cell.

To apply drop-down lists and input messages, follow these steps:

1. Open the *MEE-S7challenge* workbook, if necessary, and select the CH6 worksheet.

2. Select all the cells in the list that contain position data in column C (the range C32:C142).

3. Display the Data Validation dialog box.

4. Select the Settings tab and apply the List option using A12:A25 as the Source.

5. Specify the input message `Select an entry from the drop-down list`, and click OK.

   You specified data validation for the Position data field. You can check your specifications by selecting any cell in the field and displaying the drop-down list. Visually check that your message is correct.

6. Select all the cells in the list that contain department data (the range D32:D142), and open the Data Validation dialog box.

7. Select the Settings tab and apply the List option using B12:B19 as the source.

8. Specify the input message `Select an entry from the drop-down list`, and click OK.

   Visually inspect the validations for the Department field in the same manner as you did the Position field.

9. Save your changes to the *MEE-S7challenge* workbook.

7. Apply Validations with Information and Warning Messages

You want to apply validation restrictions and error messages to the Shift and Hire Date fields in an employee list. Shift data should be limited to whole numbers between 1 and 3, with an input message and an Information error alert. Hire date should restrict entries to dates between August 1, 1988 and the current date, with an appropriate input message and a Warning error alert. This is a little different, because you use the =Today() function to determine the current date. The date settings will also be stored in cells rather than typed directly into the validation settings.

To apply validations with information and warning messages, follow these steps:

1. Open the *MEE-S7challenge* workbook, if necessary, and select the CH7 worksheet.

2. Select the Shift field data starting in row 32, and open the Data Validation dialog box.

3. Use the Settings tab to allow whole numbers between 1 and 3.

4. Select the Input Message tab; type **Shift** as the message Title, and type **Please enter 1, 2, or 3** as the Input message.

5. Use the Error Alert tab to display the Information message **You have entered an incorrect number. Please enter 1, 2, or 3.**

6. Click OK and check that your Input and Error messages display correctly. You can test your validation by entering an invalid shift, such as 0 or 4.

7. Enter **8-1-88** in cell C12, and enter **=TODAY()** in cell D12.

8. Select the Hire Date data starting in row 32, and open the Data Validation dialog box.

9. Use the Settings tab to allow dates. Refer to cell C12 as the Start date and to cell D12 as the End date. Make sure that the cell references are absolute.

10. Use the Input Message tab to inform users that they must enter a date between August 1, 1988 and the current date.

11. Use the Error Alert tab to display a Warning message with two messages in the Error message box:

    Please enter a date between August 1, 1988 and the current date.
    Select Yes to accept the date, No to enter another date, or Cancel to quit.

12. Click OK and test your Hire Date validation settings. Try entering the date **1-1-1980** or a date in the future.

13. Save your changes to the *MEE-S7challenge* workbook.

8. Create a Web Query

In this skill set, you created a Web query to retrieve earnings-related data from the Microsoft Corporation Web site. Now you want to import data from a site of your choice, such as one maintained by your school, a volunteer organization, or a sports organization.

To import data into an Excel worksheet by creating a Web query of your choice, follow these steps:

1. Connect to the Internet.
2. Open the *MEE-S7challenge* workbook, if necessary, and select the CH8 worksheet.
3. Choose Data, Import External Data, New Web Query.
4. Enter the URL of your choice in the Address text box, and click Go.
5. Click one or more of the yellow squares with arrows that indicate data you can select; then click the Import button.
6. Specify that you want to import the selected data starting in cell A4 of the existing worksheet, and complete the process to import.
7. Add documentation to the worksheet that includes your name, the date you obtained the information, and the URL for your data source.
8. Save your changes to the *MEE-S7challenge* workbook.

Analyzing Data

CHAPTER 15

This skill set includes

Create pivot tables, pivot charts, and pivot table/pivot chart reports

- Create a pivot table
- Expand a pivot table
- Remove, hide, and show data
- Refresh a pivot table
- Create a chart from pivot table data
- Apply predefined formats to a pivot table

Forecast values with what-if analysis

- Create an XY scatter chart
- Fit a trendline to an XY scatter chart

Create and display scenarios

Skill Set Overview

n this skill set, you learn three ways to analyze data. You begin by creating, expanding, editing, and formatting pivot tables. A *pivot table* is an interactive table that quickly summarizes large amounts of data from a data source, such as a list or another table. You also create a chart based on pivot table data.

The second topic focuses on forecasting values in the future by analyzing current and prior values. You create a chart and place a line in the chart that shows the trend over time.

The final topic introduces scenarios. A *scenario* is a set of saved values that you can recall for substitution in a worksheet.

Skill 8.1: Create Pivot Tables, Pivot Charts, and Pivot Table/Pivot Chart Reports

The *PivotTable and PivotChart Wizard* guides you through the steps to make a custom report from a list of data. The initial steps include specifying the data source, the type of report (Pivot-Table or PivotChart), and the location of the report (a new worksheet or the existing worksheet). At that point you have two options for completing the design of the pivot table: using a Layout dialog box or making selections directly on the worksheet.

You can easily set up a pivot table directly on the worksheet by dragging the names of fields listed in the PivotTable toolbar to the appropriate areas of a pivot table shell (see Figure 15.1). That way you can view the data while you arrange the fields.

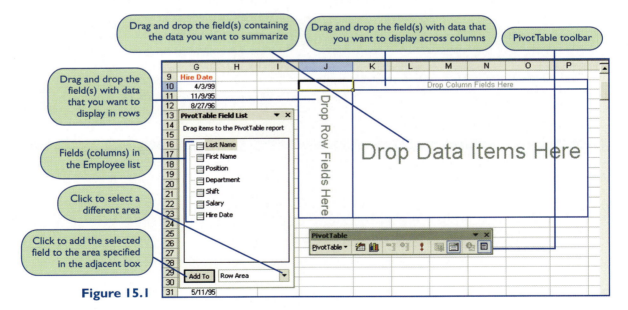

Figure 15.1

If the pivot table you have in mind is large and complex, using the on-sheet layout illustrated in Figure 15.1 can be quite time-consuming, because data updates each time you make a change. You might prefer to design the pivot table using the Layout dialog box (see Figure 15.2) and then display the results when you are done.

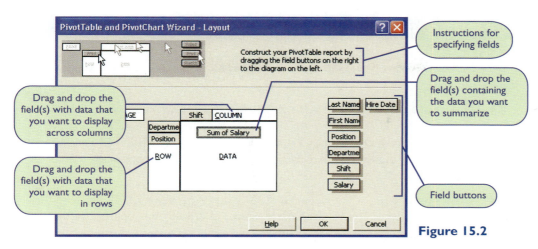

Figure 15.2

Either method generates a pivot table based on your specifications. Now begin your exploration of this powerful analysis tool by creating a simple pivot table.

Create a Pivot Table

In this skill, you design a pivot table directly on the worksheet. You create a simple table that totals salaries by department for Millennium Manufacturing.

To Create a Pivot Table

① **Open the *MEE-S801* workbook and save it as** Salary Pivots.

The workbook includes one worksheet named Employees, which contains employee-related data organized as an Excel list.

② **Click any cell within the list range A9:G120, and choose Data, PivotTable and PivotChart Report.**

The PivotTable and PivotChart Wizard–Step 1 of 3 dialog box opens (see Figure 15.3).

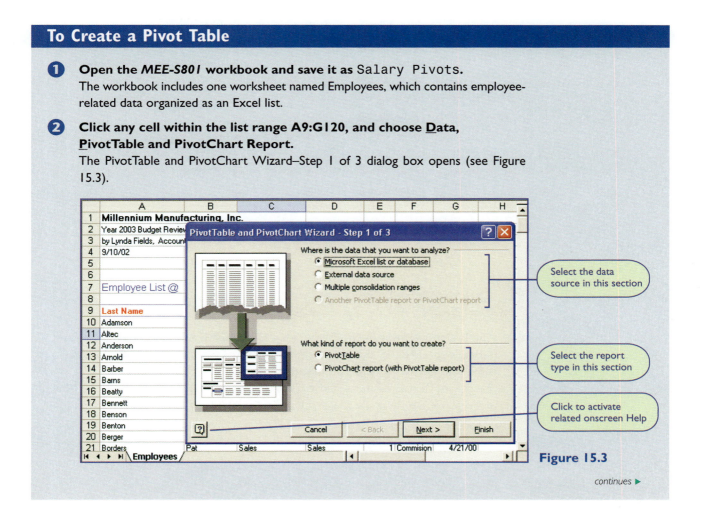

Figure 15.3

continues ▶

To Create a Pivot Table (continued)

③ Make sure that _Microsoft Excel list or database_ is selected as the data source.

④ Make sure that Pivot**T**able is selected as the report type, and click the **N**ext button.

The PivotTable and PivotChart Wizard–Step 2 of 3 dialog box opens. Because you clicked within the list before activating the Wizard, Excel automatically selects the entire list and displays $A$9:$G$120 in the **R**ange box.

⑤ Click **N**ext.

The PivotTable and PivotChart Wizard–Step 3 of 3 dialog box opens. Use this dialog box to specify whether to create the pivot table in a new worksheet or in the existing worksheet.

⑥ Select **E**xisting worksheet, and click cell J10.

This tells Excel to position the upper-left cell of the pivot table in cell J10 in the active worksheet. Employees!$J$10 displays in the box below the **E**xisting worksheet option (see Figure 15.4).

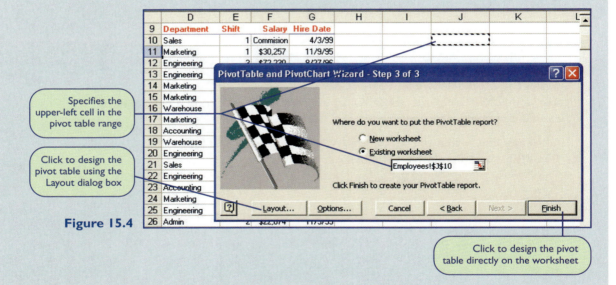

Specifies the upper-left cell in the pivot table range

Click to design the pivot table using the Layout dialog box

Figure 15.4

Click to design the pivot table directly on the worksheet

⑦ Click the **F**inish button.

Excel creates a shell for a pivot table (refer to Figure 15.1).

⑧ Click Department in the PivotTable Field List box, make sure that Row Area is selected in the lower-right corner of the PivotTable Field List box, and click the Add To button.

Excel adds the Department field as a row in the pivot table (see Figure 15.5). Alternatively, you can drag the Department field to the _Drop Row Fields Here_ section in the pivot table shell.

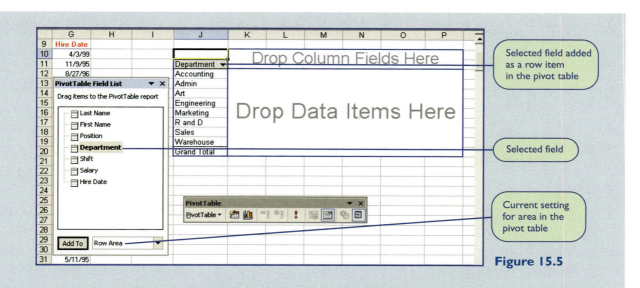

Figure 15.5

9 **Click Salary in the PivotTable Field List box, and display the Area drop-down list to the right of the Add To button (see Figure 15.6).**

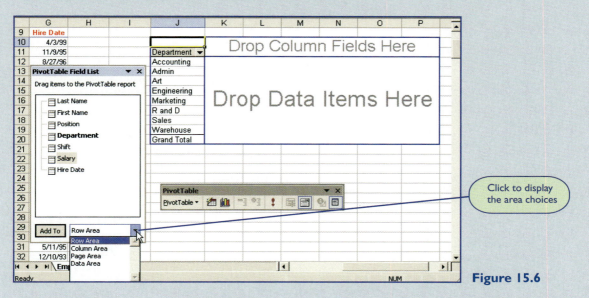

Figure 15.6

10 **Select Data Area in the drop-down list, and click the Add To button.**
Excel adds salary data to the pivot table (see Figure 15.7). You can also drag the Salary field to the *Drop Data Items Here* section in the pivot table shell. By default, the summary calculation on salary data is a count.

continues ▶

To Create a Pivot Table (continued)

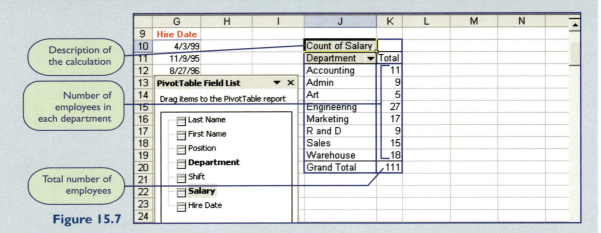

Description of the calculation

Number of employees in each department

Total number of employees

Figure 15.7

⑪ **Double-click Count of Salary (cell J10).**
The PivotTable Field dialog box opens.

⑫ **Select Sum in the Summarize by list box (see Figure 15.8).**

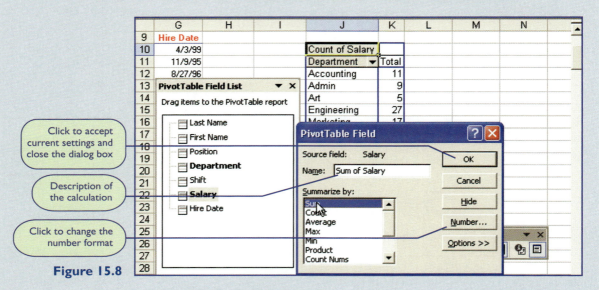

Click to accept current settings and close the dialog box

Description of the calculation

Click to change the number format

Figure 15.8

Sum of Salary replaces *Count of Salary* in the Na̲me text box.

⑬ **Click the N̲umber button to open the Format Cells dialog box. Specify Currency format without the $ sign symbol and with zero decimal places (see Figure 15.9).**

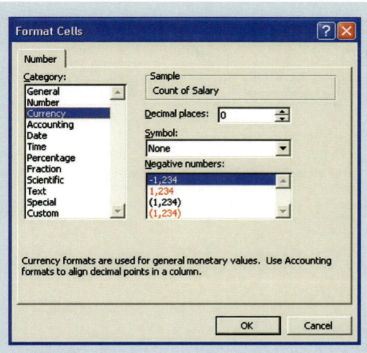

Figure 15.9

⑭ **Click OK twice to close the Format Cells and PivotTable Field dialog boxes respectively.**

The pivot table reflects the changes in type of summary and number formatting (see Figure 15.10).

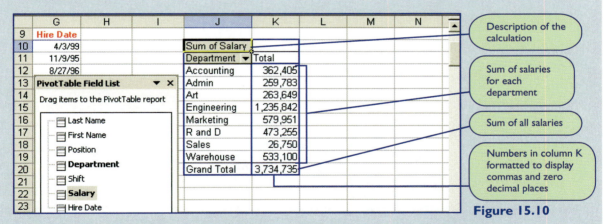

Figure 15.10

⑮ **Close the PivotTable Field List box by clicking the Close button—a large X—in the upper-right corner of that box.**

⑯ **Use a similar process to close the PivotTable toolbar, and save your changes to the *Salary Pivots* workbook.**

Keep the *Salary Pivots* workbook open for the next skill, or close the workbook and exit Excel.

In Depth:
Delete a Pivot Table

Before you can delete a pivot table, you must select it using a three-step process. Right-click within the pivot table; choose Select from the shortcut menu, and click Entire Table. After selecting the table, choose Edit, Clear, All. When you delete a pivot table, the source data is not affected.

Expand a Pivot Table

You can expand a pivot table by adding more fields to a pivot table on the worksheet or to the row, column, and data areas of the Layout dialog box. For example, instead of displaying a single column with total salary for each Millennium Manufacturing department, you can add columns that provide totals for each shift within a department. You can also add rows that provide totals for each position within a department. In this skill, you make these changes using the PivotTable and PivotChart Wizard's Layout dialog box.

To Expand a Pivot Table

① **Open the *Salary Pivots* workbook, if necessary.**
A pivot table showing salaries by department and in total displays in the range J10:K20.

② **Right-click within the pivot table, and then select Show Field List.**

③ **Click Position in the PivotTable Field List box. Display the Area drop-down list to the right of the Add To button; select Row Area, and click the Add To button.**
Excel adds position data to the pivot table (see Figure 15.11).

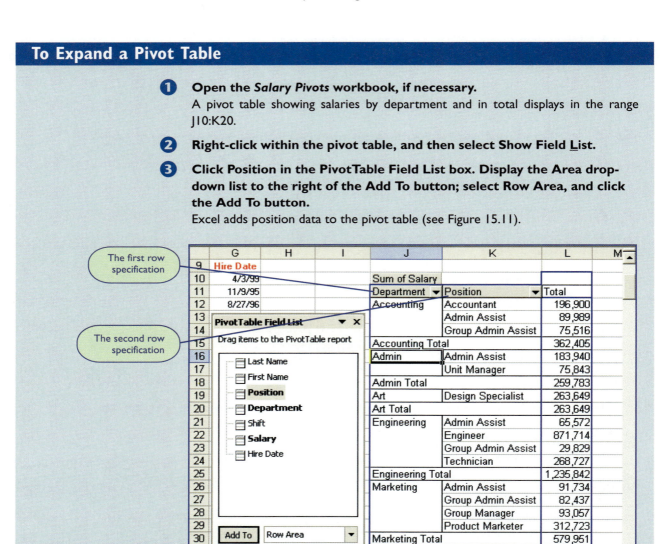

Figure 15.11

④ **Click Shift in the PivotTable Field List box. Display the Area drop-down list to the right of the Add To button; select Column Area, and click the Add To button.**

Excel adds shift data to the pivot table (see Figure 15.12). The summary information in the table more than doubles, as a result of adding data from two fields.

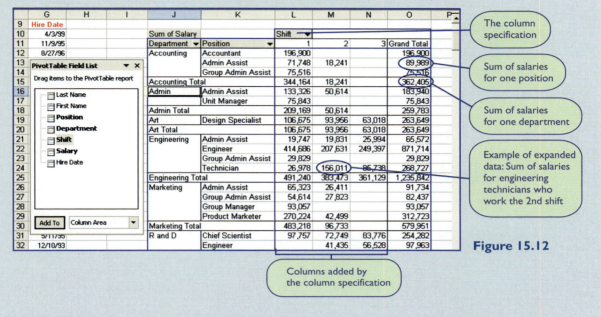

Figure 15.12

The column specification

Sum of salaries for one position

Sum of salaries for one department

Example of expanded data: Sum of salaries for engineering technicians who work the 2nd shift

Columns added by the column specification

⑤ **Close the PivotTable Field List box, and save your changes to the *Salary Pivots* workbook.**

Keep the *Salary Pivots* workbook open for the next skill, or close the workbook and exit Excel.

Remove, Hide, and Show Data

As your information needs change, you might want to display more or less summary data in a pivot table. The process for removing a field is opposite that of adding a field—drag the field away from the pivot table on the worksheet or drag the field away from the Row, Column, or Data area in the Layout dialog box. Showing or hiding detail in a field is as easy as pulling down a list of items in a field on the pivot table and checking or unchecking the field.

In this skill, you modify the pivot table in preparation for creating a chart. You remove the Shift field, and then hide data for the Engineering, R and D, and Warehouse departments. When you are done, only the Accounting, Administration, Art, Marketing, and Sales summary data display.

To Remove, Hide, and Show Data

① **Open the *Salary Pivots* workbook, if necessary.**

② **Click the Shift button in the pivot table (cell L10), and drag it upward off the pivot table.**

The three columns of Shift summary data are removed from the pivot table (see Figure 15.13). Excel keeps the removed field button accessible by positioning it just above the pivot table.

continues ▶

To Remove, Hide, and Show Data (continued)

Field removed from the pivot table

	G	H	I	J	K	L	M
7							
8				Shift	(All) ▾		
9	**Hire Date**						
10	4/3/99			Sum of Salary			
11	11/9/95			Department ▾	Position ▾	Total	
12	8/27/96			Accounting	Accountant	196,900	
13	11/8/97				Admin Assist	89,989	
14	5/9/01				Group Admin Assist	75,516	
15	2/26/01			Accounting Total		362,405	
16	7/10/97			Admin	Admin Assist	183,940	
17	5/10/01				Unit Manager	75,843	
18	3/21/94			Admin Total		259,783	
19	9/21/91			Art	Design Specialist	263,649	
20	2/25/01			Art Total		263,649	
21	4/21/00			Engineering	Admin Assist	65,572	
22	11/8/96				Engineer	871,714	
23	12/17/91				Group Admin Assist	29,829	
24	1/27/97				Technician	268,727	
25	8/26/00			Engineering Total		1,235,842	
26	11/9/93			Marketing	Admin Assist	91,734	

Figure 15.13

③ Click the drop-down arrow in cell J11.

The Department drop-down list displays. Check marks in front of department names indicate the pivot table currently displays summary data for all departments (see Figure 15.14). Clicking a check mark deselects the box and temporarily hides the related data in the pivot table.

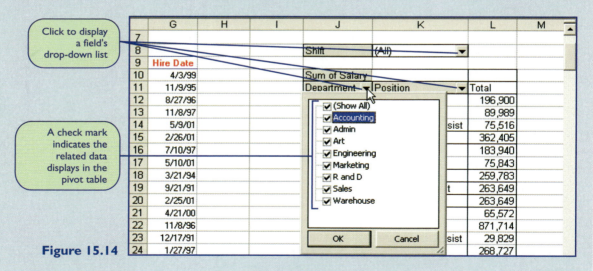

Click to display a field's drop-down list

A check mark indicates the related data displays in the pivot table

Figure 15.14

④ Uncheck the Engineering, R and D, and Warehouse items in the Department drop-down list.

⑤ Click OK.

Summary data for the Engineering, R and D, and Warehouse departments does not display in the pivot table (see Figure 15.15).

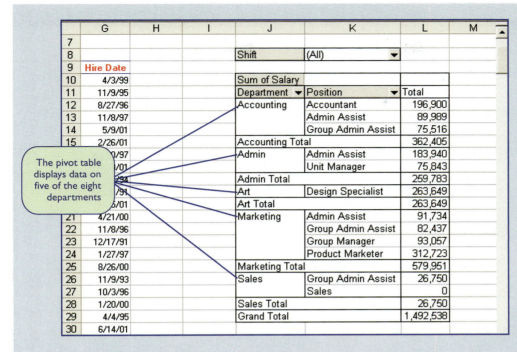

Figure 15.15

6 Save your changes to the *Salary Pivots* workbook.

Keep the *Salary Pivots* workbook open for the next skill, or close the workbook and exit Excel.

In Depth:

Display the Top or Bottom Items in a Field

You can display a user-specified number of top or bottom items in a pivot table field. Click within the pivot table; click PivotTable on the PivotTable toolbar, and select *Sort and Top 10*. Under *Top 10 AutoShow*, click On. In the Show box, select Top or Bottom, and in the spin box to the right, specify the number of items to display. In the Using field box, click the data field to use for calculating the top or bottom items, and then click OK.

Refresh a Pivot Table

If you change data in a worksheet and that data impacts a summary calculation in a pivot table, Excel does not automatically update the pivot table. After making changes to the worksheet, you must *refresh* (recalculate) the pivot table.

A word of caution is in order to avoid using invalid data to make decisions. Because you are so used to Excel recalculating a worksheet automatically, it's easy to overlook refreshing any pivot tables that incorporate the changed data. In complex pivot tables, errors in summary amounts are difficult to detect visually; therefore, acquire the habit of refreshing pivot tables after making a change in worksheet data.

In this skill, you change worksheet data, check for changes in pivot table amounts, refresh the pivot table, and check amounts again.

To Refresh a Pivot Table

① **Open the *Salary Pivots* workbook, if necessary.**

② **Scroll the worksheet to display column A, starting with row 7.**
Currently the salary for accountant Pat Collingwood is $48,968 (cell F23).

③ **Scroll right as needed to display the entire pivot table.**
The sum of salaries for accountants is $196,900 (cell L12).

④ **Change the contents of cell F23 to $50,968 instead of *$48,968*.**
You changed the salary of an accountant, but the sum of salaries for accountants in the pivot table did not change ($196,900 in cell L12). Just looking at the summary data, it is not apparent that the pivot table contains an error.

⑤ **Right-click anywhere within the pivot table.**
A shortcut menu opens (see Figure 15.16).

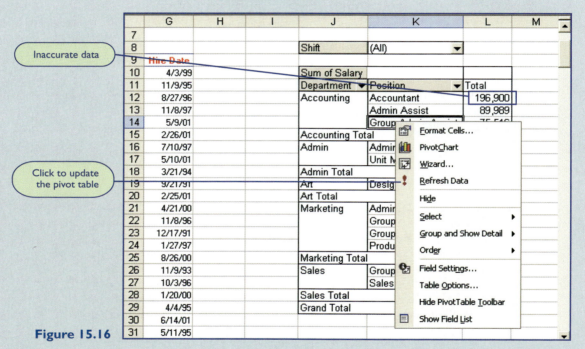

Figure 15.16

⑥ **Choose <u>R</u>efresh Data from the shortcut menu.**
The sum of salaries for accountants increases from $196,900 to $198,900 in cell L12.

⑦ **Save your changes to the *Salary Pivots* workbook.**
Keep the *Salary Pivots* workbook open for the next skill, or close the workbook and exit Excel.

Alternate Way:
Other Ways to Select Refresh
<u>R</u>efresh Data is an option on the shortcut menu that displays when you right-click within a pivot table. You can also choose the menu sequence <u>D</u>ata, <u>R</u>efresh Data, or click the Refresh Data button on the PivotTable toolbar.

Create a Chart from Pivot Table Data

A pivot table provides informative summary data in rows and columns. Creating a chart based on pivot table data can be an effective way to interpret that data. You can create a chart quickly by right-clicking within an existing pivot table, and selecting Pivot**C**hart from the shortcut menu. You can also use the PivotTable and PivotChart Wizard to create both a chart and its related table at the same time.

For either method, Excel automatically creates a column chart on a separate sheet. You can then edit the PivotChart report just as you would any Excel chart—adding and deleting data points, changing chart type, applying number formats, and so forth. You can use any chart type except XY (scatter), bubble, and stock.

In this skill, you create a column chart based on the pivot table in the *Salary Pivots* workbook. You then hide the Art department salary data, which limits the chart to Accounting, Admin, Marketing, and Sales salaries. You also convert the chart type to Line, so you can compare the effectiveness of the two chart types.

To Create and Modify a Chart Based on Pivot Table Data

1 **Open the *Salary Pivots* workbook, if necessary.**

2 **Right-click any cell in the pivot table (J10:L29), and select Pivot**C**hart on the shortcut menu.**
Excel creates a column chart based on the visible data in the pivot table (see Figure 15.17). Department and Position buttons display centered below the chart.

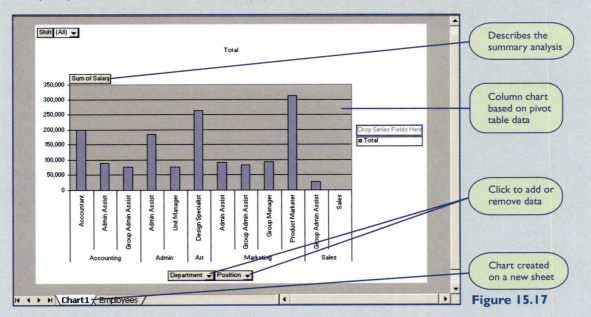

Describes the summary analysis

Column chart based on pivot table data

Click to add or remove data

Chart created on a new sheet

Figure 15.17

3 **Click the arrow on the Department button below the chart.**
The Department drop-down list displays.

4 **Deselect the Art check box, and click OK.**
The column depicting Art department data disappears from the chart.

continues ▶

To Create and Modify a Chart Based on Pivot Table Data (continued)

⑤ **Right-click a blank area within the chart, and select Chart Type from the shortcut menu.**
The Chart Type dialog box opens.

⑥ **Select Line in the Chart type list box, and click OK.**
A line chart replaces the column chart (see Figure 15.18).

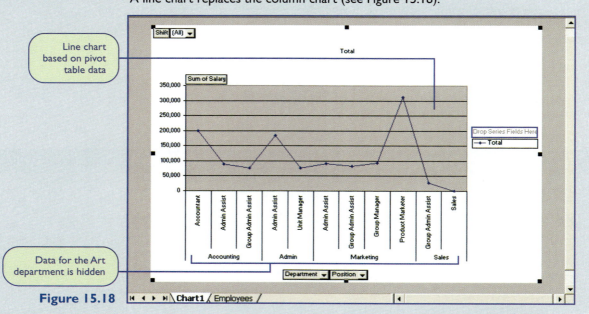

Line chart based on pivot table data

Data for the Art department is hidden

Figure 15.18

⑦ **Click outside the chart to deselect it, and save your changes to the *Salary Pivots* workbook.**
Keep the *Salary Pivots* workbook open for the next skill, or close the workbook and exit Excel.

In Depth:

How Changes in Pivot Table Data Affect a Related Chart
If a chart is based on pivot table data, which in turn summarizes worksheet data, you should understand the impact on the chart of a change in underlying worksheet data. Such a chart is only updated when its associated pivot table is refreshed.

Create a Static Chart Based on Pivot Table Data
You can convert an existing PivotChart report to a static chart—also known as a nonpivoting chart—by deleting the associated PivotTable report. You cannot change the charted data in a static chart.

Apply Predefined Formats to a Pivot Table

You can apply a variety of predefined formats to pivot tables. These formats not only improve the aesthetics of a table, they focus the reader's attention on different areas of the table. Some formats work better than others, depending on the layout and complexity of the pivot table. You should experiment with different types of formats to see which best presents your data.

In this skill, you apply a table format to a pivot table, switch to a report format, and then add a field to the table using the PivotTable and PivotChart Wizard Layout dialog box.

To Apply Predefined Formats to a Pivot Table

1 **Open the *Salary Pivots* workbook, if necessary, and select the Employees worksheet.**

2 **Scroll to display the entire pivot table in the range J10:L27, and click any cell within this range.**

The pivot table displays in the PivotTable Classic format—the default format automatically assigned to new pivot tables.

3 **Click the Format Report button on the PivotTable toolbar. If the PivotTable toolbar is not in view, right-click within the pivot table, and select Show PivotTable Toolbar.**

The AutoFormat dialog box opens (see Figure 15.19). Report formats—the indented formats—display first. An ***indented format*** supports the presentation of pivot table data in categories and subcategories. Each subcategory is offset to the right from its main category.

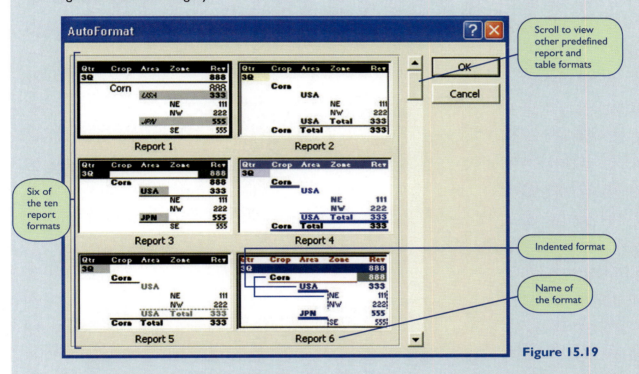

Figure 15.19

4 **Scroll down to view the remaining report formats and the table formats.**

Ten table formats—the nonindented formats—display after the report formats. A ***nonindented format*** does not offset subcategories within categories in a PivotTable report. The last two choices are PivotTable Classic (the default) and None.

5 **Double-click the Table 1 format (the description displays below the associated format). Click anywhere outside the table to deselect it, and scroll to view the entire pivot table.**

The pivot table displays in the Table 1 format (see Figure 15.20).

continues ▶

To Apply Predefined Formats to a Pivot Table (continued)

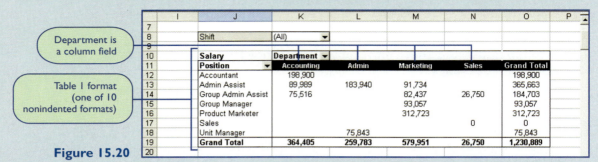

Department is a column field

Table 1 format (one of 10 nonindented formats)

Figure 15.20

6 Click a cell within the pivot table, and click the **Format Report** button on the **PivotTable** toolbar.

7 Double-click the **Report 1** format, and click anywhere outside the table to deselect it.

The pivot table displays in the Report 1 format (see Figure 15.21).

Report 1 format (one of 10 indented formats)

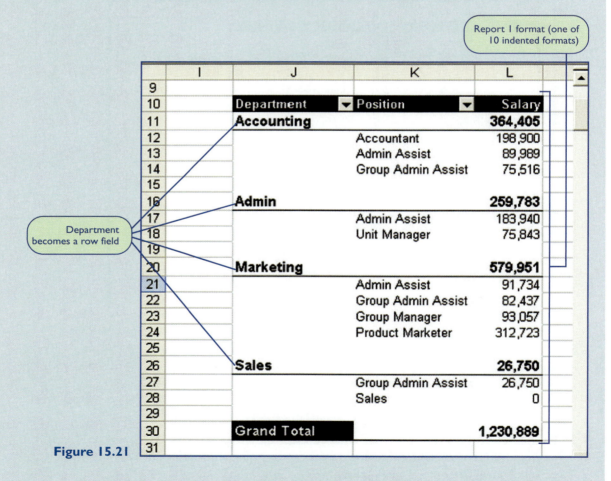

Department becomes a row field

Figure 15.21

8 Display the **Department** drop-down list (cell J10), and deselect the four check boxes: **Accounting, Admin, Marketing,** and **Sales.**

9 **Check the Engineering and R and D check boxes, and click OK.**
The pivot table continues to display the Report 1 format.

10 **Click within the pivot table; display the PivotTable drop-down list in the PivotTable toolbar, and select Wizard.**
The PivotTable and PivotChart Wizard–Step 3 of 3 dialog box opens.

11 **Click the Layout button in the lower-left corner of the dialog box.**
Now you add the Shift data as a row item in the PivotTable report.

12 **Drag the Shift field button to the Row area below the Position field.**
Three field buttons are now in the row area in the order—from top to bottom—Department, Position, and Shift (see Figure 15.22).

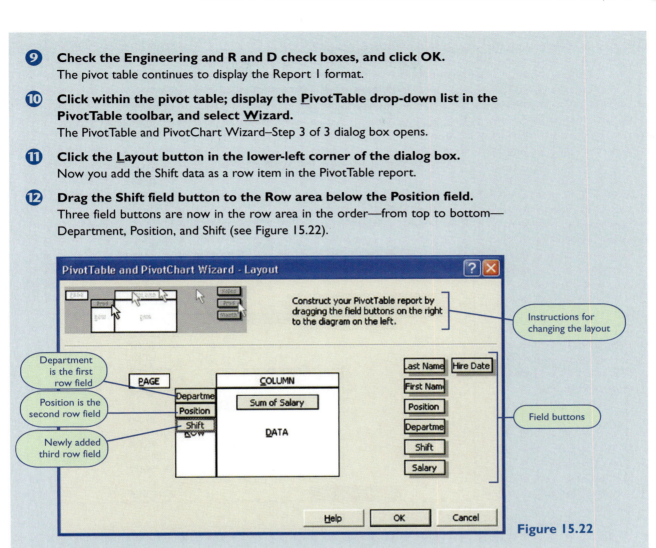

Figure 15.22

13 **Click OK and click Finish.**

14 **Close the PivotTable Field List box and the PivotTable toolbar.**
The report displays the layered (indented) layout shown in Figure 15.23.

continues ▶

To Apply Predefined Formats to a Pivot Table (continued)

First level by department

Second level by position within department

Third level by shift for each position

	I	J	K	L	M	N
10		Department ▼	Position ▼	Shift ▼	Salary	
11		**Engineering**			**1,235,842**	
12			Admin Assist		65,572	
13				1	19,747	
14				2	19,831	
15				3	25,994	
16			Engineer		871,714	
17				1	414,686	
18				2	207,631	
19				3	249,397	
20			Group Admin Assist		29,829	
21				1	29,829	
22			Technician		268,727	
23				1	26,978	
24				2	156,011	
25				3	85,738	
26						
27		**R and D**			**473,255**	
28			Chief Scientist		254,282	
29				1	97,757	
30				2	72,749	
31				3	83,776	
32			Engineer		97,963	
33				2	41,435	
34				3	56,528	
35			Group Admin Assist		86,317	
36				1	33,320	
37				2	27,344	
38				3	25,653	
39			Technician		34,693	
40				1	34,693	
41						
42		**Grand Total**			**1,709,097**	

Figure 15.23

15 **Save your changes to the *Salary Pivots* workbook and close the workbook.**
Continue with the next skill, or exit Excel.

In Depth:
Remove a Predefined Format

To remove a predefined format, and any other character and cell formats applied manually, display the gallery of predefined formats, and choose None. You might not get the results you want, however, because Excel simply removes effects, such as borders, shading, italics, and changes in font size. Because cell contents remain in place, the action does not move any fields, change display to indented or nonindented format, or remove blank lines inserted between items in rows.

You can use the Undo button to revert to the previous format immediately after changing it. You can also reproduce the original layout of a pivot table by saving the workbook before you apply a predefined format. If using the None option produces unwanted effects, you can close the workbook without saving your changes and then reopen the workbook as it was before you applied the predefined format.

*For immediate reinforcement, work Skill Drills 1 through 6
and Challenges 1 through 4.*

Skill 8.2: **Forecast Values with What-if Analysis**

Narrowly defined, *what-if analysis* is the process of changing the values in cells to see how those changes affect the outcome of one or more formulas. For example, you might set up a worksheet with separate cells for amount borrowed, loan term, annual interest rate, and a PMT function. Changing one or more values in the first three cells enables you to see the change in payment calculated by the PMT function.

In a broader sense, what-if analysis refers to a wide range of Excel tools that enable you to interpret data and communicate results. Interpreting current and prior data can be useful in forecasting values.

Charts provide an excellent means for interpreting data and communicating results. The graphical presentation of data makes it easy for users to see trends and make comparisons. In this skill, you create an XY scatter chart, and place a line in the chart that shows the trend over time.

Create an XY Scatter Chart

One of the most useful charts for statistical purposes is the *XY (Scatter) chart* that plots two groups of numbers as one series of xy coordinates. You can use a scatter chart to show a relationship, if any, between two variables, such as hours studied compared to grade earned (see Figure 15.24). The arrangement of data points in that chart seems to suggest that those who study more hours earn higher grades.

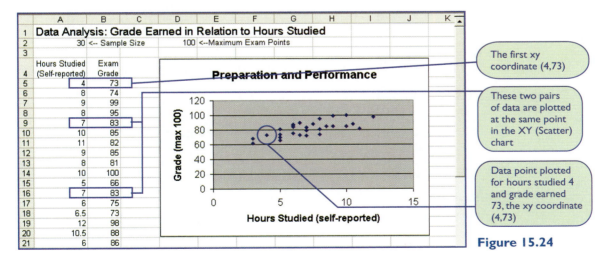

Figure 15.24

In this section, you create the chart shown in Figure 15.24. In the next section, you learn to interpret the results.

To Create an XY Scatter Chart

1 **Open the *MEE-S802* workbook and save it as** Trend.
The workbook includes one worksheet named *XY Scatter*.

2 **Select cells A4:B34.**

3 **Choose Insert, Chart, or click the Chart Wizard button on the toolbar. Check that Standard Types is the current tab in the Chart Type dialog box.**

4 **In the Chart type list box, select XY (Scatter); then check that the top option, *Scatter*, is the selected sub-type.**

5 **Click the Next button twice to display the Chart Options dialog box, and select the Titles tab.**

6 **Replace the default chart title *Exam Grade* with** Preparation and Performance, **and enter** Hours Studied (self-reported) **for the X-axis title and** Grade (max 100) **for the Y-axis title (see Figure 15.25).**

Preview of the XY scatter chart

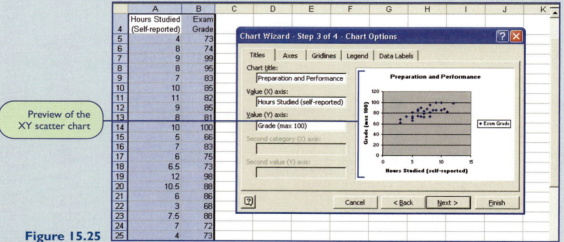

Figure 15.25

7 **Click the Legend tab and deselect the Show legend check box.**
Because only one series is plotted, there is no need for a legend.

8 **Click Finish; then move and size the chart as shown in Figure 15.24.**

9 **Save your changes to the *Trend* workbook.**
Keep the workbook open for the next skill, or close the workbook and exit Excel.

Fit a Trendline to an XY Scatter Chart

In the previous section, you created an XY (Scatter) chart to show the relationship between hours spent studying for an exam and the grade earned on the exam. The pattern of data points seemed to cluster along an invisible line slanting upward from left to right. This suggests that the data is *linear*—that is, the y value (grade earned) increases at a steady rate in proportion to the x value (hours spent studying). Rather than relying solely on visual inspection to draw conclusions about a relationship, you can fit a trendline to the data.

A *trendline* is a graphical representation of the direction or trend of data. Excel supports the creation of six types of trendlines, one of which is linear. A *linear trendline* is a best-fit straight line applied to simple linear data (see Figure 15.26).

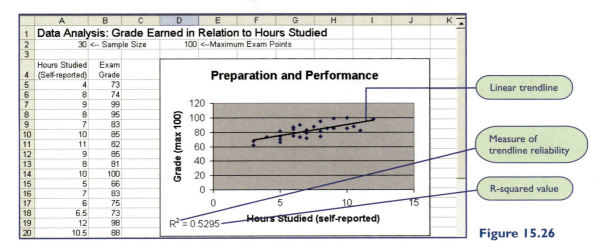

Figure 15.26

When you create a trendline, Excel computes an R-squared value. *R-squared* is a measure of how well the line fits the data points. If it is near 1.00, the fit is good; if it approaches 0, the fit is poor. In the following steps, you add the trendline shown in Figure 15.26.

To Fit a Trendline

1 **Open the *Trend* workbook, if necessary.**
The worksheet includes an XY (Scatter) chart in the range D4:J20.

2 **Click within a blank area of the chart to select it, and choose C̲hart, Add T̲rendline.**
The Add Trendline dialog box opens.

Alternate Way:
Using Advanced Search
You can also right-click any data point, and choose Add T̲rendline from the shortcut menu to display the dialog box.

3 **Select the Type tab, and make sure that L̲inear is the selected Trend/Regression type (see Figure 15.27).**

continues ▶

To Fit a Trendline (continued)

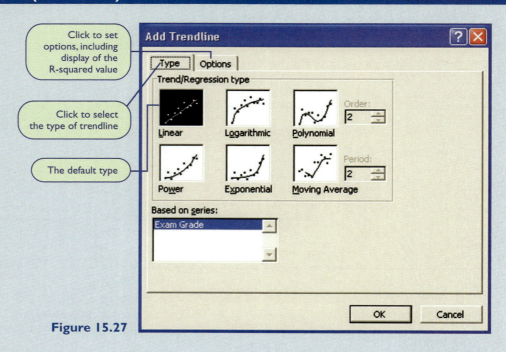

Figure 15.27

4 **Click the Options tab, and select the *Display R-squared value on chart* check box (see Figure 15.28).**

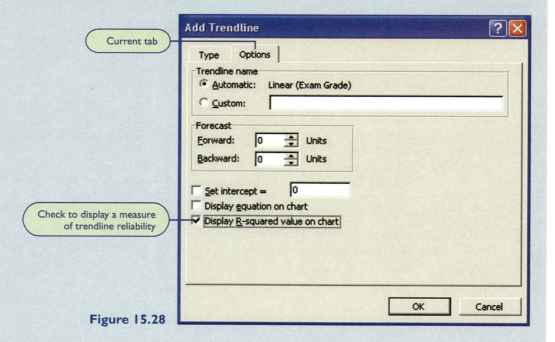

Figure 15.28

5 **Click OK.**

Excel inserts a trendline and displays an R-squared value of 0.5295 above the trendline (see Figure 15.29).

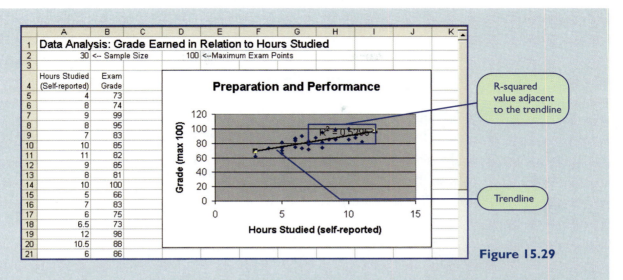

Figure 15.29

6 Click the R-squared box and drag it by its border to a spot on the chart where it is not on top of the data points, such as the lower-left corner of the chart area.

The scatter chart displays the trendline and R-squared value (refer to Figure 15.26). The R-squared value of 0.5295 is slightly closer to a good fit (1.0) than a poor fit (0). This indicates that hours studied bear some relationship to grade earned, but other factors must be influencing performance. You can draw general conclusions from the chart, but the degree of reliability is too low to predict a grade earned based on the number of hours studied.

7 Change the background color of the chart to white, and remove the gridlines.

8 Save your changes to the *Trend* workbook and close the workbook.
Continue with the next skill, or exit Excel.

In Depth:
Limits on Trendlines
You cannot apply trendlines to doughnut, pie, radar, or surface charts. You can apply the feature to other chart types—area, bar, bubble, column, line, stock, and XY (Scatter)—as long as you do not select a three-dimensional or stacked subtype.

For immediate reinforcement, work Challenge 5.

Skill 8.3: **Create and Display Scenarios**

A *scenario* is a set of saved values that you can recall for substitution in a worksheet. Creating scenarios is useful when you have several what-if assumptions and want to present the results of all of them. For example, you might want to summarize the effects of various interest rate and loan term combinations on the size of a loan payment.

In this skill, you analyze loan data. You create four scenarios—two loan periods (15- and 20-year) each at two interest rates (7 percent and 8 percent). You also generate a scenario summary.

To Create Scenarios

1 **Open the *MEE-S803* workbook and save it as** Scenarios.
The workbook includes the worksheet named Loan Terms.

2 **Choose Tools, Scenarios.**
The Scenario Manager dialog box opens (see Figure 15.30).

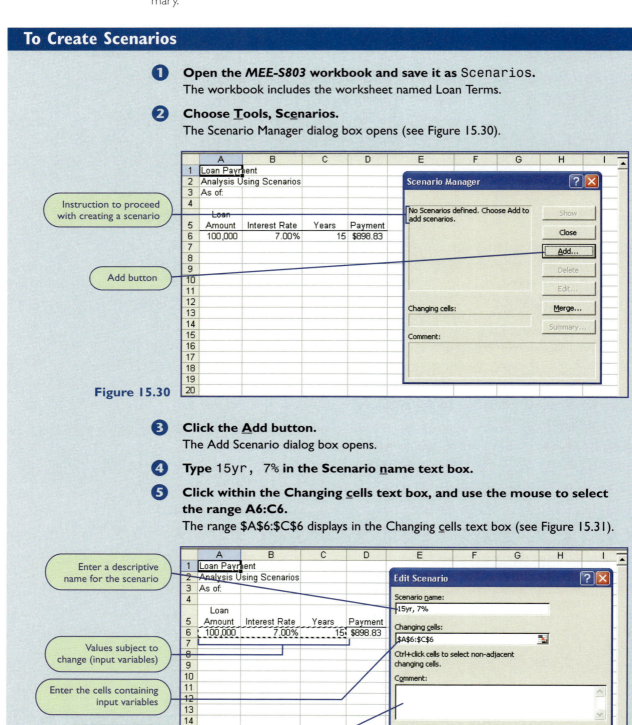

Figure 15.30

3 **Click the Add button.**
The Add Scenario dialog box opens.

4 **Type** 15yr, 7% **in the Scenario name text box.**

5 **Click within the Changing cells text box, and use the mouse to select the range A6:C6.**
The range $A$6:$C$6 displays in the Changing cells text box (see Figure 15.31).

Figure 15.31

Excel automatically inserts the name assigned to your computer system and the current date in the Comment text box. You can edit or delete the contents of the text box as desired.

⑥ Make sure that your specifications for scenario name and changing cells match those in Figure 15.31, and click OK.
The Scenario Values dialog box opens (see Figure 15.32).

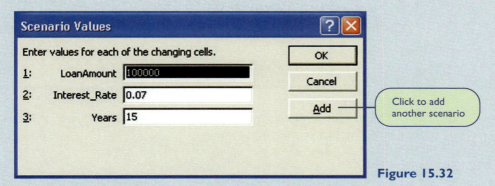

Figure 15.32

The current specifications for scenario name and changing cells define the first scenario. Now, you set up a second scenario.

⑦ Click the Add button.
The Add Scenario dialog box opens.

⑧ Type 15yr, 8% in the Scenario name text box, and make sure that A6:C6 displays in the Changing cells text box. Delete any existing comments, and click OK.
The Scenario Values dialog box opens.

⑨ Type 0.08 in the Interest_Rate text box.
You entered specifications for the second scenario. Now you set up a third scenario.

⑩ Click Add, type 20yr, 7% in the Scenario name text box, and make sure that A6:C6 displays in the Changing cells text box. Delete any existing comments, and click OK.

⑪ Make sure that 0.07 displays in the Interest_Rate text box of the Scenario Values dialog box, and type 20 in the Years box.
You entered specifications for the third scenario. Now you set up a fourth scenario.

⑫ Click Add, type 20yr, 8% in the Scenario Name text box, and make sure that A6:C6 displays in the Changing cells text box. Delete any existing comments, and click OK.

⑬ Type 0.08 in the Interest_Rate text box and type 20 in the Years text box.
You entered the scenario values for the fourth of four scenarios (see Figure 15.33).

continues ▶

To Create Scenarios (continued)

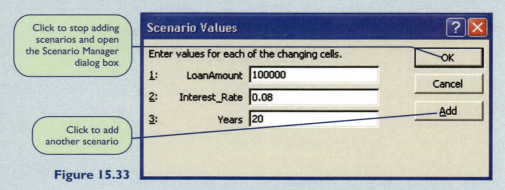

Click to stop adding scenarios and open the Scenario Manager dialog box

Click to add another scenario

Figure 15.33

14 **Click OK. (Make sure that you click OK instead of Add when you complete the last scenario.)**
The Scenario Manager dialog box opens and lists four scenarios.

15 **Make sure that the scenario *20yr, 8%* is selected, and click the Show button.**
The results of this scenario display on the worksheet—a payment of $836.44 in cell D6 (see Figure 15.34).

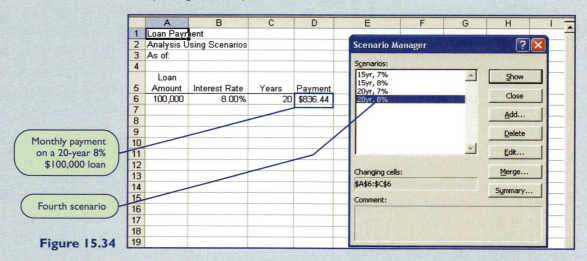

Monthly payment on a 20-year 8% $100,000 loan

Fourth scenario

Figure 15.34

16 **Click the scenario name** 15yr, **8%, and click the Show button.**
The results of this scenario display on the worksheet—a payment of $955.65 in cell D6. You can view the results of any scenario by selecting its name in the Scenario Manager dialog box and clicking Show. Now, you create a summary of the current scenarios.

17 **Click the Summary button in the Scenario Manager dialog box.**
The Scenario Summary dialog box opens.

18 **Select Scenario summary as the report type; enter** D6 **in the Result cells text box, and click OK.**
Excel inserts a new worksheet named Scenario Summary. Plus and minus outlining symbols enable you to expand and contract the level of detail about the four scenarios (see Figure 15.35).

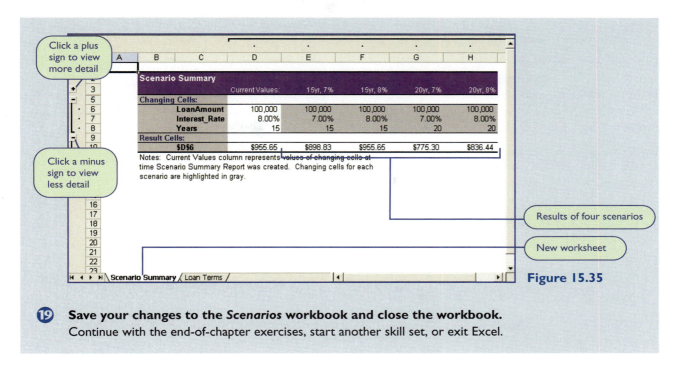

Figure 15.35

19 **Save your changes to the *Scenarios* workbook and close the workbook.**
Continue with the end-of-chapter exercises, start another skill set, or exit Excel.

In Depth:
Modify and Delete a Scenario
In this skill, you used the Add and Show buttons in the Scenario Manager dialog
box. You can also use this dialog box to edit or delete a scenario. Select the
name of the scenario, and click the Delete or Edit button as desired.

For immediate reinforcement, work Skill Drill 7.

Summary

You began this skill set with a glimpse of the power of pivot tables. By creating a variety of pivot
tables, you learned how to add and remove fields, hide and show fields, refresh a pivot table,
create a chart from pivot table data, and apply a predefined format to a pivot table.

You continued with two methods to analyze data. You created an XY scatter chart, and fitted a
trendline to the charted results. You also created four scenarios, displayed different scenarios in
a worksheet, and generated a summary of the scenarios on a new worksheet.

Skill Drill

Skill Drill exercises *reinforce* skills. Each skill reinforced is the same, or nearly the same, as a skill
presented in the skill set. Detailed instructions are provided in a step-by-step format.

Before beginning your Excel Expert Skill Set 8 Skill Drill exercises, complete the following steps:

I. Open the file named *MEE-S804*, and immediately save it as **MEE-S8drill**.

The workbook contains eight sheets: an overview and seven exercise sheets labeled
SD1 through SD7.

2. Click the Overview sheet to view the organization and content of the Skill Drill workbook for Excel Expert Skill Set 8.

Each exercise is independent of the others, so you may complete the exercises in any order. Be sure to save the workbook after completing each exercise. If you need a paper copy of one or more completed exercises, enter your name, centered in a header, before printing. Print options have already been set to print compressed to one page and to display the filename, sheet name, and current date in a footer.

Be sure to save your changes and close the workbook if you need more than one work session to complete the desired exercises. Continue working on *MEE-S8drill* instead of starting over in the original *MEE-S804* file.

1. Create a Pivot Table

You keep track of your contributions in an Excel list. Now you want to find out how much you gave to each agency during the year. To get the information you need by creating a pivot table, follow these steps:

1. Open the *MEE-S8drill* workbook, if necessary, and select the SD1 worksheet.

2. Click any cell in the list range A13:E42.

3. Choose Data, PivotTable and PivotChart Report, and click the Next button.

This accepts the default settings for data and type of report—a pivot table based on an Excel list.

4. Verify that the specified range is $A$13:$E$42, and click the Next button.

5. Click Existing worksheet; click cell G14, and click Finish.

Excel creates a shell for a pivot table on the worksheet.

6. Click *Agency* in the PivotTable Field List box, make sure that Row Area is selected in the lower-right corner of the PivotTable Field List box, and click the Add To button.

Excel adds the Agency field as a row in the pivot table.

7. Click *Declared Value* in the PivotTable Field List box. Display the Area drop-down list to the right of the Add To button, select Data Area, and click the Add To button.

A pivot table showing a summary of contributions by agency displays in the range G14:H22. The Grand Total of contributions is **4685**.

8. Click outside the table to deselect it, and save your changes to the *MEE-S8drill* workbook.

2. Expand a Pivot Table

You can expand a pivot table by adding one or more column, row, and data fields. Assume that you created a simple pivot table to sum contributions by agency. Now expand that table to show subtotals by agency based on whether a receipt was provided. To expand a pivot table, follow these steps:

1. Open the *MEE-S8drill* workbook, if necessary, and select the SD2 worksheet.

2. Click within the pivot table.

The PivotTable Field List box displays.

3. Click *Receipt* in the PivotTable Field List box.

4. Display the Area drop-down list to the right of the Add To button in the PivotTable Field List box; select Column Area, and click the Add To button.

Two new columns display between the Agency and Grand Total columns. The total of contributions for which no receipt was provided is **685**. Contributions confirmed by receipts total **4000**.

5. Save your changes to the *MEE-S8drill* workbook.

3. Display Counts in a Pivot Table

As you analyze your contributions during the past year, you want to know how many times you made a contribution to each agency. To display counts in a pivot table, follow these steps:

1. Open the *MEE-S8drill* workbook, if necessary, and select the SD3 worksheet.
2. Right-click any cell in the pivot table, and select Wizard from the shortcut menu.
3. Click the Layout button.
4. Drag the Declared Value field button onto the DATA area.

   Two *Sum of Declared Value* buttons display in the DATA area.
5. Double-click the upper of the two *Sum of Declared Value* buttons.

   The PivotTable Field dialog box opens.
6. Select Count and click OK.

   Count of Declared Value displays in the DATA area above *Sum of Declared Value*.
7. Click OK and then click Finish.

   The table expands to include counts of contributions. You made three contributions to the Salvation Army with a total declared value of **135**. You made seven contributions to Goodwill with a total declared value of **2660**.
8. Save your changes to the *MEE-S8drill* workbook.

4. Refresh a Pivot Table

After creating a pivot table, you discover an error in the amount of a contribution to the Girl Scouts. You need to edit the worksheet data and refresh the pivot table. To create a pivot table, change data, and refresh the pivot table, follow these steps:

1. Open the *MEE-S8drill* workbook, if necessary, and select the SD4 worksheet.
2. Click any cell in the list range A13:E42.
3. Choose Data, PivotTable and PivotChart Report, and click the Next button.
4. Verify that the specified range is $A$13:$E$42, and click the Next button.
5. Click Existing worksheet; click cell G14, and click Finish.
6. Click *Agency* in the PivotTable Field List box, make sure that Row Area is selected in the lower-right corner of the PivotTable Field List box, and click the Add To button.
7. Click *Declared Value* in the PivotTable Field List box. Display the Area drop-down list to the right of the Add To button; select Data Area, and click the Add To button.

   The total for contributions to the Girl Scouts (**100**) displays in cell H18 of the pivot table.
8. Click cell B16 in the list of contributions, and change *100* to **200**.

   Note that cell H18 still displays *100* as the total for contributions to the Girl Scouts organization.

9. Right-click any cell in the pivot table, and select Refresh Data from the shortcut menu. Alternatively, click within the pivot table, and then click the Refresh Data button on the PivotTable toolbar.

   Now cell H18 displays the correct amount—*200*.

10. Save your changes to the *MEE-S8drill* workbook.

5. Apply a Predefined Format to a Pivot Table

Your pivot table format is acceptable for your personal or inter-office use; however, to prepare your table for use with presentation graphics, you want to apply one of Excel's AutoFormats. To apply a predefined format to a pivot table, follow these steps:

1. Open the *MEE-S8drill* workbook, if necessary, and select the SD5 worksheet.

2. Set zoom level to 75%, and scroll to view the pivot table to the right of the data.

   The pivot table is wider than it is tall, displaying agencies in columns and categories in rows. Now apply a report format to produce an indented effect that is easier to view and print.

3. Click any cell in the pivot table, and click the Format Report button on the PivotTable toolbar. If the PivotTable toolbar is not in view, right-click within the pivot table and select Show PivotTable Toolbar.

4. Select Report 4; click OK, and click outside the pivot table to deselect it.

   Data display in three columns, with indenting that clearly defines the levels of detail in rows.

5. Save your changes to the *MEE-S8drill* workbook.

6. Create a Chart Based on Pivot Table Data

You think it might be easier to compare the amounts donated to various agencies if you see the data in a column chart. To create a chart based on data in a pivot table, follow these steps:

1. Open the *MEE-S8drill* workbook, if necessary, and select the SD6 worksheet.

2. Right-click any cell in the pivot table.

3. Choose PivotChart.

   A column chart displays on a new worksheet named Chart1. Much higher amounts were contributed in total to church and Goodwill than to the other four categories.

4. Display the Field drop-down list for Agency at the bottom of the chart.

5. Deselect the Church and Goodwill agencies, and click OK.

   Excel hides the data for the two agencies receiving the largest contributions. The Y-axis scale shifts to illustrate more clearly the differences between amounts contributed to the other four agencies.

6. Select the SD6 worksheet.

   Hiding data in a chart also hides the data in the associated pivot table.

7. Save your changes to the *MEE-S8drill* workbook.

7. Analyze Investment Options Using Scenarios

You are the financial consultant for a homeowners' association. The association collects a monthly maintenance fee from each homeowner and in return provides various services including painting, lawn care, and snow removal. The association has a surplus each month and needs to invest part of that in a fund that will provide money needed for replacing roofs on all of the homes. The association tentatively plans to invest between $900 and $1,200 a month for this purpose, but must have $300,000 at the end of 15 years when the first roofs are scheduled for replacement. Minimum-risk, fixed-interest investments are expected to yield between 4 and 8 percent.

You have already set up a FV (future value) function to calculate the future value of a 15-year investment plan. Now you want to create and save four scenarios for investing that would generate the minimum amount needed. Follow these steps:

1. Open the *MEE-S8drill* workbook, if necessary, and select the SD7 worksheet.

2. Choose Tools, Scenarios.

   The Scenario Manager dialog box opens.

3. Click the Add button.

   The Add Scenario dialog box opens.

4. Type **$900, 7.6%** in the Scenario name text box.

5. Click within the Changing cells text box, and use the mouse to select the range B6:D6.

   The range $B$6:$D$6 displays in the Changing cells text box.

6. Delete any existing comments, and click OK.

   The Scenario Values dialog box opens. The current specifications for scenario name and changing cells define the first scenario. Now, you set up a second scenario.

7. Click the Add button.

   The Add Scenario dialog box opens.

8. Type **$1000, 6.35%** in the Scenario name text box, and make sure that *B6:D6* displays in the Changing cells text box. Delete any existing comments, and click OK.

   The Scenario Values dialog box opens.

9. Type **1000** in the Monthly_Deposit text box, and type **0.0635** in the Interest_Rate text box.

   You entered specifications for the second scenario. Now you set up a third scenario.

10. Click Add; type **$1100, 5.25%** in the Scenario name text box, and make sure that *B6:D6* displays in the Changing cells text box. Delete any existing comments, and click OK.

11. Type **1100** in the Monthly_Deposit text box, and type **0.0525** in the Interest_Rate text box.

    You entered specifications for the third scenario. Now you set up a fourth scenario.

12. Click Add; type **$1200, 4.2%** in the Scenario Name text box, and make sure that *B6:D6* displays in the Changing cells text box. Delete any existing comments, and click OK.

13. Type **1200** in the Monthly_Deposit text box, and type **0.042** in the Interest_Rate text box.

    You entered the scenario values for the fourth of four scenarios.

14. Click OK. (Make sure that you click OK instead of Add when you complete the last scenario.)

    The Scenario Manager dialog box opens and lists four scenarios.

15. Make sure that the scenario *$1200, 4.2%* is selected, and click the Show button.

    The results of this scenario display on the worksheet—a future value of $300,187.36 in cell E6.

16. View the results of each scenario by selecting its name in the Scenario Manager dialog box and clicking <u>S</u>how.

Other scenarios produce futures values of $300,630.55, $299,656.15, and $300,236.60.

17. Click the S<u>u</u>mmary button in the Scenario Manager dialog box.

The Scenario Summary dialog box opens.

18. Select Scenario <u>s</u>ummary as the report type; enter **E6** in the <u>R</u>esult cells text box, and click OK.

Excel inserts a new worksheet named Scenario Summary. Plus and minus outlining symbols enable you to expand and contract the level of detail about the four scenarios.

19. Save your changes to the *MEE-S8drill* workbook.

Challenge

Challenge exercises expand on or are somewhat related to skills presented in the skill sets. Each exercise provides a brief narrative introduction, followed by instructions in a numbered-step format that are not as detailed as those in the Skill Drill section.

Before beginning your Excel Expert Skill Set 8 Challenge exercises, complete the following steps:

1. Open the file named *MEE-S805*, and immediately save it as **MEE-S8challenge**.

The workbook contains six sheets: an overview and five exercise sheets labeled CH1 through CH5.

2. Click the Overview sheet to view the organization and content of the Challenge workbook for Excel Expert Skill Set 8.

Each exercise is independent of the others, so you may complete the exercises in any order. Be sure to save the workbook after completing each exercise. If you need a paper copy of one or more completed exercises, enter your name, centered in a header, before printing. Other print options have already been set to print compressed to one page, and to display the filename, sheet name, and current date in a footer.

Be sure to save your changes and close the workbook if you need more than one work session to complete the desired exercises. Continue working on *MEE-S8challenge* instead of starting over in the original *MEE-S805* file.

1. Use MAX or MIN in a Pivot Table

As you analyze current residential real estate listings, you decide to display the highest selling price for a home in each area. Next, you want to switch the display to the lowest price at which someone could buy into each area. To do this, you can use Max and Min summary calculations respectively. To create summary data using Max or Min and format the results to Currency with zero decimal places, follow these steps:

1. Open the *MEE-S8challenge* workbook, if necessary, and select the CH1 worksheet.

2. Click any cell within the database, and activate the PivotTable and PivotChart Wizard.

3. Specify that you want to create a pivot table in the current worksheet starting in cell K5.

4. Lay out the pivot table to include Area as a row field and Price as the data item.

5. Specify Max as the summary calculation on price and generate the pivot table.

Max of Price displays in cell K5. The second column displays the highest asking price for a home in the corresponding area. For example, the highest asking price for a home in Champions Village is *156400*.

6. Change the summary calculation from Max to Min.

Excel replaces the prices in the second column with the lowest asking price for a home in each corresponding area. For example, the lowest asking price for a home in Champions Village is *102900*.

7. Double-click Min of Price in cell K5, and click the Number button in the PivotTable Field dialog box.

8. Specify Currency with $ sign and zero decimal places as the number format.

Numbers display with the specified format. The Grand Total (in this case, the minimum of the listed values) is *$74,500*.

9. Save your changes to the *MEE-S8challenge* workbook.

2. Modify a Pivot Table

You created a pivot table that displays the counts of homes in each area—the list of areas in one column, and the counts in the adjacent column to the right. Now you want to add counts for type of heat, and number of bedrooms within each type of heat. That way you can easily answer a question such as "How many of the three bedroom homes in Glenn Lakes have electric heat?" To change the number and location of fields in a pivot table, follow these steps:

1. Open the *MEE-S8challenge* workbook, if necessary, and select the CH2 worksheet.

2. Click within the pivot table (K5:L17). Use the PivotTable Field List box to add two fields to the Row area—first Heat; then Bed.

3. Click Area in the PivotTable Field List box, and add it to the Column area.

Adding the Area field to the Column area removes it from the Row area. Excel computes the requested counts in a pivot table that extends across many columns. Scroll to view counts at a detailed level. For example, there are five 3-bedroom homes with electric heat in the Glenn Lakes area.

4. Apply the Report 6 AutoFormat to the pivot table.

5. Deselect the pivot table, and save your changes to the *MEE-S8challenge* workbook.

3. Create a PivotChart Report Using a Wizard

You know how to create a chart from an existing pivot table. Now you want to create a chart and its associated pivot table at the same time. To create a PivotChart report, follow these steps:

1. Open the *MEE-S8challenge* workbook, if necessary, and select the CH3 worksheet.

2. Click any cell in the list range A5:I40, and activate the PivotTable and PivotChart Wizard.

3. Specify that you want to create a PivotChart report with the corresponding pivot table located at cell K5.

Excel creates a blank Chart1 worksheet.

4. Use the PivotTable Field List box in the Chart1 worksheet to set up two fields: *Price* in the Data area of the chart, and *Area* as the category axis.

5. Change *Sum of Price* to *Average of Price*.

6. Click the CH3 worksheet tab.

Excel automatically creates the pivot table on which the chart is based.

7. Format the numbers in the pivot table to show commas and zero decimal places, and deselect the pivot table.

8. Switch back to the Chart1 worksheet. Add titles and other documentation as appropriate, and change the display of Y-axis values to include commas and $ signs with zero decimal places.

9. Close the Chart toolbar; close the PivotTable Field List box, and save your changes to the *MEE-S8challenge* workbook.

4. Use Multiple Summary Calculations in a Pivot Table

For each area in the residential listings database, you want to know the number of homes available for sale and the average price of homes. To specify more than one summary calculation, follow these steps:

1. Open the *MEE-S8challenge* workbook, if necessary, and select the CH4 worksheet.
2. Click any cell within the database, and activate the PivotTable and PivotChart Wizard.
3. Specify that you want to create a pivot table in the current worksheet starting in cell K5, and access the PivotTable and PivotChart Wizard–Layout dialog box.
4. Lay out the pivot table to include Area as a ROW field and Price as a DATA item two times.
5. Specify Count as the summary calculation on the first Price data item, and specify Average as the summary calculation on the second Price data item.
6. Close or exit as needed to generate the pivot table.
7. Widen column K as desired, and change the format of numbers in the pivot table to show commas and zero decimal places.

   The table displays in PivotTable Classic format. Eight houses are listed for sale in Glenn Lakes, at an average price of *159,975*.
8. Apply a Table 6 predefined format.
9. If Excel does not retain number formatting within the pivot table when you apply the predefined format, change the display of numbers to show commas and zero decimal places.
10. Deselect the pivot table and save your changes to the *MEE-S8challenge* workbook.

5. Use a Trendline to Make a Prediction

You created a line chart showing total costs at various levels of production. You are negotiating with a customer who wants to buy 12,000 units. You decide to fit a linear trendline to the charted data and extend it forward four periods so that you can predict the cost to produce that number of units.

1. Open the *MEE-S8challenge* workbook, if necessary, and select the CH5 worksheet.
2. Select the charted data series, and fit a thin red linear trendline to it. (Display the R-squared value in the lower-right corner of the plot area.)
3. Right-click the linear trendline; select Format Trendline from the shortcut menu, and select the Options tab.
4. Type **4** in the Forecast Forward box, and close the dialog box.
5. Draw an arrow pointing to the point on the trendline that approximates the projected cost of producing 12,000 units.
6. Save your changes to the *MEE-S8challenge* workbook.

Workgroup
Collaboration

This skill set includes

Modify passwords, protections, and properties

- Protect cell contents and objects
- Unlock cells and objects
- Set a password for a worksheet range
- Set a password for a workbook
- View and set file properties

Create a shared workbook

Track, accept, and reject changes to a workbook

Merge workbooks

Skill Set Overview

This skill set encompasses four topic areas. You begin by exploring a variety of features that you can use to protect your work. You apply settings that enable users of your worksheets to enter or edit data in some cells but not others, and you set a password to view a worksheet range or open a workbook. You also view and set file properties.

The remaining topics focus on working with others to create and modify workbooks. You create a shared workbook, so that you can track changes by multiple users to that workbook, and accept or reject those changes. You also learn to merge revisions made on multiple copies of a workbook.

Skill 9.1: Modify Passwords, Protections, and Properties

A *password* is a collection of up to 255 case-sensitive characters that must be known to use a password-protected range, worksheet, or workbook. It can contain any combination of letters, numbers, spaces, and symbols. Make sure that you choose a password you can remember, because you cannot access a password-protected element without specifying it.

Excel provides another protection feature at the cell level. *Cell protection* enables you to allow changes in content or formatting for specified cells and prevent such changes in the remaining cells.

Each Excel workbook has file properties. The term *file property* describes a characteristic of a file, such as file type, file size, storage location, author's name, and date last revised.

In this skill, you set cell protection using a two-step process—unlocking the cells that users can change, and applying protection to remaining cells. You then set a password for a protected worksheet range and set a password for a workbook. You also view file properties and modify one of them.

Protect Cell Contents and Objects

If you protect the contents of a worksheet, you cannot make changes to cell contents or objects unless you unlock them before activating protection. Excel also prevents viewing hidden rows or columns and making changes to items on chart sheets. You cannot add or edit comments, move or size objects, or make any changes in formatting.

Protection is an option on the <u>T</u>ools menu. In the following steps, you protect an entire worksheet and then attempt to modify the worksheet—changing cell contents, moving an object, applying a different color, and selecting another font style—all without success. You then remove the worksheet protection. In the next skill, you learn to unlock selected cells and objects, and protect remaining elements.

To Protect Cell Contents and Objects

1 **Open the *MEE-S901* workbook and save it as** Protection.
The file contains a single worksheet named *Copy Bids*.

2 **Select <u>T</u>ools, <u>P</u>rotection, <u>P</u>rotect Sheet.**
The Protect Sheet dialog box opens (see Figure 16.1).

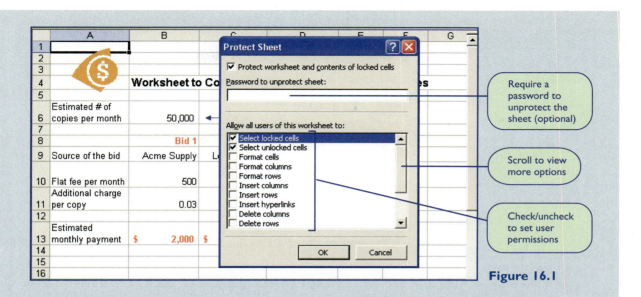

Figure 16.1

Require a password to unprotect the sheet (optional)

Scroll to view more options

Check/uncheck to set user permissions

❸ **Click OK.**

All worksheet elements are protected.

❹ **Click cell B6 and start to type 40000.**

As soon as you type the 4, a message states that the cell is protected (see Figure 16.2).

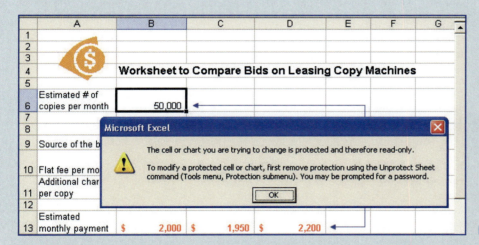

Figure 16.2

❺ **Click OK to close the message, and click within the $ sign image at the upper-left corner of the worksheet.**

Sizing handles do not appear. You cannot select the object because it is protected.

❻ **Select the range B8:D8 and display the Font Color drop-down list in the toolbar.**

A grid of sample squares displays without any colors, indicating that you cannot apply a color change (see Figure 16.3).

continues ▶

To Protect Cell Contents and Objects (continued)

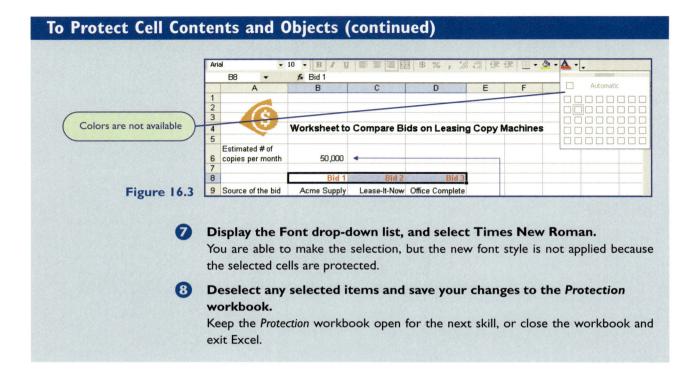

Figure 16.3

Colors are not available

7 **Display the Font drop-down list, and select Times New Roman.**
You are able to make the selection, but the new font style is not applied because the selected cells are protected.

8 **Deselect any selected items and save your changes to the *Protection* workbook.**
Keep the *Protection* workbook open for the next skill, or close the workbook and exit Excel.

Unlock Cells and Objects

In the previous skill, you protected every worksheet element. In some situations, however, you might need to unlock cells or objects that you are likely to change. As a general guideline, all formulas, and most labels and objects, should remain locked. Cells containing numbers are generally unlocked.

When you **unlock** a cell or object, you remove the default locked setting that prevents changes when worksheet protection is active. Unlocking a cell requires a four-step process: select the cell(s); open the Format Cells dialog box; select the Protection tab, and clear the Locked check box. The steps to unlock an object are similar; only the dialog box varies.

In the following steps, you disable worksheet protection, unlock several cells and an object, and restore worksheet protection.

To Unlock Cells and Objects

1 **Open the *Protection* workbook, if necessary, and select Tools, Protection, Unprotect Sheet.**
Worksheet protection is disabled. Next, you unlock the cells you want to be able to change—estimated # of copies in cell B6, and vendor data in the range B9:D11.

2 **Click cell B6; press and hold down Ctrl; select the range B9:D11, and release Ctrl.**

3 **Select Format, Cells; then select the Protection tab (see Figure 16.4).**

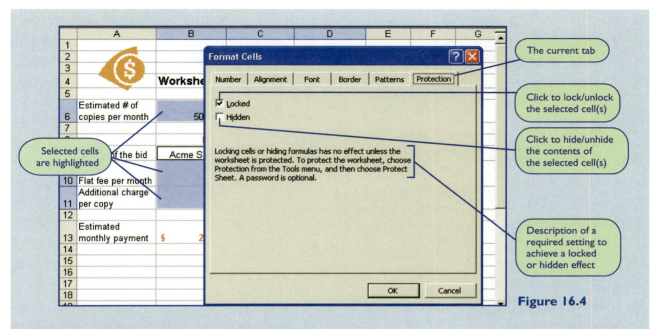

Figure 16.4

④ **Clear the Locked check box, and click OK.**

Cells B6 and B9 through D11 are unlocked; they remain selected.

⑤ **Apply a Tan fill color to the selected cells.**

Shading unlocked cells before protecting a worksheet provides a visual means of identifying cells that users can change. Next, you unlock the $ sign object just below cell A1.

⑥ **Right-click the $ sign object; select Format Picture from the shortcut menu, and select the Protection tab in the Format Picture dialog box (see Figure 16.5).**

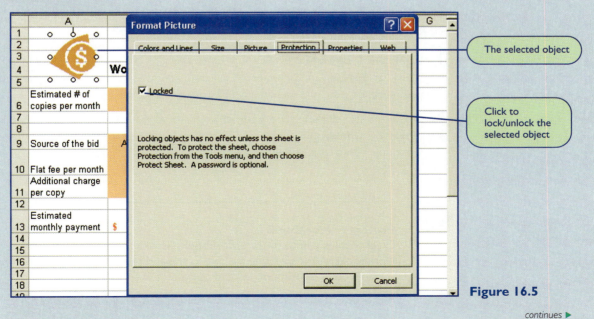

Figure 16.5

continues ▶

To Unlock Cells and Objects (continued)

7 **Clear the Locked check box; then click OK, and click outside the object to deselect it.**
The $ sign object is unlocked. Next, you activate worksheet protection, and try again to make changes.

8 **Select Tools, Protection, Protect Sheet; then leave the *Password to unprotect sheet* text box blank, and click OK.**
Worksheet protection is active for all locked cells.

9 **Enter 40000 in cell B6.**
Excel accepts the change because you unlocked cell B6 before enabling worksheet protection (see Figure 16.6).

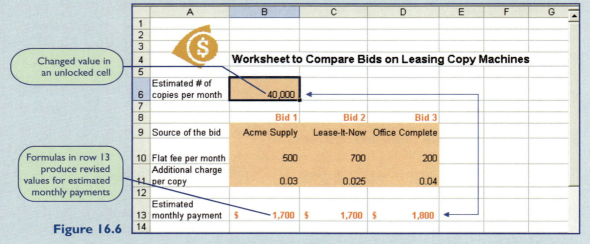

> Changed value in an unlocked cell

> Formulas in row 13 produce revised values for estimated monthly payments

Figure 16.6

10 **Press Tab⇆ repeatedly.**
You can press Tab⇆ to move the cell pointer from one unlocked cell to the next in a protected worksheet.

11 **Click the $ sign object.**
Sizing handles indicate the object is selected. You can work with the object because you unlocked it before activating worksheet protection.

12 **Deselect the object; save your changes to the *Protection* workbook, and close the workbook.**
Continue with the next skill, or exit Excel.

In Depth:
Protect a Workbook
Excel enables you to protect workbooks as well as worksheets within workbooks. After selecting the two-command sequence Tools, Protection, select Protect Workbook instead of Protect Sheet.

Protection at this level applies to structure and windows. If you protect structure, users cannot view hidden worksheets. They also cannot insert, delete, move, hide, or rename worksheets. If you protect a workbook's windows, users cannot move, resize, hide, unhide, or close windows.

Set a Password for a Worksheet Range

You can require a password to open or edit a workbook, access a worksheet, or make changes to a range within a worksheet. In the following steps, you password-protect a range—the vendor-specific data in a worksheet that compares bids on providing copier service.

To Set a Password for a Worksheet Range

1 **Open the *MEE-S902* file and save it as** Range Password.
The *Range Password* file consists of a single worksheet named Copy Bids. In this worksheet, the cells containing vendor data in the range B9:D11 are locked. Cell B6 is the only unlocked cell, and worksheet protection is turned on.

2 **Select <u>T</u>ools, <u>P</u>rotection, Un<u>p</u>rotect Sheet.**
Worksheet protection is disabled. Next, you select the range of locked cells that you want to be accessible if a password is supplied.

3 **Select the range B9:D11.**
The range containing vendor-specific data is selected.

4 **Select <u>T</u>ools, <u>P</u>rotection, <u>A</u>llow Users to Edit Ranges.**
The Allow Users to Edit Ranges dialog box opens (see Figure 16.7).

> Click to specify a range that can be unlocked by using a password

> The selected range B9:D11

Figure 16.7

5 **Click the <u>N</u>ew button in the dialog box.**
The New Range dialog box opens.

6 **Type** Bids **in the <u>T</u>itle text box, and type** 123change **in the Range password text box.**
Excel displays an asterisk for each character in the password you specify (see Figure 16.8).

continues ▶

To Set a Password for a Worksheet Range (continued)

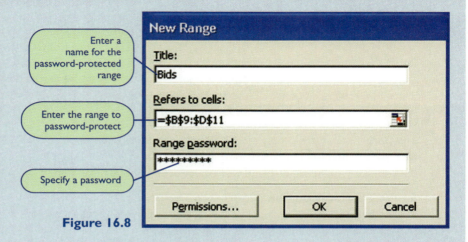

Enter a name for the password-protected range

Enter the range to password-protect

Specify a password

Figure 16.8

7 **Click OK.**
The Confirm Password dialog box opens.

8 **Type** 123change **in the Reenter password to proceed text box (see Figure 16.9).**

Type the password again

Figure 16.9

9 **Click OK.**
The Allow Users to Edit Ranges dialog box displays the newly defined range (see Figure 16.10). Next, you restore worksheet protection from within the current dialog box.

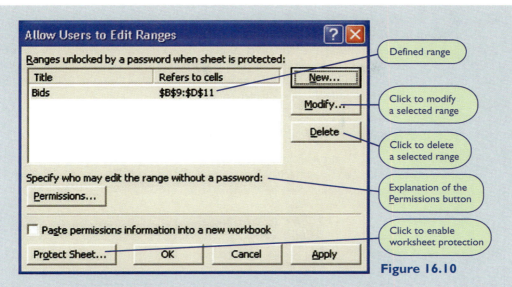

Figure 16.10

10 **Click the Protect Sheet button in the lower-left corner of the dialog box.**
The Protect Sheet dialog box opens.

11 **Click OK to restore protection without setting a password at the worksheet level.**
Worksheet protection is enabled.

12 **Click cell B10 and start to type** 600.
The Unlock Range dialog box opens (see Figure 16.11). You must enter a password, or you cannot continue with the edit.

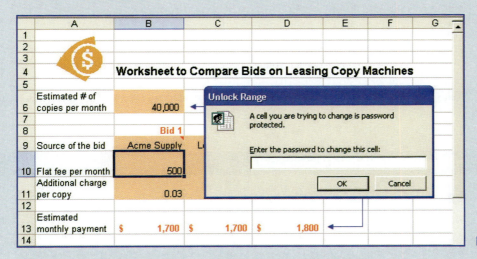

Figure 16.11

13 **Type** 123change **in the _Enter the password to change this cell_ text box, and click OK.**

14 **Type** 600 **in cell B10, and press** ⏎Enter.
Excel accepts the change because you supplied the correct password. The revised value for the Bid 1 estimated monthly payment is *$1,800.*

15 **Save and close the _Range Password_ workbook.**
Continue with the next skill, or exit Excel.

> ### *In Depth:*
> **Giving Specific Users Access to Protected Cells**
> If you are using the Windows 2000 (or later) operating system, you can enable specific users to edit locked cells in a protected worksheet without specifying a password. Use the Permissions button in the Allow Users to Edit Ranges dialog box to identify the users (refer to Figure 16.10).

Set a Password for a Workbook

Excel supports password protection of a workbook at two levels: opening a workbook, and editing a workbook (see Figure 16.12). Each is independent of the other; you can set either one or both. Password protection is set up during execution of a Save As command.

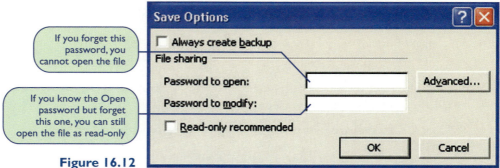

Figure 16.12

If a password is required to open a workbook but you don't know the password, you cannot access the file. If you can access a password-protected workbook but a password is required to modify it, you can at least open the file as read-only if you don't know the modify password. A *read-only* file can be viewed but not changed if you save it under the same name. You can, however, modify it if you save it under a different name or save it to a different location.

In the following steps, you set up one password to open a workbook and another to modify that workbook. Because you are just learning about this feature, you use a different file from the ones you used in previous skills. That way, if you inadvertently set up a password to open a file that doesn't match the one in the instructions, and you can't remember what you typed, you can start the skill over at Step 1.

To Set a Password for a Workbook

1 **Open the *MEE-S903* file and immediately save it as** File Password.
The *File Password* workbook consists of a single worksheet named Copy Bids. Cell B6 and cells in the range B9:D11 are unlocked. Worksheet protection is turned on.

2 **Choose File, Save As, and click the small arrow to the right of Tools near the upper-right corner of the Save As dialog box.**
The Tools drop-down list displays.

3 **Select General Options.**
The Save Options dialog box opens (refer to Figure 16.12).

4   **Type** `abc123` **in the Password to o̲pen text box.**
Be sure to type in the first text box, and type the letters in the password in lower-case.

5   **Type** `xyz999` **in the Password to m̲odify text box.**
Be sure to type in the second text box, and type the letters in the password in low-ercase.

6   **Click OK.**
The Confirm Password dialog box opens, with a message to reenter the password to proceed (which is the same as the password to open).

7   **Type** `abc123` **in the text box, and click OK.**
The Confirm Password dialog box reopens again, with a message telling you to reenter the password to modify.

8   **Type** `xyz999` **in the text box, and click OK.**
The Save As dialog box reopens.

9   **Click S̲ave in the Save As dialog box.**
A warning message displays, asking whether you want to replace the existing file.

10   **Click Yes and then close the workbook.**
The workbook is saved with password protection at two levels. Next, you verify that the passwords work as intended.

11   **Open the *File Password* workbook.**
The Password dialog box opens with a message that the file is protected (see Figure 16.13).

Figure 16.13

12   **Type** `abc123` **in the P̲assword text box, and click OK.**
The Password dialog box opens again with a message telling you to enter the pass-word for write access or open the file as read-only (see Figure 16.14). Write access means you can modify a file.

The name assigned to the user's system displays here

Figure 16.14

continues ▶

To Set a Password for a Workbook (continued)

 If you have problems...

If you do not enter the correct password to open the file, which should be abc123, Excel displays a message that the password supplied is not correct. Repeat the process to open the password-protected file and supply the correct password, including lowercase letters. If you still have problems, start the skill over.

13 **Type** xyz999 **as the password for write access, and click OK.**
The Copy Bids worksheet in the *File Password* workbook displays onscreen.

 If you have problems...

If you enter text other than xyz999, Excel displays a message that the password supplied is not correct. If you cannot remember the modify password, you can open the file as read-only and make changes as long as you save it under another name.

14 **Close the *File Password* workbook.**
Continue with the next skill, or exit Excel.

 In Depth:
Change or Remove a Password
To change or remove a password, start the process to set up a password—that is, select Save As from the File menu, display the Tools drop-down list, and select General Options. The Save Options dialog box opens, and you see asterisks representing the current passwords. To change a password, select (highlight) the asterisks for the password you want to change, and type a new password. To remove a password, select the asterisks for the password you want to remove, and press Del.

View and Set File Properties

A file property describes a characteristic of a file, such as file type, file size, storage location, author's name, and date last revised. You can view the properties of the active workbook by selecting File, Properties and choosing one of five tabs in the Properties dialog box: General, Summary, Statistics, Contents, and Custom. You can also view the properties of any Microsoft Excel or Office file through the Open dialog box.

In the following steps, you display the Properties dialog box, view assorted information, and specify your name as the author of the current workbook.

To View and Set File Properties

1 **Open the *MEE-S901* workbook and save it as** File Property.

2 **Select File, Properties; then click the General tab in the Properties dialog box.**
Excel displays information about the current workbook's name, type, location, and size. You also see the equivalent MS-DOS name (restricted to eight characters and a three-character extension) and the dates created, modified, and accessed.

3 **Select the Summary tab, and delete any existing text (see Figure 16.15).**

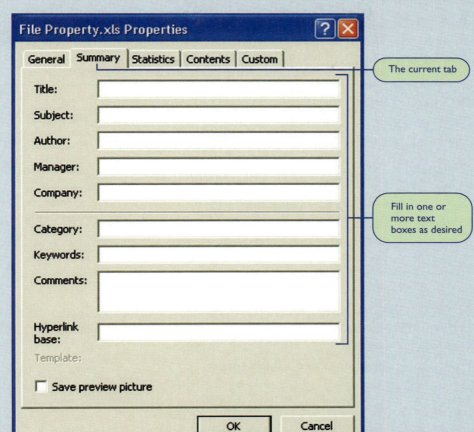

File Property.xls Properties   ? ✕

| General | Summary | Statistics | Contents | Custom |

The current tab

Title:

Subject:

Author:

Manager:

Company:

Fill in one or more text boxes as desired

Category:

Keywords:

Comments:

Hyperlink base:

Template:

☐ Save preview picture

OK   Cancel

Figure 16.15

4 **Click within the Author text box, and type your name.**

5 **Click the Statistics tab.**
Excel displays information about key dates and editing time.

6 **Click the Contents tab.**
Excel lists the worksheets and named ranges in the workbook.

7 **Click the Custom tab.**
You can use the Custom tab to display information about the current file that you do not want to enter in the file itself. The items you specify—such as Checked by, Date completed, Disposition, Received from, or Source—display in the Properties area when the Custom tab is active.

8 **Click OK.**
The Properties dialog box closes, and revised settings are in effect. If you click the Cancel button or the dialog box's Close button instead of OK, any revisions to settings are not saved.

9 **Save and close the *File Property* workbook.**
Continue with the next skill or exit Excel.

In Depth:
View the Properties of Any Workbook
In this skill, you viewed the properties of the active workbook. You can also view the properties of any workbook from the Open dialog box. Select <u>O</u>pen from the <u>F</u>ile menu; display the folder containing the file you want to review, and click the filename to select it (but do not click the Open button yet). Click the Too<u>l</u>s button in the Open dialog box menu bar and select <u>P</u>roperties.

For immediate reinforcement, work Skill Drills 1 through 5 and Challenges 1, 2, 3.

Skill 9.2: **Create a Shared Workbook**

In a work environment, it is common practice for two or more people to collaborate on developing or editing a workbook. Each user needs to know what changes the others have made.

A *shared workbook* enables one or more users to make and track changes in the same workbook. When the setting to track changes is active, the word *[Shared]* displays to the right of the filename in the title bar. While in shared mode, certain operations are not available. For example, you cannot delete a worksheet while a workbook is shared.

Change tracking records row and column insertions and deletions, moves and copies, and changes to cell contents. The feature does not track formatting changes to cells or data, hiding or unhiding rows or columns, and adding or changing comments.

To explore tracking changes in a shared workbook, you use a worksheet for ordering office supplies. Imagine that you want to make the worksheet available to many users on a network. In this skill, you create a shared workbook by turning on the track changes feature. In the next skill, you track changes made by different users and accept or reject those changes.

To Save a Workbook as a Shared Workbook

1 **Open the *MEE-S904* workbook, and save it as** Track Changes.
The workbook includes one worksheet named Tracking.

2 **Choose <u>T</u>ools, <u>T</u>rack Changes, <u>H</u>ighlight Changes.**
The Highlight Changes dialog box opens (see Figure 16.16).

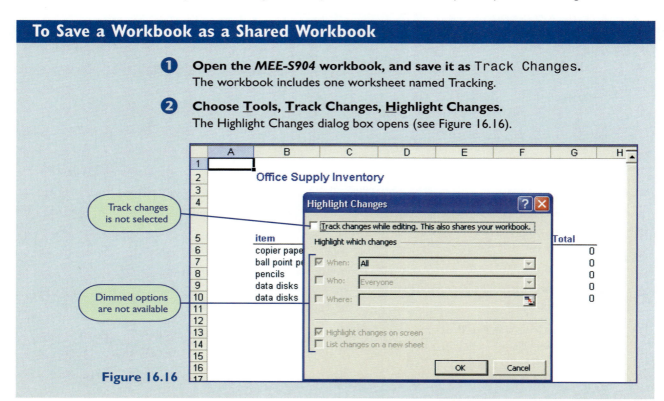

Figure 16.16

3 **Click the _Track changes while editing_ check box at the top of the dialog box.**

Options to select the changes to track are now available.

4 **Check the When check box and select All from the drop-down list, if necessary.**

The _When_ check box determines the extent of tracking changes. Selecting All (the default) causes all changes to be tracked. Other options include _Since I last saved_, _Not yet reviewed_, and _Since date_. If you select the last option, a date displays in the When text box. You can change the date, if necessary.

5 **Check the Who check box; then select Everyone from the drop-down list.**

Options on the Who drop-down list include _Everyone_ and _Everyone but Me_. You might use the latter if you are a supervisor or want to monitor only changes other people in your workgroup make to the workbook.

6 **Leave the Where check box unchecked.**

If you check Where, you can select specific cells to be monitored.

7 **Check the _Highlight changes on screen_ check box, if necessary.**

Specifications to track changes are complete (see Figure 16.17). When the _Highlight changes on screen_ check box is selected, Excel creates a cell comment for every cell that is changed.

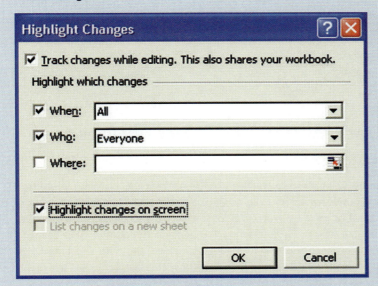

Figure 16.17

8 **Click OK. If a message box appears asking whether you want to continue the save operation, click OK.**

The word _[Shared]_ displays in the title bar (see Figure 16.18). Tracking changes automatically shares the workbook even though you might be the only one making changes.

continues ▶

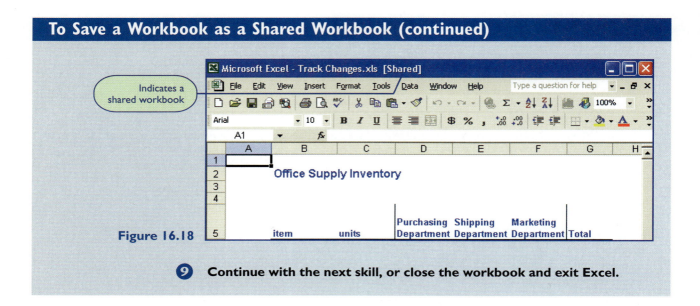

To Save a Workbook as a Shared Workbook (continued)

Indicates a shared workbook

Figure 16.18

Microsoft Excel - Track Changes.xls [Shared]

Office Supply Inventory

| item | units | Purchasing Department | Shipping Department | Marketing Department | Total |

⑨ Continue with the next skill, or close the workbook and exit Excel.

In Depth:
Remove a Workbook from Shared Use

To remove a workbook from shared use, choose Tools, Share Workbook, and then select the Editing tab. Make sure that you are the only person listed in the *Who has this workbook open now* section. Remove the check mark from the *Allow changes by more than one user at the same time* check box, and click OK. Click Yes in response to the prompt about effects on other users.

For immediate reinforcement, work Skill Drill 6.

Skill 9.3: Track, Accept, and Reject Changes to a Workbook

Excel provides three ways to view tracked changes—onscreen highlighting, a History worksheet, and a dialog box in which you can accept or reject each change. You are using the first method when you view a shared workbook onscreen. Excel outlines changes with a different color for each user, and displays a note when you position the pointer on a changed cell. The note includes the name of the user who made the change, the date and time of the change, and a description of the change.

A *History worksheet* is a separate worksheet that provides detailed information about changes —one change per row. You can print the list of changes. You can also analyze changes by filtering records in the list.

You can also view each change in sequence in a dialog box that enables you to accept or reject each change. When multiple users revise a tracked document, generally one person makes the final decision about whether to keep or discard the suggested changes. It is a good idea to accept or reject changes on a regular basis to keep the display of changes made to other revisions at a minimum.

In this skill, you use the first and third methods to view tracked changes as you complete two sets of hands-on steps. In the first set, you open a shared workbook, make a change in the worksheet that lists inventory orders, and view information about the change onscreen. You then make a second change, and use the Accept or Reject Changes dialog box to accept one change and reject another. You are the only one making changes, but your actions enable you to learn the process to accept and reject changes.

In the second set of hands-on steps, you simulate changes made by two users—the Purchasing department and the Shipping department—in the same workbook. You view the changes and end the simulation of multiple users.

To Track Changes and Accept or Reject Changes

1 **Open the *Track Changes* workbook, if necessary.**
The word *[Shared]* displays after the filename in the title bar.

2 **Enter the number 7 in cell D7.**
Excel automatically displays a border around the cell and inserts a comment, as evidenced by the small triangular comment indicator in the upper-left corner of the cell.

 ### If you have problems...
If you closed and reopened the file prior to starting these hands-on steps, the comment indicator does not appear. To display the indicator, choose <u>T</u>ools, <u>T</u>rack changes, <u>H</u>ighlight Changes; then deselect the Whe<u>n</u> check box if necessary, and click OK.

3 **Position the pointer on cell D7.**
The attached comment displays. It identifies the user—by name or computer number—who made the change, specifies the date and time the change was made, and provides a description of the change (see the sample in Figure 16.19).

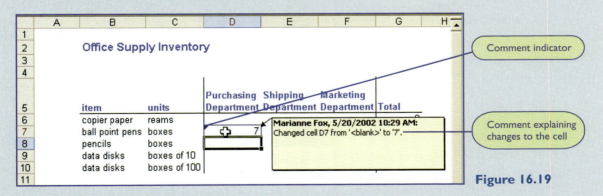

Comment indicator

Comment explaining changes to the cell

Figure 16.19

4 **Enter the number 5 in cell D9.**

5 **Choose <u>T</u>ools, <u>T</u>rack Changes, <u>A</u>ccept or Reject Changes.**
A message box displays with the following text: *This action will now save the workbook. Do you want to continue?*

6 **Click OK.**
The *Select Changes to Accept or Reject* dialog box opens (see Figure 16.20).

continues ▶

To Track Changes and Accept or Reject Changes (continued)

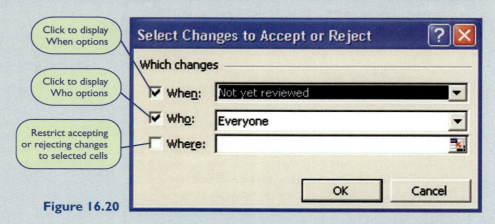

Click to display When options

Click to display Who options

Restrict accepting or rejecting changes to selected cells

Figure 16.20

7 If necessary, check the We**n** box, and select *Not yet reviewed* from the drop-down list.

8 If necessary, check the Wh**o** box, and select Everyone from the drop-down list.

9 Click OK.
The Accept or Reject Changes dialog box opens (see the sample in Figure 16.21).

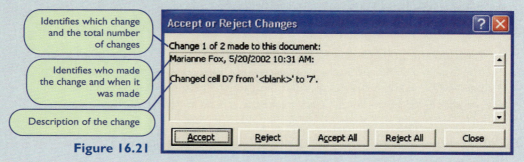

Identifies which change and the total number of changes

Identifies who made the change and when it was made

Description of the change

Figure 16.21

10 Click the **A**ccept button to accept the first change.
Information about the second change displays in the Accept or Reject Changes dialog box (see Figure 16.22).

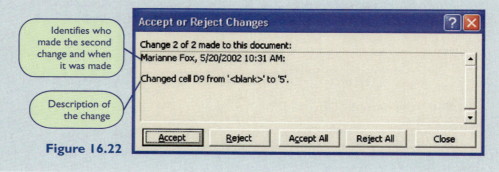

Identifies who made the second change and when it was made

Description of the change

Figure 16.22

⑪ **Click the Reject button to reject the second change.**
Because you rejected the change, the contents of cell D9 revert to the value that was previously in the cell. The Accept or Reject Changes dialog box closes automatically after the last change is accepted or rejected.

⑫ **Save your changes to the *Track Changes* workbook.**
Continue with the next skill, or close the workbook and exit Excel.

In the previous set of steps, you learned the process to accept or reject changes by evaluating changes made by a single user in one workbook. In the next set of steps, you simulate changes made by two users—the Purchasing department and the Shipping department—in the same workbook. If you are working in a computer lab or networked environment, you might not be able to change the user name on your system and complete this skill. Refer to instructions within the steps if you encounter this problem.

To Edit a Shared Workbook

① **Open the *Track Changes* workbook, if necessary.**
The word *[Shared]* displays after the filename in the title bar. Now you create the simulation by revising the User name on the General tab in the Options dialog box.

 ### If you have problems...
If the workbook is not currently shared, choose Share Workbook on the Tools menu, click the Editing tab, and check that the *Allow changes by more than one user at the same time* check box is selected.

② **Choose Tools, Options.**

③ **Click the General tab, and make note of the current entry in the User name text box at the bottom of the Options dialog box.**
Make sure that you remember this original user name. You restore the original user name near the end of this lesson.

④ **Change the User name to Purchasing, and click OK.**

 ### If you have problems...
If you are working in a computer lab or networked environment, you might not be able to change the user name on your system and complete this skill. Instead, read the remaining steps and the *In Depth* section at the end of this skill to gain an understanding of related processes.

⑤ **Enter the number 50 in cell D6, and position the pointer on cell D6.**
The comment indicates that the change was made by *Purchasing* (see Figure 16.23). The borders around cells D6 and D7 are different colors, indicating that different users made the changes.

continues ▶

To Edit a Shared Workbook (continued)

Information about the second change

Color differences indicate different users made changes

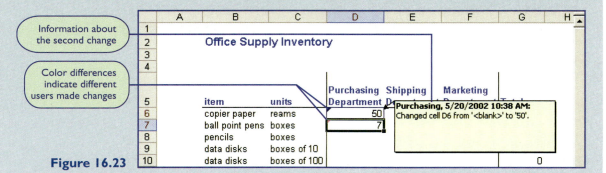

Figure 16.23

6 Choose **Tools, Options; click the General tab; change the User name to** `Shipping`, **and click OK.**

7 Enter the number `10` in cell E7, and position the pointer on cell E7.
The comment indicates that *Shipping* made the change (see Figure 16.24).

Information about the third change

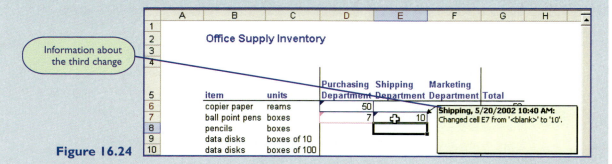

Figure 16.24

8 Choose **Tools, Track Changes, Accept or Reject Changes; then click OK twice.**
The Accept or Reject Changes dialog box opens (see Figure 16.25).

Figure 16.25

At this point, you could proceed to accept or reject changes made by multiple users the same way you accepted or rejected changes made by a single user in the previous lesson. Instead, restore the appropriate user name, and save your changes to the shared workbook.

⑨ **Click Close.**
The Accept or Reject Changes dialog box closes without accepting or rejecting any change. Now end the simulation of multiple users by restoring the original user name, and save your changes.

⑩ **Choose Tools, Options; then select the General tab, if necessary.**

⑪ **Change the User name to its original specification, and click OK.**

⑫ **Save your changes to the *Track Changes* workbook, and close the workbook.**
Continue with the next skill or exit Excel.

In Depth:
Resolve Conflicting Changes to a Shared Workbook
When change tracking is active, Excel displays a Resolve Conflicts dialog box if you try to save changes to a cell that has already been changed by another user. After you read the information about each change and the conflicting changes made by others, you can select Accept Mine, Accept All Mine, Accept Other, and Accept All Others. You can see how you and others resolved past conflicts by viewing the History worksheet.

Set the Number of Days to Track Changes
When you turn on change tracking, the history is kept for 30 days. When you turn off change tracking or stop sharing the workbook, all change history is deleted.

You can increase or decrease the number of days that changes are tracked. Choose Tools, Share Workbook and then select the Advanced tab in the Share Workbook dialog box. Type the desired number of days in the *Keep change history for* spinner box, and click OK.

For immediate reinforcement, work Challenges 4 and 5.

Skill 9.4: Merge Workbooks

In the previous skill, you worked with changes made by users in a single file. Often two or more people collaborate on the development of a workbook by working on different copies of the file. If you want to merge copies of a shared workbook in which users have made changes, Excel requires that each copy be set up to maintain the history of changes.

If you intend to merge workbooks, set up Shared mode in the original workbook and make copies for others to edit. All copies of the workbook must remain in the Shared mode while being modified. Collaborators can work on their copies from remote locations on a network or download them to their computers. When editing is complete, you must merge all the workbooks into one before you accept or reject changes.

Merging copies of a shared workbook takes only a few steps. Choose Compare and Merge Workbooks from the Tools menu; save the shared workbook if prompted; hold down Ctrl and click the name of each copy of the shared workbook listed in the *Select Files to Merge Into Current Workbook* dialog box that you want to merge, and click OK. You can then accept or reject changes as usual.

In the following steps, you open a shared workbook that contains only the labels and formulas for displaying annual sales data from three stores (see Figure 16.26).

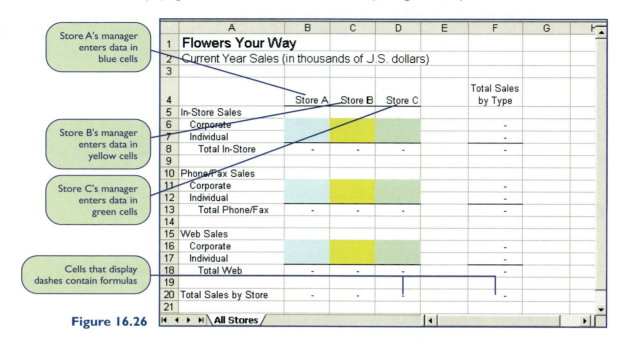

Figure 16.26

Assume that you previously distributed copies of this shared workbook to the managers of three stores. You requested that each manager keep the Shared mode active and fill in the appropriate data in column B (Store A), column C (Store B), or column D (Store C). Now each store manager has returned a copy with numbers added, and you want to merge those three copies into the original workbook.

In the following steps, you open the four files involved in the merge and save them under different names. Doing so enables you to work through the steps more than once. You then merge the changes in workbooks that contain store-specific data into the original workbook.

To Merge Workbooks

① **Open the *MEE-S905* workbook, and save it as** Store A.

Shared mode is active. The blue cells display data entered by the manager of store A (see Figure 16.27).

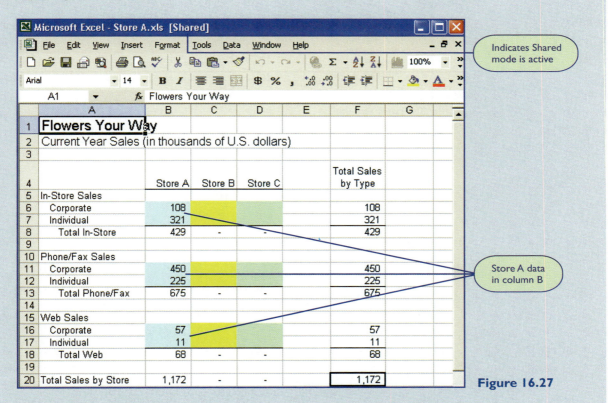

Indicates Shared mode is active

Store A data in column B

Figure 16.27

② **Close the *Store A* workbook.**

③ **Open the *MEE-S906* workbook and save it as** Store B.

Shared mode is active. The yellow cells display data entered by the manager of store B (see Figure 16.28).

continues ▶

To Merge Workbooks (continued)

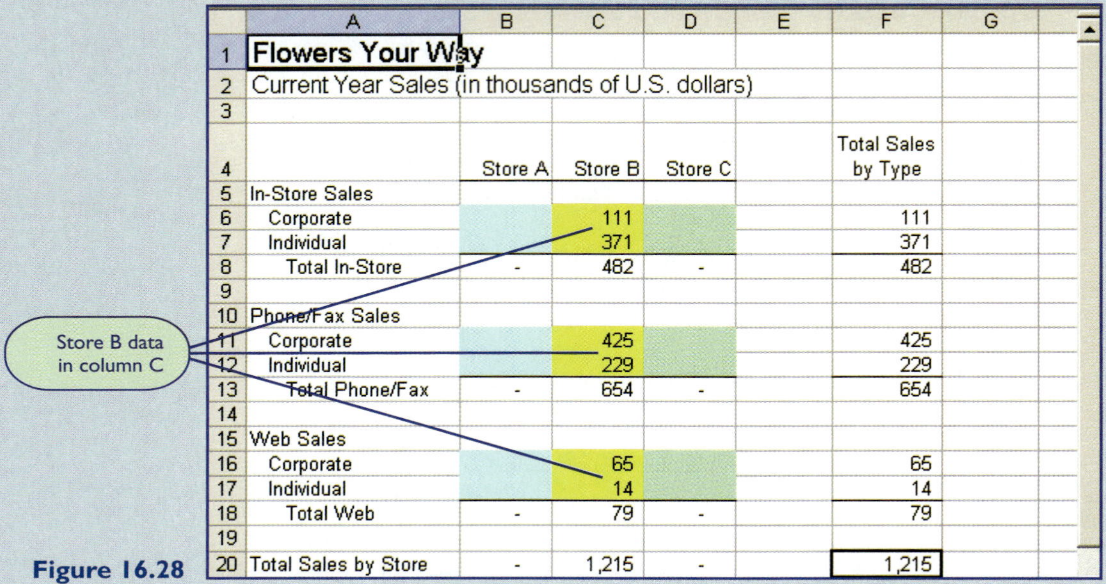

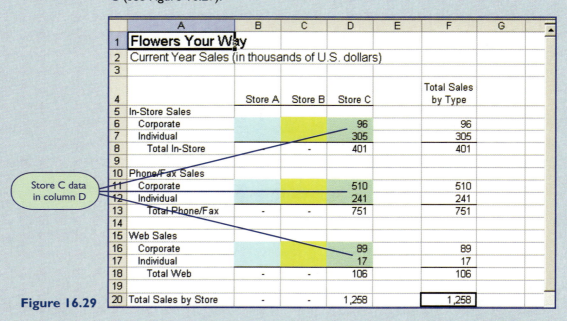

Figure 16.28

4 **Close the Store B workbook.**

5 **Open the *MEE-S907* workbook and save it as** Store C.
Shared mode is active. The green cells display data entered by the manager of store C (see Figure 16.29).

Figure 16.29

6 **Close the Store C workbook.**
The previous steps enabled you to create copies of original student data files and to view the data that you will merge into a fourth workbook. Next, you begin the merge process.

7 **Open the _MEE-S908_ workbook and save it as** Merge Workbooks.

Shared mode is active. The workbook includes one worksheet named All Stores. Labels and formulas are in place, and colors indicate cells that will hold data about each store's sales (refer to Figure 16.26).

8 **Choose Tools, Compare and Merge Workbooks.**

The _Select Files to Merge Into Current Workbook_ dialog box opens.

9 **In the Look in box, display the folder containing your Store A, Store B, Store C, and Merge Workbooks files (see the sample in Figure 16.30).**

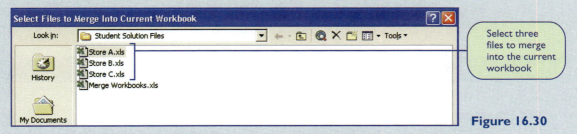

Select three files to merge into the current workbook

Figure 16.30

10 **Hold down** Ctrl **; then click each of the three files your want to merge (refer to Figure 16.30) and release** Ctrl **.**

You selected the files named Store A, Store B, and Store C.

11 **Click OK.**

The dialog box closes and Excel executes the merge. Data displays for each store, one column at a time, in the _Merge Workbooks_ file (see the complete results in Figure 16.31).

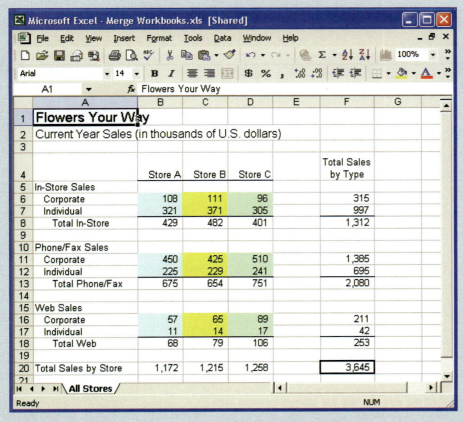

Figure 16.31

continues ▶

To Merge Workbooks (continued)

⑫ **Activate Excel's change tracking feature, and accept all changes.**

⑬ **Save your changes to the *Merge Workbooks* file, and close the workbook.**
Continue with Skill Drill and Challenge exercises, review another skill set, or exit Excel.

For immediate reinforcement, work Skill Drill 7 and Challenge 6.

Summary

The initial portion of this skill set focused on two ways to protect your work: cell protection, and passwords. You set cell protection using a two-step process—unlocking the cells that users can change, and then applying protection to remaining cells. You then set a password for a protected worksheet range and set a password for a workbook.

You also learned that each Excel workbook has file properties, including file type, file size, author's name, and date last revised. You used the Properties option on the File menu to view assorted properties, and you changed author's name.

Remaining coverage in the skill set enabled you to explore powerful collaborating tools. First, you created a shared workbook. In Shared mode, you tracked changes made by one or more users, and you accepted or rejected several changes. You also learned to merge revisions made on multiple copies of a shared workbook.

Skill Drill

Skill Drill exercises *reinforce* skills. Each skill reinforced is the same, or nearly the same, as a skill presented in the skill set. Detailed instructions are provided in a step-by-step format.

Before beginning your Excel Expert Skill Set 9 Skill Drill exercises, complete the following steps:

1. Open the file named *MEE-S909*, and immediately save it as **MEE-S9drill**.

The workbook contains four sheets: an overview and three exercise sheets labeled SD1, SD2, and SD6.

2. Click the Overview sheet to view the organization and content of the Skill Drill workbook for Excel Expert Skill Set 9.

Each exercise is independent of the others, so you may complete the exercises in any order. Be sure to save the workbook after completing each exercise. If you need a paper copy of one or more completed exercises, enter your name, centered in a header, before printing. Print options have already been set to print compressed to one page and to display the filename, sheet name, and current date in a footer.

Be sure to save your changes and close the workbook if you need more than one work session to complete the desired exercises. Continue working on *MEE-S9drill* instead of starting over in the original *MEE-S909* file.

1. Protect Formulas and Labels

You completed a worksheet that budgets quarterly revenue for the year 2004. Now you want to apply worksheet protection appropriately. You decide that you want to be able to change only the numbers used as revenue projections.

To unlock the cells subject to change and protect the rest of the worksheet—the labels, the formulas, and the AutoShape describing the scenario—follow these steps:

1. Open the *MEE-S9drill* workbook, if necessary. If prompted for a password, enter `drill999`.
2. Select the SD1 worksheet.
3. Select the range B10:E12, and choose Format, Cells.
4. Select the Protection tab in the Format Cells dialog box.
5. Clear the Locked check box.
6. Click OK; apply a Light Yellow fill to the range B10:E12, and deselect the range.

    Applying a fill color is not required, but it does help show a user which cells are unlocked.
7. Select Tools, Protection, Protect Sheet; then click OK without specifying a password.
8. Make sure that you can change any estimated quarterly revenue in the range B10:E12, and undo each change.
9. Make sure that you cannot select the AutoShape, change a label, or change a formula.
10. Save your changes to the *MEE-S9drill* workbook.

2. Unlock an AutoShape

Assume that you unlocked cells containing numbers in a budget worksheet and protected the rest of the worksheet. Now you want to unlock the AutoShape, so that in the future you can edit its description, if necessary (such as changing it from "Best Case" Scenario to "Worst Case" Scenario).

To turn protection off, unlock the AutoShape, and then turn protection back on, follow these steps:

1. Open the *MEE-S9drill* workbook, if necessary. If prompted for a password, enter `drill999`.
2. Select the SD2 worksheet.
3. Select Tools, Protection, Unprotect Sheet.
4. Click within the star-shaped AutoShape, and right-click the border that appears around the star-shaped AutoShape.

    The sizing handles display. You can select the object because protection is turned off.
5. Select Format AutoShape from the shortcut menu.
6. Select the Protection tab in the Format AutoShape dialog box, and clear the Locked check box.
7. Clear the Lock text check box; click OK, and deselect the AutoShape.
8. Select Tools, Protection, Protect Sheet; then click OK without specifying a password.
9. Make sure that you can select the AutoShape and change its text, even though protection is turned on again.
10. Save your changes to the *MEE-S9drill* workbook.

3. Get Help on Protection Features in Excel

You want to know more about protection features in Excel. To use onscreen Help to get an overview of protection features, follow these steps:

1. Display any Excel worksheet; then type **protection** in the Ask a Question box, and press ⏎Enter).

   Help topics associated with the phrase *protection* display in the Ask a Question drop-down list.

2. Select *About worksheet and workbook protection*.

   A window titled Microsoft Excel Help opens.

3. Read the short introductory paragraphs about *Worksheet protection* and *Workbook-level protection*.

4. Click the blue link titled *Protecting worksheet elements*, and scroll to view the related information.

5. Click the blue link titled *Protecting workbook elements and files*, and scroll to view the related information.

6. Click the Show button, if necessary, to display the Contents, Answer Wizard, and Index tabs.

7. Click the Contents tab, if necessary; then click and read other topics listed in the *Worksheet and Workbook Protection* subtopic under *Security* on the Contents tab.

8. When you finish, close the Help window.

4. Set a Password to Open a Workbook

You want to set a password to open the *MEE-S9drill* workbook. Follow these steps:

1. Open the *MEE-S9drill* workbook, if necessary.

2. Choose File, Save As, and click the small arrow to the right of Tools near the upper-right corner of the dialog box.

   The Tools drop-down list displays.

3. Select General Options to display the Save Options dialog box.

4. Type **drill999** in the Password to open text box.

   Be sure to type in the first text box, and type the letters in the password in lowercase.

5. Click OK.

   The Confirm Password dialog box opens with a message telling you to reenter the password to proceed (which is the same as the password to open).

6. Type **drill999** and click OK.

7. Click Save in the Save As dialog box.

8. If the message displays stating that *MEE-S9drill* already exists, click Yes to replace the file.

5. View the Properties of an Unopened Excel Workbook

You decide to view the properties of an unopened workbook while working in Excel. Follow these steps:

1. Display any Excel worksheet, which can be a blank worksheet; then choose File, Open.

2. Select the folder containing the student files for this skill set.

3. Click *MEE-S901* (but do not click the Open button).

4. Select Tools in the Open dialog box menu bar, and select Properties from the drop-down list.

5. View the information on the General, Summary, Statistics, and Contents tabs.

6. Close the Properties dialog box.

7. Click *MEE-S902* (but do not click the Open button).

8. Select Tools in the Open dialog box menu bar, and select Properties from the drop-down list.

9. View the information on the General, Summary, Statistics and Contents tabs.

10. Close the Properties dialog box.

11. View the properties for any other unopened file as desired, and close the Open dialog box.

6. Create a Shared Workbook and Track Changes

You work for Real Estate for Tomorrow, Inc., and you manage a listing of residential real estate for sale. You want to track changes in the selling prices of several homes, so that a co-worker can easily double-check your work. To create a shared workbook and track a change, follow these steps:

1. Open the *MEE-S9drill* workbook, if necessary. If prompted for a password, enter **drill999**.

2. Select the SD6 worksheet.

3. Choose Tools, Track Changes, Highlight Changes.

   The Highlight Changes dialog box opens.

4. Click the *Track changes while editing* check box at the top of the dialog box.

5. Check the When check box and select All from the drop-down list, if necessary.

6. Check the Who check box, and select Everyone from the drop-down list.

7. Leave the Where check box unchecked.

8. Check the *Highlight changes on screen* check box, if necessary, and click OK.

9. If a message box appears asking whether you want to continue the save operation, click OK.

   The word *[Shared]* displays in the title bar. The change-tracking feature is active.

10. Change the amount in cell B22 from *225,000* to **219,900**.

    Excel automatically displays a border around the cell and inserts a comment, as evidenced by the small triangular comment indicator in the upper-left corner of the cell.

11. Position the pointer on cell B22.

    The attached comment displays. It identifies the user—by name or computer number—that made the change, specifies the date and time the change was made, and provides a description of the change.

12. Save your changes to the *MEE-S9drill* workbook.

7. Get Help with Merging Workbooks

You work for Real Estate for Tomorrow, Inc., and you manage a listing of residential real estate for sale. You want to learn more about merging workbooks. To view information about merging workbooks in onscreen Help, follow these steps:

1. Display any Excel worksheet; then type **merge workbooks** in the Ask a Question box in the upper-right corner of the screen, and press ⏎Enter.

2. Select the topic *Merge workbooks*; read the related information, and close the Microsoft Excel Help window.

3. Click the small down arrow at the right end of the Ask a Question box, and select *merge workbooks* from the list of recently requested Help topics.

4. Select the topic *Troubleshoot merging workbooks*.

5. Click the Show All button in the right pane, if necessary, and read the extensive information on dealing with merge problems.

6. Close the Microsoft Excel Help window.

Challenge

Challenge exercises expand on or are somewhat related to skills presented in the skill sets. Each exercise provides a brief narrative introduction, followed by instructions in a numbered-step format that are not as detailed as those in the Skill Drill section.

Use the MEE-S911 workbook for Challenge Exercise 6 on merging workbooks. Before beginning your Excel Expert Skill Set 9 Challenge exercises 1 through 5, complete the following steps:

1. Open the file named *MEE-S910*, and immediately save it as **MEE-S9challenge**.

   The workbook contains six sheets: an overview and five exercise sheets labeled CH1 through CH5.

2. Click the Overview sheet to view the organization and content of the Challenge workbook for Excel Expert Skill Set 9.

Each exercise is independent of the others, so you may complete the exercises in any order. Be sure to save the workbook after completing each exercise. If you need a paper copy of one or more completed exercises, enter your name, centered in a header, before printing. Other print options have already been set to print compressed to one page, and to display the filename, sheet name, and current date in a footer.

Be sure to save your changes and close the workbook if you need more than one work session to complete the desired exercises. Continue working on *MEE-S9challenge* instead of starting over in the original *MEE-S910* file.

1. Delete an Embedded Chart in a Protected Worksheet

You decide to delete an embedded chart, but it is part of a protected worksheet. Follow these steps:

1. Open the *MEE-S9challenge* workbook, if necessary, and select the CH1 worksheet.

2. Disable worksheet protection.

3. Select the column chart below the monthly data, and delete it.

4. Restore worksheet protection, and do not assign a password.

5. Save your changes to the *MEE-S9challenge* workbook.

2. Decide Which Cells to Unlock and Protect the Rest

Assume that you completed a worksheet showing monthly and annual revenues, expenses, net income, and gross profit percentages. Now you want to apply protection to the worksheet. Follow these steps:

1. Open the *MEE-S9challenge* workbook, if necessary; then select the CH2 worksheet.

2. Set up worksheet protection so that you can change only raw numbers, date last revised, and the name of the person who revised it. Apply a light fill color to the unprotected cells.

3. Make sure that you cannot change formulas and labels, with the exception of date last revised and the name of the person who made the latest revisions.

4. Save your changes to the *MEE-S9challenge* workbook.

3. Require a Password to Unprotect a Sheet

Assume that you created a list of employees that includes a column for last name, a column for first name, and a hidden column with the related wage per hour data. You unlocked cells in the name columns so that your assistant can enter the full name of a new employee. Now you want to enable worksheet protection and require a password to turn off protection. Follow these steps:

1. Open the *MEE-S9challenge* workbook, if necessary; then select the CH3 worksheet.

2. Display the Protect Sheet dialog box.

3. Enter **FWFwages** in the *Password to unprotect sheet* box.

4. Complete the process to apply worksheet protection and save your changes to the *MEE-S9challenge* workbook.

5. Try to unhide column C.

   You cannot unhide a column when worksheet protection is enabled.

6. Choose Tools, Protection, Unprotect Sheet.

   The Unprotect Sheet dialog box opens. The flashing cursor in the Password box indicates a password is required to remove worksheet protection.

7. Enter the appropriate password; then unhide column C.

8. Hide column C again, protect the sheet with the same password, and save your changes to the *MEE-S9challenge* workbook.

4. Accept or Reject Tracked Changes

You are managing a Transportation Model worksheet. You want to track changes in that worksheet as you make them and then accept or reject each change when you are done. To activate Excel's change-tracking feature, make changes, and accept or reject each change, follow these steps:

1. Open the *MEE-S9challenge* workbook, if necessary, and select the CH4 worksheet.

2. Turn on tracking of all changes by everyone.

3. Change the shipping cost per unit in cell H8 to **3.40**.

4. Replace all occurrences of Chicago with **St. Louis**.

5. Change the capacity value in cell J17 from *20,000* to **22,000**.

6. Activate accepting and rejecting changes for changes by everyone not yet reviewed.

7. Accept the change in city and shipping cost per unit, but reject the change in capacity.

8. Disable tracking changes while editing, which removes the *MEE-S9challenge* workbook from shared use and saves the file.

5. Display and Print a History Worksheet

You want to make several changes in a workbook and view the changes in a History worksheet. Follow these steps:

1. Open the *MEE-S9challenge* workbook, if necessary; then select the CH5 worksheet.

2. Turn on tracking of all changes by everyone, and make the following changes:

    Center the column headings in row 5.
    Change the contents of cell B6 from *145,000* to **150,000**.
    Change the name of the worksheet from *CH5* to **CH5budget**.
    Insert a row between *Golf Lessons* (row 7) and *Other Revenue* (row 8).

3. Save your changes to the *MEE-S9challenge* workbook.

4. Display and read onscreen Help about History worksheets.

5. Display and print a History worksheet.

    Note that centering the column headings in row 3—a formatting change—is not listed. You cannot save the History worksheet. Saving the workbook removes it, as does closing the workbook without saving your changes.

6. Disable change tracking.

    You removed the workbook from shared use.

6. Merge Workbooks

You (Person #1) are going to make changes to a workbook. Select someone else (Person #2) to make changes to a copy of the same workbook. After all changes are made, merge the workbooks. Follow the instructions in this exercise in three stages—prepare to edit (Person #1), make changes (Persons #1 and #2), and merge the workbooks (Person #1).

 If you have problems...
If you are not able to work with another person, you can simulate merging changes from two people by completing all the steps yourself.

Prepare to Edit and Make Changes (Person #1):

1. Open the *MEE-S911* workbook and save it as **Edit 1**.

2. Enable change tracking for all changes by everyone.

3. Make a copy of the *Edit 1* workbook; change the name of the copy to **Edit 2**, and distribute the copy to Person #2.

4. Open the *Edit 1* workbook, if necessary, and make sure that change tracking is enabled.

5. Change the contents of cell B6 from *145,000* to **150,000**, and save your change.

Make Changes (Person #2):

1. Open the *edit2* workbook, and make sure that change tracking is enabled for all changes by everyone.

2. Insert a row between *Golf Lessons* (row 7) and *Other Revenue* (row 8).

3. Enter **Pro Shop Sales** in column A of the newly inserted row.

4. Save your changes to the *Edit 2* workbook; close it, and return a copy of the revised workbook to Person #1.

Merge Workbooks (Person #1):

1. Make sure that the revised workbooks *Edit 1* and *Edit 2* are in the same folder.

2. Open the *Edit 1* workbook, if necessary, and select the option on the Tools menu to merge workbooks.

3. Select the *Edit 2* workbook to merge into the current workbook.

4. Complete the merge and save the workbook as *MEE-S9challenge-merge*.

   The results include revisions by two reviewers—the $150,000 revised amount in cell B6, and the label *Pro Shop Sales* in the newly inserted row below Golf Lessons.

5. Close the *MEE-S9challenge-merge* workbook.

Glossary

3-D formula A formula that refers to cells in multiple worksheets. [pg. 309]

3-D reference A reference to the same cell in multiple worksheets. [pg. 138]

absolute cell reference Specifies that the row and/or column cell references do not change as a formula is copied. For example, copying the formula =$A$1*A5 in cell A6 to cells B6 and C6 results in the formulas =$A$1*B5 and =$A$1*C5, respectively. You can create an absolute reference by placing a dollar sign ($) in front of the part(s) of the cell reference that you do not want to change during the copy operation. (See also **relative cell reference**.) [pg. 162]

adjustment handle A yellow diamond-shaped handle used to adjust the appearance, but not the size, of most AutoShapes. [pg. 239]

Advanced Filter A list-management feature that enables you to specify more complex criteria and to copy filtered records to another location. [pg. 51]

AND search criteria Search criteria in which two or more conditions must all be met to select a record for inclusion in search results. [pg. 422]

annuity An investment that provides fixed payments at equal intervals. The term appears in explanations of the arguments for several functions, including the future value (FV) function. [pg. 179]

argument A specific component in a function, such as a range of cells. For example, the function =SUM(B5:B20) has one argument—the range of cells from B5 through B20. The function =IF(B5>B2,"Goal Met","Keep Trying") has three arguments within parentheses, separated by commas. [pg. 170]

arithmetic operators Symbols in formulas that specify the type of calculation; symbols include +, −, *, and / (to add, subtract, multiply, and divide, respectively). [pg. 31]

array A set of items operated on as a group or individually. A one-dimensional array can be stored in a range that consists of one row (a horizontal array) or one column (a vertical array). A two-dimensional array can be stored in a rectangular range of cells. [pg. 340]

array constant A group of constants arranged in a special way and used as an argument in a formula. [pg. 341]

ascending order An order in which records are organized on the sort field A to Z, lowest to highest value, earliest to most recent date, and so on. [pg. 410]

AutoComplete A feature that compares text you are typing into a cell with text already entered in the same column and automatically completes the word or phrase if a match is found. You can accept the suggested entry or continue typing. [pg. 25]

AutoCorrect A feature that can correct common errors as you type, such as changing *adn* to *and*. [pg. 40]

AutoFill A feature that enables you to fill in a series of numbers, dates, or other items automatically in a specified range. [pg. 30]

AutoFilter Limits the display of records in a list, based on simple search conditions. [pg. 51]

AutoFormat A feature that enables you to apply one of 16 predefined formats to lists and cell ranges. [pg. 119]

AutoShape A predefined shape that you create using the Drawing toolbar. [pg. 230]

AutoSum A feature that you can use to insert a formula that sums a range of cells automatically. Excel suggests a formula that you can accept or edit. [pg. 31]

AVERAGE function A predefined formula that calculates the average of specified values. [pg. 170]

border A solid or dashed line that is applied to one or more sides of a cell, or to a range of cells. [pg. 100]

built-in template A template provided by Excel that contains content and formatting designed to meet a common business need. [pg. 80]

built-in toolbar A toolbar provided by Microsoft Office programs that includes buttons for performing common tasks. [pg. 356]

callout A text-filled object that points to other text or another object. [pg. 239]

cell The intersection of a column and a row in a worksheet. You can enter text, a number, or a formula in a cell. [pg. 2]

cell address Describes which column and row intersect to form the cell; for example, A1 is the address for the cell in the first column (column A) and the first row (row 1). [pg. 5]

cell protection Enables a user to allow changes in content or formatting for specified cells and prevent such changes in remaining cells. [pg. 500]

change tracking An Excel feature that records row and column insertions and deletions, moves and copies, and changes to cell contents. [pg. 512]

chart A graphical representation of data that makes it easy for users to see trends and make comparisons. [pg. 200]

clip A drawing, photograph, or other media type, such as sound, animation, or movies. [pg. 241]

clip art Drawings as well as photographs and sound files. [pg. 241]

Clipboard   A temporary storage area for data that you want to copy or move to another location. [pg. 21]

clustered column chart   A chart that presents multiple data series as side-by-side columns. [pg. 212]

column chart   A chart in which each data point is reflected in the height of its column, in relation to the scale shown on the Y-axis. [pg. 203]

column letter   Lettered A through Z, AA through AZ, and so on through IV, up to 256 columns. [pg. 6]

combination chart   Includes two or more chart types, such as showing one data series as a column and another as a line. Create a combination chart if the values in the data series vary widely or you want to emphasize differences in the data. [pg. 224]

comment   An annotation attached to a cell that displays within a box whenever the mouse pointer rests on the cell. [pg. 263]

comment indicator   A small red triangle in the cell's upper-right corner indicating that supplementary information is stored in the cell, but is not visible unless the comment is opened. [pg. 263]

comparison operator   Used to test the relationship between two items, such as finding out whether the items are equal (=) or if one is greater than (>) the other. [pg. 156]

concatenation operator   The & symbol in a formula that joins one or more text entries to form a single entry. [pg. 156]

conditional formatting   Cell formatting that returns a result based on whether the value in the cell meets a specified condition. [pg. 323]

consolidate   Combine the values from multiple cells or ranges using common math operations such as sum, count, or average. [pg. 309]

constants   Text values (also called labels), numeric values (numbers), or date and time values. Constants do not change unless you edit them. [pg. 25]

current (or active) cell   The selected cell where the next action you take, such as typing, happens. An outline appears around the cell to indicate that it is the current cell. [pg. 5]

custom menu   Includes one or more user-specified menu options that you can select to perform a designated task. [pg. 363]

custom number format   A user-defined format created for a unique situation in which a predefined number format is not available. [pg. 320]

custom template   A template that you create and save with your preferred content and/or formatting in one or more worksheets. (See also **template**.) [pg. 80]

custom toolbar   A toolbar created by the user. [pg. 356]

data marker   An area, bar, dot, slice, or other symbol that represents a data point or value that originates from a worksheet cell. [pg. 201]

data series   A set of related values that are entered in a row or column of the worksheet. [pg. 201]

data validation   Options that enable you to set up data entry instructions, drop-down lists of allowable entries, and error messages. [pg. 428]

database   An organized collection of related data. [pg. 50]

default   A setting that a program uses unless you specify another setting. [pg. 3]

descending order   An order in which records are organized on the sort field Z to A, highest to lowest value, most recent to earliest date, and so on. [pg. 410]

destination file   A file that contains linked or embedded data. [pg. 281]

diagram   A drawing that generally illustrates relationships. [pg. 241]

discussion comment   A remark associated with a Web page or Office application file that is stored on a discussion server. [pg. 265]

dynamic Web page   An alternative term for an *interactive Web page*. [pg. 289]

embedded chart   A graphical representation of data created within the worksheet rather than as a separate worksheet. [pg. 200]

embedded object   An object in a destination file that does not update when the data in the source file changes. [pg. 281]

error alert message   A data validation option applied to a cell that displays an error alert message if a user attempts to enter invalid data. There are three styles of error alert messages: Stop, Warning, or Information. [pg. 433]

error value   A message that displays in a cell to indicate a specific type of error. [pg. 396]

export   Output Excel data for use in another program or data source. [pg. 274]

external data   Data stored outside the current application software. [pg. 438]

field   A data item in each database record, such as order number or order date in a database that tracks catalog sales. In an Excel list, each field is set up in a column. [pg. 50]

file property   Describes a characteristic of a file, such as file type, file size, storage location, author's name, or date last revised. [pg. 500]

fill handle   Displays as a small black square in the lower-right corner of the current (active) cell. You can drag the fill handle to copy cell contents to adjacent cells. [pg. 65]

filter   To hide rows in a list, except those that meet specified criteria. This is a temporary view of your list. Canceling the filter operation displays all of the records again. [pg. 51]

folder   A storage location on disk that enables you to store multiple files by type or subject. [pg. 70]

font   The type style, type size, and type attributes that you apply to text and numbers. As a specific command in Excel, font refers to the **typeface**—a style of print, such as Arial, Courier, or Times New Roman. The default font in an Excel worksheet is Arial. [pg. 97]

footer   Displays at the bottom of each printed page. [pg. 121]

format   To apply attributes to cells that alter the display of cell contents. For example, you can format a worksheet by italicizing text and displaying a border around a cell or group of cells. [pg. 14]

Formatting toolbar   Provides, in button form, shortcuts to frequently used commands for changing the appearance of data. The Formatting and Standard toolbars can share one row or display on two rows. [pg. 3]

formula   Produces a calculated result, usually based on a reference to one or more cells in the worksheet. The results of a formula change if you change the contents of a cell referenced in the formula. [pg. 25]

formula bar   Displays the contents of the current or active cell. [pg. 6]

Formula error checker   A feature that uses rules to check for errors in formulas. [pg. 395]

Formula Watch Window   Enables users to view cells containing formulas even when the cells are out of view. [pg. 390]

function   A predefined formula in Excel. [pg. 31]

FV function   Calculates the future value of an investment based on fixed payments (deposits) earning a fixed rate of interest across equal time periods. [pg. 179]

grouped objects   Two or more objects that can be manipulated as a single object. [pg. 234]

header   Displays at the top of each printed page. [pg. 121]

History worksheet   A separate worksheet that provides detailed information about tracked changes, one change per row. [pg. 514]

HLOOKUP function   Looks for a specified value in the top row of a table array. When that value is found in a cell within the table, the function displays the contents of another cell in that same column from the row you specify. [pg. 345]

hotkey   The underlined letter in a menu or dialog box option. Enables you to select a menu or dialog box option by typing the underlined letter. [pg. 10]

HTML (Hypertext Markup Language)   The standard language for creating and displaying Web pages. [pg. 448]

hyperlink   Text or an object that you can click to jump to another location, open another file, or start a process, such as sending an e-mail or transferring a file. [pg. 258]

IF function   A logical function used to perform one of two operations in a single cell, based on the evaluation of some condition being true or false. [pg. 181]

import   Add data to a worksheet that originates outside of Excel. [pg. 274]

indented format   A report layout that offsets subcategories within categories in a PivotTable report. [pg. 479]

input message   A data validation option attached to a cell that displays user-specified instructions when the mouse pointer rests on the cell. [pg. 429]

landscape orientation   Produces a printed page that is wider than it is long. [pg. 121]

legend   Displays the colors, patterns, or symbols that identify data categories in a chart. [pg. 202]

line chart   Plots one or more data series as connected points along an axis. [pg. 202]

linear   A type of relationship in which one value changes at a steady rate in proportion to another value. [pg. 484]

linear trendline   A best-fit straight line applied to simple linear data. [pg. 485]

linked object   An object in a destination file that updates whenever the data in the source file changes. [pg. 281]

list   An Excel database in which columns are fields and rows are records. [pg. 50]

long label   Text that exceeds the width of its cell. Overflow text displays if the adjacent cells are blank. [pg. 27]

macro   A tool that enables you to combine multiple commands and keystrokes, and then execute them as a single command. [pg. 356]

macro button   A button to which a macro has been assigned. Clicking the macro button activates the macro. [pg. 367]

MAX function   Displays the largest value among specified values. [pg. 170]

menu bar   Contains common menu names that, when activated, display a list of related commands. The File menu, for example, contains such commands as Open, Close, Save, and Print. [pg. 2]

Microsoft Query   An optional feature accessible from within Excel that enables you to perform specialized query tasks. [pg. 439]

MIN function   Displays the smallest value among specified values. [pg. 170]

mouse pointer   Selects items and positions the insertion point (cursor). [pg. 3]

name box   Displays the cell address of the current cell or the name of a cell or range of cells. [pg. 2]

nested subtotals   Subtotals within subtotals. [pg. 418]

nonindented format   A report layout that does not offset subcategories within categories in a PivotTable report. [pg. 479]

NOW function   Enters the serial number of the current date and time—numbers to the left of the decimal point represent the date, and numbers to the right of the decimal point represent the time. [pg. 186]

object   A workbook, worksheet, range of cells, chart, clip art, or WordArt element that has properties, and can be referenced and used by another program. [pg. 280]

Object Linking and Embedding (OLE)   A method of sharing data that is supported by many different programs, including all Office XP applications. [pg. 280]

Office Assistant   A component of onscreen Help in the form of an animated graphics image that can be turned on or off; brings up a list of subjects related to a question you type. [pg. 3]

operand   An item on either side of an operator in a formula. For example, in the formula =B5*C5, B5 and C5 are operands located before and after the multiplication operator. [pg. 399]

OR search criteria   Search criteria where only one condition must be met to select a record for inclusion in search results. [pg. 419]

order of precedence   The order in which Excel performs calculations. For example, multiplication and division take place before addition and subtraction. [pg. 156]

password   A collection of up to 255 case-sensitive characters that must be known to use a password-protected range, worksheet, or workbook. [pg. 500]

pattern   Repeats an effect such as a horizontal, vertical, or diagonal stripe. [pg. 100]

Personal Macro Workbook   A Microsoft Excel file named *Personal.xls* that contains macros that are available to all workbooks. [pg. 372]

pie chart   A circular chart in which each piece (wedge) shows a data segment and its relationship to the whole. [pg. 200]

pivot table   An interactive table that quickly summarizes large amounts of data from a data source, such as a list or another table. [pg. 466]

PivotTable and PivotChart Wizard   Guides you through the steps to make a custom report from a list of data. [pg. 466]

PMT function   Calculates the payment due on a loan, assuming equal payments and a fixed interest rate. [pg. 172]

point   A unit of measurement used in printing and publishing to designate the height of type. There are 72 points in an inch. The default type size in a worksheet is 10 points. [pg. 97]

portrait orientation   Produces a printed page that is longer than it is wide. [pg. 120]

publish with interactivity   Enables users to modify as well as view the content and formatting of an Excel element— such as a workbook, worksheet, range of cells, or chart— from within a Web browser. They can also enter, analyze, sort, and filter data on the Web page. [pg. 254]

publish without interactivity   Enables users to view, but not change, the content and formatting of a published element from within a Web browser. [pg. 254]

query   A tool for extracting and displaying data that meets the condition(s) you specify. [pg. 439]

R-squared   A measure of how well a trendline fits the data points. [pg. 485]

range   One cell or a rectangular group of adjacent cells. [pg. 18]

range name   A word or string of characters that refers to a cell or range of cells. [pg. 334]

read-only   A file attribute that prevents a user from saving changes to a file unless the name or storage location of the file is also changed. [pg. 508]

record   A collection of related data in a database. In an Excel list, each record is set up in a row. [pg. 50]

reference operator   Used to combine cell references in calculations. The colon (:), which connects the first and last cells of the range to be summed, is an example of a reference operator. [pg. 156]

refresh   A required action that recalculates a pivot table to reflect changes in the associated worksheet. [pg. 475]

relative cell reference   Specifies that the row and/or column cell references change as a formula is copied. For example, copying the formula =A1+A2 in cell A3 to cells B3 and C3 results in the formulas =B1+B2 and =C1+C2, respectively. (See also **absolute cell reference**.) [pg. 162]

root directory   The first level of storage on a drive. [pg. 73]

row number   Numbered 1 through 65,536. [pg. 6]

scenario   A set of saved values that you can recall for substitution in a worksheet. [pg. 466]

scrollbars   Enable you to move the worksheet window vertically and horizontally so that you can see other parts of the worksheet. [pg. 6]

shared workbook   Enables one or more users to make and track changes in the same workbook. [pg. 512]

sheet tab   A means to access each sheet in a workbook. Click a sheet tab to quickly move to that sheet. [pg. 6]

shortcut key   Enables you to execute a command by typing one or more keys instead of making selections from menus. For example, the key combination Ctrl+C is an alternative for the Edit, Copy command. [pg. 10]

shortcut menu   Pops up in the worksheet and displays common commands after you right-click an area in a worksheet, chart, or object. [pg. 23]

sizing handles   Small black squares at the corners and midpoints of a selected object. The handles indicate that the object can be moved and sized. [pg. 208]

sort   To rearrange the records in a list, based on the contents of one or more fields in the list. [pg. 410]

sort field A column you want Excel to use in sorting a list or table. [pg. 410]

source file The file providing the data to link or embed. [pg. 281]

spelling checker A feature that highlights words that are not in its dictionary and lets you change or ignore any highlighted word. [pg. 40]

spreadsheet A work area—called a **worksheet** in Excel—comprised of rows and columns. [pg. 2]

stacked column chart Displays multiple data series as stacked components of a single column instead of as side-by-side columns. The stacked column subtype is appropriate if the multiple data series total to a meaningful number. [pg. 212]

Standard toolbar Provides, in button form, shortcuts to frequently used commands including Save, Print, Cut (move), Copy, and Paste. The Formatting and Standard toolbars can share one row or display on two rows. [pg. 3]

static Web page An alternative term for a *noninteractive Web page*. [pg. 289]

status bar Provides information about the current operation or workspace, such as displaying *CAPS* if you turn on Caps Lock. [pg. 2]

style A means of combining more than one format, such as font type, size, and color, into a single definition that can be applied to one or more cells. [pg. 116]

subfolder A folder within a folder in a multiple-level file storage system. [pg. 70]

task pane Provides a quick means to execute commands. The task pane that displays when you start Excel enables you to create new workbooks or to select a workbook to open from a list of files used in recent work sessions. [pg. 4]

template A workbook containing standardized content and/or formatting that you can use as the basis for other workbooks. A template has an .xlt extension. [pg. 70]

text box An object that contains words and is shaped like a square or rectangle. [pg. 232]

thumbnail A miniature representation of an image. [pg. 242]

title bar Displays the name of the software and the name of the active workbook—either a default name, such as *Book1*, or a saved filename. [pg. 2]

toolbar A set of buttons that can be displayed using the View, Toolbars menu. [pg. 2]

trace dependents An audit feature that shows which other cells use the results of the current cell. [pg. 392]

trace precedents An audit feature that shows which cells provide data to the current cell. [pg. 390]

tracer arrow Shows the relationship between the current cell and its related cells. A tracer arrow is blue when it points from a cell that provides data to another cell, and red if a cell contains an error. [pg. 392]

trendline A graphical representation of the direction or trend of data. [pg. 485]

typeface A style of print, such as Arial, Courier, or Times New Roman. The default typeface in an Excel worksheet is Arial. (See also **font**.) [pg. 97]

unlock Remove the default locked setting that prevents change when worksheet protection is active. [pg. 502]

variable data Amounts that are subject to change, such as the interest rate or amount borrowed in a loan situation. [pg. 172]

Visual Basic Editor A program used to view and edit macros. [pg. 367]

Visual Basic for Applications (VBA) The software language used to create macros. [pg. 366]

VLOOKUP function Looks for a specified value in the leftmost column of a table array. When that value is found in a cell within the table, the function displays the contents of another cell in that same row from the column you specify. [pg. 340]

Web query Retrieves data stored on the Internet or your company's intranet or extranet. [pg. 443]

what-if analysis The process of changing the values in cells to see how those changes affect the outcome of one or more formulas. [pg. 483]

Windows Explorer A utility program that you can use to access programs and documents, as well as create folders and copy, move, delete, and rename files. [pg. 70]

WordArt An object that contains user-specified text in one of 30 predefined styles. [pg. 227]

workbook An Excel file that contains one or more worksheets. [pg. 2]

worksheet Excel's term for a work area comprised of rows and columns; also known as a **spreadsheet**. [pg. 2]

worksheet frame The row and column headings that appear along the top and left edge of the worksheet. [pg. 7]

worksheet model Generally contains labels and formulas, but the cells that hold variable data are left blank. [pg. 172]

worksheet window Contains the current worksheet—the work area. [pg. 2]

workspace A file that saves information about all open workbooks, including filenames, screen positions, and window sizes. [pg. 307]

XML (Extensible Markup Language) The standard language for describing and delivering data on the Web. [pg. 448]

XY (Scatter) chart Plots two groups of numbers as one series of xy coordinates. [pg. 483]

X-axis The horizontal axis of a chart that generally appears at the bottom edge of the chart. [pg. 202]

Y-axis A vertical axis of a chart that usually appears at the left edge of the chart. Some chart types support creation of a second Y-axis at the right edge of the chart. [pg. 202]

Index